GOVERNMENT

Energy:
Natural Gas

The Production and Use of Natural Gas, Natural Gas Imports and Exports, EPAct Project, Liquefied Natural Gas (LNG) Import Terminals and Infrastructure Security, Underground Working Gas Storage, Fischer-Tropsch Fuels from Coal, Natural Gas, and Biomass, Gas Hydrates, Gas Shales, Hydraulic Fracturing, Alaska Natural Gas Pipelines

Compiled by TheCapitol.Net

Authors: Gene Whitney, Carl E. Behrens, Carol Glover, William F. Hederman, Anthony Andrews, Peter Folger, Marc Humphries, Claudia Copeland, Mary Tiemann, Robert Meltz, Cynthia Brougher, Jeffrey Logan, Henry A. Waxman, Edward J. Markey, Stephen Cooney, Robert Pirog, Paul W. Parfomak, Adam Vann, Salvatore Lazzari, Brent D. Yacobucci, and Stan Mark Kaplan

TheCapitol.Net

For over 30 years, TheCapitol.Net and its predecessor, Congressional Quarterly Executive Conferences, have been training professionals from government, military, business, and NGOs on the dynamics and operations of the legislative and executive branches and how to work with them.

Our training and publications include congressional operations, legislative and budget process, communication and advocacy, media and public relations, research, business etiquette, and more.

TheCapitol.Net is a non-partisan firm.

Our publications and courses, written and taught by *current* Washington insiders who are all independent subject matter experts, show how Washington works.™ Our products and services can be found on our web site at <*www.TheCapitol.Net*>.

Additional copies of *Energy: Natural Gas* can be ordered online: <*www.GovernmentSeries.com*>.

Design and production by Zaccarine Design, Inc., Evanston, IL; 847-864-3994.

v 1

Energy: Natural Gas, softbound:
ISBN: 158733-189-6
ISBN 13: 978-1-58733-189-3

Summary Table of Contents

iv

Table of Contents

Chapter 4:
"High Natural Gas Prices: The Basics," Federal Energy
Regulatory Commission (FERC), February 1, 2006

Chapter 5:
"Natural Gas Markets: An Overview of 2008," by William F.
Hederman, CRS Report for Congress R40487, March 31, 2009

Chapter 7:
"EPAct Project: Valuing Domestically Produced Natural Gas and Oil, Final Report," National Energy Technology Laboratory (NETL), December 31, 2008

Chapter 8:
"Unconventional Gas Shales: Development, Technology, and Policy Issues," by Anthony Andrews, Peter Folger, Marc Humphries, Claudia Copeland, Mary Tiemann, Robert Meltz, and Cynthia Brougher, CRS Report for Congress R40894, October 30, 2009

Chapter 11:

Chapter 12:

Chapter 13:

xvi

xviii

Chapter 21:

Chapter 22:

Chapter 23:

Chapter 24:

xxii

Introduction

Energy: Natural Gas

The Production and Use of Natural Gas, Natural Gas Imports and Exports, EPAct Project, Liquefied Natural Gas (LNG) Import Terminals and Infrastructure Security, Underground Working Gas Storage, Fischer-Tropsch Fuels from Coal, Natural Gas, and Biomass, Gas Hydrates, Gas Shales, Hydraulic Fracturing, Alaska Natural Gas Pipelines

The main ingredient in natural gas is methane, a gas (or compound) composed of one carbon atom and four hydrogen atoms. Millions of years ago, the remains of plants and animals (diatoms) decayed and built up in thick layers. This decayed matter from plants and animals is called organic material— it was once alive. Over time, the sand and silt changed to rock, covered the organic material, and trapped it beneath the rock. Pressure and heat changed some of this organic material into coal, some into oil (petroleum), and some into natural gas—tiny bubbles of odorless gas.

Discussions of U.S. and global energy supply refer to oil, natural gas, and coal using several terms that may be unfamiliar to some. The terms used to describe different types of fossil fuels have technically precise definitions, and misunderstanding or misuse of these terms may lead to errors and confusion in estimating energy available or making comparisons among fuels, regions, or nations.

For oil and natural gas, a major distinction in measuring quantities of energy commodities is made between proved reserves and undiscovered resources.

Proved reserves are those amounts of oil, natural gas, or coal that have been discovered and defined, typically by drilling wells or other exploratory measures, and which can be economically recovered. In the United States, proved reserves are typically measured by private companies, who report their findings to the Securities and Exchange Commission because they are considered capital assets.

In addition to the volumes of proved reserves are deposits of oil and gas that have not yet been discovered, and those are called undiscovered resources. The term has a specific meaning: undiscovered resources are amounts of oil and gas estimated to exist in unexplored areas. If they are considered to be recoverable using existing production technologies, they are referred to as undiscovered technically recoverable resources (UTRR). In-place resources are intended to represent all of the oil, natural gas, or coal contained in a formation or basin without regard to technical or economic recoverability.

Natural gas provided about 22% of U.S. energy requirements in 2007. It will continue to be a major element of the overall U.S. energy market for the foreseeable future. Given its environmental advantages, it will likely maintain an important market share in the growing electricity generation applications, along with other clean power sources.

In 2008, the United States natural gas market experienced a tumultuous year, and market forces appeared to guide consumers, producers and investors through rapidly changing circumstances. Natural gas continues to be a major fuel supply for the United States, supplying about 24% of total energy in 2008.

In the past, the oil and gas industry considered gas locked in tight, impermeable shale uneconomical to produce. However, advances in directional well drilling and reservoir stimulation have dramatically increased gas production from unconventional shales. The United States Geological Survey estimates that 200 trillion cubic feet of natural gas may be technically recoverable from these shales. Recent high natural gas prices have also stimulated interest in developing gas shales. Although natural gas prices fell dramatically in 2009, there is an expectation that the demand for natural gas will increase. Developing these shales comes with some controversy, though.

The hydraulic fracturing treatments used to stimulate gas production from shale have stirred environmental concerns over excessive water consumption, drinking water well contamination, and surface water contamination from both drilling activities and fracturing fluid disposal.

Solid gas hydrates are a potentially huge resource of natural gas for the United States. The U.S. Geological Survey estimated that there are about 85 trillion cubic feet (TCF) of technically recoverable gas hydrates in northern Alaska. The Minerals Management Service estimated a mean value of 21,000 TCF of in-place gas hydrates in the Gulf of Mexico. By comparison, total U.S. natural gas consumption is about 23 TCF annually.

As the price of crude oil sets a record high, liquid transportation fuels synthesized from coal, natural gas, and biomass are proposed as one solution to reducing dependency on imported petroleum and strained refinery capacity. The technology to do so developed from processes that directly and indirectly convert coal into liquid fuel.

As Congress seeks to address energy security issues, the increasing importation of liquefied natural gas (LNG) is also a matter deserving careful attention. In 2007, LNG imports reached a record high and plans are to increase this fuel source.

Links to Internet resources are available on the book's web site at <www.TCNNaturalGas.com>.

U.S. Department of the Interior
Bureau of Land Mangagement

ENERGY FACTS

Onshore Federal Lands

BLM

The Bureau of Land Management manages over 261 million acres of surface land and 700 million acres of subsurface mineral estate, most being in the western states, including Alaska. Its multiple-use mission is to sustain the health, diversity, and productivity of the public lands, including energy and mineral development that helps meet the nation's energy needs. The Bureau plays a critical role in facilitating the development of energy resources such as oil and gas, coal, geothermal, hydropower, solar, wind, and biomass in its implementation of the President's National Energy Policy. The Bureau is also the leasing agent for all energy minerals on all Federal lands, and as trustee, manages mineral development on over 56 million acres of Indian lands.

2 703-739-3790 TCNNaturalGas.com

OIL and GAS

BLM Photo

- Provides 62 percent of nation's energy and almost 100 percent of its transportation fuels
- Onshore Federal oil production– 5% of total domestic production
- Onshore Federal gas production– 11% of total domestic production
- Estimated 60 billion barrels of oil nationwide on all lands potentially recoverable through enhanced oil recovery projects
- Coal bed natural gas or CBNG (included in the production figures below); found associated with coal and recovered by removing water in coal beds, which lowers hydrostatic pressure in the coal, thus allowing the gas to escape
- Coal bed natural gas- In conterminous U.S., estimated resources at 700 trillion cubic feet (TCF); about 100 TCF economically recoverable with existing technology
  -Technically recoverable CBNG at 30 (TCF) (mean) in six Rocky Mountain provinces

  -Accounts for about 7.5 percent of total natural gas production in the United States
- One billion cubic feet (BCF) of natural gas supplies approximately 3.9 million households
- U.S. consumption of natural gas (2001) – 22,190 billion cubic feet
- Petroleum consumption (2001) – 19,649,000 barrels per day
- U.S. energy consumption: oil – 40%; natural gas – 25%
- About 19% of total U.S. generating capacity of 724 billion kWh from oil and gas (2000)
- Total oil sales volume produced (FY 2003) from onshore Federal lands = 600 trillion Btus
- Total gas sales volume produced (FY 2003) from onshore Federal lands = 2.2 quadrillion Btus

OIL AND GAS ACTIVITIES *(BLM Public Land Statistics, FY 2004)*

State	Producible and Service Holes*	Producible Leases	Acres in Producing Status
Alabama	27	18	6,474
Alaska	129	38	67,350
Arizona	1	0	0
Arkansas	113	151	71,588
California	5,887	304	70,339
Colorado	3,573	2,039	1,340,546
Florida	2	2	3,468
Illinois	16	8	1,581
Kansas	447	432	109,649
Kentucky	160	43	26,039
Louisiana	294	154	64,945
Maryland	9	0	0
Michigan	81	63	30,490
Mississippi	110	63	36,506
Montana	2,156	1,360	736,958
Nebraska	27	18	6,069

State	Producible and Service Holes*	Producible Leases	Acres in Producing Status
Nevada	102	29	15,498
New Mexico	25,112	6,598	3,769,487
New York	5	6	1,284
North Dakota	746	562	299,487
Ohio	495	202	36,542
Oklahoma	335	806	120,582
Pennsylvania	145	67	4,894
South Dakota	65	72	33,377
Tennessee	9	3	2,296
Texas	332	181	113,398
Utah	3,745	1,235	916,106
Virginia	15	11	10,555
Washington	1	0	0
West Virginia	290	161	54,987
Wyoming	18,943	7,263	3,719,919
Total	63,370	21,889	11,671,414

*Wells with one or more producible oil or gas service completions.

ONSHORE FEDERAL LANDS ENERGY FACTS

1

OIL AND GAS SALES AND REVENUES *(MMS Mineral Review, FY 2004)*

State	Oil Sales Volume (bbls)	Royalty Revenues ($)	Gas Sales Volume (MCF)	Royalty Revenues ($)
Alabama	262,249	929,356	681,990	406,837
Alaska	297,556	1,000,456	30,438,714	8,241,241
Arkansas	2,214	7,081	6,902,885	4,083,430
California	15,827,500	21,924,000	6,733,922	4,279,993
Colorado	3,998,996	15,188,924	111,355,670	43,703,409
Florida	1,200	3,619	-----	-----
Illinois	45,925	142,300	-----	-----
Kansas	28,126	84,802	13,907,928	6,957,948
Kentucky	9,639	3,292	294,578	109,379
Louisiana	657,931	2,100,178	13,462,837	8,469,430
Michigan	37,329	101,153	2,424,989	1,294,944
Mississippi	470,049	1,374,627	629,599	382,126
Montana	3,434,518	10,195,884	21,371,718	8,647,005
Nebraska	41,871	130,936	----	---
Nevada	598,796	1,498,428		
New Mexico	30,336,794	91,858,280	930,158,803	400,848,183
New York	-----	-----	18,310	10,913
North Dakota	5,038,396	17,776,148	7,282,857	2,996,728
Ohio	28,501	31,216	845,674	397,899
Oklahoma	150,201	390,635	12,070,082	6,047,082
Pennsylvania	69	179	93,769	24,380
South Dakota	172,609	567,068	262,814	81,748
Texas	438,329	1,481,649	24,018,895	12,933,238
Utah	4,121,756	10,636,752	126,362,710	47,053,522
Virginia	-----	-----	73,380	37,611
West Virginia	-----	-----	759,958	346,731
Wyoming	33,345,702	84,547,529	911,199,107	357,110,212
Total	99,346,256	261,974,494	2,221,352,097	914,103,989

OIL AND GAS ACTIVITY OVER FIVE-YEAR PERIOD *(BLM PUBLIC LAND STATS, FY 2004)*

Year	Competitive Leases No.	Acres	Non-Competitive Leases No.	Acres	Other Types of Leases No.	Acres
2000	24,339	16,792,130	23,171	18,022,788	2,524	810,430
2001	26,330	17,031,579	23,051	18,478,799	2,525	796,977
2002	28,317	20,781,874	23,327	19,443,008	2,511	768,574
2003	28,799	21,461,003	23,121	19,299,378	2,515	768,628
2004	21,646	16,744,795	21,669	17,934,651	2,521	766,998

Year	Total Leases in Effect No.	Acres	Total Leases Issued No.	Acres	APD's* Approved No.	Producible Leases No.
2000	50,034	35,625,348	2,900	2,650,493	3,066	21,531
2001	51,870	37,990,113	3,289	3,997,271	3,439	21,531
2002	54,200	40,993,429	2,384	2,812,606	3,372	21,529
2003	54,435	41,529,009	2,022	2,064,289	3,802	21,729
2004	45,836	35,446,444	2,699	4,157,121	6,130	21,851

*Application Permit to Drill

ENERGY FACTS · ONSHORE FEDERAL LANDS

2

BLM Photo

COAL

- Coal used almost exclusively to generate electricity
- Coal power plants accounting for over 51 percent of all U.S. electricity generation of 1,966 billion kWh (2000)
- U.S. energy consumption: coal – 22%
- Total coal demonstrated reserve base in U.S. – 501.1 billion tons (2001)
- Total short tons of coal produced (FY 2003) from Federal lands - 10.2 quadrillion Btus

FEDERAL COAL LEASES (BLM PUBLIC LAND STATISTICS, FY 2004)

State	Number of Leases	Acres
Alabama	3	1,730
Alaska	2	5,148
Colorado	54	78,704
Kentucky	6	5,378
Montana	29	44,081
New Mexico	13	31,716
North Dakota	13	5,408
Oklahoma	9	14,086
Utah	85	106,805
Washington	2	521
Wyoming	84	163,001
Total	301	456,578

COAL SALES AND REVENUES (MMS MINERAL REVIEW, FY 2003)

State	Sales Volume* (short tons)	Royalties/ Revenues ($)
Alabama	---	---
Colorado	21,168,432	28,010,112
Kentucky	---	---
Montana	23,164,925	36,973,528
New Mexico	112,837,091	42,020,459
North Dakota	361,326	167,323
Oklahoma	709,058	567,732
Utah	17,440,361	21,595,527
Washington	2,260,822	4,768,258
Wyoming	380,177,079	321,076,791
Total	458,119,094	455,179,730

*Sales volumes are edited cursorily due to resource constraints

ONSHORE FEDERAL LANDS ENERGY FACTS

3

GEOTHERMAL

BLM Photo

- Geothermal energy accounting for 17 percent of renewable electricity generation, and 0.4 percent of total U.S. electricity supply of 14 billion kWh (2000)
- Most activity in California and Nevada; other active states– Utah, New Mexico, and Oregon
- California: geothermal energy displaces need for over 9 million barrels of oil per year
- California: 40 percent of world's geothermal-generated energy produced in Federal land non-Federal power plants
- Percent of production from BLM leases of the nation's Federal geothermal production energy from geothermal resources:

California	87%	Nevada	9%
New Mexico	<1%	Utah	3%

GEOTHERMAL ACTIVITIES *(BLM PUBLIC LAND STATISTICS, FY 2004)*

State	Producing Wells	Injection Wells	Producing Leases	Direct Use[1] (BTUs)	Total Electrical Generation (GW-hr)
California	273	90	23	140,000	4,109 [23]
Nevada	45	20	24	1,174 [1]	1,120 [9]
New Mexico	1	0	2	0 [2]	0
Utah	4	4	6	0	217 [2]
Total	323	114	55	141,174	6,446

( ) Indicates the number of Direct Use facilities or power plants.

(1) Provides an alternative source of energy for greenhouses, tilapia farms, and other commercial uses

GEOTHERMAL REVENUES *(MMS MINERAL REVIEW, FY 2003)*

State	Sales Volume (in millions of BTU)	Royalties/ Revenues($)
California	8,448,976	5,866,852
Nevada	6,981,462	3,323,176
Utah	779,684	175,429
Total	16,210,124	9,365,457

4

GEOTHERMAL REVENUES FROM HOT WATER OR DIRECT USE
(MMS MINERL REVIEW, FY 2003)

State	Sales Volume* (in millions of BTU)	Royalties/ Revenues ($)
California	278,102	62,935
Nevada	19,773	8,880
New Mexico	779,958	93,595
Total	1,077,833	165,410

GEOTHERMAL LEASES
(Competitive & Non-Competitive Public Domain & Acquired Lands)
(BLM PUBLIC LAND STATISTICS, FY2004)

State	Number	Acres
California	70	98,865
Idaho	3	2,465
Nevada	242	356,861
New Mexico	4	4,581
Oregon	57	54,151
Utah	9	8,047
Total	385	522,970

BLM Photo

WIND

- Accounts for 6 percent of renewable electricity generation and 0.1 percent of total energy supply of 6 billion kWh (2000)
- About 20 percent of installed energy capacity on Federal lands
- Abundant wind energy potential: West, Great Plains, and New England
- Nevada: largest potential for wind development; approximately 46 percent of 22 million acres of BLM administered land with commercial energy development potential
- California wind energy project: 2,960 wind turbines installed on public lands with capacity to generate 315 megawatts of electrical power; can supply needs of about 300,000 people
- Currently 22 wind-energy right-of-way authorizations for wind energy production on public lands in California and Wyoming covering approximately 5,000 acres; can generate about 500 megawatt hours of electrical power
- Additional 9 right-of-way authorizations for wind energy site testing and monitoring activities in Idaho, Nevada, Oregon, and Washington
- Extension of Federal wind energy production tax credit and State-level tax credits generating renewed interest in commercial wind energy projects on public lands
- 60 new applications in Arizona, Nevada, Idaho, California, Utah, New Mexico, and Wyoming

ONSHORE FEDERAL LANDS ENERGY FACTS

5

BLM Photo

RIGHTS OF WAY

- Provides access for electrical transmission lines, oil and gas pipelines, roads, telephone/ telegraph lines, water pipelines, and communication sites.

NUMBER OF EXISTING RIGHTS OF WAY *(BLM PUBLIC LAND STATISTICS, FY 2004)*

Administrative State	*MLA	**FLPMA/ Other	Total	Rents($)
Alaska	10	1,093	1,103	276,474.18
Arizona	290	4,326	4,616	1,074,172.77
California	243	5,577	5,820	2,401,884.78
Colorado	1,201	4,866	6,067	691,351.53
Eastern States	18	47	65	1,374.52
Idaho	110	4,885	4,995	750,372.62
Montana	308	3,239	3,547	141,244.34
Nevada	112	7,338	7,450	2,471,473.94
New Mexico	17,776	8,328	26,104	1,448,680.64
Oregon	22	8,975	8,997	562,256.17
Utah	788	4,231	5,019	708,527.95
Wyoming	5,833	9,453	15,286	1,476,824.80
Total	26,711	62,385	89,069	12,005,257.98

*Mineral Leasing Act
**Federal Land Policy and Management Act of 1976 (Public Law 94-597)

Of these ROWs:

- 13,400 are electric transmission linear
  25,401 are oil and gas pipelines
  4,638 are telephone/telegraph lines
  44,527 other other ROWs for roads, water pipelines, communication sites, et al
- Total length of authorized ROWs (assumes average width of 100 feet):

Transmission lines	71,613 miles
Oil and gas pipelines	36,310 miles
Telephone/telegraph	4,638 miles

- Total area of electrical transmission lines — 868,035 acres
- Total area of oil and gas pipelines — 220,062 acres
- Total area of telephone/telegraph lines — 54,274 acres
- Total area of non-linear and other types of ROWs — 5,484,347 acres

ENERGY FACTS   ONSHORE FEDERAL LANDS

6

8 703-739-3790 TCNNaturalGas.com

SOLAR

- Solar energy from the sun used to generate electricity, heat water, and heat, cool and light buildings
- Accounts for 1 percent of renewable electricity generation and 0.02 percent of total U.S. electricity supply of 0.5 billion kWh (2000)
- No pending applications or existing right-of-way authorization on BLM public lands for large concentrated solar power commercial generating facilities
- BLM generating 177 megawatt hours of electricity from photovoltaic systems each year from over 600 installations
- BLM a leader in implementing cost effective photovoltaic systems and demonstrating appropriate use of the technology

BIOMASS

- Organic matter can be used to provide heat, make fuel, and generate electricity
- Accounting for 76 percent of renewable electricity generation and 1.6 percent of total U.S. electricity supply of 61 billion kWh (2000)
- BLM managing 55 million acres of forest and woodlands
- Primary focus of biomass thinning treatments – restore long-term ecological function
- BLM developing biomass utilization strategy to address forest health and restoration concerns; reduce hazardous fuels
- Estimated 12 million acres in need of restoration which could lead to biomass removal
- Estimated 120,000 acres per year needing biomass treatments- could lead to an estimated 650 gigawatt hours of electricity per year

HYDROPOWER

- BLM - the primary agency with responsibility for the initial identification and evaluation of potential waterpower sites
- The Federal Power Act of 1920 (FPA) – the principal authority for authorizing non-Federal development of water on Federal lands
- BLM - permits non-government agencies to build dams and reservoirs on Federal lands through issuance of rights-of-way
- Currently 40 hydroelectric projects on BLM lands subject to license renewal over next 10 years
- Accounting for about 7 percent of total power generation; fourth largest source of U.S. electricity generation of 276 billion kWh (2000)
- States depending heavily on waterpower as source of energy: Idaho, Washington, Oregon, Maine, South Dakota, California, Montana, and New York
- Energy production from Bureau of Reclamation dams not included

ONSHORE FEDERAL LANDS ENERGY FACTS

7

ENERGY FACTS ONSHORE FEDERAL LANDS

OIL SHALE

- Oil shale resources in the U.S. enormous; over 50% of world's estimate of 2.6 trillion barrels of oil from oil shale resource
- Green River oil shale deposits largest with estimated 1.5 trillion barrels of oil
- Federal Government owns approximately 72% of oil shale acreage
- In Colorado; Federal Government owns approximately 78% of surface acreage and 82% of shale oil in-place
- Original oil shale leases, Ca, Cb, Ua, and Ub relinquished
- No Federal oil shale leases at this time
- Research and development leasing proposal is underway

BLM Photo

URANIUM/ NUCLEAR

- Uranium (U3O8) reserves and resources - 268 million pounds @ $30 per pound forward cost (operating and capital costs); 1,422 million pounds @ $100 forward costs (2001)
- Total production of uranium in U.S. - estimated 2,344,107 pounds (2002)
- No exploratory holes drilled; 1,000 development holes drilled in 2002
- U.S. energy consumption; nuclear – 8%
- Mining claims are located on Federal Lands but there is no leasing
- Almost 20% share of total U.S. generating capacity of 754 billion kWh (2000)
- Nuclear fuel costs low and well below that of major competing fossil fuels

TAR SANDS

- Estimated resource in U.S.- 40 to 76 billion barrels of oil
- Economics and technology hinder development
- No tar sands leases on Federal lands at present

8

10

US ENERGY CONSUMPTION BY ENERGY SOURCE: 2000 ACTUAL AND EIA FORECAST for 2025

	Actual 2000		EIA Forcast for 2025	
	Quadrillion BTU	% of Total	Quadrillion BTU	% of Total
Traditional Sources				
Petroleum Products	38.39	38.60%	56.22	40.40%
Natural Gas	24.07	24.20%	25.81	25.73%
Coal	22.64	22.76%	29.42	21.14%
Nuclear Power	7.87	7.91%	8.43	6.06%
Conventional Hydropower	2.84	2.86%	3.12	2.24%
Other	0.31	0.31%	0.07	0.05%
Sub Total-Traditional	96.12	96.64%	133.07	95.62%
Non-Hydro Renewables				
Geothermal	0.30	0.30%	1.02	0.73%
Wood	0.41	.41%	0.40	0.29%
Other Biomass	2.07	2.08%	3.42	2.46%
Municipal Solid Waste	0.31	0.31%	0.44	0.32%
Solar Thermal, Electric & Hot Water	0.06	0.06%	0.09	0.06%
Solar Photovoltaic	0.00	0.00%	0.01	0.01%
Ethanol	0.14	0.14%	0.34	0.24%
Wind	0.05	0.05%	0.37	0.27%
Sub Total-Non Hydro Renew.	3.34	3.36%	6.09	4.38%
Total	99.46	100.00%	139.16	100.00%

Title based on Energy Information Administration's (EIA) Annual Energy Outlook 2003 and from Meridian Clan Fuels, LLC

DEFINITIONS

BLM Photo

Megawatt: 1 million watts.

Gigawatt: a unit of power equal to 1 billion watts

MCF: 1,000 cubic feet

TCF: trillion cubic feet

Bbls (barrels of liquid, i.e. oil): one barrel equals 42 U.S. gallons

BTU: British Thermal Units: amount of energy to raise temperature of 1 pound of water 1 degree Fahrenheit

CREDITS

SOURCES OF INFORMATION:

BLM Public Affairs Office

National Energy Policy Report, 2001

BLM Public Land Statistics, 2004

MMS Minerals Review FY 2004

Coalbed Methane Development Information, Powder River Information Council

U.S Department of the Interior: Interim Report of the Oil Shale Advisory Board to the Secretary of the Interior, February 1965

U.S. Department of Energy, Tar Sands Program Plan, FY 1989, June 1989 (DOE/FE 0133)

U.S. Department of Energy, Energy Information Administration

ONSHORE FEDERAL LANDS ENERGY FACTS

9

Interesting Facts

1 barrel of crude oil = 6 million Btus

•

1 billion Btus = 45 tons of coal

•

5 trillion Btus = enough energy to heat 100,000 single family homes per year in the U.S.

•

1 quadrillion (1x1015) Btus = 170 million barrels of crude oil; 45 million tons of coal;
1 trillion cubic feet of natural gas

•

Per person energy consumption in the U.S. = 323 million Btus

•

Total energy consumed in U.S. yearly = 88 quadrillion Btus

•

Worldwide energy production (1995) = 363 quadrillion Btus

•

One thousand megawatts can supply 1 million people with electrical power.

•

Coal, nuclear energy, natural gas, and hydropower account for about 95 percent of total electricity
generation; oil and renewable energy contribute remainder

Cover Photo: Alaska Pipeline
BLM Photo

Bureau of Land Management
Minerals, Realty, and Resource Protection Directorate
Mail Stop 5235 MIB
1849 C Street N.W.
Washington, DC 20240

202.208.4201

http://www.blm.gov

Natural Gas *Explained*

Basics

How Was Natural Gas Formed?

The main ingredient in natural gas is methane, a gas (or compound) composed of one carbon atom and four hydrogen atoms. Millions of years ago, the remains of plants and animals (diatoms) decayed and built up in thick layers. This decayed matter from plants and animals is called organic material — it was once alive. Over time, the sand and silt changed to rock, covered the organic material, and trapped it beneath the rock. Pressure and heat changed some of this organic material into coal, some into oil (petroleum), and some into natural gas — tiny bubbles of odorless gas.

PETROLEUM & NATURAL GAS FORMATION

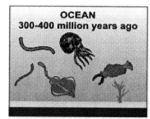

OCEAN
300-400 million years ago

Tiny sea plants and animals died and were buried on the ocean floor. Over time, they were covered by layers of silt and sand.

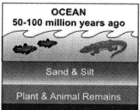

OCEAN
50-100 million years ago

Sand & Silt

Plant & Animal Remains

Over millions of years, the remains were buried deeper and deeper. The enormous heat and pressure turned them into oil and gas.

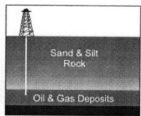

Sand & Silt
Rock

Oil & Gas Deposits

Today, we drill down through layers of sand, silt, and rock to reach the rock formations that contain oil and gas deposits.

Source: Energy Information Administration (Public Domain)

How Do We Get Natural Gas?

The search for natural gas begins with geologists, who study the structure and processes of the Earth. They locate the types of rock that are likely to contain gas and oil deposits.

Today, geologists' tools include seismic surveys that are used to find the right places to drill wells. Seismic surveys use echoes from a vibration source at the Earth's surface (usually a vibrating pad under a truck built for this purpose) to collect information about the rocks beneath. Sometimes it is necessary to use small amounts of dynamite to provide the vibration that is needed.

Scientists and engineers explore a chosen area by studying rock samples from the earth and taking measurements. If the site seems promising, drilling begins. Some of these areas are on land but many are offshore, deep in the ocean. Once the gas is found, it flows up through the well to the surface of the ground and into large pipelines.

Some of the gases that are produced along with methane, such as butane and propane (also known as "by-products"), are separated and cleaned at a gas processing plant. The by-products, once removed, are used in a number of ways. For example, propane can be used for cooking on gas grills.

Natural gas withdrawn from a well may contain liquid hydrocarbons and nonhydrocarbon gases. This is called "wet" natural gas. The natural

Did You Know?
Because natural gas is colorless, odorless, and tasteless, mercaptan (a chemical that smells like sulfur) is added before distribution, to give it a distinct unpleasant odor (it smells like rotten eggs). This added smell serves as a safety device by allowing it to be detected in the atmosphere, in cases where leaks occur.

Operators Preparing a Hole for the Explosive Charges Used in Seismic Exploration

gas is separated from these components near the site of the well or at a natural gas processing plant. The gas is then considered "dry" and is sent through pipelines to a local distribution company, and, ultimately, to the consumer.

Dry natural gas is also known as consumer-grade natural gas. In addition to natural gas production, the U.S. gas supply is augmented by imports, withdrawals from storage, and by supplemental gaseous fuels.

Most of the natural gas consumed in the United States is produced in the United States. Some is imported from Canada and shipped to the United States in pipelines. Increasingly, natural gas is also being shipped to the United States as liquefied natural gas (LNG).

We can also use machines called "digesters" that turn today's organic material (plants, animal wastes, etc.) into natural gas. This process replaces waiting for millions of years for the gas to form naturally.

Learn More

- Natural Gas Data — http://www.eia.doe.gov/oil_gas/natural_gas/info_glance/natural_gas.html
- American Gas Association — http://www.aga.org/
- Natural Gas Production — http://tonto.eia.doe.gov/dnav/ng/ng_prod_sum_dcu_NUS_a.htm
- State-level production — http://tonto.eia.doe.gov/dnav/ng/ng_prod_sum_a_EPG0_FPD_mmcf_a.htm
- What Is LNG? — http://tonto.eia.doe.gov/energy_in_brief/liquefied_natural_gas_lng.cfm
- Weekly Natural Gas Storage — http://www.eia.doe.gov/oil_gas/natural_gas/ngs/ngs.html

eia U.S. Energy Information Administration
Independent Statistics and Analysis

Last Reviewed: October 1, 2009

http://tonto.eia.doe.gov/energyexplained/index.cfm?page=natural_gas_home

Natural Gas Statistics

2008 data except where noted:

U.S. Production (Dry gas production)	20,561 billion cubic feet
U.S. Consumption	23,210 billion cubic feet
U.S. Imports	3,981 billion cubic feet
U.S. Exports	1,006 billion cubic feet
Wellhead Price	$8.07 per thousand cubic feet (Nominal)
Average City Gate Price	$9.18 per thousand cubic feet
Average Price Delivered to Consumers	
Residential	$13.68 per thousand cubic feet
Commercial	$11.99 per thousand cubic feet
Industrial	$9.58 per thousand cubic feet
Electric Power	$9.35 per thousand cubic feet
Ranking of State Residential Prices	#1 — Hawaii
Consumers:	
* industrial * residential * commercial * electric power * transportation (pipeline & vehicle fuel) & other	34% 21% 13% 29% 3%
LNG Imports	352 billion cubic feet
Number of U.S. Producing Gas and Gas Condensate Wells (2007)	452,768
Pipeline Miles (Lower 48 States)	305,954 miles
Dry Natural Gas Proved Reserves as of December 31, 2008	244,700 billion cubic feet
Natural Gas Percentage of Electricity Generation (2007)	21.6%
Natural Gas Percentage of Electric Industry Capacity (2007)	39.5%
Top Producing States (2007)	#1 — Texas
Top U.S. Gas Fields (2007) (PDF)	#1 — San Juan Basin (Colorado and New Mexico)
Top Producing Companies (PDF)	#1 — ConocoPhillips Co.
World Production (2007)	106.4 trillion cubic feet
World Consumption (2007)	108.5 trillion cubic feet

Source: U.S. Energy Information Administration, last updated July 15, 2009

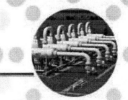

Natural Gas *Explained*

Delivery and Storage of Natural Gas – Basics

Natural Gas Is Often Stored Before It Is Delivered

Natural gas is moved by pipelines from the producing fields to consumers. Because natural gas demand is greater in the winter, it is stored along the way in large underground storage systems, such as old oil and gas wells or caverns formed in old salt beds. The gas remains there until it is added back into the pipeline when people begin to use more gas, such as in the winter to heat homes.

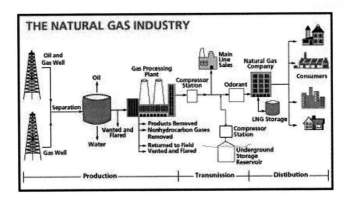

When the gas gets to the communities where it will be used (usually through large pipelines), it flows into smaller pipelines called "mains." Very small lines, called "services," connect to the mains and go directly to homes or buildings where it will be used.

Natural Gas Can Also Be Stored and Transported as a Liquid

When chilled to very cold temperatures, approximately -260°F, natural gas changes into a liquid and can be stored in this form. Because it takes up only 1/600th of the space that it would in its gaseous state, liquefied natural gas (LNG) can be loaded onto tankers (large ships with several domed tanks) and moved across the ocean to other countries. When this LNG is received in the United States, it can be shipped by truck to be held in large chilled tanks close to users or turned back into gas when it's ready to put in the pipelines.

Natural Gas *Explained*

Natural Gas Pipelines – Basics

An intricate transportation system, made up of about 1.5 million miles of mainline and other pipelines, links production areas and natural gas markets. The U.S. natural gas transportation network delivered more than 23 trillion cubic feet of natural gas during 2008 to about 70 million customers.

What Makes Up This Transportation Network?

Transporting natural gas from the production field to the consumer involves a series of steps, generally carried out in order:

- Gathering systems, primarily made up of small-diameter, low-pressure pipelines, move raw natural gas from the wellhead to a natural gas processing plant or to an interconnection with a larger mainline pipeline.
- Processing plants separate natural gas liquids and impurities from the natural gas stream before the natural gas is delivered into a mainline transmission system.
- About 306,000 miles of wide-diameter, high-pressure interstate and intrastate transmission pipelines transport natural gas from the producing area to market areas. Compressor stations (or pumping stations), located strategically along the length of the pipeline network, keep the natural gas flowing forward along the pipeline system. More than 200 companies operate mainline transmission pipelines.
- Underground storage facilities, fashioned from depleted oil, natural gas, or aquifer reservoirs or salt caverns, are used to store natural gas as a seasonal backup supply. In 2007, about 125 natural gas storage operators managed roughly 400 active storage fields. When needed, this reserve is withdrawn to meet additional customer demand during peak usage periods. Aboveground liquefied natural gas storage facilities are also used for this purpose. More than 200 companies operate
- More than 1,300 local distribution companies deliver natural gas to end users through hundreds of thousands of miles of small-diameter service lines. Local distribution companies reduce the pressure of the natural gas received from the high-pressure mainline transmission system to a level that is acceptable for use in residences and commercial establishments.

How Did This Transmission and Distribution Network Become So Large?

About 142,000 miles of the current 306,000 miles of the mainline natural gas transmission network were installed in the 1950s and 1960s as consumer demand for low-priced natural gas more than doubled following World War II. In fact, about half of the natural gas pipeline mileage currently installed in Texas and Louisiana, two of the largest natural gas production areas in the country, was constructed between 1950 and 1969. By the close of 1969, marketed natural gas production exceeded 20 trillion cubic feet for the first time.

A large portion of the 1.2 million miles of local distribution pipelines, which receive natural gas from the mainline transmission grid and

Nearly one-fifth of all natural gas transmission pipelines, by mileage, are located in Texas. More than half of all transmission pipelines are located in Texas and eight other States.

Percent of U.S. Natural Gas Transmission Pipeline Mileage in Each State (2008)

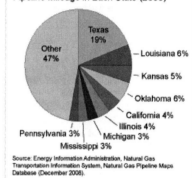

Source: Energy Information Administration, Natural Gas Transportation Information System, Natural Gas Pipeline Maps Database (December 2008).

The national natural gas mainline transmission grid is made up of approximately 217,000 miles of interstate pipelines and 89,000 miles of intrastate pipeline.

Legend
—— Interstate Pipelines
—— Intrastate Pipelines

Source: Energy Information Administration, Natural Gas Transportation Information System, Natural Gas Pipeline Maps Database (December 2008).

Did You Know?

Customers in more than half of the Lower 48 States are totally dependent upon the interstate natural gas pipeline system to supply their natural gas needs.

Natural Gas Pipelines

deliver it to consumers, was also installed during the same period. However, the period of greatest local distribution pipeline growth has been more recent. In the 1990s, more than 225,000 miles of new local distribution lines were installed to provide service to the many new commercial facilities and housing developments that wanted access to natural gas supplies during that period of economic growth.

The demand for natural gas has grown in recent years in part because it is considered a relatively environmentally-friendly energy source. Its use as an electric power generation fuel also has grown steadily with a decline in the capital costs of producing electric power from natural gas as technology in the area has improved.

Natural gas prices, along with oil prices, increased substantially between 2003 and 2008. Higher prices gave natural gas producers the incentive to expand development of new natural gas fields. Consequently, new pipelines have been and are being built to link these new production sources to the existing mainline transmission network. Construction of new transmission and local distribution mainline pipeline mileage during the current decade, 2000-2009, is projected to surpass that of any other decade since the 1950s.

Based on data compiled by the U.S. Department of Transportation's Office of Pipeline Safety through 2005 and proposed pipeline project data maintained by the Energy Information Administration.

Learn More

- About U.S. Natural Gas Pipelines — http://www.eia.doe.gov/pub/oil_gas/natural_gas/analysis_publications /ngpipeline/index.html
- Additions to Capacity on the U.S. Natural Gas Pipeline Network: 2007 — http://www.eia.doe.gov/pub/oil_gas /natural_gas/feature_articles/2008/ngpipelinenet/ngpipelinenet.pdf
- Interstate Natural Gas Association of America (INGAA) — http://www.ingaa.org
- Office of Pipeline Safety — http://www.phmsa.dot.gov/pipeline/about/contact
- Natural Gas Pipelines — http://www.eia.doe.gov/pub/oil_gas/natural_gas/feature_articles/2009/pipelinenetwork /pipelinenetwork.pdf
- How does natural gas travel to consumers? — http://tonto.eia.doe.gov/energy_in_brief/natural_gas_pipeline.cfm

U.S. Energy Information Administration
Independent Statistics and Analysis

Last Reviewed: July 15, 2009

http://tonto.eia.doe.gov/energyexplained/index.cfm?page=natural_gas_pipelines

Natural Gas *Explained*

Liquefied Natural Gas – Basics

What Is LNG?

Liquefied natural gas (LNG) is natural gas that has been cooled to about -260°F for shipment and/or storage as a liquid. The volume of the liquid is about 600 times smaller than in its gaseous form. In this compact form, natural gas can be shipped in special tankers to receiving terminals in the United States and other importing countries. At these terminals, the LNG is returned to a gaseous form and transported by pipeline to distribution companies, industrial consumers, and power plants.

Liquefying natural gas provides a means of moving it long distances where pipeline transport is not feasible, allowing access to natural gas from regions with vast production potential that are too distant from end-use markets to be connected by pipeline.

Read more about LNG's role as a U.S. energy source.

Did You Know?

Even though the United States is primarily an importer of liquefied natural gas (LNG), it is also an exporter. The oldest active LNG marine terminal in the United States is located in Kenai, Alaska. The terminal has exported LNG to Japan almost continuously since beginning operations in 1969.

Learn More

- Natural Gas Imports and Exports — http://tonto.eia.doe.gov/dnav/ng/ng_move_top.asp
- U.S. Natural Gas Imports by Country of Origin — http://tonto.eia.doe.gov/dnav/ng/ng_move_impc_s1_m.htm
- DOE's Office of Fossil Energy — http://www.fe.doe.gov/programs/oilgas/storage/index.html
- What Role Does Liquefied Natural Gas (LNG) Play as an Energy Source for the United States? — http://tonto.eia.doe.gov/energy_in_brief/liquefied_natural_gas_lng.cfm

 U.S. Energy Information Administration
Independent Statistics and Analysis

Last Reviewed: October 1, 2009

http://tonto.eia.doe.gov/energyexplained/index.cfm?page=natural_gas_lng

Natural Gas *Explained*

Natural Gas Imports and Exports – Basics

Most of the natural gas consumed in the United States is produced in the United States. Some is imported from Canada and shipped to the United States in pipelines. Natural gas is also being shipped to the United States as liquefied natural gas (LNG).

In 2008, 90% of net imports of natural gas came by pipeline, primarily from Canada, and 10% came by liquefied natural gas (LNG) tankers with gas from five different countries.

At the end of 2008, the United States had 58 locations where natural gas can be exported or imported.

- 20 locations are for imports only
- 16 locations are for exports only
- 13 locations are for both imports and exports
- 9 LNG terminals — 8 for LNG imports and 1 for LNG exports

Pipeline Imports of Natural Gas are Mostly from Canada

In 2008, net pipeline imports totaled 2,673 billion cubic feet, or 11.5% of total natural gas consumption.

In 2008, the United States received almost 99% of its pipeline-imported natural gas from Canada with the remainder from Mexico. Canada also accounted for 62% of pipeline natural gas exports, and Mexico, 38%.

Forty-eight natural gas pipelines, representing approximately 28 billion cubic feet per day of capacity, import and export natural gas between the United States and Canada or Mexico.

Imports of Liquefied Natural Gas (LNG) Are Mostly from Trinidad and Tobago

In 2008, LNG imports totaled 352 billion cubic feet, or about 1.5% of total natural gas consumption, most from Trinidad and Tobago. In recent years, several African countries, including Egypt, Nigeria, and Algeria, also have been suppliers of LNG to the United States.

As of the end of 2008, the United States had seven LNG import terminals.

Most Natural Gas Exports Go to Mexico and Canada

The United States also has exported increased volumes of natural gas in recent years to its trading partners. In spite of a decline in pipeline exports to Mexico, overall U.S. pipeline exports in North America increased in 2008 to 956 billion cubic feet.

Trinidad and Tobago provided 75% of our LNG imports in 2008.

Sources of LNG to the United States, 2008 (Percent)

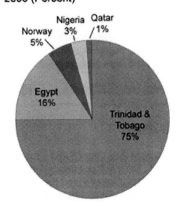

Source: Energy Information Administration, Office of Oil and Gas, based on data from the Office of Fossil Energy, U.S. Department of Energy.

Did You Know?

Natural gas is transported on specially designed ships as liquefied natural gas (LNG). LNG is natural gas that is cooled to -260°F at which point the gas becomes a liquid. The volume of the liquid is 600 times smaller than the gaseous form.

Learn More

- Natural Gas Imports and Exports — http://tonto.eia.doe.gov/dnav/ng/ng_move_top.asp

20 TCNNaturalGas.com

Natural Gas *Explained*

How Much Natural Gas Is Left – Basics

Underground Reservoirs Hold Oil and Gas

A "reservoir" is a place where large volumes of methane, the major component of natural gas, can be trapped in the subsurface of the Earth at places where the right geological conditions occurred at the right times. Reservoirs are made up of porous and permeable rocks that can hold significant amounts of oil and gas within their pore spaces.

What Are Proved Reserves?

Proved reserves of natural gas are estimated quantities that analyses of geological and engineering data have demonstrated to be economically recoverable in future years from known reservoirs.

Proved reserves are added each year with successful exploratory wells and as more is learned about fields where current wells are producing. For this reason those reserves constantly change and should not be considered a finite amount of resources available.

How Much Natural Gas Reserves Are in the United States?

As of December 31, 2007, estimated proved reserves of "dry natural gas" (consumer-grade natural gas) in the United States were 237.7 trillion cubic feet (Tcf). The United States consumed 23.2 Tcf of natural gas in 2007.

Record-high additions to U.S. dry natural gas proved reserves in 2007 totaled 46.1 Tcf. The dry natural gas reserve additions mostly reflected the rapid development of unconventional gas resources including shale, coalbed methane, and tight, low-permeability formations. Many of these unconventional resources are cost effective to develop because of advances in drilling technologies and in techniques to increase gas yields from these formations and because of increases in market prices for natural gas.

What Are Undiscovered Technically Recoverable Resources?

In addition to proved natural gas reserves, there are large volumes of natural gas classified as undiscovered technically recoverable resources. Undiscovered technically recoverable resources are expected to exist because the geologic settings are favorable despite the relative uncertainty of their specific location. Undiscovered technically recoverable resources are also assumed to be producible over some time period using existing recovery technology.

As of January 1, 2007, EIA assumes that domestic natural gas undiscovered technically recoverable resources are approximately 1,536 trillion cubic feet.[1] Almost half of all onshore undiscovered

A Drilling Rig Near Downtown Fort Worth

Source: Cheasapeake Energy, 2007 Annual Report
Photo: Gary Wilson

Did You Know?
In 1821, William Hart dug the first well specifically to produce natural gas in the United States in the Village of Fredonia on the banks of Canadaway Creek in Chautauqua County, New York. It was 27 feet deep, excavated with shovels by hand, and its gas pipeline was hollowed-out logs sealed with tar and rags.

Dry Natural Gas Proved Reserves by Area, 2007

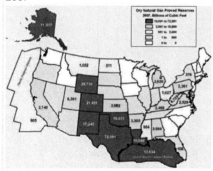

recoverable gas resources are believed to be located in the Alaska and Gulf Coast regions. Over one-third of all undiscovered gas resources are estimated to be in Federal offshore areas, primarily near Alaska, in the Gulf of Mexico, and along the Atlantic Coast.

Source: Energy Information Administration, *U.S. Crude Oil, Natural Gas, and Natural Gas Liquids Reserves 2007 Annual Report*

1. EIA resource assumptions are based on estimates of technically recoverable resources from the United States Geological Survey (USGS), the Minerals Management Service (MMS) of the Department of the Interior, and supplemented by outside experts.

Learn More

- Natural Gas Exploration & Reserves — http://tonto.eia.doe.gov/dnav/ng/ng_enr_top.asp
- Total U.S. Technically Recoverable Natural Gas Resources — http://www.eia.doe.gov/oiaf/aeo/assumption/pdf/tbl9.2.pdf
- U.S. Crude Oil, Natural Gas, and Natural Gas Liquids Reserves Report — http://www.eia.doe.gov/oil_gas/natural_gas/data_publications/crude_oil_natural_gas_reserves/cr.html

U.S. Energy Information Administration
Independent Statistics and Analysis

Last Reviewed: July 15, 2009

http://tonto.eia.doe.gov/energyexplained/index.cfm?page=natural_gas_reserves

Use of Natural Gas – Basics

Natural Gas Is a Major Energy Source for the United States

About 24% of energy used in the United States came from natural gas in 2008. The United States used 23.8 trillion cubic feet (Tcf) of natural gas, matching the record high set in 2000.

How Natural Gas Is Used

Natural gas is used to produce steel, glass, paper, clothing, brick, electricity and as an essential raw material for many common products. Some products that use natural gas as a raw material are: paints, fertilizer, plastics, antifreeze, dyes, photographic film, medicines, and explosives.

Slightly more than half of the homes in the United States use natural gas as their main heating fuel. Natural gas is also used in homes to fuel stoves, water heaters, clothes dryers, and other household appliances.

The major consumers of natural gas in the United States in 2008 included:

- Electric power sector — 6.7 trillion cubic feet (Tcf)
- Industrial sector — 7.9 Tcf
- Residential sector — 4.9 Tcf
- Commercial sector — 3.1 Tcf

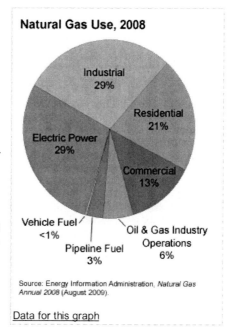

Natural Gas Use, 2008

Industrial 29%
Residential 21%
Electric Power 29%
Commercial 13%
Vehicle Fuel <1%
Pipeline Fuel 3%
Oil & Gas Industry Operations 6%

Source: Energy Information Administration, *Natural Gas Annual 2008* (August 2009).

Data for this graph

Where Natural Gas Is Used

Natural gas is used throughout the United States, but the top natural gas consuming States in 2007 were:

- Texas
- California
- Louisiana
- New York
- Illinois
- Florida

Learn More

- Natural Gas Consumption — http://tonto.eia.doe.gov/dnav/ng/ng_cons_top.asp
- DOE's Office of Fossil Energy — http://www.fe.doe.gov/
- What role does LNG play as an energy source? — http://tonto.eia.doe.gov/energy_in_brief /liquefied_natural_gas_lng.cfm
- How does natural gas travel to consumers? — http://tonto.eia.doe.gov/energy_in_brief/natural_gas_pipeline.cfm

eia U.S. Energy Information Administration
Independent Statistics and Analysis

Last Updated: July 15, 2009

http://tonto.eia.doe.gov/energyexplained/index.cfm?page=natural_gas_use

Natural Gas *Explained*

Natural Gas Prices – Basics

The price of natural gas has two main parts (all cost components include a number of taxes):

Commodity costs — the cost to the natural gas itself.

Transmission and distribution costs — the cost of move the natural gas by pipeline from where it is produced to the customer's local gas company, and to bring the natural gas from the local gas company to your house.

Since the winter of 2001-2002, the natural gas commodity cost (the cost at the wellhead) has constituted more than half of the residential price. This relative cost pattern differs from earlier years in which the commodity cost was consistently less than half the total residential price. The large commodity cost share has resulted from increasingly high prices for natural gas during most of this decade.

The increasing price trend reflects market conditions that have included:

- Colder-than-normal weather for long periods during some heating seasons
- Increasing use of natural gas for electric generation
- Production disruptions from hurricane activity in the Gulf of Mexico
- Fluctuating net import levels
- Record-high crude oil prices over much of the last two years

Average Natural Gas Prices in the United States

Between 1999 and 2008, the national annual average residential natural gas price more than doubled, from $6.69 per thousand cubic feet (Mcf) to $13.68 per Mcf. The national average price of natural gas is only part of the story, as the prices in individual States can differ greatly. These differences are often related to a market's proximity to the producing areas, the number of pipelines in the State, average consumption per residence receiving service, and the transportation charges associated with them, as well as State regulations and degree of competition.

For example, based on 2008 data, residential consumers along the Atlantic Coast tend to pay the most, with prices ranging from $15 to more than $20 per Mcf. By contrast, States in the rest of the country benefit from either indigenous production or the presence of major trunk lines traversing the State. The availability of relatively abundant supplies results in prices between $10 and $15 per Mcf.

Breakdown of Natural Gas Price Paid by Residential Consumers During the Heating Season, 2003-2009

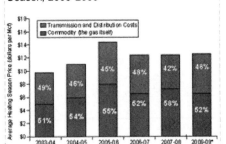

Mcf = Thousand cubic feet.

Source: History: Energy Information Administration, Natural Gas Monthly (October 2008).
Projections: Energy Information Administration, Short Term Energy Outlook (November 2008).

24 703-739-3790 TCNNaturalGas.com

How Can Residential Customers Reduce Their Natural Gas Bills?

To cope with or reduce their natural gas bills, residential customers can:

- Shop for lower-priced natural gas, if their State has customer choice programs. Find more information on the status of natural gas residential choice programs in each State.
- Participate in their local gas company's yearly budget plan to spread gas costs evenly throughout the year, thereby lessening the impact of higher prices.
- Check natural gas appliances and space-heating equipment for efficient operation.
- Obtain a home energy audit to identify ways to conserve energy.
- Reduce thermostat settings, especially when they are not at home.

U.S. Residential Natural Gas Prices by State, 2008 (dollars per thousand cubic feet)

$8.72 - $11.32	$15.19 - $16.75
$11.52 - $13.06	$17.11 - $44.75
$13.33 - $14.61	Data unavailable

Source. Energy Information Administration, *Natural Gas Monthly*, Table 18: Average Price of Natural Gas Sold to Residential Consumers, by State (August 2009).

Data for this figure.

In addition, both Federal and State energy assistance programs are available to natural gas customers who have a limited budget. For example, the Low Income Home Energy Assistance Program (LIHEAP) is a Federal program that distributes funds to States to help low-income households pay heating bills.

Additional State energy assistance and fuel fund programs may be available to help households pay energy bills during a winter emergency. To find out if you qualify for assistance in your State, contact your State public utility commission or your local gas company.

Learn More

- Natural Gas Prices — http://tonto.eia.doe.gov/dnav/ng/ng_pri_top.asp
- Historical U.S. Natural Gas Prices — http://www.eia.doe.gov/emeu/aer/natgas.html
- International Outlook — http://www.eia.doe.gov/oiaf/ieo/index.html
- Short-Term Energy Outlook — http://www.eia.doe.gov/emeu/steo/pub/contents.html

eia U.S. Energy Information Administration
Independent Statistics and Analysis

Last Reviewed: July 13, 2009

http://tonto.eia.doe.gov/energyexplained/index.cfm?page=natural_gas_prices

Natural Gas *Explained*

Factors Affecting Natural Gas Prices – Basics

Natural gas prices are a function of market supply and demand. Due to limited alternatives for natural gas consumption or production in the short run, changes in supply or demand over a short period often result in large price movements to bring supply and demand back into balance.

Factors on the supply side that may affect prices include variations in natural gas production, net imports, or storage levels. Increases in supply tend to pull prices down, while decreases in supply tend to push prices up.

Factors on the demand side include economic growth, winter and summer weather, and oil prices. Higher demand tends to lead to higher prices, while lower demand can lead to lower prices.

Tropical Storm Katrina Over the Bahamas and East of Florida, August 24, 2005

Source: NASA image courtesy Jeff Schmaltz, MODIS Land Rapid Response Team (Public Domain)

Domestic Supply and Prices Can Be Cyclical

Most of the natural gas consumed in the United States comes from domestic production. Lower production can lead to higher prices, but those higher prices, in turn, can lead to increased drilling for natural gas and eventually increased production.

Beginning in the second half of 2008, natural gas prices declined significantly with the economic downturn and a decline in natural gas consumption. These lower prices were accompanied by a steep decline in the number of drilling rigs drilling for gas. That erosion of drilling activity, combined with production cutbacks in response to current and projected low demand, are expected to lead to a drop in natural gas production. As economic recovery leads to increasing demand for natural gas in the industrial sector, natural gas prices are expected to rise again.

Severe Weather Can Disrupt Production

Hurricanes and other severe weather can affect the supply of natural gas. For example, in the summer of 2005, hurricanes along the U.S. Gulf Coast caused the equivalent of about 4% of U.S. total production to be shut in between August 2005 and June 2006.

Pipeline Imports from Canada Are the Second Largest Source of Supply

In 2008, pipeline imports amounted to almost 16% of total natural gas consumption. About 99% of the pipeline-imported natural gas came from Canada with the remainder from Mexico. U.S. pipeline imports are expected to decline in 2009 because of a robust U.S. production, especially relative to demand that has been reduced by the current economic downturn. Canadian production is also expected to decline reflecting both a slowdown in drilling for gas and declining productivity of existing gas wells in Canada.

Liquefied Natural Gas (LNG) Imports May Increase

In 2008, LNG imports totaled 352 billion cubic feet or about 2% of total natural gas consumption, most from Trinidad and Tobago. U.S. LNG imports are projected to rise in 2009. Increasing world LNG export capacity, along with expected weak natural gas demand and limited natural gas storage capacity in Asia and Europe, are expected to increase the availability of LNG for the United States.

Strong Economic Growth Can Drive Up Natural Gas Demand and Prices

Economic activity is a major factor influencing natural gas markets. When the economy improves, the increased demand for goods and services from the commercial and industrial sectors generates an increase in natural gas demand. This is particularly true in the industrial sector, which is the leading consumer of natural gas as both a plant fuel and as a feedstock for many products such as fertilizer and pharmaceuticals.

Winter Weather Strongly Influences Residential and Commercial Demand

During cold months, residential and commercial end users consume natural gas for heating, which places upward pressure on prices. If unexpected or severe weather occurs, the effect on prices intensifies because supply is often unable to react quickly to the short-term increased level of demand. These effects of weather on natural gas prices may be exacerbated if the natural gas transportation system is operating at full capacity. Under these conditions, prices must increase enough to reduce the overall demand for natural gas.

Hot Summer Weather Can Increase Power Plant Demand for Gas

Temperatures also can have an effect on prices in the cooling season as many electric power plants that are operated to meet air conditioning needs in the summer are fueled by natural gas. Hotter-than-normal temperatures can increase gas demand and push up prices.

Natural Gas Supplies Held in Storage Play a Key Role in Meeting Peak Demand

The overall supply picture is also influenced by the level of gas held in underground storage fields. Natural gas in storage is a critical supply component during the heating season that helps satisfy sudden shifts in supply and demand, accommodates stable production rates, and supports pipeline operations and hub services. Levels of natural gas in storage typically increase during the refill season (April through October), when demand for natural gas is low, and decrease during the heating season (November through March), when space heating demand for natural gas is high. Natural gas in storage represents an incremental source of supply immediately available to the market, which can ameliorate the effects of increased demand for natural gas, or other supply disruptions, on prices.

Oil Prices Can Influence Natural Gas Prices

Some large-volume gas consumers (primarily industrial consumers and electricity generators) can switch between natural gas and oil, depending on the prices of each.

Natural gas and coal markets can also interact when the price of natural gas falls significantly. Electricity generation using natural gas can even become attractive relative to coal-fired electricity generation in some areas of the Country.

Because of this interrelation between fuel markets, when oil prices fall, the shift in demand from natural gas to oil pulls gas prices downward. When oil prices rise relative to natural gas prices, there may be switching from oil to natural gas, pushing gas prices upward.

Learn More

- Short-Term Energy Outlook — http://www.eia.doe.gov/emeu/steo/pub/contents.html
- Long Term Outlook — http://www.eia.doe.gov/oiaf/aeo/index.html

 U.S. Energy Information Administration
Independent Statistics and Analysis

Last Updated: July 15, 2009

http://tonto.eia.doe.gov/energyexplained/index.cfm?page=natural_gas_factors_affecting_prices

Natural Gas *Explained*

Natural Gas and the Environment – Basics

Natural Gas Use Contributes to Air Pollution

Natural gas burns more cleanly than other fossil fuels. It has fewer emissions of sulfur, carbon, and nitrogen than coal or oil, and when it is burned, it leaves almost no ash particles. Being a cleaner fuel is one reason that the use of natural gas, especially for electricity generation, has grown so much.

However, as with other fossil fuels, burning natural gas produces carbon dioxide which is a greenhouse gas. Greenhouse gases contribute to the "greenhouse effect."[1]

As with other fuels, natural gas also affects the environment when it is produced, stored, and transported. Because natural gas is made up mostly of methane (another greenhouse gas), small amounts of methane can sometimes leak into the atmosphere from wells, storage tanks, and pipelines. The natural gas industry is working to prevent any methane from escaping.

Technology Helps Reduce Drilling's "Footprint"

Exploring and drilling for natural gas will always have some impact on land and marine habitats. But new technologies have greatly reduced the number and size of areas disturbed by drilling, sometimes called "footprints." Plus, the use of horizontal and directional drilling make it possible for a single well to produce gas from much bigger areas than in the past.

> **Did You Know?**
> Advanced technologies like satellites, global positioning systems, remote sensing devices, and 3-D and 4-D seismic technologies make it possible to discover natural gas reserves while drilling fewer wells.

Natural gas pipelines and storage facilities have a good safety record. This is important because when natural gas leaks it can cause explosions. Since raw natural gas has no odor, natural gas companies add a smelly substance to it so that people will know if there is a leak. If you have a natural gas stove, you may have smelled this "rotten egg" smell of natural gas when the pilot light has gone out.

1. Scientists know with virtual certainty that increasing greenhouse gas concentrations tend to warm the planet, according to the U.S. Environmental Protection Agency, Climate Change State of Knowledge.

Learn More

- Emissions of Greenhouse Gases — http://www.eia.doe.gov/oiaf/1605/ggrpt/index.html
- Environmental Protection Agency — http://www.epa.gov/

 U.S. Energy Information Administration
Independent Statistics and Analysis

Last Reviewed: October 1, 2009

http://tonto.eia.doe.gov/energyexplained/index.cfm?page=natural_gas_environment

Natural Gas *Explained*

Natural Gas Customer Choice Programs – Basics

Natural gas customer choice programs let households and small commercial establishments purchase natural gas from someone other than their traditional utility company. However, utility companies still deliver the natural gas to consumers.

How Choice Programs Work

Customer choice programs give consumers the option of purchasing natural gas from an unregulated supplier (marketer) rather than a local utility company. If a consumer chooses to buy from a marketer, the marketer purchases the natural gas and arranges for its delivery to the local utility. The local natural gas utility, generally referred to as a local distribution company or LDC, continues to provide local transportation and distribution services. Local distribution companies are regulated by State utility commissions and cannot earn a profit on natural gas sales, whereas sales by marketers are unregulated.

Most natural gas customer choice programs began in the 1990s in an effort to introduce more competition into local energy markets. Traditionally, local distribution companies provide natural gas to their customers as part of a bundled service that includes both the price of the natural gas (sometimes called sales service) and the price of distributing the gas. In customer choice programs, gas sales are unbundled from distribution and other delivery-related services.

The characteristics and availability of existing choice programs vary markedly. Some States allow all customers to choose, while some limit choice to specific service areas or a specific number of customers. In some cases, even though choice is allowed statewide, no programs are being offered or no marketers are participating.

Choice Enrollment Reached a New High in 2008

Overall, more than 13%, or about 4.7 million, of the approximately 35 million residential natural gas customers with access to choice (55% of U.S. residential customers) were buying natural gas from marketers in 2008, up from 4.4 million in 2007. Enrollment totaled 6% more than in 2007 and 12% more than in 2006, although the number of States allowing choice has remained the same since 2002.

The State of Georgia has by far the most comprehensive choice program, in that all residential customers in Atlanta Gas Light Company's service territory (more than 80% of Georgia's residential gas customers) purchase their natural gas from marketers. Atlanta Gas Light still delivers the gas but no longer provides sales service. Ohio has the second largest program with about 48% of all eligible households participating and enrollment levels of nearly 1.4 million. Together Georgia and Ohio accounted for nearly 60% of the residential customer enrollment total in 2008.

Customer participation is determined by a variety of factors, such as the customer's potential to save money and the terms of service. In the same way, marketers' participation is influenced by the potential to earn a profit on natural gas

As of December 2008, 21 States and the District of Columbia Had Legislation or Programs Allowing Residential Customer Choice

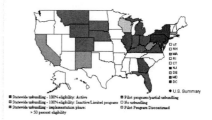

Source: Energy Information Administration, *Natural Gas Residential Choice Programs* (2009)

Did You Know?

Large commercial and industrial consumers have had the option of purchasing the natural gas commodity separately from other natural gas services for many years.

Natural Gas Residential Choice Programs by State, 2008

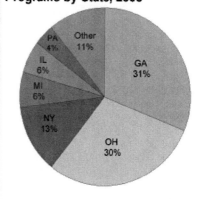

Source: Energy Information Administration, *Natural Gas Residential Choice Programs* (2009).

sales. In 2008, 133 marketers were authorized to serve residential customers, of which 99 were actively serving customers. Many marketers have expanded their price offerings to attract customers. Besides month-to-month variable rates or fixed rates for longer terms, some marketers offer introductory rates, rebates, budget plans, or capped rates.

Learn More

- Natural Gas Residential Choice Programs — http://www.eia.doe.gov/oil_gas/natural_gas/restructure/state/us.html
- DOE's Natural Gas Regulatory Responsibilities — http://www.fe.doe.gov/programs/gasregulation/index.html
- American Gas Association — http://www.aga.org/
- Natural Gas Customer Choice Programs — http://tonto.eia.doe.gov/energy_in_brief/natural_gas_customer_choice.cfm

(eia) U.S. Energy Information Administration
Independent Statistics and Analysis

Last Updated: July 15, 2009

http://tonto.eia.doe.gov/energyexplained/index.cfm?page=natural_gas_customer_choice

U.S. Fossil Fuel Resources:
Terminology, Reporting, and Summary

Gene Whitney
Section Research Manager

Carl E. Behrens
Specialist in Energy Policy

Carol Glover
Information Research Specialist

October 28, 2009

Congressional Research Service

7-5700

www.crs.gov

R40872

CRS Report for Congress —————————————————————
Prepared for Members and Committees of Congress

Summary

Discussions of U.S. and global energy supply refer to oil, natural gas, and coal using several terms that may be unfamiliar to some. The terms used to describe different types of fossil fuels have technically precise definitions, and misunderstanding or misuse of these terms may lead to errors and confusion in estimating energy available or making comparisons among fuels, regions, or nations.

Fossil fuels are categorized, classified, and named using a number of variables. Naturally occurring deposits of any material, whether it is fossil fuels, gold, or timber, comprise a broad spectrum of concentration, quality, and accessibility (geologic, technical, and cultural). Terminology is adopted to reflect those characteristics.

For oil and natural gas, a major distinction in measuring quantities of energy commodities is made between proved reserves and undiscovered resources. Proved reserves are those amounts of oil, natural gas, or coal that have been discovered and defined, typically by drilling wells or other exploratory measures, and which can be economically recovered. In the United States, proved reserves are typically measured by private companies, who report their findings to the Securities and Exchange Commission because they are considered capital assets. In addition to the volumes of proved reserves are deposits of oil and gas that have not yet been discovered, and those are called undiscovered resources. The term has a specific meaning: undiscovered resources are amounts of oil and gas estimated to exist in unexplored areas. If they are considered to be recoverable using existing production technologies, they are referred to as undiscovered technically recoverable resources (UTRR). In-place resources are intended to represent all of the oil, natural gas, or coal contained in a formation or basin without regard to technical or economic recoverability.

In the United States, certain institutions are designated to determine and report quantities of oil, natural gas, and coal reserves and undiscovered resources. Other institutions also estimate these values, but differences in estimating methodology can produce significantly different values.

U.S. proved reserves of oil total 21.3 billion barrels and reserves of natural gas are 237.7 trillion cubic feet. Undiscovered technically recoverable oil in the United States is 145.5 billion barrels, and undiscovered technically recoverable natural gas is 1,162.7 trillion cubic feet. The demonstrated reserve base for coal is 489 billion short tons, of which 262 billion short tons are considered technically recoverable.

Comparisons of different fuel types can be made by converting all of them to a common unit, such as barrels of oil equivalent, based on their heat content. The amounts of fossil fuels found in other nations as reserves and undiscovered resources are much more difficult to determine reliably because data are sometimes lacking or unreliable, but gross comparisons of national endowments can be made using available data.

Contents

Figures

Tables

U.S. Fossil Fuel Resources: Terminology, Reporting, and Summary

Appendixes

Contacts

Congressional Research Service

Introduction

Current discussions of U.S. and global energy supply refer to oil, natural gas, and coal using several terms that may be unfamiliar to some. The terms used to describe different types of fossil fuels have technically precise definitions, and misunderstanding or misuse of these terms may lead to errors and confusion in estimating energy available or making comparisons among fuels, regions, or nations. This report describes the characteristics of fossil fuels that make it necessary to use precise terminology, summarizes the major terms and their meanings, and provides a brief summary of U.S. endowment of fossil fuels and the relationship between the U.S. fossil fuel energy endowment and those of other nations.

Characteristics of Fossil Fuels

Fossil fuels are categorized, classified, and named using a number of variables. It is important to keep in mind that naturally occurring deposits of any material, whether it is fossil fuels, gold or timber, comprise a broad spectrum of concentration, quality, and accessibility (geologic, technical, and cultural). These characteristics are graphically portrayed in **Figure 1** as a resource pyramid. At the top of the pyramid are the deposits that are high-quality, and easy to access. These deposits have been generally discovered and produced first. Examples of the deposits at the top of the resource pyramid are the large oil deposits of Saudi Arabia and the enormous natural gas deposits of Qatar. Moving down the pyramid, the quality and/or accessibility declines, and production becomes more difficult and expensive. A large oil deposit in the deep waters of the Gulf of Mexico would be further down the pyramid than a comparable deposit on land because of the added expense and technology required to produce it.

It is important to note that the deposits at the bottom of the pyramid may be quite extensive. Deposits may be of poor quality or diffuse, but may occur in vast quantities. Examples of fossil fuel deposits that would be found at the bottom of the pyramid are oil shale and methane hydrates (both discussed further below). Oil shale and methane hydrate deposits contain massive amounts of oil and natural gas, but their mode of occurrence, poor accessibility, and difficult recovery make them sub-economic. The economic threshold for producing deposits further down the pyramid is partly a function of commodity price. That threshold is also moved by the development of new extraction technologies that make production feasible at lower cost.

Figure 1. The Resource Pyramid Concept
All resources are not equal

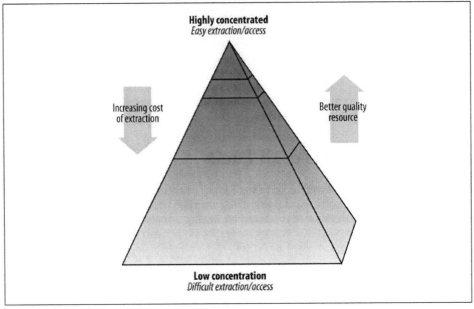

Source: Michael Lardelli, "Earth as a Magic Pudding," October 20, 2008, http://www.energybulletin.net/node/46956, modified from Thomas Ahlbrandt and Peter J. McCabe, "Global Petroleum Resources: A View to the Future," Geotimes, November 2002, http://www.geotimes.org/nov02/feature_oil.html

For U.S. oil deposits, the resource pyramid (**Figure 2**) indicates that many of the high quality, easy to find deposits have already been produced. Current proved reserves (terminology is discussed below) include many deposits that are of lower quality or with poorer access than some historical production, but which are still economic under current market conditions. As long as demand for oil continues, the exploration and production process will move down the pyramid under the influences of price (including environmental costs in some cases) and technology. Whether the vast deposits of oil shale that are lower on the pyramid will be produced depends on the price of oil, the cost of production (including environmental cost), and the availability of technology to produce it. Although this example is for oil, similar relationships exist for natural gas and coal.

Figure 2. Resource Pyramid for U.S. Oil

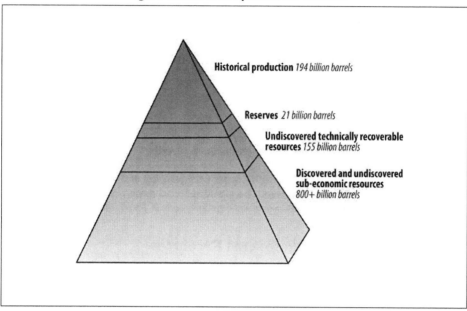

Source: Historical production and proved reserves figures are from Energy Information Administration, undiscovered technically recoverable resource value is from U.S. Geological Survey, and discovered and undiscovered sub-economic resources uses the lower estimate for oil shale resources from RAND as a minimum.

Notes: Discovered and undiscovered sub-economic resources would include poor quality or small deposits of conventional oil, some deposits of oil sands, and various other forms of oil deposits such as oil shale. Reserves and Undiscovered Technically Recoverable Resource numbers are for 2007 and 2008, respectively.

Terminology

A search for energy statistics in the literature quickly reveals a large number of terms used to describe amounts of fossil fuels. Most of these terms have precise and legitimate definitions, and even a careful comparison of statistics for diverse forms of fossil fuels can become quite difficult to reconcile or understand. Not only do oil, natural gas, and coal occur in many diverse geologic environments, but each commodity may occur in different modes or in different geologic settings that impose vastly different economics on their recovery and delivery to market.

Examples of terms used for fossil fuel deposits (not an exhaustive list) include:

- Proved reserves
- Probable reserves
- Possible reserves
- Unproved reserves
- Demonstrated reserve base

- Undiscovered resources
- Probable resources
- Possible resources
- Speculative resources
- Potential resources
- Technically recoverable resources
- Economically recoverable resources

Definitions for several of these terms are included in the **Appendix**.

Two particularly important distinctions afford a better understanding of fossil fuel statistics. The first key distinction is between proved reserves and undiscovered resources; the second key distinction is between conventional and unconventional deposits of fossil fuels.

Proved Reserves and Undiscovered Resources

For oil and natural gas, a major distinction in measuring quantities of energy commodities is made between proved reserves and undiscovered resources. Understanding these terms will help avoid confusion about statistical energy data.

Proved reserves are those amounts of oil, natural gas, or coal that have been discovered and defined, typically by drilling wells or other exploratory measures, and which can be economically recovered. In the United States, proved reserves are typically measured by private companies, who report their findings to the Securities and Exchange Commission because they are considered capital assets. Because proved reserves are defined by strict rules, they do not include all of the oil or gas in a region, but only those amounts that have been carefully confirmed.[1] Because proved reserves are, by definition, economically recoverable, the proportion of the oil in the ground that qualifies as proved reserves grows when prices are high, and shrinks when prices are low. That is, even without new discoveries, oil that may be sub-economic at $30 per barrel becomes economic at $60 per barrel and so the total proved reserves increase simply because price increases.

In addition to the volumes of proved reserves are deposits of oil and gas that have not yet been discovered, and those are called undiscovered resources.[2] The term "resource" has often been used in a generic sense to refer to quantities of energy commodities in general. Observers may refer to resource-rich nations, or speak about a large resource base, for example. But the term "undiscovered resources" has a specific meaning. Undiscovered resources are amounts of oil and gas estimated to exist in unexplored areas. Estimates of undiscovered resources for the United States are made by the U.S. Geological Survey for resources on land, and by the U.S. Minerals

---

[1] The Securities and Exchange Commission has recently modified their classification of reserves to include proved reserves, probable reserves, and possible reserves, adding precision of language to the degree of certainty associated with a particular volume of oil or gas, but also requiring increased attention to the terms used in energy statistics.

[2] The historic question is "If they are undiscovered, how do we know they exist?" The answer is that there is a probability that such deposits exist based on the geologic characteristics of a region, even if they have not been discovered yet. The exploration process is predicated on the probability that such deposits exist.

Management Service for resources offshore. These assessments are based on observation of geological characteristics similar to producing areas and many other factors. Reported statistics for undiscovered resources may vary greatly in precision and accuracy (determined retrospectively), which are directly dependent upon data availability, and their quality may differ for different fuels and different regions. Because estimates of undiscovered resources are based partly on current production practices, they are generally reported as undiscovered technically recoverable resources.

Another term sometimes used in the fossil fuels literature is "in-place" resources. In-place resources are intended to represent all of the oil, natural gas, or coal contained in a formation or basin without regard to technical or economic recoverability. Because only a small proportion of the total amount of the fossil fuel in a deposit is ever recovered, there are large discrepancies between technically recoverable resources and estimates of in-place resources. In-place resource estimates sometimes result in very large numbers, which may be misleading if the reader does not appreciate that the in-place volume of resource can never be completely produced or recovered.

The Importance of Terminology: The Example of the Bakken Formation

Research by a USGS geologist during the 1980s and 1990s revealed that a rock formation in the Williston Basin of North Dakota, South Dakota, Montana, and southern Canada contained an abundance of hydrocarbons dispersed throughout layers of shale and sandstone.[3] Though the author, Dr. Leigh Price, died before publishing his results, the numbers reported were quite impressive: estimates of 271 to 503 billion barrels of oil attracted the attention of the oil industry. However, those estimates, while huge, represented "in place" oil. That is, the total volume of oil was huge, but it was disseminated throughout thousands of square miles of shale and only a small portion of that total would be recoverable. At that time, production of unconventional (or continuous) oil was not being done at large scales, so the technically recoverable volumes of oil were modest.

Subsequently, the USGS has conducted a more detailed and thorough estimate of the technically recoverable resources using modern directional drilling techniques and estimate that the Bakken Formation contains 3.65 billion barrels of undiscovered technically recoverable oil and 1.85 trillion cubic feet (tcf) of undiscovered technically recoverable natural gas.[4] These estimates are still substantial in volume, and production in the Bakken Formation is proceeding. But the gap between estimates of in-place oil and technically recoverable oil demonstrates vividly the importance of knowing what the numbers represent.

Conventional Versus Unconventional Oil and Natural Gas Deposits

The first oil and gas deposits discovered consisted of porous reservoirs in geologic formations, capped by an impervious rock "trap" within which migrating fluids such as oil, natural gas, and

---

[3] Leigh Price, Origins and Characteristics of the Basin-Centered Continuous Reservoir Unconventional Oil-Resource Base of the Bakken Source System, Williston Basin, unpublished but available at http://www.undeerc.org/Price/.

[4] Richard Pollastro, Assessment of Undiscovered Oil Resources in the Devonian-Mississippian Bakken Formation, Williston Basin Province, Montana and North Dakota, 2008, U.S. Geological Survey Fact Sheet 2008-3021, http://pubs.usgs.gov/fs/2008/3021/.

water would accumulate. Within the reservoir, natural gas would be the least dense fluid and would have accumulated at the top of the reservoir. Oil is more dense than gas, but less dense than water and would pool in a layer below the gas cap. Below the oil and gas, water would fill the confined reservoir. This layered arrangement of natural gas, oil, and water within a reservoir is called a conventional deposit and has historically provided most of the oil and natural gas that has been produced.

In recent decades, geologists began to realize that considerable volumes of oil and natural gas exist outside conventional reservoirs in sedimentary rocks situated in geologic basins. The distribution of oil or natural gas throughout a geologic formation over a wide area, but not in a reservoir, is called an unconventional deposit (sometimes called a continuous deposit). The amounts of oil and gas contained in unconventional deposits may be very large, but recovering those deposits is sometimes difficult and expensive. An example of an unconventional oil deposit is oil sand, in which the oil is distributed widely through the sandstone formation. Recovering the oil from oil sands requires special technologies and treatments such as heating, steam flooding, or even excavation. An example of an unconventional natural gas deposit is coalbed methane. The natural gas (methane) does not exist in a discrete reservoir but is distributed throughout the pore spaces of coal. When water is removed from the coal, the gas is released and can be produced. Another type of unconventional natural gas deposit is shale gas, which is discussed below.

There is no direct correlation between the economic recoverability of a deposit and whether it is conventional or unconventional. Some conventional deposits are not economically recoverable because they are too small, too deep, or lack surface access. On the other hand, unconventional deposits such as oil sands and coalbed methane are economically recoverable in some locations. For example, coalbed methane production was 1.75 tcf in 2007[5] out of a total U.S. natural gas production of 19.3 tcf (approximately 9%), and is an important component of U.S. natural gas supply.

Authoritative Data Sources for U.S. Fossil Fuel Reserves and Resources

Many individuals and institutions have attempted to compile and publish estimates of resources. However, the statutory responsibility for collecting and publishing authoritative statistical information on the various types of energy sources in the United States has been given to specific Federal agencies. The Energy Information Administration (EIA) was originally created as the Federal Energy Administration (FEA)[6] and is charged with the responsibility of monitoring and reporting U.S. energy reserves and production.

> The Energy Information Administration (EIA) was created in response to the need for additional Federal initiatives to collect and disseminate energy-related information, and to evaluate and analyze this information. These needs were revealed as the United States sought to respond to the energy crises of the 1970s. The first law to address these needs was the

---

[5] http://tonto.eia.doe.gov/dnav/ng/xls/NG_ENR_CBM_A_EPG0_R52_BCF_A.xls

[6] The Federal Energy Administration would later become the Energy Information Administration, http://tonto.eia.doe.gov/abouteia/legislative_timeline.cfm.

Federal Energy Administration Act of 1974 and, over the years, many subsequent laws have contributed to EIA's evolution and growth.

[The law] Created the FEA and mandated it to collect, assemble, evaluate, and analyze energy information; provide energy information and projections to the Federal Government, State Governments, and the public; and provide Congress with an annual report summarizing these activities. It also provided FEA with data collection enforcement authority for gathering data from energy producing and consuming firms.[7]

Likewise, the responsibility for assessing onshore undiscovered technically recoverable oil and gas resources in the United States resides with the U.S. Geological Survey (USGS), in the Department of the Interior.[8] The USGS has conducted a number of national assessments of undiscovered technically recoverable oil and natural gas resources over several decades. The most recent complete national assessment for onshore oil and gas was completed in 1995, but USGS updates that assessment on an ongoing basis as new data become available. Responsibility for assessment of offshore undiscovered technically recoverable oil and gas resources belongs to the Minerals Management Service, also within the Department of the Interior.[9] EIA and USGS have similar responsibilities for evaluating the nation's endowment of coal.

In addition to purely governmental assessments, several expert groups provide perspectives on individual fuels, geographic areas, or industry sector. Some of these groups are composed of government, industry, and academic experts (e.g., the Potential Gas Committee[10]), expert advisory committees for federal agencies (e.g., National Petroleum Council[11]), independent study groups (e.g., the National Research Council, Committee on Earth Resources[12]), or professional societies (e.g., American Association of Petroleum Geologists[13] or the Society of Petroleum Engineers[14]). Each of these groups provides considerable expertise to the assessment and evaluation of oil and gas reserves and resources, and their reports are considered to be serious, but none have the responsibility to provide a consistent, timely statistical review of U.S. oil and natural gas resources. When using estimates generated by these expert groups, it is important to look for clear and transparent explanation of assessment methodology; in the absence of explanation, it will not be clear what is being estimated and the value and usefulness of the statistics will be diminished.

---

[7] 1974: Federal Energy Administration (FEA) Act (P.L. 93-275, 15 USC 761)

[8] http://energy.cr.usgs.gov/oilgas/noga/

[9] http://www.mms.gov/offshore/

[10] http://www.mines.edu/Potential-Gas-Committee-reports-unprecedented-increase-in-magnitude-of-U.S.-natural-gas-resource-base

[11] http://www.npc.org/

[12] http://dels.nas.edu/besr/

[13] http://www.aapg.org/

[14] http://www.spe.org/spe-app/spe/index.jsp

U.S. Oil and Natural Gas Reserves and Resources

Proved Reserves

U.S. proved reserves of oil as reported by EIA total 21.317 billion barrels.[15] The data are from the latest full compilation, at the end of calendar year 2007. There is generally a delay of over a year between the end of a reporting year and the compilation of the data because the process is time-consuming and quality control is essential. The EIA value for proved reserves includes both onshore and offshore reserves.

Compiling oil reserves is not a simple arithmetic exercise. Each year, volumes of individual components change significantly. Below is a list of how the reserves changed during 2007 as a function of the normal exploration, production, and business processes conducted by oil companies. A more detailed description of these terms is in the **Appendix**.

- Adjustments (+,-) 65 million barrels

- Revision Increases (+) 2,278 million barrels

- Revision Decreases (-) 1,078 million barrels

- Sales (-) 811 million barrels

- Acquisitions (+) 792 million barrels

- Extensions (+) 651 million barrels

- New Field Discoveries (+) 66 million barrels

- New Reservoir Discoveries in Old Fields (+) 73 million barrels

- Estimated Production (-) 1,691 million barrels

U.S. proved reserves of natural gas, also reported by EIA for 2007 total 237.726 tcf.[16] Like oil, the compilation of proved reserves of natural gas involved keeping track of several kinds of production and adjustments. The liquid components (natural gas liquids) are reported with oil production.[17] Total proved reserves are reported as dry natural gas and includes both onshore and offshore reserves. The following list shows a breakdown of how natural gas production is reported prior to separation into its gas and liquid components.

- Natural Gas, Wet After Lease Separation 247.789 tcf

- Natural Gas Nonassociated, Wet After Lease Separation 215.121 tcf

- Natural Gas Associated-Dissolved, Wet After Lease Separation 32.668 tcf

- Natural Gas Liquids (Million Barrels) 9.143

---

[15] Energy Information Administration, Data as of 12/31/2007, Release Date: 2/10/2009, http://tonto.eia.doe.gov/dnav/pet/pet_crd_pres_dcu_NUS_a.htm

[16] Energy Information Administration, Data as of 12/31/2007, Release Date: 2/10/2009, http://tonto.eia.doe.gov/dnav/ng/ng_enr_sum_dcu_NUS_a.htm

[17] http://tonto.eia.doe.gov/cfapps/ipdbproject/docs/IPMNotes.html#p1

Undiscovered Oil and Natural Gas Resources

As mentioned previously, the responsibility for assessing the undiscovered technically recoverable resources of oil and natural gas is split between the USGS for onshore resources, and the MMS for offshore resources. USGS and MMS use somewhat different assessment methodologies. The combined results of the onshore and offshore assessments are based on the availability of geologic data, which may be quite limited, especially for certain offshore areas. Nevertheless, the estimates are complementary and are tabulated in **Tables 1 and 2**. The USGS distinguishes between conventional and unconventional undiscovered resources and they are reported separately for oil, natural gas, and natural gas liquids. MMS reports their estimates for each offshore planning region but does not distinguish between conventional and unconventional deposits.

Table 1. Onshore U.S. Oil, Natural Gas, and Natural Gas Liquids

Undiscovered Technically Recoverable Resources (UTRR)

	Oil (Bbo)	Natural Gas (Tcf)	Natural Gas Liquids (BOE)
Conventional	41.38	378.60	7.38
Unconventional (continuous)	6.16	364.20	4.77
TOTAL U.S. ONSHORE UTRR	47.53	742.88	12.11

Source: U.S. Geological Survey, Department of the Interior, 2008: http://certmapper.cr.usgs.gov/data/noga00/natl/tabular/2008/summary_08.pdf.

Notes: Unconventional natural gas includes coalbed methane; Bbo = billion barrels of oil, Tcf = trillion cubic feet, BOE = billion barrels of oil equivalent.

Table 2. Offshore U.S. Oil and Natural Gas

Undiscovered Technically Recoverable Resources (UTRR), mean values

U.S. OCS Region	Oil (Bbo)	Natural Gas (Tcf)
Alaska	26.6	132.0
Atlantic	3.8	36.9
Gulf of Mexico	44.9	232.5
Pacific	10.5	18.2
TOTAL U.S. OFFSHORE UTRR	85.8	419.8

Source: Minerals Management Service, Department of the Interior, 2006: http://www.mms.gov/revaldiv/PDFs/2006NationalAssessmentBrochure.pdf

Notes: Bbo = billion barrels of oil; Tcf = trillion cubic feet; BOE = billion barrels of oil equivalent

The total endowment of technically recoverable oil and natural gas for the United States is obtained by summing proved reserves from EIA with the onshore and offshore undiscovered technically recoverable resources from USGS and MMS, as shown in **Table 3**.

The value for total technically recoverable natural gas (1,400.49 tcf) does not include much of the newly prospective shale gas being explored in the United States. According to a 2009 report by the Potential Gas Committee, a consortium of industry, academic, and government experts, the total "future supply" of natural gas is 2,074 tcf, which includes substantial volumes of shale gas (see description of shale gas below).

Table 3. Total U.S. Endowment of Technically Recoverable Oil and Natural Gas
(sum of EIA reserves, USGS, and MMS UTRR values)

	Oil (Bbo)	Natural Gas (Tcf)
Total U.S. UTRR	145.5[a]	1,162.7
Proved reserves	21.3	237.7
Total U.S. endowment	166.7	1,400.4

Note: Bbo = billion barrels of oil, Tcf = trillion cubic feet.

a. Represents the total of technically recoverable oil plus natural gas liquids from Tables 1 and 2.

Sub-Economic[18] Oil and Natural Gas Resources

Shale Oil

After coal, shale oil represents the most abundant fossil fuel in the United States. However, despite government programs in the 1970s and early 1980s to stimulate development of the resource, production of shale oil is not yet commercially viable. The need for massive capital investment and the cost of production itself have been the major barriers. A further economic factor lies in the fact that shale oil has a unique chemical composition and, unlike conventional crude oil, cannot be distilled to produce gasoline, but would be primarily a source of other liquid middle distillate fuels such as jet fuel or diesel oil, fuels for which there is significant national demand.

In addition, production of shale oil requires large amounts of water, an important factor since most of the resource is located in water-scarce regions of western Colorado, Utah, and Wyoming. Other environmental problems include the difficulty in disposing of tailings if excavation is used as the extraction process, and the production of greenhouse gases.

In light of these difficulties, efforts to aid in the development of shale oil are focused on pilot projects to test alternative technologies of production.[19]

Estimates of the amount of hydrocarbon fuel in U.S. shale oil resources are highly speculative, given the small amount of development that has taken place. The Department of Energy (DOE) Office of Naval Petroleum and Oil Shale estimates that approximately 1.38 trillion barrels of shale oil are potentially recoverable from the roughly 7.8 million acres of federal oil shale.[20] A

---

[18] The amount of resources considered "sub-economic" changes with economic conditions and extraction technologies.

[19] For more details about shale oil development, see CRS Report RL34748, *Developments in Oil Shale*, by Anthony Andrews1.

[20] U.S. DOE, Office of Petroleum and Oil Shale Reserves, *National Strategic Unconventional Resource Model*, April 2006.

more conservative estimate by the RAND Corporation is that 800 billion barrels may be recoverable.[21]

Shale Gas

Shale gas is an emerging type of natural gas deposit, and exploration for and production of shale gas is increasing. Shale gas is currently marginally economic, and production is therefore sensitive to the price of natural gas; if natural gas prices increase, production of shale gas would likely increase. Shale gas is a classical unconventional type of deposit; the gas is distributed throughout the low permeability shale formations rather than accumulating in a more permeable reservoir. The occurrence of gas in this manner requires special production techniques that often involve horizontal drilling into the gas-bearing formation, followed by hydrofracturing of the rock (exerting pressure in the gas well so high that it causes brittle rock to fracture) to release the gas from the rock. The use of hydrofracturing has caused some environmental concerns arising from the injection of large amounts of water into the well, concerns about the chemical composition of the injected fluids, fears that the fractured rock will expose local water wells to non-potable waters, and the observation that some hydrofracturing jobs have apparently created small earthquakes. However, industry officials insist that any environmental concerns could be mitigated through careful production practices.

No systematic assessment of shale gas resources has been conducted for the United States, though industry and academic experts estimate that the technically recoverable volumes of natural gas from these shale deposits are very large. Recently, the Potential Gas Committee estimated that the United States has 616 tcf of "potential natural gas resources" occurring as shale gas.[22] The proportion of that resource that will actually be produced will depend on further development of exploration and production technology, the price of natural gas, and the ways in which states deal with potential environmental issues.

Methane Hydrates

Another form of fossil fuel with potentially vast resources is natural gas in the form of methane hydrate. Methane hydrate (sometimes called natural gas hydrate, or just gas hydrates) are being investigated as an energy source by both DOE[23] and USGS.[24] Methane hydrate is a crystalline solid composed of methane and water which forms in porous rocks under very specific conditions of temperature and pressure. Deposits occur most commonly offshore in the sediments or rocks of the continental shelf and slope, or in cold climates such as northern Alaska and Canada. Although considered a scientific oddity until the 1990s, methane hydrates are now known to exist in hundreds of locations around the world, often in small isolated deposits, but sometimes in massive quantities. Total worldwide in-place resources of methane hydrates are probably huge, perhaps thousands of trillion cubic feet, but hydrates have never been produced commercially. Currently efforts by the United States, Canada, Japan, India, and several other nations are aimed at developing technologies to exploit this large and widespread form of natural gas.

---

[21] J. T. Bartis, T. LaTourrette, L. Dixon, D.J. Peterson, and G. Cecchine, *Oil Shale Development in the United States Prospects and Policy Issues* (MG-414-NETL), RAND Corporation, 2005.

[22] http://geology.mines.edu/pgc/index.html

[23] http://www.fossil.energy.gov/programs/oilgas/hydrates/

[24] http://energy.usgs.gov/other/gashydrates/

The mean in-place gas hydrate resource for the entire United States is estimated to be 320,000 tcf of gas, with approximately half of this resource occurring offshore of Alaska and most of the remainder occurring beneath the continental margins of the lower 48 states.[25] The USGS estimates that there are about 85 tcf of undiscovered, technically recoverable gas resources within gas hydrates in northern Alaska, and recent studies have shown that methane hydrates are more abundant in the sediments of the Gulf of Mexico than previously believed.[26] Improved understanding of the occurrence and behavior of these important natural gas deposits, and improved technology for producing them, may make methane hydrates a viable source of natural gas in the future.

Heavy Oil

Heavy oil, so-named because its specific gravity and viscosity are higher than those of light crude oil, constitutes substantial deposits of oil in Canada, Venezuela, and other parts of the world. Canada's Athabasca oil sands and Venezuela's Orinoco oil sands are the largest deposits of this type. Canada's oil sands contain an estimated 173 billion barrels of technically recoverable oil and accounts for more than half of Canada's oil production. The Orinoco oil sands are estimated to contain 1.36 trillion barrels of extra heavy oil in-place, of which approximately 270 billion barrels are technically recoverable.[27] Oil sands generally require special production techniques such as excavation or steam flooding, and the oil produced is often limited to certain refineries equipped to handle the heavy oil. U.S. heavy oil is found in California, Alaska, and Wyoming, and is estimated to constitute in-place resources of up to 100 billion barrels of oil, though production of heavy oil in the United States is declining because of the depth of the resource and the cost of production.[28]

---

[25] Statement of Dr. Timothy S. Collett, Research Geologist, U.S. Geological Survey, U.S. Department of the Interior, Before the House Committee on Resources Subcommittee on Energy and Mineral Resources: On Unconventional Fuels II: The Promise of Methane Hydrates, July 30, 2009.

[26] http://www.usgs.gov/newsroom/article.asp?ID=2227

[27] http://www.eia.doe.gov/oiaf/aeo/otheranalysis/aeo_2006analysispapers/nlf.html

[28] http://fossil.energy.gov/programs/reserves/npr/Heavy_Oil_Fact_Sheet.pdf

U.S. Coal Reserves and Resources

EIA is the authoritative source for coal reserves and resource estimates for the United States. EIA compiles data on coal reserves and resources from state sources and federal sources, including from work done by the USGS.[29] The terminology used for coal is slightly different than for oil and natural gas. The primary statistic reported by EIA is the demonstrated reserve base (DRB), which is comprised of coal resources that have been identified to specified levels of accuracy and may support economic mining under current technologies.[30] For the latest reporting period, calendar year 2007, the U.S. demonstrated reserve base was 489 billion short tons.[31] Because the United States produces and consumes about 1.2 billion short tons of coal per year, the demonstrated reserve base would appear to provide hundreds of years' supply of coal, if U.S. users continue to consume it at the same rate. However, because coal production often requires ground disturbance, especially for open-pit mining, the amount that is technically recoverable is not always available. EIA has applied an availability factor that reduces the technically recoverable amount to 262 billion short tons that would actually be available for mining.[32] Detailed availability studies by the USGS have indicated that, at least in some cases, the available and economically recoverable coal might be even substantially less than the technically recoverable amount:[33]

> ... a significant portion of the coal resources less than 4,000 ft (1,219.2 m) in depth are also typically subeconomic due to a number of restrictions that further limit their availability and recoverability. Some of these restrictions are technical constraints (using existing technology) such as coal beds too thin to recover or dipping too steeply. Many societal or environmental restrictions such as the presence of towns, wetlands, or other environmentally sensitive areas may also preclude coal recovery. Both regional mine planning and economic studies are necessary to derive estimates of the coal reserves for any given area.

For example, in one specific case in Wyoming, 47% of the in-place coal is technically recoverable, but the available, economically recoverable coal is only about 6% of the in-place coal.[34] While these proportions may vary between 5% and 20%, depending upon the specific conditions for each coal mining area, very large coal numbers are viewed with some caution because in-place numbers, or even recoverable numbers, may not provide a realistic assessment of the coal that could actually be produced.

---

[29] http://energy.cr.usgs.gov/coal/coal_assessments/summary.html

[30] http://www.eia.doe.gov/cneaf/coal/reserves/reserves.html

[31] A short ton is 2,000 pounds. A metric tonne is 2,204 pounds.

[32] http://www.eia.doe.gov/cneaf/coal/reserves/reserves.html

[33] James A. Luppens, Timothy J. Rohrbacher, Lee M. Osmonson, and M. Devereux Carter, Coal Resource Availability, Recoverability, and Economic Evaluations in the United States—A Summary, U.S. Geological Survey Professional Paper 1625-F, Chapter D, 2009.

[34] http://pubs.usgs.gov/of/2008/1202/pdf/ofr2008-1202.pdf

Expressing Fossil Fuels as Barrels of Oil Equivalent (BOE)

It is sometimes useful to equate the different types of fossil fuels in order to compare the energy content or to gauge the magnitude of one type of fossil fuel in terms of another. Fossil fuels may be liquid, gas, and solid; oil is a liquid measured in barrels, natural gas is a gas measured in cubic feet, coal is a solid measured in pounds or short tons, and all three types of fossil fuels vary in composition, quality, and heat content. Therefore, converting one type of fossil fuel to an equivalent amount of another is a slightly problematic calculation. For example, the energy content of coal varies by at least a factor of three depending on grade.[35] However, government and industry sources commonly use rule-of-thumb measures to make these conversions. For example, EIA provides a conversion tool on their website[36] that assumes the following heat contents (based on U.S. consumption, 2008):

Coal	1 Short Ton = 19,988,000 Btu[37]
Natural gas	1 Cubic Foot = 1,028 Btu
Oil	1 Barrel = 42 U.S. gallons = 5,800,000 Btu

Using these rule-of-thumb heat values, we can express natural gas and coal units in terms of barrels of oil equivalent (BOE):

Coal	1 Short Ton = 3.45 BOE
Natural gas	1 million cubic feet = 1,028,000,000 Btu = 177.2 BOE = 5,643 cubic feet/barrel

Using these conversion factors, we present a crude comparison of U.S. energy reserves plus resources in **Table 4**.

Table 4. U.S. fossil fuel reserves and resources expressed as BOE

BOE = Barrels of oil equivalent

Fossil Fuel	Native units	BOE
Technically recoverable oil[a]	166.7 billion barrels	166.7 billion BOE
Technically recoverable natural gas	1,400.4 trillion cubic feet	248.2 billion BOE
Recoverable reserve base of coal	262 billion short tons	903.9 billion BOE
TOTAL U.S. fossil fuel endowment		1,318.8 billion BOE

a. Technically recoverable oil and natural gas includes proved reserves plus undiscovered technically recoverable resources.

[35] http://www.aps.org/policy/reports/popa-reports/energy/units.cfm

[36] http://tonto.eia.doe.gov/kids/energy.cfm?page=about_energy_conversion_calculator-basics

[37] Btu is the abbreviation for British thermal units, a common measure of heat content. One Btu is the amount of energy in the form of heat required to raise the temperature of one pound of water one degree Fahrenheit.

A Brief Overview of Global Fossil Fuel Resources

Reliable values for proved reserves and undiscovered resources outside the United States are less available than for the United States. The only source of data for some countries is one of the nation's ministries (energy, resource, interior, commerce, etc.), and those data may not be completely accurate because of the lack of good geologic data and assessment methodology, or because the information is purposely withheld. In fact, even if all nations wished to report their resource estimates reliably, it would not be possible to collect uniform data because different methods, accounting rules, and terminology are used in each country. Therefore, some reserve statistics reported outside the United States are not consistent with the U.S. data. Furthermore, only reserves and production statistics are reported for most nations. There has been no reliable source for estimates of undiscovered oil and natural gas resources internationally since the U.S. Geological Survey completed its World Petroleum Assessment in 2000.[38]

Data for proved reserves and production in all countries are most reliable. Production statistics can be obtained for the Organization of the Petroleum Exporting Countries (OPEC)[39] and for the Organization for Economic Cooperation and Development (OECD) countries from the International Energy Agency,[40] an arm of OECD. For international statistics, the EIA relies on the Oil & Gas Journal (a publication of PennWell Corporation) or World Oil (a publication of Gulf Publishing Company) for foreign oil and natural gas reserves. These energy industry trade publications monitor individual national sources for information, as described by the Oil & Gas Journal:

> OGJ does not make its own estimates of a country's reserves but rather compiles the estimates of proved reserves from an annual survey of official sources, including government agencies and ministries. Since most countries do not assess their reserves annually, many of the figures in this report are unchanged from a year ago.[41]

World Oil summarizes their data sources this way:

> World Oil's tables are produced with data from a variety of sources, including governmental agencies. Operating companies with drilling programs also contributed to this year's survey. Our survey is not scientifically randomized, and new environmental and political challenges may emerge at any time. In some cases, a country may not have responded to our surveys, in which case we might use proxies such as rig counts and third-party sources, both public and private.[42]

A source of global oil and gas information commonly used by a number of analysts is the BP Statistical Review of World Energy.[43] Some of BP's data also comes from Oil & Gas Journal and World Oil, but is supplemented with additional data:

---

[38] U.S. Geological Survey, World Petroleum Assessment, 2000, http://certmapper.cr.usgs.gov/rooms/we/index.jsp.

[39] http://www.opec.org/home/.

[40] http://www.iea.org/index.asp.

[41] Marilyn Radler, *Oil & Gas Journal*, "New estimates boost worldwide oil, gas reserves," December 22, 2008.

[42] World Oil, Production and reserves lag as world drilling grows, September, 2008.

[43] http://www.bp.com/productlanding.do?categoryId=6929&contentId=7044622.

The reserve numbers published in the BP Statistical Review of World Energy are an estimate of proved reserves, drawn from a variety of official primary sources and data provided by the OPEC Secretariat, Cedigaz, World Oil and the Oil & Gas Journal and an independent estimate of Russian oil reserves based on information in the public domain. Oil reserves include field condensate and natural gas liquids as well as crude oil. They also include an estimate of Canadian oil sands 'under active development' as a proxy for proved reserves. This inclusive approach helps to develop consistency with the oil production numbers published in the Review, which also include these categories of oil.

The BP Statistical Review of World Energy uses data from the World Energy Council (WEC)[44] for coal reserves. The WEC is a global consortium of national committees that compile energy statistics for their own countries. WEC estimates for oil and natural gas reserves differ somewhat from the Oil & Gas Journal and World Oil values, but not dramatically. For the United States, the U.S. Energy Association (USEA)[45] is the WEC national committee, and USEA cites EIA sources for its estimates for the United States. When using any international fossil fuel statistics, users should be cognizant of ultimate sources of data among these energy data organizations.

Using the best-available data, it is possible to draw a comparison of the total endowment of fossil fuels for nations. **Table 5** includes the basic data for oil, natural gas, and coal for selected nations, with calculations of the total fossil fuels in each nation, expressed in billions of barrels of oil equivalent (billion BOE).

---

[44] http://www.worldenergy.org/

[45] http://www.usea.org/

Table 5. Total Fossil Fuel Reserves of Selected Nations

(expressed in native units and as billions of barrels of oil equivalent (BOE))

	Oil Reserves[a]	Natural Gas Reserves	Natural Gas As BOE	Coal	Coal As BOE	Total Fossil Fuels in BOE
	(billions of barrels)	(trillion cubic feet)		(billion short tons)		(billions of barrels)
World	1,332.0	6,212.3	1,100.8	929.3	3,206.1	5,638.9
Saudi Arabia	266.8	253.1	44.8	0.0	0.0	311.6
Canada	178.6	58.2	10.3	7.3	25.2	214.1
Iran	138.4	948.2	168.0	1.5	5.2	311.6
Iraq	115.0	111.9	19.8	0.0	0.0	134.8
Kuwait	104.0	56.0	9.9	0.0	0.0	113.9
United Arab Emirates	97.8	214.4	38.0	0.0	0.0	135.8
Venezuela	87.0	166.3	29.5	0.5	1.8	118.3
Russia	60.0	1,680.0	297.7	173.1	597.2	954.9
Libya	41.5	54.4	9.6	0.0	0.0	51.1
Nigeria	36.2	184.0	32.6	0.2	0.7	69.5
Kazakhstan	30.0	100.0	17.7	34.5	119.0	166.7
United States	21.3	237.7	42.1	262.7	906.3	969.7
China	16.0	80.0	14.2	126.2	435.4	465.6
Qatar	15.2	905.3	160.4	0.0	0.0	175.6
Brazil	12.2	12.9	2.3	7.8	26.9	41.4
Algeria	12.2	159.0	28.2	0.1	0.2	40.6
Mexico	11.7	13.2	2.3	1.3	4.5	18.5
Angola	9.0	9.5	1.7	0.0	0.0	10.7
Azerbaijan	7.0	30.0	5.3	0.0	0.0	12.3
Norway	6.9	79.1	14.0	0.0	0.0	20.9
Turkmenistan	0.6	100.0	17.7	0.0	0.0	18.3
Indonesia	4.0	106.0	18.8	4.8	16.5	39.2
Malaysia	4.0	83.0	14.7	0.0	0.0	18.7
Uzbekistan	0.6	65.0	11.5	3.3	11.4	23.5
Egypt	3.7	58.5	10.4	0.0	0.1	14.1
Australia and New Zealand	1.6	31.2	5.5	85.1	293.6	300.7
India	5.6	38.0	6.7	62.3	214.9	227.3

Source: Energy Information Administration, http://www.eia.doe.gov/emeu/international/contents.html.

Note: All values are for 2007 or latest available data. Countries are listed in order of oil reserve ranking.

a. Oil and natural gas reserve numbers are from the EIA tables, using only the Oil & Gas Journal values.

Using only proved reserve numbers for the United States and other nations shows that the United States remains among the top nations in proved reserves of all fossil fuels taken together.

Values for technically recoverable oil and natural gas resources estimated by the USGS contain greater uncertainty than the statistics for proved reserves. Nevertheless, adding the estimates for undiscovered technically recoverable oil and natural gas provides a more inclusive estimate of total endowment of technically recoverable fossil fuels. **Table 6** adds technically recoverable oil and natural gas resources to the proved reserve figures of **Table 5** to provide a more complete tabulation of technically recoverable fossil fuels. Values for total fossil fuels in **Table 6** include the estimates for coal reserves in the first column but do not include any estimates for undiscovered coal resources; those data simply do not exist in any consistent form for various nations.

As an example of how such undiscovered coal resources might affect the ultimate total endowment of fossil fuels, the U.S. coal resource estimates do not include some potentially massive deposits of coal that exist in northwestern Alaska. These currently inaccessible coal deposits have been estimated to be more than 3,200 billion short tons of coal.[46] Only a portion of that coal would likely be technically recoverable even if development were pursued but, nevertheless, it suggests other fossil fuel deposits in many parts of the world that have not been estimated or are not available for extraction.

---

[46] Romeo M. Flores, Gary D. Stricker, and Scott A. Kinney, "Alaska Coal Resources and Coalbed Methane Potential," U.S. Geological Survey Bulletin 2198, 2003.

Table 6. Reserves of Fossil Fuels Plus Technically Recoverable Undiscovered Oil and Natural Gas

	Total Fossil Fuel Proved Reserves (from **Table 5**)	Estimated Undiscovered Oil and Gas (Billion BOE, USGS[a])	Total Fossil Fuels[b] (Billion BOE)
Saudi Arabia	311.6	231.3	543.0
Canada	214.1	7.2	221.3
Iran	311.6	114.3	425.9
Iraq	134.8	68.4	203.3
Kuwait	113.9	4.7	118.6
United Arab Emirates	135.8	16.2	152.0
Venezuela	118.3	38.1	156.4
Russia	954.9	293.7	1,248.6
Libya	51.1	10.8	61.9
Nigeria	69.5	63.4	133.0
Kazakhstan	166.7	33.7	200.4
United States	969.7	351.5	1,321.3
China	465.6	28.4	494.0
Qatar	175.6	12.1	187.7
Brazil	41.4	79.4	120.8

a. U.S. Geological Survey, World Petroleum Assessment, 2000, http://energy.cr.usgs.gov/WEcont/WEMap.pdf; mean values of estimates are used for foreign countries. U.S. number is taken from values in **Table 3**.

b. Total Fossil Fuels in this table include the technically recoverable reserves of oil, natural gas, and coal from **Table 5**, plus estimates of undiscovered oil and natural gas from the USGS World Petroleum Assessment. No global estimates of undiscovered coal exist.

A meaningful comparison of the ultimate endowments of fossil fuels among nations would include the important deposits of oil, natural gas, and coal that are lower on the resource pyramid in **Figure 1**, and that might be exploited in the future given the appropriate technology, economic viability, and environmental acceptability. However, the uncertainty associated with estimates of those deposits is too great to produce meaningful comparisons. For example, the values in **Table 6** could be amended further by including estimates of oil shale or methane hydrate resources, but the final tally would have very little meaning considering the difficulties in estimating those resources. The United States has considerable amounts of fossil fuels, both conventional and unconventional, both discovered and undiscovered, that are not currently economically viable. However, it is likely that other nations contain similar deposits but lack any comprehensive assessment of those resources.

U.S. Production and Consumption of Oil, Natural Gas, and Coal

To provide some scale for the reserves and undiscovered resource values reported above, **Table 7** lists production and consumption of oil, natural gas, and coal by the United States. For a more complete summary of U.S. energy supply and demand, see CRS Report R40187, *U.S. Energy: Overview and Key Statistics*, by Carl E. Behrens and Carol Glover.

Table 7. United States Annual Consumption of Oil, Natural Gas, and Coal

Values are for year-end, 2008

	Production	Consumption
Oil	2.46 billion barrels/year (2.46 billion BOE)	7.1 billion barrels/year (7.1 billion BOE)
Natural Gas	20.6 trillion cubic feet/year (3.7 billion BOE)	23.2 trillion cubic feet/year (4.1 billion BOE)
Coal	1.17 billion short tons/year (4.0 billion BOE)	1.04 billion short tons/year (3.6 billon BOE)

Source: Energy Information Administration, http://www.eia.doe.gov/.

Notes: Natural gas is reported on a dry basis, BOE = barrels of oil equivalent.

Appendix. Definition of Terms

Reserves and Resources Terms

Definitions of terms taken from U.S. Department of the Interior, Survey of Available Data on OCS Resources and Identification of Data Gaps, Report to the Secretary, OCS Report MMS 2009-015, Appendix A, List of Terms Used, http://www.doi.gov/ocs/report.pdf.

Proved reserves. The quantities of hydrocarbons estimated with reasonable certainty to be commercially recoverable from known accumulations under current economic conditions, operating methods, and government regulations. Current economic conditions include prices and costs prevailing at the time of the estimate. Estimates of proved reserves do not include reserves appreciation.

Reserves. The quantities of hydrocarbon resources anticipated to be recovered from known accumulations from a given date forward. All reserve estimates involve some degree of uncertainty.

Reserves appreciation. The observed incremental increase through time in the estimates of reserves (proved and unproved) of an oil and/or natural gas field as a consequence of extension, revision, improved recovery, and the additions of new reservoirs.

Resources. Concentrations in the earth's crust of naturally occurring liquid or gaseous hydrocarbons that can conceivably be discovered and recovered.

Undiscovered resources. Resources postulated, on the basis of the geologic knowledge and theory, to exist outside of known fields or accumulations.

Undiscovered technically recoverable resources (UTRR). Oil and gas that may be produced as a consequence of natural pressure, artificial lift, pressure maintenance, or other secondary recovery methods, but without any consideration of economic viability. They are primarily located outside of known fields.

Undiscovered economically recoverable resources (UERR). The portion of the undiscovered technically recoverable resources that is economically recoverable under imposed economic and technologic conditions.

Unproved reserves. Quantities of hydrocarbon resources that are assessed based on geologic and engineering information similar to that used in developing estimates of proved reserves, but technical, contractual, economic, or regulatory uncertainty precludes such reserves from being classified as proved.

Key Terms Used in Oil Statistics

Acquisitions	The volume of proved reserves gained by the purchase of existing fields or properties, from the date of purchase or transfer.
Adjustments	The quantity which preserves an exact annual reserves balance within each State or State subdivision of the following form:
	Adjustments + Revision Increases - Revision Decreases - Sales + Acquisitions + Extensions + New Field Discoveries + New Reservoir Discoveries in Old Fields - Report Year Production = Published Proved Reserves at End of Report Year
	These adjustments are the yearly changes in the published reserve estimates that cannot be attributed to the estimates for other reserve change categories because of the survey and statistical estimation methods employed. For example, variations as a result of changes in the operator frame, different random samples or imputations for missing or unreported reserve changes, could contribute to adjustments.
Crude Oil	A mixture of hydrocarbons that exists in the liquid phase in natural underground reservoirs and remains liquid at atmospheric pressure after passing through surface separating facilities. Crude oil may also include:
	Small amounts of hydrocarbons that exist in the gaseous phase in natural underground reservoirs but are liquid at atmospheric pressure after being recovered from oil well (casinghead) gas in lease separators, and that subsequently are comingled with the crude stream without being separately measured.
	Small amounts of non-hydrocarbons produced with the oil.
	When a State regulatory agency specifies a definition of crude oil which differs from that set forth above, the State definition is to be followed.
Extensions	The reserves credited to a reservoir because of enlargement of its proved area. Normally the ultimate size of newly discovered fields, or newly discovered reservoirs in old fields, is determined by wells drilled in years subsequent to discovery. When such wells add to the proved area of a previously discovered reservoir, the increase in proved reserves is classified as an extension.
New Field Discoveries	The volumes of proved reserves of crude oil, natural gas and/or natural gas liquids discovered in new fields during the report year.
New Reservoir Discoveries in Old Fields	The volumes of proved reserves of crude oil, natural gas, and/or natural gas liquids discovered during the report year in new reservoir(s) located in old fields.
Production, Crude Oil	The volumes of crude oil which are extracted from oil reservoirs during the report year. These volumes are determined through measurement of the volumes delivered from lease storage tanks, (i.e., at the point of custody transfer) with adjustment for (1) net differences between opening and closing lease inventories, and for (2) basic sediment and water. Oil used on the lease is considered production.

Proved Reserves of Crude Oil	Proved reserves of crude oil as of December 31 of the report year are the estimated quantities of all liquids defined as crude oil, which geological and engineering data demonstrate with reasonable certainty to be recoverable in future years from known reservoirs under existing economic and operating conditions.

Reservoirs are considered proved if economic producibility is supported by actual production or conclusive formation test (drill stem or wire line), or if economic producibility is supported by core analyses and/or electric or other log interpretations. The area of an oil reservoir considered proved includes: (1) that portion delineated by drilling and defined by gas—oil and/or gas—water contacts, if any; and (2) the immediately adjoining portions not yet drilled, but which can be reasonably judged as economically productive on the basis of available geological and engineering data. In the absence of information on fluid contacts, the lowest known structural occurrence of hydrocarbons is considered to be the lower proved limit of the reservoir.

Volumes of crude oil placed in underground storage are not to be considered proved reserves.

Reserves of crude oil which can be produced economically through application of improved recovery techniques (such as fluid injection) are included in the "proved" classification when successful testing by a pilot project, or the operation of an installed program in the reservoir, provides support for the engineering analysis on which the project or program was based.

Estimates of proved crude oil reserves do not include the following: (1) oil that may become available from known reservoirs but is reported separately as "indicated additional reserves"; (2) natural gas liquids (including lease condensate); (3) oil, the recovery of which is subject to reasonable doubt because of uncertainty as to geology, reservoir characteristics, or economic factors; (4) oil that may occur in undrilled prospects; and (5) oil that may be recovered from oil shales, coal, gilsonite, and other such sources. It is necessary that production, gathering or transportation facilities be installed or operative for a reservoir to be considered proved. |
| **Revisions** | Changes to prior year-end proved reserves estimates, either positive or negative, resulting from new information other than an increase in proved acreage (extension). Revisions include increases of proved reserves associated with the installation of improved recovery techniques or equipment. They also include correction of prior report year arithmetical or clerical errors and adjustments to prior year-end production volumes to the extent that these alter reported prior year reserves estimates. |
| **Sales** | The volume of proved reserves deducted from an operator's total reserves when selling an existing field or property, during the calendar year. |

Source: EIA, http://tonto.eia.doe.gov/dnav/pet/TblDefs/pet_crd_pres_tbldef2.asp.

Key Terms Used in Natural Gas Statistics

Dry Natural Gas	Natural gas which remains after: (1) the liquefiable hydrocarbon portion has been removed from the gas stream (i.e., gas after lease, field, and/or plant separation); and (2) any volumes of non-hydrocarbon gases have been removed where they occur in sufficient quantity to render the gas unmarketable. (Note: Dry natural gas is also known as consumer-grade natural gas. The parameters for measurement are cubic feet at 60 degrees Fahrenheit and 14.73 pounds per square inch absolute.)
Natural Gas Associated-Dissolved	The combined volume of natural gas which occurs in crude oil reservoirs either as free gas (associated) or as gas in solution with crude oil (dissolved).
Natural Gas Liquids	Those hydrocarbons in natural gas which are separated from the gas through the processes of absorption, condensation, adsorption, or other methods in gas processing or cycling plants. Generally such liquids consist of propane and heavier hydrocarbons and are commonly referred to as condensate, natural gasoline, or liquefied petroleum gases. Where hydrocarbon components lighter than propane are recovered as liquids, these components are included with natural gas liquids.
Natural Gas Non-associated	Natural gas not in contact with significant quantities of crude oil in a reservoir.
Natural Gas, Wet After Lease Separation	The volume of natural gas remaining after removal of lease condensate in lease and/or field separation facilities, if any, and after exclusion of non-hydrocarbon gases where they occur in sufficient quantity to render the gas unmarketable. Natural gas liquids may be recovered from volume of natural gas, wet after lease separation, at natural gas processing plants.
Proved Reserves of Natural Gas	Proved reserves of natural gas as of December 31 of the report year are the estimated quantities which analysis of geological and engineering data demonstrate with reasonable certainty to be recoverable in future years from known reservoirs under existing economic and operating conditions.
	Reservoirs are considered proved if economic producibility is supported by actual production or conclusive formation test (drill stem or wire line), or if economic producibility is supported by core analyses and/or electric or other log interpretations.
	The area of a gas reservoir considered proved includes: (1) that portion delineated by drilling and defined by gas—oil and/or gas—water contacts, if any; and (2) the immediately adjoining portions not yet drilled, but which can be reasonably judged as economically productive on the basis of available geological and engineering data. In the absence of information on fluid contacts, the lowest known structural occurrence of hydrocarbons is considered to be the lower proved limit of the reservoir.
	Volumes of natural gas placed in underground storage are not to be considered proved reserves.
	For natural gas, wet after lease separation, an appropriate reduction in the reservoir gas volume has been made to cover the removal of the liquefiable portions of the gas in lease and/or field separation facilities and the exclusion of non-hydrocarbon gases where they occur in sufficient quantity to render the gas unmarketable.
	For dry natural gas, an appropriate reduction in the gas volume has been made to cover the removal of the liquefiable portions of the gas in lease and/or field separation facilities, and in natural gas processing plants, and the exclusion of non-hydrocarbon gases where they occur in sufficient quantity to render the gas unmarketable.
	It is not necessary that production, gathering, or transportation facilities be installed or operative for a reservoir to be considered proved. It is to be assumed that compression will be initiated if and when economically justified.

Source: EIA, http://tonto.eia.doe.gov/dnav/ng/TblDefs/ng_enr_sum_tbldef2.asp.

U.S. Fossil Fuel Resources: Terminology, Reporting, and Summary

Author Contact Information

Gene Whitney
Section Research Manager
gwhitney@crs.loc.gov, 7-7231

Carl E. Behrens
Specialist in Energy Policy
cbehrens@crs.loc.gov, 7-8303

Carol Glover
Information Research Specialist
cglover@crs.loc.gov, 7-7353

FEDERAL ENERGY REGULATORY COMMISSION

HIGH NATURAL GAS PRICES:
THE BASICS

"Given weather conditions this winter, supply overall appears to be adequate for U.S. needs through the winter, though prices could still spike on cold weather and local deliveries could be affected by local prices."

Winter 2005-2006 Natural Gas Market Update

January 19, 2006

EDITION 2   02•01•2006

FEDERAL ENERGY REGULATORY COMMISSION

Natural gas prices have fallen in recent weeks.

Natural gas prices rose significantly in 2005, trading for as much as $16.00 per MMBtu in national production-area spot markets after hurricanes Rita and Katrina. Since then, prices have fluctuated with changing weather – lower during a warm November, higher during cold weather in early December and lower again during mild weather through January. As of January 23, prices were at $8.25 per MMBtu at the Henry Hub, slightly higher in consuming areas of the East and lower in the rest of the country. These prices are much lower than peak prices in 2005, but still high by historical standards.

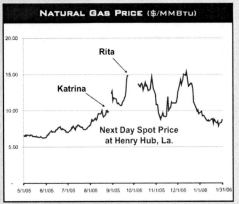

DERIVED FROM INTERCONTINENTAL EXCHANGE.

Natural gas prices have fallen to the point where oil prices appear to be holding them up. Except during weather-driven periods, gas prices normally fall between those for residual fuel oil (as a low) and heating oil (as a high). After the hurricanes, and again during cold weather in December 2005, gas prices rose above that range. Recently, however, the gas price has fallen near the bottom of that range and may not fall much further at current oil prices. In New York, for example, the gas price has not dropped far below residual fuel oil for any significant length of time in years.

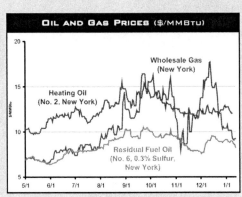

DERIVED FROM INTERCONTINENTAL EXCHANGE.

Production recovery in the Gulf of Mexico is strong.

Recovery efforts in the Gulf of Mexico have returned almost three-quarters of the supplies shut in by storm damage, both offshore and onshore, in Louisiana. Today, about 2.4 billion cubic feet (Bcf) remains shut-in, 1.8 Bcf offshore and 0.6 Bcf onshore in Louisiana. Combined with lower consumption because of weather, this recovery has alleviated most of the immediate supply concerns for the winter of 2005-2006.

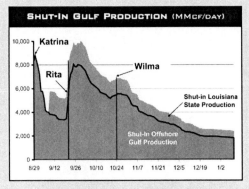

DERIVED FROM MINERALS MANAGEMENT SERVICE (MMS) AND THE LOUISIANA DEPARTMENT OF NATURAL RESOURCES.

FEDERAL ENERGY REGULATORY COMMISSION

The natural gas industry entered the winter with high levels of gas storage, despite the supply interruptions from the hurricanes. This was a sensible insurance policy against the possibility of a cold winter. As weather has remained warm in January, storage levels have remained high (near the top of the five-year range). Withdrawals from storage have been relatively low – consistent with warm weather and high prices. As a result, storage inventories are as high as they have been at this time of the year in any of the last five years.

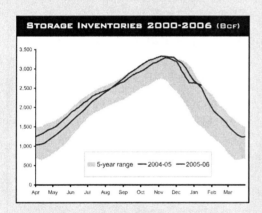

STORAGE INVENTORIES 2000-2006 (BCF)

5-year range — 2004-05 — 2005-06

DERIVED FROM ENERGY INFORMATION ADMINISTRATION THROUGH 1/20/06.

What is the Commission doing to respond to high gas prices?

The Commission is acting to make sure that natural gas prices reflect the true balance between supply and demand, and not artificial constraints in the system or the exercise of market power. It has:

- Strengthened its enforcement policy, adopting new market manipulation rules and implementing its new civil penalty authority (up to $1 million per day, per violation) in a manner to encourage a strong compliance program.

- Improved its ability to detect new market manipulation by implementing a Memorandum of Understanding with the Commodity Futures Trading Commission.

- Established a strong monitoring system for the market to make sure that the Commission detects any market manipulation that might arise during this time of high prices.

- Issued orders immediately after the hurricanes that let market participants move gas in new ways that avoided bottlenecks caused by the hurricane damage.

- Approved applications for a substantial expansion of the Nation's LNG terminals for receipt of imported gas.

- Shown a strong record of approving applications for new pipelines in a swift and environmentally responsible way.

- Approved changes to pipeline tariffs to help pipelines force compliance with operational flow orders to maintain system reliability.

It is important to remember that the Commission does not directly regulate most wholesale natural gas prices, which were decontrolled in 1989 to prevent the severe inefficiencies and shortages of the 1970s from recurring. It has no jurisdiction over retail gas prices.

3 02•01•2006

FEDERAL ENERGY REGULATORY COMMISSION

Where are gas prices headed from here?

Before the hurricanes, natural gas prices had reached levels that reflected an ongoing tightness between supply and demand. Despite the warm weather this winter, markets appear to expect natural gas prices to remain high in historical terms for some years to come.

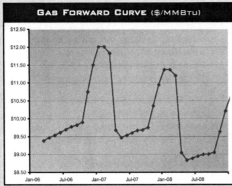

GAS FORWARD CURVE ($/MMBTU)

DERIVED FROM NYMEX DATA FROM 1/30/06.

In the near term, the best guess from the market is that prices will probably remain near current levels for the next month or two and then trend higher through the summer as the electric power load picks up. The relatively low price for the rest of this winter reflects high gas storage inventories resulting from warm weather so far. Forward prices for next winter are 30 percent to 40 percent higher than current prices. In future years, forward prices anticipate slightly lower prices each year, with recurring peaks in the winter.

These forward prices are not price predictions – only what the market is willing to trade at now for the future. In practice, weather will continue to be the most important factor in determining prices. A very hot summer or cold winter would tend to increase gas prices, while mild weather would do the opposite.

How will imports affect the American market?

The United States produces 84 percent of the natural gas it consumes. The United States imports the remainder from Canada and from overseas as liquefied natural gas (LNG). Canada is part of the same basic market with the United States and sees the same tightness between demand and supply that we do. For overseas shipments, the United States competes with other consuming countries in Europe and Asia. Even where spot markets are active (for example, in the United Kingdom), prices can be higher than in North America. This winter, Europe has seen very cold weather and much higher prices than the United States. As a result, where contracts permit, gas sellers have diverted LNG deliveries to Europe to take advantage of the high prices, and deliveries to the United States have been lower than last year.

In the future, more natural gas producing countries will be building plants to liquefy natural gas, increasing overall supply. As a result, LNG is likely to be an increasing part of natural gas supply in the United States.

What can you as a customer do about high natural gas prices?

You can cut your own natural gas bill through conservation – see (for example) the Department of Energy's website http://energysavers.gov for practical suggestions on conservation. When you conserve, you also help everyone else, since reduced consumption lowers stress on the whole gas industry and tends to lower prices.

FEDERAL ENERGY REGULATORY COMMISSION
888 FIRST STREET NE • WASHINGTON DC 20426

For further information on natural gas:
WWW.FERC.GOV/INDUSTRIES/GAS.ASP

If you have any questions please contact:
OFFICE OF EXTERNAL AFFAIRS • 202-502-6088
1-866-208-3372 (TOLL FREE) • 202-502-8371 (TTY)
CUSTOMER@FERC.GOV

Disclaimer: This document reflects the views of the Commission staff and not necessarily the views of the Commission itself or any individual Commissioner.

4 02•01•2006

Congressional Research Service

Natural Gas Markets: An Overview of 2008

William F. Hederman
Specialist in Energy Policy

March 31, 2009

Congressional Research Service

7-5700

www.crs.gov

R40487

CRS Report for Congress
Prepared for Members and Committees of Congress

Summary

In 2008, the United States natural gas market experienced a tumultuous year, and market forces appeared to guide consumers, producers and investors through rapidly changing circumstances. Natural gas continues to be a major fuel supply for the United States, supplying about 24% of total energy in 2008.

The year began with a relatively tight demand/supply balance, and this generated upward spot price movement. For the 2007-2008 heating season, the Energy Information Administration (EIA) reported a price increase of more than 30% (beginning to end of season). The key "benchmark" price for the United States, the Henry Hub spot price, generally rose through the first half of 2008 to a peak of $13.32 per million British thermal units (Btu) on July 3, 2008. By the end of 2008, the Henry Hub spot price had decreased 56% to $5.83 per million Btu, lower than the $7.83 per million Btu price on January 2, 2008.

Closer to consumers, the EIA average citygate price increased 47% from January to $12.08 per million Btu in July and then decreased to $7.94 per million Btu as of December, a 2% drop from the start of 2008. Residential consumers saw a 68% increase through July and then a decline that had December 5% above January's average price.

The supply outlook for the lower-48 states began a potentially important change in 2008. Onshore production in Texas and the Rocky Mountain region increased by 15%, especially because of the production of unconventional natural gas (e.g., deep shale gas).

Noteworthy events in 2008:

- The national natural gas market experienced an unusual price pattern in the first half of the year, with EIA reporting average citygate (delivery area) prices lower than Henry Hub (supply area) spot prices. The normal pattern is the prices in delivery areas, which include transportation costs, are higher than supply area prices.

- Lower-48 onshore natural gas production increased 10% to reach more than 20.5 trillion cubic feet, a level not achieved since 1974. This production, along with other factors such as the weakened economy, appear to have prevented the 350 Bcf of lost gas production due to Hurricanes Gustav and Ike in the Gulf of Mexico from increasing prices.

- Liquefied natural gas (LNG) imports decreased 54% from the record level in 2007. Average use was less than 10% of reported capacity at operational LNG import facilities. The Federal Energy Regulatory Commission (FERC) approved another 2 Bcf per day of new import facilities in 2008.

- Gas for power use decreased 2.4% from 2007 and electric power remained the largest end use category for natural gas consumption for a second year.

Going forward, current economic turbulence may contribute to natural gas market challenges, in terms of investment or attempts at market mischief. Vigilance in market oversight could grow in importance.

Congressional Research Service

Contents

Figures

Tables

Appendixes

Contacts

Introduction

Natural gas markets in North America had a tumultuous year in 2008. This contrasted with the relative stability of 2007. In early 2008, the market tightened and prices moved up. In the summer, supply area spot prices went much higher than in the past, then decreased through the rest of the year to end lower than at the start of the year.

This report examines current conditions and trends in the U.S. natural gas markets. Key market elements examined include prices, consumption, production, imports, and infrastructure. Expectations about the future, as reflected in recent official forecasts, are also incorporated here.

Natural gas remains an important and environmentally attractive energy source for the United States and supplied approximately 24% of total U.S. energy in 2008. Domestic supply has recently increased significantly. New developments in Alaska increase the likelihood that a pipeline from the North Slope will proceed, although uncertainty remains regarding this undertaking. The natural gas industry continues to attract capital for new pipeline and storage infrastructure to link shifting loads and supply sources.

In 2008, liquefied natural gas (LNG) imports decreased 54% from the record levels of 2007, decreasing already low utilization factors at import facilities. The Federal Energy Regulatory Commission (FERC) approved two more major import terminals in 2008.

Given the generally adequate functioning of natural gas markets, congressional attention may address development of new supply sources (such as deep shale gas), unexpected price volatility or behavior, or import and other supply issues. In the longer term, industry pressure for increased access to public lands for exploration and production may continue as a policy concern.

This report reviews key factors likely to affect market outcomes. These factors include weather, the economy, oil prices, and infrastructure development. **Table A-1** to **Table A-6** (in **Appendix A**) present selected highlight statistics that illustrate current market status.

Briefly, important developments in natural gas markets during 2008 include the following:

- Domestic natural gas production increased to 20.5 trillion cubic feet, the most since 1974.[1] Hurricanes Gustav and Ike reduced Gulf of Mexico production but did not affect market prices significantly.

- There was an unusual price pattern in the first half of 2008, with citygate (delivered) prices lower than Henry Hub spot prices. Citygate prices have seldom exceeded Henry Hub prices.

- The natural gas spot price at Henry Hub peaked on July 3, 2008, at $13.32 per million Btu and declined to under $6 by end of year.[2]

---

[1] EIA, *Natural Gas Monthly*, February 2009, Table 1, Annual Summary of Natural Gas Production.

[2] Federal Energy Regulatory Commission, *Market Snapshot*, January 2009, p.4.

- During the 2007-2008 heating season (October to March), average wellhead prices increased more than 30%, according to the U.S. Energy Information Administration (EIA) estimates.[3]

- Natural gas for power has reduced seasonal variation in use because gas-for-power peaks in summer, versus the total natural gas use peak in winter.

- The power generation sector used more natural gas than any other sector in 2008 and 2007.

- Storage levels towards the end of the 2007-2008 heating season dropped below five year averages. In the first storage report after the 2007-2008 heating season, working gas storage was at 1,234 billion cubic feet (Bcf) – the lowest level since April 30, 2004.[4] However, as of December 2008, working gas storage was at 2,840 Bcf.[5]

- LNG imports in 2008 dropped 54% from the 2007 record level of 77.1 billion cubic feet. The future outlook is uncertain. FERC approved 2 import facilities in 2008, with an import capacity increase of 2 billion cubic feet per day.

- Natural gas infrastructure development continued to advance, with more pipeline and storage projects successfully completed in 2007 and more underway in 2008.

- Industrial gas use had some growth in 2008, continuing increases since 2006.

Background

Unlike the global oil market, natural gas markets remain generally regional, with global trade in LNG growing. For the most part, North America has a continent-wide market that is integrated through a pipeline network that connects the lower-48 states, the most populous provinces of Canada, and parts of Mexico. Prices throughout this integrated market are influenced by demand (which may be influenced by weather, economic conditions, alternative fuel prices, and other factors), supply, and the capacity available to link supply sources and demand loads (transmission and distribution systems).

The U.S. natural gas market is the major component of the North American natural gas market. It accounts for about 81% of North American consumption and about 70% of North American supply.

The key price point in North America is Henry Hub. Henry Hub is a major pipeline hub near Erath, Louisiana, that is used as the designated pricing and delivery point for the New York Mercantile Exchange (NYMEX) gas futures contracts and other transactions. The price difference between other locations and Henry Hub is called the "basis differential." When there is spare capacity available to move natural gas from Henry Hub, or the Gulf of Mexico region in general, to the relevant price point area, the basis differential tends to be low, approximating the costs of fuel used to move the gas to the location. When capacity availability is tight, basis differentials

---

[3] EIA, *Natural Gas Weekly Update*, February 5, 2009.

[4] EIA, *Natural Gas Weekly Update*, February 5, 2009.

[5] EIA, *Natural Gas Navigator*, Underground Natural Gas Storage by All Operators, February 26, 2009.

can grow because the driving force can become the value of the natural gas at the delivery point, rather than the cost of getting the natural gas to that point.

Natural gas prices also incorporate costs for distributing the gas from the wholesale marketplace to retail customers. These rates are generally determined by state regulators and involve both (1) the approval of costs and rates of return and (2) the allocation of costs among customer classes (e.g., residential, commercial, industrial firm, industrial interruptible).

Although the North American natural gas market remains a distinct regional market, it is connecting to a global gas marketplace through international LNG trade. Oil prices still affect U.S. natural gas prices and this evolving relationship is discussed later in this report.

Market Conditions

The key elements of the market are prices, consumption, and supply. This section provides highlights from recent market developments relating to these factors.

Prices

The price stability of 2006 and 2007 ended in 2008. Early 2008 prices increased at a faster pace than in 2007. According to EIA figures, spot prices at Henry Hub increased about 70% from January 1 to July 3, 2008, peaking at $13.31 per million Btu (MMBtu).[6] The price then decreased to $5.83 per MMBtu by the end of December 2008,[7] ending the year about 28% below the start-of-year price. (See **Figure 1** for price graph.)

The U.S. Energy Information Administration reports producer price data for its wellhead price series. During the 2007-2008 heating season (October to March), EIA estimates the average wellhead price increased more than 30%, to $8.06 per MMBtu.[8] The highest monthly value was $10.52 per MMBtu in June.

The EIA citygate price series reflects the unit prices delivered to consuming areas.[9] The average U.S. citygate price increased $1.03 to $9.15 per thousand cubic feet (mcf) from 2007 to 2008.[10]

From 2006 to 2007, LNG import prices continued to decrease, from $7.19 per mcf to $7.07. (EIA full year 2008 LNG price data are not yet available.)

---

[6] EIA data is recorded as dollars per thousand cubic feet; the EIA provided conversion factor for 2008 (based on 2007 consumption) is 1 Cubic Foot = 1,028 Btu.

[7] Energy Information Administration (EIA), *Short-Term Energy Outlook*, February 2009, Table 5c.

[8] EIA, *Natural Gas Weekly Update*, February 5, 2009.

[9] The "citygate" is the transfer point from a high pressure natural gas pipeline to a local distribution company.

[10] EIA, *Natural Gas Monthly*, February 2009, Table 3.

Figure 1. U.S. Natural Gas Wholesale Price Overview

($ per million Btu)

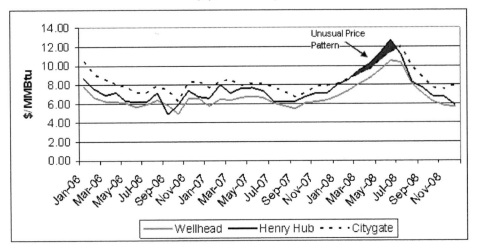

Source: EIA, *Natural Gas Monthly* (NGM), January 2009, Table 3 for citygate and wellhead; EIA, *Short-Term Energy Outlook*, February 2009, Figure 4 and archive, for Henry Hub.

Notes: See **Table A-1** for source data.

At the retail level, average U.S. residential natural gas prices were $13.52 per MMBtu in 2008, with a high of $19.74 in July. This average was about 5% increase from 2007. The average commercial price was $11.76 per MMBtu, an increase of about 6% from 2007. Industrial prices increased about 25% to $9.61 per MMBtu. Yearly totals are not yet available for natural gas sold for electric power; as of September 2008, prices had increased 25% versus September 2007 however. (See **Figure 2** for price chart)

An Anomalous Price Pattern

The spot price of natural gas is a key indicator of the price that producers or LNG importers are receiving for spot sales in the major producing area of the Gulf of Mexico. From there, the gas generally moves to markets to the north (e.g. Chicago), to the east (e.g. New York), or around the Gulf (e.g. Florida). This transmission to market generally leads to a transport cost add-on and a higher price at the delivery point.

Since the Henry Hub spot price was first reported in 1993 until 2008, this price has exceeded the EIA citygate (delivered price) in only eleven months (see **Figure A-1** in **Appendix A**). In the first half of 2008, the Henry Hub spot price exceeded the EIA reported citygate price in three consecutive months (April, May, and June).

The spot price at Henry Hub appears to have increased quickly in the first half of 2008, and this price at Henry Hub (a supply area price benchmark) actually exceeded the EIA estimated average citygate (the "delivery points" in consumption areas) price. CRS has found no discussion of this price anomaly in market monitoring documents from that period. One possible explanation for this anomaly is that the citygate price includes multi-month contracted-for supplies that would include natural gas from earlier months when prices were lower than the current spot price.

Greater production from shale areas near markets or storage gas withdrawal could be other explanations.

Figure 2. U.S. End Use Price Overview

($ per million Btu)

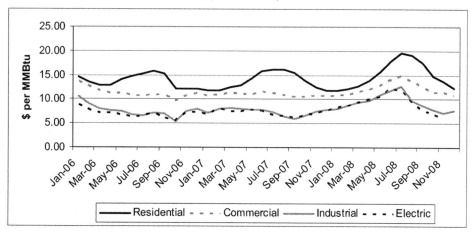

Source: EIA, Natural Gas Monthly, February 2009, Table 3.

Notes: See **Table A-3** for source data.

Consumption

Total U.S. consumption of natural gas grew almost 1% from 2007 to 2008, according to EIA. Power sector use of natural gas decreased about 2.8% in 2008. Commercial and residential sectors grew more than 3% each and industrial use (without lease and plant use) increased 0.3%. The power sector led end-use consumption for the first time in 2007 and maintained its position as the sector using the most gas in 2008. Power and industrial use were essentially equal for 2008. (**Table 1** shows the consumption data.)

Table 1. U.S. Natural Gas Consumption Overview

Billion cubic feet (Bcf)

Year	Residential	Electric	Commercial	Industrial	Other	Total
2006	4,368	6,222	2,832	6,512	1,750	21,685
2007	4,717	6,841	3,017	6,625	1,847	23,047
2008	4,879	6,649	3,126	6,644	1,944	23,242
% change 2006/07	8.0%	10.0%	6.5%	1.7%	N.A.	6.3%
% change 2007/08	3.4%	-2.8%	3.6%	0.3%	N.A.	0.8%

Source: EIA, *Natural Gas Monthly*, February 2009, Table 2 and CRS calculations.

Supply

U.S. natural gas supply comes from domestic production, pipeline imports, imported LNG, and net withdrawals from storage. In a major shift, domestic supplies increased more than 7% between 2007 and 2008. Total production for 2008 exceeded 20.5 trillion cubic feet, the most since 1974.[11] Net imports decreased in 2008.

The dry gas production increased 7.8% to 20,571 billion cubic feet in 2008,[12] reflecting in part the increase in drilling activity in response to price increases, as indicated in the natural gas rig count. The U.S. natural gas rig count has trended upward since 2002. In 2002, the average monthly rig count was about 600. The count reached 1,606 in September 2008, before decreasing to 1,366 late in the year.[13] Recent news accounts report that natural gas rigs have declined about 45% since September 2008, the most rapid decline since 2002.[14]

In 2008, U.S. consumers received most of their supply, 91%, from domestic production. Net imports (pipeline and LNG) decreased over 20% to 2,996 Bcf in 2008. Imports via pipeline from Canada decreased 5%. LNG imports in 2008 decreased 54% from 2007 after increasing 32%, to a record level, between 2006 and 2007.[15] (See **Table 2**.)

Table 2. U.S. Natural Gas Supply Overview
(Bcf)

Year	Dry Gas Production	Net Imports	Net Storage Withdrawals	Other/ balancing	Total
2005	18,051	3,612	52	296	22,011
2006	18,504	3,462	-436	155	21,685
2007	19,089	3,785	193	-19	23,047
2008	20,571	2,996	32	-357	23,242
% change 2006/07	3.2%	9.3%	N.A.	N.A.	6.3%
% change 2007/08	7.8%	-20.8%	N.A.	N.A.	0.8%

Source: EIA, *Natural Gas Monthly*, February 2009, Table 1 and CRS calculations

In 2008, available LNG supplies were sometimes bid away to European terminals for higher prices. Nevertheless, new U.S. LNG infrastructure went into service in 2008 and still more received approvals from FERC. To compete effectively for supply in the global LNG market, natural gas prices at the U.S. delivery points would have to increase to attract LNG deliveries.

---

[11] EIA, *Natural Gas Monthly*, February 2009, Table 1, Annual Summary of Natural Gas Production.

[12] EIA, *Natural Gas Monthly*, February 2009, Table 1.

[13] Baker Hughes, *North American Rotary Rig Count*, U.S. Oil & Gas Split.

[14] Bloomberg.com, March 16, 2009, available at http://www.bloomberg.com/apps/news?pid=20670001&refer=home&sid=a3PoNVnytrgo.

[15] EIA, *Natural Gas Imports by Country*, available at http://tonto.eia.doe.gov/dnav/ng/ng_move_impc_s1_m.htm.

Location of import facilities is an important factor in the value of landed LNG.[16] The United States appears more likely to be receiver-of-last-resort for LNG shipments in the near-to-mid term than to outbid Europeans, given the recent interruptions in Russian supplies. On the other hand, lack of storage in Europe and Asia may lead to continued U.S. receipts of LNG, even at relatively low prices, because new LNG export facilities serving the Atlantic Basin are expected to reach completion soon.

Table 3. Lower-48 LNG Overview
(Bcf/d)

Terminal	Average Deliveries 2008	Deliverability EOY 2008	Average Deliveries 2007	Deliverability EOY 2007
Cove Point, MD	N.A.	1.00	0.41	1.00
Everett, MA	N.A.	1.04	0.50	1.04
Elba Island, GA	N.A.	1.20	0.47	1.20
Lake Charles, LA	N.A.	2.10	0.69	1.80
Gulf Gateway, TX[a]	N.A.	0.50	0.05	0.50
Northeast Gateway, MA[a]	N.A.	0.80	N.A.	0.80
Freeport, TX	N.A.	1.50	N.A.	N.A.
Sabine, LA	N.A.	2.60	N.A.	N.A.
Total	0.96	10.74	2.11	7.34

Source: EIA, Short-Term Energy Outlook Supplement: U.S. LNG Imports – The Next Wave, January 2007, pp.9-10; FERC, North American LNG Terminals, Existing, Office of Energy Projects, February 6, 2009; EIA.

a.   Offshore

EIA forecasts an increase of less than 20 Bcf of LNG for 2009 to 369 Bcf.[17] In addition, an LNG import facility in eastern Canada largely focused on exporting to the United States was originally expected to enter service in 2008, but remains under construction. It may enter service in 2009.

Market Trends

There are several trends under way in natural gas markets of interest to policy makers. They include:

- strong lower-48 onshore production

- a decrease in seasonal demand swings

- strong gas-for-power use

- changing international trade in LNG

---

[16] This siting issue is discussed in greater detail in CRS Report RL32386, *Liquefied Natural Gas (LNG) in U.S. Energy Policy: Infrastructure and Market Issues*, by Paul W. Parfomak

[17] EIA, *Short-Term Energy Outlook*, February 10, 2009, p.5.

- continuing progress in natural gas infrastructure development

Strong Production

The natural gas supply picture for the lower-48 improved during 2008. Advances in unconventional gas production led to a 7.7% increase in lower-48 production, even though outer continental shelf (OCS) production lost almost 350 billion cubic feet due to hurricanes Gustav and Ike.

Figure 3. Estimated Recoverable Natural Gas for Select Shale Basins
(trillion cubic feet)

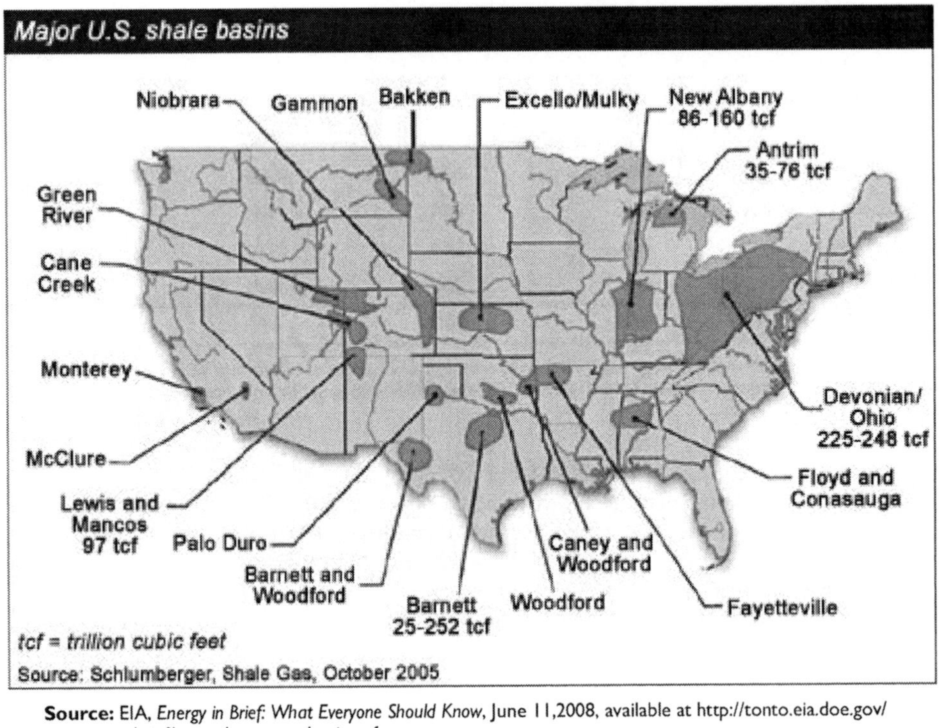

Major U.S. shale basins

tcf = trillion cubic feet

Source: Schlumberger, Shale Gas, October 2005

Source: EIA, *Energy in Brief: What Everyone Should Know*, June 11, 2008, available at http://tonto.eia.doe.gov/energy_in_brief/natural_gas_production.cfm.

The domestic supply has shifted from shallow Gulf of Mexico to deep Gulf of Mexico and unconventional sources in Texas, the Rocky Mountains and elsewhere.[18] As new resources grow in importance, the need for increased gas leasing of on- and offshore federal lands is evolving.[19]

---

[18] Conventional natural gas supplies are produced by conventional drilling and extraction. Unconventional gas involves more advanced technology, such as extraction of methane from coal beds or from tight formations and shales requiring fracturing and other techniques.

[19] For more discussion, see CRS Report RL33493, *Outer Continental Shelf: Debate Over Oil and Gas Leasing and Revenue Sharing*, by Marc Humphries.

The U.S. natural gas reserve base has recently continued to increase. EIA reserves and production data indicate that the latest reserves-to-production ratio[20] (2007) is 12.2, an increase from the prior year's ratio of 11.4 and 2000's ratio of 9.2.[21]

The Potential Gas Committee (PGC) is expected to release an assessment of the nation's natural gas supplies in the Spring of 2009. This will provide an authoritative update on the natural gas supply situation for the United States. The PGC consists of more than 100 "voluntary experts" from industry, academia, and government. They are primarily geologists or engineers recruited because of their experience preparing resource estimates within their area. It was created in 1964 to address conflicting predictions of long term gas supply at that time.[22]

Seasonality

Consumption of natural gas in the United States remains highly seasonal for three major sectors, reflecting the importance of space heating; residential and commercial use of natural gas peaks in winter. Reflecting the importance of air conditioning load and the role of natural gas as the marginal fuel source for power generation, electric power use of natural gas peaks in summer. (Industrial use is relatively stable throughout the year.)

Figure 4. Monthly Natural Gas Consumption: Total and Electric Power Use
(Tcf/month)

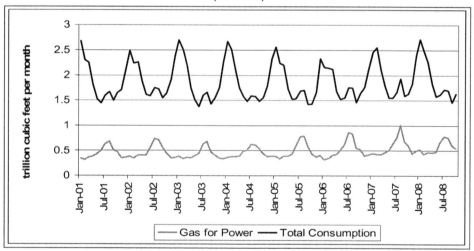

Source: EIA, *Natural Gas Navigator*, Consumption for End Use, December 2008.

Figure 4 illustrates that the combination of these seasonal patterns has led to a decrease in the overall seasonal swing and the development of a secondary peak in the summer due to gas-for-

---

[20] The reserves-to-production ratio divides the nation's proven reserve figure by the annual production to calculate this metric of supply inventory.

[21] EIA, *Dry Natural Gas Proved Reserves*, available at http://tonto.eia.doe.gov/dnav/ng/ng_enr_dry_dcu_NUS_a.htm.

[22] Potential Gas Committee, *History and Present Status*, available at http://inside.mines.edu/research/pga/aboutpgc.html.

power use. Interestingly, some continue to call for more storage because of the growing consumption of natural gas, thinking that higher consumption levels require more storage volume. The decrease in the seasonal swing, however, through a decrease in the high month volume and an increase in the low month volume, means that less storage may be capable of serving the annual seasonal cycling needs of the U.S. markets. Those trading natural gas may want additional storage for arbitrage uses, but the fundamental needs related to system reliability may decrease somewhat with a decrease in the difference between minimum and maximum consumption rates.

The secondary peak in gas for power was less in 2008 than in the previous years. This is explained by a decrease in the number of cooling degree days for summer 2008, ending a trend of increasing cooling degree days for several years. (See **Table A-7** for data.)

Another noteworthy seasonal feature observed by EIA was that as of 2007, natural gas price volatility was "considerably higher" in colder months than in other times.[23] The pattern in 2008, however, appears contrary to this observation.

Gas-for-Power Use

From 2006 to 2007 deliveries to electric power customers increased by 615 Bcf, more than 45% of the consumption growth for the year. For the first time, electric power use of natural gas became the largest end use sector for natural gas.[24] In 2008, gas-for-power use declined but this sector remained the largest gas user.

The relative increase in electric generator use of natural gas during winter is also significant. In 2007, FERC's Division of Energy Market Oversight noted that November-March volumes increased 14% between winter 2005/06 and winter 2006/07.[25] More recent data are not yet available.

Industrial Gas Use

Industrial gas use in 2006 was approximately 13% lower than the 7,507 Bcf consumed in 2002. In 2007, industrial use increased by 2% over the 2006 level. In 2008, industrial gas increased about 0.3%.

Global LNG Trade

LNG monthly imports in 2008 varied from a high of 35.4 Bcf in August to a low of 22.8 Bcf in November. Because little of the LNG is imported under long term contracts, U.S. importers compete on the global LNG spot market for deliveries.

In December 2008, European natural gas prices were in the $7.80-$9.50 per MMBtu range. New England citygates were at $10.06 per MMBtu and Henry Hub was at $8.85 per MMBtu. Thus,

---

[23] EIA, *An Analysis of Price Volatility in Natural Gas Markets*, August 2007, p.2.

[24] This excludes lease and plant gas use from the industrial sector, where it sometimes is included.

[25] FERC, Division of Market Oversight, *Winter 2007/2008 Energy Market Assessment*, Item No.: A-3, October 18, 2007, "Electric Generators Using More Winter Gas," no page.

some import points could compete successfully in the global spot market for LNG and others could not.[26] There is excess physical capacity at existing LNG import facilities to handle about ten times the imports of 2008.

Infrastructure Progress

The North American natural gas industry has continued to add new infrastructure to the system. As noted in **Table 4** and **Table 5**, FERC identifies facilities that went into service in 2007 and 2008. These facilities appear responsive to serving fundamental market needs, such as new capacity from the growing production areas.

Table 4. Infrastructure Completed in 2007

Type of Project	Number of Projects	Capacity
Pipelines	more than 50	14.9 Bcf/d
LNG import terminals	0	—
Storage facilities	9	1.8 Bcf/d

Source: EIA, Office of Oil and Gas, *Natural Gas Year-In-Review,*, March 2008, p.5 and FERC, *Winter 2007/2008 Energy Market Assessment*, Item No.: A-3, October 18, 2007, "What has been placed into service," no page.

Table 5. Infrastructure Completed in 2008

Type of Project	Number of Projects	Capacity
Pipelines	N.A.[a]	15.4 Bcf/d
LNG import terminals	3[b]	5.7 Bcf/d
Storage Facilities	N.A.[a]	4.6 Bcf/d

Source: FERC, by CRS request.

a.   Despite CRS requests for an update on the 2007 project data, FERC has not provided these figures.

b.   These new LNG import terminals are Northeast Gateway Deepwater Port, Freeport Texas and Sabine, LA. Additionally, the Lake Charles, LA facility was expanded in 2008; that new capacity is included in the 5.7 Bcf/d.

Forecasts

Given the major economic shock to the energy markets during 2008, forecasts mean even less today than they usually do.

In its Short Term Energy Outlook, EIA forecasts a 1% decrease in natural gas use for 2009, relative to 2008 because of weak economic conditions. A small increase in residential use will be offset by a larger decrease in commercial, industrial, and electric power demand. EIA forecasts increased U.S. production of less than 1%, primarily because of lower natural gas prices and

---

[26] FERC, Division of Market Oversight, Office of Enforcement, *OE Energy Market Snapshot*, February 6, 2009, National Version, p. 13.

decreased demands because of the economic downturn. EIA expects LNG imports to increase 20% in 2009, rebounding somewhat from the 42% drop in 2008. However, low summer demand in Europe could mean the United States will receive more LNG than forecast. EIA forecasts average Henry Hub prices to decrease roughly 35% in 2009, to $5.62 per MMBtu, due to weak economic conditions, increased U.S. production, and lower demand.

Uncertainties

EIA's forecast of natural gas prices depends on certain assumptions embedded in the forecast. These factors have uncertainty associated with them, as discussed next.

Weather

Weather affects natural gas consumption through both the significant space heating loads in the residential and commercial sectors and the cooling load served by gas-fired power generation. EIA incorporates National Oceanic Atmospheric Administration (NOAA) weather forecasts in its short and long term forecasts. To the extent that actual heating degree days exceed the temperature scenario from NOAA, that will tend to increase demand for natural gas in the heating season and increase prices for natural gas during those periods. Similarly, if the actual cooling degree day requirements exceed those incorporated in the EIA scenario, then this will increase natural gas use in the cooling season via increased gas-fired power for air conditioning and increase the price for natural gas in the relevant cooling season.

Oil Prices

Natural gas prices and oil prices have long had a correlation. As the extent of oil/gas fuel switching has declined, this linkage has changed. For many years, the key relationship was between the delivered price of natural gas to New York and the price of alternative fuels (residual fuel oil, No. 6, or distillate fuel oil, No. 2). Historically, when natural gas prices in the northeast market area reached a price at which a significant industrial or utility load could save fuel costs by switching to a petroleum alternative, the users would switch fuel. This would limit the price to this alternative. There was a time when almost 1 trillion cubic feet of natural gas load could switch. As illustrated in **Figure 5**, natural gas prices have generally been lower than either alternative fuel since the beginning of 2007. The exceptions have been limited periods of extreme cold in the Northeast. This suggests a delinkage in prices that may have resulted from environmental restrictions limiting the quantity of fuel-switchable load.

The convergence of No. 6 oil and natural gas prices appears more likely to be due to oil prices falling more drastically than natural gas prices in the second half of 2008.

Figure 5. Comparison of Natural Gas and Competing Oil Product Prices

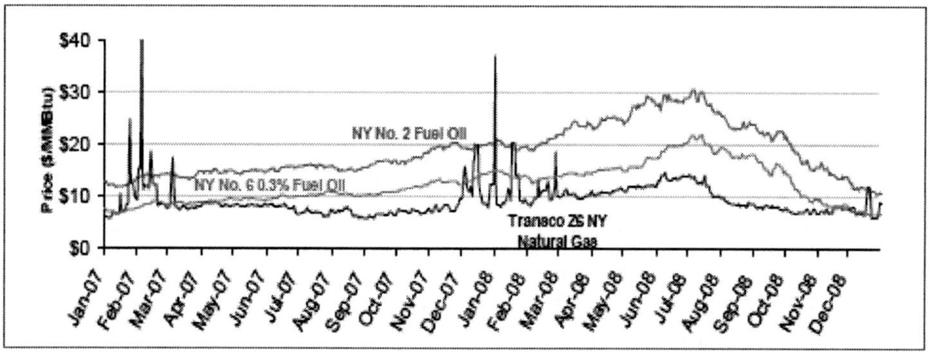

Source: FERC, Division of Market Oversight, *OE Energy Market Snapshot*, National Version - December 2008 data, January 2009, p.41

Economy

Economic growth affects consumers' demand for natural gas and their ability to purchase it. EIA appears to have incorporated an economic outlook that expects less growth than in its recent forecasts. Given the relative stability in the residential and commercial sector consumption, the changed economic outlook would most likely affect industrial and power generation natural gas use most directly.

Conclusion

Natural gas markets in North America continue to function well relative to other energy markets. Consumers and producers managed the tumultuous prices of 2008 without suffering major apparent damage.

This market appears to continue responding appropriately to price signals. New pipelines and storage facilities have been built where price differentials have indicated need and value for these facilities.

Current investment in LNG import capacity may prove excessive for the 2008-2009 heating season.

There is the potential, given the higher prices in summer than in the heating season, that retail customers may face prices higher than spot prices because of risk management contracts signed by local gas utilities during the 2008 period of high prices.

Weather and the overall economy remain important factors for natural gas demand and price levels. These factors remain uncertain and beyond human forecasting capability.

Appendix A. Selected Statistics

Table A-1. U.S. Natural Gas Wholesale Price Overview
($ per MMBtu)

Month	2008			2007		
	Henry Hub	Wellhead	Citygate	Henry Hub	Wellhead	Citygate
January	8.02	6.80	8.11	6.56	5.76	7.68
February	8.53	7.34	8.63	8.02	6.48	8.36
March	9.48	8.06	9.19	7.12	6.38	8.57
April	10.20	8.70	9.59	7.62	6.65	7.97
May	11.34	9.54	10.66	7.65	6.79	8.16
June	12.71	10.53	11.40	7.36	6.67	8.15
July	11.13	10.33	12.03	6.23	6.02	7.72
August	8.27	8.09	9.88	6.20	5.74	7.26
September	7.66	7.07	8.72	6.26	5.46	6.70
October	6.75	6.19	7.67	6.75	6.08	7.16
November	6.68	5.81	7.54	7.11	6.20	7.83
December	5.83	5.65	7.94	7.12	6.35	7.91
Average	8.88	7.84	9.28	7.00	6.22	7.79

Source: EIA, *Natural Gas Monthly*, February 2009, Table 3 for Wellhead and Citygate; EIA, *Short Term Energy Outlook*, February 2009, Figure 4 for Henry Hub.

Notes: EIA provides data in dollars per thousand cubic feet; EIA conversion factor for 2008 (based on 2007 consumption) is 1 Cubic Foot = 1,028 Btu.

Table A-2. U.S. Natural Gas Wholesale Price Overview

($ per mcf)

Month	2008			2007		
	Henry Hub	Wellhead	Citygate	Henry Hub	Wellhead	Citygate
January	8.25	6.99	8.34	6.75	5.92	7.89
February	8.76	7.55	8.87	8.24	6.66	8.59
March	9.74	8.29	9.45	7.32	6.56	8.81
April	10.49	8.94	9.86	7.83	6.84	8.19
May	11.65	9.81	10.96	7.87	6.98	8.39
June	13.06	10.82	11.72	7.57	6.86	8.38
July	11.45	10.62	12.37	6.40	6.19	7.94
August	8.51	8.32	10.16	6.37	5.90	7.46
September	7.88	7.27	8.96	6.44	5.61	6.89
October	6.94	6.36	7.88	6.94	6.25	7.36
November	6.87	5.97	7.75	7.31	6.37	8.05
December	5.99	5.81	8.16	7.32	6.53	8.13
Average	9.13	8.06	9.54	7.20	6.39	8.01

Source: EIA, *Natural Gas Monthly*, February 2009, Table 3 for Wellhead and Citygate; EIA, *Short Term Energy Outlook*, February 2009, Figure 4 for Henry Hub.

Figure A-1. Henry Hub and EIA Citygate Prices (1995-2008)

$ per thousand cubic feet

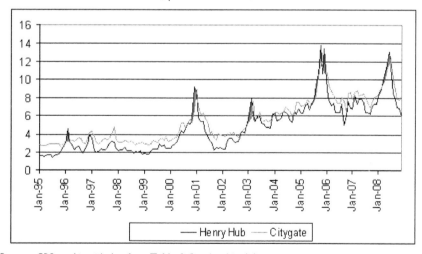

Source: CRS graphic with data from **Table A-2** and archived data.

Notes: Shaded area indicates times when Henry Hub spot prices exceeded citygate prices.

Natural Gas Markets: An Overview of 2008

Table A-3. U.S. End Use Price Overview

($ per MMBtu)

Month	2008				2007			
	Residential	Commercial	Industrial	Electric Power	Residential	Commercial	Industrial	Electric Power
January	11.77	10.76	7.97	8.25	11.76	10.84	7.14	6.86
February	12.10	11.04	8.68	8.66	11.79	10.93	8.01	7.94
March	12.62	11.46	9.37	9.30	12.51	11.50	8.17	7.43
April	13.91	12.11	9.75	9.99	12.91	11.20	7.92	7.55
May	15.58	12.87	11.02	10.66	14.21	11.20	7.89	7.74
June	17.82	14.02	11.74	12.26	15.76	11.55	7.77	7.59
July	19.65	15.01	12.71	11.83	16.20	11.31	7.35	6.82
August	19.10	13.68	9.68	9.08	16.19	10.88	6.40	6.61
September	17.45	12.68	8.67	7.81	15.51	10.60	5.95	6.18
October	14.82	11.50	7.86	6.83	13.86	10.51	6.67	6.85
November	13.36	11.15	7.00	6.48	12.47	10.74	7.43	7.07
December	12.30	11.00	7.63	N.A.	11.84	10.72	7.77	7.71
Average	15.04	12.27	9.34	9.20	13.75	11.00	7.37	7.20

Source: EIA, *Natural Gas Monthly*, February 2009, Table 3.

Table A-4. U.S. End Use Price Overview

($ per mcf)

Month	2008				2007			
	Residential	Commercial	Industrial	Electric Power	Residential	Commercial	Industrial	Electric Power
January	12.10	11.06	8.19	8.48	12.09	11.14	7.34	7.05
February	12.44	11.35	8.92	8.90	12.12	11.24	8.23	8.16
March	12.97	11.78	9.63	9.56	12.86	11.82	8.40	7.64
April	14.30	12.45	10.02	10.27	13.27	11.51	8.14	7.76
May	16.02	13.23	11.33	10.96	14.61	11.51	8.11	7.96
June	18.32	14.41	12.07	12.60	16.20	11.87	7.99	7.80
July	20.20	15.43	13.07	12.16	16.65	11.63	7.56	7.01
August	19.63	14.06	9.95	9.33	16.64	11.18	6.58	6.80
September	17.94	13.04	8.91	8.03	15.94	10.90	6.12	6.35
October	15.23	11.82	8.08	7.02	14.25	10.80	6.86	7.04
November	14.11	11.78	7.40	6.66	12.82	11.04	7.64	7.27
December	12.64	11.31	7.84	N.A.	12.17	11.02	7.99	7.93
Average	15.49	12.64	9.62	9.45	14.14	11.31	7.58	7.40

Congressional Research Service

Source: EIA, *Natural Gas Monthly*, February 2009, Table 3

Table A-5. Selected Natural Gas Market Regional Prices
($ per mcf)

	2008		2007		5-year range (2003-2007) (annual average)
	Annual Average	December	Annual Average	December	
Wellhead	8.07	5.87	6.39	6.53	4.88-7.33
NY citygate	10.07a	9.24	8.61	7.35	4.91-12.40
IL citygate	8.48	6.73	7.89	7.82	4.98-10.89
CA citygate	8.16	5.86	6.82	7.35	4.03-12.98
U.S. citygate	9.15	8.16	8.11	8.13	5.85-8.67

Source: EIA, *Natural Gas Prices*, Area: US, CA, IL, NY, available at http://tonto.eia.doe.gov/dnav/ng/ng_pri_sum_dcu_nus_m.htm.

a. Excluding November 2008; Data not available according to EIA.

Table A-6. Consumption of Natural Gas
(Trillion cubic feet)

	2008	2007	5 year range (2003-2007)
Total	23.2	23.0	21.7-23.0
Electric Power	6.6	6.8	5.1-6.8
Residential	4.9	4.7	4.4-5.1
Commercial	3.1	3.0	2.8-3.2
Industrial	6.7	6.6	6.5-7.2

Source: EIA, *Short Term Energy Outlook*, February 10, 2009, Table 5a.

Table A-7. Heating and Cooling Degree Days

	2008	2007	Normal
Heating Degree Days (Oct.-Jan.)	2,579	2,388	2,555
Cooling Degree Days (April-Sept.)	1,174	1,246	1,128

Source: EIA, *Short-Term Energy Outlook*, February 10, 2009; Figure 23 and 24.

Table A-8. Supply of Natural Gas
(Trillion cubic feet)

	2008	2007	5 year range (2003-2007)
U.S. Dry Gas Production	20.5	19.1	18.1-19.3
Net Imports	2.9	3.8	3.3-3.8

Source: EIA, *Short Term Energy Outlook*, February 10, 2009, Table 5a.

Appendix B. Acronyms

Bcf	Billion cubic feet
Bcf/d	Billion cubic feet per day
Btu	British thermal units
EIA	U.S. Energy Information Administration
FERC	Federal Energy Regulatory Commission
LNG	liquefied natural gas
mcf	thousand cubic feet
MMBtu	Million British thermal units
NOAA	National Oceanic and Atmospheric Administration
NYMEX	New York Mercantile Exchange
OCS	outer continental shelf
PGC	Potential Gas Committee
Tcf	Trillion cubic feet

Author Contact Information

William F. Hederman
Specialist in Energy Policy
whederman@crs.loc.gov, 7-7738

Acknowledgments

Stephen Meehan, an intern at CRS from the University of Notre Dame, made valuable contributions to the update of this report.

Order Code RL34508

CRS Report for Congress

Natural Gas Markets:
Overview and Policy Issues

May 23, 2008

William F. Hederman, Jr.
Specialist in Energy Policy
Resources, Science, and Industry Division

Congressional
Research
Service

**Prepared for Members and
Committees of Congress**

Natural Gas Markets: Overview and Policy Issues

Summary

The functioning of the natural gas market in 2007 appeared relatively stable and infrastructure development continued at an appropriate pace. A tighter demand/supply balance for 2008, however, has generated more upward spot price movement in this latest period. From the beginning to the end of the 2007-2008 heating season, the average wellhead price rose more than 30%, according to Energy Information Administration estimates. In the foreseeable future, weather and economic performance appear most likely to influence prices.

Natural gas provided about 22% of U.S. energy requirements in 2007. It will continue to be a major element of the overall U.S. energy market for the foreseeable future. Given its environmental advantages, it will likely maintain an important market share in the growing electricity generation applications, along with other clean power sources.

As Congress seeks to address energy security issues, the increasing importation of liquefied natural gas (LNG) is also a matter deserving careful attention. In 2007, LNG imports reached a record high and plans are to increase this fuel source.

This report provides an update to Congress on recent natural gas market developments and trends that have implications for important energy policy considerations, such as prices, natural gas use for power generation, and liquefied natural gas imports.

From 2006 to 2007, the average wellhead price reported to the U.S. Energy Information Administration (EIA) remained essentially unchanged at $6.39 per thousand cubic feet (mcf), down $0.01. The average citygate price increased about 3% to $6.98 per mcf. Domestic production grew, up about 0.8 trillion cubic feet, and domestic consumption increased more than 1 trillion cubic feet. This was the first increase in end-use consumption since 2004, according to EIA.

Natural gas use for electric power generation increased in 2007 by 10.5% and for the first time became the largest sector for natural gas consumption in the period covered by EIA records. Residential use increased 8.2%, with weather as a major factor. Commercial and industrial consumption also increased, by 6% and 2%, respectively. The industrial growth reversed a decline of 1.5% from 2005 to 2006.

On the supply side, onshore production in areas such as the Rocky Mountains and the Barnett Shales of Texas grew and liquefied natural gas (LNG) imports increased. LNG imports reached a record level of 0.8 trillion cubic feet.

EIA's Short Term Energy Outlook anticipates the Henry Hub spot price increasing almost 20% in 2008, reflecting strong demand, relatively low working gas in storage, and domestic production growth of almost 3%. The Henry Hub spot price did increase about 20% between the first quarter 2007 and first quarter 2008.

This report will be updated. This report supersedes CRS Report RL33714.

Contents

List of Figures

List of Tables

Natural Gas Markets: Overview and Policy Issues

Introduction

Natural gas markets in North America remained relatively stable compared to oil markets in 2007. The situation has tightened and prices have regained some upward momentum in 2008.

This report examines current conditions and trends in the U.S. natural gas markets. Key market elements examined include prices, consumption, production, imports, and infrastructure. Expectations about the future, as reflected in recent official forecasts, are also incorporated here.

Natural gas remains an important and environmentally attractive energy source for the United States. Its share of the power generation market has grown. Domestic supply has remained stable and even increased in recent months. New developments in Alaska increase the likelihood that a pipeline from the North Slope will proceed. The natural gas industry continues to attract capital for new pipeline and storage infrastructure. Liquefied natural gas (LNG) imports hit a record level in 2007, even as import facilities continue to have low utilization rates. Weather and the economy remain important factors in natural gas prices, as well.

Given the generally adequate functioning of natural gas markets, congressional interest in the near term is likely to focus on unexpected price volatility or importation (or other supply) issues. In the longer term, industry pressure for increased access to public lands for exploration and production is expected to continue receiving congressional attention.

This report reviews key factors likely to affect market outcomes. These factors include weather, the economy, oil prices, and infrastructure development. **Tables A1 to A4** (in the Appendix) present selected highlight statistics that illustrate current market status.

Briefly, important developments in natural gas markets include the following:

- The growth in natural gas for power generation has contributed to increased consumption and reduced seasonal variation in use because gas-for-power peaks in summer, versus the total natural gas use winter peak.

- In 2007, for the first time, the power generation sector used more natural gas than any other sector.

CRS-2

- The first quarter 2008 average spot price at Henry Hub increased 20% from the first quarter 2007 to $8.92 per thousand cubic feet (mcf), versus a 6% year-to-year increase from 2006 to 2007.[1] During the 2007-2008 heating season (October to March), average wellhead prices increased more than 30%, according to EIA estimates.[2]

- Storage levels towards the end of the heating season dropped below five year averages. In the first storage report after the 2007-2008 heating season, working gas storage was at 1,234 billion cubic feet — the lowest level since April 30, 2004.[3] This may indicate that slack in the supply side is decreasing.

- The United States had record LNG imports in 2007, and increased LNG imports appear likely.

- Natural gas infrastructure development continued to advance, with many pipeline and storage projects successfully completed in 2007 and more underway in 2008 (including LNG import facilities).

- Industrial natural gas use had a small rebound in 2007.

Background

Unlike the global oil market, natural gas markets remain generally regional, with global trade in LNG growing. For the most part, North America has a continent-wide market that is integrated through a pipeline network that connects the lower-48 states, the most populous provinces of Canada, and parts of Mexico. Prices throughout this integrated market are influenced by demand (which may be influenced by weather, economic conditions, alternative fuel prices, and other factors), supply, and the capacity available to link supply sources and demand loads (transmission and distribution systems).

The U.S. natural gas market is the major component of the North American natural gas market. It accounts for about 81% of North American consumption and about 69% of North American supply.

The key price point in North America is Henry Hub. Henry Hub is a major pipeline hub in Erath, Louisiana, that is used as the designated pricing and delivery point for the New York Mercantile Exchange (NYMEX) gas futures contract and

---

[1] Energy Information Administration (EIA), *Short-Term Energy and Summer Fuel Outlook*, April 2008, Table 5c.

[2] EIA, *Natural Gas Weekly Update*, April 10, 2008, p. 3.

[3] Ibid., p. 3.

CRS-3

other transactions. The price difference between other locations and Henry Hub is called the "basis differential." When there is spare capacity available to move natural gas from Henry Hub, or the Gulf of Mexico region in general, to the relevant price point area, the basis differential tends to be low, approximating the costs of fuel used to move the gas to the location. When capacity availability is tight, basis differentials can grow because the driving force can become the value of the natural gas at the delivery point, rather than the cost of getting the natural gas to that point.

Natural gas prices also incorporate costs for distributing the gas from the wholesale marketplace to retail customers. These rates are generally determined by state regulators and involve both (1) the approval of costs and rates of return and (2) the allocation of costs among customer classes (e.g., residential, commercial, industrial).

Although the North American natural gas market remains a distinct regional market, it is increasingly connecting to a global gas marketplace through international LNG trade. Oil prices still affect U.S. natural gas prices and this relationship is changing.

Market Conditions

The key elements of the market are prices, consumption, and supply. This section provides highlights from recent market developments relating to these factors.

Prices

Prices remained fairly stable between 2006 and 2007. Early 2008 prices have increased at a faster pace than in 2007. According to EIA figures, average spot prices at Henry Hub increased about 6% between 2006 and 2007. (See **Table 1** for price data.)

The U.S. Energy Information Administration (EIA) reports producer price data for its wellhead price series. This price remained stable from 2006 to 2007, decreasing by $0.01 to $6.39 per mcf in 2007 (average). During the 2007-2008 heating season (October to March), EIA estimates the average wellhead price increased more than 30%, to $8.29 per mcf.[4]

The EIA citygate price series reflects the unit prices delivered to consuming areas.[5] The U.S. average citygate price decreased $0.49 to $8.11 per mcf from 2006 to 2007.

Complete import price data for 2007 are not yet available from EIA. From 2005 to 2006, LNG import prices decreased 11.6% to $7.14 per mcf.

---

[4] Ibid., p.3.

[5] The "citygate" is the transfer point from a high pressure natural gas pipeline to a local distribution company.

CRS-4

Table 1. U.S. Natural Gas Wholesale Price Overview
($ per thousand cubic feet)

Month	2007			2006		
	Henry Hub	Wellhead	Citygate	Henry Hub	Wellhead	Citygate
January	6.75	5.92	7.89	8.92	8.02	10.80
February	8.24	6.66	8.59	7.76	6.86	9.34
March	7.32	6.56	8.81	7.10	6.44	8.81
April	7.83	6.84	8.19	7.38	6.38	8.29
May	7.87	6.98	8.39	6.45	6.24	7.99
June	7.57	6.86	8.38	6.39	5.78	7.39
July	6.40	6.19	7.94	6.35	5.92	7.40
August	6.37	5.90	7.46	7.35	6.56	8.10
September	6.26	5.61	6.89	5.04	6.06	7.68
October	6.94	6.25	7.36	6.02	5.09	6.42
November	7.31	6.37	8.05	7.61	6.72	8.47
December	7.32	6.53	8.13	6.90	6.76	8.66
Average	7.17	6.39	8.11	6.74	6.37	8.60

Source: EIA, *Natural Gas Monthly* (NGM), April 2008, Table 3, for citygate and wellhead; EIA, *Short-Term Energy Outlook*, May 2008, Table 2 and backup data, for Henry Hub 2007 and May 2007, Table 4 for Henry Hub 2006.

At the retail level, average U.S. residential natural gas prices were $13.01 per mcf in 2007, with a high of $16.65 in July. This average was a 5.4% decrease from 2006. The average commercial price was $11.31 per mcf, a decrease of 5.7% from 2006. Industrial prices decreased 4.6% on average to $7.58 per mcf. Natural gas sold for electric power use increased prices 2.8% to average $7.30 per mcf. See **Table 2** for these data.

CRS-5

Table 2. U.S. Retail Price overview
($ per thousand cubic feet)

Month	2007				2006			
	Residential	Commercial	Industrial	Electric power	Residential	Commercial	Industrial	Electric power
January	12.09	11.14	7.33	7.05	14.94	14.15	10.84	9.15
February	12.12	11.21	8.23	8.16	14.00	12.95	9.35	8.00
March	12.86	11.81	8.40	7.64	13.29	12.07	8.23	7.36
April	13.27	11.51	8.13	7.76	13.29	11.57	7.91	7.32
May	14.61	11.50	8.10	7.96	14.43	11.60	7.62	6.89
June	16.20	11.87	7.98	7.80	15.09	11.09	6.90	6.69
July	16.65	11.63	7.54	7.01	15.73	10.98	6.77	6.69
August	16.64	11.18	6.57	6.80	16.19	11.20	7.35	7.56
September	15.94	10.90	6.11	6.35	15.73	11.16	7.20	6.27
October	14.25	10.80	6.85	7.04	12.52	10.04	5.62	5.76
November	12.82	11.04	7.63	7.27	12.47	11.05	7.74	7.48
December	12.17	11.02	7.97	7.93	12.54	11.61	8.23	7.57
Aver	13.01	11.31	7.58	7.30	13.75	11.99	7.86	7.11

Source: EIA, NGM, April 2008, Table 3.

CRS-6

Consumption

Power sector use of natural gas increased most rapidly in 2007, followed by the weather-sensitive residential and commercial sectors. Total U.S. consumption of natural gas grew 6.5% from 2006 to 2007, according to EIA. Gas-for-power led the sectoral growth, increasing 10.5%. Residential consumption increased about 8.2%, primarily due to colder weather than 2006. The commercial and industrial (without lease and plant use) sectors also had modest increases in consumption, reversing drops in use in these sectors for 2005 to 2006. The power sector led end-use consumption for the first time in 2007.

Table 3 shows these consumption data.

Table 3. U.S. Natural Gas Consumption Overview
Billion cubic feet (Bcf)

Year	Residential	Electric power	Commercial	Industrial	Other	Total
2005	4,827	5,869	2,999	6,597	1,719	22,011
2006	4,368	6,222	2,835	6,495	1,733	21,653
2007	4,724	6,874	3,008	6,635	1,817	23,058
% change 2006/07	8.2%	10.5%	6.1%	2.2%	N.A.	6.5%

Source: EIA, NGM, April 2008, Table 2.

Supply

U.S. natural gas supply comes from domestic production, pipeline imports, imported LNG, and net withdrawals from storage. Both domestic and imported supplies increased between 2006 and 2007.

Dry gas production increased by 4.3% from 2006 to 2007, to 19,278 billion cubic feet (Bcf). This reflects the increase in drilling activity in response to price increases, as indicated in the natural gas rig count. The U.S. natural gas rig count has trended upward since 2002. In 2002, the average monthly rig count was about 600. Recent data show the count at approximately 1,500.[6]

---

[6] FERC, *Division of Market Oversight, OE, Winter 2007/2008 Energy Market Assessment*, Item No. A-3, October 18, 2007, "Gas Drilling Continues to Rise," no page, citing Baker Hughes and EIA.

CRS-7

The U.S. natural gas reserve base increased recently. EIA reserves and production data indicate the latest reserves-to-production ratio[7] (2006) is 11.4, an increase from the prior year's ratio of 11.1 and 2000's ratio of 9.2.[8]

In 2007, U.S. consumers received most of their supply, 84%, from domestic production. The domestic supply has shifted from shallow Gulf of Mexico to deep Gulf of Mexico and unconventional sources, in the Rocky Mountains and elsewhere.[9] As these new resources grow in importance, industry pressure for increased gas leasing of on- and offshore federal lands is likely to be a continuing issue.[10]

Net imports (pipeline and LNG) increased almost 10%, to 3,793 Bcf. Imports via pipeline from Canada increased 5%. LNG imports increased more than 32%, growing from 584 Bcf in 2006 to 771 Bcf in 2007.[11]

Table 4 show these data.

Table 4. U.S. Natural Gas Supply Overview
(Bcf)

Year	Dry Gas production	Net imports	Net storage withdrawals	Other/ balancing	Total
2005	18,051	3,612	52	296	22,011
2006	18,476	3,462	-436	151	21,653
2007	19,278	3,793	177	-193	23,055
% change 2006/07	4.3%	9.6%	N.A.	N.A.	6.6%

Source: EIA, NGM, April 2008, Table 1 and CRS calculations.

In 2007, the available spot LNG supplies were sometimes bid away to European terminals for higher prices. Nevertheless, new U.S. LNG infrastructure went into service in early 2008 and still more received approvals from the Federal Energy Regulatory Commission (FERC). To compete effectively for supply in the global LNG market, natural gas prices at the delivery points may have to increase further to

---

[7] The reserves-to-production ratio divides the nation's proven reserve figure by the annual production to get this metric of supply inventory.

[8] EIA, available at [http://tonto.eia.doe.gov/dnav/ng/ng_enr_dry_dcu_NUS_a.htm].

[9] Conventional natural gas supplies are produced by conventional drilling and extraction. Unconventional gas involves more advanced technology, such as extraction of methane from coal beds or from tight formations requiring fracturing and other techniques.

[10] For more discussion, see CRS Report RL33493, *Outer Continental Shelf: Debate over Oil and Gas Leasing and Revenue Sharing*, by Marc Humphries.

[11] EIA, NGM, April 2008, Table 4.

CRS-8

attract LNG deliveries. Location of import facilities is an important factor in the value of landed LNG.[12]

Table 5. Lower-48 LNG Overview
(Bcf/d)

Terminal	Deliver-ability EOY 2006	Average delivery 2006	Deliver-ability EOY 2007	Average delivery 2007	Estimated deliver-ability 2008
Cove Point, MD	1.0	0.32	1.0	N.A.	1.0
Everett, MA	0.725	0.48	1.035	N.A.	1.035
Elba Island, GA	1.2	0.40	1.2	N.A.	1.2
Lake Charles, LA	1.8	0.39	1.8	N.A.	1.8
Northeast Gateway, MA (offshore)	-	-	0.8	N.A.	0.8
Gulf Gateway, TX (offshore)	0.5	N.A.	0.5	N.A.	0.5
Freeport, TX	-	-	-	-	1.5
Sabine Pass, LA	-	-	-	-	2.6
Hackberry Cameron, LA	-	-	-	-	1.8

Source: EIA, *US Natural Gas Imports and Exports:2006*, March 2008, figure 1 and EIA, *Short-Term Energy Outlook Supplement: U.S. LNG Imports - The Next Wave*, January 2007, pp. 9-10.

EIA forecasts U.S. imports of 1,080 Bcf LNG for 2008, including regasified LNG from Mexico's Costa Azul terminal in Baja California.[13] In addition, an LNG import facility in eastern Canada largely focused on exporting to the United States is expected to enter service in 2008.

---

[12] This siting issue is discussed in greater detail in CRS Report RL32386, *Liquefied Natural Gas (LNG) in U.S. Energy Policy: Infrastructure and Market Issues*, by Paul Parfomak, updated January 31, 2006.

[13] EIA, *Short-Term Energy Outlook*, January 2007, p. 8.

CRS-9

Market Trends

There are several trends under way in natural gas markets of interest to policy makers. They include:

- a decrease in seasonal demand swings
- a growth in gas-for-power use
- a small rebound in industrial use of natural gas
- a growing international trade in LNG
- continuing progress in natural gas infrastructure development.

Seasonality

Consumption of natural gas in the United States remains highly seasonal for three important sectors. Reflecting the importance of space heating, residential and commercial use of natural gas peaks in winter. Reflecting the importance of air conditioning load and the role of natural gas as the marginal fuel source for power generation, electric power use of natural gas peaks in summer.

Figure 1. Monthly Natural Gas Consumption: Total and Electric Power Use

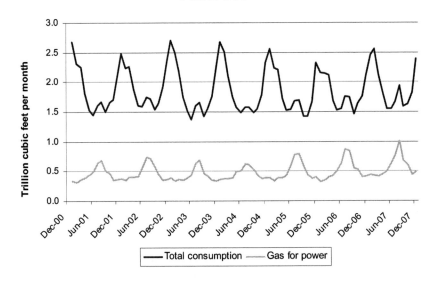

Source: CRS graphic, data from U.S. Energy Information Administration, Natural Gas Navigator, available at [http://tonto.eia.doe.gov/dnav/ng/ng_cons_sumc_duc_nus_m.htm]

Figure 1 illustrates that the combination of these seasonal patterns has led to a decrease in the overall seasonal swing and the development of a secondary peak in the summer due to gas-for-power use. Interestingly, while some continue to call for more storage because of the growing consumption of natural gas, the decrease in the seasonal swing (through a decrease in the high month volume and an increase in the

CRS-10

low month volume) means that less storage may be able to serve the annual cycling needs of the U.S. markets. Those trading natural gas may want additional storage for arbitrage uses, but the fundamental needs related to system reliability may decrease somewhat with a decrease in the difference between the minimum and maximum consumption rates.

Another noteworthy seasonal feature observed in 2007 by EIA found that natural gas price volatility is "considerably higher" in colder months than in other times.[14]

Increasing Gas-for-Power Use

The natural gas consumption sector with the greatest increase from 2006 to 2007 was electric power. Deliveries to electric power customers increased by 615 Bcf, more than 45% of the consumption growth for the year. For the first time, electric power use of natural gas became the largest end-use sector for natural gas.[15]

Perhaps even more striking is the relative increase in electric generator use of natural gas during winter. In 2007, FERC's Division of Energy Market Oversight noted that November-March volumes increased 14% between winter 2005/06 and winter 2006/07.[16]

Industrial Gas Use Rebound

Industrial natural gas use in 2006 was approximately 13% lower than the 7,507 Bcf consumed in 2002. In 2007, industrial use increased by 2% over the 2006 level. The decrease in price to industrial users may have played a role in this effect.

Global LNG Trade

In 2007, LNG monthly imports varied from a high of 98.7 Bcf in April to a low of 20.8 Bcf in December. Because little of the LNG is imported under long term contracts, U.S. importers compete on the global LNG spot market for deliveries.

In December 2007, European natural gas prices were in the $10.20-$10.66 per million Btu range. U.S. prices varied above and below this. New England citygates were at $12.16 per million Btu and Henry Hub was at $7.15 (the Algonquin citygate figure represents several citygates in New England). Thus, some import points could compete successfully in the global spot market for LNG and others could not.[17] There is excess physical capacity at existing LNG import facilities to handle more than three times the record imports of 2007.

---

[14] EIA, *An Analysis of Price Volatility in Natural Gas Markets*, August 2007, p.2.

[15] This excludes lease and plant gas use from the industrial sector, where it sometimes is included.

[16] FERC, Division of Market Oversight, *Winter 2007/2008 Energy Market Assessment*, Item No.: A-3, October 18, 2007, "Electric Generators Using More Winter Gas," no page.

[17] FERC, Division of Market Oversight, Office of Enforcement, *OE Energy Market Snapshot*, February 2008, National Version, p. 28.

CRS-11

Infrastructure Progress

During 2007, the North American natural gas industry continued its progress in adding new infrastructure to the system. According to EIA and the FERC, the following facilities went into service in the United States in 2007. These facilities appear responsive to serving fundamental market needs, such as new capacity from the growing Rocky Mountains production area. Although no new LNG facilities became operational in 2007, facilities are expected to achieve commercial operation in 2008.

Table 6. Infrastructure Complete in 2007

Type of project	Number of projects	Capacity
Pipelines	more than 50	14.9 Bcf/d
LNG import terminals	0	-
Storage facilities	9	1.8 Bcf/d

Sources: EIA, Office of Oil and Gas, *Natural Gas Year-In-Review*, March 2008, p.5 and FERC, *Winter 2007/2008 Energy Market Assessment, Item No.: A-3,* October 18, 2007, "What has been placed into service," no page.

Forecasts

There are a few noteworthy elements of recent EIA forecasts for the natural gas markets.

In its Short Term Energy Outlook, EIA forecasts a 1% increase in natural gas use for 2008, relative to 2007. Weather changes and economic conditions are the reasons EIA mentioned for the slowed growth. Prices are also likely to reinforce a short term slowdown in use. EIA forecasts record U.S. consumption of 23.4 trillion cf in 2009. EIA forecasts increased U.S. production in 2008 of almost 3%, primarily from growth in deepwater Gulf of Mexico and unconventional gas production. LNG imports are expected to decline about 14% from 2007. EIA forecasts supply area natural gas prices (Henry Hub) to increase almost 20% in 2008 to $8.34 per million Btu.

In EIA's long term forecast (through 2030), the reference case forecasts natural gas prices at the wellhead gradually decreasing to $5.27 per mcf during the 2015 to 2020 period before gradually increasing to $6.42 per mcf (2006 dollars) in 2030. EIA forecasts natural gas consumption growth to 24.4 trillion cubic feet (tcf) in 2015, declining to 23.4 tcf by 2030. Most of this increased use and the drop come from growth, then decline, in natural gas for power generation. EIA forecasts the arrival

CRS-12

of Alaska Natural Gas to the lower-48 via pipeline in 2020, with deliveries reaching 2.4 tcf per year by 2030. This is a two year delay from EIA's 2007 forecast.[18]

Uncertainties

EIA's forecast of gradual reductions in natural gas prices depends on certain assumptions embedded in the forecast. These factors have uncertainty associated with them, as discussed next.

Weather

Weather affects natural gas consumption through both the significant space heating loads in the residential and commercial sectors and the cooling load served by gas-fired power generation. EIA incorporates National Oceanic Atmospheric Administration (NOAA) weather forecasts in its short and long term forecasts. To the extent that actual heating degree days exceed the temperature scenario from NOAA, that will tend to increase demand for natural gas in the relevant heating seasons and increase prices for natural gas during those periods. Similarly, if the actual cooling degree day requirements exceed those incorporated in the EIA scenario, then this will increase natural gas use in the cooling season via increased gas-fired power for air conditioning and increase the price for natural gas in the relevant cooling season.

Oil Prices

Natural gas prices and oil prices have long had a correlation. As the extent of oil/gas fuel switching has declined, this linkage has changed. During 2007, as crude oil and petroleum product prices increased, relative prices for natural gas became lower than the historical pattern. In the recent past, natural gas and oil product price competition tended to exhibit itself most clearly around the New York metropolitan area, where there remained a fair amount of fuel switching capability. This fuel switching capability tended to keep natural gas prices at the New York citygate in a range bounded on the high side by distillate fuel oil prices and on the low side by low sulfur residual fuel oil prices. In 2007, the relevant natural gas prices tended to be below this range (see **Figure 2**).

---

[18] EIA, *Annual Energy Outlook 2008*, p.10.

CRS-13

Figure 2. Comparison of Natural Gas and Competing Oil Product Prices

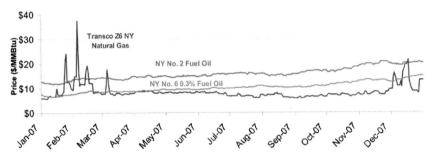

Source: FERC, Division of Market Oversight, Office of Enforcement, *OE Energy Market Snapshot*, National Version - December 2007 data, January 2008, p. 23.

The shift to outside this fuel price range suggests that the consumers had done all the fuel switching to natural gas that remained feasible. Then, as oil prices moved above the relevant range, gas-on-gas competition could have become the market force determining the natural gas prices.

Economy

Economic growth affects consumers' demand for natural gas and their ability to purchase it. EIA appears to have incorporated an economic outlook for 2008 that expects less growth than in its recent forecasts. Given the relative stability in the residential and commercial sector demand, any change in economic outlook would most likely affect industrial natural gas use most directly, but it could also affect commodity prices and world oil prices.

Recent Developments

Since the end of 2007, several noteworthy developments have occurred in the natural gas markets:

- EIA reports natural gas price increases in 2008. For the 2007-2008 heating season (November-March), the average spot price at the wellhead increased more than 30% from the beginning to the end of heating season, to $8.06 per million Btu.[19]

- Storage levels towards the end of the heating season dropped below five year averages. In the first storage report after the 2007-2008 heating season, working gas storage was at 1,234 billion cubic feet,

---

[19] EIA, *Natural Gas Weekly*, April 10, 2008, p. 3.

CRS-14

the lowest level since April 30, 2004.[20] This may indicate that slack in the supply side is decreasing.

- The opening of the Rockies Express natural gas pipeline out of the Rocky Mountain production region appears to have relieved transmission congestion there. This improved the net back price within the production area.[21] The wellhead price in the Rockies area increased from $4.82 per million Btu in November 2007 to $8.41 in March 2008.[22] This improves the incentives for producers to find and develop new supplies in this area.

- The natural gas pipeline from the North Slope of Alaska has made progress. In January 2008, the Governor of Alaska announced that one of the pipeline project applications under the state Alaska Gasline Inducement Act (AGIA) was judged complete. In April 2008, two of the North Slope gas producers, BP and ConocoPhillips, announced that they had joined together to start a potentially competing effort, the Denali Alaska Gas Pipeline, which has an open season target date (date when capacity will be offered to potential shippers) of 2010 and an in-service target of 2018 (stated by the producers as a 10-year target).[23]

- In early April, the Independence Trail pipeline that serves the Independence Hub platform in the Gulf of Mexico was taken out of service for pipeline repairs that could take until mid-year to complete. Independence Hub produces almost 1 billion cubic feet per day, roughly 10% of U.S. Gulf of Mexico production.

- In May, the North American Electric Reliability Corporation concluded the natural gas supply outlook for the summer of 2008 is "healthy."[24]

Generally, these developments indicate that the nation's natural gas market is functioning in tune with fundamental supply and demand conditions.

---

[20] Ibid., p.3.

[21] The "net back price" is the price a producer receives based on the price at the end-use market minus the cost of transmission to that market.

[22] Ibid., p.4.

[23] Denali, presentation, April 8, 2008.

[24] North American Electric Reliability Corporation, *2008 Summer Reliability Assessment*, May 2008, p. 12.

703-739-3790 TCNNaturalGas.com **105**

CRS-15

Conclusion

Despite the problems arising in some parts of the energy system, natural gas fuel markets in North America have operated relatively well. The smooth natural gas market situation of 2007 appears to have evolved into different, tighter circumstances for 2008. If gas-on-gas competition declines and natural gas prices shift back into a competitive range with petroleum products, this will intensify the adverse effects of high oil prices.

The decline in seasonal consumption swings, primarily due to the increased use of gas-for-power, can improve the efficiency with which the nation's natural gas pipeline and storage infrastructure is used. Construction of new pipeline and storage infrastructure has continued to progress in a way apparently consistent with supply and demand fundamentals.

Finally, LNG infrastructure development also continues. The low current capacity factors at the capital-intensive existing LNG import facilities may indicate that the U.S. LNG purchasing power is not proving as competitive in the international LNG market as project developers or those reviewing the projects had anticipated. The location of LNG facilities has an important effect on this potential competitiveness, and this factor may require greater consideration for future projects.

How weather and the economy perform will play an important role in whether prices continue to increase or downward pressure develops for natural gas as a commodity.

106 703-739-3790 TCNNaturalGas.com

CRS-16

Appendix

Table A1. Selected Natural Gas Market Statistics Prices
(\$/mcf)

	2007		2006		5-year range (2003-2007)
	Annual Average	December	Annual Average	December	
Wellhead	6.39	6.53	6.40	6.76	4.88-7.33
NY citygate	8.61	7.35	9.22	10.09	N.A.
IL citygate	7.89	7.82	8.26	8.15	N.A.
CA citygate	6.82	7.35	6.76	7.13	N.A.
U.S. Citygate	8.11	8.13	8.61	8.66	5.85-8.67
Residential consumer	13.01	12.17	13.75	12.54	9.63-13.75

Table A2. Consumption
(trillion cubic feet)

	2007	2006	5-year range (2003-2007)
Total	23.0	21.7	21.7-23.0
Electric power	6.8	6.2	5.1-6.8
Residential	4.7	4.4	4.4-5.1
Commercial	3.0	2.8	2.8-3.2
Industrial	6.6	6.5	6.5-7.2
	2007	2006	Normal
Heating degree days (Nov-Jan)	2,392	2,157	2,465

Table A3. Supply
(trillion cubic feet)

	2007	2006	5-year range (2003-2007)
U.S. dry gas production	19.3	18.5	18.1-19.3
Net imports	3.8	3.5	3.3-3.8

CRS-17

Table A4. Infrastructure Projects into Service in 2007

	Number	Capacity
Pipeline	50	14.9 Bcf/d
LNG	0	-
Storage	9	1.8 Bcf/d

Sources: Energy Information Administration (EIA) and Federal Energy Regulatory Commission (FERC), various documents, detailed in body of report.

EPAct Project:
Valuing Domestically Produced Natural Gas and Oil
Final Report

DOE/NETL-2009/1355

December 31, 2008

109

Disclaimer

This report was prepared as an account of work sponsored by an agency of the United States Government. Neither the United States Government nor any agency thereof, nor any of their employees, makes any warranty, express or implied, or assumes any legal liability or responsibility for the accuracy, completeness, or usefulness of any information, apparatus, product, or process disclosed, or represents that its use would not infringe privately owned rights. Reference therein to any specific commercial product, process, or service by trade name, trademark, manufacturer, or otherwise does not necessarily constitute or imply its endorsement, recommendation, or favoring by the United States Government or any agency thereof. The views and opinions of authors expressed therein do not necessarily state or reflect those of the United States Government or any agency thereof.

EPAct Project:
Valuing Domestically Produced Natural Gas and Oil
Final Report

DOE/NETL-2009/1355

December 31, 2008

NETL Contact:

Lisa Phares
Office of Systems, Analyses and Planning

National Energy Technology Laboratory
www.netl.doe.gov

Table of Contents

iii

List of Figures and Tables

iv

v

vi

115

Prepared by:

Randall Jackson
West Virginia University

Lisa Phares
National Energy Technology Laboratory

Christa Jensen
West Virginia University

Contract Information: 404.03.02

vii

Acknowledgements

This work is funded by the U.S. Department of Energy's National Energy Technology Laboratory (U.S. DOE-NETL). The NETL sponsors for this project are John Duda, Director of NETL's Strategic Center for Natural Gas and Oil, and Joseph P. DiPietro, Task Manager for the Office of Systems, Analysis and Planning (OSAP). Kristin Gerdes of OSAP provided valuable information and guidance related to well, plant and pipeline construction costs. The NETL management team provided guidance and technical oversight for this study. The authors acknowledge the significant role played by U.S. DOE/NETL in providing the programmatic guidance and review of this report.

The participation of the following individuals, who served as merit reviewers for the methodology of this project, is gratefully acknowledged: Dr. Larry Leistritz (North Dakota State University), Thomas Murphy (Penn State University), Scott Rotruck (Chesapeake Energy), David Taylor (University of Wyoming) and Kent Perry (Gas Technology Institute).

Executive Summary

In accordance with research called for under Section 999 of the Energy Policy Act (EPAct) of 2005, the National Energy Technology Laboratory (NETL) collaborated with West Virginia University (WVU) to develop and conduct this project – EPAct Project: Valuing Domestically Produced Natural Gas and Oil.

The primary goal of this project was to develop a model that facilitates a national and regional economic analysis of the potential impacts of offsetting oil and/or natural gas foreign imports by increasing domestic natural gas and/or oil production in areas that are likely to be impacted by EPAct 999 related technologies. The development of these models allows NETL to analyze increases in domestic production using present-day technologies to serve as a baseline for potential future impacts.

This report documents the development of the model that incorporates input output modeling frameworks for five sub-national regions and one national region consisting of the US Lower-48. Because the model was developed to identify and quantify the potential impacts of increasing domestic production of oil and natural gas to offset foreign imports, the sub-national regions represent areas in the US with large reservoirs and production levels.

This project expands NETL's analytical capabilities by producing an economic model that allows for the calculation of direct, indirect and income-induced impacts to both output and employment as well as tax impacts. The model also lays the groundwork for future analyses through extensions and additions to the already existing consistent framework.

The economic modeling framework developed within this project provides a user friendly, flexible interface that allows for a wide range of target audiences – government officials, industry researchers and decision makers, and energy researchers. These audiences can use this model to conduct their own impact analyses on one region or the nation as a whole. Constructing a modeling framework that consistently models import substitution and structural change within an economy presented three key challenges:

- Identifying a sensible industry aggregation scheme that maintained detail in all energy-related production and support industries while aggregating other industries to keep the model manageable.
- Selecting a definition of the five sub-national regions so that they coincide with large production basins of the US and allow for data collection on all relative economic parameters.
- Selecting a methodology that would allow import substitution and structural changes without sacrificing consistency or theoretical foundation.

As noted, this project uses input-output (IO) models as the foundation of the modeling framework. In developing the model, the project team compiled resource production and processing data that reflect region-specific domestic production and trade levels and developed a consistent approach to modeling import substitution within the IO framework. As opposed to

1

118

conventional, final demand driven impacts assessments, import substitution is modeled through a table editing procedure that allows the model to be driven by unchanged final demand. Differences between the unedited and edited solutions reflect the impacts of substituting increased domestic production for imports. More detail on the table-editing procedure and the modeling framework in general is given in Section 6 of this report.

To generate the regional tables for the five sub-national regions of the US, the average regional purchase coefficient (RPC) method was used in conjunction with region-specific data on many of the production and economic parameters. The RPC method estimates trade flows based on econometric equations that rely on a number of regional-to-national variables including wage, output, and commodity weight/value ratios, the ratio of the number of users of a good, the ratio of the number of producers of a good, and the land area ratio.

Results are reported within two contexts. The first represents estimating the impacts of a standardized 10 percent change in production. These impacts are shown in two parts, an analysis of a 10 percent increase in oil production and an analysis of a 10 percent increase in natural gas production. These impacts provide a benchmark to facilitate comparisons of impacts within and across regions.

The second context reflects the production level changes forecasted by the Energy Information Administration's National Energy Modeling System (NEMS) in 2010, 2020 and 2030 assuming the implementation of the Lieberman-Warner Climate Security Act of 2007 (S.2191). Under this context, forecasted regional production impacts were compared to production levels forecasted under a business-as-usual (BAU) scenario, also through the NEMS. When forecasted production under S.2191 was lower than the BAU levels, the impacts are reported as an opportunity cost of implementing the legislation. In contrast, when forecasted production under S.2191 was higher than the BAU levels, the impacts are reported as a benefit of implementing the legislation. The analysis under this context was conducted to illustrate the potential uses of the model developed under this project and to provide guidance on how to model projected production declines.

The impact analyses results under the two contexts described above are listed in Section 9.2 of this report.

2

Section 1:0 Objective, Scope, and Key Assumptions of the Impact Analysis Project

1.1 Objective

In August 2005, President Bush signed the Energy Policy Act (EPAct) into law; EPAct was the first national energy legislation in more than a decade. EPAct Sections 965, 968 and 999 all support oil and gas research and development (R&D). Sections 965 and 968 relate to programs that DOE's Office of Fossil Energy and the National Energy Technology Laboratory (NETL) are already implementing. Section 999 (EPAct 999), however, adds a new dimension to the overall DOE oil and gas R&D effort, enhancing opportunities to demonstrate ultra-deepwater and unconventional technologies in the field and accelerate their implementation in the marketplace.[1] In addition to the direct support of technology development, Section 999 also provides for benefits and impact analyses to be conducted in support of the technology development programs.

Technologies supported and advanced by EPAct 999 funding are expected to increase the United States' natural gas and oil production while lowering production costs. The goal of this project is to develop a model that will facilitate a national and regional economic analysis of the potential impacts of offsetting natural gas and or oil imports by increasing domestic natural gas and oil production in areas likely to be impacted by this R&D program. Because this project is conducted prior to the development of EPAct 999-related technologies, it does not intend to capture the impact of deploying new, potentially game-changing technologies into the market. Rather, this analysis intends to serve as a baseline of potential impacts that could be derived using present-day technologies.

Ultimately, this project is aimed at capturing the economic impacts of industry-based activity associated with converting new and existing reserves into production and moving this product to the point of refinement or processing. In the case of natural gas, processing is included within the scope of this project. The incremental value of these activities is defined as the net value of the new domestic production activities less the value of imported supply activities within the United States.[2]

This research is distinguished from other research efforts in three major dimensions. First, this project rests on a foundation of comprehensive oil and gas production-and-demand data specific to five primary production basins. Model data are drawn from a wide range of sources and compiled under a comprehensive framework. Second, this project conjoins the foundation data

---

[1] NETL, 2007, p. 10.
[2] Earlier definitions of incremental value included the possibility of incorporating an aspect of loss of economic activity associated with imports-handling activities such as operation and maintenance of liquefied natural gas (LNG) facilities, natural gas pipelines and port off-loading of crude oil. Subsequent research, however, suggests they not be incorporated for two reasons. First, many of the related imports-handling activities are insubstantial, such as coupling a pipeline connector and throwing a switch. Activity levels this small, in and of themselves, are effectively beyond the accuracy of most macroeconomic models and would be completely overwhelmed by the positive impacts of increased domestic production. Second, even if the associated direct impacts were more substantial, there is effectively no data available with which to quantify them.

3

above with a macroeconomic modeling framework at both national and sub-national regional scales. Third, the method of modeling import substitution that was developed and implemented in this project differs from previous approaches, both by the design and of the focus on sub-national regional economic impacts.

1.2 Scope

The scope of the project is the economic analysis of regional and national impacts of the substitution of domestic oil and natural gas production for imports on a variety of economic factors, including output, jobs, income and Federal and State taxes. The impacts will cover those derived from direct, indirect and induced economic activity. Additionally, if possible, the model will estimate level changes to total governmental spending (due to increased tax and/or royalties revenue[3]) and consumer expenditures. This analysis will be conducted for five state or multi-state sub-national regions and for the United States as a whole. Detailed discussion concerning the selection of the sub-national regions can be found in Section 4.0.

This project is focused on capturing the incremental, comparative value of replacing imports with domestically sourced onshore oil and natural gas in various regions of the United States as well as in the national context. Because the goal of this project is specific, the project must employ scope boundaries. Thus, a critical decision point in this project is the determination of what will and will not be included in the model and the resulting analysis.

For both natural gas and oil, the project boundary encompasses raw material extraction and transmission of this raw material to a processing facility. It is acknowledged that increased domestic production of natural gas and oil may overwhelm existing transportation modes that move supply from new or existing extraction sources to the processing site. Therefore, the analysis will incorporate pipeline construction costs on a per-well and average-distance basis.[4]

Because additional domestic production is displacing current dry natural gas and crude oil production in a 1:1 ratio, new transportation infrastructure is not expected to be required to move processed natural gas or processed crude oil out of a refinery. Should such infrastructure be required by the region, this impact is not captured within the boundary of this project. For this reason, the existing transportation system (pipelines, trucks, etc.) will be analyzed to determine if additional resources would be needed to satisfy only the movement of natural gas and crude oil to a processing plant or refinery.[5] The costs of land acquisition and subsequent impacts on real estate and development values, however, lie beyond the project scope.

---

[3] Royalties revenue will not be calculated as part of this project. Should royalties revenue be reported with this project's results, they will be an exogenous input from the presently on-going DOE/NETL project 402.02.01.
[4] Operation and maintenance (O&M) costs for pipelines are embedded into the production function of the natural gas and oil extraction industry and therefore will automatically be captured in the analysis of increased production.
[5] Data required to incorporate pre-processing transportation impacts include, but may not be limited to, existing refinery and pipeline capacity locations and utilization rates and distinct construction and O&M costs. Consideration of impacts on the trucking industry may be limited to capacity additions in the form of demand for additional tanker trucks and possibly fuel demand. Modeling the impacts of increased truck transportation comprehensively can be an exceedingly complex process, the majority of which lies beyond the scope of this project.

4

Because domestically produced natural gas is oftentimes less pure than imported natural gas, it is important to include the gas processing facility within the boundary of the project.[6,7] A portion of marketed natural gas does not require processing and is sent straight to the transmission and distribution system. Pipelines that move unprocessed natural gas to end users are outside the scope of this project.

For the purposes of this study, we assume that domestically produced crude oil is immaterially different from imported crude oil with respect to the amount of processing required and thus is processed with the same level of ease or difficulty as current imported volumes. This assumption supports the exclusion of refineries from the project boundary. Shipments of crude oil from the field to a collection station, however, are still within project bounds. Pipelines that move crude oil from a collection station to the refinery are outside the project boundary.

Once natural gas is cleaned at a processing plant or crude oil is refined at a petroleum refinery, these products are considered ready for distribution to end users. At this point in the life cycle of natural gas and oil, no distinction is made between domestic and imported supplies. Therefore, because shifting supply from imported to domestic sources has no bearing on the post-processing system, the transportation system that moves supply from the processing site to the end user is not within the system boundary.

---

[6] Gas-processing plants yield by-products that can be sold and thus increase total gas processing industry output. This output will be higher when domestic natural gas production increases because imported LNG has been processed prior to shipment to remove impurities.
[7] Imported LNG is received at pipeline quality and does not require further processing at domestic natural gas processing plants.

5

Figure 1. System Boundary for Valuing the Incremental Value of Producing Natural Gas and Oil Domestically

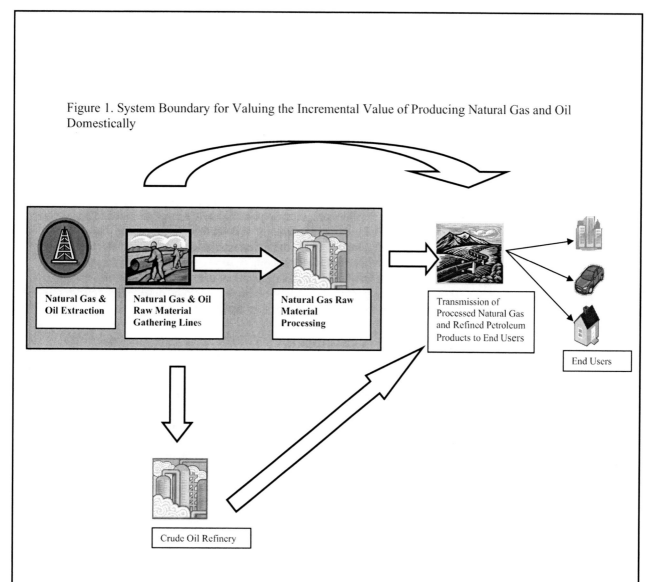

The scope of this project is also bounded by assumptions on supply displacement. In the model constructed and the subsequent analysis, it is assumed that domestic production will only displace natural gas imported via pipelines or as liquefied natural gas (LNG) and crude oil and will not impact refined oil product imports. A review of major project assumptions is provided in Section 1.3.

The project will also incorporate an element of time. EPAct 999 activities began in 2007, though many of the technologies aimed at increasing domestic production are not expected to become commercially available until after 2009. However, this project is focused on impacts of increasing production in regions that are home to resources targeted by EPAct 999, such as unconventional natural gas and oil reserves and does not attempt to estimate the impacts derived from EPAct 999 technologies, per se. Although EPAct 999, in part, focuses on the development of technologies for use in ultra-deep water (UDW) extraction, impacts of increased production

6

123

from UDW activities are not analyzed in this study due to project resource constraints. There is, however, a potential area for future work following the demonstration of the methodology developed here for onshore production impacts. The analysis conducted through this project covers increased production that begins prior to EPAct technology deployment. As a result, the scenario impact analysis, presented in Section 9.0 presents an analysis of incremental production impacts for the years 2010, 2020 and 2030. This section also presents the results of an alternative production forecast.

As an additional point, effects on prices and behavioral responses to relative price changes lie outside the project system boundary. Furthermore, electric power industry employment and output data are typically reported for the industry as a whole. It is reasonable to assume that changes in fuel prices due to increased domestic fuel production would lead to shifts in electric generation shares from one fuel to another, potentially leading to impacts on end-user average electricity prices. However, given the level of industry aggregation, the shift in generation shares would occur within the same aggregate sector, thus no impact could be detected. Impacts on end-user average electricity prices therefore will not be captured.

1.3 Design Parameters and Assumptions

This section provides information on various components of the study process and model design that must be clearly defined to ensure the goals of the project are met. Some study parameters are discussed in other sections of this report. Specifically, Section 1.2 lists the economic variables that will be analyzed by the model. Section 4.0 discusses the geographic level of detail that will be used in this study and presents map-based presentations of the project's analysis regions. Appendix B defines the industry detail that is maintained in the model. Lastly, a list of preliminary data sources is presented in Section 5.0, while Section 6.0 discusses the project methodology and Section 7.0 reviews the model construction and calculation methodology.

This project incorporates several assumptions into the study design. These assumptions impact the results and should be taken into consideration when analyzing, interpreting and applying the results generated from the project model.

To isolate the value of increasing domestically produced natural gas and oil, a primary assumption is that increased domestic production replaces imported supplies in a one-to-one relationship, thus leaving the total supply of energy resources within a region and/or the United States unaffected by increased domestic production.

Specifically, the modeling approach assumes the following:

- Domestic crude displaces imported crude only.
- Domestic crude is materially equivalent to imported crude in terms of processing requirements.
- Domestic natural gas displaces imported LNG and pipeline imports.[8]

---

[8] Energy Information Administration (EIA) data show that none of the sub-national regions currently import LNG and only California has LNG exports.

- New regional production will be used within the region to the extent that the region is under-supplied; beyond this point, new production will be exported beyond the region's borders in proportion to the existing export destination distribution.

Average transportation distances will be applied to the analysis to facilitate the calculation of required pipeline distances for new and displaced oil and natural gas supplies. These averages were developed during the course of the project and are based on a review of available data and literature.

This project's researchers recognize that oil and natural gas supplies are often purchased from suppliers through long-term contracts. Therefore, to accommodate the injection of new domestic supply and the displacement of imports, it is assumed that a significant portion of imported supply is held under short- to medium-range contracts such that new domestic supply can displace imports without causing implied contractual infractions.

It is also assumed that resources exist to meet employment, material and service demand of increased domestic production. Other assumptions consistent with the economic input-output (IO) modeling framework will be adopted for this analysis.

The output of the model will be in monetary terms. It is expected that all output will be in 2006 constant dollars, which is consistent with the model's input data. If, and as needed, deflators will be based on IMPLAN[9] data.[10]

Section 2.0 Comparison to Other Production Impact Studies

Agencies such as the Interstate Oil and Gas Compact Commission (IOGCC) and the Independent Petroleum Association of America (IPAA) conduct single-year studies on the economic activity and resulting economic impacts of activity within the oil and natural gas industries. While the project outlined in this report addresses issues within the same problem domain as research reported in the IOGCC and IPAA reports, this project does not intend to duplicate these external efforts but rather aims to complement and expand the information and insights provided by them. This project quantifies the impacts of import substitution (a) with a different geographical breakdown and coverage, and (b) by using a fundamentally different methodological approach than the studies accessed and reviewed to date. Without exception, the studies reviewed use final demand-based estimates to drive their assessment models. The approach used here relies more directly on table editing procedures that emphasize the impacts of domestic output changes rather than changes in final demand (although the latter also enter into our analyses, as described in greater detail in later sections).

---

[9] IMPLAN (IMpact analysis for PLANning) is an input-output-based analysis framework produced by the Minnesota IMPLAN Group (MIG), Inc.
[10] IMPLAN provides deflator estimates through 2020. These deflators will be extrapolated to estimate deflators for later years.

8

The IOGCC publishes an annual report on the number of and production from marginal oil and gas wells. These reports, entitled *Marginal Wells*,[11] focus on the availability and production of oil and gas resources from marginal wells[12] as well as the economic activity that arises from increasing production from these marginal wells. Two key differences between the IOGCC report and DOE's project *Valuing Domestically Produced Natural Gas and Oil* are (a) the geographic breakdown and coverage and (b) the production process coverage.

In the IOGCC report, production and economic impacts are reported on a state-level basis for 11 states. The 11 states selected for the IOGCC study are those deemed to be the top oil producers in the country, excluding Alaska. These states are responsible for more than 90 percent of marginal oil well production.[13] When marginal gas production was added to the IOGCC study, the 11 states selected based on oil production were maintained for consistency, even though they only have about 43 percent of the total marginal gas wells in the United States.[14] Furthermore, the 11 states selected exclude the Appalachian states even though the Appalachian Basin accounts for about 51 percent of the marginal gas well count and almost 29 percent of the marginal gas produced.[15]

In contrast, all contiguous continental United States will be included in the research area for the DOE project – some are covered through single- or multi-state regions, while all are covered in the U.S.-Lower 48 model region. This difference will allow for a more comprehensive coverage of both oil and gas production, though this is more notable for gas production. Additionally, in the DOE project, selected states will be grouped into five state or multi-state sub-national regions of particular interest.

The IOGCC report includes production and activity data for marginal wells. According to the latest IOGCC report, these wells contributed 18 percent of oil and 9 percent of natural gas produced in this country in 2006.[16] The DOE report will provide a broader view of impacts from increased activity in the oil and natural gas industries by modeling impacts derived from increased domestic oil and natural gas production, regardless of reserve type or production method.

The IPAA publishes an annual report[17] detailing domestic oil and natural gas production, cost, price, consumption and other economic data. The IPAA report provides these data on a state and national level. The primary distinctions between this project and the IPAA report are the goals of the projects and consequently, the reported data. The IPAA report provides point information on the number of wells, levels of production and reserves, unit costs for drilling wells and selling a barrel of oil or mcf of gas, average number of employees per related sector and so on. This

---

[11] IOGCC. *Marginal Wells: 2007 Report*, August 2007. http://www.iogcc.state.ok.us/PDFS/2007-Marginal-Well-Report.pdf.
[12] Marginal oil wells are those producing 10 or fewer barrels of oil per day. Marginal gas wells are those producing 60 or fewer thousands of cubic feet of gas per day.
[13] IOGCC, 2007. p. 24.
[14] IOGCC, 2007. p. 25.
[15] IOGCC, 2007. p. 25.
[16] IOGCC, 2007. p. 6.
[17] IPAA, *The Oil and Gas Producing Industry in Your State*, July 2005. http://www.ipaa.org/reports/econreports/IPAAOPI.pdf.

9

project, *Valuing Domestically Produced Natural Gas and Oil*, will use such data as guidance and calculation inputs for the valuation of domestic production that will be conjoined with a macroeconomic modeling framework. This approach will provide both point impacts and downstream impacts of increased production at both national and sub-national regional levels. Furthermore, the IPAA report reflects the industries' current production and market status while this project aims to estimate the incremental value of increasing domestic production as an offset to imports, thus capturing potential benefits from altering industries' current production.

Section 3.0 Model Evaluation and Selection

3.1 Model Review

A review of general modeling frameworks and several specific models ultimately led to the selection of the IO model as the analysis framework for this project. In addition to the IO framework and IO models such as the Job and Economic Development Impact Model (e.g., JEDI and JEDI II), the computable general equilibrium framework and existing models, such as the All-Modular Industry Growth Assessment Model (AMIGA) and National Energy Modeling System (NEMS) were also evaluated. Each of these frameworks and specific models were evaluated along a number of dimensions, including methodological basis, strengths, weaknesses, geographical scale, data requirements, model outputs and representative applications. The following section presents a brief description of the input-output modeling framework to be used in this project. A general and comprehensive introduction to and description of the fundamental input-output model is included as an Appendix to this report.[18]

The description below extends that description to more accurately reflect the specific data that forms the IO foundation of the analyses of this project.

3.2 The Input-Output Model and Accounting Framework

The foundation for an input-output (IO) model is an accounting framework that characterizes the purchases and sales of industries within an economy. Early input-output accounting frameworks divided the activities in an economy into industries, final demand activities and payment sectors. Final demand activities include consumption, investment, government expenditures and net exports. Payments sectors are those activities to which industries make payments and include households, profits, indirect business taxes and imports. Both final demands and payments sectors can be more finely disaggregated. One difficulty in characterizing purchase and sales relationships for modeling purposes is that industries often produce more than a single commodity output. Most will produce a dominant commodity output along with some number of secondary commodity byproducts. In 1972, governments began to publish IO accounting data in a commodity-by-industry format to provide a more comprehensive and accurate mechanism for modeling the relationships among industries and activities. This section presents an overview

---

[18] The appendix and complete evaluation of alternative modeling frameworks can be found in NETL DOE/NETL-404.03.02/020408, *Modeling Options for EPAct Project: Valuing Domestically Produced Natural Gas and Oil.*

10

of this framework and of the computational algorithms that produce the kinds of impact analyses on which this project focuses.

The table below is a schematic diagram of the generalized commodity-by-industry accounting framework.

Table 1. Commodity-by-Industry Accounting Framework

	Commodities	*Industries*	*Final Demand*	*Total Output*
Commodities		U	E	q
Industries	V			g
Value Added		W		
Total Input	q'	g'		

Four tables define the information generally included in published data sources. These are U, V, E, and W. U is called the Use table—all of these tables are generally represented in matrix format, so are often referred to as matrices rather than tables—and represents the use of commodities by industries. The number of industries and commodities is not required to be equal, but in practice there is a one-to-one correspondence among them. Table V is called the Make table and represents the commodities produced by industries. (The Use table is also called an absorption table, and the Make table is often called the byproducts table.) The sum across any commodities row of U and E equals total commodity output. The sum down any industry's column of U and W equals total industry input. The sum across an industry row of the Make table equals total industry output, while the sum of any commodity column of the Make table equals total commodity output. By definition, total commodity or industry inputs equal total commodity or industry output. These identities are reflected mathematically in the first six equations below:

1) $Ui + E = q$

2) $Vi = g$

3) $V'i = q$

4) $B = U\hat{g}^{-1}$

5) $U = B\hat{g}$

6) $q = Bg + E$

7) $D = V\hat{q}^{-1} \rightarrow d_{ij} = v_{ij} / q_j$

B is a standardized version of the Use table that depicts dollars worth of commodity input per dollar of industry output. Its use embodies the linear technology assumption and defines the input-output coefficients. Equation 7 reflects the industry-based technology assumption, which implies that an industry's output product mix is variable, and that the total output of a commodity is produced by industries in fixed proportions. Hence, D is the standardized version of V that describes the commodity output distribution of industries.

11

The total commodity or industry requirements to satisfy a given level of commodity or industry final demand can be derived from these basic equations. For example, the total commodity requirements necessary to meet a given commodity final demand can be derived as:

8) $V = D\hat{q}$

9) $D\hat{q}i = g$ (from 2)

10) $g = Dq$

11) $q = BDq + E$ (from 6)

12) $\left(I - BD\right)^{-1} E = q$

Likewise, total commodity requirements to meet a specified industry-based final demand are derived as:

13) $Y = DE$

14) $E = D^{-1}Y$

15) $\left(I - BD\right)^{-1} D^{-1}Y = q$

Total industry requirements to meet a specified commodity final demand are shown in equation 17 and total industry requirements to meet industry-based final demand are shown in equation 21, below.

16) $\left(I - BD\right)^{-1} E = D^{-1}g$

17) $D\left(I - BD\right)^{-1} E = g$

18) $E = (I - BD)D^{-1}$ (from 16)

19) $E = (D^{-1} - B)g$

20) $DE = \left(I - DB\right)g$

21) $\left(I - DB\right)^{-1} Y = g$ (from 13: $Y = DE$)

The formats in which the data are published therefore provide a great deal of flexibility in modeling choices. The expression most compatible with and supportive of the analysis for this project is the industry-by-commodity relationship represented in equation 17. Our base model will provide commodity final demand and the Use and Make tables that will be edited as described in Section 6.2 on the table-editing procedures for the model.

12

Section 4.0 Definitions of Regions Used in the Model

The analysis conducted through this project will explore the potential impacts of domestic natural gas and oil production on a regional and national basis. Therefore, a key decision point in this project was the definition of analytical regions. The project models six U.S. regions—five sub-national regions and one national region. The nation as a whole is modeled separately because there are interregional interactions that are not captured when modeling impacts within one region. Thus, the sum of the impacts over the five sub-national regions will not correspond to the sum of the impacts on the nation. The difference between the national impacts estimate and the sum of the region-specific impacts is attributable to interregional economic interaction.

The results of this analysis include incremental impacts of producing natural gas and oil domestically on gross output, jobs and taxes. Current data on these economic factors are generally reported on a state-level basis. Additionally, natural gas and oil supply and demand data are also on a state-level basis. As such, it was important to define the analytical regions along state lines.

The primary focus of this analysis is the impacts associated with increased domestic natural gas and oil production. Therefore, the regions, in addition to following state lines, also needed to represent states with large reservoirs and production levels. The primary resource used to guide the construction of the regions was the "Major Oil and Natural Gas Basins of the United States" map[19] that is based on data from the Energy Information Administration (EIA). Additionally, resource areas that are the focus of EPAct 999-directed research were also considered in the development of the final regions. To the greatest extent possible, large resource reservoirs that cross state lines were kept within the same region, although this wasn't always feasible. States with little or no natural gas or oil production were not included in any of the sub-national regions and will only be included in the national-level analysis.

---

[19] The "Major Oil and Natural Gas Basins of the United States" map is Figure 9 in the Design Basis Document.

13

The final regional delineation is shown in the region-level maps below.

Region 1. Marcellus Shale (New York, Pennsylvania, Ohio, West Virginia)

Region 2. Bakken Shale (Montana, North Dakota)

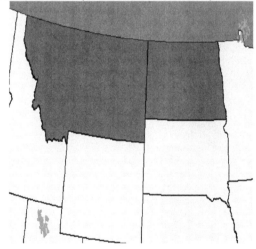

14

Region 3. Barnett Shale (Texas)

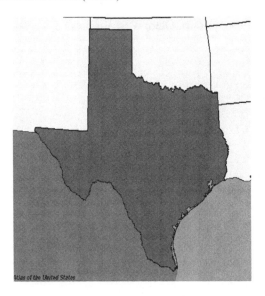

Region 4. Greater Green River/Pinedale Anticline/Jonah Field (Wyoming, Colorado, Utah)

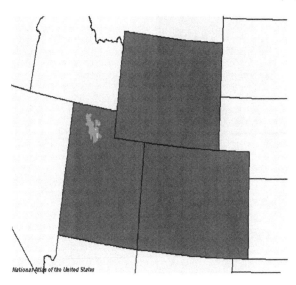

15

Region 5. California (California)

Region 6. United States – Lower 48

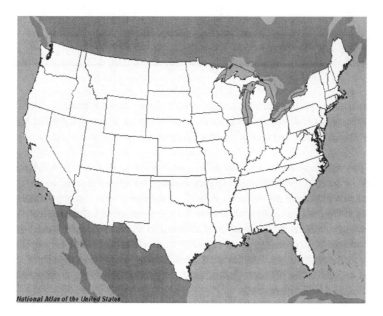

16

133

Section 5.0 Model Data Sources

As noted in Section 1.0, this project will analyze potential impacts from increased domestic natural gas and oil production using the IMPLAN input-output database. This project uses the latest version of IMPLAN, which is for 2006. More information on the IMPLAN model and its use in this project is provided in Section 6.0.

To assess potential impacts from increased domestic natural gas and oil production, it is imperative to understand the regions' current activities related to demand, production, supply, prices, and employment, as well as the natural gas and oil industry's inter-industry relationships. Because they provide the majority of natural gas and oil market data (demand, production, supply and prices), the EIA is the primary data source for this project. Annual 2006[20] data were collected and aggregated to the regional level for inclusion in the model. Import and export data were arranged to identify the volumes of interregional and international flows and average trade prices were calculated by aggregating and averaging state-level data as shown in Table 2.

Table 2. Example of International Trade Price Calculations

Region	State	Import Volume (Natural Gas, MMcf/yr)	Import Price ($/tcf)	Value of Imported Natural Gas (volume x price) (thousand $)	Regional Average Import Price ($/tcf)
2	Montana	684,279	$6.75	$ 4,616,768	Calculated as regional value divided by regional volumes
2	North Dakota	514,053	$6.71	$ 3,451,307	
2		1,198,332		$ 8,068,074	$6.73

Market prices for processing plant byproduct output were drawn from Barnes & Click, Inc. and margin ratios for converting producer and purchaser prices were extracted from the Bureau of Economic Analysis' (BEA) 2002 Benchmark Input-Output Tables.

The boundaries for this study, as noted in Section 1.2, extend from the field to the back end of the processing plant for natural gas that requires processing and from the field to the gathering center for natural gas not requiring processing, as well as for crude oil. Once production increases, impacts on field-level activity and the industry's supporting infrastructure will be calculated. These calculations, more thoroughly discussed in Section 7.1, are based on data such as per well production levels; processing plant capacity and utilization rates; oil pipeline capacity and utilization rates; and construction data for wells, processing plants and pipelines. As with the market data, the EIA serves as the primary data source for production rates, well counts and plant and pipeline capacities and utilization rates.

---

[20] 2006 data were used because these are consistent with the data in the model's framework data from IMPLAN and because 2006 is the most current complete year available for nearly all required data sets required for this study.

17

Construction data for natural gas and oil wells are derived from the 2003 Joint Association Survey on Drilling Costs (JAS). These costs are provided by state and by well depth. In IO accounts, such as those provided by BEA, well construction is part of fixed investment. Following BEA's approach of using the Producer Price Index (PPI) to deflate costs associated with well construction, the 2003 drilling costs provided by the JAS were inflated to 2006 costs using the PPI for industry 213111 (Drilling Oil and Gas Wells), product 213111213111 (Drilling Oil and Gas Wells).

Gathering pipeline costs are based on onshore data provided in the *O&G Journal's* 2007 U.S. Pipeline Costs Survey. These data (capital cost/well) are combined with data on existing gathering pipeline mileage,[21,22] EIA data on onshore wells and production and an estimate for the percent of existing lines that are useful (set at 80 percent for calculation purposes).

State-level data on processing plant construction costs are derived from cost data in Kidnay and Parrish, *Fundamentals of Natural Gas Processing*, 2006; EIA's *U.S Crude Oil, Natural Gas, and Natural Gas Liquids Reserves Report;* and the United States Geological Survey's *2006 Mineral Yearbook (Sulfur)*.

Section 6.0 Regional and National Table Construction Methodology

6.1 Input-Output Model Obtained from IMPLAN

Software and data purchased from the Minnesota IMPLAN Group, Inc. forms the foundation for the regional IO models and for the national IO model. All of the models have been constructed with the IMPLAN software, using 2006 structural and region-specific data.

Within each model, trade flows—the transfer of goods and services between the region and the rest of the world—are estimated using the average regional purchase coefficient (RPC) method. The RPC method estimates trade flows based on econometric equations internal to IMPLAN. These equations are based upon a number of regional-to-national variables, including the wage ratio, "other costs" ratios, output ratios, the commodity weight/value ratio, the ratio of the number of users of a good, the ratio of the number of producers of a good and the land area ratio. The baseline and impacts estimates of relevant variables will be generated using the independent modeling framework developed in this project. The following data are extracted from IMPLAN and saved in spreadsheet form for use in the impacts assessment model:

- Regional Use Table – contains information on the use of commodities by industry (the dollar value of purchases of goods and services by each industry for use in the production process)

---

[21] Natural Gas: http://www.naturalgas.org/naturalgas/processing_ng.asp and Pipeline and Hazardous Materials Safety Administration, US DOT http://ops.dot.gov/stats/stats.htm.

[22] Oil: http://www.pipeline101.com/Overview/crude-pl.html.

18

- Regional Make Table – contains the information on the output distribution of commodities by industry (the dollar value of each good and service produced by each industry)
- Total Commodity Imports – sum of intermediate and institutional imports of commodities (goods and services)
- Total Commodity Final Demand – institutional demand for the final use of commodities (includes the household consumption portion of final demand)
- Employment by Industry – total employment (number of jobs) for each industry (sector)
- Tax Multipliers – multipliers for all tax variables, including business taxes (expressed in dollars by type per dollar of industry output)

6.2 Table Editing Procedure

The IO modeling framework forms the analytical basis for this project. However, unlike most conventional final demand-driven IO applications, this project focuses on the changes that can be expected to occur in response to increased domestic (intraregional) production replacing previously imported oil and gas (commonly referred to as *import substitution*). Whereas the former analyses are implemented by driving an existing structural model with a new final demand or final demand change vector, the latter are implemented by driving a model based on an edited IO structure by unchanged final demand. Our analytical model will accommodate both modes of analysis, along with combinations of modes when needed. Import substitution impacts will be computed as differences in model outputs between the initial baseline outputs and those of the edited model.

There are two general categories of impacts our model will assess. These are the impacts of increased domestic production and the impacts of any new construction necessitated by the shift from imports to domestic production. Whereas construction impacts are associated with one-time events, production impacts are considered to be long run and annually recurring. Hence, the two impacts categories are reported separately. The modeling approach for each of these impacts categories will be addressed separately below.

6.2.1 Import Substitution Impacts

As domestic production increases, the first and most direct impact will be on the output-increasing industry (or industries). This output increase results in greater numbers of employees and their associated income in the producing industry (and region), and it results in increased demand for intermediate materials and supplies used in the industry's production process. A second impact will be reflected in larger dollar transactions associated with sales from the output-increasing industry to any other domestic sectors that previously had to import supplies now available from domestic sources. The latter changes also imply potential changes in transport costs (margins), particularly when transportation distances have changed markedly. However, margins were also associated with the previous import purchases. Hence, there may in fact be no detectable change in the margins associated with import substitution. Were cases to arise in which there is high confidence that margins associated with domestic production are substantially

19

different from those associated with imports, and in instances where these differences were quantified with high levels of certainty, the table could be edited to reflect the new margin values. To date, however, no such instances have been identified. Therefore, this mechanism is not included in the prototype model and not expected to be a feature of the final model.

Sub-national regional IO models differ most markedly from national IO models in their greater reliance on imports because sub-national regions are typically more open to trade than their national counterparts. This is reflected through the values in supplying rows of the regional IO coefficients table being less than (or at most equal to) their national counterpart values, such that the regional trade coefficient plus the imports coefficient equals the corresponding national coefficient. Table editing for import substitution therefore proceeds by effectively increasing the intraregional coefficients in the output-increasing row in proportion to the increases in domestic supply. These regional trade coefficient increases will continue until the point at which they equal their national counterpart values. At this point, all domestic (intraregional) demand for the industry's output will have been satisfied. Any additional output over and above the intraregional demand will be added to the baseline final demand vector in the appropriate industry row. The appropriately adjusted baseline, final demand vector will then be used to drive the newly edited model.

In actual implementation, table editing takes place in a byproducts matrix. Modern IO accounts are published in what is known as commodity-by-industry format; this is also the format of the IMPLAN data that forms the basis of our analyses. Rather than the more traditional inter-industry IO tables, the foundations of the commodity-by-industry accounts are the Use and Make tables. The Use table is organized as a series of columns, one per industry, with each row corresponding to a commodity used as an input to the column industry's production process. Commodities and industries generally share common names, with the industry being named according to its primary commodity output. This table, populated by the dollar value of commodities used by each industry, represents the technical requirements of each industry for the production of its output over the course of a one-year period. When the columns of the Use table are standardized by corresponding industry output values, the values in each cell of the table can be interpreted as cost shares and can be referred to as input-output technical coefficients.

The Make table is also referred to as a byproducts table. The rows of this table refer to industries, while the columns refer to commodities. The dollar values along any row represent the primary and secondary commodities produced by the row industry. In addition to the regional industries represented as rows in a byproducts table, there will be a final row that refers to a rest-of-world industry, which is the source of commodity imports. Because this row is present, the sum of the values in any commodity column will be equal to the total supply of the commodity available for the satisfaction of regional and export demand. As an industry increases domestic (regional) production and reduces its imports of a commodity, the element in that industry's row for the commodity whose output is being increased will take on a larger value, and the rest-of-

20

world industry value for that commodity will be decreased. When used to generate an inter-industry table, the mathematical operations will have the effect of increasing intraregional cost shares for the strengthening domestic industry and decreasing import cost shares, which is the goal of modeling import substitution.

Should the commodity output increase exceed the amount of commodity formerly imported for satisfying regional demand, the excess will be added to the baseline final demand vector. The edited IO matrix will be post-multiplied by the final demand vector to generate a counterfactual activity level, which will be compared to the baseline activity level to estimate the impacts of the import substitution. Activity levels will include industry output, employment, income and tax revenues.

A final consideration in the substitution of domestic production for imports concerns the characteristics of the domestically sourced natural gas. Imported natural gas is considered "clean." Domestically produced gas requires an additional processing step to separate byproduct gases in the cleaning process. This results in a moderate shift in the distribution of outputs of the gas processing sector away from the dominant output and toward the byproducts. This shift can be reflected in an edited Make table to the extent that this shift can be quantified.

6.2.2 Construction Impacts

Because the IO model is a current accounts modeling framework, the investment in construction of new production facilities should not be included in a model intended to identify ongoing, annually recurring impacts. The impacts of these investments, however, can be captured separately. These impacts will occur once, but not continue in subsequent years. To model these construction impacts, total construction dollar investments are translated into final demands for goods and services necessary for the particular kinds of production facilities involved. For this model, we are interested in the construction impacts associated with natural gas and oil wells. Final demand vectors constructed in this way drive the IO model computation in the conventional fashion.

While there will be new operating and maintenance expenditures associated with the operation of the new natural gas and oil wells, these expenditures are already effectively captured by increased output values that result from the increases in intraregional inter-industry interaction. They are implicitly embedded in the IO structure for the region and need not be handled separately.

6.3 International Trade Feedback Effects

As U.S. imports of oil and gas are offset by increased domestic production, countries that formerly exported to the United States will either export to other countries or will simply export less. In the latter case, the loss of income to such countries could result in decreased imports of U.S. goods. The maximum decrease in their imports from the United States would correspond to a U.S. export decline equal to the value of the formerly imported oil and gas. The maximum possible impact is unlikely, since those countries would be expected to find other markets for some portion of the oil and gas formerly sold to the United States, and since some portion of the

21

declines in their imports would be expected to impact countries other than the United States. Even with detailed historical trade data, the proportion of the displaced import value not received and consequently not re-spent by foreign countries on U.S. goods would be virtually impossible to predict with accuracy. Hence, the model allows for this proportion to be specified by the user, with values ranging from zero to a maximum of 20 percent of the value of displaced imports. Let P^X denote this "feedback" proportion, whose default value will be set at 0.2.

The value of the reduction in U.S. exports will equal the product of the feedback proportion and the value of displaced imports. We assume that the reduction in national exports of each commodity will be proportionate to each commodity's share of total base year national exports. The region's share of the reduction in foreign exports for a given commodity will be proportionate to the region's share of national exports of that commodity. If we let Δ denote *change in*, X_i^r denote region, r be commodity i exports, X_i be commodity i national exports, and X be total national exports, then

$$\Delta X_i^r = \left(P^X\right)\left(IS_i\right)\left(\frac{X_i^r}{X_i}\right)\left(\frac{X_i}{X}\right) = \left(P^X\right)\left(IS_i\right)\left(\frac{X_i^r}{X}\right)$$

where IS_i is the value of displaced imports. Changes in exports are then subtracted from the baseline final demand vector to generate the impact final demand vector in non-oil and gas commodity sectors.

Section 7.0 Spreadsheet Model Construction

The model used to assess the impacts of increased natural gas and oil production is an Excel spreadsheet model. The model is comprised of a region map sheet, a user-interface sheet, a results sheet and multiple data and calculation sheets. All data, unless otherwise noted, are for calendar year 2006. Natural gas is presented in million cubic feet per year (MMcf/yr) and oil is presented in thousand barrels per year (thbbls/yr) unless otherwise noted.

The user interface tab, "Inputs," allows the user to select the region for analysis and enter the volumes of increased wellhead production and the well depth for the region. As the user makes selections on well depth, the model presents the per-well drilling costs for that region (thousand $/well). Producer prices for natural gas and oil are also presented to the user. Lastly, this portion of the model presents the user the option to set an international trade feedback rate. This percentage, bound to a range of 0 percent to 20 percent reflects the impacts of increased regional production that leads to a decline in international natural gas and/or oil import. These reduced imports could cause a decline in revenue by the exporting country. The decline in international revenue could then cause a downstream decline in imports of U.S. goods by impacted countries.

Below the user input section of this tab, data on the current (2006) state of activity within the region are presented to the user as guidance for the user's selection of increased regional production. The data presented as informational guidance and the calculations used to convert user production inputs into model inputs (converting production volumes into dollars) are based on data held in the tabs "NG Data Sheet" and "Oil Data Sheet." The following section details how the informational values and the model input values are calculated (more information on the

22

base data in tabs "NG Data Sheet" and "Oil Data Sheet" will be explained in greater detail later in this section). Detailed instructions for this tab are in the section *User Instructions*.

7.1 Calculations

7.1.1 Regional Information

The box "Regional Information" on the tab "Inputs" provides the user with information on the current industry-related activities within the region. These data are provided to inform the user's entries for increased production based on the region's current supply-and-demand balance.

a. Regional Demand: $\sum_{S1}^{Sx} C$ where C = consumption in all sectors, S = state within region

b. Regional Imports: $\sum_{R1}^{R5} M$ where M = imports from all other regions and international sources, R = importing region. Imports between states in the same region are considered regional production and are not counted as regional imports.

c. Current Well Withdrawals:

Natural Gas: $\sum_{S1}^{Sx} NGP_{ng,o}$ where NGP = wet production of natural gas, ng = gas wells, o = oil wells, S = state within region

Crude Oil: $\sum_{S1}^{Sx} OP_{ng,o}$ where OP = crude production of oil, ng = gas wells, o = oil wells, S = state within region

d. Number of Wells: $\sum_{S1}^{Sx} W$ where W = fuel specific producing wells, S = state within region

e. Current Marketed Production (applies only to natural gas): $\sum_{S1}^{Sx} Pg - PLg$ where Pg = wet production of natural gas from gas and oil wells, PLg = production losses from re-pressuring, venting/flaring and removal of non-hydrocarbon gases, S = state within region

23

f. Natural Gas Processing Plant Capacity: $\sum\limits_{S1}^{Sx}\left(\sum\limits_{Plant1}^{Plantx} NGC * 365\right)$ where NGC = natural gas processing capacity per day, Plant = processing plant facility, S = state within region

g. Average Utilization Rate:

$$\left.\left(\sum\limits_{S1}^{Sx}(NGProcessed)\right)\middle/ NaturalGasProcessingPlantCapacity\right.$$

h. Current Dry Production (applies only to natural gas): $\sum\limits_{S1}^{Sx} Pg - PLg - NGLg$

where Pg = wet production of natural gas from gas and oil wells; PLg = production losses from re-pressuring, venting/flaring and removal of non-hydrocarbon gases; NGLg = natural gas liquid constituents such as ethane, propane and butane removed at natural gas processing plants; S = state within region

i. Average Natural Gas Processing Plant Capacity: $\left.\sum\limits_{S1}^{Sx}\left(\sum\limits_{Plant1}^{Plantx} NGC * 365\right)\middle/ \sum\limits_{S1}^{Sx}(Plants)\right.$

7.1.2 Production Results

Input values for input-output-based models must be in dollar format and in producer's prices. Therefore the production level values entered by a user must be converted to producer's price dollars to drive the impacts assessment model. Calculations shown in Sections 7.1.2 through 7.1.4 provide a walk-through of the calculations used to do this production-to-value conversion.

As noted in Section 1.3, the scope of this project includes natural gas processing. This allows the impacts to encompass the production of natural gas liquids that are produced when wet natural gas is cleaned to pipeline quality levels. Prior to the production-to-value conversion, the volume of additional natural gas produced at the wellhead must be converted to the volume of natural gas that reaches the processing plant market (marketed production). This volume must then be stripped of natural gas liquids, leaving the volume of natural gas that will enter the transmission and distribution system (dry natural gas).

a. Increased Marketed Production (natural gas): Increased market production is defined as the gross withdrawals of natural gas less gas used for re-pressuring, quantities vented and flared and non-hydrocarbon gases removed in treating or

24

processing operations.[23] The EIA provides state-level data on gross withdrawals and process losses. These data were aggregated into the model regions and the regional process-losses percentage, the parameter directly used by the model, was calculated as a percent loss of regional wet production volumes.

$$\text{Source Data Process Losses}_R = \sum_{S1}^{Sx} ProcessLosses$$

$$\text{Source Data Marketed Production}_R =$$
$$\sum_{S1}^{Sx} Current\ Well\ Withdrawal\ s - ProcessLos\ ses$$

$$\text{Source Data Regional Process Loss Percent} =$$
$$ProcessLoc\ sses\ _R \Big/ Marketed\ Production\ _R$$

In the model, increased marketed production from increased regional natural gas production is calculated as:

Increased Marketed Production = Increased Regional Production$_{NG}$
* (1- Regional Process Loss Percent)

b. Natural Gas Sent to Processing: According to EIA data, 23.5 Tcf[24] of wet natural gas was produced in the United States in 2006. This production yielded 19.4 Tcf[19] of marketed production of which 14.7 Tcf[25] (76 percent) was sent to natural gas processing plants for further processing. These data were also available on a state level and were used to calculate the regional volumes of marketed production that were and were not sent to natural gas processing plants.

$$\text{Source Data Processed Volumes}_R = \sum_{S1}^{Sx} (ProcessedVolumes)$$

NG Not Requiring Processing$_R$ = *Increased Marketed Production*
* *[1-(Source Data Processed Volumes$_R$ ÷ Source Data Marketed Production$_R$)]*

Processed NG$_R$ = *Increased Marketed Production * (Source Data Processed Volumes$_R$ ÷ Source Data Marketed Production$_R$)*

---

[23] EIA Glossary, Marketed Production, http://www.eia.doe.gov/glossary/glossary_m.htm.
[24] EIA. Natural Gas Gross Withdrawals and Production.
http://tonto.eia.doe.gov/dnav/ng/ng_prod_sum_dcu_NUS_a.htm.
[25] *U.S. Crude Oil, Natural Gas, and Natural Gas Liquids Reserves Report.* Appendix E, Table E4. Natural Gas Processed and Liquids Extracted at Natural Gas Processing Plants, 2006.

25

c. Natural Gas Processing Plant Output: Once the volume of natural gas that is sent to processing is determined (by calculation of Processed NG_R), the volumes of extraction losses,[26] extracted liquids and dry natural gas[27] output must be calculated. EIA presents state-level data on the volume of natural gas processed (MMcf), the total liquids extracted (thbbls) and the extraction loss (MMcf) of natural gas.[28] The relationship between these data is used to calculate the losses, liquids and dry natural gas from the increased natural gas sent through a processing plant.

$Extraction\ Loss_R = Processed\ NG_R * (Source\ Data\ Extraction\ Loss_R \div Source\ Data\ Processed\ Volumes_R)$

$where\ Source\ Data\ Extraction\ Loss_R = \sum_{S1}^{Sx} ExtractionLosses$

$Extracted\ Liquids_R = Extraction\ Loss_R * Percent\ Liquids\text{-}to\text{-}Extracted\ Liquids_R$

$\qquad where\ Percent\ Liquids\text{-}to\text{-}Extracted\ Liquids_R = Source\ Data\ Extracted\ Liquids_R \div Source\ Data\ Extraction\ Loss_R$

$\qquad where\ Source\ Data\ Extracted\ Liquids_R = \sum_{S1}^{Sx} ExtractionLiquds$

$Dry\ Natural\ Gas\ from\ Processing\ Plants_R = Processed\ NG_R - Extraction\ Loss_R$

d. Total Dry Natural Gas to Market: The amount of dry natural gas that is sent to the natural gas transmission and distribution market represents both the volumes that did not require additional processing and the dry natural gas output by the processing plant industry.

$Total\ Dry\ Natural\ Gas\ to\ Market_R = NG\ Not\ Requiring\ Processing_R + Dry\ Natural\ Gas\ from\ Processing\ Plants_R$

---

[26] Extraction losses are the reduction in volume of natural gas due to the removal of natural gas liquid constituents such as ethane, propane and butane at natural gas processing plants. http://tonto.eia.doe.gov/dnav/ng/TblDefs/ng_prod_sum_tbldef2.asp.

[27] Dry natural gas is consumer-grade natural gas and is the natural gas which remains after the liquefiable hydrocarbon portion has been removed from the gas stream (i.e., gas after lease, field and/or plant separation) and any volumes of non-hydrocarbon gases have been removed where they occur in sufficient quantity to render the gas unmarketable. EIA Glossary, Marketed Production, http://www.eia.doe.gov/glossary/glossary_d.htm.

[28] EIA, Natural Gas Processing. http://tonto.eia.doe.gov/dnav/ng/ng_prod_pp_dcu_nus_a.htm.

26

e. Crude Oil Production: As previously noted, the boundary of this project, with respect to crude oil production, ends at the gathering line that then sends crude oil to the refinery. Therefore, the only production volume reported for crude oil is the increase in crude oil production without any processes having taken place.

$$\text{Crude Oil Production}_R = \text{Increased Regional Production}_O$$

7.1.3 Impact on Supply Allocation

Once the conversion of increased wellhead production to increased marketed production is complete, the role of this increased production must be determined.

a. Allocation of Increased Production to Regional Demand: A key assumption to this portion of the model is that total regional demand is constant. Given constant demand, increases in production either meet current demand, thus offsetting current imports, or increase regional exports. The allocation of increased production to current demand or increased exports is determined by the region's ability to meet demand given baseline (current) production. Therefore, if regional demand exceeds baseline dry production (natural gas) or well withdrawals (crude oil), then increased production goes toward meeting regional demand up to the point that regional demand is satisfied. The volume applied to regional demand offsets regional imports while any excess production volumes are exported (see Example 1).

Example 1: Regional Demand (D) = 500,000 MMcf/yr
Regional Production (P) = 375,000 MMcf/yr
Regional Production Variance = 500,000
                                    - 375,000
                                    = 125,000 MMcf/yr

Increased Regional Production set at 300,000 MMcf/yr
Increased Production to Regional Demand
                        = Region Production Variance
                        = Offset Imports
                        = 125,000 MMcf/yr

Increased Production Exported = 300,000
                                    - 125,000
                                    = 175,000 MMcf/yr

If baseline production levels already satisfy the regional demand, then any increase in regional production is exported (see Example 2).

27

Example 2: Regional Demand (D) = 300 thbbl/yr
Regional Production (P) = 475 thbbl/yr
Regional Production Variance = 300
  - 475
  = -175 thbbl/yr

Increased Production Exported = 175 thbbl/yr

b. Determining Interregional and International Shares of Offset Imports and Increased Exports: Each sub-national model region is supplied by regional and/or imported natural gas and oil.[29] Additionally, each sub-national region exports natural gas and oil to other sub-national regions and to international markets. When increased domestic production meets the regional demand, thus offsetting imports, it must be determined whether these offset imports are imported from other sub-national U.S. regions or if they are international imports. Additionally, when increased production within a region exceeds the region's demand (e.g., Example 1 above) or when the increased production is not needed within the region(e.g., Example 2), the excess supply will be exported and it must be determined whether these exports will supply other sub-national U.S. regions or if they will enter the international markets. The split between sub-national and international markets for both offset imports and increased exports is determined by the aggregation of state-level proportions as reported by the EIA.

Example 3. From Example 1, offset imports = 125,000 MMcf/yr and EIA data show that in 2006, Region X imported 775,000 MMcf/yr from other sub-national regions and 1,120,000 MMcf/yr from the international market, for total imports of 1,895,000 MMcf/yr.
Region X regional imports = 775,000/ 1,895,000 = 41%
Region X international imports = 1,120,000/1,895,000 = 59%

Given these data points, the model will calculate:
Offset imports (U.S. Regions) = 51,121 MMcf/yr, (125,000*41%)
Offset imports (International) = 73,879 MMcf/yr, (125,000*59%)

---

[29] For the United States-Lower 48 region, all imports and exports are sourced from and sent to the international market with no allocations to sub-national regions.

28

Example 4. From Example 2, increased exports = 175 thbbl/yr and EIA data show that in 2006, Region X exported 250 thbbl/yr to other sub-national regions and 75 thbbl/yr to international markets, for a total exported volume of 325 thbbl/yr.

Region X regional exports = 250/325 = 77%

Region X international exports = 75/325 = 23%

Given these data points, the model will calculate:

Increased exports (U.S. Regions) = 135 thbbl/yr, (175*77%)

Increased exports (International) = 40 thbbl/yr, (175*23%)

7.1.4 Calculating Increased Regional Industry Output and Reduced Import Payments

The calculations shown in steps 7.1.2 and 7.1.3 move the production volumes from raw production to volumes that will either enter the transmission and distribution system (natural gas) or be sent to a refinery (crude oil). The final step needed before executing the model is to convert both the production volumes used to meet demand and the volumes being exported into industry output valued in producer prices (million $). Additionally, the value of offset imports must be captured by converting offset import volumes to offset import payments.

a. Natural Gas Industry Output: Output for the natural gas industry is comprised of three components – natural gas sold for regional consumption, natural gas exports and sales of natural gas liquids.

NG Regional Demand (Million $) = *Total Dry Natural Gas to Market$_R$ (MMcf/yr) * (Imputed Wellhead Price$_R$ ($/tcf)^{30,31}) ÷ 1,000*

NG Regional Exports (Million $) = *[(Increased exports (United States Regions) + Increased exports (International)) * (Imputed Wellhead Price$_R$ ($/tcf))] ÷ 1,000*

NG Plant Liquids (Million $) = *[Extracted Liquids$_R$ (th bbls/yr) * Avg. NGPL Market Value$_R$($/bbl)^{32} * Avg. Industry Ratio of Producer's Prices to Purchaser's Prices (%)^{33}] ÷ 1,000*

---

[30] EIA. Natural Gas Prices, wellhead price.
http://tonto.eia.doe.gov/dnav/ng/ng_pri_sum_a_EPG0_FWA_DMcf_a.htm.
[31] No adjustment is made to wellhead prices – assumed to be producer prices.
[32] Regional average NGPL production: EIA, Natural Gas Plant Field Production, state-level data; NGPL prices: Barnes and Click: http://www.engineers1.com/pdf/PriceCorr.pdf.
[33] Bureau of Economic Analysis (BEA), Benchmark Input-Output Data, Table 2. "The Use of Commodities by Industries before Redefinitions, 2002 Benchmark, at the detail level." Average United States Purchaser-to-Producer ratio for purchases of NAICS 211000 (Oil & Natural Gas Extraction) by chemical industries; NAICS 324191 (Petroleum Lubricating Oil and Grease Manufacturing); 324199 (All Other Petroleum and Coal Products Manufacturing); 325110 (Petrochemical Manufacturing); and 325190 (Other Basic Organic Chemical Manufacturing).

29

b. Reduction in NG Import Payments: This value represents the value of a region's reduced payments for natural gas imports from other sub-national regions and the international market.

Reduced NG Import Payments$_1$ (Million $) =

$$\sum_{R1}^{R6}\left(OffsetImports(MMcf\,/\,yr) * ImputedWellheadPrice(\$\,/\,tcf)\right) * Avg.$$

Industry Ratio of Purchaser's Prices to Producer's Prices (%)[34],[35] ÷ 1,000

Reduced NG Import Payments$_2$ (Million $) = [*Offset imports (International)* *
Avg. Natural Gas Import Price$_R$ ($/tcf)[36]*] ÷ 1,000*

c. Oil Industry Output: Output for the oil industry is comprised of two components – oil sold for regional consumption and oil for export.

Oil Regional Demand (Million $) = [*Crude Oil Production$_R$ (thbbl/yr)* *
Domestic Price to Refiners$_R$ ($/bbl)[37] * *Avg. Industry Ratio of Producer's
Prices to Purchaser's Prices (%)*[38]*] ÷ 1,000*

Oil Regional Exports (Million $) =
  i. *[Increased exports (U.S. Regions) * Domestic Price to
      Refiners$_R$ ($/bbl) * Avg. Industry Ratio of Producer's Prices to
      Purchaser's Prices (%)] ÷ 1,000*   +
  ii. *[Increased exports (International) * F.O.B. Costs of Imported
      Crude Oil$_{US}$ ($/bbl)*[39]*] ÷ 1,000*

---

[34] BEA, Benchmark Input-Output Data, Table 2. Average U.S. Producer-to-Purchaser ratio for purchases of NAICS 211000 (Oil & Natural Gas Extraction) by NAICS 211000 (Oil & Natural Gas Extraction).
[35] Import payments must be in purchaser prices, so wellhead prices had to be increased to account for transportation margins (largely pipeline transportation costs).
[36] EIA, United States Natural Gas Imports by Point of Entry, Pipeline Prices and LNG Prices.
[37] EIA. Refiner Acquisition Cost of Crude Oil, domestic. http://tonto.eia.doe.gov/dnav/pet/pet_pri_rac2_a_EPC0_PDT_dpbbl_a.htm.
[38] BEA, Benchmark Input-Output Data, Table 2. Average U.S. Purchaser-to-Producer ratio for purchases of NAICS 211000 (Oil & Natural Gas Extraction) by NAICS 324110 (Petroleum Refineries).
[39] EIA, F.O.B. Costs of Imported Crude Oil by Area, http://tonto.eia.doe.gov/dnav/pet/pet_pri_imc1_k_a.htm.

30

    d. Reduction in Oil Import Payments: This value represents the value of a region's reduced payments for oil imports from other sub-national regions and the international market. The calculations are done similarly to the reduced natural gas import payment calculations.

Reduced Oil Import Payments$_1$ (Million \$) =

$$\sum_{R1}^{R6}\left(OffsetImports(thbbl\,/\,yr) * Domestic\ Price\ to\ Refiners_R\,(\$/bbl)\right) \div 1{,}000$$

Reduced Oil Import Payments$_2$ (Million \$) = [*Offset international imports (thbbl/yr) * Landed Cost of Imported Crude Oil$_{US}$ (\$/bbl)*[40]] ÷ *1,000*

7.1.5 Construction Cost Results

    a. Number of New Wells: Increased domestic production will lead to the construction of new wells given the assumption that none of the new production is due to increased recovery rates from existing wells. Additionally, although each region obtains both natural gas and oil from the wells within the region, the model calculates the number of new wells needed using the assumption that only natural gas wells will produce natural gas and only oil wells will produce oil.

New Natural Gas Wells (#) =

$$Increased\ Regional\ Production_{NG} \Bigg/ \left(\frac{\sum_{S1}^{Sx} GasWithdrawals}{\sum_{S1}^{Sx} GasWells} \right)$$

New Oil Wells (#) =

$$Increased\ Regional\ Production_{O} \Bigg/ \left(\frac{\dfrac{\sum_{S1}^{Sx} OilWithdrawals}{1{,}000}}{\sum_{S1}^{Sx} OilWells} \right)[41]$$

---

[40] EIA, Landed Costs of Imported Crude by Area. http://tonto.eia.doe.gov/dnav/pet/pet_move_land1_k_a.htm.
[41] Oil well withdrawals are divided by 1,000 because regional withdrawals in the source data are in thousand bbls/yr while increased regional production held in the model are in million bbls/yr.

31

b. New Well Construction: Total construction costs for new natural gas and oil wells are derived by multiplying the number of new wells required by the average regional construction costs per well, plus any cost adjustment entered by the user.

Well Construction Costs$_R$ (Million \$) = (New Natural Gas Wells (#), New Oil Wells (#)) * Avg. By-depth Well Construction Cost$_R$ (thousand \$/well) ÷ 1,000

c. New Gas Processing Plants (#): In 2006, there were 491 natural gas processing plants across 22 states.[42] These processing plants had a reported daily processing capacity that was extrapolated to an annual processing capacity for use in the model.[43] State-level processed volumes were used along with the capacity data to generate regional plant utilization rates and maximum regional utilization rates. The number of new processing plants required in each model region is a function of the region's processing plant maximum utilization rate, the new volume of natural gas requiring processing (see function Processed NG$_R$ [step 2.b. shown above]) and the displaced processed inter-regional imports. The calculation for the number of new natural gas processing plants is a two-step process. The first step compares the excess regional processing capacity and the volume of inter-regional natural gas that is processed within the region to the new volume of natural gas. If the new volume exceeds the displaced imports or the excess regional capacity, the second step then determines the number of new plants required within the region.

i. New Natural Gas Processing Plants Required (yes/no):
If Processed NG$_R$ ≤ Source Data Inter-Region Processed Import Volumes$_R$
OR Processed NG$_R$ ≤ Excess Processing Capacity,
Then no new plants are required; Else

ii. New Natural Gas Processing Plants$_R$ (#) =
If *Processed NG$_R$ > Source Data Inter-Region Processed Import Volumes$_R$*
Then
$$\frac{\left(ProcessedNG_R - SourceDataInter\,Re\,gional\,Processed\,Im\,ports_R\right)}{\left(\dfrac{MaxUtilizationVolume_R}{Plants_R}\right)}$$

Else $\dfrac{\left(ProcessedNG_R\right)}{\left(\dfrac{MaxUtilizationVolume_R}{Plants_R}\right)}$

---

[42] *U.S. Crude Oil, Natural Gas, and Natural Gas Liquids Reserves Report.* Appendix E, Table E5. Form EIA-64A 2006 Plant Frame Activity.

[43] *Natural Gas Processing: The Crucial Link Between Natural Gas Production and Its Transportation to Market,* Table 1. Natural Gas Processing Plant Capacity in the Lower 48 States, 1995 and 2004. These data were extrapolated to 2006 based on the capacity-to-plant ratio in 2004.

32

d. New Gas Processing Plant Construction: Total construction costs for new natural gas processing plants are derived by multiplying the net volume of new natural gas requiring processing by the average regional construction costs per MMcf processed per day.

Gas Plant Construction Costs$_R$ (Million $) = *Net Natural Gas Requiring New Processing Capacity$_R$ (MMcf/yr) /365/ Max Plant Utilization Rate$_R$ * Avg. construction costs per MMcf Capacity$_R$ (Million $)*

e. Pipeline Construction: Pipeline construction cost source data are based on the national average capital cost per well.[44] Therefore, pipeline construction costs due to the construction of new wells is calculated as the number of new wells multiplied by the average regional pipeline construction cost per well.

Pipeline Construction Costs$_R$ (Million $) = *(New Natural Gas Wells (#), New Oil Wells (#)) * Avg. Pipeline Construction Cost per Well$_R$ (Million $)*

7.2 Results Presentation

The third tab in the model, "Results," presents a summary of the user inputs and both a summary and detailed listings of the results of the import substitution and construction impacts by aggregated industries. Examples of the four results tables are shown below (Tables 3–6). The tables shown here correspond to the prototype model using aggregated sample data from Region 1: New York, Ohio, Pennsylvania, and West Virginia. The prototype model and its corresponding results tables were aggregated into 6 industries, but the final model for this project and its corresponding results include 33 industries (see Appendix B).

Table 3 reports import substitution impacts. This includes total output impacts for each industry, which are divided into the two components of intermediate inputs and value added. Value added is further sub-divided into its separate components of employment compensation, proprietor's income, other property type income and indirect business taxes.

---

[44] See Section 5 for data source references.

33

Table 3. Import Substitution Impacts

Table 4 reports construction impacts. Once again, results are reported for total output impacts but have also been sub-divided into their respective components as in the table above.

Table 4. Construction Impacts

Tables 5 and 6 report the tax impacts for import substitution and construction, respectively. Impacts are given for enterprises (corporations), Federal Government Non-Defense, and State/Local Government Non-Education categories. The sources of these impacts are given in the columns and include employee compensation, proprietary income, household expenditures, enterprises and indirect business taxes which can be summed to get the total tax impact.

34

Table 5. Import Substitution Tax Impacts

Table 6. Construction Tax Impacts

35

7.3 Other Model Tabs

There are two primary data tabs, "NG Data Sheet" and "Oil Data Sheet." These tabs hold state-level source data on production volumes, prices, well counts, trade activity and processing capacities, all of which have been aggregated to the model regions. These tabs also hold industry-level data used to transform producer prices to purchaser prices and vice versa.

The "Data Link" tab is used as the bridge between the user inputs entered on the "Inputs" tab and the IO modeling which occurs within the model. A key component of this tab is the Oil and Gas Price Ratio (cells B9:C9). This ratio is necessary to adjust the composite price of oil and natural gas used in the model. The total consumption of oil and natural gas in the original setup is made up of both domestic oil and natural gas and internationally imported oil and natural gas. Domestic prices are not equal to the prices of the international imports; therefore, the overall price of oil and natural gas is a weighted average of the domestic price and the price of international imports. When the model is run to determine potential impacts, the overall price of oil and natural gas will change because the amount of domestic oil and natural gas being produced is now larger and international imports have declined. Thus, the weights on the overall price of oil and natural gas will be different. These changes should be reflected in an adjustment

of the overall price. The calculation for the ratio is: $\dfrac{P_n}{P_0}$ where $P_n =$

$$\left[\frac{Pi(Qi + \Delta Qi) + Pd(Qd + \Delta Qd)}{(Qi + Qd)} \right] \text{ and } P_0 = \left[\frac{PiQi + PdQd}{(Qi + Qd)} \right]$$

Table 7. Price Ratio Parameter Definitions

	Natural Gas	Oil
Pi	Weighted Average of Domestic and International Import Prices	
Qi	Demand - Domestic Production	
Pd	Wellhead Price	Refiner Price minus Margins
Qd	Minimum of Domestic Production and Domestic Demand	
ΔQi	Offset Imports	
ΔQd	Domestic Production minus Change in Exports	

All remaining tabs represent various steps in the IO modeling of the impacts related to increased natural gas and oil production and the generation of the results tabs presented above.

36

Section 8.0 User Instructions

The model allows for the analysis of increased natural gas and/or oil production within a single region. The current version of the model, as noted in Section 4.0, does not capture the impact on a region caused by production increases in a different region. Therefore, the model is run, and the impacts should be assessed, on an isolated, single-region basis.

Exercising the model requires five steps:

1. Select a region.
2. Enter levels of increased natural gas and/or oil production.
3. Select average well depths for natural gas and/or oil.
4. Enter rate for international trade feedback percentage.
5. Generate and view results.

To begin using the model, users have two options. First, the user can select a region map shown on the tab titled "Regions." This will jump the user to the region selection drop-down on the "Inputs" tab, but will not alter the region selection based on the map selected; the user still must select a region. Alternatively, as shown in Figure 2, the user can begin on the "Inputs" tab in cell F10 (located in the box "Increased Regional Production") and select an analysis region from the drop-down menu.

Figure 2. Region Selection Drop-Down Menu

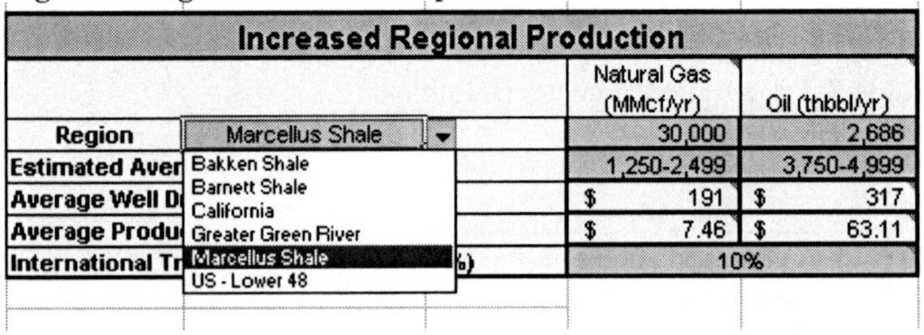

Increased Regional Production			
		Natural Gas (MMcf/yr)	Oil (thbbl/yr)
Region	Marcellus Shale ▾	30,000	2,686
Estimated Aver Bakken Shale		1,250-2,499	3,750-4,999
Average Well D Barnett Shale California		$ 191	$ 317
Average Produ Greater Green River		$ 7.46	$ 63.11
International Tr Marcellus Shale		10%	
US - Lower 48			

All user inputs are entered in the box "Increased Regional Production" located on the "Inputs" tab. In this box, all cells requiring user inputs are highlighted in orange; yellow fields represent source and/or calculated data.

To calculate the potential impacts of increased domestic natural gas and oil production within the selected region, users first determine the level of increased production for which they want to assess the impacts and enter these values in cells H10 and I10 for natural gas (MMcf/yr) and/or oil (thbbl/yr), respectively. It is important to note that the values to be entered are levels of production *increases* and are not levels of total production. Additionally, the model limits production increases to 25 percent of 2006 well withdrawals (cells I123:I124). If the user enters a production increase that is greater than 25 percent of the existing well withdrawals, the model provides a warning that a new production level must be entered (Figure 3).

37

Figure 3. Warning Showing User-Entered Production Level Exceeds Constraint

Increased Regional Production				
			Natural Gas (MMcf/yr)	Oil (thbbl/yr)
Region	Marcellus Shale		155,000	2,686
Estimated Average Well Depth (ft/well)			5,000-7,499	3,750-4,999
Average Well Drilling Cost (th$ per well)			$ 469	$ 317
Average Producer Price ($/tcf, $/bbl)			$ 7.46	$ 63.11
International Trade Feedback Percent (%)			10%	
			INCREASED PRODUCTION TOO HIGH, RE-ENTER	

In the next row down (cells H11:I11), the user can select the average well depth for the analysis region from a drop-down list. For natural gas wells, there are 11 depth options ranging from 0–20,000+ feet/well as well as the option of a coal bed methane (CBM) site. For oil wells, the user can select from the same well depth options available under natural gas. Once the user selects the average well depth for the region, the model returns the regional average well construction cost (thousand $/well) for the selected depth (cells H12:I12). This cost information will flow to the new-well-construction cost calculations that drive the construction impacts in the model. If the underlying source data indicate that the selected region does not have any wells at the selected depth, cost per well cell will be shaded in red (Figure 4). If this should happen, the user must select an alternate average well depth.

Figure 4. Example of Region with No Data to Support Selection of Depth Ranging from 5,000 to 7,499 Feet

Increased Regional Production				
			Natural Gas (MMcf/yr)	Oil (thbbl/yr)
Region	Bakken Shale		30,000	2,686
Estimated Average Well Depth (ft/well)			5,000-7,499	3,750-4,999
Average Well Drilling Cost (th$ per well)			$ -	$ 2,140
Average Producer Price ($/tcf, $/bbl)			$ 5.86	$ 60.04
International Trade Feedback Percent (%)			10%	

Lastly, the user enters the international trade feedback percent (H14). This rate is arbitrarily set to a range of 0–20 percent. The model applies this rate to the value of offset international imports and reduces the region's foreign export final demand for each of the modeled industries (see Section 6.3).

38

Figure 5. User Entry Cell for International Trade Feedback Percent

Increased Regional Production			Natural Gas (MMcf/yr)	Oil (thbbl/yr)
Region	Bakken Shale		30,000	2,686
Estimated Average Well Depth (ft/well)			1,250-2,499	3,750-4,999
Average Well Drilling Cost (th$ per well)			$ 204	$ 2,140
Average Producer Price ($/tcf, $/bbl)			$ 5.86	$ 60.04
International Trade Feedback Percent (%)			10%	←

As noted in the previous section describing the construction of the model, data on regional production, supply and demand are located in the box "Regional Information." Calculation steps that convert user-entered production increases (volume units) to industry output (dollars) that will drive the model are in the box "Production Results." Lastly, information on new wells and plants, as well as construction costs, is in the box "Construction Cost Results." It is important to note that the values presented in "Production Results" and "Construction Cost Results" do not represent full production impacts.

To calculate economy-wide potential impacts of increased natural gas and/or oil production and related construction costs, the user must click the button "Generate & View Impact Results" located at the top of the "Inputs" tab. This button runs the IO model to estimate total impacts and redirects the user to the top of the "Results" tab. While users can view results without clicking the "Generate & View Impact Results" button, clicking this button allows the spreadsheet model to (1) access the input data from previous computations, (2) edit the appropriate Use and Make tables along with appropriate final demand and output values, and (3) carry out the computations described in the above Input-Output Model and Accounting Framework section to generate the total impacts of the increase in domestic production.

As shown in Section 7.2, the "Results" tab summarizes the results in tabular form. One set of output tables will present annually occurring impacts by industry,[45] and a second set will present construction impacts stimulated by the initial expansion in domestic output. Output table information includes:

1. Input data summary
2. Summary impact results
3. Output impacts by industry
4. Value added by industry
5. Income impacts by industry
6. Employment impacts by industry
7. Tax effects by type and source of tax

---

[45] The prototype model and its corresponding results tables are aggregated into 6 industries, but the final models for this project and their corresponding results will include 33 industries. Industry aggregation schema is detailed in Appendix B.

Section 9.0 Scenario and Results Analysis

This section provides an overview of the two impacts estimation contexts used to demonstrate the model, a summary analysis and interpretation of the results.

9.1 Scenarios

The large volume of output data from the impacts model presents a challenge for presentation. However, impacts distributions across industries and tax types are relatively consistent for oil and gas productions within a region, and indeed across regions and over time. Based on this realization, the impacts subsections are organized by region and provide results from two types of analyses.

The first context for analysis represents estimating the impacts of a standardized 10 percent change in production. The impacts from these modeled impacts, shown in two parts, represent analyses of a 10 percent increase in oil, and then a 10 percent increase in natural gas production, respectively, to provide a benchmark for and to facilitate comparisons of impacts within and across regions. This context corresponds directly to, and can be most accurately interpreted as the impacts of the substitution of domestic production for previously imported oil or gas.

The second estimation context involved developing a production baseline and alternative level forecasts. This context allowed for the analysis of potential impacts due to changes in forecasted production levels.

9.1.1 The Baseline

For this context, which demonstrates the versatility of the model developed, the EIA's Annual Energy Outlook, 2008 (AEO2008), serves as a baseline estimate of future regional natural gas and oil production levels. Because the model is founded on EIA's 2006 disposition and price data and 2006 economic data, industry characterization and regional proportions of supply sources are held constant.[46] The AEO2008 was selected as the baseline scenario for a number of reasons. First, as noted in Section 5.0, the EIA serves as the primary data source for this project and the model. The data collected from EIA for this project is also represented in the AEO2008, so using this forecast series enhances data consistency. Second, the AEO2008 constitutes EIA's projection of production, total supply (including trade), demand and prices of the various fuel and energy sources produced and/or consumed within the United States. Hence, it provides annual forecasts through 2030 under the assumption of continuing the existing regulatory framework. This assumption means that any legislation that has been enacted at the time of the AEO's development is incorporated and any pending or potential legislation is excluded. In addition, the AEO assumes technologies will continue to develop at established learning rates and that no additional resource sinks will be discovered. These characteristics allow scenario analysis to cover an array of years and potential production levels and support the general definition of a baseline (i.e., a control data set used for

---

[46] Estimating future impacts based on a static industry and economic framework is not ideal. FY 2009 plans for extending this project include incorporating price sensitivities and final demand forecasts into the model.

40

comparison). The third reason the AEO2008 was used as a baseline is because it is generated through the National Energy Modeling System (NEMS)[47] and regional disposition data were available, thus supporting the regional aspect of this project.

AEO2008 regional natural gas and oil production data are generated in NEMS' Oil and Gas Supply Module (OGSM) and reported by three prime regions: Lower-48 onshore, Lower-48 offshore and Alaska.[48] The Lower-48 data were used in the lower-48 region of the model and the sub-regional data, based on the regional delineation shown in Figure 1, were collected for use in the sub-national regions of the model. The 2006 sub-national data were then mapped to the state level to match the data used as the model base data. The state-level production forecasts were then aggregated to match the model's regional definitions and 2006 production levels, which are equal to EIA state-level reports. The ratios developed in mapping the lower-48 OGSM regional data to the state level were held constant across all forecast years.

Figure 6. OGSM Lower-48 Regions

The last steps in establishing the baseline were to define the regions' average well depths for natural gas and oil wells and to set the international trade feedback share.[49] In order to maintain consistency with the model's source data, well depth data by state (as provided by the Joint Association Survey [JAS]) serve as the basis for setting each region's average well depth for both natural gas and oil in the baseline scenario. Table 8 illustrates how the regional average well depths were calculated in Region 5 for natural

---

[47] EIA. "Overview of NEMS." March 4, 2003. http://www.eia.doe.gov/oiaf/aeo/overview/overview.html. Annually updated module documentation: http://tonto.eia.doe.gov/reports/reports_kindD.asp?type=model%20documentation.
[48] EIA. "Documentation of the Oil and Gas Supply Module (OGSM)." DOE/EIA-M063(2008). October 2008. p. 2-1.
[49] The international feedback share represents the decline in exports of all U.S. goods caused by the decline in revenue from countries whose exports of crude oil and natural gas to the U.S. are displaced by domestic production.

41

gas; the same methodology was applied to oil wells. The regional average well depths were held constant across all forecast years.

Table 8. Regional Average Well Depth Calculation

Region	Well Type	Depth Range (ft)	Number of Wells	Total Footage (ft)	Average Footage (ft)
CA	NATURAL GAS	2,500 – 3,749	10	33,075	
CA	NATURAL GAS	3,750 – 4,999	10	44,538	
CA	NATURAL GAS	5,000 – 7,499	26	149,459	
CA	NATURAL GAS	7,500 – 9,999	3	24,296	
CA	NATURAL GAS	10,000 – 12,499	1	10,550	
CA	**NATURAL GAS**	----------------	**50**	**261,918**	**5,238; Range 5,000 – 7,499**

For the baseline, the international trade feedback share was set at 10 percent. The model is set to accept a share ranging from 0 to 20 percent. Ten percent was selected for the baseline run to serve as a mid-point estimate (neither liberal nor conservative in estimation).

9.1.2 The Counterfactual

The original plan for this project indicated that the alternative, or production impact, scenario would reflect production changes due to the deployment of EPAct-999 supported technologies, provided these data were available. The original plan also recognized that these data may not yet be available and offered an alternative analysis of running varying rates of production increases to exemplify the potential applications of the model. Because data on new technologies is not yet available, the latter alternative was taken and the results are shown in subsequent subsections. The alternative scenario generated through the NEMS model provides a realistic demonstration of the model application.

The alternative production scenario, or "counterfactual," reflects the estimated impact of America's Climate Security Act of 2007 (or S.2191) coupled with (1) advanced nuclear technology total plant costs set to approximately $4,000/kW[50] and (2) the availability of CO_2 capture retrofit technology for existing pulverized coal power plants beginning in 2014—this case's acronym is S2191HNR. The S.2191 bill proposed establishing a carbon trading system, beginning in 2012, aimed at reducing greenhouse gas (GHG) emissions from facilities within the electric power and industrial sectors. Additionally, the legislation covered GHGs emitted from facilities that produce, or entities that import, petroleum- or coal-based transportation fuel or chemicals; this legislation specifically covers natural gas and oil suppliers.[51] Both natural gas and oil domestic production decline in nearly all years and in all regions as end users reduce their demand for both natural gas and oil, due to rising prices created by legislation costs passed down from

---

[50] The increased capital cost price point is based on the capital cost range of $3,108/kW and $4,540/kW estimated by Florida Power & Light for Turkey Point units 6 and 7. Florida Public Service Commission, Docket 070650-EI, p. 24.

[51] U.S. Library of Congress, THOMAS, S.2191 summary, http://thomas.loc.gov/cgi-bin/query/z?c110:S.2191.

42

suppliers. See Table 9 for examples of the national level impact of the legislation on natural gas and oil product prices, domestic production and consumption.

Table 9. Natural Gas and Oil Price and Consumption Data, AEO2008 and S2191HNR

	2010		2020		2030	
	AEO2008	S2191HNR	AEO2008	S2191HNR	AEO2008	S2191HNR
Delivered Energy Prices						
Motor gasoline, transport (per gallon)	2.55	2.54	2.36	2.58	2.45	2.85
Jet fuel (per gallon)	2.13	2.12	1.79	2.09	2.07	2.66
Diesel (per gallon)	2.70	2.82	2.50	2.82	2.68	3.26
Natural gas (per thousand cubic feet)						
Residential	12.52	12.47	11.74	13.81	13.30	18.29
Electric Power	7.16	7.10	6.11	7.90	7.13	11.44
Domestic Production[52]						
Natural gas (dry, tcf/yr)	19.29	19.20	19.67	18.92	19.43	19.05
Crude oil (MMbbl/yr)	1,133	1,133	1,197	1,192	1,233	1,229
Energy Consumption (Quads)						
Liquid Fuels	40.5	40.4	42.2	41.2	44.0	42.0
Natural Gas	23.9	23.8	24.0	22.9	23.4	22.7
Electricity Generation (BkWh)						
Petroleum	57	55	60	33	66	27
Natural Gas	908	894	832	832	737	896

The S2191HNR scenario average natural gas and oil well depths are set equal to those used in the baseline (AEO2008) scenario. Additionally, the international feedback loop was also set equal to the baseline scenario at 10 percent. With the baseline and alternative scenarios defined and developed, impact estimates reflecting the change in production become possible.

9.2 Model Analysis Results

To address both scenario contexts developed above and to demonstrate the flexibility and utility of the model, impact results from the scenarios described above are reported and analyzed in this subsection. Results for those industries most heavily affected are presented in detail, which also identifies those industries with the strongest intra-regional, inter-industry relationships within the oil and gas economy. For the standardized 10-percent analyses, no international trade feedback effects are included (feedback effect set equal to zero) and baseline values are used for average

---

[52] Natural Gas production presented here reflects national, dry production from onshore, offshore and Alaska; oil production presented here reflects national withdrawals from onshore sources only.

43

well-depth by region.[53] Disaggregated results tables of output and employment impacts for strongly linked industries are presented for both import substitution and construction.

Each counterfactual scenario represents the impacts differences to the AEO baseline due to the adoption of America's Climate Security Act of 2007, or S.2191. Along with summary input data, summary results are presented for the resulting import substitution and construction impacts for each region for the years 2010, 2020, and 2030.[54] These results are reported as either legislation benefits or the opportunity costs of legislation. When the production levels in the baseline scenario (AEO2008) are less than those in the S.2191 scenario, the resulting impacts are considered to be legislation benefits that would not have occurred absent the 2007 legislation. However, when the production levels in the S.2191 scenario are less than those in the AEO baseline scenario, the resulting impacts represent opportunity costs of legislation, in the form of impacts that do not occur as a result of passing this particular legislation.

The results for Region 1, the Marcellus Shale region, are presented in greatest detail. Impacts distributions across industries, tax types and regions are quite similar. This result reflects the fact that the industries most strongly linked to the energy economy are the same from region to region. Industry impacts across regions differ primarily in the extent to which this set of industries is present or absent within each region. Likewise, the distribution of tax impacts across tax types will appear strongly similar from region to region. For this reason, discussion of subsequent regions will be limited to a description of the nature of the impacts scenarios in terms of benefits versus opportunity costs.

9.2.1 Region 1 (Marcellus Shale) – Standardized Production Increase

Oil. In 2006, onshore oil withdrawals for the Marcellus Shale Region totaled 11,116 kbbl/yr. A 10 percent increase in this value yields a new production level of 12,228 kbbl/yr, or an increase of 1,112 kbbl/yr. Table 10 reports the regional impacts from import substitution for this particular increase in domestic production ranked by output impact.

---

[53] The interregional feedback effect used in the subsequent scenario analyses is quite small and has very little impact on the industry or tax-type distribution of impacts.

[54] Scenario analyses tables for which results are effectively zero are not reported in the document. This occurred for Bakken Shale, 2010 (Oil Only) and Greater Green River, 2010 (Oil Only).

44

Table 10. Major Import Substitution Impacts from a 10 Percent Oil Increase for Region 1

Import Substitution Impacts (In Millions of US Dollars)		Output Components		Value Added Components				
Industry	Output	Intermediate Inputs	Value Added	Employment Compensation	Proprietor's Income	Other Property Type Income	Indirect Business Taxes	Employment (FTE's)
Oil and Gas Extraction	$70	$27	$43	$3	$15	$22	$4	124
Finance and Insurance, Real Estate, Rental and Leasing Services	$4	$1	$3	$1	$0	$1	$0	16
Other Manufacturing	$4	$3	$1	$1	$0	$0	$0	10
Other Professional, Scientific & Tech Services	$1	$0	$1	$0	$0	$0	$0	7
Educational Services, Health Care, and Social Assistance	$1	$0	$0	$0	$0	$0	$0	9
Operations	$1	$0	$1	$0	$0	$0	$0	4
Enterprises	$1	$0	$0	$0	$0	$0	$0	3
Government & Non NAICs	$1	$0	$1	$0	$0	$0	$0	6
Wholesale Trade	$1	$0	$0	$0	$0	$0	$0	3
Information	$1	$0	$0	$0	$0	$0	$0	1
Total	$86	$34	$52	$7	$15	$25	$5	216

*Results displayed for the top 10 sectors in terms of total output impacts. Total values still include all 33 sectors.

As expected, "Oil and Gas Extraction" is the most heavily impacted sector both in terms of output and employment import substitution impacts. While it might appear counter-intuitive at first glance, other detailed oil and gas industries, such as "Drilling Oil and Gas Wells" and "Support Activities for Oil and Gas Operations," have little to no impact based on this analysis. However, this result is due first to the fact that the import substitution impacts do not include the construction impacts of increased production; the impacts identified here are annual and ongoing. Second, support activities for oil and gas operations simply do not account for a large portion of average annual costs per dollar of sector output.

Industries that are somewhat more heavily impacted both in terms of output and employment are "Finance and Insurance, Real Estate, Rental and Leasing Services" and "Other Manufacturing," which account for much larger cost shares per dollar of oil and gas sector output. The "Leasing Services" category likely accounts for the bulk of the former impact, while the "Other Manufacturing" category includes a wide and varied set of industries in which its cumulative cost share is large enough to be noted. Together with "Oil and Gas Extraction," these four industries account for over 90 percent of output impacts and 69 percent of employment impacts in the region. Indeed, few industries constitute major per dollar costs for this industry, reflecting the fact that this is a highly capital-intensive industry, with much of the production costs playing an early role during installation of the production facilities. The industry impacts of these one-time construction investment expenditures are shown in Table 11, again sorted by output impact size.

45

Table 11. Major Construction Impacts from a 10 Percent Oil Increase for Region 1

Construction Impacts (In Millions of US Dollars)		Output Components		Value Added Components				
Industry	Output	Intermediate Inputs	Value Added	Employment Compensation	Proprietor's Income	Other Property Type Income	Indirect Business Taxes	Employment (FTE's)
Water, Sewer, and Pipeline Construction	$305	$160	$145	$94	$27	$22	$2	2,388
Drilling Oil and Gas Wells	$968	$691	$277	$77	$19	$148	$32	1,687
Other Manufacturing	$483	$344	$140	$82	$7	$47	$4	1,273
Arts, Entertainment, Recreation, Accomodation, and Food Services	$65	$30	$35	$22	$2	$7	$4	1,138
Educational Services, Health Care, and Social Assistance	$69	$27	$42	$34	$4	$4	$0	865
Retail Trade	$54	$18	$36	$20	$2	$7	$7	770
Finance and Insurance, Real Estate, Rental and Leasing Services	$152	$54	$98	$47	$8	$35	$8	616
Other Professional, Scientific & Tech Services	$92	$37	$55	$34	$12	$8	$1	601
Government & Non NAICs	$55	$5	$50	$27	$0	$20	$3	493
Administrative and Support & Waste Managment and Remediation Services	$30	$11	$19	$13	$1	$3	$1	469
Total	$2,734	$1,578	$1,156	$594	$104	$376	$82	12,781

*Results displayed for the top 10 sectors in terms of total output impacts. Total values still include all 33 sectors.

Recall that construction impacts reflect the sum total of impacts from the construction investment activity and do not recur annually. Construction impacts clearly affect a larger proportion and more even distribution of industry sectors in the regional economy than do import substitution impacts. In terms of output, the directly linked "Drilling Oil and Gas Wells" sector has the largest impact, while "Water, Sewer and Pipeline Construction" yields the largest employment impact, with "Drilling Oil and Gas Wells" coming in second. "Drilling Oil and Gas Wells," "Water, Sewer and Pipeline Construction," and "Other Manufacturing" alone account for over 64 percent of output impacts and over 41 percent of employment impacts. It can also be seen from the table that a larger number of consumer-related sectors, such as "Educational Services, Health Care and Social Assistance" or "Wholesale" or "Retail" services are notably affected. This result is attributed to the large portion of construction expenditures that translate to income and subsequently income-induced impacts. The sector rankings differ when sorted by output or by employment. This result reflects inter-sectoral differences in wages per dollar of output.

Gas. In 2006, onshore natural gas withdrawals for the Marcellus Shale Region totaled 526,180 MMcf/yr. A 10 percent increase in this value yields a new production value of 578,798 MMcf/yr, or an increase of 52,618 MMcf/yr. Table 12 reports the regional impacts from import substitution ranked by output impacts.

46

Table 12. Major Import Substitution Impacts for a 10 Percent Natural Gas Increase for Region 1

| Import Substitution Impacts (In Millions of US | Output Components | | Value Added Components | | | | |
Industry	Output	Intermediate Inputs	Value Added	Employment Compensation	Proprietor's Income	Other Property Type Income	Indirect Business Taxes	Employment (FTE's)
Oil and Gas Extraction	$386	$147	$239	$14	$81	$121	$23	684
Other Manufacturing	$50	$35	$14	$8	$1	$5	$0	131
Finance and Insurance, Real Estate, Rental and Leasing Services	$31	$11	$20	$10	$2	$7	$2	125
Educational Services, Health Care, and Social Assistance	$8	$3	$5	$4	$0	$1	$0	103
Retail Trade	$6	$2	$4	$2	$0	$1	$1	81
Arts, Entertainment, Recreation, Accomodation, and Food Services	$4	$2	$2	$1	$0	$0	$0	76
Other Professional, Scientific & Tech Services	$11	$4	$6	$4	$1	$1	$0	70
Government & Non NAICs	$7	$1	$6	$3	$0	$2	$0	60
Administrative and Support & Waste Managment and Remediation Services	$3	$1	$2	$1	$0	$0	$0	51
Wholesale Trade	$8	$3	$5	$3	$0	$1	$1	43
Total	$581	$246	$335	$66	$88	$150	$32	1,679

*Results displayed for the top 10 sectors in terms of total output impacts. Total values still include all 33 sectors.

Note that the top ranked sectors in the Gas Import Substitution table coincide approximately with the top import substitution sectors for oil import substitution, although "Natural Gas Distribution" rises in importance while "Support Activities for Oil and Gas Operations" falls in relative importance, and other minor re-orderings occur. The differences between the Oil and the Gas Import Substitution results tables are due primarily to the differences in sheer size of the dollar impact, which translates into much larger output impacts and payments to households in the form of employment compensation, which in turn translates to larger income-induced impacts.

Table 13. Construction Impacts from a 10 Percent Natural Gas Increase for Region 1

| Construction Impacts (In Millions of US Dollars) | Output Components | | Value Added Components | | | | |
Industry	Output	Intermediate Inputs	Value Added	Employment Compensation	Proprietor's Income	Other Property Type Income	Indirect Business Taxes	Employment (FTE's)
Drilling Oil and Gas Wells	$5,023	$3,586	$1,437	$401	$99	$769	$168	8,753
Arts, Entertainment, Recreation, Accomodation, and Food Services	$274	$125	$149	$93	$10	$30	$16	4,800
Other Manufacturing	$1,813	$1,289	$523	$309	$27	$175	$13	4,774
Educational Services, Health Care, and Social Assistance	$231	$90	$141	$113	$12	$14	$2	2,910
Other Professional, Scientific & Tech Services	$397	$159	$238	$148	$51	$34	$4	2,597
Retail Trade	$178	$61	$118	$65	$6	$23	$24	2,537
Finance and Insurance, Real Estate, Rental and Leasing Services	$561	$198	$363	$175	$28	$129	$30	2,279
Management of Companies and Enterprises	$463	$169	$294	$229	-$1	$61	$5	1,975
Government & Non NAICs	$194	$18	$177	$95	$1	$70	$10	1,739
Administrative and Support & Waste Managment and Remediation Services	$106	$40	$66	$47	$5	$12	$2	1,652
Total	$10,617	$6,367	$4,250	$2,021	$314	$1,567	$348	41,470

*Results displayed for the top 10 sectors in terms of total output impacts. Total values still include all 33 sectors.

As with the increase in oil production, the construction impacts are much larger overall in Table 13, and have larger relative effects on more regional industries than do the corresponding import substitution impacts. The natural gas import substitution impacts are also more widespread than the oil import substitution impacts. The directly linked "Drilling Oil and Gas Wells" still accounts for the largest impacts in terms of both output and employment.

47

Tax Impacts.

Tax impacts are estimated from data that relates regional tax receipts by type to output totals and to the various components of value added, including employee compensation, proprietary income (profit), other property income and indirect business taxes. Because these data are related at a highly aggregated level, they should be taken as coarse estimates of impacts on tax revenues. As was the case with industry impacts, the distribution of sizable tax impacts is wider ranging for construction compared to import substitution impacts.

IMPLAN provides the following definitions:[55]

> Employee Compensation in IMPLAN is the total payroll cost of the employee paid by the employer. This includes wage and salary, all benefits (e.g., health, retirement, etc.) and employer paid payroll taxes (e.g., employer side of social security, unemployment taxes, etc.).

> Proprietor income consists of payments received by self-employed individuals and unincorporated business owners. This income also includes the capital consumption allowance.

> Other property income represents property income minus proprietor income. It includes corporate profits, capital consumption allowance, payments for rent, and interest income. It may also be referred to as "other property type income."

> Indirect Business Taxes […] consist of tax and nontax liabilities that are chargeable to business expenses when calculating profit-type incomes and certain other business liabilities to government agencies that are treated like taxes. Thus, IBT includes taxes on sales, property and production, but it excludes employer contributions for social insurance and taxes on income. As part of the NIPA revision, this component was modified and termed "taxes on production and imports less subsidies." The major differences between the two are attributable to the treatments of subsidies and non-taxes. (BEA)

---

[55] For complete definitions of types of taxes, see http://implan.com/index.php?option=com_glossary&Itemid=108. For a comprehensive treatment of the IMPLAN tax estimation procedures, see http://implan.com/index.php?option=com_docman&task=doc_download&gid=97&Itemid=65.

48

Table 14. Import Substitution Tax Impacts from a 10 Percent Oil Increase for Region 1

Import Substitution Tax Impact (In Millions of US Dollars)		Sources					
		Employee Compensation	Proprietary Income	Household Expenditures	Enterprises (Corporations)	Indirect Business Tax	Total
Federal Government NonDefense	Corporate Profits Tax	$0	$0	$0	$2	$0	$2
	Personal Tax: Income Tax	$0	$0	$2	$0	$0	$2
	Social Insurance Tax-Employee Contribution	$0	$1	$0	$0	$0	$1
	Total	$1	$1	$2	$2	$1	$6
State/Local Government NonEducation	Corporate Profits Tax	$0	$0	$0	$1	$0	$1
	Dividends	$0	$0	$0	$1	$0	$1
	Indirect Business Tax: Property Tax	$0	$0	$0	$0	$2	$2
	Indirect Business Tax: Sales Tax	$0	$0	$0	$0	$2	$2
	Personal Tax: Income Tax	$0	$0	$1	$0	$0	$1
	Total	$0	$0	$1	$1	$4	$7
Total		$1	$1	$3	$4	$5	$13

*Results are not displayed for tax categories that experience no impact.

Table 15. Construction Tax Impacts from a 10 Percent Oil Increase for Region 1

Construction Tax Impact (In Millions of US Dollars)		Sources					
		Employee Compensation	Proprietary Income	Household Expenditures	Enterprises (Corporations)	Indirect Business Tax	Total
Enterprises (Corporations)	Transfers	$1	$0	$0	$0	$0	$1
	Total	$1	$0	$0	$0	$0	$1
Federal Government NonDefense	Corporate Profits Tax	$0	$0	$0	$36	$0	$36
	Indirect Business Tax: Custom Duty	$0	$0	$0	$0	$2	$2
	Indirect Business Tax: Excise Taxes	$0	$0	$0	$0	$5	$5
	Indirect Business Tax: Fed Non Taxes	$0	$0	$0	$0	$2	$2
	Personal Tax: Income Tax	$0	$0	$55	$0	$0	$55
	Social Insurance Tax-Employee Contribution	$34	$5	$0	$0	$0	$39
	Social Insurance Tax-Employer Contribution	$34	$0	$0	$0	$0	$34
	Total	$68	$5	$55	$36	$9	$174
State/Local Government NonEducation	Corporate Profits Tax	$0	$0	$0	$10	$0	$10
	Dividends	$0	$0	$0	$12	$0	$12
	Indirect Business Tax: Motor Vehicle License	$0	$0	$0	$0	$1	$1
	Indirect Business Tax:	$0	$0	$0	$0	$6	$6
	Indirect Business Tax: Property Tax	$0	$0	$0	$0	$33	$33
	Indirect Business Tax: S/L Non Taxes	$0	$0	$0	$0	$2	$2
	Indirect Business Tax: Sales Tax	$0	$0	$0	$0	$31	$31
	Personal Tax: Income Tax	$0	$0	$22	$0	$0	$22
	Personal Tax: Motor Vehicle License	$0	$0	$1	$0	$0	$1
	Personal Tax: Non Taxes (Fines-Fees)	$0	$0	$4	$0	$0	$4
	Social Insurance Tax-Employee Contribution	$1	$0	$0	$0	$0	$1
	Social Insurance Tax-Employer Contribution	$2	$0	$0	$0	$0	$2
	Total	$3	$0	$27	$22	$73	$125
Total		$72	$5	$82	$58	$82	$299

*Results are not displayed for tax categories that experience no impact.

These general tax results hold with little variation for oil and gas, and across all regions.

49

Table 16. Import Substitution Tax Impacts from a 10 Percent Gas Increase for Region 1

Import Substitution Tax Impact (In Millions of US Dollars)		Sources					
		Employee Compensation	Proprietary Income	Household Expenditures	Enterprises (Corporations)	Indirect Business Tax	Total
Enterprises (Corporations)	Transfers	$3	$0	$0	$0	$0	$3
	Total	$3	$0	$0	$0	$0	$3
Federal Government NonDefense	Corporate Profits Tax	$0	$0	$0	$438	$0	$438
	Indirect Business Tax: Custom Duty	$0	$0	$0	$0	$29	$29
	Indirect Business Tax: Excise Taxes	$0	$0	$0	$0	$77	$77
	Indirect Business Tax: Fed Non Taxes	$0	$0	$0	$0	$35	$35
	Personal Tax: Income Tax	$0	$0	$429	$0	$0	$429
	Social Insurance Tax- Employee Contribution	$182	$91	$0	$0	$0	$273
	Social Insurance Tax- Employer Contribution	$184	$0	$0	$0	$0	$184
	Total	$366	$91	$429	$438	$141	$1,465
State/Local Government NonEducation	Corporate Profits Tax	$0	$0	$0	$73	$0	$73
	Dividends	$0	$0	$0	$112	$0	$112
	Indirect Business Tax: Motor Vehicle License	$0	$0	$0	$0	$9	$9
	Indirect Business Tax: Other Taxes	$0	$0	$0	$0	$72	$72
	Indirect Business Tax: Property Tax	$0	$0	$0	$0	$395	$395
	Indirect Business Tax: S/L Non Taxes	$0	$0	$0	$0	$44	$44
	Indirect Business Tax: Sales Tax	$0	$0	$0	$0	$446	$446
	Indirect Business Tax: Severance Tax	$0	$0	$0	$0	$11	$11
	Personal Tax: Income Tax	$0	$0	$112	$0	$0	$112
	Personal Tax: Motor Vehicle License	$0	$0	$4	$0	$0	$4
	Personal Tax: Non Taxes (Fines-Fees)	$0	$0	$26	$0	$0	$26
	Personal Tax: Other Tax (Fish/Hunt)	$0	$0	$2	$0	$0	$2
	Personal Tax: Property Tax	$0	$0	$3	$0	$0	$3
	Social Insurance Tax- Employee Contribution	$2	$0	$0	$0	$0	$2
	Social Insurance Tax- Employer Contribution	$9	$0	$0	$0	$0	$9
	Total	$11	$0	$146	$185	$977	$1,320
Total		$381	$91	$575	$624	$1,118	$2,788

*Results are not displayed for tax categories that experience no impact.

50

Table 17. Construction Tax Impacts from a 10 Percent Natural Gas Increase for Region 1

Construction Tax Impact (In Millions of US Dollars)		Employee Compensation	Proprietary Income	Household Expenditures	Enterprises (Corporations)	Indirect Business Tax	Total
Enterprises (Corporations)	Transfers	$14	$0	$0	$0	$0	$14
	Total	$14	$0	$0	$0	$0	$14
Federal Government NonDefense	Corporate Profits Tax	$0	$0	$0	$1,214	$0	$1,214
	Indirect Business Tax: Custom Duty	$0	$0	$0	$0	$73	$73
	Indirect Business Tax: Excise Taxes	$0	$0	$0	$0	$197	$197
	Indirect Business Tax: Fed Non Taxes	$0	$0	$0	$0	$89	$89
	Personal Tax: Income Tax	$0	$0	$1,286	$0	$0	$1,286
	Social Insurance Tax-Employee Contribution	$812	$77	$0	$0	$0	$890
	Social Insurance Tax-Employer Contribution	$824	$0	$0	$0	$0	$824
	Total	$1,637	$77	$1,286	$1,214	$359	$4,573
State/Local Government NonEducation	Corporate Profits Tax	$0	$0	$0	$203	$0	$203
	Dividends	$0	$0	$0	$310	$0	$310
	Indirect Business Tax: Motor Vehicle License	$0	$0	$0	$0	$23	$23
	Indirect Business Tax: Other Taxes	$0	$0	$0	$0	$183	$183
	Indirect Business Tax: Property Tax	$0	$0	$0	$0	$1,006	$1,006
	Indirect Business Tax: S/L Non Taxes	$0	$0	$0	$0	$111	$111
	Indirect Business Tax: Sales Tax	$0	$0	$0	$0	$1,136	$1,136
	Indirect Business Tax: Severance Tax	$0	$0	$0	$0	$29	$29
	Personal Tax: Income Tax	$0	$0	$336	$0	$0	$336
	Personal Tax: Motor Vehicle License	$0	$0	$18	$0	$0	$18
	Personal Tax: Non Taxes (Fines-Fees)	$0	$0	$78	$0	$0	$78
	Personal Tax: Other Tax (Fish/Hunt)	$0	$0	$6	$0	$0	$6
	Personal Tax: Property Tax	$0	$0	$8	$0	$0	$8
	Social Insurance Tax-Employee Contribution	$10	$0	$0	$0	$0	$10
	Social Insurance Tax-Employer Contribution	$40	$0	$0	$0	$0	$40
	Total	$50	$0	$446	$514	$2,487	$3,496
Total		$1,701	$77	$1,732	$1,728	$2,846	$8,084

*Results are not displayed for tax categories that experience no impact.

9.2.2 Region 1 (Marcellus Shale) – Scenario Analysis

Three scenario analyses for the Marcellus Shale Region are performed and reported, one for each time period, 2010, 2020, and 2030. For this region, future production in all time periods is expected to be less after adopting the S.2191 legislation in 2007 than it is for the AEO2008 estimate under the 2006 legislative environment. Therefore, all of the following impacts estimated for this region are considered opportunity costs of the S.2191 legislation.

In 2010, there is no difference in the future production of oil in the baseline (AEO2008) estimation and S.2191 estimation, but 2008 MMcf/yr of natural gas was not produced due to the new legislation. Table 18 gives a summary report of the data input and the total impacts from import substitution and construction that are not realized due to the adoption of S.2191.[56]

Table 18. Input Data and Summary Results for Marcellus Shale, 2010

Input Data Summary for Marcellus Shale		
	Natural Gas	Oil
Production Increases	2008 MMcf/yr	0 thbbl/yr
Estimated Average Well Depth	3,750-4,999 ft/well	2,500-3,749 ft/well
Well Construction Cost	352 th$/well	228 th$/well
Average Producer Price	7.46 $/tcf	63.11 $/bbl
Industry Output	16 Million $	0 Million $
Reduced Import Payments	15 Million $	0 Million $
International Trade Feedback Share	10%	10%
Year Dollars	2006	2006

Summary Results for Marcellus Shale			
(Millions of US Dollars)	Output	FTEs	Taxes
Import Substitution Impacts	$22	61	$3
Construction Impacts	$405	1,580	$43

In 2020, due to the new legislation, 22,370 MMcf/yr of natural gas and 6 thbbl/yr of oil are not produced. The following impacts, shown in Table 19, are not realized and reflect the opportunity costs of the legislation.

---

[56] With the duplication of input data included in this report and the ease of impacts model use, interested readers can easily duplicate any of the scenario analyses to obtain results at the level of industry detail. Likewise, the readers can contact the authors for more detailed and disaggregated results. Again, however, the distributions of impacts across industries and tax types will strongly resemble those of the standard 10 percent analyses presented for each region.

Table 19. Input Data and Summary Results for Marcellus Shale, 2020

Input Data Summary for Marcellus Shale		
	Natural Gas	Oil
Production Increases	22370 MMcf/yr	6 thbbl/yr
Estimated Average Well Depth	3,750-4,999 ft/well	2,500-3,749 ft/well
Well Construction Cost	352 th$/well	228 th$/well
Average Producer Price	7.46 $/tcf	63.11 $/bbl
Industry Output	177 Million $	0 Million $
Reduced Import Payments	172 Million $	0 Million $
International Trade Feedback Share	10%	10%
Year Dollars	2006	2006

Summary Results for Marcellus Shale			
(Millions of US Dollars)	Output	FTEs	Taxes
Import Substitution Impacts	$242	687	$36
Construction Impacts	$4,526	17,680	$478

Finally, a similar scenario exists for the year 2030. Once again, there is no difference in the amount of oil produced under the S.2191 legislation, but 3,982 fewer MMcf/yr of natural gas are produced. The results displayed below in Table 20 represent the opportunity costs in the year 2030 of the S.2191 legislation.

Table 20. Input Data and Summary Results for Marcellus Shale, 2030

Input Data Summary for Marcellus Shale		
	Natural Gas	Oil
Production Increases	3982 MMcf/yr	0 thbbl/yr
Estimated Average Well Depth	3,750-4,999 ft/well	2,500-3,749 ft/well
Well Construction Cost	352 th$/well	228 th$/well
Average Producer Price	7.46 $/tcf	63.11 $/bbl
Industry Output	31 Million $	0 Million $
Reduced Import Payments	31 Million $	0 Million $
International Trade Feedback Share	10%	10%
Year Dollars	2006	2006

Summary Results for Marcellus Shale			
(Millions of US Dollars)	Output	FTEs	Taxes
Import Substitution Impacts	$43	122	$6
Construction Impacts	$803	3,134	$85

53

9.2.3 Region 2 (Bakken Shale) – Standardized Production Increase

Oil.

Table 21. Major Import Substitution Impacts from a 10 Percent Oil Increase for Region 2

Import Substitution Impacts (In Millions of US Dollars)	Output	Output Components		Value Added Components				Employment (FTE's)
Industry	Output	Intermediate Inputs	Value Added	Employment Compensation	Proprietor's Income	Other Property Type Income	Indirect Business Taxes	Employment (FTE's)
Oil and Gas Extraction	$457	$167	$291	$29	$87	$147	$28	781
Other Manufacturing	$62	$52	$10	$5	$1	$4	$0	122
Finance and Insurance, Real Estate, Rental and Leasing Services	$61	$25	$36	$9	$4	$19	$4	375
Other Professional, Scientific & Tech Services	$17	$8	$8	$5	$2	$1	$0	183
Educational Services, Health Care, and Social Assistance	$11	$5	$6	$5	$1	$1	$0	158
Support Activities for Oil and Gas Operations	$10	$1	$10	$3	$0	$6	$0	52
Management of Companies and Enterprises	$10	$5	$5	$4	$0	$1	$0	68
Wholesale Trade	$9	$3	$6	$3	$0	$1	$1	70
Government & Non NAICs	$9	$1	$8	$5	$0	$2	$0	114
Information	$8	$5	$4	$2	$0	$1	$0	39
Total	$705	$296	$409	$85	$97	$189	$37	2,551

*Results displayed for the top 10 sectors in terms of total output impacts. Total values still include all 33 sectors.

Table 22. Major Construction Impacts from a 10 Percent Oil Increase for Region 2

Construction Impacts (In Millions of US Dollars)	Output	Output Components		Value Added Components				Employment (FTE's)
Industry	Output	Intermediate Inputs	Value Added	Employment Compensation	Proprietor's Income	Other Property Type Income	Indirect Business Taxes	Employment (FTE's)
Drilling Oil and Gas Wells	$2,668	$1,742	$926	$309	$14	$495	$108	4,051
Other Manufacturing	$1,375	$1,145	$230	$121	$20	$83	$6	2,693
Finance and Insurance, Real Estate, Rental and Leasing Services	$400	$163	$237	$60	$25	$126	$25	2,469
Management of Companies and Enterprises	$344	$171	$173	$135	$0	$36	$3	2,309
Other Professional, Scientific & Tech Services	$270	$136	$134	$81	$29	$21	$3	2,966
Wholesale Trade	$202	$66	$136	$70	$6	$30	$30	1,510
Arts, Entertainment, Recreation, Accomodation, and Food Services	$194	$103	$91	$55	$5	$21	$11	4,338
Educational Services, Health Care, and Social Assistance	$145	$63	$82	$65	$8	$9	$1	2,030
Information	$144	$83	$60	$30	$3	$23	$5	676
Retail Trade	$118	$42	$76	$41	$6	$13	$16	2,022
Total	$6,781	$4,142	$2,639	$1,221	$172	$1,011	$235	32,797

*Results displayed for the top 10 sectors in terms of total output impacts. Total values still include all 33 sectors.

54

Gas.

Table 23. Major Import Substitution Impacts from a 10 Percent Natural Gas Increase for Region 2

Import Substitution Impacts (In Millions of US Dollars)		Output Components		Value Added Components				Employment
Industry	Output	Intermediate Inputs	Value Added	Employment Compensation	Proprietor's Income	Other Property Type Income	Indirect Business Taxes	(FTE's)
Oil and Gas Extraction	$93	$34	$59	$6	$18	$30	$6	160
Natural Gas Distribution	$30	$20	$10	$4	$1	$3	$3	40
Other Manufacturing	$17	$14	$3	$2	$0	$1	$0	34
Finance and Insurance, Real Estate, Rental and Leasing Services	$16	$6	$9	$2	$1	$5	$1	96
Other Professional, Scientific & Tech Services	$4	$2	$2	$1	$0	$0	$0	49
Educational Services, Health Care, and Social Assistance	$3	$1	$2	$1	$0	$0	$0	46
Management of Companies and Enterprises	$3	$1	$1	$1	$0	$0	$0	17
Wholesale Trade	$3	$1	$2	$1	$0	$0	$0	19
Support Activities for Oil and Gas Operations	$3	$0	$2	$1	$0	$1	$0	13
Pipeline Transportation	$2	$2	$1	$0	$0	$0	$0	4
Total	$191	$90	$101	$25	$21	$44	$11	686

*Results displayed for the top 10 sectors in terms of total output impacts. Total values still include all 33 sectors.

Table 24. Major Construction Impacts from a 10 Percent Natural Gas Increase for Region 2

Construction Impacts (In Millions of US Dollars)		Output Components		Value Added Components				Employment
Industry	Output	Intermediate Inputs	Value Added	Employment Compensation	Proprietor's Income	Other Property Type Income	Indirect Business Taxes	(FTE's)
Drilling Oil and Gas Wells	$218	$143	$76	$25	$1	$41	$9	331
Other Manufacturing	$115	$95	$19	$10	$2	$7	$1	225
Finance and Insurance, Real Estate, Rental and Leasing Services	$33	$14	$20	$5	$2	$10	$2	206
Management of Companies and Enterprises	$28	$14	$14	$11	$0	$3	$0	189
Other Professional, Scientific & Tech Services	$22	$11	$11	$7	$2	$2	$0	245
Wholesale Trade	$17	$6	$11	$6	$1	$2	$2	126
Arts, Entertainment, Recreation, Accomodation, and Food Services	$16	$8	$8	$5	$0	$2	$1	359
Educational Services, Health Care, and Social Assistance	$12	$5	$7	$5	$1	$1	$0	170
Information	$12	$7	$5	$2	$0	$2	$0	56
Retail Trade	$10	$4	$6	$3	$0	$1	$1	170
Total	$564	$345	$220	$102	$15	$84	$19	2,759

*Results displayed for the top 10 sectors in terms of total output impacts. Total values still include all 33 sectors.

55

Tax Impacts.

Table 25. Import Substitution Tax Impacts from a 10 Percent Oil Increase for Region 2

Import Substitution Tax Impact (In Millions of US Dollars)		Sources					
		Employee Compensation	Proprietary Income	Household Expenditures	Enterprises (Corporations)	Indirect Business Tax	Total
Federal Government NonDefense	Corporate Profits Tax	$0	$0	$0	$18	$0	$18
	Indirect Business Tax: Custom Duty	$0	$0	$0	$0	$1	$1
	Indirect Business Tax: Excise Taxes	$0	$0	$0	$0	$3	$3
	Indirect Business Tax: Fed Non Taxes	$0	$0	$0	$0	$1	$1
	Personal Tax: Income Tax	$0	$0	$10	$0	$0	$10
	Social Insurance Tax- Employee Contribution	$5	$4	$0	$0	$0	$10
	Social Insurance Tax- Employer Contribution	$5	$0	$0	$0	$0	$5
	Total	$11	$4	$10	$18	$6	$49
State/Local Government NonEducation	Corporate Profits Tax	$0	$0	$0	$3	$0	$3
	Dividends	$0	$0	$0	$3	$0	$3
	Indirect Business Tax: Motor Vehicle License	$0	$0	$0	$0	$1	$1
	Indirect Business Tax: Other Taxes	$0	$0	$0	$0	$1	$1
	Indirect Business Tax: Property Tax	$0	$0	$0	$0	$15	$15
	Indirect Business Tax: S/L Non Taxes	$0	$0	$0	$0	$3	$3
	Indirect Business Tax: Sales Tax	$0	$0	$0	$0	$6	$6
	Indirect Business Tax: Severance Tax	$0	$0	$0	$0	$5	$5
	Personal Tax: Income Tax	$0	$0	$3	$0	$0	$3
	Personal Tax: Non Taxes (Fines-Fees)	$0	$0	$1	$0	$0	$1
	Personal Tax: Other Tax (Fish/Hunt)	$0	$0	$1	$0	$0	$1
	Total	$0	$0	$4	$6	$32	$43
Total		$11	$4	$15	$24	$37	$92

*Results are not displayed for tax categories that experience no impact. Totals still reflect all tax categories.

56

Table 26. Construction Tax Impacts from a 10 Percent Oil Increase for Region 2

Construction Tax Impact (In Millions of US Dollars)		Sources					
		Employee Compensation	Proprietary Income	Household Expenditures	Enterprises (Corporations)	Indirect Business Tax	Total
Enterprises (Corporations)	Transfers	$1	$0	$0	$0	$0	$1
	Total	$1	$0	$0	$0	$0	$1
Federal Government NonDefense	Corporate Profits Tax	$0	$0	$0	$96	$0	$96
	Indirect Business Tax: Custom Duty	$0	$0	$0	$0	$7	$7
	Indirect Business Tax: Excise Taxes	$0	$0	$0	$0	$19	$19
	Indirect Business Tax: Fed Non Taxes	$0	$0	$0	$0	$9	$9
	Personal Tax: Income Tax	$0	$0	$74	$0	$0	$74
	Social Insurance Tax- Employee Contribution	$77	$8	$0	$0	$0	$85
	Social Insurance Tax- Employer Contribution	$79	$0	$0	$0	$0	$79
	Total	$156	$8	$74	$96	$35	$368
State/Local Government NonEducation	Corporate Profits Tax	$0	$0	$0	$14	$0	$14
	Dividends	$0	$0	$0	$18	$0	$18
	Indirect Business Tax: Motor Vehicle License	$0	$0	$0	$0	$4	$4
	Indirect Business Tax: Other Taxes	$0	$0	$0	$0	$9	$9
	Indirect Business Tax: Property Tax	$0	$0	$0	$0	$97	$97
	Indirect Business Tax: S/L Non Taxes	$0	$0	$0	$0	$19	$19
	Indirect Business Tax: Sales Tax	$0	$0	$0	$0	$41	$41
	Indirect Business Tax: Severance Tax	$0	$0	$0	$0	$30	$30
	Personal Tax: Income Tax	$0	$0	$22	$0	$0	$22
	Personal Tax: Motor Vehicle License	$0	$0	$3	$0	$0	$3
	Personal Tax: Non Taxes (Fines-Fees)	$0	$0	$5	$0	$0	$5
	Personal Tax: Other Tax (Fish/Hunt)	$0	$0	$4	$0	$0	$4
	Personal Tax: Property Tax	$0	$0	$1	$0	$0	$1
	Social Insurance Tax- Employee Contribution	$1	$0	$0	$0	$0	$1
	Social Insurance Tax- Employer Contribution	$4	$0	$0	$0	$0	$4
	Total	$5	$0	$34	$33	$200	$271
Total		$162	$8	$107	$129	$235	$641

*Results are not displayed for tax categories that experience no impact. Totals still reflect all tax categories.

Table 27. Import Substitution Tax Impacts from a 10 Percent Natural Gas Increase for Region 2

Import Substitution Tax Impact (In Millions of US Dollars)		Sources					
		Employee Compensation	Proprietary Income	Household Expenditures	Enterprises (Corporations)	Indirect Business Tax	Total
Federal Government NonDefense	Corporate Profits Tax	$0	$0	$0	$4	$0	$4
	Indirect Business Tax: Excise Taxes	$0	$0	$0	$0	$1	$1
	Personal Tax: Income Tax	$0	$0	$3	$0	$0	$3
	Social Insurance Tax- Employee Contribution	$2	$1	$0	$0	$0	$3
	Social Insurance Tax- Employer Contribution	$2	$0	$0	$0	$0	$2
	Total	$3	$1	$3	$4	$2	$12
State/Local Government NonEducation	Corporate Profits Tax	$0	$0	$0	$1	$0	$1
	Dividends	$0	$0	$0	$1	$0	$1
	Indirect Business Tax: Property Tax	$0	$0	$0	$0	$5	$5
	Indirect Business Tax: S/L Non Taxes	$0	$0	$0	$0	$1	$1
	Indirect Business Tax: Sales Tax	$0	$0	$0	$0	$2	$2
	Indirect Business Tax: Severance Tax	$0	$0	$0	$0	$1	$1
	Personal Tax: Income Tax	$0	$0	$1	$0	$0	$1
	Total	$0	$0	$1	$1	$9	$12
Total		$3	$1	$4	$6	$11	$24

*Results are not displayed for tax categories that experience no impact. Totals still reflect all tax categories.

Table 28. Construction Tax Impacts from a 10 Percent Natural Gas Increase for Region 2

Construction Tax Impact (In Millions of US Dollars)		Sources					
		Employee Compensation	Proprietary Income	Household Expenditures	Enterprises (Corporations)	Indirect Business Tax	Total
Federal Government NonDefense	Corporate Profits Tax	$0	$0	$0	$8	$0	$8
	Indirect Business Tax: Custom Duty	$0	$0	$0	$0	$1	$1
	Indirect Business Tax: Excise Taxes	$0	$0	$0	$0	$2	$2
	Indirect Business Tax: Fed Non Taxes	$0	$0	$0	$0	$1	$1
	Personal Tax: Income Tax	$0	$0	$6	$0	$0	$6
	Social Insurance Tax- Employee Contribution	$6	$1	$0	$0	$0	$7
	Social Insurance Tax- Employer Contribution	$7	$0	$0	$0	$0	$7
	Total	$13	$1	$6	$8	$3	$31
State/Local Government NonEducation	Corporate Profits Tax	$0	$0	$0	$1	$0	$1
	Dividends	$0	$0	$0	$2	$0	$2
	Indirect Business Tax: Other Taxes	$0	$0	$0	$0	$1	$1
	Indirect Business Tax: Property Tax	$0	$0	$0	$0	$8	$8
	Indirect Business Tax: S/L Non Taxes	$0	$0	$0	$0	$2	$2
	Indirect Business Tax: Sales Tax	$0	$0	$0	$0	$3	$3
	Indirect Business Tax: Severance Tax	$0	$0	$0	$0	$3	$3
	Personal Tax: Income Tax	$0	$0	$2	$0	$0	$2
	Total	$0	$0	$3	$3	$17	$22
Total		$14	$1	$9	$11	$19	$53

*Results are not displayed for tax categories that experience no impact. Totals still reflect all tax categories.

58

9.2.4 Region 2 (Bakken Shale) – Scenario Analysis

Four scenario analyses were performed for the Bakken Shale Region, however, only three are reported. The analyses reported here are for natural gas impacts in 2010 and oil and gas impacts for both 2020 and 2030. Future production in these three analyses is expected to be less after adopting the S.2191 legislation in 2007 and all impacts reported for this region are considered opportunity costs of the legislation. For the oil industry in 2010, future production was expected to be greater after adopting the S.2191 legislation, but the analysis of this legislation benefit did not yield any significant results as the change in production was very small. Tables 29–31 give summary reports of the data inputs and the total impacts from import substitution and construction for Region 2 that are not realized due to the adoption of S.2191.

Table 29. Input Data and Summary Results for Bakken Shale, 2010 (Natural Gas Only)

Input Data Summary for Bakken Shale		
	Natural Gas	Oil
Production Increases	1346 MMcf/yr	
Estimated Average Well Depth	1,250-2,499 ft/well	
Well Construction Cost	204 th$/well	
Average Producer Price	5.86 $/tcf	
Industry Output	9 Million $	
Reduced Import Payments	0 Million $	
International Trade Feedback Share	10%	
Year Dollars	2006	

Summary Results for Bakken Shale			
(Millions of US Dollars)	Output	FTEs	Taxes
Import Substitution Impacts	$14	51	$2
Construction Impacts	$43	210	$4

Table 30. Input Data and Summary Results for Bakken Shale, 2020

Input Data Summary for Bakken Shale		
	Natural Gas	Oil
Production Increases	9181 MMcf/yr	640 thbbl/yr
Estimated Average Well Depth	1,250-2,499 ft/well	12,500-14,999 ft/well
Well Construction Cost	204 th$/well	3496 th$/well
Average Producer Price	5.86 $/tcf	60.04 $/bbl
Industry Output	64 Million $	38 Million $
Reduced Import Payments	0 Million $	38 Million $
International Trade Feedback Share	10%	10%
Year Dollars	2006	2006

Summary Results for Bakken Shale			
(Millions of US Dollars)	Output	FTEs	Taxes
Import Substitution Impacts	$156	553	$20
Construction Impacts	$861	4,180	$81

59

Table 31. Input Data and Summary Results for Bakken Shale, 2030

Input Data Summary for Bakken Shale		
	Natural Gas	Oil
Production Increases	1050 MMcf/yr	741 thbbl/yr
Estimated Average Well Depth	1,250-2,499 ft/well	12,500-14,999 ft/well
Well Construction Cost	204 th$/well	3496 th$/well
Average Producer Price	5.86 $/tcf	60.04 $/bbl
Industry Output	7 Million $	44 Million $
Reduced Import Payments	0 Million $	44 Million $
International Trade Feedback Share	10%	10%
Year Dollars	2006	2006

Summary Results for Bakken Shale			
(Millions of US Dollars)	Output	FTEs	Taxes
Import Substitution Impacts	$77	267	$10
Construction Impacts	$689	3,334	$65

9.2.5 Region 3 (Barnett Shale) – Standardized Production Increase

Oil.

Table 32. Major Import Substitution Impacts from a 10 Percent Oil Increase for Region 3

Import Substitution Impacts (Millions of US Dollars)		Output Components		Value Added Components				
Industry	Output	Intermediate Inputs	Value Added	Employment Compensation	Proprietor's Income	Other Property Type Income	Indirect Business Taxes	Employment (FTE's)
Oil and Gas Extraction	$2,364	$861	$1,503	$248	$354	$757	$144	2,658
Other Manufacturing	$724	$578	$146	$68	$15	$58	$5	952
Finance and Insurance, Real Estate, Rental and Leasing Services	$636	$249	$386	$112	$42	$193	$39	2,995
Other Professional, Scientific & Tech Services	$178	$74	$104	$67	$22	$14	$2	1,316
Government & Non NAICs	$123	$12	$111	$62	$0	$43	$6	1,271
Educational Services, Health Care, and Social Assistance	$119	$45	$74	$55	$9	$9	$1	1,491
Wholesale Trade	$116	$38	$78	$40	$4	$17	$17	590
Retail Trade	$110	$38	$73	$41	$5	$11	$15	1,603
Management of Companies and Enterprises	$107	$46	$61	$48	-$1	$13	$1	588
Information	$103	$53	$50	$19	$5	$21	$4	292
Total	$5,158	$2,230	$2,927	$920	$493	$1,256	$258	18,804

*Results displayed for the top 10 sectors in terms of total output impacts. Total values still include all 33 sectors.

60

Table 33. Major Construction Impacts from a 10 Percent Oil Increase for Region 3

Construction Impacts (In Millions of US Dollars)		Output Components		Value Added Components				
Industry	Output	Intermediate Inputs	Value Added	Employment Compensation	Proprietor's Income	Other Property Type Income	Indirect Business Taxes	Employment (FTE's)
Drilling Oil and Gas Wells	$12,158	$7,508	$4,651	$1,489	$132	$2,488	$542	16,868
Other Manufacturing	$6,799	$5,425	$1,374	$638	$145	$547	$44	8,932
Finance and Insurance, Real Estate, Rental and Leasing Services	$1,990	$781	$1,209	$350	$133	$603	$123	9,378
Management of Companies and Enterprises	$1,562	$674	$888	$704	-$15	$185	$14	8,595
Other Professional, Scientific & Tech Services	$1,269	$526	$743	$474	$156	$99	$14	9,369
Water, Sewer, and Pipeline Construction	$1,154	$610	$544	$333	$121	$82	$8	9,158
Wholesale Trade	$1,027	$334	$692	$356	$33	$152	$152	5,241
Arts, Entertainment, Recreation, Accomodation, and Food Services	$850	$403	$446	$277	$27	$93	$50	15,672
Information	$728	$376	$352	$134	$37	$152	$29	2,070
Oil and Gas Extraction	$707	$257	$450	$74	$106	$226	$43	795
Total	$33,284	$18,932	$14,352	$6,526	$1,155	$5,435	$1,237	134,595

*Results displayed for the top 10 sectors in terms of total output impacts. Total values still include all 33 sectors.

Gas.

Table 34. Import Substitution Impacts for a 10 Percent Natural Gas Increase for Region 3

Import Substitution Impacts (Millions of US Dollars)		Output Components		Value Added Components				
Industry	Output	Intermediate Inputs	Value Added	Employment Compensation	Proprietor's Income	Other Property Type Income	Indirect Business Taxes	Employment (FTE's)
Oil and Gas Extraction	$3,390	$1,235	$2,156	$355	$508	$1,086	$206	3,812
Other Manufacturing	$1,480	$1,181	$299	$139	$32	$119	$10	1,944
Finance and Insurance, Real Estate, Rental and Leasing Services	$1,247	$489	$758	$219	$83	$378	$77	5,878
Natural Gas Distribution	$1,046	$546	$500	$93	$106	$157	$144	894
Other Professional, Scientific & Tech Services	$359	$149	$210	$134	$44	$28	$4	2,653
Government & Non NAICs	$251	$24	$227	$126	$1	$88	$12	2,601
Educational Services, Health Care, and Social Assistance	$245	$93	$153	$113	$19	$19	$2	3,085
Wholesale Trade	$235	$77	$159	$82	$7	$35	$35	1,200
Retail Trade	$227	$78	$150	$84	$11	$23	$32	3,308
Information	$209	$108	$101	$39	$11	$44	$8	595
Total	$10,150	$4,594	$5,556	$1,817	$907	$2,247	$585	37,525

*Results displayed for the top 10 sectors in terms of total output impacts. Total values still include all 33 sectors.

Table 35. Construction Impacts from a 10 Percent Natural Gas Increase for Region 3

Construction Impacts (In Millions of US Dollars)		Output Components		Value Added Components				
Industry	Output	Intermediate Inputs	Value Added	Employment Compensation	Proprietor's Income	Other Property Type Income	Indirect Business Taxes	Employment (FTE's)
Drilling Oil and Gas Wells	$14,568	$8,995	$5,572	$1,784	$159	$2,981	$649	20,210
Other Manufacturing	$7,868	$6,278	$1,590	$739	$168	$633	$51	10,336
Finance and Insurance, Real Estate, Rental and Leasing Services	$2,301	$903	$1,398	$405	$153	$698	$143	10,842
Management of Companies and Enterprises	$1,858	$802	$1,057	$837	-$17	$220	$17	10,226
Other Professional, Scientific & Tech Services	$1,489	$617	$872	$557	$183	$116	$16	10,997
Wholesale Trade	$1,190	$388	$803	$413	$38	$176	$176	6,076
Arts, Entertainment, Recreation, Accomodation, and Food Services	$997	$473	$524	$325	$31	$109	$58	18,395
Information	$845	$436	$409	$155	$43	$176	$34	2,402
Oil and Gas Extraction	$818	$298	$520	$86	$123	$262	$50	920
Government & Non NAICs	$738	$70	$667	$372	$3	$259	$34	7,650
Total	$38,047	$21,704	$16,344	$7,333	$1,231	$6,332	$1,448	148,450

*Results displayed for the top 10 sectors in terms of total output impacts. Total values still include all 33 sectors.

61

Tax Impacts.

Table 36. Import Substitution Tax Impacts from a 10 Percent Oil Increase for Region 3

Import Substitution Tax Impact (In Millions of US Dollars)		Sources					
		Employee Compensation	Proprietary Income	Household Expenditures	Enterprises (Corporations)	Indirect Business Tax	Total
Enterprises (Corporations)	Transfers	$1	$0	$0	$0	$0	$1
	Total	$1	$0	$0	$0	$0	$1
Federal Government NonDefense	Corporate Profits Tax	$0	$0	$0	$120	$0	$120
	Indirect Business Tax: Custom Duty	$0	$0	$0	$0	$7	$7
	Indirect Business Tax: Excise Taxes	$0	$0	$0	$0	$20	$20
	Indirect Business Tax: Fed Non Taxes	$0	$0	$0	$0	$9	$9
	Personal Tax: Income Tax	$0	$0	$115	$0	$0	$115
	Social Insurance Tax- Employee Contribution	$50	$22	$0	$0	$0	$73
	Social Insurance Tax- Employer Contribution	$51	$0	$0	$0	$0	$51
	Total	$102	$22	$115	$120	$36	$395
State/Local Government NonEducation	Dividends	$0	$0	$0	$17	$0	$17
	Indirect Business Tax: Motor Vehicle License	$0	$0	$0	$0	$2	$2
	Indirect Business Tax: Other Taxes	$0	$0	$0	$0	$13	$13
	Indirect Business Tax: Property Tax	$0	$0	$0	$0	$99	$99
	Indirect Business Tax: S/L Non Taxes	$0	$0	$0	$0	$7	$7
	Indirect Business Tax: Sales Tax	$0	$0	$0	$0	$92	$92
	Indirect Business Tax: Severance Tax	$0	$0	$0	$0	$9	$9
	Personal Tax: Motor Vehicle License	$0	$0	$1	$0	$0	$1
	Personal Tax: Non Taxes (Fines-Fees)	$0	$0	$7	$0	$0	$7
	Personal Tax: Other Tax (Fish/Hunt)	$0	$0	$1	$0	$0	$1
	Personal Tax: Property Tax	$0	$0	$1	$0	$0	$1
	Social Insurance Tax- Employee Contribution	$1	$0	$0	$0	$0	$1
	Social Insurance Tax- Employer Contribution	$2	$0	$0	$0	$0	$2
	Total	$3	$0	$10	$17	$222	$251
Total		$105	$22	$125	$137	$258	$647

*Results are not displayed for tax categories that experience no impact. Totals still reflect all tax categories.

62

Table 37. Construction Tax Impacts from a 10 Percent Oil Increase for Region 3

Construction Tax Impact (In Millions of US Dollars)		Sources					
		Employee Compensation	Proprietary Income	Household Expenditures	Enterprises (Corporations)	Indirect Business Tax	Total
Enterprises (Corporations)	Transfers	$7	$0	$0	$0	$0	$7
	Total	$7	$0	$0	$0	$0	$7
Federal Government NonDefense	Corporate Profits Tax	$0	$0	$0	$520	$0	$520
	Indirect Business Tax: Custom Duty	$0	$0	$0	$0	$35	$35
	Indirect Business Tax: Excise Taxes	$0	$0	$0	$0	$94	$94
	Indirect Business Tax: Fed Non Taxes	$0	$0	$0	$0	$43	$43
	Personal Tax: Income Tax	$0	$0	$615	$0	$0	$615
	Social Insurance Tax- Employee Contribution	$358	$52	$0	$0	$0	$410
	Social Insurance Tax- Employer Contribution	$363	$0	$0	$0	$0	$363
	Total	$721	$52	$615	$520	$172	$2,080
State/Local Government NonEducation	Dividends	$0	$0	$0	$74	$0	$74
	Indirect Business Tax: Motor Vehicle License	$0	$0	$0	$0	$9	$9
	Indirect Business Tax: Other Taxes	$0	$0	$0	$0	$60	$60
	Indirect Business Tax: Property Tax	$0	$0	$0	$0	$476	$476
	Indirect Business Tax: S/L Non Taxes	$0	$0	$0	$0	$35	$35
	Indirect Business Tax: Sales Tax	$0	$0	$0	$0	$442	$442
	Indirect Business Tax: Severance Tax	$0	$0	$0	$0	$42	$42
	Personal Tax: Motor Vehicle License	$0	$0	$9	$0	$0	$9
	Personal Tax: Non Taxes (Fines-Fees)	$0	$0	$40	$0	$0	$40
	Personal Tax: Other Tax (Fish/Hunt)	$0	$0	$3	$0	$0	$3
	Personal Tax: Property Tax	$0	$0	$5	$0	$0	$5
	Social Insurance Tax- Employee Contribution	$4	$0	$0	$0	$0	$4
	Social Insurance Tax- Employer Contribution	$16	$0	$0	$0	$0	$16
	Total	$19	$0	$56	$74	$1,064	$1,214
Total		$747	$52	$671	$593	$1,237	$3,300

*Results are not displayed for tax categories that experience no impact. Totals still reflect all tax categories.

63

Table 38. Import Substitution Tax Impacts from a 10 Percent Natural Gas Increase for Region 3

Import Substitution Tax Impact (In Millions of US Dollars)		Sources					
		Employee Compensation	Proprietary Income	Household Expenditures	Enterprises (Corporations)	Indirect Business Tax	Total
Enterprises (Corporations)	Transfers	$2	$0	$0	$0	$0	$2
	Total	$2	$0	$0	$0	$0	$2
Federal Government NonDefense	Corporate Profits Tax	$0	$0	$0	$215	$0	$215
	Indirect Business Tax: Custom Duty	$0	$0	$0	$0	$17	$17
	Indirect Business Tax: Excise Taxes	$0	$0	$0	$0	$45	$45
	Indirect Business Tax: Fed Non Taxes	$0	$0	$0	$0	$20	$20
	Personal Tax: Income Tax	$0	$0	$222	$0	$0	$222
	Social Insurance Tax- Employee Contribution	$100	$41	$0	$0	$0	$141
	Social Insurance Tax- Employer Contribution	$101	$0	$0	$0	$0	$101
	Total	$201	$41	$222	$215	$82	$760
State/Local Government NonEducation	Dividends	$0	$0	$0	$30	$0	$30
	Indirect Business Tax: Motor Vehicle License	$0	$0	$0	$0	$4	$4
	Indirect Business Tax: Other Taxes	$0	$0	$0	$0	$28	$28
	Indirect Business Tax: Property Tax	$0	$0	$0	$0	$225	$225
	Indirect Business Tax: S/L Non Taxes	$0	$0	$0	$0	$16	$16
	Indirect Business Tax: Sales Tax	$0	$0	$0	$0	$209	$209
	Indirect Business Tax: Severance Tax	$0	$0	$0	$0	$20	$20
	Personal Tax: Motor Vehicle License	$0	$0	$2	$0	$0	$2
	Personal Tax: Non Taxes (Fines-Fees)	$0	$0	$14	$0	$0	$14
	Personal Tax: Other Tax (Fish/Hunt)	$0	$0	$1	$0	$0	$1
	Personal Tax: Property Tax	$0	$0	$2	$0	$0	$2
	Social Insurance Tax- Employee Contribution	$1	$0	$0	$0	$0	$1
	Social Insurance Tax- Employer Contribution	$4	$0	$0	$0	$0	$4
	Total	$5	$0	$19	$30	$503	$558
Total		$208	$41	$241	$245	$585	$1,320

*Results are not displayed for tax categories that experience no impact. Totals still reflect all tax categories.

64

Table 39. Construction Tax Impacts from a 10 Percent Natural Gas Increase for Region 3

Construction Tax Impact (In Millions of US Dollars)		Sources					
		Employee Compensation	Proprietary Income	Household Expenditures	Enterprises (Corporations)	Indirect Business Tax	Total
Enterprises (Corporations)	Transfers	$7	$0	$0	$0	$0	$7
	Total	$7	$0	$0	$0	$0	$7
Federal Government NonDefense	Corporate Profits Tax	$0	$0	$0	$605	$0	$605
	Indirect Business Tax: Custom Duty	$0	$0	$0	$0	$41	$41
	Indirect Business Tax: Excise Taxes	$0	$0	$0	$0	$111	$111
	Indirect Business Tax: Fed Non Taxes	$0	$0	$0	$0	$50	$50
	Personal Tax: Income Tax	$0	$0	$685	$0	$0	$685
	Social Insurance Tax- Employee Contribution	$402	$56	$0	$0	$0	$458
	Social Insurance Tax- Employer Contribution	$408	$0	$0	$0	$0	$408
	Total	$810	$56	$685	$605	$202	$2,358
State/Local Government NonEducation	Dividends	$0	$0	$0	$86	$0	$86
	Indirect Business Tax: Motor Vehicle License	$0	$0	$0	$0	$10	$10
	Indirect Business Tax: Other Taxes	$0	$0	$0	$0	$70	$70
	Indirect Business Tax: Property Tax	$0	$0	$0	$0	$557	$557
	Indirect Business Tax: S/L Non Taxes	$0	$0	$0	$0	$40	$40
	Indirect Business Tax: Sales Tax	$0	$0	$0	$0	$518	$518
	Indirect Business Tax: Severance Tax	$0	$0	$0	$0	$50	$50
	Personal Tax: Motor Vehicle License	$0	$0	$10	$0	$0	$10
	Personal Tax: Non Taxes (Fines-Fees)	$0	$0	$44	$0	$0	$44
	Personal Tax: Other Tax (Fish/Hunt)	$0	$0	$3	$0	$0	$3
	Personal Tax: Property Tax	$0	$0	$5	$0	$0	$5
	Social Insurance Tax- Employee Contribution	$4	$0	$0	$0	$0	$4
	Social Insurance Tax- Employer Contribution	$17	$0	$0	$0	$0	$17
	Total	$22	$0	$63	$86	$1,246	$1,416
Total		$839	$56	$748	$691	$1,448	$3,782

*Results are not displayed for tax categories that experience no impact. Totals still reflect all tax categories.

65

9.2.6 Region 3 (Barnett Shale) – Scenario Analysis

Four scenario analyses were performed for the Barnett Shale Region and all are reported below. All analyses except for the Natural Gas Only scenario in 2030 are reported as opportunity costs of S.2191 legislation. The Natural Gas Only scenario in 2030 has impacts reported as benefits of the legislation. These analyses are included in Tables 40–43 where summary reports of the data inputs and the total impacts from import substitution and construction are given for Region 3.

Table 40. Input Data and Summary Results for Barnett Shale, 2010

Input Data Summary for Barnett Shale		
	Natural Gas	Oil
Production Increases	31658 MMcf/yr	45 thbbl/yr
Estimated Average Well Depth	7,500-9,999 ft/well	5,000-7,499 ft/well
Well Construction Cost	1588 th$/well	758 th$/well
Average Producer Price	6.63 $/tcf	59.57 $/bbl
Industry Output	224 Million $	3 Million $
Reduced Import Payments	0 Million $	3 Million $
International Trade Feedback Share	10%	10%
Year Dollars	2006	2006

Summary Results for Barnett Shale			
(Millions of US Dollars)	Output	FTEs	Taxes
Import Substitution Impacts	$514	1,887	$67
Construction Impacts	$1,962	7,669	$195

Table 41. Input Data and Summary Results for Barnett Shale, 2020

Input Data Summary for Barnett Shale		
	Natural Gas	Oil
Production Increases	31658 MMcf/yr	45 thbbl/yr
Estimated Average Well Depth	7,500-9,999 ft/well	5,000-7,499 ft/well
Well Construction Cost	1588 th$/well	758 th$/well
Average Producer Price	6.63 $/tcf	59.57 $/bbl
Industry Output	224 Million $	3 Million $
Reduced Import Payments	0 Million $	3 Million $
International Trade Feedback Share	10%	10%
Year Dollars	2006	2006

Summary Results for Barnett Shale			
(Millions of US Dollars)	Output	FTEs	Taxes
Import Substitution Impacts	$514	1,887	$67
Construction Impacts	$1,962	7,669	$195

66

Table 42. Input Data and Summary Results for Barnett Shale, 2030 (Oil Only)

Input Data Summary for Barnett Shale	Natural Gas	Oil
Production Increases		1473 thbbl/yr
Estimated Average Well Depth		5,000-7,499 ft/well
Well Construction Cost		758 th$/well
Average Producer Price		59.57 $/bbl
Industry Output		88 Million $
Reduced Import Payments		87 Million $
International Trade Feedback Share		10%
Year Dollars		2006

Summary Results for Barnett Shale			
(Millions of US Dollars)	Output	FTEs	Taxes
Import Substitution Impacts	$189	684	$24
Construction Impacts	$1,235	4,992	$122

Table 43. Input Data and Summary Results for Barnett Shale, 2030 (Gas Only)

Input Data Summary for Barnett Shale	Natural Gas	Oil
Production Increases	12954 MMcf/yr	
Estimated Average Well Depth	7,500-9,999 ft/well	
Well Construction Cost	1588 th$/well	
Average Producer Price	6.63 $/tcf	
Industry Output	92 Million $	
Reduced Import Payments	0 Million $	
International Trade Feedback Share	10%	
Year Dollars	2006	

Summary Results for Barnett Shale			
(Millions of US Dollars)	Output	FTEs	Taxes
Import Substitution Impacts	$208	763	$27
Construction Impacts	$786	3,072	$78

9.2.7 Region 4 (Greater Green River/Jonah Field/Pinedale Anticline) – Standardized Production Increase

Oil.

Table 44. Import Substitution Impacts from a 10 Percent Oil Increase for Region 4

Import Substitution Impacts (In Millions of US		Output Components		Value Added Components				
Industry	Output	Intermediate Inputs	Value Added	Employment Compensation	Proprietor's Income	Other Property Type Income	Indirect Business Taxes	Employment (FTE's)
Ag, Forestry, Fish & Hunting	$5	$4	$1	$1	$0	$0	$0	50
Oil and Gas Extraction	$540	$197	$343	$44	$93	$173	$33	690
Coal, Metal Ores & Nonmetalic Mineral Mining, Quarrying & Support Activites	$1	$1	$1	$0	$0	$0	$0	4
Drilling Oil and Gas Wells	$1	$1	$0	$0	$0	$0	$0	2
Support Activities for Oil and Gas Operations	$23	$1	$22	$7	$1	$13	$1	106
Power Generation and Supply and Water, Sewage and Other Systems	$9	$2	$7	$2	$0	$4	$1	18
Natural Gas Distribution	$2	$1	$1	$0	$0	$0	$0	2
Other New Construction, Including Maintenance and Repair Construction	$2	$1	$1	$1	$0	$0	$0	18
Manufacturing and Industrial Buildings	$0	$0	$0	$0	$0	$0	$0	0
Water, Sewer, and Pipeline Construction	$0	$0	$0	$0	$0	$0	$0	0
Total	$1,129	$477	$653	$199	$119	$277	$58	4,518

*Results displayed for the top 10 sectors in terms of total output impacts. Total values still include all 33 sectors.

67

184 703-739-3790 TCNNaturalGas.com

Table 45. Construction Impacts from a 10 Percent Oil Increase for Region 4

Construction Impacts (In Millions of US Dollars)	Output	Output Components		Value Added Components				Employment (FTE's)
Industry	Output	Intermediate Inputs	Value Added	Employment Compensation	Proprietor's Income	Other Property Type Income	Indirect Business Taxes	Employment (FTE's)
Ag, Forestry, Fish & Hunting	$48	$35	$13	$5	$2	$4	$1	461
Oil and Gas Extraction	$121	$44	$77	$10	$21	$39	$7	155
Coal, Metal Ores & Nonmetalic Mineral Mining, Quarrying & Support Activites	$14	$7	$7	$3	$1	$2	$1	41
Drilling Oil and Gas Wells	$2,718	$1,753	$965	$298	$38	$516	$112	4,045
Support Activities for Oil and Gas Operations	$59	$3	$55	$18	$2	$33	$2	272
Power Generation and Supply and Water, Sewage and Other Systems	$38	$7	$31	$7	$1	$18	$4	82
Natural Gas Distribution	$22	$12	$10	$4	$1	$3	$3	19
Other New Construction, Including Maintenance and Repair Construction	$17	$9	$8	$5	$2	$1	$0	127
Manufacturing and Industrial Buildings	$0	$0	$0	$0	$0	$0	$0	0
Water, Sewer, and Pipeline Construction	$178	$93	$86	$51	$21	$13	$1	1,379
Total	$7,416	$4,194	$3,222	$1,549	$237	$1,160	$276	33,443

*Results displayed for the top 10 sectors in terms of total output impacts. Total values still include all 33 sectors.

Gas.

Table 46. Import Substitution Impacts for a 10 Percent Natural Gas Increase for Region 4

Import Substitution Impacts (In Millions of US	Output	Output Components		Value Added Components				Employment (FTE's)
Industry	Output	Intermediate Inputs	Value Added	Employment Compensation	Proprietor's Income	Other Property Type Income	Indirect Business Taxes	Employment (FTE's)
Ag, Forestry, Fish & Hunting	$24	$18	$7	$3	$1	$2	$0	234
Oil and Gas Extraction	$1,934	$704	$1,230	$157	$335	$620	$118	2,472
Coal, Metal Ores & Nonmetalic Mineral Mining, Quarrying & Support Activites	$6	$3	$3	$1	$0	$1	$0	17
Drilling Oil and Gas Wells	$5	$3	$2	$1	$0	$1	$0	7
Support Activities for Oil and Gas Operations	$99	$5	$94	$30	$4	$56	$4	458
Power Generation and Supply and Water, Sewage and Other Systems	$39	$7	$32	$7	$1	$18	$4	84
Natural Gas Distribution	$303	$162	$141	$50	$9	$43	$39	273
Other New Construction, Including Maintenance and Repair Construction	$11	$6	$5	$3	$1	$1	$0	85
Manufacturing and Industrial Buildings	$0	$0	$0	$0	$0	$0	$0	0
Water, Sewer, and Pipeline Construction	$0	$0	$0	$0	$0	$0	$0	0
Total	$4,968	$2,172	$2,797	$926	$463	$1,135	$272	20,515

*Results displayed for the top 10 sectors in terms of total output impacts. Total values still include all 33 sectors.

Table 47. Construction Impacts from a 10 Percent Natural Gas Increase for Region 4

Construction Impacts (In Millions of US Dollars)	Output	Output Components		Value Added Components				Employment (FTE's)
Industry	Output	Intermediate Inputs	Value Added	Employment Compensation	Proprietor's Income	Other Property Type Income	Indirect Business Taxes	Employment (FTE's)
Ag, Forestry, Fish & Hunting	$65	$47	$18	$7	$3	$6	$1	627
Oil and Gas Extraction	$167	$61	$106	$14	$29	$54	$10	214
Coal, Metal Ores & Nonmetalic Mineral Mining, Quarrying & Support Activites	$19	$9	$10	$4	$1	$3	$1	56
Drilling Oil and Gas Wells	$3,802	$2,452	$1,350	$417	$53	$722	$157	5,659
Support Activities for Oil and Gas Operations	$82	$4	$78	$25	$3	$46	$3	382
Power Generation and Supply and Water, Sewage and Other Systems	$52	$10	$42	$10	$2	$25	$6	112
Natural Gas Distribution	$32	$17	$15	$5	$1	$4	$4	29
Other New Construction, Including Maintenance and Repair Construction	$23	$12	$10	$6	$3	$1	$0	174
Manufacturing and Industrial Buildings	$0	$0	$0	$0	$0	$0	$0	0
Water, Sewer, and Pipeline Construction	$154	$80	$74	$44	$18	$11	$1	1,195
Total	$10,141	$5,744	$4,397	$2,103	$314	$1,599	$380	45,122

*Results displayed for the top 10 sectors in terms of total output impacts. Total values still include all 33 sectors.

68

Tax Impacts.

Table 48. Import Substitution Tax Impacts from a 10 Percent Oil Increase for Region 4

Import Substitution Tax Impact (In Millions of US Dollars)		Sources					
		Employee Compensation	Proprietary Income	Household Expenditures	Enterprises (Corporations)	Indirect Business Tax	Total
Federal Government NonDefense	Corporate Profits Tax	$0	$0	$0	$26	$0	$26
	Indirect Business Tax: Custom Duty	$0	$0	$0	$0	$2	$2
	Indirect Business Tax: Excise Taxes	$0	$0	$0	$0	$5	$5
	Indirect Business Tax: Fed Non Taxes	$0	$0	$0	$0	$2	$2
	Personal Tax: Income Tax	$0	$0	$26	$0	$0	$26
	Social Insurance Tax-Employee Contribution	$11	$5	$0	$0	$0	$17
	Social Insurance Tax-Employer Contribution	$11	$0	$0	$0	$0	$11
	Total	$23	$5	$26	$26	$8	$89
State/Local Government NonEducation	Corporate Profits Tax	$0	$0	$0	$2	$0	$2
	Dividends	$0	$0	$0	$5	$0	$5
	Indirect Business Tax: Other Taxes	$0	$0	$0	$0	$1	$1
	Indirect Business Tax: Property Tax	$0	$0	$0	$0	$17	$17
	Indirect Business Tax: S/L Non Taxes	$0	$0	$0	$0	$4	$4
	Indirect Business Tax: Sales Tax	$0	$0	$0	$0	$23	$23
	Indirect Business Tax: Severance Tax	$0	$0	$0	$0	$3	$3
	Personal Tax: Income Tax	$0	$0	$6	$0	$0	$6
	Personal Tax: Non Taxes (Fines-Fees)	$0	$0	$1	$0	$0	$1
	Total	$0	$0	$8	$7	$49	$65
Total		$23	$5	$35	$33	$58	$154

*Results are not displayed for tax categories that experience no impact. Totals still reflect all tax categories.

69

Table 49. Construction Tax Impacts from a 10 Percent Oil Increase for Region 4

Construction Tax Impact (In Millions of US Dollars)		Sources					
		Employee Compensation	Proprietary Income	Household Expenditures	Enterprises (Corporations)	Indirect Business Tax	Total
Enterprises (Corporations)	Transfers	$2	$0	$0	$0	$0	$2
	Total	$2	$0	$0	$0	$0	$2
Federal Government NonDefense	Corporate Profits Tax	$0	$0	$0	$111	$0	$111
	Indirect Business Tax: Custom Duty	$0	$0	$0	$0	$8	$8
	Indirect Business Tax: Excise Taxes	$0	$0	$0	$0	$22	$22
	Indirect Business Tax: Fed Non Taxes	$0	$0	$0	$0	$10	$10
	Personal Tax: Income Tax	$0	$0	$145	$0	$0	$145
	Social Insurance Tax- Employee Contribution	$87	$11	$0	$0	$0	$98
	Social Insurance Tax- Employer Contribution	$89	$0	$0	$0	$0	$89
	Total	$176	$11	$145	$111	$39	$482
State/Local Government NonEducation	Corporate Profits Tax	$0	$0	$0	$7	$0	$7
	Dividends	$0	$0	$0	$22	$0	$22
	Indirect Business Tax: Motor Vehicle License	$0	$0	$0	$0	$2	$2
	Indirect Business Tax: Other Taxes	$0	$0	$0	$0	$7	$7
	Indirect Business Tax: Property Tax	$0	$0	$0	$0	$83	$83
	Indirect Business Tax: S/L Non Taxes	$0	$0	$0	$0	$20	$20
	Indirect Business Tax: Sales Tax	$0	$0	$0	$0	$111	$111
	Indirect Business Tax: Severance Tax	$0	$0	$0	$0	$13	$13
	Personal Tax: Income Tax	$0	$0	$35	$0	$0	$35
	Personal Tax: Motor Vehicle License	$0	$0	$2	$0	$0	$2
	Personal Tax: Non Taxes (Fines-Fees)	$0	$0	$7	$0	$0	$7
	Personal Tax: Other Tax (Fish/Hunt)	$0	$0	$2	$0	$0	$2
	Personal Tax: Property Tax	$0	$0	$1	$0	$0	$1
	Social Insurance Tax- Employee Contribution	$1	$0	$0	$0	$0	$1
	Social Insurance Tax- Employer Contribution	$3	$0	$0	$0	$0	$3
	Total	$4	$0	$46	$29	$236	$316
Total		$182	$11	$191	$140	$276	$799

*Results are not displayed for tax categories that experience no impact. Totals still reflect all tax categories.

70

Table 50. Import Substitution Tax Impacts from a 10 Percent Natural Gas Increase for Region 4

Import Substitution Tax Impact (In Millions of US Dollars)		Employee Compensation	Proprietary Income	Household Expenditures	Enterprises (Corporations)	Indirect Business Tax	Total
				Sources			
Enterprises (Corporations)	Transfers	$1	$0	$0	$0	$0	$1
	Total	$1	$0	$0	$0	$0	$1
Federal Government NonDefense	Corporate Profits Tax	$0	$0	$0	$108	$0	$108
	Indirect Business Tax: Custom Duty	$0	$0	$0	$0	$8	$8
	Indirect Business Tax: Excise Taxes	$0	$0	$0	$0	$21	$21
	Indirect Business Tax: Fed Non Taxes	$0	$0	$0	$0	$10	$10
	Personal Tax: Income Tax	$0	$0	$114	$0	$0	$114
	Social Insurance Tax- Employee Contribution	$52	$21	$0	$0	$0	$73
	Social Insurance Tax- Employer Contribution	$53	$0	$0	$0	$0	$53
	Total	$105	$21	$114	$108	$39	$388
State/Local Government NonEducation	Corporate Profits Tax	$0	$0	$0	$7	$0	$7
	Dividends	$0	$0	$0	$21	$0	$21
	Indirect Business Tax: Motor Vehicle License	$0	$0	$0	$0	$2	$2
	Indirect Business Tax: Other Taxes	$0	$0	$0	$0	$7	$7
	Indirect Business Tax: Property Tax	$0	$0	$0	$0	$82	$82
	Indirect Business Tax: S/L Non Taxes	$0	$0	$0	$0	$20	$20
	Indirect Business Tax: Sales Tax	$0	$0	$0	$0	$109	$109
	Indirect Business Tax: Severance Tax	$0	$0	$0	$0	$13	$13
	Personal Tax: Income Tax	$0	$0	$28	$0	$0	$28
	Personal Tax: Motor Vehicle License	$0	$0	$1	$0	$0	$1
	Personal Tax: Non Taxes (Fines-Fees)	$0	$0	$5	$0	$0	$5
	Personal Tax: Other Tax (Fish/Hunt)	$0	$0	$2	$0	$0	$2
	Personal Tax: Property Tax	$0	$0	$1	$0	$0	$1
	Social Insurance Tax- Employer Contribution	$2	$0	$0	$0	$0	$2
	Total	$2	$0	$36	$28	$233	$300
Total		$109	$21	$151	$137	$272	$689

*Results are not displayed for tax categories that experience no impact. Totals still reflect all tax categories.

71

Table 51. Construction Tax Impacts from a 10 Percent Natural Gas Increase for Region 4

Construction Tax Impact (In Millions of US Dollars)		Sources					
		Employee Compensation	Proprietary Income	Household Expenditures	Enterprises (Corporations)	Indirect Business Tax	Total
Enterprises (Corporations)	Transfers	$2	$0	$0	$0	$0	$2
	Total	$2	$0	$0	$0	$0	$2
Federal Government NonDefense	Corporate Profits Tax	$0	$0	$0	$153	$0	$153
	Indirect Business Tax: Custom Duty	$0	$0	$0	$0	$11	$11
	Indirect Business Tax: Excise Taxes	$0	$0	$0	$0	$30	$30
	Indirect Business Tax: Fed Non Taxes	$0	$0	$0	$0	$14	$14
	Personal Tax: Income Tax	$0	$0	$196	$0	$0	$196
	Social Insurance Tax- Employee Contribution	$119	$14	$0	$0	$0	$133
	Social Insurance Tax- Employer Contribution	$120	$0	$0	$0	$0	$120
	Total	$239	$14	$196	$153	$54	$656
State/Local Government NonEducation	Corporate Profits Tax	$0	$0	$0	$10	$0	$10
	Dividends	$0	$0	$0	$30	$0	$30
	Indirect Business Tax: Motor Vehicle License	$0	$0	$0	$0	$2	$2
	Indirect Business Tax: Other Taxes	$0	$0	$0	$0	$10	$10
	Indirect Business Tax: Property Tax	$0	$0	$0	$0	$115	$115
	Indirect Business Tax: S/L Non Taxes	$0	$0	$0	$0	$28	$28
	Indirect Business Tax: Sales Tax	$0	$0	$0	$0	$152	$152
	Indirect Business Tax: Severance Tax	$0	$0	$0	$0	$18	$18
	Personal Tax: Income Tax	$0	$0	$47	$0	$0	$47
	Personal Tax: Motor Vehicle License	$0	$0	$2	$0	$0	$2
	Personal Tax: Non Taxes (Fines-Fees)	$0	$0	$9	$0	$0	$9
	Personal Tax: Other Tax (Fish/Hunt)	$0	$0	$3	$0	$0	$3
	Personal Tax: Property Tax	$0	$0	$1	$0	$0	$1
	Social Insurance Tax- Employee Contribution	$1	$0	$0	$0	$0	$1
	Social Insurance Tax- Employer Contribution	$4	$0	$0	$0	$0	$4
	Total	$5	$0	$63	$40	$326	$434
Total		$246	$14	$258	$193	$380	$1,092

*Results are not displayed for tax categories that experience no impact. Totals still reflect all tax categories.

72

9.2.8 Region 4 (Greater Green River/Jonah Field/Pinedale Anticline) – Scenario Analysis

Three scenario analyses for the Greater Green River Region were performed and two are reported. The analysis for 2010 involved future production of oil that was not large enough to create any significant impacts. The two analyses reported below for oil and gas in 2020 and 2030 consider opportunity costs of the S.2191 legislation. Tables 52–53 give a summary report of the data inputs and the total impacts from import substitution and construction in Region 4 that are not realized due to the adoption of S.2191.

Table 52. Input Data and Summary Results for GGR/JF/PA, 2020

Input Data Summary for Greater Green River		
	Natural Gas	Oil
Production Increases	197733 MMcf/yr	786 thbbl/yr
Estimated Average Well Depth	3,750-4,999 ft/well	5,000-7,499 ft/well
Well Construction Cost	699 th$/well	1099 th$/well
Average Producer Price	5.93 $/tcf	57.34 $/bbl
Industry Output	1200 Million $	45 Million $
Reduced Import Payments	0 Million $	48 Million $
International Trade Feedback Share	10%	10%
Year Dollars	2006	2006

Summary Results for Greater Green River			
(Millions of US Dollars)	Output	FTEs	Taxes
Import Substitution Impacts	$2,721	11,121	$377
Construction Impacts	$6,044	26,883	$651

Table 53. Input Data and Summary Results for GGR/JF/PA, 2030

Input Data Summary for Greater Green River		
	Natural Gas	Oil
Production Increases	22623 MMcf/yr	910 thbbl/yr
Estimated Average Well Depth	3,750-4,999 ft/well	5,000-7,499 ft/well
Well Construction Cost	699 th$/well	1099 th$/well
Average Producer Price	5.93 $/tcf	57.34 $/bbl
Industry Output	137 Million $	52 Million $
Reduced Import Payments	0 Million $	56 Million $
International Trade Feedback Share	10%	10%
Year Dollars	2006	2006

Summary Results for Greater Green River			
(Millions of US Dollars)	Output	FTEs	Taxes
Import Substitution Impacts	$404	1,626	$56
Construction Impacts	$1,315	5,834	$142

73

9.2.9 Region 5 (California) – Standardized Production Increase

Oil.

Table 54. Import Substitution Impacts from a 10 Percent Oil Increase for Region 5

Import Substitution Impacts (In Millions of US	Output	Output Components		Value Added Components				Employment (FTE's)
Industry	Output	Intermediate Inputs	Value Added	Employment Compensation	Proprietor's Income	Other Property Type Income	Indirect Business Taxes	Employment (FTE's)
Ag, Forestry, Fish & Hunting	$2	$1	$1	$1	$0	$0	$0	22
Oil and Gas Extraction	$1,197	$436	$761	$176	$129	$383	$73	2,033
Coal, Metal Ores & Nonmetalic Mineral Mining, Quarrying & Support Activites	$0	$0	$0	$0	$0	$0	$0	1
Drilling Oil and Gas Wells	$0	$0	$0	$0	$0	$0	$0	1
Support Activities for Oil and Gas Operations	$8	$0	$7	$2	$0	$4	$0	36
Power Generation and Supply and Water, Sewage and Other Systems	$3	$1	$2	$0	$0	$1	$0	4
Natural Gas Distribution	$1	$1	$0	$0	$0	$0	$0	1
Other New Construction, Including Maintenance and Repair Construction	$1	$0	$0	$0	$0	$0	$0	6
Manufacturing and Industrial Buildings	$0	$0	$0	$0	$0	$0	$0	0
Water, Sewer, and Pipeline Construction	$0	$0	$0	$0	$0	$0	$0	0
Other Manufacturing	$57	$43	$14	$10	$1	$4	$0	121
Construction and Mining Machinery Manufacturing	$2	$1	$0	$0	$0	$0	$0	2
Total	$1,439	$545	$894	$246	$141	$423	$83	3,500

*Results displayed for the top 10 sectors in terms of total output impacts. Total values still include all 33 sectors.

Table 55. Major Construction Impacts from a 10 Percent Oil Increase for Region 5

Construction Impacts (In Millions of US Dollars)	Output	Output Components		Value Added Components				Employment (FTE's)
Industry	Output	Intermediate Inputs	Value Added	Employment Compensation	Proprietor's Income	Other Property Type Income	Indirect Business Taxes	Employment (FTE's)
Ag, Forestry, Fish & Hunting	$46	$21	$24	$12	$5	$7	$1	494
Oil and Gas Extraction	$95	$34	$60	$14	$10	$30	$6	161
Coal, Metal Ores & Nonmetalic Mineral Mining, Quarrying & Support Activites	$9	$4	$5	$3	$0	$2	$0	43
Drilling Oil and Gas Wells	$3,539	$2,260	$1,279	$423	$23	$684	$149	5,184
Support Activities for Oil and Gas Operations	$77	$4	$73	$25	$1	$44	$3	362
Power Generation and Supply and Water, Sewage and Other Systems	$30	$6	$24	$4	$3	$14	$3	39
Natural Gas Distribution	$26	$15	$11	$3	$1	$3	$3	27
Other New Construction, Including Maintenance and Repair Construction	$17	$9	$8	$5	$2	$1	$0	115
Manufacturing and Industrial Buildings	$0	$0	$0	$0	$0	$0	$0	0
Water, Sewer, and Pipeline Construction	$318	$152	$166	$102	$36	$25	$2	2,173
Total	$8,345	$4,653	$3,692	$1,819	$254	$1,311	$307	33,102

*Results displayed for the top 10 sectors in terms of total output impacts. Total values still include all 33 sectors.

74

Gas.

Table 56. Major Import Substitution Impacts for a 10 Percent Natural Gas Increase for Region 5

Import Substitution Impacts (In Millions of US)	Output	Output Components		Value Added Components				Employment (FTE's)
Industry	Output	Intermediate Inputs	Value Added	Employment Compensation	Proprietor's Income	Other Property Type Income	Indirect Business Taxes	Employment (FTE's)
Ag, Forestry, Fish & Hunting	$2	$1	$1	$1	$0	$0	$0	27
Oil and Gas Extraction	$195	$71	$124	$29	$21	$62	$12	331
Coal, Metal Ores & Nonmetalic Mineral Mining, Quarrying & Support Activites	$0	$0	$0	$0	$0	$0	$0	2
Drilling Oil and Gas Wells	$0	$0	$0	$0	$0	$0	$0	0
Support Activities for Oil and Gas Operations	$1	$0	$1	$0	$0	$1	$0	7
Power Generation and Supply and Water, Sewage and Other Systems	$1	$0	$1	$0	$0	$1	$0	1
Natural Gas Distribution	$47	$27	$20	$6	$3	$6	$6	48
Other New Construction, Including Maintenance and Repair Construction	$1	$0	$0	$0	$0	$0	$0	4
Manufacturing and Industrial Buildings	$0	$0	$0	$0	$0	$0	$0	0
Water, Sewer, and Pipeline Construction	$0	$0	$0	$0	$0	$0	$0	0
Total	$365	$159	$206	$69	$30	$86	$22	1,089

*Results displayed for the top 10 sectors in terms of total output impacts. Total values still include all 33 sectors.

Table 57. Construction Impacts from a 10 Percent Natural Gas Increase for Region 5

Construction Impacts (In Millions of US Dollars)	Output	Output Components		Value Added Components				Employment (FTE's)
Industry	Output	Intermediate Inputs	Value Added	Employment Compensation	Proprietor's Income	Other Property Type Income	Indirect Business Taxes	Employment (FTE's)
Ag, Forestry, Fish & Hunting	$6	$3	$3	$1	$1	$1	$0	61
Oil and Gas Extraction	$12	$4	$7	$2	$1	$4	$1	20
Coal, Metal Ores & Nonmetalic Mineral Mining, Quarrying & Support Activites	$1	$0	$1	$0	$0	$0	$0	5
Drilling Oil and Gas Wells	$470	$300	$170	$56	$3	$91	$20	689
Support Activities for Oil and Gas Operations	$10	$1	$10	$3	$0	$6	$0	48
Power Generation and Supply and Water, Sewage and Other Systems	$4	$1	$3	$1	$0	$2	$0	5
Natural Gas Distribution	$3	$2	$1	$0	$0	$0	$0	3
Other New Construction, Including Maintenance and Repair Construction	$2	$1	$1	$1	$0	$0	$0	14
Manufacturing and Industrial Buildings	$0	$0	$0	$0	$0	$0	$0	0
Water, Sewer, and Pipeline Construction	$18	$9	$9	$6	$2	$1	$0	123
Total	$1,044	$586	$458	$222	$29	$167	$39	3,989

*Results displayed for the top 10 sectors in terms of total output impacts. Total values still include all 33 sectors.

75

Tax Impacts.

Table 58. Import Substitution Tax Impacts from a 10 Percent Oil Increase for Region 5

Import Substitution Tax Impact (In Millions of US Dollars)		Employee Compensation	Proprietary Income	Household Expenditures	Enterprises (Corporations)	Indirect Business Tax	Total
Federal Government NonDefense	Corporate Profits Tax	$0	$0	$0	$40	$0	$40
	Indirect Business Tax: Custom Duty	$0	$0	$0	$0	$2	$2
	Indirect Business Tax: Excise Taxes	$0	$0	$0	$0	$6	$6
	Indirect Business Tax: Fed Non Taxes	$0	$0	$0	$0	$3	$3
	Personal Tax: Income Tax	$0	$0	$34	$0	$0	$34
	Social Insurance Tax-Employee Contribution	$15	$6	$0	$0	$0	$21
	Social Insurance Tax-Employer Contribution	$15	$0	$0	$0	$0	$15
	Total	$29	$6	$34	$40	$11	$121
State/Local Government NonEducation	Corporate Profits Tax	$0	$0	$0	$10	$0	$10
	Dividends	$0	$0	$0	$15	$0	$15
	Indirect Business Tax: Motor Vehicle License	$0	$0	$0	$0	$1	$1
	Indirect Business Tax: Other Taxes	$0	$0	$0	$0	$6	$6
	Indirect Business Tax: Property Tax	$0	$0	$0	$0	$24	$24
	Indirect Business Tax: S/L Non Taxes	$0	$0	$0	$0	$3	$3
	Indirect Business Tax: Sales Tax	$0	$0	$0	$0	$37	$37
	Personal Tax: Income Tax	$0	$0	$11	$0	$0	$11
	Personal Tax: Non Taxes (Fines-Fees)	$0	$0	$3	$0	$0	$3
	Social Insurance Tax-Employer Contribution	$1	$0	$0	$0	$0	$1
	Total	$2	$0	$15	$26	$72	$114
Total		$31	$6	$49	$66	$83	$235

*Results are not displayed for tax categories that experience no impact. Totals still reflect all tax categories.

76

Table 59. Construction Tax Impacts from a 10 Percent Oil Increase for Region 5

Construction Tax Impact (In Millions of US Dollars)		Sources					
		Employee Compensation	Proprietary Income	Household Expenditures	Enterprises (Corporations)	Indirect Business Tax	Total
Enterprises (Corporations)	Transfers	$2	$0	$0	$0	$0	$2
	Total	$2	$0	$0	$0	$0	$2
Federal Government NonDefense	Corporate Profits Tax	$0	$0	$0	$125	$0	$125
	Indirect Business Tax: Custom Duty	$0	$0	$0	$0	$8	$8
	Indirect Business Tax: Excise Taxes	$0	$0	$0	$0	$23	$23
	Indirect Business Tax: Fed Non Taxes	$0	$0	$0	$0	$10	$10
	Personal Tax: Income Tax	$0	$0	$177	$0	$0	$177
	Social Insurance Tax- Employee Contribution	$108	$12	$0	$0	$0	$120
	Social Insurance Tax- Employer Contribution	$110	$0	$0	$0	$0	$110
	Total	$218	$12	$177	$125	$42	$573
State/Local Government NonEducation	Corporate Profits Tax	$0	$0	$0	$33	$0	$33
	Dividends	$0	$0	$0	$47	$0	$47
	Indirect Business Tax: Motor Vehicle License	$0	$0	$0	$0	$2	$2
	Indirect Business Tax: Other Taxes	$0	$0	$0	$0	$24	$24
	Indirect Business Tax: Property Tax	$0	$0	$0	$0	$91	$91
	Indirect Business Tax: S/L Non Taxes	$0	$0	$0	$0	$11	$11
	Indirect Business Tax: Sales Tax	$0	$0	$0	$0	$138	$138
	Personal Tax: Income Tax	$0	$0	$60	$0	$0	$60
	Personal Tax: Motor Vehicle License	$0	$0	$2	$0	$0	$2
	Personal Tax: Non Taxes (Fines-Fees)	$0	$0	$16	$0	$0	$16
	Personal Tax: Property Tax	$0	$0	$1	$0	$0	$1
	Social Insurance Tax- Employee Contribution	$2	$0	$0	$0	$0	$2
	Social Insurance Tax- Employer Contribution	$9	$0	$0	$0	$0	$9
	Total	$11	$0	$79	$79	$266	$435
Total		$231	$12	$256	$204	$307	$1,010

*Results are not displayed for tax categories that experience no impact. Totals still reflect all tax categories.

77

Table 60. Import Substitution Tax Impacts from a 10 Percent Natural Gas Increase for Region 5

Import Substitution Tax Impact (In Millions of US Dollars)		Sources					
		Employee Compensation	Proprietary Income	Household Expenditures	Enterprises (Corporations)	Indirect Business Tax	Total
Federal Government NonDefense	Corporate Profits Tax	$0	$0	$0	$8	$0	$8
	Indirect Business Tax: Custom Duty	$0	$0	$0	$0	$1	$1
	Indirect Business Tax: Excise Taxes	$0	$0	$0	$0	$2	$2
	Indirect Business Tax: Fed Non Taxes	$0	$0	$0	$0	$1	$1
	Personal Tax: Income Tax	$0	$0	$9	$0	$0	$9
	Social Insurance Tax- Employee Contribution	$4	$1	$0	$0	$0	$5
	Social Insurance Tax- Employer Contribution	$4	$0	$0	$0	$0	$4
	Total	$8	$1	$9	$8	$3	$29
State/Local Government NonEducation	Corporate Profits Tax	$0	$0	$0	$2	$0	$2
	Dividends	$0	$0	$0	$3	$0	$3
	Indirect Business Tax: Other Taxes	$0	$0	$0	$0	$2	$2
	Indirect Business Tax: Property Tax	$0	$0	$0	$0	$7	$7
	Indirect Business Tax: S/L Non Taxes	$0	$0	$0	$0	$1	$1
	Indirect Business Tax: Sales Tax	$0	$0	$0	$0	$10	$10
	Personal Tax: Income Tax	$0	$0	$3	$0	$0	$3
	Personal Tax: Non Taxes (Fines-Fees)	$0	$0	$1	$0	$0	$1
	Total	$0	$0	$4	$5	$19	$29
Total		$9	$1	$12	$13	$22	$58

*Results are not displayed for tax categories that experience no impact. Totals still reflect all tax categories.

Table 61. Construction Tax Impacts from a 10 Percent Natural Gas Increase for Region 5

Construction Tax Impact (In Millions of US Dollars)		Sources					
		Employee Compensation	Proprietary Income	Household Expenditures	Enterprises (Corporations)	Indirect Business Tax	Total
Federal Government NonDefense	Corporate Profits Tax	$0	$0	$0	$16	$0	$16
	Indirect Business Tax: Custom Duty	$0	$0	$0	$0	$1	$1
	Indirect Business Tax: Excise Taxes	$0	$0	$0	$0	$3	$3
	Indirect Business Tax: Fed Non Taxes	$0	$0	$0	$0	$1	$1
	Personal Tax: Income Tax	$0	$0	$21	$0	$0	$21
	Social Insurance Tax- Employee Contribution	$13	$1	$0	$0	$0	$15
	Social Insurance Tax- Employer Contribution	$13	$0	$0	$0	$0	$13
	Total	$27	$1	$21	$16	$5	$71
State/Local Government NonEducation	Corporate Profits Tax	$0	$0	$0	$4	$0	$4
	Dividends	$0	$0	$0	$6	$0	$6
	Indirect Business Tax: Other Taxes	$0	$0	$0	$0	$3	$3
	Indirect Business Tax: Property Tax	$0	$0	$0	$0	$12	$12
	Indirect Business Tax: S/L Non Taxes	$0	$0	$0	$0	$1	$1
	Indirect Business Tax: Sales Tax	$0	$0	$0	$0	$18	$18
	Personal Tax: Income Tax	$0	$0	$7	$0	$0	$7
	Personal Tax: Non Taxes (Fines-Fees)	$0	$0	$2	$0	$0	$2
	Social Insurance Tax- Employer Contribution	$1	$0	$0	$0	$0	$1
	Total	$1	$0	$10	$10	$34	$55
Total		$28	$1	$31	$26	$39	$126

*Results are not displayed for tax categories that experience no impact. Totals still reflect all tax categories.

78

9.2.10 Region 5 (California) – Scenario Analysis

Three scenario analyses for California were performed and all are reported. These analyses for 2010 and 2020 are evaluated as opportunity costs of the S.2191 legislation whereas the 2030 scenario estimates impacts that are considered to be benefits of the legislation. Tables 62–64 give a summary report of the data inputs and the total impacts from import substitution and construction in Region 5.

Table 62. Input Data and Summary Results for California, 2010

Input Data Summary for California		
	Natural Gas	Oil
Production Increases	398 MMcf/yr	6 thbbl/yr
Estimated Average Well Depth	5,000-7,499 ft/well	1,250-2,499 ft/well
Well Construction Cost	1014 th$/well	803 th$/well
Average Producer Price	7.31 $/tcf	57.43 $/bbl
Industry Output	3 Million $	0 Million $
Reduced Import Payments	3 Million $	0 Million $
International Trade Feedback Share	10%	10%
Year Dollars	2006	2006

Summary Results for California			
(Millions of US Dollars)	Output	FTEs	Taxes
Import Substitution Impacts	$5	15	$1
Construction Impacts	$15	58	$2

Table 63. Input Data and Summary Results for California, 2020

Input Data Summary for California		
	Natural Gas	Oil
Production Increases	2823 MMcf/yr	26 thbbl/yr
Estimated Average Well Depth	5,000-7,499 ft/well	1,250-2,499 ft/well
Well Construction Cost	1014 th$/well	803 th$/well
Average Producer Price	7.31 $/tcf	57.43 $/bbl
Industry Output	23 Million $	1 Million $
Reduced Import Payments	20 Million $	2 Million $
International Trade Feedback Share	10%	10%
Year Dollars	2006	2006

Summary Results for California			
(Millions of US Dollars)	Output	FTEs	Taxes
Import Substitution Impacts	$36	106	$6
Construction Impacts	$108	415	$13

79

Table 64. Input Data and Summary Results for California, 2030

Input Data Summary for California		
	Natural Gas	Oil
Production Increases	487 MMcf/yr	1151 thbbl/yr
Estimated Average Well Depth	5,000-7,499 ft/well	1,250-2,499 ft/well
Well Construction Cost	1014 th$/well	803 th$/well
Average Producer Price	7.31 $/tcf	57.43 $/bbl
Industry Output	4 Million $	66 Million $
Reduced Import Payments	3 Million $	68 Million $
International Trade Feedback Share	10%	10%
Year Dollars	2006	2006

Summary Results for California			
(Millions of US Dollars)	Output	FTEs	Taxes
Import Substitution Impacts	$83	198	$14
Construction Impacts	$479	1,896	$58

9.2.11 Region 6 (U.S. Lower 48) – Standardized Production Increase

Oil.

Table 65. Major Import Substitution Impacts from a 10 Percent Oil Increase for Region 6

Import Substitution Impacts (In Millions of US		Output Components		Value Added Components				
Industry	Output	Intermediate Inputs	Value Added	Employment Compensation	Proprietor's Income	Other Property Type Income	Indirect Business Taxes	Employment (FTE's)
Ag. Forestry, Fish & Hunting	$20	$12	$7	$3	$2	$2	$0	233
Oil and Gas Extraction	$6,310	$2,398	$3,912	$538	$1,027	$1,973	$374	8,660
Coal, Metal Ores & Nonmetalic Mineral Mining, Quarrying & Support Activites	$4	$2	$2	$1	$0	$1	$0	16
Drilling Oil and Gas Wells	$6	$4	$2	$1	$0	$1	$0	9
Support Activities for Oil and Gas Operations	$120	$6	$113	$37	$4	$67	$5	532
Power Generation and Supply and Water, Sewage and Other Systems	$47	$9	$39	$8	$3	$22	$5	79
Natural Gas Distribution	$8	$5	$3	$1	$0	$1	$1	10
Other New Construction, Including Maintenance and Repair Construction	$11	$6	$5	$3	$1	$1	$0	85
Manufacturing and Industrial Buildings	$0	$0	$0	$0	$0	$0	$0	0
Water, Sewer, and Pipeline Construction	$0	$0	$0	$0	$0	$0	$0	0
Total	$9,277	$3,759	$5,518	$1,374	$1,147	$2,503	$494	26,944

*Results displayed for the top 10 sectors in terms of total output impacts. Total values still include all 33 sectors.

80

Table 66. Major Construction Impacts from a 10 Percent Oil Increase for Region 6

Construction Impacts (In Millions of US Dollars)		Output Components		Value Added Components				Employment (FTE's)
Industry	Output	Intermediate Inputs	Value Added	Employment Compensation	Proprietor's Income	Other Property Type Income	Indirect Business Taxes	
Ag, Forestry, Fish & Hunting	$280	$174	$106	$37	$29	$35	$4	3,294
Oil and Gas Extraction	$632	$240	$392	$54	$103	$198	$38	868
Coal, Metal Ores & Nonmetalic Mineral Mining, Quarrying & Support Activites	$79	$39	$41	$19	$4	$12	$5	281
Drilling Oil and Gas Wells	$38,236	$24,736	$13,499	$4,296	$410	$7,221	$1,572	57,195
Support Activities for Oil and Gas Operations	$768	$40	$728	$240	$24	$432	$32	3,421
Power Generation and Supply and Water, Sewage and Other Systems	$311	$58	$253	$50	$20	$147	$36	515
Natural Gas Distribution	$151	$92	$59	$17	$7	$18	$17	175
Other New Construction, Including Maintenance and Repair Construction	$121	$66	$55	$37	$11	$7	$1	956
Manufacturing and Industrial Buildings	$0	$0	$0	$0	$0	$0	$0	0
Water, Sewer, and Pipeline Construction	$3,024	$1,593	$1,431	$919	$276	$215	$20	23,895
Total	$75,623	$43,683	$31,939	$14,838	$1,928	$12,403	$2,770	288,466

*Results displayed for the top 10 sectors in terms of total output impacts. Total values still include all 33 sectors.

Gas.

Table 67. Major Import Substitution Impacts for a 10 Percent Natural Gas Increase for Region 6

Import Substitution Impacts (In Millions of US		Output Components		Value Added Components				Employment (FTE's)
Industry	Output	Intermediate Inputs	Value Added	Employment Compensation	Proprietor's Income	Other Property Type Income	Indirect Business Taxes	
Ag, Forestry, Fish & Hunting	$83	$52	$31	$11	$9	$10	$1	976
Oil and Gas Extraction	$9,828	$3,735	$6,093	$838	$1,599	$3,073	$583	13,489
Coal, Metal Ores & Nonmetalic Mineral Mining, Quarrying & Support Activites	$18	$9	$9	$4	$1	$3	$1	66
Drilling Oil and Gas Wells	$12	$8	$4	$1	$0	$2	$0	18
Support Activities for Oil and Gas Operations	$230	$12	$218	$72	$7	$130	$9	1,026
Power Generation and Supply and Water, Sewage and Other Systems	$112	$21	$91	$18	$7	$53	$13	185
Natural Gas Distribution	$2,131	$1,300	$831	$246	$98	$254	$233	2,468
Other New Construction, Including Maintenance and Repair Construction	$31	$17	$14	$9	$3	$2	$0	242
Manufacturing and Industrial Buildings	$0	$0	$0	$0	$0	$0	$0	0
Water, Sewer, and Pipeline Construction	$0	$0	$0	$0	$0	$0	$0	0
Total	$19,559	$8,649	$10,910	$3,188	$2,006	$4,598	$1,118	62,221

*Results displayed for the top 10 sectors in terms of total output impacts. Total values still include all 33 sectors.

Table 68. Major Construction Impacts from a 10 Percent Natural Gas Increase for Region 6

Construction Impacts (In Millions of US Dollars)		Output Components		Value Added Components				Employment (FTE's)
Industry	Output	Intermediate Inputs	Value Added	Employment Compensation	Proprietor's Income	Other Property Type Income	Indirect Business Taxes	
Ag, Forestry, Fish & Hunting	$267	$166	$101	$36	$28	$33	$4	3,142
Oil and Gas Extraction	$607	$231	$376	$52	$99	$190	$36	833
Coal, Metal Ores & Nonmetalic Mineral Mining, Quarrying & Support Activites	$79	$38	$40	$19	$4	$12	$5	279
Drilling Oil and Gas Wells	$41,394	$26,780	$14,614	$4,650	$444	$7,818	$1,702	61,919
Support Activities for Oil and Gas Operations	$831	$44	$787	$260	$25	$468	$34	3,701
Power Generation and Supply and Water, Sewage and Other Systems	$302	$57	$245	$49	$19	$143	$35	500
Natural Gas Distribution	$156	$95	$61	$18	$7	$19	$17	181
Other New Construction, Including Maintenance and Repair Construction	$116	$63	$53	$35	$11	$6	$1	917
Manufacturing and Industrial Buildings	$0	$0	$0	$0	$0	$0	$0	0
Water, Sewer, and Pipeline Construction	$795	$419	$376	$241	$73	$57	$5	6,279
Total	$75,540	$44,006	$31,534	$14,247	$1,699	$12,742	$2,846	268,136

*Results displayed for the top 10 sectors in terms of total output impacts. Total values still include all 33 sectors.

81

198 703-739-3790 TCNNaturalGas.com

Tax Impacts.

Table 69. Import Substitution Tax Impacts from a 10 Percent Oil Increase for Region 6

Import Substitution Tax Impact (In Millions of US Dollars)		Sources					
		Employee Compensation	Proprietary Income	Household Expenditures	Enterprises (Corporations)	Indirect Business Tax	Total
Enterprises (Corporations)	Transfers	$1	$0	$0	$0	$0	$1
	Total	$1	$0	$0	$0	$0	$1
Federal Government NonDefense	Corporate Profits Tax	$0	$0	$0	$239	$0	$239
	Indirect Business Tax: Custom Duty	$0	$0	$0	$0	$13	$13
	Indirect Business Tax: Excise Taxes	$0	$0	$0	$0	$34	$34
	Indirect Business Tax: Fed Non Taxes	$0	$0	$0	$0	$15	$15
	Personal Tax: Income Tax	$0	$0	$209	$0	$0	$209
	Social Insurance Tax-Employee Contribution	$78	$52	$0	$0	$0	$130
	Social Insurance Tax-Employer Contribution	$80	$0	$0	$0	$0	$80
	Total	$158	$52	$209	$239	$62	$720
State/Local Government NonEducation	Corporate Profits Tax	$0	$0	$0	$40	$0	$40
	Dividends	$0	$0	$0	$61	$0	$61
	Indirect Business Tax: Motor Vehicle License	$0	$0	$0	$0	$4	$4
	Indirect Business Tax: Other Taxes	$0	$0	$0	$0	$32	$32
	Indirect Business Tax: Property Tax	$0	$0	$0	$0	$175	$175
	Indirect Business Tax: S/L Non Taxes	$0	$0	$0	$0	$19	$19
	Indirect Business Tax: Sales Tax	$0	$0	$0	$0	$197	$197
	Indirect Business Tax: Severance Tax	$0	$0	$0	$0	$5	$5
	Personal Tax: Income Tax	$0	$0	$55	$0	$0	$55
	Personal Tax: Motor Vehicle License	$0	$0	$2	$0	$0	$2
	Personal Tax: Non Taxes (Fines-Fees)	$0	$0	$13	$0	$0	$13
	Personal Tax: Other Tax (Fish/Hunt)	$0	$0	$1	$0	$0	$1
	Personal Tax: Property Tax	$0	$0	$1	$0	$0	$1
	Social Insurance Tax-Employee Contribution	$1	$0	$0	$0	$0	$1
	Social Insurance Tax-Employer Contribution	$4	$0	$0	$0	$0	$4
	Total	$5	$0	$71	$101	$432	$609
Total		$164	$52	$280	$339	$494	$1,330

*Results are not displayed for tax categories that experience no impact. Totals still reflect all tax categories.

82

Table 70. Construction Tax Impacts from a 10 Percent Oil Increase for Region 6

Construction Tax Impact (In Millions of US Dollars)		Sources					
		Employee Compensation	Proprietary Income	Household Expenditures	Enterprises (Corporations)	Indirect Business Tax	Total
Enterprises (Corporations)	Transfers	$15	$0	$0	$0	$0	$15
	Total	$15	$0	$0	$0	$0	$15
Federal Government NonDefense	Corporate Profits Tax	$0	$0	$0	$1,182	$0	$1,182
	Indirect Business Tax: Custom Duty	$0	$0	$0	$0	$71	$71
	Indirect Business Tax: Excise Taxes	$0	$0	$0	$0	$191	$191
	Indirect Business Tax: Fed Non Taxes	$0	$0	$0	$0	$87	$87
	Personal Tax: Income Tax	$0	$0	$1,353	$0	$0	$1,353
	Social Insurance Tax-Employee Contribution	$846	$88	$0	$0	$0	$934
	Social Insurance Tax-Employer Contribution	$859	$0	$0	$0	$0	$859
	Total	$1,705	$88	$1,353	$1,182	$349	$4,677
State/Local Government NonEducation	Corporate Profits Tax	$0	$0	$0	$198	$0	$198
	Dividends	$0	$0	$0	$302	$0	$302
	Indirect Business Tax: Motor Vehicle License	$0	$0	$0	$0	$22	$22
	Indirect Business Tax: Other Taxes	$0	$0	$0	$0	$178	$178
	Indirect Business Tax: Property Tax	$0	$0	$0	$0	$979	$979
	Indirect Business Tax: S/L Non Taxes	$0	$0	$0	$0	$108	$108
	Indirect Business Tax: Sales Tax	$0	$0	$0	$0	$1,106	$1,106
	Indirect Business Tax: Severance Tax	$0	$0	$0	$0	$28	$28
	Personal Tax: Income Tax	$0	$0	$353	$0	$0	$353
	Personal Tax: Motor Vehicle License	$0	$0	$19	$0	$0	$19
	Personal Tax: Non Taxes (Fines-Fees)	$0	$0	$82	$0	$0	$82
	Personal Tax: Other Tax (Fish/Hunt)	$0	$0	$6	$0	$0	$6
	Personal Tax: Property Tax	$0	$0	$8	$0	$0	$8
	Social Insurance Tax-Employee Contribution	$10	$0	$0	$0	$0	$10
	Social Insurance Tax-Employer Contribution	$41	$0	$0	$0	$0	$41
	Total	$52	$0	$469	$500	$2,421	$3,442
Total		$1,771	$88	$1,822	$1,682	$2,770	$8,133

*Results are not displayed for tax categories that experience no impact. Totals still reflect all tax categories.

83

Table 71. Import Substitution Tax Impacts from a 10 Percent Natural Gas Increase for Region 6

Import Substitution Tax Impact (In Millions of US Dollars)		Employee Compensation	Proprietary Income	Household Expenditures	Enterprises (Corporations)	Indirect Business Tax	Total
				Sources			
	Transfers	$3	$0	$0	$0	$0	$3
Enterprises (Corporations)	Total	$3	$0	$0	$0	$0	$3
	Corporate Profits Tax	$0	$0	$0	$438	$0	$438
	Indirect Business Tax: Custom Duty	$0	$0	$0	$0	$29	$29
	Indirect Business Tax: Excise Taxes	$0	$0	$0	$0	$77	$77
	Indirect Business Tax: Fed Non Taxes	$0	$0	$0	$0	$35	$35
Federal Government NonDefense	Personal Tax: Income Tax	$0	$0	$429	$0	$0	$429
	Social Insurance Tax- Employee Contribution	$182	$91	$0	$0	$0	$273
	Social Insurance Tax- Employer Contribution	$184	$0	$0	$0	$0	$184
	Total	$366	$91	$429	$438	$141	$1,465
	Corporate Profits Tax	$0	$0	$0	$73	$0	$73
	Dividends	$0	$0	$0	$112	$0	$112
	Indirect Business Tax: Motor Vehicle License	$0	$0	$0	$0	$9	$9
	Indirect Business Tax: Other Taxes	$0	$0	$0	$0	$72	$72
	Indirect Business Tax: Property Tax	$0	$0	$0	$0	$395	$395
	Indirect Business Tax: S/L Non Taxes	$0	$0	$0	$0	$44	$44
	Indirect Business Tax: Sales Tax	$0	$0	$0	$0	$446	$446
	Indirect Business Tax: Severance Tax	$0	$0	$0	$0	$11	$11
State/Local Government NonEducation	Personal Tax: Income Tax	$0	$0	$112	$0	$0	$112
	Personal Tax: Motor Vehicle License	$0	$0	$4	$0	$0	$4
	Personal Tax: Non Taxes (Fines-Fees)	$0	$0	$26	$0	$0	$26
	Personal Tax: Other Tax (Fish/Hunt)	$0	$0	$2	$0	$0	$2
	Personal Tax: Property Tax	$0	$0	$3	$0	$0	$3
	Social Insurance Tax- Employee Contribution	$2	$0	$0	$0	$0	$2
	Social Insurance Tax- Employer Contribution	$9	$0	$0	$0	$0	$9
	Total	$11	$0	$146	$185	$977	$1,320
Total		$381	$91	$575	$624	$1,118	$2,788

*Results are not displayed for tax categories that experience no impact. Totals still reflect all tax categories.

84

Table 72. Construction Tax Impacts from a 10 Percent Natural Gas Increase for Region 6

Construction Tax Impact (In Millions of US Dollars)		Sources					
		Employee Compensation	Proprietary Income	Household Expenditures	Enterprises (Corporations)	Indirect Business Tax	Total
Enterprises (Corporations)	Transfers	$14	$0	$0	$0	$0	$14
	Total	$14	$0	$0	$0	$0	$14
Federal Government NonDefense	Corporate Profits Tax	$0	$0	$0	$1,214	$0	$1,214
	Indirect Business Tax: Custom Duty	$0	$0	$0	$0	$73	$73
	Indirect Business Tax: Excise Taxes	$0	$0	$0	$0	$197	$197
	Indirect Business Tax: Fed Non Taxes	$0	$0	$0	$0	$89	$89
	Personal Tax: Income Tax	$0	$0	$1,286	$0	$0	$1,286
	Social Insurance Tax- Employee Contribution	$812	$77	$0	$0	$0	$890
	Social Insurance Tax- Employer Contribution	$824	$0	$0	$0	$0	$824
	Total	$1,637	$77	$1,286	$1,214	$359	$4,573
State/Local Government NonEducation	Corporate Profits Tax	$0	$0	$0	$203	$0	$203
	Dividends	$0	$0	$0	$310	$0	$310
	Indirect Business Tax: Motor Vehicle License	$0	$0	$0	$0	$23	$23
	Indirect Business Tax: Other Taxes	$0	$0	$0	$0	$183	$183
	Indirect Business Tax: Property Tax	$0	$0	$0	$0	$1,006	$1,006
	Indirect Business Tax: S/L Non Taxes	$0	$0	$0	$0	$111	$111
	Indirect Business Tax: Sales Tax	$0	$0	$0	$0	$1,136	$1,136
	Indirect Business Tax: Severance Tax	$0	$0	$0	$0	$29	$29
	Personal Tax: Income Tax	$0	$0	$336	$0	$0	$336
	Personal Tax: Motor Vehicle License	$0	$0	$18	$0	$0	$18
	Personal Tax: Non Taxes (Fines-Fees)	$0	$0	$78	$0	$0	$78
	Personal Tax: Other Tax (Fish/Hunt)	$0	$0	$6	$0	$0	$6
	Personal Tax: Property Tax	$0	$0	$8	$0	$0	$8
	Social Insurance Tax- Employee Contribution	$10	$0	$0	$0	$0	$10
	Social Insurance Tax- Employer Contribution	$40	$0	$0	$0	$0	$40
	Total	$50	$0	$446	$514	$2,487	$3,496
Total		$1,701	$77	$1,732	$1,728	$2,846	$8,084

*Results are not displayed for tax categories that experience no impact. Totals still reflect all tax categories.

85

9.2.12 Region 6 (U.S. Lower 48) – Scenario Analysis.

Three scenario analyses for the U.S.-Lower 48 Region were performed and all are reported. All three of these analyses are evaluated as opportunity costs of the S.2191 legislation. Tables 73–75 give a summary report of the data inputs and the total impacts from import substitution and construction for the U.S.-Lower 48.

Table 73. Input Data and Summary Results for U.S. – Lower 48, 2010

Input Data Summary for US - Lower 48		
	Natural Gas	Oil
Production Increases	95973 MMcf/yr	60 thbbl/yr
Estimated Average Well Depth	5,000-7,499 ft/well	3,750-4,999 ft/well
Well Construction Cost	843 th$/well	911 th$/well
Average Producer Price	6.56 $/tcf	59.05 $/bbl
Industry Output	672 Million $	4 Million $
Reduced Import Payments	580 Million $	4 Million $
International Trade Feedback Share	10%	10%
Year Dollars	2006	2006

Summary Results for US - Lower 48			
(Millions of US Dollars)	Output	FTEs	Taxes
Import Substitution Impacts	$988	2,905	$145
Construction Impacts	$4,187	14,522	$447

Table 74. Input Data and Summary Results for U.S. – Lower 48, 2020

Input Data Summary for US - Lower 48		
	Natural Gas	Oil
Production Increases	573692 MMcf/yr	3056 thbbl/yr
Estimated Average Well Depth	5,000-7,499 ft/well	3,750-4,999 ft/well
Well Construction Cost	843 th$/well	911 th$/well
Average Producer Price	6.56 $/tcf	59.05 $/bbl
Industry Output	4018 Million $	180 Million $
Reduced Import Payments	3465 Million $	181 Million $
International Trade Feedback Share	10%	10%
Year Dollars	2006	2006

Summary Results for US - Lower 48			
(Millions of US Dollars)	Output	FTEs	Taxes
Import Substitution Impacts	$6,122	17,987	$896
Construction Impacts	$27,261	96,366	$2,916

Table 75. Input Data and Summary Results for U.S. – Lower 48, 2030

Input Data Summary for US - Lower 48		
	Natural Gas	Oil
Production Increases	84802 MMcf/yr	2686 thbbl/yr
Estimated Average Well Depth	5,000-7,499 ft/well	3,750-4,999 ft/well
Well Construction Cost	843 th$/well	911 th$/well
Average Producer Price	6.56 $/tcf	59.05 $/bbl
Industry Output	594 Million $	159 Million $
Reduced Import Payments	512 Million $	159 Million $
International Trade Feedback Share	10%	10%
Year Dollars	2006	2006

Summary Results for US - Lower 48			
(Millions of US Dollars)	Output	FTEs	Taxes
Import Substitution Impacts	$1,071	3,078	$157
Construction Impacts	$5,563	19,939	$596

86

9.3 Comparison to Other Studies

In anticipation of technological data for new technologies, the original intent was to provide a comparison of the results of these impacts analyses to those reported elsewhere. However, because other technological data remain undeveloped to date, there are no other reports that are directly comparable. Hence, the data reported here result from the necessity of generating alternate scenarios for analysis. Therefore, no model comparisons beyond those already presented in Section 2.0 of this document are reported.

87

Appendix A: The Input-Output Model

Input-output (IO) analysis is based on the inter-industry sales and purchases relationships that exist in every economy. IO analysis characterizes an economy by describing these flows of goods and services between industries, institutions and the final market.

François Quesnay (1694–1774), a French physician turned economist, was the first to use this type of system to describe the economy. One of his main works, *Le Tableau Économique* (1758), contained an early, much less sophisticated version of a multi-sector IO system. He aimed to show diagrammatically the flow of money in a primarily agrarian economy. Later, forms of this technique would be expounded upon by such great economic minds as David Ricardo, Karl Marx, and Léon Walras.

It wasn't until the late 1930s that Wassily Leontief (1906–1999), a Russian-born American economist, developed the analytical framework that would become modern IO analysis. For this substantial contribution to the field, he was awarded the Nobel Prize in Economic Science in 1973. In more recent years, IO analysis has been extended to cover items such as energy consumption, environmental factors, and employment impacts. It can now also be extended to consider interregional and multiregional analyses.

Methodological Basis

The statistical foundation of IO analysis is essentially an accounting framework. The basis of any type of IO system is the transactions matrix. The transactions matrix is a means of ordering all inter-industry sales (outputs) and purchases (inputs)—the economic transactions that occur in the economy—during a given time period. Each column of this matrix consists of the values of the inputs required by a given industry to produce its output. Each row consists of the values of the industry's outputs distributed throughout the economy. This transactions matrix only reports the intermediate goods and services being exchanged among industries.

Additionally, a full IO table also includes a few additional rows (value added) and additional columns (final demand). The value added rows include information about the non-industrial inputs of production, such as labor. The final demand columns show the sales by each industry to a final market, such as consumption, investment, government purchases and net exports. An example of an IO table is produced below in Figure A1.

Transactions Table

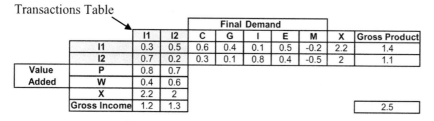

Figure A1: *Accounting Foundations of IO Analysis*

88

Notation:

$\mathbf{Z}$: transactions matrix

$\mathbf{z_{ij}} \in \mathbf{Z}$: dollar flow of commodities from industry i to industry j on current account

$\mathbf{P_j}$: profits for industry j

$\mathbf{W_j}$: wages and salaries for industry j

$\mathbf{v_j}$: value added for industry j

$\mathbf{C_i}$: value of flows of commodities from industry i to consumption

$\mathbf{G_i}$: value of flows of commodities from industry i to government expenditures

$\mathbf{I_i}$: value of flows of commodities from industry i to investment

$\mathbf{E_i}$: value of flows of commodities from industry i to export sales

$\mathbf{M_i}$: value of imports of commodities for industry i

$\mathbf{f_i}$: value of flows of commodities from industry i to category k of final demand (consumption, government expenditures, investment and export sales)

$\mathbf{X_i}$: output of industry i

$v_j = P_j + W_j$

$f_i = C_i + G_i + I_i + E_i$

Balance Equation for Output:

$$\left(\sum_j z_{ij} \right) + C_i + G_i + I_i + E_i = X_i \; \forall \, i, i = 1, ..., \; n$$

Balance Equation for Input:

$$\left(\sum_i z_{ij} \right) + P_j + W_j + M_j = X_j \; \forall \, j, j = 1, ..., \; n$$

Total Output:

$$\sum_i \sum_j z_{ij} + \sum_i \left(C_i + G_i + I_i + E_i \right) = \sum_i X_i$$

Total Input:

$$\sum_j \sum_i z_{ij} + \sum_j \left(P_j + W_j + M_j \right) = \sum_j X_j$$

To make economic sense, total outputs must equal total inputs. Then we can see that:

$$\sum_i \sum_j z_{ij} + \sum_i \left(C_i + G_i + I_i + E_i \right) = \sum_j \sum_i z_{ij} + \sum_j \left(P_j + W_j + M_j \right)$$

$$\sum_i \left(C_i + G_i + I_i + E_i \right) = \sum_j \left(P_j + W_j + M_j \right)$$

89

$$C + I + G + E = P + W + M$$

$$C + I + G + E - M = P + W$$

The left hand side of this final equation is gross national product and the right hand side is gross national income.

Technical Coefficients (a_{ij})

<u>Assumptions</u>

1. Inter-industry flows from i to j in a given time period depend solely on the total output for sector j in that same time period.
2. The technical coefficients are constant and measure fixed relationships between an industry's output and its inputs.
3. Production operates under constant returns to scale.
4. IO analysis requires that an industry uses inputs in fixed proportions.

$$a_{ij} = \frac{z_{ij}}{X_j}$$

The technical coefficient, a_{ij}, can be interpreted as the dollar's worth of input from industry i per dollar's worth of output of industry j. We can now define the technical coefficients matrix for an n-industry economy, A:

$$A = \begin{bmatrix} a_{11} & a_{12} & . & . & . & a_{1n} \\ a_{21} & a_{22} & . & . & . & a_{2n} \\ . & . & . & & & . \\ . & . & & . & & . \\ . & . & & & . & . \\ a_{n1} & a_{n2} & . & . & . & a_{nn} \end{bmatrix}$$

Using the numbers above in Figure 1, the technical coefficients matrix is defined as:

$$A = \begin{bmatrix} .1364 & .25 \\ .3182 & .1 \end{bmatrix}$$

Now, if Y_i is designated as industry i's sales to final demand:

$$Y_i = C_i + G_i + I_i + E_i$$

90

Then we can write that:

$$X_i = z_{i1} + z_{i2} + \ldots + z_{in} + Y_i$$

Using the equation for technical coefficients above:

$$X_i = a_{i1}X_1 + a_{i2}X_2 + \ldots + a_{in}X_n + Y_i$$

By manipulating this equation in matrix form we can define the complete system as:

$$(I-A)X = Y \qquad \text{or} \qquad X = (I-A)^{-1}Y$$

where I corresponds to the (nxn) identity matrix and $(I-A)^{-1}$ is called the Leontief inverse.

The Leontief inverse referencing Figure 1 is:

$$(I - A)^{-1} = L = \begin{bmatrix} 1.28997 & .3583 \\ .45608 & 1.2378 \end{bmatrix}$$

To show the dependence of the gross outputs on the values of the final demands we can define the elements of the Leontief inverse as l_{ij} and write the equation:

$$X_i = l_{i1}Y_1 + l_{i2}Y_2 + \ldots + l_{in}Y_n$$

Open or Closed Model

The IO model can either be open or closed with respect to households. If our project goal is to model the direct, indirect and induced impacts of domestic oil and natural gas consumption, then we are necessarily considering a model that is closed with respect to households.

The difference between an open model and a closed model is that households are exogenous in the open model and endogenous in the closed model. In a closed model, households are treated as part of the production sector and are therefore economically connected with all other parts of the transactions matrix. This addition adds one extra row and column to the transactions matrix, the matrix of technical coefficients, and the Leontief inverse. The household sector can be thought of as buying consumer goods from and selling labor to all other industries.

Strengths

- IO models provide a large amount of information in a concise and easy to understand form. They present a comprehensive picture of the economy and its inter-industry relations.
- IO analysis is transparent; it does not rest on as many assumptions and parameters as some of the models that are discussed later in this document.
- IO models are extremely useful in analyzing the impact of a change in any sector on the output of others.

91

- One main attribute of IO analysis is its descriptive analytical power. It has predictive capabilities in that it can estimate both direct and indirect impacts as they are tracked through the economy.

- IO analysis analyzes changes and impacts on an industry-by-industry level, tracing the flow of dollars between industries; thus, making it possible to have a very precise calculation of the economic impacts to the economy.

- The extension of an IO model to an interregional or multiregional framework is straightforward.

Weaknesses

- Constructing transactions matrices can be costly and time-consuming. These data, however, are often collected by government agencies and are available for use but with some significant time lag.

- An IO matrix gives a static view of the economy and can make structural projection difficult. Even so, with a significant level of complication, IO models can be transformed into dynamic models. With required data and economic assumptions, it is also possible to make changes to the initial IO model in order to model different time periods by assuming that technical coefficients are stable over time.

- IO analysis does not allow for interaction between supply and demand. Prices are fixed in both goods and labor.

- IO models are not set up for any supply or capacity constraints; however, these could be handled with the external processing of data.

- The linear relationships assumed in IO analysis do not allow for externalities or increasing/decreasing returns to scale.

- There is no statistical test to check the model specification.

Geographical Scale

Most available IO data are collected and published on a national scale. These national data can be used to estimate regional data using one of several regionalization techniques. The regionalization technique of greatest relevance to this project is the regional purchase coefficient (RPC) technique used in Impact Analysis for Planning (IMPLAN), from whom project data have been obtained.

RPC Method

The regional purchase coefficient is the proportion of the regional demand for a good or service that is fulfilled by production within the region, as opposed to being fulfilled by imports from other regions.

92

Notation:

R^M : regional purchase coefficient for region M

S^{MM} : amount of good produced locally in region M (amount shipped from region M to itself)

S^{LM} : amount of the same good produced in region L and shipped to region M. (If this were a multi-region setup, L corresponds to the rest of the "world," not just one other region.)

A general equation of an RPC for a region M can then be defined as:

$$R^M = \frac{S^{MM}}{S^{MM} + S^{LM}}$$

IMPLAN uses a more sophisticated form of this equation that estimates the RPC as a function of the wage ratio, the ratio of "other costs," the output ratio, the weight/value ratio of the good, the ratio of the number of users of a good, the ratio of the number of producers of a good and the land area ratio of each region.

Data Requirements

- Sales and purchases data, disaggregated by industry and region
- Final demand data by industry and region
- Household consumption data by industry and region
- Household compensation data by industry and region
- Data on the impact scenario

Applications

There is voluminous literature available on the uses and applications of IO analysis. The literature ranges from many different policy implications to environmental applications (Duchin 1992, Hubacek et al. 2002) with general studies on many different countries (e.g., Haddad and Hewings 2000, Cho et al. 2000). Studies have even been conducted predicting the effects of sudden changes to the economy (Okuyama et al. 1997, Lahr et al. forthcoming). There is also literature in which IO analysis techniques are advanced and changes in regional structure are further explored (Rey and Jackson 1999, Jackson et al. 1989).

93

Appendix B: Assessment of Tax Impact Estimation

The following assessment of the tax impact estimates in this project is provided by Dr. Brian Cushing, Associate Professor in West Virginia University's Department of Economics.

As it is with most impact analyses, estimation of tax impacts is an important component of the DOE/NETL project, "Valuing Domestically Produced Natural Gas and Oil." This note explains how tax impacts come out of the IMPLAN model. It then evaluates this method of estimating tax impacts, discussing advantages and disadvantages. The bottom line is simple: while tax impact estimates from IMPLAN may not be perfect, they are likely to be reasonable. Given the normal limitations in knowledge and data, it is unlikely that one could find a better (and feasible) method to handle tax impacts.

For this project, tax impacts are developed as they normally come out of an IMPLAN impact model:

(1) For each of the six models (five regions and the national model), the research team begins with social accounts for the base year, which show the distribution of receipts and disbursements for all the different industries, institutional sectors (households, Federal Government, ...), etc.

(2) Given a shock to the system (in this case, increased domestic production of oil and natural gas), IMPLAN's impact analysis generates changes in the four components of value added (employee compensation, proprietor's income, indirect business taxes, and other property income), as well as for enterprises;

(3) These changes are applied to the (normalized) social accounts, which yields estimated tax impacts;

(4) The researchers assume that any marginal changes (impacts) flow through the system according to the base year distribution discussed above;

(5) The researchers also assume that the detailed distribution of expenditures by employment compensation, proprietor's income, other property income, indirect business taxes, and enterprise holds, no matter what the mix of affected industries.

For the first step, a typical IMPLAN model begins by developing a set of social accounts for each state that will be part of the analysis. If impacts are desired at the county level, the each state model is used as the basis for developing models for its counties. The DOE/NETL model does not need county-level detail.

The key data used to develop tax impacts for IMPLAN models come from four primary sources: 1) the *National Income and Product Accounts (NIPA)* [U.S. Bureau of Economic Analysis]; 2) the *Consumer Expenditure Survey (CES)* [U.S. Bureau of the Census]; 3) the *Annual Survey of State and Local Government Finances (SLGF)* [U.S. Bureau of the Census]; and 4) the *Regional Economic Information System (REIS)* [U.S. Bureau of Economic Analysis]. Most of the tax

94

information for states comes directly from these sources. For example, personal income taxes paid to the Federal Government come directly from the *REIS* data, with *NIPA* used as a control for the total. Some tax information must be estimated even at the state level of analysis. For example, corporate profit taxes paid to the Federal Government are based on the national total from NIPA, which is allocated to states based on each state's proportion of US Other Property Income.

Rather than a collection of individual states, the DOE/NETL model was developed to separately analyze six regions. These six regions include two large (in terms of magnitude of the data) individual states (California and Texas), one four state region (New York, Ohio, Pennsylvania, and West Virginia) that includes three large states, one three-state region (Colorado, Utah, and Wyoming) that includes two moderate-sized states, one region with two small states (Montana and North Dakota), and one region that encompasses the lower 48 states. For the multi-state regions, the individual state models are integrated into a single regional model, with imports and exports adjusted accordingly. As will be discussed later, integrating states into regions has some favorable implications for tax impact estimation.

Once the social accounts are developed for the region or regions used in an impact analysis, actually generating the estimated impacts is straightforward, following the procedure briefly described in (2) and (3) above. The assumptions listed in (4) and (5) assure that estimating impacts will be easy. (4) is the same assumption used to generate predictive multipliers in any input-output analysis – that the current structure of the local economy does not change during the impact period. It is this assumption that allows the modelers to generate all of the detailed tax impacts based on estimated impacts for just the value added and enterprise components of the model, which can then be applied to the unchanged normalized social accounts matrix. Without the assumption, the information requirements to generate detailed tax impacts or just about any other impacts would be prohibitive. The second assumption reveals an aggregation issue implicit in IMPLAN's impact estimations. For impact estimation, it does not matter whether the initial impact takes place in the extraction industries (as in the DOE/NETL model), manufacturing, various service industries, or some other industry. The model initially estimates impacts on the four value-added components and on enterprises for each of the impacted industries. Once the model gets these initial impacts, however, each component is distributed based on the normalized social accounts, regardless of the initial source of the impacts. For example, the model does not differentiate the distribution of initial tax impacts originating in the retail industry from those originating in the oil and gas industry, even though the former would likely yield a relatively greater sales tax impact while the latter would yield a relatively greater severance tax impact. In IMPLAN, these two taxes are both treated generically as "indirect business taxes" and distributed accordingly. This simplifying assumption is necessary in order to keep the impact analysis manageable.

Ultimately, we want to know how accurate the tax impact estimates are likely to be. The answer is that, in general, the impact estimates are likely to be good. First, while the researchers do not have ready access to accurate primary-source data, the IMPLAN model generates the social accounts matrix using comprehensive secondary-source data gathered by the Federal Government that is widely accepted as high quality data. Whether one uses the type of model

95

employed for the DOE/NETL project or some other method, such as an econometric forecast model, this is the most accurate and comprehensive data available.

Second, the social accounts matrix that is the basis for generating impacts in the DOE/NETL model provides a highly-detailed structure for each region's economy. Thus, the initial impacts on value added, including the initial indirect business taxes, account for hundreds or even thousands of relationships. Even though the tax impacts of these initial value-added (and enterprise) changes are distributed based on region-wide coefficients, these coefficients are also built in a bottom-up fashion that accounts for hundreds or thousands of relationships. No other method could provide such rich and precise detail in tracing the initial oil and natural gas impacts through the regional economies. One outcome of this detailed structure should be highly robust impact estimates. A small error or a peculiarity in the base-year data is unlikely to have much impact on the overall impact estimates by the time it makes its way through the detailed relationships of the model. In methods that have less detail and thus far fewer data points, an outlier in the data has a much greater chance of significantly affecting model outcomes.

Third, the regional structure of the model makes it more likely that the model's coefficients and predictions are representative for each region. Two of the regions are two of the largest individual states (California and Texas). Data for both states are based on a very large number of household, government, and business transactions, which should average out any outlier data. Together, the four states of the Marcellus Shale Region are much larger than either California or Texas. The states in Region 4 (Colorado, Utah, and Wyoming) are not so large, but with three different states, including two moderate-sized states, this region can still benefit from averaging out any oddities. The Bakken Shale Region, with two less populous states (North Dakota and Montana), is the most susceptible to any peculiarities in the base year, but still benefits from having two states to diminish the impact of any atypical data.

The only other issue with predicting tax impacts is the assumption that the base-year structure and coefficients hold throughout the impact period. This issue has been addressed at length in many forums. There may indeed be ways to account better for system dynamics over time, but they would come at a cost, primarily a cost of sacrificing much of the rich detail regarding the structure of the regional economy that is the strength of Input-Output models. Especially since much of the impact of shocks occurs relatively early in the impact period, assuming that the system's structure does not change is generally a good approximation. This assumption might be more problematic if the regions were single counties or even single small states. However, given the current structure, with two regions being large states and the rest being multi-state regions, small changes in the structure of one or a few relationships are not likely to have much of an effect on predicted tax impacts. If structural changes are major, but anticipated, then the modified structure can be built into the impact model. Major structural changes that are not anticipated could cause significant errors in the projected impact, but such changes would also be problematic for any other way of projecting tax impacts.

No tax impact estimation will be perfect. The rich, detailed structure of the Input-Output model used for the DOE/NETL project should provide reasonable tax impact estimates in the absence of unanticipated major structural changes that would significantly change the coefficients used to generate tax impacts. These tax impact estimates should be as good as, and likely better than,

96

estimates that alternative methodologies could provide. If unanticipated major structural changes related to tax impacts did occur, the methodology used here might not work so well, but then neither would other methodologies since a model can never predict well without adequate information. The detailed structure of an Input-Output model and the deeper understanding it enables of a regional economy make these large unanticipated changes less likely. All-in-all, while not perfect, the methodology used for the DOE/NETL model is likely the best available for providing tax impact estimates.

Bibliography

Hewings, Geoffrey. 1986. *Regional Input-Output Analysis.* Sage Publications: Scientific Geography Series, Vol. 6.

King, B.B. 1985. "What is a SAM?" In Pyatt, G., & Round, J. I. (eds.), *Social Accounting Matrices: A Basis for Planning.* Washington, D.C.: The World Bank.

Loveridge, Scott, "A Typology and Assessment of Multi-sector Regional Economic Impact Model," *Regional Studies*, 83, 305-317.

Miller, Ronald E. and Peter D. Blair. 1985. *Input-Output Analysis: Foundations and Extensions.* Englewood Cliffs, NJ: Prentice-Hall.

Minnesota IMPLAN Group, "Elements of the Social Accounting Matrix (Elements of the IMPLAN SAM)" MIG IMPLAN Technical Report TR-98002, Stillwater, MN: Minnesota IMPLAN Group, Inc., url: http://implan.com/index2.php?option=com_docman&task=doc_view&gid=91&Itemid=65

Olson, Douglas, "Using Social Accounts to Estimate Tax Impacts," Stillwater, MN: Minnesota IMPLAN Group, Inc., url: http://implan.com/index2.php?option=com_docman&task=doc_view&gid=97&Itemid=65

Schaffer, William. 1999. "Regional Impact Models." In Scott Loveridge (ed.), *The Web Book of Regional Science* (www.rri.wvu.edu/regscweb.htm). Morgantown, WV: Regional Research Institute, West Virginia University.

Biographical Sketch
December 2008

Brian Cushing is Associate Professor of Economics and Faculty Research Associate of the Regional Research Institute at West Virginia University. He obtained a B.A. in economics from University of Notre Dame (1975) and an M.A. (1979) and Ph.D. (1981) in economics from University of Maryland – College Park. His primary research and teaching interests include population migration, poverty, and regional policy, but also touch on a variety of other urban/regional issues. Cushing's most recent work has focused on analysis of Appalachian poverty, consideration of appropriate methods to measure the true extent of poverty, the effects of poverty, and of public policy - especially social welfare programs - on migration decisions of low-income households, the role of race relations in population migration, the relationship between amenities and migration, and technical aspects of migration modeling. He has taught urban economics and regional economics at both the undergraduate and graduate level. Cushing developed the initial version of the West Virginia State Economic Forecast Model – an expanded version of the model is still used today, 20 years after its initial development. He has published on a range of economics and regional science journals such as the *Annals of Regional Science*, *Journal of Econometrics*, *Journal of Regional Science*, *Journal of Urban Economics*, *Papers in Regional Science*, *Socio-Economic Planning Sciences*, *Southern Economic Journal*, and *Urban Studies,* among others.

98

Appendix C: Industry Aggregation Schema

Project Model Sector #	Sector Name	IMPLAN Sector Code	Related BEA Sectors
1	Agriculture, Forestry, Fishing and Hunting	1-18	11
2	Oil and Gas Extraction	19	2110
3	Coal, Metal Ores and Non-Metallic Mineral Mining, Quarrying and Support Activities	20-26, 29	212X
4	Drilling Oil and Gas Wells	27	213111
5	Support Activities for Oil and Gas Operations	28	213112
6	Power Generation and Supply, and Water, Sewage and Other Systems	30, 32	221X
7	Natural Gas Distribution	31	2212
8	Manufacturing and Industrial Buildings	37	23621
9	Water-, Sewer- and Pipeline Construction	40	23711, 23712
10	Other New Construction, including Maintenance and Repair Construction	33-36, 38-39, 41-45	23X
11	Construction and Mining Machinery Manufacturing	259-260	3331X
12	Oil and Gas Field Machinery and Equipment Manufacturing	261	333132
13	Motor Vehicle Manufacturing	344-345	3361
14	Other Manufacturing	46-258, 262-343, 346-389	3X
15	Wholesale Trade	390	42
16	Retail Trade	401-412	4A
17	Air, Rail and Water Transportation	391-393	481-483
18	Truck Transportation	394	484
19	Pipeline Transportation	396	486
20	Transit and Sightseeing Transportation and Transportation Support Services	395, 397	485, 487
21	Postal Services, Couriers, and Messengers and Warehousing and Storage	398-400	49
22	Information	413-424	51
23	FIRE and Rental and Leasing Services, excluding Commercial and Industrial Machinery and Equipment Rental and Leasing	425-433, 435-436	52_3X
24	Commercial and Industrial Machinery and Equipment Rental and Leasing	434	5324
25	Architectural, Engineering and Related Services	439	5413
26	Environmental and Other Technical Consulting	445	5416X
27	Other Professional, Scientific and Technical Services	440-444, 446-450	541X
28	Management of Companies and Enterprises	451	55
29	Administrative and Support and Waste Management and Remediation Services	452-460	56
30	Educational Services, Health Care and Social Assistance	461-470	6
31	Arts, Entertainment, Recreation, Accommodation and Food Services	471-481	7
32	Other Services, except Government	482-493	8
33	Government and Non-NAICS	494-509	92

Appendix D: Acronyms

AEO	Annual Energy Outlook
AMIGA	All-Modular Industry Growth Assessment Model
BEA	Bureau of Economic Analysis
CBM	Coal Bed Methane
DOE	Department of Energy
EIA	Energy Information Administration
EPAct	Energy Policy Act
FERC	Federal Energy Regulatory Commission
IMPLAN	Impact Analysis for Planning
IO	Input-Output
IOGCC	Interstate Oil and Gas Compact Commission
IPAA	Independent Petroleum Association of America
JAS	Joint Association Survey
JEDI	Job and Economic Development Impact
LNG	Liquefied Natural Gas
NAICS	North American Industry Classification System
NEMS	National Energy Modeling System
NETL	National Energy Technology Laboratory
NGPL	Natural Gas Plant Liquids
O&M	Operation and Maintenance
OSAP	Office of Systems, Analyses and Planning (NETL)
RPC	Regional Purchase Coefficient

101

Appendix E: Glossary

Absorption Table – A coefficient form of the Use table derived by dividing each element of the Use table by total industry output.

Byproducts Table – A coefficient form of the Make table derived by dividing each element by the Make table row totals.

Crude Oil – Unprocessed oil that has come out of the ground.

Direct Impact – The initial change in the industries to which a final demand change was made.

Final Demand – The purchases of goods and services for final consumption.

Import Substitution – The process of replacing imports with domestic production.

Indirect Business Taxes – These taxes include sales, excise, fees, licenses and other taxes that are paid during the normal operation of a business. This includes all payments to the government except for income taxes.

Indirect Impact – The changes in inter-industry purchases that occur as they respond to the new demands of the industries that were directly affected.

Induced Impact – The changes that typically reflect the changes in spending from households as income changes due to the changes in production.

Input-Output Analysis – The manner in which an input-output model is used to perform an economy-wide analysis for a given time period. The model is capable of examining inter-industry relationships as well as relationships between industries and final consumption.

Liquefied Natural Gas – Natural gas that has been converted to liquid form for ease of storage or transport.

Make Table – The matrix that contains the dollar value of each commodity or service that is produced by each industry. In this matrix, the rows are the industries and the columns are commodities.

Marginal Wells – Marginal wells can be either oil or gas wells. Marginal oil wells are those producing 10 or fewer barrels of oil per day. Marginal gas wells are those producing 60,000 or fewer cubic feet of gas per day.

Margins – The difference between producer and purchaser prices.

Producer Prices – The selling price received by a producer for goods and/or services produced.

102

Purchaser Prices – The price paid by the purchaser for a good or service. This price reflects the producer's price plus all applicable retail, wholesale and transportation costs.

Regional Purchase Coefficient – A coefficient representing the proportion of local demand that is purchased from local producers.

Social Accounting Matrix – A set of economic accounts which describe inter-industry relationships and transfers between institutions, as well as value added components for a given time period.

Use Table – The matrix that contains the dollar value of commodities and services purchased by each industry for use in the production process. In this matrix, the rows are the commodities and the columns are industries.

Value Added – Payments made by industries to workers, interest, profits and indirect business taxes.

103

References

Cho, Byung-Do, Jungyul Sohn, and Geoffrey J.D. Hewings. (2000). "Industrial Structural Change in the Korean Economy between 1975 and 1995: Input-Output Analysis," *Economic Papers (Bank of Korea)* 3: 109–136. [Korean version in *Quarterly Economic Analysis*, 5: 136–162. (1999)].

Duchin, Faye. (1992). "Industrial Input-Output Analysis: Implications for Industrial Ecology," *Proc. Natl. Acad. Sci.* USA. 89(3): 851–855.

Driscoll, Daniel, George Richards, and Brad Tomer. (2007). "LNG Interchangeability/Gas Quality: Results of the National Energy Technology Laboratory's Research for the FERC on Natural Gas Quality and Interchangeability." DOE/NETL-2007/1290.

Haddad, Eduardo A., and Geoffrey J.D. Hewings. (2000). "Linkages and Interdependence in the Brazilian Economy: An Evaluation of the Inter-Regional Input-Output System, 1985," *Revista Econômia do Nordeste*, 31:330–367.

Hewings, Geoffrey J.D. (1985). *Regional Input-Output Analysis*. Beverly Hills: Sage Publications.

Hubacek, Klaus, Jon D. Erickson, and Faye Duchin. (2002). "Input-Output Modeling of Protected Landscapes: The Adirondack Park," *The Review of Regional Studies*, 32(2): 207–222.

Isard, Walter, et al. (1998). *Methods of Interregional and Regional Analysis*. Brookfield, VT: Ashgate.

Jackson R.W., G.J.D. Hewings, and M. Sonis. (1989). "Decomposition Approaches to the Identification of Change in Regional Economies," *Economic Geography*, 65: 216–231.

Kidnay and Parrish. (2006). *Fundamentals of Natural Gas Processing.*

Lahr, Michael, Michael Greenberg, and Nancy Mantell. "Understanding the Economic Costs and Benefits of Catastrophes and Their Aftermath: A Review and Suggestions for the U.S. Federal Government," forthcoming in *Risk Analysis*.

Miller, Ronald E., and Peter D. Blair. (1985). *Input-Output Analysis: Foundations and Extensions*. Englewood Cliffs, NJ: Prentice Hall.

NETL. (2007). *2007 Annual Plan for the Ultra-Deepwater and Unconventional Natural Gas and Other Petroleum Resources Research and Development Program.* DOE/NETL-2007/1294.

Okuyama, Yasuhide, Geoffrey J.D. Hewings, and Michael Sonis. (1997). "Economic Impacts of an Unscheduled Event: Interregional Input-Output Approach," *Journal of Applied Regional Science*, 2: 79–93.

104

Rey, S., and R.W. Jackson. (1999). "Interindustry Employment Demand and Labor Productivity in Regional Econometric+Input-Output Models," *Environment and Planning, A*, 31: 1583–1599.

Stevens, Benjamin H., et al. (1983). "A New Technique for the Construction of Non-Survey Regional Input-Output Models," *International Regional Science Review.* 8(3): 271–86.

105

Congressional Research Service

Unconventional Gas Shales: Development, Technology, and Policy Issues

Anthony Andrews, Coordinator
Specialist in Energy and Energy Infrastructure Policy

Peter Folger
Specialist in Energy and Natural Resources Policy

Marc Humphries
Analyst in Energy Policy

Claudia Copeland
Specialist in Resources and Environmental Policy

Mary Tiemann
Specialist in Environmental Policy

Robert Meltz
Legislative Attorney

Cynthia Brougher
Legislative Attorney

October 30, 2009

Congressional Research Service

7-5700

www.crs.gov

R40894

CRS Report for Congress —————
Prepared for Members and Committees of Congress

Unconventional Gas Shales: Development, Technology, and Policy Issues

Summary

In the past, the oil and gas industry considered gas locked in tight, impermeable shale uneconomical to produce. However, advances in directional well drilling and reservoir stimulation have dramatically increased gas production from unconventional shales. The United States Geological Survey estimates that 200 trillion cubic feet of natural gas may be technically recoverable from these shales. Recent high natural gas prices have also stimulated interest in developing gas shales. Although natural gas prices fell dramatically in 2009, there is an expectation that the demand for natural gas will increase. Developing these shales comes with some controversy, though.

The hydraulic fracturing treatments used to stimulate gas production from shale have stirred environmental concerns over excessive water consumption, drinking water well contamination, and surface water contamination from both drilling activities and fracturing fluid disposal.

The saline "flowback" water pumped back to the surface after the fracturing process poses a significant environmental management challenge in the Marcellus region. The flowback's high content of total dissolved solids (TDS) and other contaminants must be disposed of or adequately treated before discharged to surface waters. The federal Clean Water Act and state laws regulate the discharge of this flowback water and other drilling wastewater to surface waters, while the Safe Drinking Water Act (SDWA) regulates deep well injection of such wastewater. Hydraulically fractured wells are also subject to various state regulations. Historically, the EPA has not regulated hydraulic fracturing, and the 2005 Energy Policy Act exempted hydraulic fracturing from SDWA regulation. Recently introduced bills would make hydraulic fracturing subject to regulation under SDWA, while another bill would affirm the current regulatory exemption.

Gas shale development takes place on both private and state-owned lands. Royalty rates paid to state and private landowners for shale gas leases range from 12½% to 20%. The four states (New York, Pennsylvania, Texas, and West Virginia) discussed in this report have shown significant increases in the amounts paid as signing bonuses and increases in royalty rates. Although federal lands also overlie gas shale resources, the leasing restrictions and the low resource-potential may diminish development prospects on some federal lands. The practice of severing mineral rights from surface ownership is not unique to the gas shale development. Mineral owners retain the right to access surface property to develop their holdings. Some landowners, however, may not have realized the intrusion that could result from mineral development on their property.

Although a gas-transmission pipeline-network is in place to supply the northeast United States, gas producers would need to construct an extensive network of gathering pipelines and supporting infrastructure to move the gas from the well fields to the transmission pipelines, as is the case for developing any new well field.

Congressional Research Service

Contents

Figures

Unconventional Gas Shales: Development, Technology, and Policy Issues

Tables

Appendixes

Contacts

Background

Until recently, many oil and gas companies considered natural gas locked in tight, impermeable shale uneconomical to produce. Advanced drilling and reservoir stimulation methods have dramatically increased the gas production from "unconventional shales." The Barnett Shale formation in Texas has experienced the most rapid development. The Marcellus Shale formation of the Appalachian basin, in the northeastern United States, potentially represents the largest unconventional gas resource in the United States. Other shale formations, such as the Haynesville shale, straddling Texas and Louisiana, have also attracted interest, as have some formations in Canada. The resource potential of the shales has significantly increased the natural gas reserve estimates in the United States.[1]

Recent high natural gas prices had stimulated interest in gas shales, although prices fell below $4.00 per million Btu (mmBtu) in the summer of 2009.[2] Despite the currently low natural gas prices, there is an expectation that the demand for natural gas will increase and that unconventional gas shales will play a major role in meeting the increased demand for natural gas.

The shale's development is a subject of controversy, however. The potential economic benefits from both the drilling activities and the lease and royalty payments compete with the public's concern for environmentally safe drilling practices and protection of groundwater and surface water.

Directional drilling and "hydraulic fracturing" are instrumental in exploiting this resource. Although oil and gas developers have applied these technologies in conventional oil fields for some time, they have only recently begun applying them to unconventional gas shales. As with oil and gas production generally, gas shale development is primarily subject to state law and regulation, although provisions of two relevant federal laws—the Safe Drinking Water Act (SDWA) and the Clean Water Act (CWA)—also apply. Regulation of well construction differs by state, and federal law currently exempts from regulation the underground injection of fluids for hydraulic fracturing purposes. Two recently introduced bills would subject hydraulic fracturing to regulation under the Safe Drinking Water Act, while a third bill would affirm the current SDWA exemption. There has been an increase in reports of public concerns that hydraulic fracturing poses a potential risk to water wells and thus domestic drinking water supply. The concern is that the chemicals used pose a potential risk to groundwater quality, and the fracturing may damage aquifers. Critics maintain that the large quantities of water that hydraulic fracturing consumes may tax local and regional water supplies and that disposing the "flowback" extracted from the shale after fracturing may affect surface water and groundwater quality. Understanding the technical principles of well drilling, well construction, and stimulation methods are important to assessing the concerns that have arisen over the shale's development.

---

[1] "Reserves are those quantities of petroleum, which, by analysis of geoscience and engineering data, can be estimated with reasonable certainty to be commercially recoverable ... " in: Society of Petroleum Engineers: *Petroleum Resources Management System,* 2007, p. 3, http://www.spe.org/spe-app/spe/industry/reserves/prms.htm.

[2] See Energy Information Administration, *Natural Gas page,* http://www.eia.doe.gov/oil_gas/natural_gas/info_glance/natural_gas.html.

Gas shale development takes place on both private and state lands. Royalty rates, rents, and signing bonuses paid to state and private landowners vary. In Texas, where similar gas shale development takes place, the rates are generally higher. Although federal lands overlie some portions of the Marcellus, restrictions to drilling and low resource potential may make them less desirable to develop. In the case of split-estate lands, which sever mineral rights from surface ownership, the mineral-owner retains the right to access the land for development. Landowners may not be aware of the mineral-owners' access rights, and are not due compensation for access. Furthermore, they may have to contend with long-term easements for the gathering pipelines that connect the wells to natural gas transmission lines. The states do regulate reclamation of the drilling sites to varying degrees.

This report does not discuss all unconventional gas shales. Rather, this report limits discussion to the Barnett and Marcellus Shale formations, which are most representative of the resource. Both formations also serve to illustrate the technical and policy issues that are most likely common to developing all gas shales.

Unconventional Gas Shale Resources in the United States

Unconventional gas shales are fine grained, organic rich, sedimentary rocks. The shales are both the source of and the reservoir for natural gas, unlike conventional petroleum reservoirs. In the shales, gas occupies pore spaces, and organic matter adsorbs gas on its surface. The Society of Petroleum Engineers describes "unconventional resources" as petroleum accumulations that are pervasive throughout a large area and that are not significantly affected by hydrodynamic influences (they are also called "continuous-type deposits"). In contrast, conventional petroleum and natural gas occur in porous sandstone and carbonate reservoirs. Under hydrodynamic pressure exerted by water, the petroleum migrated upward from its organic source until an impermeable cap-rock (such as shale) trapped it in the reservoir rock. The "gas-cap" that accumulated over the petroleum has been the source of most produced natural gas.

Though the shales may be as porous as other sedimentary reservoir rocks, their extremely small pore sizes make them relatively impermeable to gas flow, unless natural or artificial fractures occur. Major gas shale basins exist throughout the lower-48 United States. There are at least 21 shale basins in more than 20 states (see **Figure 1**).[3]

Based on a recent assessment of natural gas resources, the United States has a base of 1,836 trillion cubic-feet (tcf).[4] Shale gas made up an estimated one-third of the resource base, roughly 616 tcf. Stated in other terms, shale gas represents the equivalent of approximately 102 billion barrels of crude oil.

---

[3] *North American Natural Gas Supply Assessment*, Prepared for Clean Skies Foundation, Navigant Consulting, July 4, 2008.

[4] Colorado School of Mines, *Potential Gas Committee reports unprecedented increase in magnitude of U.S. natural gas resource base*, June 18, 2009, http://www.mines.edu/Potential-Gas-Committee-reports-unprecedented-increase-in-magnitude-of-U.S.-natural-gas-resource-base.

Unconventional Gas Shales: Development, Technology, and Policy Issues

Figure 1. Major Shale Basins in the Conterminous United States

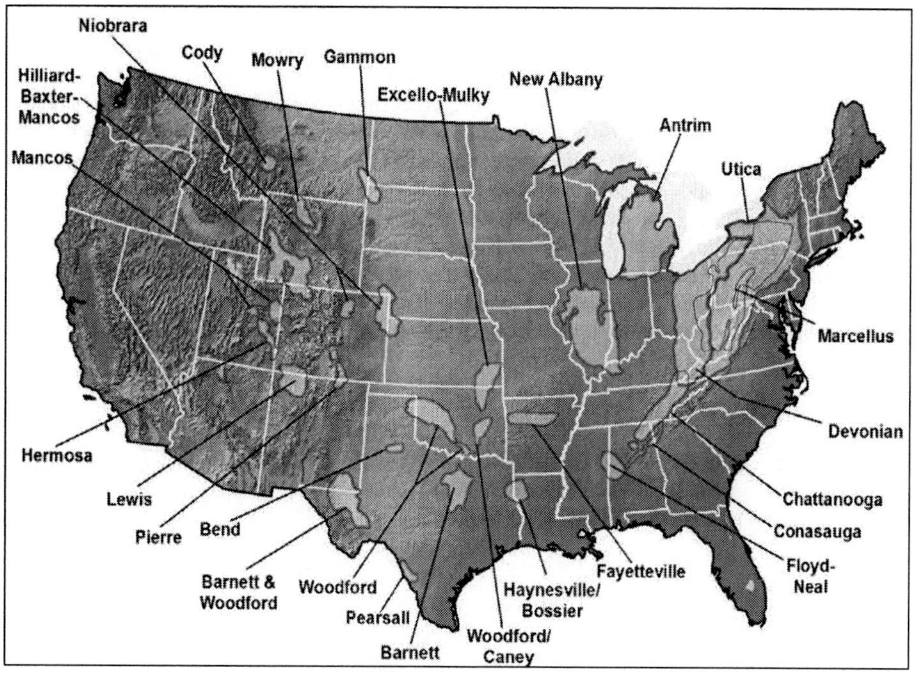

Source: U.S. DOE Office of Fossil Energy, *Modern Shale Gas Development in the United States: A Primer.*

Natural gas production in the United States had been declining until recently. After peaking at nearly 24.2 tcf in 2000, production declined to 23.5 tcf by 2005.[5] The decline had reversed by 2008 when production rose to over 26 tcf. (Gulf of Mexico offshore gas production continues to decline, however, and the 2.3 tcf produced in 2008 was only 47% of the 2000 Gulf production level.)

Since 1990, U.S. gas production increased in large part due to steadily increasing production of unconventional sources. The U.S. Geological Survey (USGS) estimates that about 200 tcf of natural gas may be technically recoverable from the shale with a recovery factor of 10% to 15%.[6] These sources include shale gas, coal-bed methane, and tight sands. Unconventional gas production increased 65% from 1998 (5.4 tcf/year) to 2007 (8.9 tcf/year).[7]

---

[5] U.S. DOE Energy Information Administration, *Natural Gas Navigator*, Natural Gas Summary, June 29, 2009, http://tonto.eia.doe.gov/dnav/ng/ng_sum_lsum_a_EPG0_FGW_mmcf_a.htm.

[6] U.S. DOE Energy Information Administration, Is *U.S. natural gas production increasing?*, June 11, 2008, http://tonto.eia.doe.gov/energy_in_brief/natural_gas_production.cfm.

[7] Navigant Consulting, *Unconventional Gas Supply*, TransCanada Pipelines Customer Meeting, San Francisco, CA,

(continued...)

Congressional Research Service 3

Natural gas production in the "big 7" shale plays (Antrim, Barnett, Devonian, Fayetteville, Woodford, Haynesville, Marcellus) could reach an estimated 27 to 39 bcf/day within 10 to 15 years.[8] Development, however, has been uneven in the Marcellus. Although production data are incomplete at best, reports indicate that Pennsylvania leads the region in producing wells, with West Virginia and Ohio trailing. Navigant expects that the Marcellus basin will be the next significant gas shale play. It appears potentially larger than the other basins already developed.

In 2006, the Bank of America estimated break-even costs for shale gas production to be within a range of $4.20 to $11.50 per thousand cubic feet (mcf).[9] The estimated median break-even cost was $6.64 per mcf. Leading shale gas producers include Chesapeake Energy Corporation, Devon Energy, XTO Energy, Inc., Southwestern Energy, Newfield Exploration Company, and Encana. In late 2008, StatoilHydro, the second largest natural gas supplier to Europe, and Chesapeake Energy Corporation, the largest U.S. natural gas producer, announced a joint agreement to explore unconventional gas opportunities. Under these agreements StatoilHydro will initially acquire a 32.5% interest in Chesapeake's Marcellus Shale gas acreage covering 1.8 million net acres (StatoilHydro's share equals approximately 0.6 million net acres of the leasehold).[10]

Barnett Shale Formation

The Barnett Shale formation is Mississippian-age black shale that has a high organic content.[11] It underlies 5,000 square miles of the Dallas/Fort Worth area of Texas (primarily in the Fort Worth Basin) to depths of 6,500 to 8,500 feet. (See **Figure 2**.)

Natural Gas Resource Potential

The Barnett Shale play is reportedly the most active natural gas play in the United States with as many as 173 drilling rigs at work in the past year. The USGS estimated that as much as 26.7 tcf of natural gas could be present in continuous accumulations as nonassociated gas trapped in strata of two of the three Barnett Shale Assessment Units (AU)—the Greater Newark East Frac-Barrier Continuous Barnett Shale Gas AU and the Extended Continuous Barnett Shale Gas AU.[12] Collectively, the units as comprise the Bend Arch–Fort Worth Basin.

(...continued)

August 26, 2008, http://www.navigantconsulting.com/downloads/knowledge_center/Unconventional_Natural_Gas_RWelch_Aug_08.pdf.

[8] See Navigant Consulting.

[9] See Navigant Consulting.

[10] StatoilHydro, "Forms strategic alliance with major US gas player," press release, November 11, 2008, http://www.statoilhydro.com/en/NewsAndMedia/News/2008/Pages/Chesapeake.aspx.

[11] Mississippian-aged shale dates back to the Paleozoic era of around 345 to 320 million years ago.

[12] Richard M. Pollastro (Task Leader), Ronald J. Hill, and Thomas A. Albrandt, et al., Assessment of Undiscovered Oil and Gas Resources of the Bend Arch-Fort Worth Basin Province of North-Central Texas and Southwestern Oklahoma, 2003, U.S. Geological Survey, Fact Sheet 2004-3022, March 2004. http://pubs.usgs.gov/fs/2004/3022/

The area has produced oil and gas since the early 1900s, but mostly from conventional reservoirs.[13] There are over 8,000 wells producing gas from the Barnett formation.[14] Gas production increased from 94 million cubic feet per day (mmcf/day) in 1998 to over 3 billion cubic feet/day (bcf/day) in 2007; an increase of over 3,000%.

Figure 2. Bend Arch-Fort Worth Basin Area

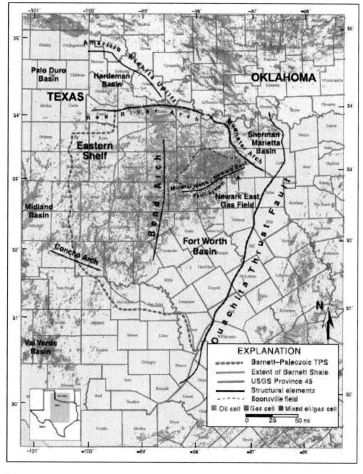

Source: Pollastro et al, *Geologic Framework of the Mississippian Barnett Shale, Barnett-Paleozoic Total Petroleum System, Bend Arch-Fort Worth Basin, Texas*, AAPG Bulletin, V. 91, No. 4 (April 2007), pp 405-436.

---

[13] Richard M. Pollastro, Daniel M. Jarvie, and Ronald J. Hill, et al., "Geologic Framework of the Mississippian Barnett Shale, Barnett-Paleozoic total petroleum system, Bend arch-Fort Worth Basin, Texas," *American Association of Petroleum Geologists*, vol. 91, no. 4 (April 2007), pp. 405-436.

[14] Personal communication with Eric Potter, Jackson School of Geosciences, University of Texas, October 2008.

The Newark East field of the Barnett has been the largest gas-producing field in Texas since 2000, and ranked as the second highest U.S. gas-producing field in 2005. Gas production rose from less than 11 bcf of natural gas in 1993 to about 480 bcf by 2005.[15] From January 1993 to January 2006, cumulative gas production measured about 1.8 tcf. The Newark East field proven gas reserve estimates range from between 2.5 and 3.0 tcf.

Southwest Regional Gas Supply and Demand

Several major pipeline corridors transport natural gas in the United States. Five major pipeline routes extend from the producing areas in the Southwest, and more than 20 of the major interstate pipelines originate in the Southwest Region.[16] (See **Figure 3**.) In particular, major pipeline networks, constructed after World War II, transport gas from the Gulf of Mexico region to the Northeast, from the Southwest to the Northeast, and from the Southwest to the Midwest.[17] Current pipelines have the capacity to transport as much as 45.2 bcf per day from the region: 62% to the Southeast Region, 20% to the Central Region, 13% to the Western Region, and the rest to Mexico. In response to increased natural gas production and supply, particularly from the Barnett Shale, the Southwest region recently expanded its pipeline infrastructure on a large-scale. In 2008, 30 new pipelines comprising 1,382 miles reached completion; nearly double the previous year's. Thirteen of the new pipelines related to or expanded the northeast Texas area to new development of gas supplies from the Barnett, Woodford, or Fayetteville Shale formations. The remaining pipelines support increased liquefied natural gas (LNG) imports through Texas marine terminals.

---

[15] Pollastro, et al., *Geologic framework of the Mississippian Barnett Shale.*

[16] Energy Information Administration, Office of Oil and Gas, Natural Gas Division , *About U.S. Natural Gas Pipelines,* Major Natural Gas Transportation Corridors, http://www.eia.doe.gov/pub/oil_gas/natural_gas/analysis_publications/ngpipeline/transcorr.html.

[17] Damien Gaula, *Expansion of the U.S. Natural Gas Pipeline Network: Additions in 2008 and Projects through 2011,* Energy Information Administration, Office of Oil and Gas, September 2009, http://www.eia.doe.gov/pub/oil_gas/natural_gas/feature_articles/2009/pipelinenetwork/pipelinenetwork.pdf.

Unconventional Gas Shales: Development, Technology, and Policy Issues

Figure 3. Major Natural Gas Transportation Corridors in the Conterminous United States, 2008

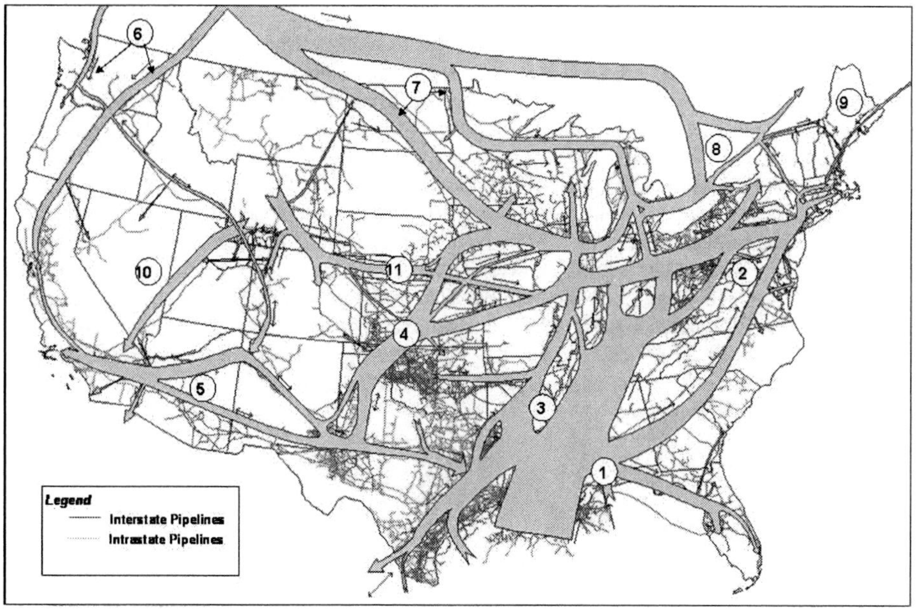

Source: EIA, Gas Tran Gas Transportation Information System http://www.eia.doe.gov/pub/oil_gas/natural_gas/analysis_publications/ngpipeline/transcorr_map.html.

Notes: major pipeline networks originating from the Southwest are: (1) Southwest-Southeast, (2) Southwest-Northeast, (3) Southwest-Midwest, (4) Southwest Panhandle-Midwest, and (5) Southwest-Western. The EIA has determined that this informational map does not raise security concerns, based on the application of the Federal Geographic Data Committee's *Guidelines for Providing Appropriate Access to Geospatial Data in Response to Security Concerns.*

Groundwater Resource Issues

As gas development in the Barnett Shale increased over the past decade, water use also increased. One study estimated that water used for Barnett Shale gas development increased from approximately 700 acre-feet (AF) in 2000 to more than 7,000 AF in 2005.[18] Barnett Shale development uses both surface water and groundwater resources, primarily for hydraulically fracturing vertical and horizontal wells. Depending on the well type, from 1.2 to 3.5 million gallons (4 to 11 AF) of water may be consumed in hydraulically fracturing a gas well. Of the approximately 7,000 AF used in 2005, about 60% came from groundwater in the Trinity and

---

[18] James Bene et al., *Northern Trinity/Woodbine Groundwater Availability Model: Assessment of Groundwater Use in the Northern Trinity Aquifer Due to Urban Growth and Barnett Shale Development*, R.W. Harden & Associates, prepared for the Texas Water Development Board, Austin, TX, January 2007, p. 2-21, at http://www.twdb.state.tx.us/RWPG/rpgm_rpts/0604830613_BarnetShale.pdf. Hereafter referred to as R.W. Harden & Associates, 2007.

Woodbine aquifers in north central Texas.[19] The deeper Trinity aquifer (underlying 61 counties) is much more extensive than the shallower Woodbine aquifer (underlying 17 counties).[20] The state of Texas also considers Trinity a major aquifer compared to the minor Woodbine.[21]

The Trinity Aquifer extends from south-central Texas to southeastern Oklahoma in a 550 mile-long arc-like band.[22] (See **Figure 4**.) It is an important water source for many communities, particularly rural, in north-central Texas where Barnett Shale development is most intense. Groundwater use varies across the Barnett Shale development area; for example, groundwater provides approximately 85% of the total water supply in Cooke County but only 1% for Dallas County.[23] Extensive development of the Trinity Aquifer in the Dallas-Ft. Worth metropolitan areas had caused groundwater levels to drop over 500 feet in some areas. However, when their populations began increasing after the 1970s, local communities abandoned many public supply wells in favor of surface water supplies. This resulted in a recovery of groundwater levels to some extent.[24] For many rural areas, however, groundwater from the Trinity Aquifer remains the sole water source. The Woodbine Aquifer, which is shallower than the Trinity, offers another groundwater supply for the region. The lowest of its three water-bearing layers yields the most water. Though the Woodbine is a minor aquifer, it could be locally important to Barnett Shale development given its proximity.

---

[19] R.W. Harden & Associates, 2007, p. 2.

[20] Texas Water Development Board, *2007 State Water Plan, Chapter 7, Groundwater Resources*.

[21] In Texas, a minor aquifer is defined as one that supplies large quantities of water in small areas or small quantities of water in large areas; a major aquifer is generally defined as supplying large quantities of water over a large areas of the state. See John B. Ashworth and Janie Hopkins, *Major and Minor Aquifers of Texas*, Texas Water Development Board, Report 345, November 1995, p. 1. The state of Texas recognizes 7 major and 21 minor aquifers, see Texas Water Development Board, *2007 State Water Plan, Chapter 7, Groundwater Resources*, at http://www.twdb.state.tx.us/wrpi/swp/swp.htm.

[22] Paul D. Ryder, U.S. Geological Survey, *Ground Water Atlas of the United States*, Oklahoma, Texas; HA 730-E, 1996, at http://pubs.usgs.gov/ha/ha730/ch_e/index.html.

[23] R.W. Harden & Associates, 2007, p. 2.

[24] John B. Ashworth and Janie Hopkins, *Major and Minor Aquifers of Texas: Trinity Aquifer*, Texas Water Development Board, Report 345, November 1995.

Unconventional Gas Shales: Development, Technology, and Policy Issues

Figure 4. Aquifers in the Bend Arch-Fort Worth Basin Area

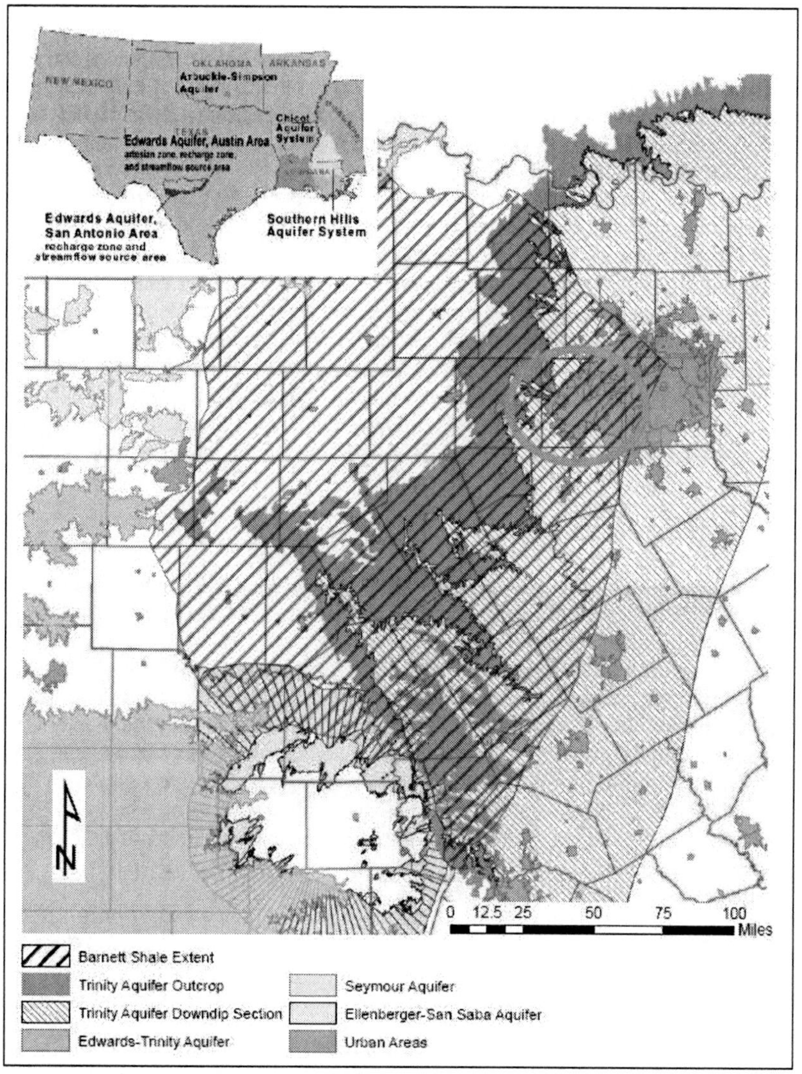

Source: James Bene et al., Northern Trinity/Woodbine Groundwater Availability Model: Assessment of Groundwater Use in the Northern Trinity Aquifer Due to Urban Growth and Barnett Shale Development, R.W. Harden & Associates. p. 2-5 Corner Inset Map: U.S. EPA, *Sole Source Aquifer Protection Program*, Regions VI (modified by CRS) .

Notes: Green circled area represents the so-called "core area" where most of the Barnett Shale gas development has taken place.

A study that modeled groundwater use in the area concluded that about 3% of the use was associated with the Barnett Shale's development in 2005.[25] Depending on the pace of shale development, water use (which is essential to hydraulic fracturing) could vary widely.[26] According to the study, low natural gas prices would slow interest in development and thus slightly decrease groundwater use by 2025. High natural gas prices could stimulate accelerated development and thus increase groundwater demand for development to about 10,000 to 25,000 AF by 2025, or from 3% in 2005 to 7% to 13% by 2025.

Increasing shale development could compete with other users for the same groundwater resources, particularly in rural areas where groundwater is a significant fraction of water supplies. It is uncertain how urban areas may react to groundwater well drilling in support of shale development (that is, for hydraulic fracturing), even though groundwater comprises a smaller fraction of the water supply compared to some more rural areas. The modeling study pointed out, as well, that the Trinity and Woodbine aquifers underlie only the eastern portion of the Barnett Shale; no major or minor aquifers underlie the western portions.[27] Development of western portions raises the possibility of transporting groundwater pumped from the Trinity and Woodbine aquifers in the east to the western portion of the Barnett Shale, which could raise estimates of potential groundwater use above those presented in the model results.

Marcellus Shale Formation

The Marcellus Shale is sedimentary rock formation deposited over 350 million years ago during the middle-Devonian period on the geologic timescale. Geologic strata deposited in the Appalachian basin during this period are likely to produce more gas than oil. Regional oil production is associated with Pennsylvanian age strata (of the later Carboniferous period). Most of this black, organic-rich shale lies beneath much of West Virginia, western and northeastern Pennsylvania, southern New York, eastern Ohio, and parts of Virginia and Maryland (see **Figure 5**). It is an estimated 95,000 square miles in areal extent and ranges from 4,000 feet to 8,500 feet in depth.[28] The shale's non-uniform thickness varies from 50 feet to 250 feet as shown by the isopach map of **Figure 5**.[29] Some reports indicate that shale's thickness may be as much as 900 feet in places, however. As shown in **Figure 6**, the Marcellus plunges in depth the further north it goes along the cross section.

---

[25] James Bene et al., *Northern Trinity/Woodbine Groundwater Availability Model: Assessment of Groundwater Use in the Northern Trinity Aquifer Due to Urban Growth and Barnett Shale Development*, R.W. Harden & Associates, p.2.

[26] Other factors could include the thickness and maturity of the shale, the ability to drill horizontally or vertically, the number of well completions per year, availability of water, and regulatory factors, among others.

[27] James Bene et al., *Northern Trinity/Woodbine Groundwater Availability Model: Assessment of Groundwater Use in the Northern Trinity Aquifer Due to Urban Growth and Barnett Shale Development*, R.W. Harden & Associates, p.15.

[28] U.S. Department of Energy Office of Fossil Energy and National Technology Laboratory, *Modern Shale Gas Development in the United States: A Primer*, DE-FG26-04NT15455, April 2009, http://fossil.energy.gov/programs/oilgas/publications/naturalgas_general/Shale_Gas_Primer_2009.pdf.

[29] An isopach is a continuous line connecting points of equal thickness.

Unconventional Gas Shales: Development, Technology, and Policy Issues

Figure 5. Marcellus Shale Formation Thickness

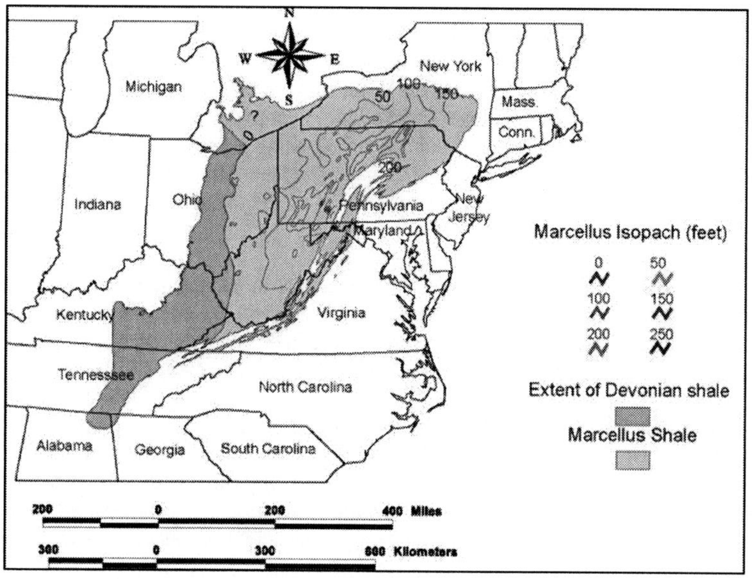

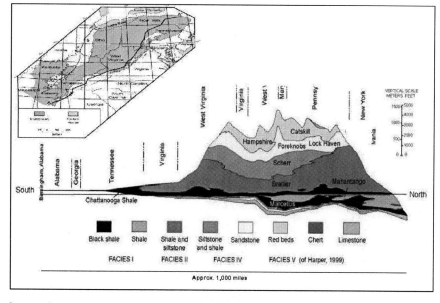

Source: U.S. Geological Survey, *Assessment of Undiscovered Natural Gas Resources in Devonian Black Shales, Appalachian Basin, Eastern U.S.A.,* Open-File Report 200-1268, 2005.

Figure 6. Devonian Shale Cross Section

Source: Compiled from USGS Open File Report 200-1268, 2005.

Notes: Cross section from Alabama to New York. Vertical scale is exaggerated.

Unconventional Gas Shales: Development, Technology, and Policy Issues

Natural Gas Resource Potential

The USGS indicates that the Marcellus Shale may have a mean undiscovered natural gas resource potential of nearly 2 tcf. Considering the total extent of Devonian/Ohio basin shales (which include the Marcellus formation), an estimated 12 tcf may be present, although not all of it may be economically recoverable. (See **Figure 7**.) The USGS estimate, however, is considerably lower than a 2008 "conservative" estimate of 516 tcf made by geoscience professors Terry Engelder (Pennsylvania State University) and Gary Lash (State University of New York). The two professors believe that there could be at least 50 tcf of gas technically recoverable from the Marcellus Shale.[30]

Typically, thicker shales with greater organic material yield more gas, and thus, are more economically desirable to produce. Shale in northeast Pennsylvania and southeast New York has these characteristics and produces dry natural gas. Shale in western Pennsylvania and New York produces a wetter gas that contains petroleum liquids.

StatoilHydro assumes that each well drilled in the Marcellus may have an average estimated ultimate recovery (EUR) of 3.1 bcf.[31] The EUR per well will depend on the length of the horizontal well drilled, the number of fractures in the well, and the quality of the shale. StatoilHydro assumes that each horizontal well would measure 3,000 feet in length with 6 hydraulic fractures intervals in each well. An average well might produce for upwards of 60 years.

---

[30] "Marcellus Shale Play's Vast Potential Creating Stir in Appalachia," by Terry Engelder and Gary Lash, Professors of Geosciences, The American Oil and Gas Reporter, May 2008.

[31] StatoilHydro, "StatoilHydro's acquisition of 32.5% of Chesapeake interest in the Marcellus shale," press release, 2008, http://www.statoilhydro.com/en/NewsAndMedia/News/2008/Downloads/Frequently%20asked%20questions.pdf.

Figure 7. Devonian Shale Undiscovered Resource Potential

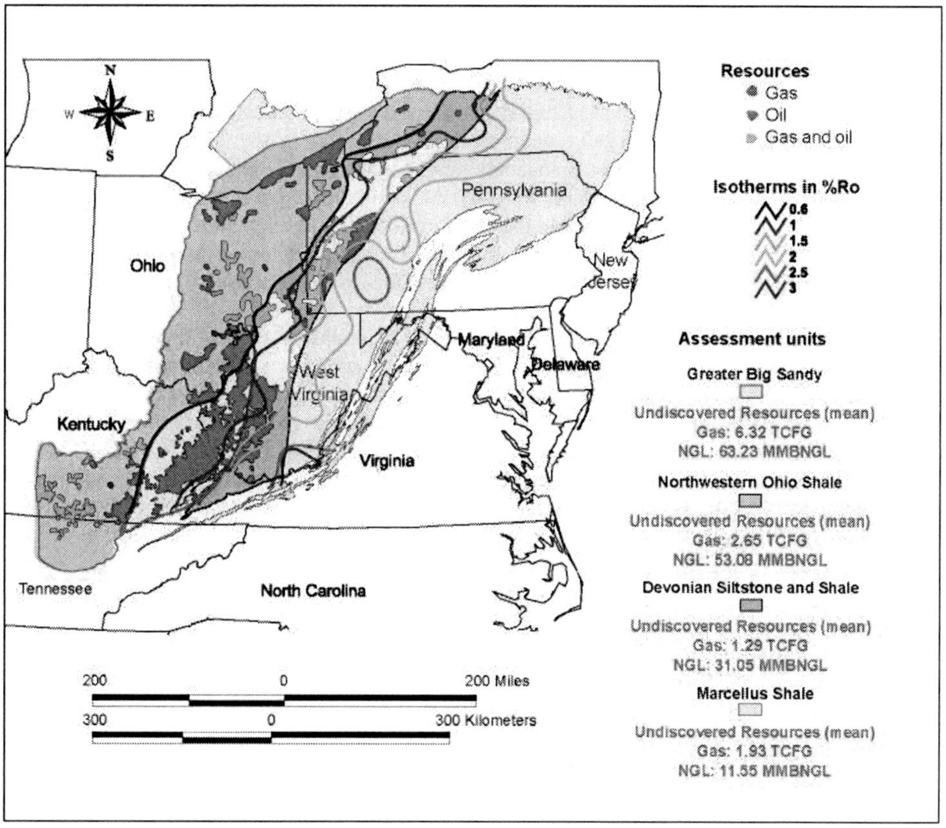

Source: USGS Open File Report 2005-1268.

Notes: NGL: natural gas liquids include butane and propane.

Northeast Regional Natural Gas Supply and Demand

In 2007, the northeast region consumed roughly 4 tcf of natural gas.[32] New York led the region in consumption with over 1.19 tcf. The United States as a whole consumed more than 23 tcf.[33] The region produced roughly 580 bcf of natural gas from some 113,000 operating gas wells. Pennsylvania and West Virginia combined made up nearly 89% of the production, with New York and Virginia making up the balance. In summary, the region consumes about seven times as much natural gas as it currently produces. The 50-tcf of gas, estimated by Engelder and Lash as

---

[32] U.S. DOE Energy Information Administration, *Natural Gas Consumption by End Use*, http://tonto.eia.doe.gov/dnav/ng/ng_cons_sum_dcu_nus_a.htm.

[33] Reported by EIA as 23,047,641 million cubic feet, http://tonto.eia.doe.gov/dnav/ng/ng_cons_sum_dcu_nus_a.htm.

Unconventional Gas Shales: Development, Technology, and Policy Issues

technically recoverable from the Marcellus Shale, would be sufficient to supply the region for 13 years at the current rate of consumption. Taking the entire 513-tcf resource-potential into account and assuming that recovery methods would improve might extend the supply further.

Currently, 20 interstate natural gas transmission pipelines serve the northeast region of the United States (see **Figure 8**).[34] This pipeline system delivers natural gas to several intrastate natural gas pipelines and at least 50 local distribution companies in the region. In addition to the natural gas produced in the region, several long-distance natural gas transmission pipelines supply the region from the southeast into Virginia and West Virginia, and from the Midwest into West Virginia and Pennsylvania. Canadian imports come into the region principally through New York, Maine, and New Hampshire. Liquefied natural gas (LNG) supplies also enter the region through import terminals located in Massachusetts, Maryland, and New Brunswick, Canada.

The natural gas produced from the eastern portion of the Marcellus Shale is of high enough quality that it requires little or no treatment for injection into transmission pipelines.[35] A gas transmission pipeline already serves the northeast United States. The Millennium Pipeline project in southern New York could accommodate any increased shale gas production from New York and parts of Pennsylvania to serve the natural gas needs of the region. However, the terrain in West Virginia presents an obstacle to developing additional pipeline capacity and other support infrastructure. Gas producers would also have to construct an extensive network of gathering pipelines to bring the gas out of the well fields.

---

[34] U.S. DOE Energy Information Administration, *Natural Gas Pipelines in the Northeast Region,* http://www.eia.doe.gov/pub/oil_gas/natural_gas/analysis_publications/ngpipeline/northeast.html.

[35] The natural gas received and transported by the major intrastate and interstate mainline transmission systems must meet the quality standards specified by pipeline companies in the "General Terms and Conditions (GTC)" section of their tariffs. These quality standards vary from pipeline to pipeline and are usually a function of a pipeline system's design, its downstream interconnecting pipelines, and its customer base. In general, these standards specify that the natural gas: be within a specific Btu content range (1,035 Btu per cubic foot, +/- 50 Btu); be delivered at a specified hydrocarbon dew point temperature level (below which any vaporized gas liquid in the mix will tend to condense at pipeline pressure); contain no more than trace amounts of elements such as hydrogen sulfide, carbon dioxide, nitrogen, water vapor, and oxygen; and be free of particulate solids and liquid water that could be detrimental to the pipeline or its ancillary operating equipment. U.S. DOE Energy Information Administration, *Natural Gas Processing: The Crucial Link Between Natural Gas Production and Its Transportation to Market,* http://www.eia.doe.gov/pub/oil_gas/natural_gas/feature_articles/2006/ngprocess/ngprocess.pdf.

Figure 8. Northeast Region Natural Gas Pipeline Network

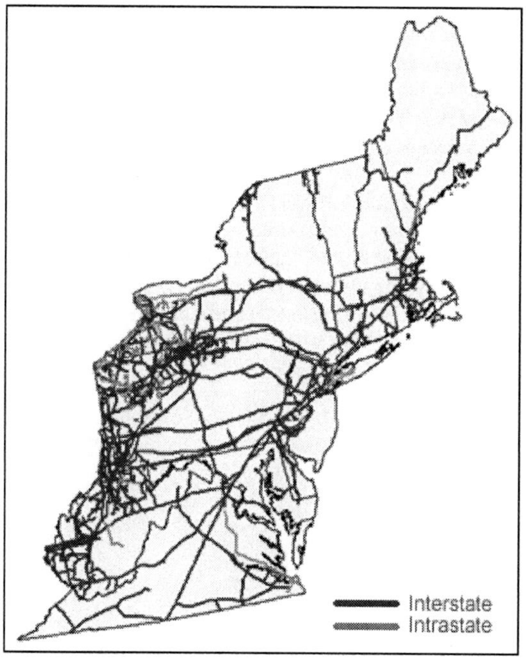

Source: Energy Information Administration, Office of Oil & Gas, Natural Gas Division, Gas Transportation Information System, http://www.eia.doe.gov/pub/oil_gas/natural_gas/analysis_publications/ngpipeline/northeast.html.

Notes: Includes Connecticut, Delaware, Massachusetts, Maine, New Hampshire, New Jersey, New York, Pennsylvania, Rhode Island, Virginia, and West Virginia.

Groundwater Resource Issues

The U.S. Geological Survey identifies three principal hydrogeological environments overlying the Marcellus Shale: (1) glacial sand and gravel aquifers in New York, northern Pennsylvania, and northeastern Ohio, (2) valley-and-ridge carbonate rock and other aquifers in Pennsylvania and eastern West Virginia, and (3) Mississippian aquifers in northern Pennsylvania and northeastern Ohio. These aquifer systems are important supplies of fresh water for communities, especially in more rural areas, although in general most residents of these states obtain their drinking water from surface water sources. Typically, these aquifers are much closer to the ground surface than the Marcellus Shale, which can be thousands of feet deep. The groundwater wells in these states may reach only several hundred feet in depth.

The layers of rocks separating most fresh water aquifers from the Marcellus Shale are typically siltstones and shales layered with minor sandstones and limestone. Siltstones and shales generally act as barriers to fluid flow. These intervening layers of rocks can be several thousand feet thick in the eastern and northern portions of the area where the Marcellus Shale is deepest. On the western and southern portions of the area, the Marcellus Shale is shallower, as separated by a thinner package of siltstones and shales.

Unconventional Gas Shales: Development, Technology, and Policy Issues

Many of the surficial sand and gravel aquifers form valley-fill deposits, in low-lying areas or stream valleys, and are recharged by precipitation that runs off surrounding, less permeable uplands.[36] As such, they would be particularly susceptible to leaky surface impoundments or careless surface disposal because of the relatively short distance and travel time from the land surface to the top of the water table. New York, for example, has deemed these unconsolidated sand and gravel aquifers "primary" or "principal" aquifers, which are highly productive and presently used as a significant source of water, or are a potentially abundant water supply.[37]

The EPA defines an aquifer that supplies at least 50 % of the drinking water consumed in the area overlying the aquifer as a "sole or principal source aquifer" (referred to, for convenience, as sole source aquifers).[38] Those who depend on the aquifer for drinking water may have no alternative drinking water source (physically, legally or economically). The EPA has designated at least four sole source aquifers in New York (EPA Region II) and one in Pennsylvania (Region III) that overlie the Marcellus Shale.[39] (See **Figure 9**). It is uncertain whether these areas would be targets for Marcellus Shale development.

---

[36] Henry Trapp, Jr. and Marilee A. Horn, "U.S. Geological Survey Ground Water Atlas of the United States," HA 730-L (1997).

[37] See New York State, Department of Environmental Conservation, "Primary & Principal Aquifers," at http://www.dec.ny.gov/lands/36119.html.

[38] U.S. Environmental Protection Agency, *Sole Source Aquifer Protection Program*, http://cfpub.epa.gov/safewater/sourcewater/sourcewater.cfm?action=SSA.

[39] Cattaraugus Creek Basin Aquifer, Cortland Homer-Preble Aquifer System, Clinton Street-Ballpark Valley Aquifer System, and Schenectady/Niskanyuna Aquifers in New York, and Steven Valleys Aquifer in Pennsylvania.

Figure 9. Sole Source Aquifers in the Appalachian—Northeast Region

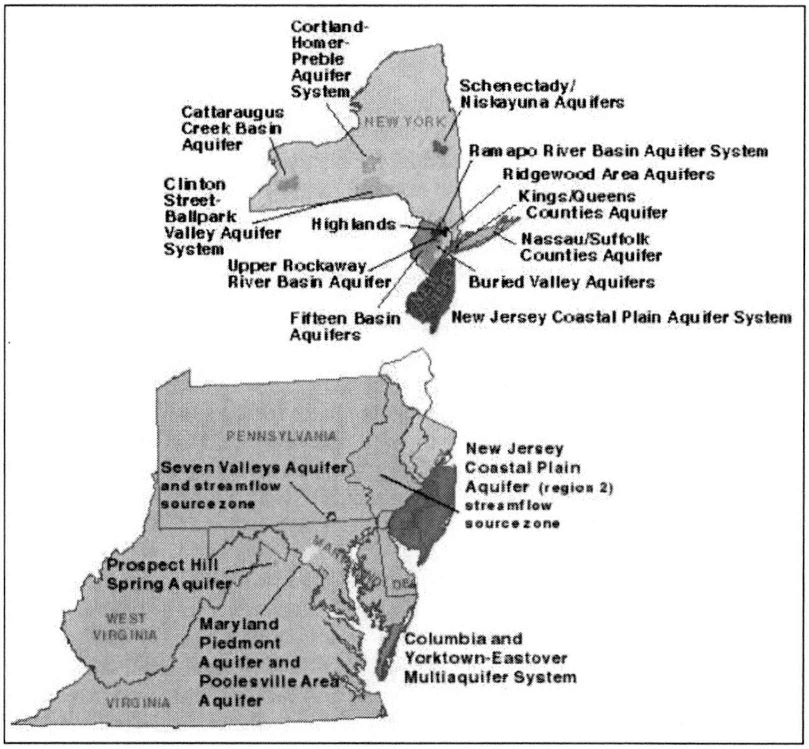

Source: U.S. EPA, *Sole Source Aquifer Protection Program*, Regions II and III, http://cfpub.epa.gov/safewater/sourcewater/sourcewater.cfm?action=SSA (modified by CRS).

Notes: EPA defines a sole or principal source aquifer as an aquifer that supplies at least 50 % of the drinking water consumed in the area overlying the aquifer.

Drilling and Development Technology

In their early stages of development, conventional petroleum reservoirs depend on the pressure of their gas-cap and oil-dissolved gas to lift the oil to the surface (i.e., gas drive). Water trapping the petroleum from below also exerts an upward hydraulic pressure (water-drive). Petroleum reservoirs produced by the pressure of their natural gas and water drives are thus termed "conventional drive." As a reservoir's production declines, lifting further petroleum to the surface requires pumping—giving rise to the term "artificial lift." In the late 1940s, drilling companies began inducing hydraulic pressure in wells to fracture the producing formation. This stimulated further production by effectively increasing a well's contact with a formation. Advances in directional drilling technology now enable wells to deviate from nearly vertical to extend horizontally into the reservoir formation, which increases the well's contact with the reservoir. Directional drilling technology also enables drilling a number of wells from a single well pad, thus cutting costs while reducing environmental disturbance. Combining hydraulic fracturing with directional drilling has opened up production of tighter (less permeable) petroleum and natural gas reservoirs, and in particular, unconventional gas shales like the Marcellus.

Drilling

Well drilling has progressed from an art to a science. Originally, drillers used "cable-tool" rigs and a percussion bit. The drill operator would raise the bit and release it to pulverize the sediment. From time to time, the driller would stop and "muck out" the pulverized rock cuttings to advance the well. Though time-consuming, this method was simple and required minimal labor. Some drillers still use this method for water-wells and even some shallow gas-wells. The introduction of rotary-drill rigs at the beginning of the 20th century marked a big advance in drilling, particularly with the development of the "tri-cone rotary bit."[40] This method, as the name implies, uses a weighted rotating bit to penetrate the sediment (see **Figure 10**).

The key to a rotary drill's speed is the relative ease of adding new sections of drill pipe (or drill string) while the drill-bit continues turning. Circulating fluids (drilling mud) down through the center of the hollow drill pipe and up through the well bore lifts the drill cuttings to the surface. Modern drill bits studded with industrial diamonds gives them an abrasive property to grind through any rock type. However, from time to time the drill string must be removed (a process termed "tripping") to replace the dulled drill bit.

To function properly, drilling fluids must lubricate the drill bit, keep the well bore from collapsing, and remove cuttings. The weight of the mud column prevents a "blow-out" from occurring when encountering high-pressure reservoir fluids. Drillers base the mud's composition on natural bentonite clay, a "thixotropic" material that is solid when still and fluid when disturbed. This essential rheological property keeps the drill cuttings suspended in the mud. The mud's chemistry and density must be carefully monitored and adjusted as the drilling deepens (for example, adding a barium compound increases mud density). "Mud pits," excavated adjacent to the drill rig provide a reservoir for mixing and holding the mud. The mud pits also serve as settling ponds for the cuttings. At the completion of drilling, the mud may be recycled at another drilling operation, but the cuttings will be disposed of in the pit. Several environmental concerns over drilling stem from the (hazardous) composition of the drilling mud and cuttings, and the potential for mud pits overflowing and contaminating surface water.

---

[40] Howard Hughes, Jr. of the Hughes Tool Company developed the modern tri-cone rotary bit. His father, Howard Robert Hughes, Sr. had invented the bit's ancestor, a two-cone rotary bit.

Unconventional Gas Shales: Development, Technology, and Policy Issues

Figure 10. Rotary Drilling Rig

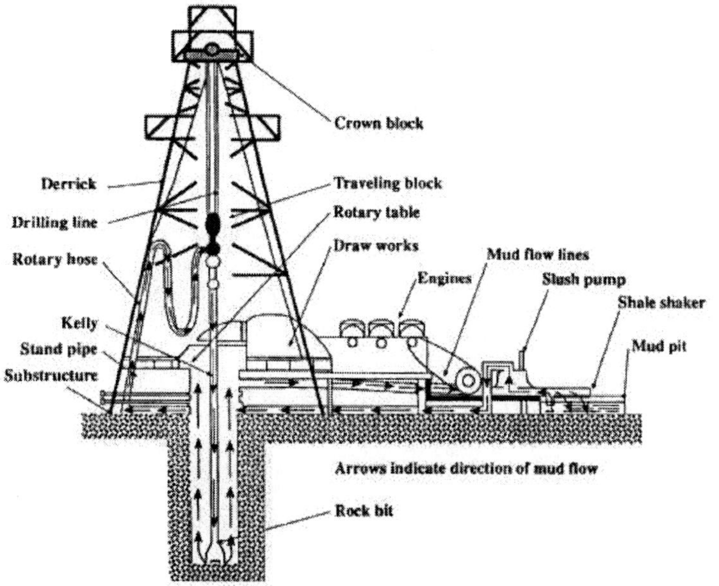

Source: Bureau of Land Management, http://www.blm.gov/rmp/wy/rawlins/documents/RMO/figures/FigureA-5.gif.

The most recent advance in drilling is the ability to direct the drill bit beyond the region immediately beneath the drill rig. Early directional drilling involved placing a steel wedge down-hole (whipstock) that deflected the drill toward the desired target, but lacked control and consumed time. Advances such as steerable down-hole drill motors that operated on the hydraulic pressure of the circulating drilling mud offered improved directional control. However to change drilling direction the operator had to halt drill string rotation in such a position that a bend in the motor pointed in the direction of the new trajectory (referred to as the sliding mode). Newer rotary steerable systems introduced in the 1990s eliminated the need to slide a steerable down-hole motor.[41] The newer tools drill directionally while continuously rotated from the surface by the drilling rig. This enables a much more complex, and thus accurate, drilling trajectory. Continuous rotation also leads to higher rates of penetration and fewer incidents of the drill-string sticking. (See **Figure 11**.)

---

[41] Schlumberger, *Better Turns for Rotary Steerable Drilling: Overview*, http://www.slb.com/content/services/resources/oilfieldreview/ori002/01.asp?.

Unconventional Gas Shales: Development, Technology, and Policy Issues

Directional drilling offers another significant advantage in developing gas shales. In the case of thin or inclined shale formations, a long horizontal well increases the length of the well bore in the gas-bearing formation and therefore increases the surface area for gas to flow into the well. However, the increased well surface (length) is often insufficient without some means of artificially stimulating flow. In some sandstone and carbonate formations, injecting dilute acid dissolves the natural cement that binds sand grains thus increasing permeability. In tight formations like shale, inducing fractures can increase flow by orders of magnitude. However, before stimulation or for that matter production can take place, the well must be completed and cased.

Figure 11. Directional Drilling
Steerable Down-hole Motor vs. Rotary Steerable System

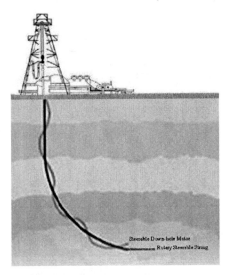

Source: Schlumberger, modified by CRS.

Well Construction and Casing

Commercial gas and oil, and municipal water-supply wells have in common a series of telescoping steel well casings that prevent well-bore collapse and water infiltration while drilling. The casing also conducts the produced reservoir fluids to the surface (see **Figure 12**). A properly designed and cemented casing also prevents reservoir fluids (gas or oil) from infiltrating the overlying groundwater aquifers.

During the first phase of drilling, termed "spuding-in," shallow casing installed underneath the drilling platform serves to reinforce the ground surface. Drilling continues to the bottom of the water table (or the potable aquifer), at which point the drill string is "tripped" out (removed) in order to lower a second casing string, which is cemented-in and plugged at the bottom. Drillers use special oil-well cement that expands when it sets to fill the void between the casing and the wellbore.

Surface casing and casing to the bottom of the water table prevents water from flooding the well while also protecting the groundwater from contamination by drilling fluids and reservoir fluids. (The initial drilling stages may use compressed air in place of drilling fluids to avoid contaminating the potable aquifer.) Drilling and casing then continue to the "pay zone"—the formation that produces gas or oil. The number and length of the casings, however, depends on the depth and the properties of the geologic strata.

Figure 12. Hypothetical Well Casing

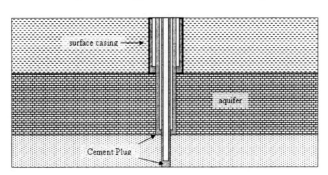

Source: CRS.

Notes: No Scale.

After completing the well to the target depth and cementing-in the final casing, the drilling operator may hire an oil-well service company to run a "cement evaluation log." An electric probe lowered into the well, measures the cement thickness. The cement evaluation log provides the critical confirmation that the cement will function as designed—preventing well fluids from bypassing outside the casing and infiltrating overlying formations.

Absent any cement voids, the well is ready for completion. A perforating tool that uses explosive shape charges punctures the casing sidewall at the pay zone. The well may then start producing under its natural reservoir pressure or, as in the case of gas shales, may need stimulation treatment.

Both domestic-use gas wells and water wells are common throughout regions experiencing recent shale gas development. In the absence of regulation, domestic-use wells (gas or water) may not meet standard practices of construction. If the wellhead of a water supply well is improperly sealed, for example, surface water may infiltrate down along the casing exterior and contaminate the drinking-water aquifer. Some domestic water wells have also produced natural gas, and some shallow gas wells have leaked into nearby building foundations. To avoid some of these problems, Pennsylvania is instituting regulations that require a minimum 2,000-foot setback between a new gas-well and an existing water-well.

Hydraulic Fracturing

Despite some shales' abundant natural gas content, they do not produce gas freely. Economic production depends on some means of artificially stimulating shale to liberate gas. In the late 1940s, Texas oil fields responded to fluids pumped down wells under pressures high enough to

Unconventional Gas Shales: Development, Technology, and Policy Issues

fracture stimulated the producing formation. Hydraulic fracture stimulation treatments have been adapted to tight gas formations such as the Barnett Shale in Texas, and more recently the Marcellus Shale.

Typical "frac" treatments or frac jobs (as commonly referred to) are relatively large operations compared to some drilling operations. The oilfield service company contracted for the work may take a week to stage the job, and a convoy of trucks to deliver the equipment and materials needed (see **Figure 13**).

A company involved in developing Texas gas shale offered the following description of a frac job:[42]

> Shale gas wells are not hard to drill, but they are difficult to complete. In almost every case, the rock around the wellbore must be hydraulically fractured before the well can produce significant amounts of gas. Fracturing involves isolating sections of the well in the producing zone, then pumping fluids and proppant (grains of sand or other material used to hold the cracks open) down the wellbore through perforations in the casing and out into the shale.

> The pumped fluid, under pressures up to 8,000 psi, is enough to crack shale as much as 3,000 ft in each direction from the wellbore. In the deeper high-pressure shales, operators pump slickwater (a low-viscosity water-based fluid) and proppant. Nitrogen-foamed fracturing fluids are commonly pumped on shallower shales and shales with low reservoir pressures.

---

[42] Schlumberger, Inc., *Shale Gas: When Your Gas Reservoir is Unconventional, So is Our Solution.* http://www.slb.com/media/services/solutions/reservoir/shale_gas.pdf.

Congressional Research Service   22

Unconventional Gas Shales: Development, Technology, and Policy Issues

Figure 13. Hydraulic Fracture Job
Marcellus Shale Well, West Virginia

Source: Chesapeake Energy Corporation, 2008.

Notes: The yellow frac tanks in the foreground and along the tree line hold water, the red tanker holds proppant; hydraulic pumps are in the center.

Fracturing Fluids

Fracturing fluid functions in two ways: opening the fracture and transporting the "propping" agent (or proppant) the length of the fracture.[43] As the term propping implies, the agent functions to prop or hold the fracture open. The fluid must have the proper viscosity and low friction pressure when pumped, it must breakdown and cleanup rapidly when treatment is over, and it must provide good fluid-loss control (not dissipate). The fluid chemistry may be water-based, oil-based or acid-based depending on the properties of the formation. Water-based fluids (sometimes referred to as slickwater) are the most widely used (especially in shale formations) because of their low cost, high performance, and ease of handling. Some fluids may also include nitrogen and carbon dioxide to help foaming. Oil-based fluids find use in hydrocarbon bearing formations susceptible to water damage, but are they expensive and difficult to use. Acid-based fluids use hydrochloric acid to dissolve the mineral matrix of carbonate formations (limestone and dolomite) and thus improve porosity; the reaction produces inert calcium chloride salt and carbon dioxide gas.

---

[43] "Chapter 7 - Fracturing Fluid Chemistry and Proppants," in *Reservoir Stimulation*, ed. Michael J. Economides and Kenneth G. Nolte, 3rd ed. (John Wiley & Sons, LTD, 2000).

Water-based fluids consist of 99% water with the remainder made up of additives. The initial fracturing stage may use hydrochloric acid (HCl) to cleanup the wellbore damage done during drilling and cementing. Gelling agents, based on water-soluble polymers such as vegetable-derived guar gum, adjust frac fluid viscosity. The most widely used additives for breaking down fluid viscosity after fracturing are oxidizers such as ammonium (NH^{+4}), potassium, and sodium salt of peroxydisulfate ($S2O_8^{-2}$); enzyme breakers may be based on hemicellulase (actually a mixture of enzymes which can hydrolyze the indigestible components of plant fibers). Silica flour serves as good fluid-loss additive. Biocides added to polymer-containing fluids prevent bacterial degradation (as the polysaccharides (sugar polymer) used to thicken water are an excellent food source for bacteria). Methanol (an alcohol) and sodium thiosulfate ($Na_2S_2O_3$) are commonly used stabilizers added to prevent polysaccharide gels degrading above temperatures of 200°F.

It is important to note that the service companies adjust the proportion of frac fluid additives to the unique conditions of each well. The Occupational Safety and Hazard Administration (OSHA) requires that material safety data sheets (MSDS) accompany each chemical used on the drill site, but the proportion of each chemical additive may be kept proprietary.[44]

Proppants hold the fracture walls apart to create conductive paths for the natural gas to reach the wellbore. Silica sands are the most commonly used proppants. Resin coating the sand grains improves their strength.

Hydraulic Fracture Process

Fracture treatments are carefully controlled and monitored operations that proceed in stages. Before beginning a treatment, the service company will perform a series of tests on the well to determine if it is competent to hold up to the hydraulic pressures generated by the fracture pumps.

In the initial stage, an HCl solution pumped down the well cleans up residue left from cementing the well casing. Each successive stage pumps discrete volumes of fluid (slickwater) and proppant down the well to open and propagate the fracture further into the formation. The treatment may last upwards of an hour or more, with the final stage designed to flush the well. Some wells may receive several or more treatments to produce multiple fractures at different depths, or further out into the formation in the case of horizontal wells.

A single fracture treatment may consume more than 500,000 gallons of water.[45] Wells subject to multiple treatments consume several million gallons of water. An Olympic-size swimming pool (164 ft x 82 ft x 6 ft deep) holds over 660,000 gallons of water, for comparison, and the average daily per capita consumption of fresh water (roughly 1,430 gallons per day) is 522,000 gallons over one year.[46]

---

[44] 29 C.F.R. §§ 1910 Subpart Z, Toxic and hazardous substances.

[45] Modern Shale Gas Development in the United States: A Primer, pp. 58-59.

[46] U.S. Geological Survey, *Summary of water use in the United States, 2000*, http://ga.water.usgs.gov/edu/wateruse2000.html.

Unconventional Gas Shales: Development, Technology, and Policy Issues

The high injection pressure not only opens and propagates the fracture but also drives fluid into the shale's pore spaces. A high volume of fluid also remains in the fracture that will impede gas flow to the well if not pumped out. The subsequent "flowback" treatment performed, attempts to recover as much of the remaining fluid as possible without removing the proppants. The "flowback" water pumped out of the well may be high in dissolved salts and frac chemicals, however, making it unsuitable for beneficial use, and requiring treatment for disposal. After the well begins producing gas, it may also produce more flowback water. Flowback disposal presents environmental issues, as discussed in the "Surface Water Quality Protection" section below.

Fracture Geometry

The fracture is ideally represented by a vertical plane that intersects the well casing (**Figure 14**). It does not propagate in a random direction, but opens perpendicular to the direction of least stress underground (which is nearly horizontal in orientation).

Figure 14. Idealized Hydraulic Fracture

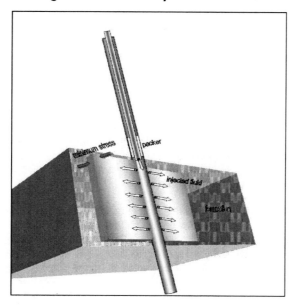

Source: CRS.

Notes: Fracture opens perpendicular to direction of minimum stress.

Hydraulic fracturing attempted at too shallow a depth develops an undesirable horizontal fracture. In the case of deep shales, such as the Marcellus, this appears unlikely. The fracture may extend outward several thousands of feet, but the fracture height is limited to the thickness of the shale formation (and controlled by the perforated zone of the well).

Fracturing Risks to Groundwater

The geologic environment that led to the deposition of the Marcellus Shale, and the overlying layers of siltstone, shale, sandstone, and limestone have kept gas from the Marcellus Shale confined at depth, and prevented it from naturally migrating upwards toward the surface. The process of developing a shale gas well (drilling through an overlying aquifer, stimulating the well via hydraulic fracturing, completing the well and producing the gas) is an issue of concern for increasing the risk of groundwater contamination. Typically, well drilling and completion practices, as described above, require sealing the well by casing throughout the aquifer interval. A properly designed and cased well will prevent drilling fluids, hydraulic fracturing fluids, or natural gas from leaking into the permeable aquifer and contaminating groundwater. The casing also prevents groundwater from leaking into the well where it could interfere with the gas production process.

An environmental concern raised by hydraulic fracturing is the possibility of introducing contaminants into aquifers. Hydraulic fracturing does induce new fractures into shale, and can propagate fractures thousands of feet along the bedding plane of a shale formation. The potential for propagating fractures to an overlying aquifer may depend on the depth separating the two. However, engineers designing and conducting frac jobs have a strong incentive to limit the fractures to the height of the gas-producing shale zones. Any fracture propagated to an overlying aquifer could allow water to flow down into the gas-producing portion of the shale, which could significantly hamper gas production.

Multiple frac treatments may pump as much as 2 to 3 million gallons of fluid down a well. Afterwards the well operator recovers a large proportion of these fluids by pumping them out of the well, and disposes of them through waster-water treatment plants or by other means as discussed below. However, any drilling fluids or frac fluids spilled on the ground surface could infiltrate downwards to shallow groundwater. This could pose a risk to surficial aquifers composed of very permeable unconsolidated sand and gravel deposits, such as those in northern Pennsylvania and southern New York (see **Figure 9**).

Another potential issue could be groundwater contamination from poorly constructed water wells. Generally, drinking water wells are shallower than natural gas wells, and their casing may not extend their entire depth. This is particularly the case for domestic water wells that may not be subject to the same level of oversight and scrutiny as natural gas well construction. A water well that is not cased from the surface, or is not constructed and cased properly, might allow contaminated water to flow from the ground surface and enter the water well, possibly compromising the quality of drinking water in the well and even the drinking water aquifer itself. In such instances, and particularly where natural gas drilling and stimulation activities are nearby, leaky surface impoundments or careless surface disposal of drilling fluids at the natural gas operation could increase the risk of contaminating the nearby water well.

Contaminated surface water unrelated to drilling could also contaminate improperly cased or constructed water well. For example, a leaky septic system, or improper disposal of domestic refuse such as car batteries or used oil, could leak from the surface into the water well. If this is the case, a dispute could ensue as to who is responsible for contaminating the water well. Resolving the dispute could involve a hydrogeological investigation to prove or disprove any linkage between natural gas development activities and water well contamination, often at considerable expense and with an uncertain outcome, given the complexity of groundwater flow at most sites.

Leasing Issues for Gas Development

The Marcellus Shale gas formation has generated considerable interest within the past two years on state-owned and private lands throughout the Appalachian region in West Virginia, Pennsylvania, and New York. Landowners who also own the subsurface mineral rights may lease their land for the development of those minerals or sell the surface or mineral rights to qualified buyers for development.[47] If the landowner decides to lease the land for mineral development, the owner may negotiate a lease agreement or contract. Common features of oil and gas leases today include signing bonuses (or up front "bonus bid" payments for competitive lease sales), royalties, rents, primary lease terms and conditions for lease renewal.

In the case of mineral rights severed from surface rights, a split-estate is established. Under a split-estate, the mineral owner has the right to reasonable access to recover the mineral. The surface owner typically has the right to protection from "unreasonable encroachment and damage" and can usually negotiate compensation for the use of the surface and for damages. On split-estates that involve private surface owners and federally owned minerals, a federal lessee must meet one of the following conditions: a surface agreement; written consent or a waiver from the private surface owner for access to the leased lands; payment for loss or damages; or the execution of a bond not less than $1,000.[48] Split-estate scenarios are common but a comprehensive discussion on the subject is beyond the scope of this report.

The state-by-state sections below describe how compensation to landowners atop the Marcellus Shale has evolved over the past few years. The discussion focuses primarily on bonus payments and royalties received by state and private landowners today compared to what they received just a few years ago. Rents are not part of the discussion because nearly all of the information available reports on signing bonuses and royalties. Further, lease agreements often roll signing bonuses into rents, and call for rents paid upfront or paid quarterly as a "delay rental." Rents appear to be much less significant to small landowners who lease a few acres. On state and private lands, as with federal lands, lessees usually pay rent until production commences and then switch to paying royalties on the value of production.

New York

In 1999, signing bonuses for leases on private lands were around $5 per acre, with royalties of 12½%. During that same time, the state received between $15 and $600 per acre in bonus payments. In today's climate, bonus payments are as much as $3,000 per acre on privately held lands with royalty rates between 15% and 20%. Lease terms are typically three to five years with renewal clauses for continued production and shut-in wells. Fewer than 10 years ago, there were only about five or six companies involved in securing leases to develop gas shale projects. By 2008 their number rose to about four dozen companies (including Exxon/Mobil, BP, and Conoco Phillips).

---

[47] The term "mineral" refers to economically recoverable resources including natural gas.

[48] This information was provided in a BLM Instructional Memorandum, No. 2003-131. Also see 43 CFR 3104, 43 CFR 3814 and 48 FR 48916 (1983) for further details.

Unconventional Gas Shales: Development, Technology, and Policy Issues

Pennsylvania

In 2002, companies were paying signing bonuses of $25 to $50 per acre and agreeing to $2 per acre annual rentals and 12½ % royalty on 10-year leases on state-owned land. Interest has grown dramatically since that time, and firms are now paying as much as $2,500 per acre in bonus payments, 16% royalty and annual rental rates of $20 per acre for years 2 through 5 and $35 per acre in years 6 through 10. Private landowners have typically issued shorter-term leases of 5 to 7 years. Private owners received about $12 per acre in signing bonuses and a 12½% royalty rate in 2003. In 2008, lessees are now paying private landowners signing bonuses of nearly $2,900 per acre with 17% to 18% royalty rates on 5- through 7-year leases. Many private leases often calculate rents as part of the signing bonus and sometimes pay them upfront or over time.

West Virginia

Some landowners in West Virginia have seen their bonus bids climb from $5 per acre in 2007 and early 2008, to more recent bonus payments of $1,000 to $3,000 per acre. Royalty rates have increased from 12½% through 16% to 18%. Rents are often included in the signing bonus or sometimes paid out in the form of a "delay rental."

State Summary

In general, Marcellus gas lease rates range for state and private lands from a low of 12½% in West Virginia to high of 20% in New York (**Table 1** and **Table 2**), but these rates are less than those paid in Texas for similar gas shale tracts. All three of Marcellus Shale states reported above have shown significant increases in the amounts paid as signing bonuses and increases in royalty rates. There are lease sales that the Natural Gas Leasing Tracking Service reported with signing bonuses as low as $100 to $200 per acre, owing to greater uncertainty and less interest among natural gas companies and/or the lack of information among landowners on what the land is worth.[49]

There are several landowner organizations that have formed in recent years to pool their land for leasing, advise landowners, and serve as information centers. Some groups seek out competitive bids from energy companies.[50]

---

[49] The Natural Gas Leasing Offer Tracking can be found at http://www.pagaslease.com/lease_tracking_2.php.

[50] Natural Gas /Oil Landowner Groups Directory, http://www.pagaslease.com/directory_public.php.

Congressional Research Service 28

Unconventional Gas Shales: Development, Technology, and Policy Issues

Table 1. Shale Gas Bonus Bids, Rents, and Royalty Rates on Selected State Lands

	Statutory Minimum or Standard Royal Rate	Royalty Rate Range	Bonus Bids (per acre)	Comments
West Virginia [a]	12½%	n.a.	n.a.	No state shale gas leases.
Pennsylvania [b]	12½%	12½% - 16%	$2,500	In many cases bonus bids were in the $25-$50 per acre range as recent as 2002. A royalty rate of 12.5% was most common.
New York [c]	12½%	15% - 20%	about $600	Bonus bids ranged from $15-$600 per acre around 1999-2000 and most royalty rates were at 12.5%.
Texas	12½%	25%	$350 - $400 (Delaware Basin) $12,000 (river tracts)	Bonus bids have been relatively consistent in recent times (within the past 5 years). Royalty rates were more common at 20%-25% about 5 years ago. Most state-owned lands are not considered to be among the best sites for shale gas development.

Source: CRS.

a. Personal communication with Joe Scarberry in the WV Department of Natural Resources, October 2008.

b. Personal communication with Ted Borawski in the PA Bureau of Forestry, who provided information on shale gas leases on both state and private lands, October 2008.

c. Personal communication with Lindsey Wickham of the NY Farm Bureau and Bert Chetuway of Cornell University, discussed lease sales on state and private land, October 2008.

Table 2. Shale Gas Bonus Bids, Rents, and Royalty Rates on Private Land in Selected States

	Royalty Rates Range	Bonus Bids (per acre)	Comments
West Virginia [a]	12½% –18 %	$1,000 – $3,000	Bonus payments were in the $5 per acre range as recently as 1-2 years ago. Royalty rates were 12½%
Pennsylvania	17% – 18%	$2,000 – $3,000	
New York	15% – 20%	$2,000 – $3,000	
Texas	25% – 28%	$10,000 – $20,000	Bonus bids were in the $1,000 range around 2000-2001. Royalty rates ranged from 20% to 25% range.

Source: CRS

a. Personal communication with David McMahon, Director of the WV Surface Owners Rights Organization, October 2008.

Lease Audit (Product Valuation and Verification)

Organizations involved with private-owned leases for shale gas development often recommend to lessors that they include provisions/clauses in their leases that require the producer to pay the wellhead price without deductions or to base the royalty on the gross proceeds at the well. Under most circumstances (in arms-length, third-party transactions), the wellhead is the point of first sale. Wellhead and spot prices are available from different sources including the EIA website. There are opportunities for a lessor to audit volume flows from the well, but more often, the producer will provide production and price data to the lessor. According to David McMahon of the West Virginia Surface Owners Rights Organization (WVSORO), there are major concerns among landowners that include the lessees deducting costs inappropriately, before the royalty is calculated.[51] This practice can deduct costs for transportation, compressors, and line loss from the wellhead price, thus reducing the royalty paid to the landowner. While metering production is typical, auditing production may be rare. The cost of an audit may be cost prohibitive for small landowners.

The state of Pennsylvania audits production from the top 100 wells of its natural gas leases using an independent auditor, or "meter truck companies" that work for the shale gas producers. The state of New York requires that natural gas producers meter production and make that information available upon request.[52] The West Virginia Department of Environmental Protection, Office of Oil and Gas, requires an annual production report from all oil and gas producers in the state.

Severance Taxes

State governments of Pennsylvania and New York have proposed a severance tax (included in the 2009-2010 budget) in order to generate revenue to address state concerns. Twenty-seven states producing natural gas (including West Virginia) already impose a severance tax. In Pennsylvania, based on the proposed severance tax, the Pennsylvania state government projected revenue increases of $107 million in 2009-2010, increasing to $632 million by 2013-2014.[53] A separate study on the economic impacts of Marcellus Shale gas development in Pennsylvania projected economic output of $3.8 billion, 48,000 jobs, and $400 million in state and local tax revenues in 2009.[54] The study also projected cumulative tax revenues reaching an estimated $12 billion (in present value dollars) in 2020. However, based on the proposed severance tax, state and local tax revenue estimates could be reduced by $880 million (in present value dollars) resulting from an estimated 30% reduction in natural gas drilling between 2009 and 2020 according to the study.

There are typically two types of severance taxes: an ad valorem or value-based tax or a unit of production-based tax. Individual states uniquely apply severance taxes to the extraction industries for the "privilege" of extracting natural resources (such as minerals and timber) in order to compensate residents for the irreplaceable loss from the extraction of the resource, sometimes described as a loss of future wealth. Revenue streams from severance taxes pay for the

---

[51] West Virginia Surface Owners' Rights Organization, http://www.wvsoro.org/.

[52] Energy Conservation Law, 23-0301-23-0305, Part 556.

[53] Pennsylvania Budget and Policy Center, *Responsible Growth, Protecting the Public Interest with a Natural Gas Severance Tax*, by Michael Wood and Sharon Ward, April 2009.

[54] Pennsylvania State University, College of Earth and Mineral Sciences, Department of Energy and Mineral Engineering, An *Emerging Giant: Prospects and Economic Impacts of Developing the Marcellus Shale Natural Gas Play*, by Timothy Considine, et al., August 5, 2009.

---

environmental and social costs associated with mining and extraction. The tax may also contribute to a state's general revenue fund.

The severance tax as other costs imposed on the oil and gas industry may affect long-term production rates. This variable cost, applied to the operator, only when production occurs, may slow extraction. A whole host of other factors, e.g., geology, price/demand, transportation costs, and capital formation, affect when and where natural gas is developed.

Federal Land Leasing and Restrictions to Leasing

Leasing federal public lands for oil and gas development is based on multiple-use/sustained yield Resource Management Plans (RMPs) prepared by the Bureau of Land Management (BLM) in the Department of the Interior. In accordance with those management plans, BLM offers tracts of public land with oil and gas potential for competitive leasing each quarter. The BLM administers oil and gas leasing and development on federally owned minerals both for BLM lands and on behalf of the U.S. Forest Service, which in turn administers the surface development within the National Forests and through its land planning process addresses surface occupancy concerns and approves or rejects any extraction of forest resources.

However, privately held mineral rights account for over 90% of the Allegheny National Forest in Pennsylvania and about 38% within the Monongahela National Forest in West Virginia. Finger Lakes National Forest in New York was withdrawn from the mineral leasing programs under section 370 the Energy Policy Act of 2005 (P.L. 109-58).

The Mineral Leasing Act and the Outer Continental Shelf Lands Act, as amended, requires that all public lands (onshore and offshore areas respectively) available for lease be offered initially to the highest responsible qualified bidder by competitive bidding. The objective of the competitive bid is to provide a "fair market value" return to the federal government for its resources. Under the two acts mentioned above, the federal government requires royalties from oil and gas producers (and other resource producers) on leasable federal lands and annual rents from non-producing lessees. Competitive oil and gas lease sales include bonus bids (upfront payments made to obtain a lease). The statutory minimum royalty rate for oil and gas leases on public lands is 12½% (also expressed as ⅛). Currently the royalty rate for onshore oil and gas leases is 12½%, while the rate for an offshore lease can range from 12½% to 18¾%. Annual rental rates established for onshore leases are at not less than $1.50 per acre for the first five years of a ten-year lease and not less than $2 per acre each year thereafter. The primary lease term for an onshore lease is 10 years and for an offshore lease is either 5, 8, or 10 years depending on the depth of the water. Annual rent paid on leases ends when production begins, then the lessor begins paying royalties on the value of production.

Of the approximately 5 million acres of federal land in the Appalachian basin (**Figure 15**), 46% (2.5 million acres) is not accessible for lease.[55] Based on resource estimates, these lands contain

---

[55] U.S Department of the Interior, Inventory of Onshore Federal Oil and Natural Gas Resources and Restrictions to Their Development, Phase III Inventory - Onshore United States, 2008, p. 225. http://www.blm.gov/pgdata/etc/medialib/blm/wo/MINERALS__REALTY__AND_RESOURCE_PROTECTION_/energy/EPCA_Text_PDF.Par.18155.File.dat/Executive%20Summary%20text.pdf

Unconventional Gas Shales: Development, Technology, and Policy Issues

41% (984.7 bcf) of the federal natural gas in the basin. Another 42% (2.2 million acres) is accessible with restrictions on oil and gas operations beyond standard lease terms. These lands contain 45% (1.1 tcf) of the federal natural gas. The remaining 13% (691.7 thousand acres) that is accessible under standard lease terms contains 14% (346.7 bcf) of the federal natural gas. Most of the undiscovered gas resource (94%) will likely occur in continuous accumulations. Coal-bed natural gas accounts for about 13% of the total undiscovered continuous gas.

Figure 15. Federal Lands Overlying Natural Gas Resources of the Appalachian Basin

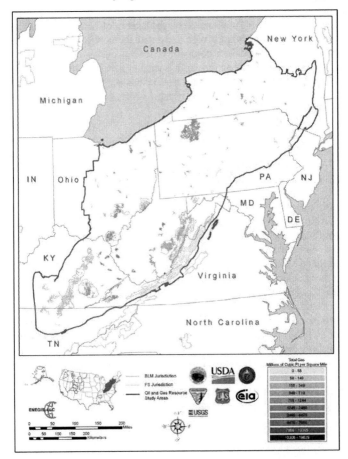

Source: U.S. Dept. of the Interior, *Inventory of Onshore Federal Oil and Natural Gas Resources and Restrictions to Their Development, Phase III Inventory,* 2008.

Notes: Approximately 5 million acres of federal lands in the Appalachian Basin region overlie natural gas resources.

Federal and State Laws and Regulations Affecting Gas Shale Development

Development of the Marcellus Shale will be subject to regulation under several federal and state laws. In particular, the large volumes of water needed to drill and hydraulically fracture the shale, and the disposal of this water and other wastewater associated with gas extraction may pose significant water quality and quantity challenges that trigger regulatory attention. As the U.S. Geological Survey noted in a recent publication, "Concerns about the availability of water supplies needed for gas production, and questions about wastewater disposal have been raised by water-resource agencies and citizens through the Marcellus Shale gas development region."[56] The following sections review key provisions of two relevant federal laws, the Safe Drinking Water Act (SDWA) and the Clean Water Act (CWA), and related state requirements.

Surface Water Quality Protection

As previously described, hydraulic fracturing involves injecting water, sand, and chemicals into the shale layer at extremely high pressures in order to release the trapped natural gas. It is a water-intensive practice. Typical projects use 1-3 million gallons of water for each well and 0.5 million pounds of sand. Large projects may require up to 5 million gallons of water.

The Texas Railroad Commission estimates that fracturing a vertical well in the Barnett Shale in Texas can use more than 1.2 million gallons of water, while fracturing a horizontal well can use more than 3.5 million gallons.[57] Moreover, the wells may be re-fractured several times, thus requiring additional water. Fracturing operations use an estimated 5 or more million gallons of water each day in the Barnett Shale, a smaller natural gas field in Texas.[58] Regarding the Marcellus Shale region, the USGS observed "many regional and local water management agencies are concerned about where such large volumes of water will be obtained, and what the possible consequences might be for local water supplies."[59]

Some of the injected fluids remain trapped underground, but the majority of the injected water— 60% to 80%—returns to the surface as "flowback" after the frac treatment. It typically contains proppant (sand), chemical residue, and trace amounts of radioactive elements that naturally occur in many geologic formations.[60] USGS notes that because the quantity of fluid used is so large, the

---

[56] Daniel J. Soeder and William M. Kappel, *Water Resources and Natural Gas Production from the Marcellus Shale*, U.S. Geological Survey, U.S. Department of the Interior, Fact Sheet 2009-3032, May 2009, http://pubs.usgs.gov/fs/ 2009/3032/pdf/FS2009-3032.pdf. Hereafter, USGS Fact Sheet.

[57] Railroad Commission of Texas, Water Use in the Barnett Shale, July 30, 2008, http://www.rrc.state.tx.us/division/og/ wateruse_barnettshale.html.

[58] Burnett, D.B. and Vavra, C.J., Desalination of Oil Field Brine—Texas A&M Produced Water Treatment. August 2006, http://www.pe.tamu.edu/gpri-new/home/BrineDesal/MembraneWkshpAug06/Burnett8-06.pdf.

[59] USGS Fact Sheet at 4.

[60] These particles, termed normally occurring radioactive materials (NORMS), can be brought to the surface on drilling equipment and in fluids. Subsurface formations may contain low levels of such materials as uranium and thorium and

(continued...)

Unconventional Gas Shales: Development, Technology, and Policy Issues

additives in a three million gallon frac job would yield about 15,000 gallons of chemicals in the waste.[61] The well service company may temporarily retain the flowback and brine in open-air, lined retention ponds before reusing it (if possible), or disposing it. The drilling operator must reclaim the temporary storage pits when the drilling and fracturing operations end. In addition, the well operator must separate, treat, and dispose the natural brine co-produced with gas. As noted below, where feasible, the produced water may be disposed through underground injection. The oil and gas industry uses this disposal method in some western states and in Ohio.[62] The industry has not yet begun using it as a disposal alternative for gas production in eastern Marcellus Shale.

In the event that underground injection is not feasible in the area of the Marcellus Shale, the well service company may discharge the flowback to surface waters if the discharge does not violate a stream or lake's water quality standards. Standards established by states under Section 303 of the Clean Water Act (CWA) protect designated beneficial uses of surface waters, such as recreation or public water supply.[63]

If contaminants present in the flowback prevent discharge to surface water without further treatment, it is likely that the service company will have to transfer the wastewater off-site to an industrial treatment facility or a municipal sewage treatment plant that is capable of handling and processing the wastewater. In this case, the operator of the publicly owned treatment works (POTW) or industrial treatment facility would assume responsibility for treating the waste before discharging it into nearby receiving water in compliance with effluent limits contained in the facility's discharge permit.[64] The chemical frac additives returned in flowback and the produced brine could cause problems for POTWs. Contaminants in industrial process wastewaters can kill off the biota essential to a POTW's operation. If contaminants pass through the POTW without adequate treatment, the discharge could violate the facility's discharge permit and could cause a violation of water quality standards. A standard POTW's effective treatment of flowback and brine is uncertain. It could require upgrading, but the cost of such an upgrade is also uncertain.

In the fall of 2008, water samples from the mid-Monongahela River valley of Pennsylvania showed high levels of total dissolved solids (TDS), which indicate salinity. Although the TDS was determined to pose little threat to health or safety, preliminary analysis suggested that the principal source was large truck deliveries of wastewater from gas well drilling sites in the Marcellus Shale to POTWs discharging, directly or indirectly, into the Monongahela River. In October 2008, state officials ordered nine sewage treatment plants to reduce their volumes of gas well drilling water, which contains high concentrations of TDS. Subsequent analysis concluded

---

(...continued)

their daughter products, radium 226 and radium 228. On gamma-ray logs, shales can be differentiated from other rocks such as clean sandstones and limestones because shales have higher concentrations of potassium-40-bearing minerals. See Commonwealth of Pennsylvania Department of Conservation and Natural Resources, Pennsylvania Geology, Vol. 38, No. 1, p. 5, Spring 2008, http://www.dcnr.state.pa.us/topogeo/pub/pageolmag/pdfs/v38n1.pdf.

[61] USGS Fact Sheet at 4.

[62] In the Barnett Shale area, most of the water is reinjected for disposal.

[63] 33 U.S. C. § 1313.

[64] Under CWA Section 301, it is illegal to discharge pollutants into the nation's waters except in compliance with substantive and procedural provisions of the law, which include obtaining a discharge permit. 33 U.S.C. § 1311.

Congressional Research Service　　　　　　　　　　　　　　　　　　　　　　**34**

that discharge from abandoned mines was more responsible for the high TDS than drilling wastewater discharges from municipal wastewater treatment plants.[65] However, state officials remain concerned about the projected need for treatment of wastewater (both initial flowback water from fracturing and longer term production brines) from gas well development—projected to be as much as 20 million gallons per day in 2011—and the capacity of the state's surface waters to assimilate associated wastewaters. In April 2009, the Pennsylvania Department of Environmental Protection issued a permitting strategy document for gas development wastewaters, requiring that any discharges will be subject to the most stringent treatment or water quality standards needed to protect aquatic life in the state's streams. Their goal is prohibiting new sources of high-TDS wastewaters from discharging into Pennsylvania's waters by January 1, 2011.[66]

Brine storage and transport are major issues in developing the Barnett Shale in Texas, and are likely to be key issues in development of the Marcellus Shale, as well. Currently, permitted treatment facilities capable of treating such wastes are not adequate. In Pennsylvania, there are five facilities designed to treat the type of industrial wastewater that is involved in producing shale gas. Most of the well sites are located in northeast Pennsylvania, while the closest treatment facilities are nearly 250 miles away.[67]

West Virginia, too, recognizes that wastewater disposal is "perhaps the greatest challenge regarding these operations."[68] State officials say that underground injection control (see discussion below) may be the best option for wastewater disposal, but the state has only permitted two commercial underground injection control (UIC) wells. The state has no centralized commercial treatment facilities available, and state officials are cautious about the capability of POTWs to handle the flow and quality of waste that they might receive.[69] The West Virginia Department of Environmental Protection has proposed both changes to the state's oil and gas drilling rules (which the state legislature must approve) and an industry guidance document to assist operators in planning for the water issues associated with drilling and operating these wells. However, local groups have criticized the proposed rules and draft non-binding guidance for failing to address disposal of wastewater, disclosure of chemicals used in hydraulic fracturing, and where the additional quantities of water required for drilling will come from.[70]

---

[65] "Minimal Impact on Total Dissolved Solids Found in Monongahela River Last Fall," Natural Gas, Tapping Pennsylvania's Potential, May 20, 2009, http://www.pamarcellus.com/news.php.

[66] Marcellus Shale Wastewater Partnership, "Permitting Strategy for High Total Dissolved Solids (TDS) Wastewater Discharges," April 11, 2009, http://www.depweb.state.pa.us/watersupply/cwp/view.asp?a=1260&Q=545730& watersupplyNav=|.

[67] Legere, Laura, "How to handle wastewater big challenge in gas drilling," The Citizens' Voice, August 25, 2008.

[68] State of West Virginia, Department of Environmental Protection, Office of Oil and Gas, "Industry Guidance, Gas Well Drilling/Completion, Large Water Volume Fracture Treatments (Draft)," March 13, 2009, p. 3, http://www.wvsoro.org/curent_events/marcellus/Marcellus_Guidance_Draft.pdf.

[69] Ibid. at 3-4. Reportedly, one company with wells in the Marcellus shale in West Virginia has its hydraulic fracturing wastewater trucked to an out-of-state commercial facility that treats the water and then injects in into depleted oil and gas reservoirs. (Kasey, Pam, *New Drilling Efforts Raise Questions*, The State Journal, August 14, 2008.)

[70] West Virginia Surface Owners' Rights Organization, "Proposed Changes to Oil & Gas Rules, Marcellus Guidance Document," http://www.wvsoro.org/curent_events/.

Unconventional Gas Shales: Development, Technology, and Policy Issues

One potential solution to off-site disposal may be on-site treatment and reuse; that is, treating and reusing flowback and produced water on-site. Some companies are reportedly considering on-site treatment options such as advanced oxidation and membrane filtration processes. On-site treatment technologies may be capable of recovering 70%-80% of the initial water to potable water standards, thus making the water immediately available for reuse. The remaining 20%-30% is very brackish and considered brine water. A portion may be further recoverable as process water, but not to achieve potable water standards. In other cases, companies send the brine water off-site for treatment and disposal. The economics of any such options are critical, and site factors such as available power and final water quality are often the determinant in treatment selection.

Other Surface Water Quality Issues

Another potential source of water pollution from oil and gas drilling sites is runoff that occurs after a rainstorm. The storm water runoff can transport sediment to nearby surface water bodies. Provisions of the CWA generally regulate storm water discharges from industrial and municipal facilities by requiring implementation of pollution prevention plans and, in some cases, remediation or treatment of runoff.[71] Industries that manufacture, process, or store raw materials and that collect or convey storm water associated with those activities are subject to the act's requirements. Furthermore, fracturing fluid chemicals and wastewater can leak or spill from injection wells, flow lines, trucks, tanks or holding pits and thus may contaminate soil, air, and water resources.

However, the act specifically exempts the oil and gas industry from these storm water management regulatory provisions. CWA Section 402(l)(2) exempts mining operations or oil and gas exploration, production, processing, or treatment operations or transmission facilities from federal storm water regulations, and Section 502(24) extends the exemption to construction activities, as well.[72] Thus, federal law contains no requirements to minimize uncontaminated sediment pollution from the construction or operation of oil and gas operations. However, the federal exemption does not hinder states from requiring erosion and sedimentation controls at well sites, under authority of non-federal law. Pennsylvania, for example, requires well drill operators to obtain a permit for implementation of erosion and sedimentation controls, including storm water management, if the site disturbance area is more than five acres in size. If the site is less than five acres, a plan for erosion and sediment control is required. Storm water requirements are part of this permit.[73] New York has similar requirements for erosion and sedimentation controls at well sites, regardless of site area. The Delaware River Basin Commission, which has jurisdiction over water quality in a portion of the area underlain by the Marcellus Shale (see section on State Water Quality Laws below) also has similar requirements regardless of site area.

---

[71] Clean Water Act section 402(p); 33 U.S.C. § 1342(p).

[72] 33 U.S.C. § 1342(l)(2); 33 U.S.C. §1362(24).

[73] The Pennsylvania permit is called an Earth Disturbance Permit (ESCGP-1).

Groundwater Quality Protection

Because development of the Marcellus Shale is dependent on the use of hydraulic fracturing, some fear it could potentially contaminate underground aquifers that provide water supplies to private wells and public water systems. The Safe Drinking Water Act in 2005 broadly excluded the underground injection of fluids used in hydraulic fracturing for oil and gas development.[74] However, the SDWA does not preempt states from imposing their own laws and regulations, and the states have long been responsible for protecting groundwater resources during oil and gas production activities.[75] For example, in New York, the Department of Environmental Conservation (DEC) has authority over oil and gas development in the state, including oversight of hydraulic fracturing activities to ensure protection of groundwater resources. Although federal laws do not regulate the injection of hydraulic fracturing fluids, states such as Pennsylvania and New York do require submission of information on hydraulic fracturing fluid composition prior to issuing a well permit. Moreover, other injection wells related to oil and gas development may be subject to federal requirements.

Safe Drinking Water Act Authority

The underground injection control provisions of the SDWA require the Environmental Protection Agency (EPA) to regulate the underground injection of fluids (including solids, liquids, and gases) to protect underground sources of drinking water. UIC program regulations specify sitting, construction, operation, closure, financial responsibility, and other requirements for owners and operators of injection wells.[76]

West Virginia, Ohio, and Texas are among the states that have assumed primacy and have lead implementation and enforcement authority for the UIC program, including primacy for injection wells associated with oil and gas development. EPA implements the programs directly for New York and Pennsylvania.[77] Most states, including Ohio and West Virginia, have received primacy for Class II oil and gas wells under Section 1425.

The Safe Drinking Water Act specifies that the UIC regulations may not interfere with the underground injection of brine or other fluids brought to the surface in connection with oil and gas production or any underground injection for the secondary or tertiary recovery of oil or natural gas

---

[74] EPA retains the authority to regulate the use of diesel fuel for the purpose of hydraulic fracturing if the agency considers such regulation necessary to protect underground sources of drinking water.

[75] SDWA § 1414(e); 42 U.S.C. § 300g-3(e).

[76] Application, construction, operating, monitoring, and reporting requirements for Class II wells are found in 40 CFR 144 and 146.

[77] To receive primacy, a state, territory, or Indian tribe must demonstrate to EPA that its UIC program is at least as stringent as the federal standards; the state, territory, or tribal UIC requirements may be more stringent than the federal requirements. For Class II wells, states must demonstrate that their programs are effective in preventing pollution of underground sources of drinking water (USDWs). Requirements for state UIC programs are established in 40 CFR §§ 144-147.

Unconventional Gas Shales: Development, Technology, and Policy Issues

unless such requirements are essential to assure that underground sources of drinking water will not be endangered by such injections.[78]

Additionally, the Energy Policy Act of 2005 amended SDWA UIC provisions to specify further that the definition of "underground injection" excludes the injection of fluids or propping agents (other than diesel fuels) used in hydraulic fracturing operations related to oil, gas, or geothermal production activities.[79]

The key statutory provisions are:[80]

- SDWA Section 1421 directs EPA to promulgate regulations for state underground injection control (UIC) programs, and mandates that the regulations contain minimum requirements for programs to prevent underground injection that endangers drinking water sources.[81]

- Section 1422 authorizes EPA to delegate primary enforcement authority (primacy) for UIC programs to the states, provided that state programs prohibit any underground injection that is not authorized by a state permit.[82]

- Section 1425 provides separate authority for states to attain primacy specifically for oil and gas (i.e., Class II) wells. The provision allows states to demonstrate that their existing programs for oil and gas wells are effective in preventing endangerment of underground sources of drinking water, providing an alternative to meeting many of the detailed requirements promulgated to implement the UIC program under Section 1421.

- Section 1431 grants the EPA Administrator emergency powers to issue orders and commence civil action to protect public water systems or underground sources of drinking water. The Administrator may take action when (1) a contaminant present in or likely to enter a public drinking water supply system or underground drinking water source poses a substantial threat to public health, and (2) state or local officials have not taken adequate action.[83]

---

[78] SDWA §1421(b)(2)

[79] P.L. 109-58, Section 322, amended SDWA section 1421(d).

[80] SDWA §§ 1421 - 1426; 42 U.S.C. §§ 300h - 300h-5. The Safe Drinking Water Act of 1974 (P.L. 93-523) authorized the UIC program at EPA.

[81] Section 1421(d)(2) states:

> underground injection endangers drinking water sources if such injection may result in the presence in underground water which supplies or can reasonably be expected to supply any public water system of any contaminant, and if the presence of such contaminant may result in such system's not complying with any national primary drinking water regulation or may otherwise adversely affect the health of persons.

[82] P.L. 93-523, SDWA §1421 (42 U.S.C. § 300h).

[83] 42 U.S.C. § 300i.

Underground Injection of Waste Fluids

As noted, nearly all of the water injected for hydraulic fracturing must come back out of the well for gas to flow out of the shale. A key issue related to Marcellus Shale gas production is safely disposing large quantities of potentially contaminated fluids recovered from the gas wells.

EPA generally categorizes injection wells associated with oil and gas production as Class II wells under its UIC regulatory program. These are wells used to inject brines and other waste fluids associated with oil and natural gas production.[84] Given the expense of treating and transporting large volumes of wastewater for disposal, it is possible that the production of gas from the Marcellus Shale will increasingly involve the use of injection wells to dispose of poor-quality formation water, flowback water resulting from hydraulic fracturing, and other waste fluids associated with gas production.

EPA reports that most of the fluid injected into Class II wells has been brine brought to the surface in producing oil and gas. This brine, a naturally occurring formation fluid, is often very saline and may contain toxic metals and naturally occurring radioactive substances. According to EPA, the brine "can be very damaging to the environment and public health if it is discharged to surface water or the land surface."[85] To prevent contamination of land and surface water, Class II wells provide a means for disposing brines by re-injecting them back into their source formation or into similar formations. Injection wells also serve as disposal means for residual water from drilling and hydraulic fracturing operations. As states have adopted rules to prevent the disposal of saline water to surface water and soil, injection has become the preferred way to dispose of this waste fluid, where the local geology permits.[86]

In New York and Pennsylvania, both EPA and the state environmental agency must issue permits if the disposal method for fracturing wastewater is deep well injection. Pennsylvania law provides that "a well operator who affects a public or private water supply by pollution or diminution shall restore or replace the affected supply with an alternate source of water adequate in quantity and quality for the purposes served by the supply."[87] Additionally, it requires a permit application for a disposal well or enhanced recovery well to include an erosion and sedimentation plan for the well site.[88]

As of now, it is unknown how much water the gas wells in the Marcellus Shale formation will produce. The amount of water produced could vary across the region. Because shale gas formations generally are impermeable, they typically produce much less water than traditional oil

---

[84] Other Class II wells include oil and natural gas storage wells and enhanced oil and gas recovery wells.

[85] U.S. Environmental Protection Agency, Underground Injection Control Program. Oil and Gas Injection Wells: Class II, http://www.epa.gov/safewater/uic/wells_class2.html.

[86] The largest subclass of Class II wells are enhanced recovery wells. These wells are used to inject various substances (including brine, water, steam, polymers, and carbon dioxide) into hydrocarbon-bearing formations to recover primarily oil, but also natural gas, that remains in previously produced areas. Class II enhanced recovery wells are regulated under the UIC program, except for their use in hydraulic fracturing operations.

[87] 25 PA Code § 78.51. Protection of water supplies.

[88] 25 PA Code § 78.18. Disposal and enhanced recovery wells.

and gas fields or coalfields. The impermeability of the shale also indicates that reinjection of wastewater from fracturing into the shale formation may not be feasible in many locations. Consequently, it is uncertain whether Class II disposal wells will find wide use in the Marcellus Shale formation. Currently, only four injection wells operate for this purpose in Pennsylvania.

Wastewater injection into the permeable Cambrian sandstones that lie beneath the Marcellus Shale appears feasible. The Cambrian Mt. Simon Sandstone, considered an ideal geologic unit in Ohio for disposal and long-term storage of liquid wastes, is relatively deep, and underlain and overlain by impervious confining layers that prevent migration of injected fluids.[89]

Although underground injection of wastewater may not be practical or economic in all areas across the Marcellus region because of the lack of suitable injection zones, the cost and environmental concerns associated with surface disposal may make Class II injection wells the preferred disposal option for flowback and other wastewater from hydraulic fracturing operations where feasible. This appears to be the trend in other shale areas. In the Fayetteville Shale in Arkansas, trucks have typically collected wastewater and hauled it to disposal wells distant from the producing areas. However, with more intense shale development, the high cost of transporting, treating, and disposing water offsite, injection well use has increased.[90] In the Barnett Shale in Texas, flowback water has been primarily disposed in Class II injection wells.

Both Class II injection and municipal and industrial water treatment facilities are under consideration for the Marcellus Shale, and more than 60 permit applications for such wells are pending in New York for Marcellus Shale development.[91] One firm active in Marcellus Shale development has been disposing of flowback water and produced water using three UIC disposal wells and two commercial water treatment facilities, but reportedly plans to use only disposal wells in the future. Based on leases already held, the firm plans to drill between 13,500 and 17,000 gas wells.[92]

Technical and practical questions regarding the development of the Marcellus Shale remain unanswered. USGS researchers have noted that while drilling and hydraulic fracturing technologies have improved over the past several decades, "the knowledge of how this extraction might affect water resources has not kept pace."[93] Consequently, environmental regulators and gas developers face new challenges and some uncertainties as the Marcellus Shale is developed.

---

[89] Ohio Department of Natural Resources, Division of Geological Survey, *The Geology of Ohio—The Cambrian*, GeoFacts No. 20, May 1998.

[90] University of Arkansas and Argonne National Lab, Reducing the Environmental Impact of Natural Gas Development, http://lingo.cast.uark.edu/LINGOPUBLIC/.

[91] J. Daniel Arthur, et al, Evaluating the Environmental Implications of Hydraulic Fracturing in Shale Gas Reservoirs, 2008, available at http://www.all-llc.com.

[92] StatoilHydro, Frequently Asked Questions: *StatoilHydro's Acquisition of 32.5% of Chesapeake Interest in the Marcellus Shale*, 2008. http://www.statoilhydro.com/en/NewsAndMedia/News/2008/Downloads/Frequently%20asked%20questions.pdf

[93] USGS Fact Sheet at 5.

State Water Quality Laws

State laws addressing the quality of surface water and groundwater also appear to apply to Marcellus Shale development. For example, in New York various aspects of such development would require a permit under the State Pollutant Discharge Elimination System (SPDES).[94] SPDES is an "approved," rather than delegated, version of the federal National Pollutant Discharge Elimination System (NPDES) permit program because, while the federal NPDES covers only discharges to surface water, SPDES covers discharges to groundwater also. The SPDES permit requirement could apply to hydraulic fracturing by meeting four conditions:

1. Most importantly, the state must determine that injection will not degrade groundwater;[95]

2. A wastewater treatment plant would likely dispose of the fluids produced from the well, in which case the plant's SPDES permit would apply;

3. SPDES permits would also cover treatment facilities built specially for disposing of flowback water, if there would be discharges into a water body; and

4. Applicable state water-quality standards would control, in part, the permit's discharge limits.[96]

New York State's Environmental Quality Review Act (SEQRA) is also relevant.[97] As with its federal counterpart, the National Environmental Policy Act, a requirement of an environmental impact statement preparation lies at the heart of the statute.[98] New York has been evaluating the environmental impact of the drilling and hydraulic fracturing activities for more than 15 years through a Generic Environmental Impact Statement (GEIS) that sets parameters that apply statewide for SEQRA review of gas well permitting. In February 2009, the state's Bureau of Oil and Gas Regulation, in the Department of Environmental Conservation, released the final scoping document under SEQRA for a Supplemental Generic Environmental Impact Statement (SGEIS) on developing the Marcellus and other gas shale regions in the state using high-volume hydraulic fracturing. On September 30, New York DEC released for comment the draft SGEIS which proposes additional parameters for SEQRA review and focuses on water supply protection and wastewater management as major issues. Until New York finalizes the supplemental GEIS, the state will only accept, but not process, permit applications for gas wells involving horizontal drilling and high-volume hydraulic fracturing.[99]

---

[94] N.Y. Envtl. Cons. Law § 17-0505.

[95] N.Y. Code of Rules and Regulations (Conservation) § 750-1.5(a)(6).

[96] N.Y. Envtl. Cons. Law § 17-0501.

[97] N.Y. Envtl. Cons. Law §§ 8-0101 – 8-0117.

[98] Id. at § 8-0109.

[99] In the announcement of the draft supplemental GEIS, the NY Department of Environmental Conservation noted that,

> While the process of preparing the Supplemental GEIS is ongoing, any entity that applies for a drilling permit for horizontal drilling in the Marcellus Shale and opts to proceed with its permit application will be required to undertake an individual, site-specific environmental review. That review must take into account the same issues being considered in the Supplemental GEIS process

(continued...)

As another example, West Virginia's NPDES permit program would apply to wastewater treatment plants to which flowback from Marcellus Shale production sites was taken and to treatment facilities built specially for the frac water that discharge into a water body.[100] Applicable state water-quality standards would control the permit's discharge limits, in part.[101] However, this program applies to surface water only, not groundwater, and the state's Groundwater Protection Act exempts "groundwater within geologic formations which are site specific to ... [t]he production ... of ... natural gas...."[102] The state's underground injection control program would regulate frac water re-injected at a second or subsequent production site.[103]

In addition to state water-quality laws, the interstate Delaware River Basin Commission (36% of whose jurisdictional land area in Pennsylvania and New York overlies the Marcellus Shale formation) would also impose water quality requirements.[104] The Commission's water quality (and other) requirements are legally separate from those of the affected states—that is, obtaining state approval does not excuse an applicant from seeking Commission approval—though in some cases the two requirements may be substantively identical.

Another interstate-compact-created commission within the Marcellus region, the Susquehanna River Basin Commission, regulates only water quantity, not water quality.

State Water Supply Management

Gas producers must arrange to procure the large volumes of water required for hydraulic fracturing in advance of their drilling and development activity. Generally, water rights and water supply regulation differ among the states. Depending on individual state resources and historic development, states may use one of two water rights doctrines, riparian or prior appropriation, or a hybrid of the two. Under the riparian doctrine, a person who owns land that borders a watercourse has the right to make reasonable use of the water on that land.[105] Traditionally, the

---

(...continued)
> and must be consistent with the requirements of the State Environmental Quality Review Act and the state Environmental Conservation Law.

See http://www.dec.ny.gov/energy/46288.html.

[100] W. Va. Code Ann. § 22-11-4(a)(16). See regulations at W. Va. Code of State Rules tit. 47, ser. 10.

[101] W. Va. Code of State Rules tit. 47, ser. 2.

[102] W. Va. Code Ann. § 22-12-5(i).

[103] W. Va. Code Ann. § 22-11-8(b)(7). See regulations at W. Va. Code of State Rules tit. 47, ser. 13.

[104] The compact creating the Delaware River Basin Commission was ratified by Congress: P.L. 87-328, 75 Stat. 688. Section 3.8 of the Compact states: "No project having a substantial effect on the water resources of the basin shall hereafter be undertaken by any person, corporation, or government authority unless it shall have been first submitted to and approved by the commission...." Section 2.3.5 B of the Delaware River Basin Comm'n Administrative Manual (Rules of Practice and Procedure) lists 18 types of projects that must be submitted to the Commission, including withdrawal of groundwater and discharge of pollutants into surface or ground waters of the Basin. Codified at 18 C.F.R. § 401.35(b).

[105] *See generally* A. Dan Tarlock, Law of Water Rights and Resources, ch. 3 "Common Law of Riparian Rights."

---

only limit to users under the riparian system is the requirement of reasonableness in comparison to other users. Under the prior appropriation doctrine, a person who diverts water from a watercourse (regardless of his location relative thereto) and makes reasonable and beneficial use of the water may acquire a right to use of the water.[106] The prior appropriation system limits users to the quantified amount of water the user secured under a state permitting process with a priority based on the date the state conferred the water right. Because of this priority system, the phrase "first in time, first in right" has sometimes substituted for appropriative rights. Some states have implemented a dual system of water rights, assigning rights under both doctrines.

Generally, states east of the Mississippi River follow a riparian doctrine of water rights, while western states follow the appropriation doctrine.[107] The system of water rights allocation in a particular state with shale resources may affect the development process, particularly in times when shortages in water supply affect the area of shale development. In areas where the Marcellus Shale is located, which are generally riparian states, water rights may not be as big a concern as in other areas of the country with shale development, such as the Barnett Shale in Texas. That is, even in times of shortage, shale development may be able to continue in the Marcellus Shale region because riparian users reduce water usage proportionally and may still receive enough for supply requirements of the development process. On the other hand, appropriative rights users in the Barnett Shale region may not be able to fill their water rights at all if other senior rights take all the water, and thus would have to postpone development. In addition, interstate compacts may apply and affect water supply for shale development processes. In the case of Marcellus Shale development, several interstate compacts are relevant, as discussed below.

New York's SPDES permit program (discussed above) governs water quality only, not water quantity. With a limited exception for pumping water on Long Island,[108] there is no proactive regulatory scheme in New York for extracting water from streams, lakes, groundwater, etc. In the case of drawing water from a public drinking water supplier, however, the state does have limited authority to make sure that the public water supplier stays within its permit terms. Otherwise, however, the state can only *respond* to water flow problems—e.g., if a fish kill occurs, it can prosecute the responsible entity for violating the flow standard that is a component of the state's water quality standards.[109] There is no requirement to notify the state in advance of a water extraction.

---

[106] *See generally id.* at ch. 5, "Prior Appropriation Doctrine."

[107] The distinction between these doctrines arises primarily from the historic availability of water geographically. In the generally wetter, eastern riparian states, water users share the water resources because water availability historically did not pose a problem to settlement and development. In the drier, western states that experience regular water shortages, the prior appropriation system provides a definitive hierarchy that allows users to acquire well-defined rights to water as a limited resource that requires planning to avoid scarcity.

[108] N.Y. Code of Rules and Regulations (Conservation) § 602.1.

[109] N.Y. Code of Rules and Regulations (Conservation) § 703.2. For certain classes of water bodies, the flow standard prohibits any "alteration that will impair the waters for their best usages."

Unconventional Gas Shales: Development, Technology, and Policy Issues

West Virginia passed the Water Resources Protection and Management Act in 2003.[110] It requires users of water resources whose withdrawals exceed 750,000 gallons in any given month for one facility to register with the Division of Water and Waste Management in the Department of Environmental Protection.[111] To protect both ground and surface waters, the state proposes to require operators to provide information about the sources of withdrawals, anticipated volumes, and the time of year of withdrawals prior to start-up.[112] State officials believe it is likely that some oil and gas industry operations in the Marcellus Shale region will exceed this threshold and will be required to submit withdrawal information.[113] The goal is to ensure that water withdrawal from ground or surface waters does not exceed volumes beyond what the waters can sustain.[114]

Texas is another relevant example, because of similarities between the Barnett Shale there and the Marcellus Shale. Texas has codified the public trust doctrine regarding ownership of state water resources. That is, water in any of the various waterbodies—including rivers, streams, lakes, etc.—within the state is the property of the state of Texas.[115] Individuals or entities may divert the state's waters for their own use only after acquiring a permit (water right) from the state through its Commission on Environmental Quality.[116] Texas does provide for the possibility of temporary water permits for a period of up to three years, if a temporary permit would not adversely affect senior rights.[117]

Other states apply surface and groundwater regulations similarly, and gas producers using fresh water for drilling and development must comply with state and local administration of water rights.

As for interstate constraints in the Marcellus Shale region and vicinity, the Delaware River Basin Commission[118] and the Susquehanna River Basin Commission[119] impose limits on the quantity of water extracted. In addition, the Great Lakes-St. Lawrence River Basin Water Resources Compact[120] prohibits inter-basin transfers of water.

---

[110] W. Va. Code Ann. § 22-26.

[111] *Id.* at § 22-26-3.

[112] *See id.*

[113] *See* State of West Virginia, Department of Environmental Protection, Office of Oil and Gas, "Industry Guidance, Gas Well Drilling/Completion, Large Water Volume Fracture Treatments (Draft)," March 13, 2009, pp. 1-2, http://www.wvsoro.org/curent_events/marcellus/Marcellus_Guidance_Draft.pdf.

[114] *Id.*

[115] Tex. Water Code § 11.021.

[116] *See* Tex. Water Code § 11.022.

[117] Tex. Water Code § 11.138.

[118] Congress ratified the compact creating the Delaware River Basin Commission in Pub. Law 87-328, 75 Stat. 688.

[119] Congress ratified the compact creating the Susquehanna River Basin Commission in Pub. Law 91-575, 84 Stat. 1509.

[120] For the text of the compact, see http://www.cglg.org/projects/water/docs/12-13-05/Great_Lakes-St_Lawrence_River_Basin_Water_Resources_Compact.pdf. Congress ratified the compact in P.L. 110-342, 122 Stat. 3739.

Congressional Interest

Recently proposed legislation would affect natural gas projects in the Marcellus Shale directly and indirectly. The 111th Congress introduced bills to amend the Safe Drinking Water Act to define hydraulic fracture as underground injection for regulatory purposes. Bills to revise the Commodity Exchange Act would place limits on the use of futures markets to hedge the risks associated with natural gas development projects. The recently enacted mandate to increase the use of renewable fuels (ethanol) has an indirect link, as fertilizer produced from natural gas is essential to producing corn — the primary feedstock for ethanol. Recently proposed low-carbon fuel standards may overlook natural gas as a substitute transportation fuel.

Current and planned projects to develop Marcellus Shale gas are apparent across the six-state region that overlies the resource (see **Figure 5**). For example, gas producers have reportedly planned over 2,000 gas wells just in West Virginia, and the state's Oil and Gas Commission estimates that, based on current information, there could be a well on every 40 acres in the state. Throughout the region, this activity is likely to put increasing demands on regulatory agencies— especially state agencies[121]—for necessary licensing, permitting, inspections, and enforcement. As noted by USGS, because of questions related to water supply and wastewater disposal, many state agencies have been cautious about granting permits, and some states have placed *de facto* moratoria on drilling until these issues are resolved.[122] New York, for example, is accepting but not processing permits until it completes a Supplemental Generic Environmental Impact Statement that will impose new environmental review requirements for permits for gas well development using high-volume hydraulic fracturing. The success of planned development activities could depend, in part, on the capacity of regulatory agencies to provide the administrative resources that supporting such plans would require.

The Energy Policy Act of 2005 (P.L. 109-58) in Section 322 (Hydraulic Fracturing) amended the Safe Drinking Water Act (42 U.S.C. 300h(d)(1)) to exclude the fluids or propping agents (other than diesel fuels) used in hydraulic fracturing operations related to oil, gas, or geothermal production activities from the definition of the term "underground injection." Several pending bills address the current exemption of hydraulic fracturing under SDWA:

- H.R. 2300 (introduced May 7, 2009, as the American Energy Innovation Act) would express the sense of Congress that the Safe Drinking Water Act was never intended to regulate natural gas and oil well construction stimulation and that the amendment of SDWA by the Energy Policy Act of 2005 to clarify that the SDWA was not intended to regulate the use of hydraulic fracturing should be maintained.

- H.R. 2766/S. 1215 (introduced June 9, 2009, as the "Fracturing Responsibility and Awareness of Chemicals Act") would amend the SDWA definition of 'underground injection' to include the underground injection of fluids or

---

[121] As discussed above, states have primary responsibility for many regulatory programs, several interstate commissions also are involved, as are federal agencies such as EPA that implements the UIC program and issues UIC permits in New York and Pennsylvania.

[122] USGS Fact Sheet at 5.

propping agents used for hydraulic fracturing operations related to oil and gas production activities. The bills would require public disclosure of the chemical constituents (but not the proprietary chemical formulas) used in the fracturing process. Disclosure of a propriety formula to the state, EPA Administrator, or treating physician or nurse would be required in the case of a medical emergency.

- The conference report for the Department of the Interior, Environment, and Related Agencies Appropriations Act, 2010 (H.R. 2996, H.Rept. 111-216) includes a provision urging the EPA, in consultation with appropriate federal, state and interstate agencies, to carry out a study on the relationship between hydraulic fracturing and drinking water.

Many industries make use of various "hedging" strategies to minimize the risk of commodity price increases. A simple hedge involves buying "futures" contracts to lock in prices. For gas exploration and development companies, hedges in effect guarantee the amount of revenue that companies will receive on a future production, thus giving them some financial stability. Two current proposed bills would limit speculation on future commodity prices. Some would argue, however, that in a time of low natural gas prices and scarce capital for financing new energy projects, restrictions on hedging could adversely these companies.

- H.R. 977 (introduced February 11, 2009, as the "Derivatives Markets Transparency and Accountability Act of 2009") would amend the Commodity Exchange Act to bring greater transparency and accountability to commodity markets. The Commodity Futures Trading Commission would establish limits on the amount of positions that a person may hold for future delivery contracts, options on such contracts or on commodities traded.

- S. 447 (introduced February 13, 2009, as the "Prevent Excessive Speculation Act") would amend the Commodity Exchange Act to prevent excessive price speculation with respect to energy commodities.

Congressional concern for energy independence that grew out of the summer 2008 oil price spikes has engendered at least one highly publicized proposal to substitute natural gas for transportation fuel.[123] Among various bills introduced to reduce consumer dependence on fossil fuels, some would establish low-carbon fuel standards. Natural gas (CH_4) has a carbon to hydrogen ratio of 1:4, the lowest of all the fossil fuels, thus leading some to argue that it has a role in newly proposed standards.

- H.R. 1787 (introduced March 30, 2009, and cited as the "Low Carbon Fuel Standard of 2009") would amend the Clean Air Act to establish a low carbon fuel standard for transportation fuels. Based on a lifecycle greenhouse gas emission baseline established for all transportation fuels, transportation fuel providers would have to reduce the annual emissions per unit of energy by 5% after 2023, and 10% after 2030.

- S. 1095 (introduced May 20, 2009, and cited as "America's Low-Carbon Fuel Standard Act of 2009") would amend the Clean Air Act to convert renewable fuel standards into low-carbon fuel standards. Low-carbon fuel would be defined

---

[123] See PickensPlan, http://www.pickensplan.com/act/.

as a transportation fuel that has lifecycle greenhouse gas emissions, equal on an annual average basis to a defined percentage less than baseline lifecycle greenhouse gas emissions. Starting at 20% in 2015, the percentage would increase to 42.5% after 2031. Regulations would insure that increasing volumes of low-carbon fuel would be sold in the United States as transportation fuel; beginning with 10% in 2015, and 32.5% by 2030.

U.S. fertilizer production has a close link to energy availability, particularly natural gas.[124] Natural gas is the key ingredient in producing anhydrous ammonia, used directly as a nitrogen fertilizer, and used as a basic building block for producing most other forms of nitrogen fertilizers (e.g., urea, ammonium nitrate, and nitrogen solutions). Natural gas also serves as a process gas in the manufacture of other nitrogenous fertilizers from anhydrous ammonia. As a result, natural gas accounts for 75% to 90% of costs of production for nitrogen fertilizers. Because fertilizer prices are closely linked to natural gas prices, higher gas prices encourage two potential responses: (1) lower fertilizer application rates on the current farm planting mix; or (2) the planting and production of crops that are less dependent on fertilizer. Among major U.S. field crops, corn uses the most fertilizer according to the U.S. Department of Agriculture's Economic Research Service.[125] Thus, ethanol production costs and thus renewable energy costs are likely to reflect natural gas availability and price. Under the Energy Independence and Security Act of 2007 (P.L. 110-140), gasoline sold in the United States must contain a minimum volume of renewable fuel. The Renewable Fuel Standard program that results from this requirement will increase the required volume of renewable fuel blended into gasoline from 9 billion gallons in 2008 to 36 billion gallons by 2022.

For Further Reading

For further reading on natural gas issues, refer to the following CRS reports:

- CRS Report R40872, *U.S. Fossil Fuel Resources: Terminology, Reporting, and Summary*, by Gene Whitney, Carl E. Behrens, and Carol Glover.

- CRS Report R40487, *Natural Gas Markets: An Overview of 2008*, by Robert Pirog.

- CRS Report R40645, *U.S. Offshore Oil and Gas Resources: Prospects and Processes*, by Marc Humphries, Robert Pirog, and Gene Whitney.

- CRS Report RL34741, *Drilling in the Great Lakes: Background and Issues*, coordinated by Pervaze A. Sheikh.

---

[124] For further information refer to CRS Report RL32677, *Energy Use in Agriculture: Background and Issues*, by Randy Schnepf.

[125] Wen-yuan Huang, William McBride, and Utpal Vasavada, *Recent Volatility in U.S. Fertilizer Prices*, USDA Economic Research Service, March 2009, http://www.ers.usda.gov/AmberWaves/March09/Features/FertilizerPrices.htm.

Appendix. Glossary

Bcf: Billion Cubic Feet; a gas measurement equal to 1,000,000,000 cubic feet. See also Mcf, Tcf, Quad.

Btu: British thermal unit; the amount of energy required to heat one pound of water by one degree Fahrenheit.

Frac: Hydraulic fracturing, as adopted by the petroleum industry.

Flowback: The fracture fluids that return to surface after a hydraulic fracture is completed.

Mcf: A natural gas measurement unit for one thousand cubic feet.

MMcf: A natural gas measurement unit for one million cubic feet.

NORM: Natural occurring radioactive material; includes naturally occurring uranium-235 and daughter products such as radium and radon.

Oil-equivalent gas (OEG): The volume of natural gas needed to generate the equivalent amount of heat as a barrel of crude oil. Approximately 6,000 cubic feet of natural gas is equivalent to one barrel of crude oil.

Slickwater: Water-based frac fluid.

Tcf: A natural gas measurement unit for one trillion cubic feet.

Thixotropy: The property of a gel to become fluid when disturbed (as by shaking).

Whipstock: A wedge-shaped piece of metal placed downhole to deflect the drill bit.

Author Contact Information

Anthony Andrews, Coordinator
Specialist in Energy and Energy Infrastructure
Policy
aandrews@crs.loc.gov, 7-6843

Peter Folger
Specialist in Energy and Natural Resources Policy
pfolger@crs.loc.gov, 7-1517

Marc Humphries
Analyst in Energy Policy
mhumphries@crs.loc.gov, 7-7264

Claudia Copeland
Specialist in Resources and Environmental Policy
ccopeland@crs.loc.gov, 7-7227

Mary Tiemann
Specialist in Environmental Policy
mtiemann@crs.loc.gov, 7-5937

Robert Meltz
Legislative Attorney
rmeltz@crs.loc.gov, 7-7891

Cynthia Brougher
Legislative Attorney
cbrougher@crs.loc.gov, 7-9121

Acknowledgments

Cynthia Brougher, Legislative Attorney

Congressional
Research
Service

Gas Hydrates: Resource and Hazard

Peter Folger
Specialist in Energy and Natural Resources Policy

January 23, 2010

Congressional Research Service

7-5700

www.crs.gov

RS22990

CRS Report for Congress

Prepared for Members and Committees of Congress

Summary

Solid gas hydrates are a potentially huge resource of natural gas for the United States. The U.S. Geological Survey estimated that there are about 85 trillion cubic feet (TCF) of technically recoverable gas hydrates in northern Alaska. The Minerals Management Service estimated a mean value of 21,000 TCF of in-place gas hydrates in the Gulf of Mexico. By comparison, total U.S. natural gas consumption is about 23 TCF annually. The in-place estimate disregards technical or economical recoverability, and likely overestimates the amount of commercially viable gas hydrates. Even if a fraction of the U.S. gas hydrates can be economically produced, however, it could add substantially to the 1,300 TCF of technically recoverable U.S. conventional natural gas reserves. To date, however, gas hydrates have no confirmed commercial production.

Gas hydrates are both a potential resource and a risk, representing a significant hazard to conventional oil and gas drilling and production operations. If the solid gas hydrates dissociate suddenly and release expanded gas during offshore drilling, they could disrupt the marine sediments and compromise pipelines and production equipment on the seafloor. The tendency of gas hydrates to dissociate and release methane, which can be a hazard, is the same characteristic that research and development efforts strive to enhance so that methane can be produced and recovered in commercial quantities.

Developing gas hydrates into a commercially viable source of energy is a goal of the U.S. Department of Energy (DOE) methane hydrate program, initially authorized by the Methane Hydrate Research and Development Act of 2000 (P.L. 106-193). The Energy Policy Act of 2005 (P.L. 109-58, Subtitle F, § 968) extended the authorization through FY2010 and authorized total appropriations of $155 million over a five-year period. Congress appropriated $15 million for the gas hydrate research and development (R&D) program in FY2009. The Obama Administration requested $25 million for the natural gas technologies program for FY2010, which includes gas hydrate R&D. Congress appropriated $17.8 million for the program in FY2010, which would also fund research and development into unconventional gas production from basins containing tight gas sands, shale gas, and coal bed methane, as well as for gas hydrates.

Contents

Figures

Contacts

G as hydrates occur naturally onshore in permafrost, and at or below the seafloor in sediments where water and gas combine at low temperatures and high pressures to form an ice-like solid substance.[1] Methane, or natural gas, is typically the dominant gas in the hydrate structure. In a gas hydrate, frozen water molecules form a cage-like structure around high concentrations of natural gas. The gas hydrate structure is very compact. When heated and depressurized to temperatures and pressures typically found on the Earth's surface (one atmosphere of pressure and 70° Fahrenheit), its volume expands by 150 to 170 times. Thus, one cubic foot of solid gas hydrate found underground in permafrost or beneath the seafloor would produce between 150 to 170 cubic feet of natural gas when brought to the surface.

Gas hydrates are a potentially huge global energy resource. The United States and other countries with territory in the Arctic or with offshore gas hydrates along their continental margins are interested in developing the resource. Countries currently pursuing national research and development programs include Japan, India, Korea, and China, among others. Although burning natural gas produces carbon dioxide (CO_2), a greenhouse gas, the amount of CO_2 liberated per unit of energy produced is less than 60% of the CO_2 produced from burning coal.[2] In addition, the United States imports 20% of its natural gas consumed each year.[3] Increasing the U.S. supply of natural gas from gas hydrates would decrease the nation's reliance on imported gas and reduce U.S. emissions of CO_2 if domestically produced gas hydrates substitute for coal as an energy source.

Gas Hydrate Resources

There are several challenges to commercially exploiting gas hydrates. How much and where gas hydrate occurs in commercially viable concentrations are not well known, and how the resource can be extracted safely and economically is a current research focus. Estimates of global gas hydrate resources, which range from at least 100,000 TCF to possibly much more, may greatly overestimate how much gas can be extracted economically. Reports of vast gas hydrate resources can be misleading unless those estimates are qualified by the use of such terms such as *in-place* resources, technically recoverable resources, and proved reserves:

- The term in-place is used to describe an estimate of gas hydrate resources without regard for technical or economical recoverability. Generally these are the largest estimates.

- Undiscovered technically recoverable resources are producible using current technology, but this does not take into account economic viability.

- Proved reserves are estimated quantities that can be recovered under existing economic and operating conditions.

---

[1] The terms *methane hydrate* and *gas hydrate* are often used interchangeably, and refer to the methane-water crystalline structure called a clathrate.

[2] U.S. Department of Energy, Energy Information Agency (EIA), at http://www.eia.doe.gov/cneaf/coal/quarterly/co2_article/co2.html.

[3] In 2007, the United States consumed approximately 23 TCF of natural gas, of which 4.6 TCF were imported. See EIA at http://tonto.eia.doe.gov/dnav/ng/ng_sum_lsum_dcu_nus_a.htm.

For example, the U.S. Department of Energy's Energy Information Agency (EIA) estimates that total undiscovered technically recoverable conventional natural gas resources in the United States are approximately 1,300 TCF, but proved reserves are only 200 TCF.[4] This is an important distinction because there are no proved reserves for gas hydrates at this time. Gas hydrates have no confirmed past or current commercial production.

Until recently, the Department of the Interior's U.S. Geological Survey (USGS) and Minerals Management Service (MMS) have reported only in-place estimates of U.S. gas hydrate resources. However, a November 12, 2008, USGS estimate of undiscovered technically recoverable gas hydrates in northern Alaska probably represents the most robust effort to identify gas hydrates that may be commercially viable sources of energy.[5] Despite a lack of a production history, the USGS report cites a growing body of evidence indicating that some gas hydrate resources, such as those in northern Alaska, might be produced with existing technology despite only limited field testing.

Gas Hydrates on the North Slope, Alaska

The USGS assessment indicates that the North Slope of Alaska may host about 85 TCF of undiscovered technically recoverable gas hydrate resources. According to the report, technically recoverable gas hydrate resources could range from a low of 25 TCF to as much as 158 TCF on the North Slope. Total U.S. consumption of natural gas in 2007 was slightly more than 23 TCF.

Of the mean estimate of 85 TCF of technically recoverable gas hydrates on the North Slope, 56% is located on federally managed lands, 39% on lands and offshore waters managed by the State of Alaska, and the remainder on Native lands.[6] The total area comprised by the USGS assessment is 55,894 square miles, and extends from the National Petroleum Reserve in the west to the Arctic National Wildlife Refuge (ANWR) in the east (**Figure 1**). The area extends north from the Brooks Range to the state-federal offshore boundary three miles north of the Alaska coastline. Gas hydrates might also be found outside the assessment area; the USGS reports that the gas hydrate stability zone—where favorable conditions of temperature and pressure coexist for gas hydrate formation—extends beyond the study boundaries into federal waters beyond the three-mile boundary (**Figure 1**).

---

[4] These estimates are as of 2006. Global proved reserves of conventional natural gas are over 6,185 TCF. See EIA at http://www.eia.doe.gov/emeu/aer/pdf/pages/sec4_3.pdf and http://www.eia.doe.gov/emeu/international/reserves.html.

[5] USGS Fact Sheet 2008-3073, Assessment of Gas Hydrate Resources on the North Slope, Alaska, 2008, at http://pubs.usgs.gov/fs/2008/3073/.

[6] USGS presentation, Timothy S. Collett, October 2008, at http://energy.usgs.gov/flash/AlaskaGHAssessment_slideshow.swf.

Figure 1. Gas Hydrate Assessment Area, North Slope, Alaska

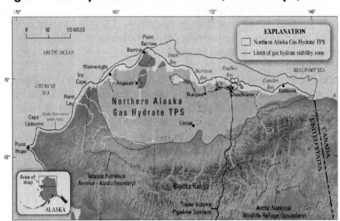

Source: USGS Fact Sheet 2008-3073, Assessment of Gas Hydrate Resources on the North Slope, Alaska, 2008, at http://pubs.usgs.gov/fs/2008/3073/.

Note: TPS refers to total petroleum system, which refers to geologic elements that control petroleum generation, migration, and entrapment.

Gas Hydrates in the Gulf of Mexico

On February 1, 2008, the MMS released an assessment of gas hydrate resources for the Gulf of Mexico.[7] The report gives a statistical probability of the volume of undiscovered *in-place* gas hydrate resources, with a mean estimate of over 21,000 TCF. The MMS report estimates how much gas hydrate may occur in sandstone and shale reservoirs, using a combination of data and modeling, but does not indicate how much is recoverable with current technology. The report notes that porous and permeable sandstone reservoirs have the greatest potential for actually producing gas from hydrates, and gives a mean estimate of over 6,700 TCF of sandstone-hosted gas hydrates, about 30% of the total mean estimate for the Gulf of Mexico.[8] Even for sandstone reservoirs, however, the in-place estimates for gas hydrates in the Gulf of Mexico likely far exceed what may be commercially recoverable with current technology. The MMS is planning similar in-place gas hydrate assessments for other portions of the U.S. Outer Continental Shelf (OCS), including Alaska.

Gas Hydrates Along Continental Margins

Globally, the amount of gas hydrate to be found offshore along continental margins probably exceeds the amount found onshore in permafrost regions by two orders of magnitude, according to one estimate.[9] With the exception of the assessments discussed above, none of the global gas

---

[7] U.S. Department of the Interior, Minerals Management Service, Resource Evaluation Division, "Preliminary evaluation of in-place gas hydrate resources: Gulf of Mexico outer continental shelf," OCS Report MMS 2008-004 (Feb. 1, 2008), at http://www.mms.gov/revaldiv/GasHydrateFiles/MMS2008-004.pdf.

[8] Ibid., table 16.

[9] George J. Moridis et al., "Toward production from gas hydrates: current status, assessment of resources, and simulation-based evaluation of technology and potential," 2008 SPE Unconventional Reservoirs Conference, Keystone, (continued...)

---

hydrate estimates is well defined, and all are speculative to some extent.[10] One way to depict the potential size and producibility of global gas hydrate resources is by using a resource pyramid (**Figure 2**).[11] The apex of the pyramid shows the smallest but most promising gas hydrate reservoir—arctic and marine sandstones—which may host tens to hundreds of TCF. The bottom of the pyramid shows the largest but most technically challenging reservoir—marine shales.

Figure 2. Gas Hydrate Reservoir Pyramid

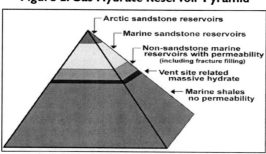

Source: Roy Boswell and Timothy S. Collett, "The Gas Hydrate Resource Pyramid," Fire in the Ice, Methane Hydrate R&D Program Newsletter, Fall 2006.

Sandstones are considered superior reservoirs because they have much higher permeability—they allow more gas to flow—than shales, which can be nearly impermeable. The marine shale gas hydrate reservoir may host hundreds of thousands of TCF, but most or all of that resource may never be economically recoverable. It is likely that continued research and development efforts in the United States and other countries will focus on producing gas hydrates from arctic and marine sandstone reservoirs.

Gas Hydrate Hazards

Gas hydrates are a significant hazard for drilling and production operations.[12] Gas hydrate production is hazardous in itself, as well as for conventional oil and gas activities that place wells and pipelines into permafrost or marine sediments. For activities in permafrost, two general categories of problems have been identified: (1) uncontrolled gas releases during drilling; and (2) damage to well casing during and after installation of a well. Similar problems could occur during offshore drilling into gas hydrate-bearing marine sediments. Offshore drilling operations that disturb gas hydrate-bearing sediments could fracture or disrupt the bottom sediments and

---

(...continued)

CO, February 10, 2008, p. 3, at http://www.netl.doe.gov/technologies/oil-gas/publications/Hydrates/reports/G308_SPE114163_Feb08.pdf.

[10] Ibid.

[11] Roy Boswell and Timothy S. Collett, "The Gas Hydrate Resource Pyramid," Fire in the Ice, Methane Hydrate R&D Program Newsletter, Fall 2006, pp. 5-7, at http://www.netl.doe.gov/technologies/oil-gas/FutureSupply/MethaneHydrates/newsletter/newsletter.htm.

[12] Timothy S. Collett and Scott R. Dallimore, "Detailed analysis of gas hydrate induced drilling and production hazards," Proceedings of the Fourth International Conference on Gas Hydrates, Yokohama, Japan, April 19-23, 2002.

compromise the wellbore, pipelines, rig supports, and other equipment involved in oil and gas production from the seafloor.[13]

Problems may differ somewhat between onshore and offshore operations, but they stem from the same characteristic of gas hydrates: decreases in pressure and/or increases in temperature can cause the gas hydrate to dissociate and rapidly release large amounts of gas into the well bore during a drilling operation.

Oil and gas wells drilled through permafrost or offshore to reach conventional oil and gas deposits may encounter gas hydrates, which companies generally try to avoid because of a lack of detailed understanding of the mechanical and thermal properties of gas hydrate-bearing sediments.[14] However, to mitigate the potential hazard in these instances, the wells are cased— typically using a steel pipe that lines the wall of the borehole—to separate and protect the well from the gas hydrates in the shallower zones as drilling continues deeper. Unless precautions are taken, continued drilling may heat up the sediments surrounding the wellbore, causing gas from the dissociated hydrates to leak and bubble up around the casing. Once oil production begins, hot fluids flowing through the well could also warm hydrate-bearing sediments and cause dissociation. The released gas may pool and build up pressure against the well casing, possibly causing damage.[15] Some observers suggest that exploiting the gas hydrate resources by intentionally heating or by depressurization poses the same risks—requiring mitigation—as drilling through gas hydrates to reach deeper conventional oil and gas deposits.[16]

Gas Hydrate Research and Development

A goal of the DOE methane hydrate research and development (R&D) program is to develop knowledge and technology to allow commercial production of methane from gas hydrates by 2015.[17] Since the Methane Hydrate Research and Development Act of 2000 (P.L. 106-193) was enacted, DOE has spent $102.3 million through FY2009, or approximately 67% of the $152.5 million authorized by law. The Omnibus Appropriations Act, 2009 (P.L. 111-8), provided $20 million in FY2009 for natural gas technologies R&D, which included $15 million for gas hydrates R&D. The Obama Administration requested $25 million for the natural gas technologies program in FY2010, or half of the $50 million authorized for methane hydrates R&D by the Energy Policy Act of 2005 (P.L. 109-58). Congress appropriated $17.8 million for natural gas technologies in FY2010, giving DOE direction to fund research into unconventional gas production from basins containing tight gas sands, shale gas, and coal bed methane, as well as for gas hydrates.[18] The gas hydrate R&D program is authorized through FY2010 under current law.

---

[13] George J. Moridis and Michael B. Kowalsky, "Geomechanical implications of thermal stresses on hydrate-bearing sediments," Fire in the Ice, Methane Hydrate R&D Program Newsletter, Winter 2006.

[14] Moridis and Kowalski (2006).

[15] Collett and Dallimore (2002).

[16] Personal communication, Ray Boswell, Manager, Methane Hydrate R&D Programs, DOE National Energy Technology Laboratory, Morgantown, WV, Nov. 5, 2008.

[17] DOE methane hydrate R&D program, at http://www.netl.doe.gov/technologies/oil-gas/FutureSupply/ MethaneHydrates/rd-program/rd-program.htm.

[18] See H.Rept. 111-278.

The DOE program completed a Gulf of Mexico offshore expedition in May 2009 and an Alaska production test in the summer of 2009. The Gulf of Mexico program was aimed at validating techniques for locating and assessing commercially viable gas hydrate deposits.[19] In Alaska, a two-year production test is expected to provide critical information about methane flow rates and sediment stability during gas hydrate dissociation.[20] Results from the two-year test in Alaska may be crucial to companies interested in producing gas hydrates commercially. Both projects have international and industry partners.

Researchers identify a need to better understand how geology in the permafrost regions and on continental margins controls the occurrence and formation of methane hydrates.[21] They underscore the need to understand fundamental aspects—porosity, permeability, reservoir temperatures—of the geologic framework that hosts the gas hydrate resource to improve assessment and exploration, to mitigate the hazard, and to enhance gas recovery.

Together with advances in R&D, economic viability will depend on the relative cost of conventional fuels, as well as other factors such as pipelines and other infrastructure needed to deliver gas hydrate methane to market. Additionally, price volatility will likely affect the level of private sector investment in commercial production of gas hydrates.

Author Contact Information

Peter Folger
Specialist in Energy and Natural Resources Policy
pfolger@crs.loc.gov, 7-1517

---

[19] See DOE, National Energy Technology Laboratory, "Fire in the Ice," Summer 2009, at http://www.netl.doe.gov/technologies/oil-gas/publications/Hydrates/Newsletter/MHNewsSummer09.pdf.

[20] See http://www.netl.doe.gov/technologies/oil-gas/FutureSupply/MethaneHydrates/projects/DOEProjects/Alaska-41332.html.

[21] Collett and Dallimore (2002); Moridis and Kowalski (2006).

Order Code RL34133

CRS Report for Congress

Fischer-Tropsch Fuels from Coal, Natural Gas, and Biomass: Background and Policy

Updated March 27, 2008

Anthony Andrews
Specialist in Energy and Energy Infrastructure Policy
Resources, Science, and Industry Division

Jeffrey Logan
Specialist in Energy Policy
Resources, Science, and Industry Division

Prepared for Members and Committees of Congress

Congressional
Research
Service

Fischer-Tropsch Fuels from Coal, Natural Gas, and Biomass: Background and Policy

Summary

As the price of crude oil sets a record high, liquid transportation fuels synthesized from coal, natural gas, and biomass are proposed as one solution to reducing dependency on imported petroleum and strained refinery capacity. The technology to do so developed from processes that directly and indirectly convert coal into liquid fuel. Congress now faces decisions on whether, and to what extent, it should support such a solution.

Lacking domestic petroleum resources, but abundant in coal, Germany built synthetic fuel plants during World War II that employed the Bergius coal hydrogenation process (direct liquefaction), and Fischer-Tropsch synthesis (indirect). The United States attempted to capitalize on the German experience after World War II. Despite considerable investment in synthetic fuel research and development, the United States cut support for commercialization when crude oil prices dropped and supplies stabilized in the mid-1980s. Since then, several synthetic fuels plants have been constructed around the world that convert coal, natural gas, or biomass to liquid fuels using the Fischer-Tropsch process. Several private ventures in the United States are now studying the feasibility of constructing Fischer-Tropsch synthetic fuel plants based on coal, natural gas, and biomass.

Proposals to expand the use of coal to synthesize transportation fuels have generated much opposition, particularly because the carbon dioxide (CO_2) produced in the Fischer-Tropsch process is a greenhouse gas associated with global warming. Also, opponents claim that coal-based synthesis, in particular, is inefficient and thus prohibitively expensive. Proponents counter that Fischer-Tropsch technology provides a means of capturing carbon dioxide for geological sequestration (though a promising solution, sequestration remains unproven on an industrial scale) and that it appears economically viable in a sustained crude oil price range above $40 to $45 per barrel.

Fischer-Tropsch synthesis is well suited to producing middle-distillate range fuels like diesel and jet. The diesel produced is superior to conventionally refined diesel in terms of higher cetane-number and low sulfur content. Overall, ~~middle~~ distillate fuels represent roughly a quarter of U.S. refinery production, which is primarily driven by the demand for gasoline. In order for a synthetic fuels industry (whether coal, natural gas, or biomass based) to begin rivaling or even supplanting conventional petroleum refining, a major shift in transportation mode toward diesel engine light-passenger vehicles would have to occur. Coal-to-liquids would also compete for the same resources needed for electric power generation, and the rail capacity currently supporting their demand.

Recent energy legislation promotes research on capturing and storing greenhouse gas emissions and improving vehicle fuel efficiency, among other goals. Fisher-Tropsch fuels present the paradox of high carbon emissions associated with production versus lower carbon emissions associated with their use.

Contents

List of Figures

List of Tables

Fischer-Tropsch Fuels from Coal, Natural Gas, and Biomass: Background and Policy

Introduction

Record high crude oil and diesel fuel prices, as well as strained refining capacity, continue to stimulate congressional and private sector interest in producing synthetic fuels from alternative resources. Current conditions almost reprise the era of the 1970s, when energy security concerns generated by oil embargoes stimulated federal spending in synthetic fuels. Despite considerable investment, federal support was withdrawn after supply concerns eased in the 1980s. The currently favored approach to producing synthetic fuels — the Fischer-Tropsch process — uses carbon monoxide and hydrogen from combustion of fossil or organically derived feedstocks. The process and has been commercially demonstrated internationally and in pilot plant demonstration in the United States. Jet fuel from a gas-to-liquids pilot plant has already been certified for use by the United States Air Force, at least one coal-to-liquids enterprise is in the planning phase, and others are being studied.

As an abundant resource in the United States, coal has long been exploited as a solid fossil fuel. As oil and natural gas supplanted coal throughout the last two centuries, technologies developed to convert coal into other fuels. Proponents of expanding the use of coal, such as the Coal-to-Liquids Coalition, argue that the United States should alleviate its dependence on imported petroleum and strained refinery capacity by converting coal to transportation fuels. Opponents, such as the Natural Resource Defense Council, argue that "considerable economic, social, and environmental drawbacks of coal-derived oil preclude it from being a sound option to move America beyond oil."[1]

Fischer-Tropsch synthesis, particularly coal based, poses several challenges. It is criticized as inefficient and thus costly. The byproduct of synthesis is carbon dioxide, a greenhouse gas associated with global warming. The use of coal and natural gas as feedstocks would compete with electric power generation — over 50% of domestic electricity generation is coal based — and gas is widely used as fuel for peak generating plants and domestic heating. The fuels produced, primarily diesel and jet, would not substitute widely for the preferred transportation fuel in the United States — gasoline. Similarly, using biomass as feedstock would compete with cellulosic ethanol production, as it is now envisioned.

Some of Fischer-Tropsch technology's comparative merits and drawbacks are presented in **Table 1**.

---

[1] NRDC, *Why Liquid Coal Is Not a Viable Option to Move America Beyond Oil*, February 2007 [http://www.nrdc.org/globalwarming/solutions].

CRS-2

Table 1. Comparative Merits and Drawbacks of Fischer-Tropsch

Abundant coal reserves available as feedstock.	↔	Competition for coal in electric power generation.
Coal-to-liquids generates significant CO_2.	↔	CO_2 separation during synthesis gas production makes capture feasible.
Produces ultra-low sulfur, high cetane diesel.	↔	Produces low-octane gasoline.
Low efficiency in converting coal to liquid.	↔	Waste heat available for electricity co-generation.
May have lower operating expenses than direct coal liquefaction.	↔	Conceptually more complex than direct liquefaction approach and higher in capital investment cost.
Deep geologic sequestration offers solution for CO_2 emissions.	↔	CO_2 sequestration not yet demonstrated on a large industrial scale.
Gas-to-liquids offers reduced CO_2 generation.	↔	Competition with domestic natural gas use.
Biomass-to-liquids offers zero carbon footprint.	↔	Competition with biomass for cellulosic ethanol production.

This report begins with a review of the synthetic fuels technology, which evolved from direct and indirect conversion of coal to liquid fuels. Attention is given to Fischer-Tropsch synthesis, as this represents the currently favored and commercially demonstrated technology. Past and currently operating synthetic fuel plants are described with comparisons of their relative efficiency. Finally, policy history and policy considerations are presented, along with bills recently introduced in Congress pertaining to coal-to-liquids research and industrial development.

Synthetic Fuel Technology

Synthetic fuels can be traced to the mid-19th century processes of making coal oil, coal gas, and the later manufacture of town gas. Coal oil was introduced as a substitute for more costly illuminating fuels, particularly premium whale oil. Originally sold under the trade name of kerosene, coal oil was in turn replaced by a similarly named, but cleaner burning, crude oil distillate. Coal gas also served as an early illuminating fuel, but burned with a yellow flame of poor quality. A process for improving coal gas was devised by passing it over a water bath. This was improved on further by passing steam through incandescent beds of charred coal (coke) to produce "water gas," a mixture of carbon monoxide (CO) and hydrogen (H_2) gases. Water gas, more commonly known as "town gas," produced a hotter, cleaner burning blue flame than coal gas. Town gas illumination eventually gave way to electric lighting, but it continued as an industrial heating fuel into the 1950s, when natural gas became more widely available.

CRS-3

Petroleum was considered a scarce commodity in the early 20th century, more suited to making illuminating fuel. Gasoline was considered too volatile a petroleum distillate and did not find widespread use until transportation modes shifted from horse and buggy to the automobile. With the growth of the automobile and aircraft industries, the demand for gasoline and thus petroleum increased. In Germany, researchers looked to coal for a petroleum substitute. The carbon monoxide and hydrogen produced in manufacturing town gas provided an essential first step in synthesizing liquid fuel from coal. The two processes developed, direct and indirect coal-to-liquids conversion, provided complementary means of producing a range of fuels and chemicals. Each offered advantages and disadvantages.

Bergius Direct Liquefaction

In the early 20th century, German researcher Friedrich Bergius developed a process to directly liquefy coal under high temperature and pressure (coal begins to dissolve above 250 degrees centigrade), and then "crack" the coal molecules into smaller molecules using hydrogen.[2] Bergius termed the process "coal hydrogenation," which was later referred to as "direct liquefaction." Coal also served as the source of hydrogen. (In modern refining, hydrogen is manufactured from methane gas (CH_4) decomposed by a process termed "steam reforming." Modern refineries rely extensively on hydrogen for hydrocracking and hydrotreating.)

Fischer-Tropsch Synthesis

As Bergius was perfecting direct liquefaction, German scientists Franz Fischer and Hans Tropsch were developing a means of indirectly converting coal into a liquid fuel. In 1926, Fischer and Tropsch reported a process to synthesize hydrocarbons using an iron or cobalt catalyst to react hydrogen (H_2) with carbon monoxide (CO) under lower temperatures and pressures than Bergius' process.

Essentially, Fischer-Tropsch (F-T) synthesizes straight molecular chains of carbon and hydrogen, whereas Bergius breaks heavier-weight hydrocarbons into lighter-weight, shorter-length molecules. Both processes involve hydrogen. Fischer-Tropsch synthesis, however, relies on carbon monoxide's potential for exchanging oxygen with hydrogen in the presence of a catalyst. As in the manufacture of water gas, coal is burned to produce the carbon monoxide and steam reacting with hot coal disassociates to produce hydrogen, as shown in the following "water gas shift" equations:[3]

$$C + H_2O \rightarrow CO + H_2 \text{ and } CO + H_2O \rightarrow CO_2 + H_2$$

The CO_2 byproduct of these reactions can be scrubbed from the "syngas" stream before it is introduced to the synthesis reactor. This provides the opportunity to capture CO_2 for sequestration as discussed below.

---

[2] A.C. Feldner, Department of Commerce Bureau of Mines, *Recent Developments in the Production of Motor Fuel from Coal*, Information Circular No. 6075, 1928.

[3] Robert Bernard Anderson, *Fischer-Tropsch Synthesis*, Academic Press Inc., 1984.

CRS-4

In the following simplification, Fischer-Tropsch synthesis occurs through two simultaneous reactions promoted by the contact of CO and H_2 with a catalyst:

$$2H_2 + CO \rightarrow -CH_2- + H_2O \text{ and } CO + H_2O \rightarrow CO_2 + H_2$$

which can be simplified as:

$$2CO + H_2 \rightarrow -CH_2- + CO_2.$$

As shown conceptually in **Figure 1**, CO and H_2 (syngas) react on the catalyst surface to form $-CH_2-$ that links up to build longer-chain hydrocarbons. As discussed later, these hydrocarbons substitute for conventional middle-distillate fuels.

Figure 1. Fischer-Tropsch Synthesis

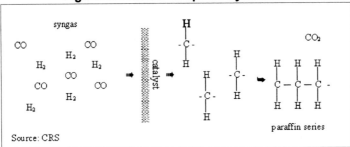

Source: CRS

A conceptual Fischer-Tropsch plant is shown in **Figure 2**. The slate of products synthesized can be adjusted by varying the temperature, pressure, and duration of reaction. F-T synthesis ideally produces straight-chain hydrocarbons in the paraffin series (also referred to as alkanes).

Figure 2. Conceptual Fischer-Tropsch Plant

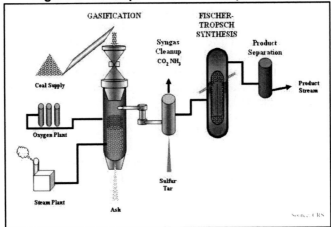

Paraffins are characterized as having carbon atoms attached by single bonds, and remaining bonds saturated with hydrogen. The paraffin series ranges from the

294 703-739-3790 TCNNaturalGas.com

CRS-5

methane (CH_4 — the principle component of natural gas) through the gasoline boiling range of C5-C10, the middle-distillate range fuels of C11-C18 (kerosene, jet, and diesel), and longer chain waxes.[4]

Comparing Fischer-Tropsch Products to Conventional Petroleum Distillates

Conventionally refined gasoline, diesel, and jet fuels are complex mixtures of hydrocarbons that include paraffins, naphthenes, and aromatics (which give diesel fuel its unique odor).[5] F-T synthesized fuels, by comparison, are composed primarily of paraffins.

Refining begins in the atmospheric distillation tower, where the "straight-run" petroleum fractions in the boiling ranges of gasoline, naphtha, kerosene, diesel and jet fuel condense and separate. Heavier fractions are cracked with catalysts and hydrogen to produce more gasoline range (C5+) blending stock, and low-octane paraffins are converted into high-octane aromatics (octane is discussed below). Other processes such as alkylation produce branched chain hydrocarbons in the gasoline range. Diesel and jet fuel are formulated by blending straight-run cut distillates with cracked stock (heavier fractions) to meet standardized specifications developed by the American Society for Testing and Materials (ASTM International) and the Environmental Protection Agency (EPA). These include octane and cetane number, sulfur content, and exhaust emissions.

The fuel specifications most familiar to motorists are "octane" and "cetane" numbers. In the case of gasoline, the octane-rating refers to the property of resisting spontaneous ignition. In contrast, diesel fuel is rated by its relative ease of ignition under compression (a desired property). This may seem a paradox — gasoline should resist ignition and diesel should ignite easily. As gasoline is more volatile than diesel, it is desirable that it not ignite before the spark plug fires.

Octane

Higher octane-number fuels better resist engine "knock" — the sound caused by fuel prematurely igniting during compression. In early gasoline research, the least knock resulted from using iso-octane, which arbitrarily received a rating of 100.[6] Iso-octane refers to a branched "isomer" in the paraffin series having eight carbons (C_8H_{18}).[7] The straight-chain isomer in this series, n-octane, has a rating -19. These isomers of paraffin are shown in **Figure 3**. Fischer-Tropsch synthesis produces primarily straight-chain paraffins, thus any gasoline produced is low in octane rating.

---

[4] The length of the carbon chain is abbreviated. For example a paraffin consisting of six carbons would be written as C6.

[5] James H. Gary and Glenn E. Handwerk, *Refining Petroleum — Technology and Economics, 4th Ed.*, Marcel Dekker, Inc., 2001.

[6] John M. Hunt, *Petroleum Geochemistry and Geology*, W. H. Freeman and Co., 1979. p. 51.

[7] Or more correctly 2,2,4-trimethylpentane.

CRS-6

Figure 3. Iso-octane vs N-octane

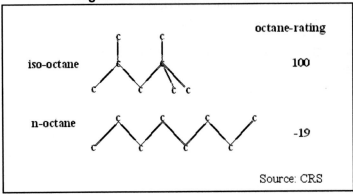

Source: CRS

Modern formulated gasolines range in octane from 87 to 93, achieved by blending various petroleum distillates, reforming gasoline-range hydrocarbons, and adding oxygenates such as MTBE or ethanol to boost octane-number. Branched paraffin series like iso-octane can not be directly produced in Fischer-Tropsch synthesis. Consequently, when Fisher-Tropsch synthesis has been used to produce gasoline, it has been blended with conventionally refined petroleum to achieve the desired octane-number.

Cetane

The standard for diesel fuel rates the ease of which auto-ignition occurs during compression in the engine cylinder, thus eliminating the need for a spark plug. The number 100 was assigned to "cetane," the more common name for n-hexadecane. Cetane's chemical formula is often written as $C_{16}H_{34}$ to represent a straight-chain hydrocarbon in the paraffin series. It consists of 16 carbon atoms with three hydrogen atoms bonded to the two end carbons, and two hydrogens bonded to each of the middle carbons. In other words, the benchmark for rating diesel fuel is a paraffin — the hydrocarbon the Fischer-Tropsch synthesis is best suited to making.

Diesel fuel cetane-numbers range from 40 to 45, and as high as 55 in Europe, where high-speed diesel engines are prevalent in light-duty passenger vehicles. The cetane-number for F-T synthesized diesel can be as high as 70. In tests conducted by the National Renewable Energy Laboratory (NREL) Fischer-Tropsch diesel fuel had a cetane-number greater than 74.[8] The diesel fuel was supplied by Shell Oil Company's gas-to-liquids plant in Bintulu, Malaysia.

---

[8] P. Norton, K. Vertin and B. Bailey (NREL); N. N. Clark and D. W. Lyons (West Virginia Univ.); S. Goguen and J. Eberhardt (U.S. DOE); *Emissions from Trucks Using Fischer-Tropsch Diesel Fuel*; Society of Automotive Engineers Technical Paper Series 982526; 1998.

CRS-7

Sulfur

As now regulated by the EPA (40 C.F.R. 80.520) diesel fuel must contain less than 15 parts-per-million (ppm) sulfur — referred to as ultra-low-sulfur diesel (ULSD). Conventionally refined aviation jet fuel may have a sulfur content as high as 3,000 ppm. However, as it has been used in blending winter diesel fuel to lower the gel point, it has had a practical limit of 500 ppm (the previous EPA limit for diesel). It is uncertain whether EPA may promulgate future rules on jet fuel sulfur content, thus limiting its use in blending winter ULSD. Fischer-Tropsch diesel fuel contains virtually no sulfur, as it must be removed before the synthesis reaction to avoid poisoning the catalysts used in the reactor. Despite its detrimental environmental effects, sulfur contributes to the "lubricity" of fuel. Under reduced sulfur, engines wear out sooner. Fuel can be blended with additives to make up for the loss of sulfur lubricity and engines can be manufactured from tougher materials, as has been the case in the EPA mandated transition from low-sulfur diesel (500 ppm) to ultra-low-sulfur diesel (15 ppm).

Exhaust Emissions

Diesel engines characteristically emit lower amounts of carbon monoxide (CO) and carbon dioxide (CO_2) than gasoline engines, but they emit higher amounts of nitrogen oxides (NOx) and particulate matter (PM). NOx is the primary cause of ground-level ozone pollution (smog) and presents a greater problem, technically, to reduce in diesel engines than PM. The CO, NOx, and PM emissions for gasoline and diesel engines are regulated by the 1990 Clean Air Act amendments (42 U.S.C. 7401-7671q). In emissions testing performed by the National Renewable Energy Laboratory (NREL), trucks using "neat" Fischer-Tropsch diesel fuel emitted about 12% lower NOx and 24% lower PM compared to trucks using conventionally refined diesel fuel (meeting California No. 2 diesel standards).[9]

Synthetic Fuel Plants

The following discussion summarizes industrial progress in synthetic fuels. As a means of comparing plant efficiencies (where possible), the energy in Btu contained in the feedstock (coal, gas, biomass) consumed is compared to the energy in the product produced.[10] Greenhouse gas emissions, primarily carbon dioxide, are also discussed as they may present regulatory challenges for future Fischer-Tropsch plants.

Germany's Synthetic Fuel Program

As part of continency planning for petroleum supply shortages, Germany built a number of coal-based synthetic fuel plants, which operated through World War II.

---

[9] P. Norton, et al., op. cit.

[10] The energy term Btu refers to British Thermal Unit, which describes the unit of heat energy required to raise 1 pound of water by 1 degree Fahrenheit.

CRS-8

Germany operated 12 coal hydrogenation plants to produce aviation gasoline (primarily), motor gasoline, diesel, heating oils, and lubricants. Peak production of 21.5 million barrels was reached in 1944.[11] According to the interrogation of a scientist who had worked on Germany's synthetic fuel program, roughly 6.7 to 7.7 metric tons of coal were required to produce one metric ton (approximately 7 barrels) of liquid product — roughly one barrel per ton of coal. [12]

Germany also built synthetic fuel plants based on Fischer-Tropsch synthesis leading up to World War II, and had completed nine by the war's end. Production was geared to low-octane motor fuel, diesel, lubricating oil, miscellaneous chemicals, and soap. Fischer-Tropsch output was low in comparison to hydrogenation at approximately 450,000 barrels annually, with the best plant capable of producing no more than 3,000 barrels per day. The plants were also about 20% more costly to operate than the hydrogenation plants, with 50% of the cost in synthesis gas production. Low-grade coal (bituminous and lignite) was used as a feedstock. From 7.1 to 8.9 metric tons of coal were required to produce one metric ton of liquid product — slightly less than one barrel per ton.

U.S. Synthetic Fuel Program

Concerns for oil supplies during World War II also prompted U.S. interest in synthetic fuels. The U.S. Synthetic Liquid Fuels Act of 1944 authorized construction and operation of plants producing synthetic liquid fuel from coal, oil shale, and agricultural and forestry products.[13] After WWII, the United States tried to capitalize on German technology and experience by sponsoring a number of research, development, and demonstration projects. The Bureau of Mines received funding for an 11-year demonstration plant program that ended in 1955. Work on Fischer-Tropsch synthesis was carried out in a pilot-scale plant at the Bureau's Morgantown, West Virginia, Laboratory. Research improved on the German fixed-bed synthesis reactor with the development of a fluidized-bed reactor.

During the 1960s, the Department of the Interior's Office of Coal Research sponsored research to directly liquefy Eastern coal, expending approximately $45.7 million (unadjusted for inflation) between 1961 and 1969.[14] Under the 1970s era DOE Synthetic Fuels program, two coal liquefaction projects were planned. Approximately $1,666 million (unadjusted for inflation) was spent between 1975 and

---

[11] Anthony N. Stranges (Texas A&M University), *Germany's Synthetic Fuel Industry 1927-1945*, AIChE Spring National Meeting, 2003.

[12] *Synthetic Oil Production in Germany — Interrogation of Dr. Butefisch* available through the Fischer-Tropsch Archive, [http://www.fischer-tropsch.org/].

[13] 30 U.S.C. Secs. 321 to 325 authorized $30 million over five years for "the construction and operation of demonstration plants to produce synthetic liquid fuels from coal, oil shales, agricultural and forestry products, and other substances, in order to aid the prosecution of the war, to conserve and increase the oil resources of the Nation, and for other purposes."

[14] Linda B. Cohen and Roger C. Noll, "Synthetic Fuels from Coal," in *The Technology Pork Barrel*, The Brookings Institution, 1991.

CRS-9

1984 on research, development, and demonstration.[15] Several processes were evaluated — noncatalytic solvent extraction, catalytic processing, and donor solvent processing — and various coals were tested.[16] In privately sponsored development, the Gulf Oil Company reported yielding three barrels of low sulfur fuel oil per ton of Eastern high-sulfur coal using its catalytic coal to liquids process. Exxon reportedly achieved a comparable yield with its donor solvent process. Accordingly, Gulf was achieving a 62% thermal conversion efficiency (see Appendix for calculations).

Efforts to move coal liquefaction beyond the demonstration phase stalled, despite federal and private funding commitments. Project cost overruns of several times the initial $700 million estimate led DOE to cancel work. Several other factors during in the 1980s also contributed to cancellation. The dramatic drop in crude oil prices, the development of new oil fields, and reduced consumption from conservation efforts all contributed to making synthetic fuels economically uncompetitive. Refineries also began converting heavy heating oil into higher value transportation fuel.

Though U.S. interest in making coal-based transportation fuel was abandoned by the mid-1980s, South Africa continued in its efforts to develop Fischer-Tropsch synthesis on a commercial scale. Several other commercial scale efforts have since succeeded in adapting Fischer-Tropsch synthesis to natural gas, where abundant supplies make it economically feasible to do so. Renewed U.S. interest in the technology includes both coal and natural gas. Consequently, the balance of this report will focus on Fischer-Tropsch.

Sasol Coal-to-Liquids Plants

The lack of petroleum resources but abundant coal resources led the Republic of South Africa to investigate establishing an oil-from-coal industry in 1927. After WWII, South Africa's government adopted German technology to build a coal-to-liquid synthetic fuel plant. The South African Coal Oil and Gas Corporation (now known as Sasol) was founded as a state owned company in 1950 to synthesize fuel from coal based on German and U.S. developed Fischer-Tropsch technology (see Bureau of Mines above). Sasol was privatized in 1979.

Sasol One started operation in 1955 at Sasolburg, South Africa. It employed two technologies. One unit used a fixed-bed catalyst similar to a German process operated during WWII, provided by the German firm Argbeit-Gemeinshaft Lurgi und Ruhrchemie (Arge).[17] It operated in the temperature range of 220-240°C at a pressure of 925 bar. Production was optimized for long-chain linear paraffins. A

---

[15] Paul F. Rothberg, CRS Report IB77105, Coal Gasification and Liquefaction, February 1, 1984.

[16] Martin A. Elliot, Ed., *Chemistry of Coal Utilization, 2nd Supplementary Volume*, John Wiley & Sons, 1981.

[17] National Academy of Sciences/National Research Council, *Chemistry of Coal Utilization*, pp. 2112-2113, John Wiley & Sons, 1981.

CRS-10

second unit used a fluid bed catalyst system developed by the U.S. firm M.W. Kellogg. Technical difficulties prevented its operation until 1957. Its higher operating temperature range of 310-340°C made it better suited to producing gasoline-range hydrocarbons. In 1970, Sasol One produced approximately 297,000 tons of liquid annually (1.9 million barrels of fuel oil equivalent), while consuming approximately 3.96 million tons of coal. This equated a yield of approximately ½ barrel per ton coal.

A second and third plant were built in Secunda, South Africa. Sasol Two was completed in 1980 at a cost of $3,200 million and Sasol Three in 1984 at a cost of $2,520 million.[18] (Costs reflect value of U.S. dollar at the time, unadjusted for inflation.) The Secunda complex is dedicated to producing liquid fuels and chemicals.

The Secunda complex originally operated 80 Lurgi fixed-bed dry-bottom gasifiers to make synthesis gas, and 16 circulating fluid bed reactors (rated at 7,500 barrels per day each). These processes gave it a capacity of 120,000 barrels per day. In 2000, Sasol replaced the fluid-bed reactors with 8 Sasol Advanced Synthol (SAS) reactors (rated at 20,000 barrels per day). The SAS reactors use a fluidized, iron-based catalyst that operates in the 300-350°C temperature range.

With the new SAS reactors, the Secunda complex production increased to 150,000 barrels per day of products in the C1-C20 range (automotive fuels and light olefin used as feedstock for chemical manufacturing).[19] In 2001, Secunda also supplied 14.3 million gigaJoules (135.54 million therms) of methane rich gas to South Africa's gas distribution network.[20]

In 2006, Secunda consumed approximately 41.8 million metric tons of low rank sub-bituminous coal supplied by Sasol Mining (the equivalent of 126,000 U.S. short tons per day).[21] At that rate of consumption, Secunda yields approximately 1.2 barrels per ton of coal, making it approximately 27% efficient in converting the coal's heat content (Btus) to liquid products. (Refer to the Appendix for calculation of the value). This does not include the heat value of the methane-rich gas that Secunda also produces, which would increase efficiency.

---

[18] Costs reflect value of U.S. dollar at the time, unadjusted for inflation. Sasol *Coal-to-Liquids Development*, presentation to the gasification technologies Council Conference, October 2005.

[19] Thi Chang, *Oil & Gas Journal*, "South African Company Commercializes New F-T Process, January 10, 2000.

[20] A gigajoule (GJ) is a standard measure used for the heating value of fuel gas supplied to South African customers. A joule is an international unit of energy defined as the energy produced from one watt flowing for one second. Giga denotes a measure of a billion (10^9). 1 GJ = 0.96 million cubic feet (mcf) of gas, under standard temperature and pressure conditions. 1 Therm = 100,000 Btu. Department of Minerals and Energy, Republic of South Africa, *Gas Infra-Structure Plan*, April 19, 2005, [http://www.dme.gov.za/pdfs/energy/gas/gas_infrastructure_plan.pdf].

[21] Platts, Coal-to-Liquids Technology, December 19, 2006 [http://www.platts.com/Coal/Resources/News%20Features/ctl/sasol.xml].

CRS-11

Sasol Sasolburg and Secunda, combined, produce 30 million metric tons of CO_2 annually. Sasol uses the Benfield process to absorb and capture 90-98% of CO_2 produced.[22] Sasol reports producing 3.04 metric tons of CO_2 per metric ton of overall product,[23] the equivalent of 0.82 metric tons elemental carbon per ton liquid.[24] This is approximately equivalent to emitting 0.48 U.S. tons of CO_2 per barrel of product produced.[25]

By the end of 1979, production costs were estimated at approximately $30 per barrel, while world spot prices for crude oil were $10 per barrel higher.[26] Until 2000, Sasol had been receiving a tariff protection when the world market oil price fell below $21.40 per barrel.[27] Crude oil prices had remained below the tariff protection level in the years 1986 through 1996, except for a brief period during the 1991 Persian Gulf War. The tariff protection lapsed in 2000. South Africa also put a sliding price scale in place to make imported refined products more costly than Sasol's, up to crude oil prices of $45 per barrel.

Shell Bintulu Gas-to-Liquids Plant

In 1993, Shell International Gas Limited began operating the first-of-its-kind full-scale commercial gas-to-liquids plant, built alongside its liquefied natural gas (LNG) plant at Bintulu in Sarawak (Malaysia).[28] Shell's Middle Distillate System (SMDS) technology was developed using natural gas as a feedstock for Fischer-Tropsch synthesis to produce middle distillates.

The Bintulu plant produces 12,500 barrels per day of product (50% middle distillates, and 50% speciality products such as detergent feedstocks and waxes), while consuming 100-120 million cubic feet per day of natural gas produced from the South China Sea. This makes it approximately 54% efficient in converting the energy content of natural gas to liquid products. (Refer to the Appendix for calculation of the value.)

Shell states that the SMDS fuels produced have virtually no aromatic and sulfur components, and when blended with conventional diesel give significant reductions

---

[22] The Benfield process uses a hot potassium carbonate solution that is diethanolamine promoted. A. Engelbrecht, A. Golding, S. Hietkamp, and B. Scholes, *The Potential for Sequestration of Carbon Dioxide in South Africa,* March 12, 2004, South Africa Department of Minerals and Energy.

[23] Sasol, *Highlights Sasol Sustainable Development Report 2006.*

[24] To convert CO_2 gas to elemental C, multiply CO_2 by 12/44. EPA Office of Transportation and Air Quality, *Metrics for Expressing Greenhouse Gas Emissions: Carbon Equivalents and Carbon Dioxide Equivalents,* EPA420-F-05-022, February 2005.

[25] 1 metric ton product ≈ 7 barrels.

[26] Sasol Ltd, *Hoovers,* [http://www.hoovers.com].

[27] "S. Africa to cut price protection for synfuel," *Oil & Gas Journal,* December 25, 1995.

[28] Shell Gas & Power External Affairs, *Gas to Liquids: Shell Middle Distillate Synthesis Process and Products,* August 2002.

CRS-12

in regulated emissions (NOx, SOx, HC, CO, and particulates). SMDS diesel can also be used as a "neat" fuel in diesel engines with minor modifications.

Oryx Gas-to-Liquids Plant

The Oryx Gas-to-Liquids (GTL) plant at Ras Laffan Industrial City, north of the Qatar capital Doha, represents a joint venture between state-owned Qatar Petroleum (51%) and Sasol Ltd. (49%).[29] Built at a cost of $950 million, operations commenced in June 2006, after 2½ years of construction. The plant uses Sasol's Fischer-Tropsch based Slurry Phase Distillate low temperature process.

Oryx is designed to produce 34,000 barrels per day of liquids (24,000 barrels diesel, 9,000 barrels naphtha, and 1,000 barrels liquefied petroleum gas). Qatar's Persian Gulf North Gas Field is expected to provide approximately 330 million cubic feet per day of "lean" gas as feedstock. This makes Oryx approximately 52% efficient. (Refer to the Appendix for calculation of the value.)

Sasol Chevron — the London-based joint venture between Sasol and Chevron Corporation — will market the Oryx GTL diesel initially in Europe and then elsewhere. The joint venture plans to expand Oryx plant capacity to about 100,000 barrels per day and is considering plans to build an integrated GTL plant with a capacity of about 130,000 barrels per day.

Syntroleum Catoosa Demonstration Facility

Syntroleum Corporation (Tulsa, Oklahoma) operates a 3-barrel-per-day Fischer-Tropsch pilot plant, used primarily to evaluate catalyst systems, and a 70-barrel-per-day demonstration plant used to produce products and evaluate technology. Syntroleum has received $31.6 million in federal government contracts since 1998 to evaluate Fischer-Tropsch technology for the Departments of Defense, Energy, and Transportation.

U.S. Air Force Coal-to-Liquids Initiative

As envisioned by the Office of the Secretary of Defense (OSD), the Assured Fuels Initiative has the intent of catalyzing commercial industry to produce clean fuels for the military from secure domestic resources.[30] Under the initiative, Fischer-Tropsch technology is under evaluation for converting coal to liquid (mobility) fuel.

In 2006, the U.S. Air Force purchased 100,000 gallons of jet fuel synthesized from natural gas, and in August 2007 certified the fuel as a blending substitute in conventionally refined JP-8 for the B52 Stratofortress. In December 2007, a C-17

---

[29] Qatar Petroleum, *Oryx GTL Inauguration - A Key Step in Qatar's Bid to Become the GTL Capital of the World* [http://www.qp.com.qa/qp.nsf/8c264276b952633c432571290026c60e/4cebdaa21d0dc4264325718600180400?OpenDocument#].

[30] William Harrison, *OSD Assured Fuels Initiative*. [http://www.trbav030.org/pdf2006/265_Harrison.pdf]

CRS-13

Globemaster III completed a transcontinental certification test flight using a synthetic fuel blend. The Air Force hopes to certify F-T fuels for its entire fleet of aircraft by 2011. The U.S. Navy will be evaluating synthetic fuel as a substitute diesel fuel.

The Air Force is now exploring the possibility of leasing property at Malmstrom Air Force Base, Montana, for construction of a coal-to-liquids plant.[31] Under its Enhanced Use Leasing authority, the Air Force would lease land to a private developer who would in turn finance and construct a facility capable of producing 25,000 barrels per day of CTL fuel. On January 30, 2008, the Air Force conducted a CTL Opportunity Community Meeting in Great Falls, Montana, to respond to community concerns about the initiative. A final request for qualifications (RFQ) for the proposed plant issued on February 29 requires proposals to be submitted to the Air Force by May 2008.

China's Coal-to-Liquids Program

China's long-term policy on coal-to-liquid deployment remains uncertain, despite the completion of many small "coal-to-chemical" facilities. While China sees unique advantages in promoting coal-based alternatives to petroleum, there are key challenges that will likely result in a period of experimental policy that "crosses the river by feeling the stones."

China's interest in CTL is driven by the country's growing sense of oil insecurity. China went from being a net oil exporter in 1993 to relying on imports for approximately half of total oil demand in 2008. Chinese decision-makers are less familiar with, and confident in, global petroleum markets than many of their industrialized country counterparts.[32] But unlike petroleum, China has abundant domestic coal supply.[33] For government planners steeped in the central planning mantra of self-sufficiency, CTL has obvious attractions. For others, its drawbacks may outweigh its advantages. Still, the technology has become one of the elements of a multi-pronged Chinese strategy to boost energy security.[34]

Chinese industry has decades of experience gasifying coal. In recent years, there has also been a mushrooming of "coal to chemicals" plants that produce methanol, dimethyl ether (DME), olefin, and other petrochemical feedstocks.[35] Experience with coal liquefaction to produce diesel, liquid petroleum gas (LPG), and naptha is more limited, but took on greater urgency in the late 1990s when it became irrefutable that domestic oil production would not be able to keep pace with surging demand.

[31] Air Force Real Property Agency, *Coal-to-Liquid Fuel Plant Opportunity Fact Sheet.* [malmstrom.ctl@afrpa.pentagon.af.mil]

[32] K. Lieberthal and M. Herberg, *China's Search for Energy Security: Implications for U.S. Policy*, National Bureau of Asian Research, 2006.

[33] China is ranked 3rd in global coal reserves behind the United States and Russia. Nevertheless, some question the accuracy of China's reported coal quantity and quality.

[34] Other measures include creation of a strategic petroleum reserve, increased vehicle fuel economy standards, and expanded investment in overseas oil assets.

[35] *Wall Street Journal*, "Coal Gasification Surging in China," December 31, 2007.

CRS-14

The National Development and Reform Commission (NDRC) has announced approval of three major CTL facilities. In 2008, China's Shenhua Group is scheduled to open a first-of-a-kind direct liquefaction plant in Inner Mongolia with initial production capacity of about 1 million tons per year. The two other approved projects are slated to be larger and use the more tested indirect liquefaction process, but their deployment remains uncertain. In late 2006, NDRC issued an ambitious draft plan for coal-based chemicals, calling for 30 million tons of diesel and LPG, 20 million tons DME, and over 60 million tons of methanol output by 2020.[36] It also issued a ban on the construction of small CTL, methanol, and olefin plants that had been mushrooming without approval or oversight. In mid-2007, China's ambitious plan was called into doubt when an NDRC official announced that the country might halt most CTL projects.[37] Like some other countries, China is wary about CTL because:

- the technology (especially direct liquefaction) is untested and still immature;
- it is capital intensive and prone to "stranded investment" should oil prices fall;
- coal supply may be insufficient to supply long-term market demand;
- increased greenhouse gas emissions will attract international concern; and perhaps most importantly,
- water is scarce where coal is plentiful.[38]

Government planners are carefully evaluating the costs and benefits of CTL deployment in China. Today they are more likely to use hard-nosed economic analysis to evaluate CTL's viability compared to earlier years when self-sufficiency could trump economic efficiency. Nevertheless, water shortages and other environmental concerns are likely to moderate China's support for CTL.

Choren Industries

Choren Industries (a partnership of Daimler AG, Volkswagen, and Shell) is finishing construction of its Beta biomass-to-liquid plant in Freiberg, Germany. The initial production goal is 15,000 metric tons (735,000 barrels) per year of diesel. Choren plans are to expand capacity to 200,000 metric tons (1,400,000 barrels) per year with its Zeta-plant (equivalent to 3,800 barrels per day). The German Energy Agency assumes that biomass-to-liquids is 42% efficient in energy conversion.[39]

---

[36] *China Daily*, "Coal Chemical Plans Announced," December 28, 2006.

[37] *Xinhua*, "China May Halt Coal-to-Liquid Projects," June 10, 2007.

[38] Chinese coal is abundant in the provinces of Shaanxi, Shanxi and Inner Mongolia. The lack of water resources in northern China is considered one of the greatest development challenges that the region faces. A general rule of thumb is that five to ten gallons of water are required for every one gallon of CTL production.

[39] Deutsche Energie-Anentur GmbH, *Biomass to Liquid - BtL, Implementation Report*, December 2006.

CRS-15

National Energy Technology Laboratory Study

The National Energy Technology Laboratory (NETL) has examined the technical and economic feasibility of a commercial scale coal-to-liquids facility using Illinois basin coal.[40] With a production goal of 50,000 barrels per day (diesel and naphtha) and consumption rate of 24,533 tons of coal per day, the plant would yield slightly more than 2 barrels per ton of coal. This would making it approximately 40.5% efficient. (Refer to the Appendix for calculation of the value.) This efficiency would not include 125 megawatts of electric power that would be generated from waste heat.

The plant is expected to produce 560 million cubic feet (32,032 tons) of CO_2 per day, which would equate to 0.64 tons of CO_2 per barrel.[41]

NETL estimated that construction could cost upwards of $4.5 billion.

Baard Energy Coal-to-Liquids Plant

Baard Energy, L.L.C., through its project company Ohio River Clean Fuels, L.L.C., is planning to build a nominal 50,000 barrel per day coal-to-liquids plant in Wellsville, Ohio. Baard's plans call for converting coal and biomass to synthesis gas, and using Fischer-Tropsch synthesis to produce diesel, jet, and naphtha hydrocarbons. The plant would also generate 250 to 300 megawatts of electricity daily. Baard expects that up to 85% of the CO_2 produced by the plant could be captured. Baard cites an Idaho National Laboratory study of the project that attributes use of Fischer-Tropsch diesel fuel with a 46% reduction in CO_2 emissions over conventionally refined diesel fuel.[42]

Comparing Efficiencies

For comparison purposes, yield and thermal conversion efficiency of the various plants discussed above are presented in **Table 2**. Yield in barrels per ton pertains to liquid fuels from coal. Thermal conversion efficiency is a term adopted in this report to compare the heating value of the feedstock to the product. It does not imply an economic comparison; that is, that one technology requiring lower Btu than another is necessarily economically superior. An economic comparison would also weigh the capital cost of construction, operation and maintenance costs, the price of

---

[40] U.S. DOE National Energy Technology Laboratory, *Baseline Technical and Economic Assessment of a Commercial Scale Fischer-Tropsch Liquids Facility* (DOE/NETL-2007/1260), April 9, 2007.

[41] 1 standard cubic foot (SCF) CO_2 = 0.1144 pounds.

[42] Richard D. Boardman, *Plant Modeling & Emissions Comparative Analysis Approach — Coal/Biomass Gasification with Fischer-Tropsch Diesel Production*, Idaho National Laboratory, May 2007. A full technical report is scheduled to be delivered by Baard Energy and the Idaho National Laboratory at the 24th Annual International Pittsburgh Coal Conference in Johannesburg, South Africa, September 10-14, 2007.

CRS-16

fuel, and the intrinsic value of environment and national security, which is beyond the scope of this report.

Table 2. Comparative Efficiencies of Processes Converting Coal, Gas, and Biomass to Liquid Fuels

	Germany WWII		Gulf DL	Sasol F-T CTL	Shell F-T GTL	Oryx F-T GTL	Choren F-T BML	NETL F-T CTL
	DL	F-T CTL						
Yield barrels/ton	1	1	3	1.2	n.a.	n.a.	n.a.	2
Thermal conversion efficiency %	—[a]	—[a]	62	27[b]	54	52	42	40.5

Note: DL: direct liquefaction; F-T CTL: Fischer-Tropsch coal-to-liquids; F-T GTL: gas to liquids, F-T BML: biomass-to-liquids.

a. insufficient information on coal heating value to determine thermal conversion efficiency
b. does not credit methane-rich gas production

Comparison might be made with the efficiency of producing other energy resources, such as petroleum, tar sands, or oil shale. The giant oil fields of North America, now depleted, produced from 50 to 1,000 barrels per acre-foot (43,560 ft³).[43] The NETL study expects to yield approximately 2 barrels per ton of Illinois bituminous coal — the equivalent of 3,806 barrels per acre-foot.[44] In further comparison, Canada's mined oil sands yield ½ barrel per ton.[45] Oil shales of the western United States could be expected to produce no more than 2/3 barrel per ton.[46]

A further comparison might be made to refining oil and generating electricity. The 5,555.3 million barrels of crude oil refined in 2005 (the equivalent of 32,221.3 trillion Btu)[47] consumed approximately 2,862.5 trillion Btu (fuel oil, still gas,

---

[43] American Association of Petroleum Geologists, *Geology of Giant Petroleum Fields*, 1970.

[44] Assumes in place density of 1,903 tons per acre-foot for bituminous coal. From James G. Speight, *The Chemistry and Technology of Coal*, Table 9.3 Expressions of the In-Place Density of Coal, CRC Press, 1994.

[45] Government of Alberta, "Oil Sand Facts," [http://www.energy.gov.ab.ca/OilSands/790.asp].

[46] CRS Report RL33359, *Oil Shale: History, Incentives, and Policy*, by Anthony Andrews.

[47] U.S. DOE EIA Petroleum Navigator, Refinery Net Input, [http://www.eia.doe.gov/].

CRS-17

petroleum coke, natural gas, coal, purchased electricity and steam).[48] (For analysis, refer to the Appendix.) Thus, on average, U.S. refineries consumed roughly 9% of the equivalent energy contained in the crude petroleum refined, making them 91% efficient. (ExxonMobile estimates, however, that its refineries require from 10%-20% of the energy in a barrel of crude oil to convert the remaining barrel into products.)[49] Coal-fired electric power plants, by comparison, average about 33% efficiency.[50]

It is emphasized that these comparisons are illustrative and do not of themselves indicate overall economic or environmental advantages.

Greenhouse Gas — CO_2

Carbon dioxide sequestration may offer a viable solution if CO_2 emissions were to be regulated. Sequestration depends on the ability to capture CO_2 after combustion, and then pump it into deep underground reservoirs. (See CRS Report RL33801, *Direct Carbon Sequestration: Capturing and Storing CO₂.*) Though considerable reservoir capacity exists in the United States, the pipeline infrastructure to facilitate sequestration would be needed on an industrial scale. (See CRS Report RL33971, *Pipelines for Carbon Sequestration: Emerging Policy Issues.*)

Congress is considering various bills aimed at reducing and stabilizing greenhouse gas emission. The Energy Independence and Security Act of 2007 (P.L. 110-140) amends the Energy Policy Act of 2005 with research and development programs to demonstrate carbon capture and sequestration, and restricts the federal government's procurement of alternative fuels that exceed the lifecycle greenhouse gas emissions associated with conventional petroleum based fuels. Carbon dioxide production associated with Fischer-Tropsch coal-to-liquids remains the primary objection by many in Congress to offering or approving legislation that promotes its development.

Of 42 states that have conducted greenhouse gas inventories, at least 30 states have either completed or are in the process of preparing climate change action plans and 12 states have set statewide greenhouse gas targets. A small, but growing, number of states have implemented or are creating mandatory emission reduction programs. (See CRS Report RL33812, *Climate Change: Action by States To Address Greenhouse Gas Emissions.*)

A recent U.S. Supreme Court decision compels the EPA to consider regulating CO_2 emissions from mobile sources under the Clean Air Act.[51] Whether EPA would

---

[48] U.S. DOE EIA, Petroleum Navigator, Fuel Consumed at Refineries, [http://www.eia.doe.gov/].

[49] Lori Ryerkerk, Beaumont Refinery Manager, Texas Industrial Energy Management Forum, April 7, 2005.

[50] President's Council of Advisors on Science and Technology, *Report on Energy Efficiency — Findings and Recommendations*, February 20, 2003.

[51] Massachusetts et al. v. Environmental Protection Agency et al. Certiorari to the United
(continued...)

CRS-18

be compelled to extend rulemaking to stationary sources, such as coal burning power plants or coal-to-liquids plants, for example, is uncertain. EPA has estimated the percentage change in lifecycle greenhouse gas emissions, relative to petroleum-based fuels that would be displaced by alternative and renewable fuels, including coal-, gas-, and biomass-to-liquids.[52] The analysis is based on work performed by the DOE Argonne National Laboratory using the *Greenhouse Gases, Regulated Emissions, and Energy Use in Transportation* (GREET) model. The fuels are compared on an energy equivalent basis. The assumptions made about Fischer-Tropsch coal-to-liquids include a plant efficiency of 52.4%, and that 85% of the carbon (exclusive of the fuel product) is captured. As shown in **Figure 4**, the impact on greenhouse gas emissions (GHG) from coal-to-liquids fuel with carbon capture and sequestration (CC&S) would represent an increase 3.7% over petroleum-based fuels; without capture and sequestration a 118.8% increase. Gas-to-liquids would increase greenhouse gas emissions by 8.6% (EPA does not state whether this factors in CC&S).

A direct comparison might be made with CO_2 emissions from refineries. In 2005, U.S. refineries emitted 277.6 million metric tons (306.11 million U.S. tons) of CO_2[53] to produce 5,686 million barrels of petroleum products in 2005[54] — or approximately 0.05 tons CO_2 per barrel. Sasol, considered the largest single global source of CO_2,[55] emits approximately 0.48 U.S. tons per barrel of product.[56] The NETL study plant would emit 0.64 tons of CO_2 per barrel.

---

[51] (...continued)
States Court of Appeals for the District of Columbia Circuit No. 05-1120. Argued November 29, 2006; decided April 2, 2007.

[52] EPA Office of Transportation and Air Quality, *Greenhouse Gas Impacts of Expanded Renewable and Alternative Fuels Use* (EPA420-F-07-035), April 2007.

[53] Mark Schipper, U.S. DOE EIA, *Energy-Related Carbon Dioxide Emissions in U.S. Manufacturing* (DOE/EIA-0573), 2005.

[54] U.S. DOE EIA, Refinery Net Production (annual-thousand barrels) [http://tonto.eia.doe.gov/dnav/pet/pet_pnp_refp2_dc_nus_mbbl_a.htm].

[55] John Yeld, Cape Argus (Cape Town), *South Africa: Sasol Plant Named as Top Culprit in Emissions* [http://allafrica.com/stories/200708080651.html].

[56] 1 metric ton product ≈ 7 barrels.

CRS-19

Figure 4. Greenhouse Gas Impacts of Expanded Renewable and Alternative Fuels Use.

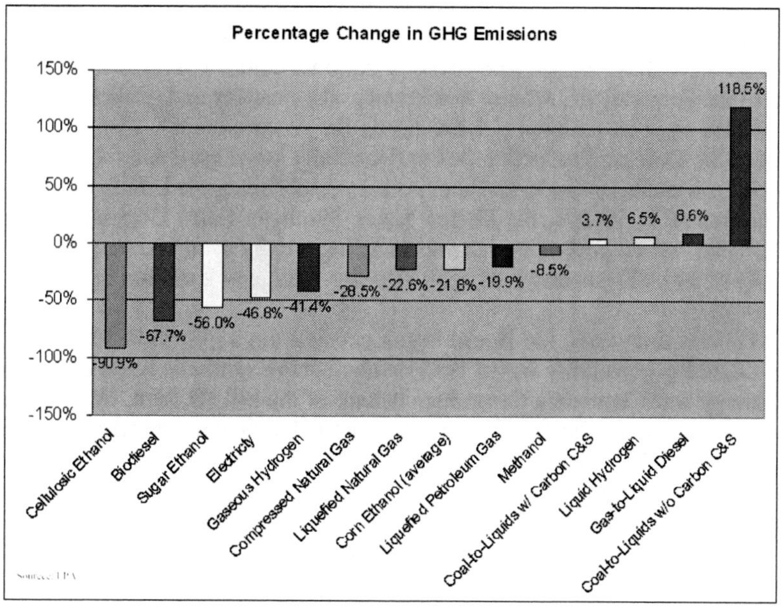

Policy History

Congress first promoted synthetic fuel from coal through the U.S. Synthetic Liquid Fuels Act of 1944.[57] Intended to aid the prosecution of World War II and conserve and increase national oil resources, the act authorized the Secretary of the Interior to construct, maintain, and operate plants producing synthetic liquid fuel from coal, oil shale, and agricultural and forestry products.[58] The Bureau of Mines received funding for an 11-year demonstration plant program that was largely completed by 1955.

During the Korean War, Section 303 of the Defense Production Act of 1950 (Ch. 932, 64 Stat. 978) authorized the President to have liquid fuels processed and refined for government use or resale, and to make improvements to government- or privately-owned facilities engaged in processing and refining liquid fuels when it would aid the national defense.[59] During the 1970s, the Department of Energy

---

[57] 30 U.S.C. Secs. 321 to 325.

[58] 30 U.S.C. Sections 321 to 325 authorized $30 million over five years for the construction and operation of demonstration plants to produce synthetic liquid fuels from coal, oil shales, agricultural and forestry products, and other substances.

[59] Ch. 932, 64 Stat. 798 (Title III Expansion of Production Capacity and Supply) intended to develop and maintain whatever military and economic strength necessary to support collective action through the United Nations. The act authorized the diversion of certain materials and facilities from civilian to military use when expansion of production facilities

(continued...)

CRS-20

(DOE) directed a synthetic fuels program toward commercializing coal liquefaction, coal gasification, and oil shale technologies. In 1980, Congress amended Section 305 of the Defense Production Act (P.L. 96-294, Energy Security Act) to authorize the President's purchase of synthetic fuels for national defense. President Carter then directed the Secretary of Defense to determine the quantity and quality of synthetic fuel needed to meet national defense needs for procurement.[60] Congress further amended the Defense Production Act to financially assist synthetic fuel production from coal, oil shale, tar sands, and heavy oils by establishing the U.S. Synthetic Fuels Corporation (P.L. 96-294, the United States Synthetic Fuels Corporation Act of 1980).[61] The stated goal of the act was reaching a daily synthetic fuels production capacity of 500,000 barrels of oil equivalent by 1987, and 2 million by 1992.

Within a few years, the House began considering a bill (H.R. 935, Synthetic Fuels Fiscal Responsibility Act of 1985) to abolish the Synthetic Fuels Corporation. The Energy and Commerce Committee debate of the bill (H.Rept. 99-196) linked abolishing the Corporation to reducing the federal deficit and viewed purchasing oil for the Strategic Petroleum Reserve as a far more cost effective defense against another oil embargo than subsidizing synthetic fuels. Congressional criticism also focused on conflicts of interest among the Corporation board members, high salaries for staff, lack of interest on the part of private industry, and the possibility of huge subsidies going to profitable oil companies.[62] The minority view noted that as late as 1983, the Department of Defense had certified that synthetic fuel was needed to meet national defense needs. Language rescinding most of the Synthetic Fuels Corporation funding was included in the FY1986 continuing appropriations resolution (H.J.Res. 465, P.L. 99-190).

Though direct federal support for synthetic fuel ended, production continued to receive indirect benefits. Section 45K (Credit for Producing Fuel From a Nonconventional Source) of the Internal Revenue Code defines a qualified fuel for the purpose of tax credit to include "liquid, gaseous, or solid synthetic fuels produced from coal (including lignite), including such fuels when used as feedstocks." The Energy Information Administration reports on production of "coal synfuels," but limits the definition to coal-based solid fuels that have been processed by a coal synfuel plant and coal-based fuels such as briquettes, pellets, or extrusions, formed from fresh or recycled coal and binding materials.[63]

---

[59] (...continued)
beyond the levels needed to meet civilian demand was required.

[60] The American Presidency Project, Executive Order 12242 Synthetic Fuels, [http://www.presidency.ucsb.edu/ws/index.php?pid=45171], signed September 30, 1980, was later revoked by President Reagan's Executive Order 12346, February 8, 1982.

[61] Title I, Part B of the Energy Security Act of 1980.

[62] CQ Almanac, "Congress Dismantles Synthetic Fuels Program," 1985.

[63] Energy Information Administration Frequently Asked Questions - Coal [http://tonto.eia.doe.gov/ask/coal_faqs. asp#coal_synfuel].

CRS-21

Authorizations Under the Energy Policy Act

The Energy Policy Act of 2005 (EPAct 2005 — P.L. 109-58) introduced several new provisions for promoting alternative fuels derived from unconventional resources and loan guarantees for facilities using Fischer-Tropsch technology to produce the fuels.

- Section 369 (Title III — Oil and Gas) amended 10 U.S.C. 141 (Miscellaneous Procurement Provisions) by inserting Section 2398a for procurement of fuel derived from coal, oil shale, and tar sands.[64] This directed the Secretary of Defense to develop a strategy to use fuel produced from coal (among other strategic unconventional fuels) to help meet the fuel requirements of the Defense Department when the Secretary determines that doing so is in the national interest. The Air Force has begun acting on Section 369 to procure coal-based fuel and encourage production of coal-based jet fuel as discussed above, and defense related legislation has gone further to encourage this procurement (see discussion below).

- Section 417 (Department of Energy Transportation Fuels from Illinois Basin Coal) directed the Energy Department to evaluate production of Fischer-Tropsch transportation fuels from Illinois basin coal (though it remained unfunded by Congress and the President's budget request).

- Section 1703 (c) (1)(D) (Eligible Projects) authorized the Energy Secretary to make loan guarantees to facilities that generate hydrogen-rich and carbon monoxide-rich product streams from the gasification of coal or coal waste and use the streams to produce ultra clean premium fuels through the Fischer- Tropsch process.

- Section 1703(c)(4) (Liquefaction Project) authorized funds awarded under the clean coal power initiative in subtitle A of Title IV for coal-to-oil liquefaction projects to finance the cost of loan guarantees (though guarantees have yet to be awarded).

EPAct 2005 also authorized coal related programs that support research in solving some technology issues related to synthesizing liquid fuels from coal.

- Title IV (Clean Coal) authorizes the annual appropriation of $200 million in FY2006 through FY2014 for the Clean Coal Power Initiative. Of the funds made available, 70% ($140 million annually) are to be used only in funding coal-based gasification technologies that includes advanced technologies capable of producing

---

[64] Energy Policy Act of 2005, P.L. 109-58, Title III, Subtitle F, Sec. 369. Oil Shale, Tar Sands, and Other Strategic Unconventional Fuels; (q) Procurement of Unconventional Fuels by the Department of Defense.

CRS-22

concentrated carbon monoxide (a component of syngas generation essential to F-T coal-to-liquids).

- Title IX (Research and Development) authorized DOE approximately $90 million for carbon capture research between FY2006 and FY2008. Carbon capture research and development has been expanded and extended under the authorization of the Energy Independence and Security Act of 2007 (P.L. 110-140), which authorizes $240 million annually from FY2008 through FY2012.

- Title XVII (42 U.S.C. 16511-16514) authorizes the Secretary of Energy, after consultation with the Secretary of the Treasury, to make loan guarantees for projects that (1) avoid, reduce, or sequester air pollutants or anthropogenic emissions of greenhouse gases; and (2) employ new or significantly improved technologies as compared to commercial technologies in service in the United States at the time. The face value of the debt guaranteed by DOE is limited to no more than 80% of total project costs. Policies, procedures, and requirements for the Title XVII loan guarantee program are promulgated in rules under 10 CFR Part 609 — Loan Guarantees for Projects That Employ Innovative Technologies.[65]

Additional Tax Incentives

Coal-based synthetic fuels benefit from certain tax incentives.

As amended by Section 11113 (Title XI) of the Safe Accountable, Flexible, Efficient Transportation Equity Act (P.L. 109-59), federal tax law imposes a 24.3¢/gallon tax on any liquid fuel (other than ethanol or methanol) derived from coal.[66] However, a 50¢/gallon allowance of credit against the imposed tax is provided for alternative fuels (which are defined to include any liquid fuel derived from coal through the Fischer-Tropsch process). The tax credit provisions expire September 30, 2009.

The American Jobs Creation Act of 2004 (P.L. 108-357) amends Section 45 of the 1986 Internal Revenue Code (relating to electricity produced from certain renewable sources) to include "refined coal," defined as a fuel which is a liquid, gaseous, or solid synthetic fuel produced from coal (including lignite) or high carbon fly ash, including such fuel used as a feedstock.

---

[65] Final rule. *Federal Register*, Vol. 72, No. 204, October 23, 2007.

[66] The Leaking Underground Storage Tank Fund Program established under Title V of the Superfund Revenue Act of 1986 (P.L. 99-149) imposes an additional 0.1¢/gallon on motor fuels which is extended to March 2011 under EPAct 2005.

CRS-23

Defense Related Authorizations and Appropriations

In addition to directing a Defense coal-based unconventional fuel strategy under EPAct 2005, Congress also authorized procurement of the fuel under Defense appropriations.

Title XXVIII (Military Construction General Provisions)[67] of the John Warner National Defense Authorization Act for FY2007 (P.L. 109-364) reorganizes 10 U.S.C. Section 2865. A new chapter: "Chapter 173 — Energy Security" is inserted, under which the new section 2914 (Energy Conservation Construction Projects) authorizes the Secretary of Defense to carry out a military construction project for energy conservation, not previously authorized, using funds appropriated or otherwise made available for that purpose, that may include procurement of fuel derived from coal.

The Joint Explanatory Statement (in H.Rept. 109-676) to the Defense Appropriations Act, 2007 (H.R. 5631, P.L.109-289)[68] notes that at the behest of Congress, the Air Force initiated research into developing coal-based and natural gas derivative jet fuel substitutes. The Navy plans to initiate a pilot program to develop alternative fuels. "Given the high costs of fuel and maintenance, the conferees are encouraged by these reports and believe that the military services should continue to pursue alternative fuels research and development. As such, the conferees encourage the Department to provide sufficient funding in its FY2008 and future budget requests to continue these important research programs."

The Energy Independence and Security Act of 2007 (P.L. 110-140), however, included language discouraging the Defense Department from procuring coal-based jet fuel. Section 526 introduces a new requirement for federal procurement of alternative or synthetic fuels. Contracts must specify that the lifecycle greenhouse gas emissions associated with the production and combustion of the alternative fuel not exceed emissions from conventionally produced petroleum based fuel. As explained by the House Oversight and Government Reform Committee Chairman, the section was included in legislation in response to proposals under consideration by the Air Force to develop coal-to-liquid fuels, and is intended to ensure that federal agencies are not spending taxpayer dollars on new fuel sources that will exacerbate global warming.[69]

Department of Defense synthetic fuel initiatives, which include CTL, fall under both Operation and Maintenance (O&M) and Research, Development, Test and Evaluation (RDT&E) budget activities. These programs are summarized in **Table 3** by budget activity, and program description.

---

[67] Division B, Subtitle E — Energy Security.

[68] "Alternative Fuels," *Congressional Record*, p. H6996.

[69] Committee on Oversight and Government Reform, Letter to Senate Energy Committee Chairman [http://oversight.house.gov /story.asp?ID=1820].

CRS-24

Table 3. DOD Synthetic Fuel Projects
($ million)

Program Element and Title	Project Number, Title, and Description	FY07	FY08	FY09
Air Force				
O&M	Synthetic fuel program to test/certify synthetic fuel to meet the goal of certifying the entire fleet for synthetic fuel use by 2011.	-	-	26.9
RDT&E 0601102F Defense Research Sciences	2308 - Propulsion: academic research coal transformation laboratory.	-	-	1.0
	2308 - Propulsion: Starting in FY2008, conduct basic research in support of Air Force priority "Energy Conservation - Assured Fuels Initiative" to identify and develop technologies that enable the use of domestic fuel sources for military energy needs.		11.1	13.7
	Congressional Add: Coal-based jet fuels - conducted research to produce coal-based jet fuels, assess military utility and suitability of this fuel.	2.8		
RDT&E 0602203F Aerospace Propulsion	3048 - Fuels and Lubrication: In FY2007, investigated performance of Fischer-Tropsch and other alternative fuels for aircraft and other field hardware.	-		1.8
	Congressional Add: Alternative Energy Research - In FY2008, perform research on alternative energy, focusing on alternative hydrocarbon fuels made from coal, biomass, oil shale. Research includes fuel property evaluation and enhancement, as well as component and engine testing of alternative fuels.		1.2	
RDT&E 0603216F Aerospace Propulsion and Power Tech.	2480 - Aerospace Fuels: Assured Fuels Initiative to characterize and demonstrate the use of alternative hydrocarbon jet fuel to comply with Air Force certifications and standards for jet fuels. Funding redirected in FY2009 due to increased emphasis on development of alternative hydrocarbon jet fuel.	-	-	2.9
Navy				
RDT&E 0603640M USMC Advanced Tech. Demo.	2223 - Marine Corps ATD: Initiate new mobility efforts in FY2009 to include Fischer-Tropsch and coal gasification processes for use in military tactical wheeled vehicles.	-	-	-

Source: Department of Defense Budget Fiscal Year 2009.

CRS-25

Bills Introduced in the 110th Congress

A number of bills promoting coal-to-liquid fuels have been introduced the 110th Congress, however non have been enacted. They include:

- H.R. 370, *Coal-to-Liquid Fuel Promotion Act of 2007*, would provide loan guarantees, and authorize the Defense Secretary to enter contracts for long term procurement of CTL fuel.

- H.R. 2208, *Coal Liquid Fuels Act*, would provide standby loans for CTL projects.

- H.R. 6, *Renewable Fuels, Consumer Protection, and Energy Efficiency Act of 2007*, enacted as P.L. 110-140, would have defined fuel derived from coal as an industrial source of carbon dioxide (for the purpose of carbon capture and sequestration). S.Amdt. 1781 (*To Provide for Corporate Average Fuel Economy (CAFE) Standards*) to H.R. 6 would have included a coal-to-liquid fuel direct loan program.

- S. 133, *American Fuels Act of 2007*, would define alternative diesel fuel to include CTL that provides for sequestration of carbon emissions, and amend 10 U.S.C. Section 2922d to authorize the Defense Secretary to enter contracts for fuels produced from coal.

- S. 155, *Coal-to-Liquid Fuel Promotion Act of 2007*, would provide loan guarantees for large scale CTL facilities, authorize the Defense Secretary to enter into contracts with companies that operate CTL facilities near military installations, and provide a tax credit for investing in qualified CTL projects.

- S. 1443, *Clean, Affordable, and Domestic Fuels for Energy Security Act of 2007*, would mandate regulations and emission standards for coal-derived fuels, provide loan guarantees for coal-derived fuel facilities.

- H.R. 2419, *Farm Bill Extension Act*, includes a tax provision that would extend an existing 50¢ per gallon fuel excise tax credit for CTL until 2010 and requires CTL producers to capture and store 50% of carbon dioxide emissions. CTL producers could be required to capture and store 75% of carbon dioxide emissions should an independent arbitration panel determine that such a level is commercially feasible. Without an extension, the tax credit, created by the Energy Policy Act of 2005, is set to expire in September 2009.

CRS-26

Additional Tax Incentives

As amended by Section 11113 (Title XI) of the Safe, Accountable, Flexible, Efficient Transportation Equity Act (P.L. 109-59), federal tax law imposes a 24.3¢/gallon tax on any liquid fuel (other than ethanol or methanol) derived from coal.[70] However, a 50¢/gallon allowance of credit against the imposed tax is provided for alternative fuels (which are defined to include any liquid fuel derived from coal through the Fischer-Tropsch process). The tax credit provisions expire September 30, 2009.

The American Jobs Creation Act of 2004 (P.L. 108-357) amends Section 45 of the 1986 Internal Revenue Code (relating to electricity produced from certain renewable sources) to include "refined coal," defined as a fuel which is a liquid, gaseous, or solid synthetic fuel produced from coal (including lignite) or high carbon fly ash, including such fuel used as a feedstock.

The Tax Relief and Health Care Act of 2006 (P.L. 109-432) amends Section 48 of the 1986 Internal Revenue Code by extending tax credits through December 31, 2008.

Policy Considerations

In the past, the precipitous drop in crude oil price and increased supply played key roles in suspending federally funded coal-based synthetic fuel programs.[71] Direct coal liquefaction was considered economically unviable and fraught with technical problems. Critics of refineries charged at that time that they were inefficient, polluting, and produced dirty fuels — much the same criticism leveled at coal-to-liquids. Meanwhile, U.S. refineries began an intense period of recapitalization in response to Clean Air Act amendments and applied much of the same technology considered too costly for direct liquefaction. For some time afterwards, refineries remained the loss-leader in vertically integrated petroleum operations. Unprofitable refining was necessary for petroleum producers in order to maintain their market access.

Proponents of coal-to-liquids point to Sasol as evidence that the Fischer-Tropsch technology is viable. However, the South Africa government protected Sasol while crude oil prices remained low. During that same economic period, Canada continued to support the development of its oil sands resources. Thus, criticism that U.S. energy policy decisions were shortsighted in abandoning synthetic fuel efforts contrast with the reality that the refining industry transformed itself under the same economic circumstances without government support.

---

[70] The Leaking Underground Storage Tank Fund Program established under Title V of the Superfund Revenue Act of 1986 (P.L. 99-149) imposes an additional 0.1¢/gallon on motor fuels which is extended to March 2011 under EPAct 2005.

[71] See section on U.S. Synthetic Fuels Program and the Synthetic Fuels Corporation in CRS Report RL33359, *Oil Shale: History, Incentives, and Policy*, by Anthony Andrews.

CRS-27

Constructing a first or even second Fischer-Tropsch synthetic facility (regardless of feedstock is coal, gas or biomass) is likely to encounter permitting as well as economic barriers. (See CRS Report RL32666, *The Gas to Liquids Industry and Natural Gas Markets*.) Advocates of developing a synthetic fuels industry argue for a variety of incentives they view necessary in helping help bridge barriers to entry; such as: loan guarantees, streamlined permitting, infrastructure improvements, and long-term contracts for purchasing coal-, gas-, or biomass- to-liquid fuels. Some might argue that offering loan guarantees for such an industry would be a misplaced incentive given the current high prices of crude oil and refined gasoline. Others might argue that the petroleum industry's reluctance to increase refining capacity justifies federal intervention. The Energy Policy Act of 2005 already includes the provisions of Section 391, *Refinery Revitalization*, for streamlining the application and permit process among federal agencies for new refineries, which arguably could be applied to Fischer-Tropsch plants.

Mandated improvements in average fuel economy standards, as provided in the Energy Independence and Security Act of 2007 (P.L. 110-140) could have some stimulus on a fledgling Fischer-Tropsch industry. (See CRS Report RL33831, *Energy Efficiency and Renewable Energy Legislation in the 110th Congress*.) Automobile manufacturers might achieve the proposed standards through increased production of diesel passenger vehicles, which at the same time consume less fuel and emit lower CO_2 than gasoline engines (partially offsetting the CO_2 emitted in producing such fuels). In that case the demand for diesel fuel might increase. U.S. refineries would be pressed to adjust their product slate toward more diesel production, and distributors would be pressed to import more diesel fuel. However, refineries may be limited to adjusting their product slates to no more than 10% to 20% diesel without making capital investments. The increased U.S. demand for imported diesel would compete with European demand, where the preference for diesel vehicles is already increasing. Either case could place upward pressure on prices and thus stimulate private investment.

Carbon dioxide's contribution to global warming represents the primary drawback to Fischer-Tropsch, particularly when using coal feedstock. It also represents the primary detraction to coal as a fuel in general, as evident in the cancellation of a number in coal-fired power plant projects (11,000 megawatts in capacity) in 2007. The Edison Electric Institute attributes the cancellation, in part, to the uncertainty over the future regulation of carbon.[72] Carbon capture and sequestration offers a promising solution. However, sceptics of the solution may go unchallenged without an industrial scale demonstration. Private interests may forestall investment in synthetic fuels over the uncertainty of future carbon emission regulations, particularly if rules are not applied evenly to existing emission sources. Policy makers may face few options in contending with the broad issue of reducing carbon emissions from existing fossil fuel users.

---

[72] Edison Electric Institute, *Q3 2007 Financial Update*.

CRS-28

Appendix

Gulf Oil Company Direct Coal Liquefaction Efficiency
Feedstock:
Pittsburgh coal @ 14,040 Btu/pound x 2,000 pounds/ton = 28,080,000 Btu per ton[a]
Product:
distillate fuel oil = 5,825,000 Btu per barrel[b]
Calculation:
(3.0 barrels x 5,825,000 Btu/barrel) ÷ 28,080,000 Btu/ton = 62%.

Sources:
a. *Marks' Standard Handbook for Mechanical Engineers* 10th Ed, Sec. 7, "Fuels and Furnaces," McGraw Hill, 1996.
b. Energy Information Administration, *Monthly Energy Review, Appendix A Thermal Conversion Factors*, 2007.

Sasol Secunda Complex Coal-to-Liquids Efficiency
Feedstock:
sub-bituminous coal: 41,800,000 metric tons/yr x 1 year/365 days x 2204 lbs/m-ton x 11,482 Btu/lb[a] = 2,898,094,549,041 Btu
Products:
liquid fuels: 150,000 barrels/day x 42 gal/bbl/ 123,600 Btu/gal[b] = 778,680,000,000 Btu
Calculation:
Product (778,680,000,000)/ Feedstock (2,898,094,549,041 = 27%

Sources:
a. Sasol coal ranges from 10,000 to 11,482 Btu/lb in calorific value, with fixed carbon ranging from 49.4% to 57.7%. Methane rich gas: 33.9 megaJoules/cubic meter) (910 Btu/ft^3) compared to natural gas: 37 to 40 MJ/m3 of (1,027 Btu/ft^3). Republic of South Africa, Department: Minerals and Energy, Operating and Developing Coal Mines in the Republic of South Africa 2005, Table 1, [http://www.dme.gov.za/pdfs/minerals/d2_2005.pdf].
b. assumed for diesel, no further information is available. Department of Minerals and Energy, Republic of South Africa, Gas Infra-Structure Plan, April 19, 2005, [http://www.dme.gov.za /pdfs/energy/gas/gas_infrastructure_plan.pdf].

Shell Bintulu Gas-to-Liquids Efficiency
Feedtsock:
natural gas: 20,000,000ft^3/day x 1,027 Btu/ft^3 = 123,240,000,000 Btu
Products:
middle distillate: 6,250 bbl/day x 42 gal/bbl x 123,600 Btu/gal[a] = 445,000,000 Btu
detergent feedstocks and waxes:

6,250 bbl/day x 5,537,000 Btu/bbl[b] =	34,606,250,000 Btu
product total =	67,051,250,000 Btu

Calculation:
Product (67,051,250,000)/Feedstock (123,240,000,000) = 54%

CRS-29

Sources:
a. Norton et al.
b. assumed based on EIA

Oryx Gas-to-Liquids Efficiency
Feedstock:
"lean" gas: 330,000,000 ft^3 /day x 1,027 Btu/ft^3 [a] = 338,910,000,000 Btu
Products:
diesel: 24,000 bbl/day x 42 gal/bbl x 123,600 Btu/gal[b] =   124,588,800,000 Btu
naphtha: 9,000 bbl/day x 5,248,000 Btu/bbl[a] =   47,232,000,000 Btu
liquified petroleum gas: 1,000 bbl/day x 4,000,000 Btu/bbl[a] =   4,000,000,000 Btu
product total =   175,820,800,000 Btu
Calculation:
Product (175,820,800,000)/ Feedstock (338,910,000,000) = 52%

Sources:
a. assumed based on EIA
b. Norton et al.

NETL Coal-to-Liquids Efficiency
Feedstock:
Illinois No. 6 coal: 24,533 tons/day x 13,126 Btu/lb. x 2000 lb./ton = 644,040,316,000 Btu
Products:
diesel: 27,819 bbl/day x 42 gal/bbl/ 123,600 Btu/gal =   144,413,992,800 Btu
naphtha: 22,173 bbl/day x 5,248,000 Btu/bbl =   116,363,904,000 Btu
product total =   260,777,896,800 Btu
Calculation:
Product (260,777,896,800) / Feedstock (644,040,316,000) = 40.5%

319

CRS-30

Table A1. Energy Consumed by Refining in 2005

	Volume by Unit	Heat Content	Energy (million BTU)
Crude Oil Refined	5,555 million barrels	5.825 million Btu/barrel	32,221,264,446
Fuels Consumed			
Liquefied Petroleum Gases	4.17 million barrels	4.000 million Btu/barrel	16,680,000
Distillate Fuel Oil	0.76 million barrels	5.825 million Btu/barrel	4,427,000
Residual Fuel Oil	2.21 million barrels	6.287 million Btu/barrel	13,894,270
Still Gas	238.24 million barrels	6.000 million Btu/barrel	1,429,440,000
Petroleum Coke	89.65 million barrels	6.024 million Btu/barrel	540,051,600
Other Petroleum Products	5.33 million barrels	5.825 million Btu/barrel	31,047,250
Natural Gas	682,919 million cubic feet	1,027 Btu/cubic foot	701,357,813
Coal	41,000 short tons	20.4 million Btu/ton	836,400
Purchased Electricity	36,594 million kilowatt hours	3,412 Btu/kilowatt-hour	124,858,728
Purchased Steam	63,591 million pounds	1,000 Btu/pound	63,591,000
TOTAL ENERGY CONSUMED IN REFINING			2,926,184,061
FUELS CONSUMED ÷ CRUDE OIL REFINED =			9.08%

Sources: U.S. DOE EIA, Petroleum Navigator, Fuel Consumed at [http://tonto.eia.doe.gov/dnav/pet/pet/pet_pnp_top.asp] (Refineriespet_pnp_capfuel_dcu_nus_a.xls); U.S. DOE EIA, Thermal Conversion Factor Source Document [http://www.eia.doe.gov/emeu/mer/pdf/pages/sec12_a_doc.pdf].

320 703-739-3790 TCNNaturalGas.com

HENRY A. WAXMAN, CALIFORNIA
CHAIRMAN

JOHN D. DINGELL, MICHIGAN
CHAIRMAN EMERITUS
EDWARD J. MARKEY, MASSACHUSETTS
RICK BOUCHER, VIRGINIA
FRANK PALLONE, JR., NEW JERSEY
BART GORDON, TENNESSEE
BOBBY L. RUSH, ILLINOIS
ANNA G. ESHOO, CALIFORNIA
BART STUPAK, MICHIGAN
ELIOT L. ENGEL, NEW YORK
GENE GREEN, TEXAS
DIANA DeGETTE, COLORADO
VICE CHAIRMAN
LOIS CAPPS, CALIFORNIA
MIKE DOYLE, PENNSYLVANIA
JANE HARMAN, CALIFORNIA
JAN SCHAKOWSKY, ILLINOIS
CHARLES A. GONZALEZ, TEXAS
JAY INSLEE, WASHINGTON
TAMMY BALDWIN, WISCONSIN
MIKE ROSS, ARKANSAS
ANTHONY D. WEINER, NEW YORK
JIM MATHESON, UTAH
G.K. BUTTERFIELD, NORTH CAROLINA
CHARLIE MELANCON, LOUISIANA
JOHN BARROW, GEORGIA
BARON P. HILL, INDIANA
DORIS O. MATSUI, CALIFORNIA
DONNA CHRISTENSEN, VIRGIN ISLANDS
KATHY CASTOR, FLORIDA
JOHN SARBANES, MARYLAND
CHRISTOPHER MURPHY, CONNECTICUT
ZACHARY T. SPACE, OHIO
JERRY McNERNEY, CALIFORNIA
BETTY SUTTON, OHIO
BRUCE BRALEY, IOWA
PETER WELCH, VERMONT

JOE BARTON, TEXAS
RANKING MEMBER

RALPH M. HALL, TEXAS
FRED UPTON, MICHIGAN
CLIFF STEARNS, FLORIDA
NATHAN DEAL, GEORGIA
ED WHITFIELD, KENTUCKY
JOHN SHIMKUS, ILLINOIS
JOHN B. SHADEGG, ARIZONA
ROY BLUNT, MISSOURI
STEVE BUYER, INDIANA
GEORGE RADANOVICH, CALIFORNIA
JOSEPH R. PITTS, PENNSYLVANIA
MARY BONO MACK, CALIFORNIA
GREG WALDEN, OREGON
LEE TERRY, NEBRASKA
MIKE ROGERS, MICHIGAN
SUE WILKINS MYRICK, NORTH CAROLINA
JOHN SULLIVAN, OKLAHOMA
TIM MURPHY, PENNSYLVANIA
MICHAEL C. BURGESS, TEXAS
MARSHA BLACKBURN, TENNESSEE
PHIL GINGREY, GEORGIA
STEVE SCALISE, LOUISIANA

ONE HUNDRED ELEVENTH CONGRESS

Congress of the United States

House of Representatives

COMMITTEE ON ENERGY AND COMMERCE

2125 RAYBURN HOUSE OFFICE BUILDING

WASHINGTON, DC 20515–6115

MAJORITY (202) 225–2927
FACSIMILE (202) 225–2525
MINORITY (202) 225–3641

energycommerce.house.gov

MEMORANDUM

February 18, 2010

To: Members of the Subcommittee on Energy and Environment

Fr: Chairman Henry A. Waxman and Subcommittee Chairman Edward J. Markey

Re: Examining the Potential Impact of Hydraulic Fracturing

Today, we are sending letters to eight oil and gas service companies regarding the chemicals they use in their hydraulic fracturing fluids. This memorandum explains why we are taking this action.

Executive Summary

One of the most promising trends in U.S. energy supplies is the development of new technologies for extracting natural gas from shale deposits and other unconventional sources. Hydraulic fracturing, along with horizontal drilling technology, has allowed oil and gas companies to reach and extract oil and natural gas once thought unattainable. As a result, proven domestic reserves of natural gas have expanded exponentially in recent years. Reliable access to this cleaner-burning fossil fuel could enhance our energy independence and reduce our reliance on more carbon-heavy sources of energy.

As the oil and gas industry applies this technology to more wells in more parts of the country, it is important to ensure that the process is safe and environmentally sound. Environmental organizations, public health groups, and local communities have expressed concerns about the potential impact of the injection of hydraulic fracturing fluids in wells located in or near underground sources of drinking water. Others have raised concerns about the quantity of water needed to hydraulically fracture oil and gas wells and the disposal of contaminated wastewater from fracturing operations. The letters that we are sending today are designed to help answer these questions.

In 2003, EPA entered into a voluntary memorandum of agreement (MOA) with the three largest hydraulic fracturing companies, Halliburton, BJ Services, and Schlumberger, to eliminate diesel fuel from hydraulic fracturing fluids injected into certain wells located in underground sources of drinking water. Aside from this MOA, there is virtually no federal regulation of hydraulic fracturing. In 2005, Congress exempted the practice of hydraulic fracturing from the Safe Drinking Water Act (SDWA), except when the injected fluids contain diesel fuel. Oil and gas companies can use additives and chemicals besides diesel fuel in their hydraulic fracturing fluids, but federal regulators have no authority to limit the types and volumes of these substances. Indeed, oil and gas companies do not need to report to federal regulators what their fracturing fluids contain or where they are used.

As Chairman of the House Committee on Oversight and Government Reform in the last Congress, Chairman Waxman requested and received some data from Halliburton, BJ Services, and Schlumberger on the chemicals used in their fracturing fluids. According to this data, two of these companies used diesel fuel as a fracturing fluid between 2005 and 2007. Halliburton reported using more than 807,000 gallons of seven diesel-based fluids, a potential violation of the MOA. BJ Services reported using 1,700 gallons of two diesel-based fluids in several fracturing jobs in Arkansas and Oklahoma. In a letter to the Oversight Committee, BJ Services acknowledged that these events were "in violation of the MOA." The companies also indicated that they used other chemicals in their fracturing fluids – such as benzene, toluene, ethylbenzene, and xylenes – that could pose environmental and human health risks.

The information provided to the Oversight Committee did not specify whether these fluids were injected into wells located in or near underground sources of drinking water. This is an important issue because injecting the chemicals in or near sources of drinking water could create contamination risks. In addition, it could be a violation of the Safe Drinking Water Act if the fluids contain diesel fuel. The information also did not address how the companies dispose of their fracturing fluids and whether this is being done in an environmentally safe manner.

Three of the letters being sent today seek additional information from Halliburton, BJ Services, and Schlumberger on these and related issues. In addition, we are seeking similar information from five smaller fracturing companies that comprise a growing share of the market.

The extraction of natural gas from unconventional sources appears to hold great potential for enhancing our energy independence and reducing air pollution, including carbon emissions. But as the development of this new technology proceeds, it should be conducted in an environmentally safe manner. The purpose of the letters is to help the Committee assess whether the new technology poses any environmental or public health risks that Congress should address.

I. Background

A. The Promise of Developing Unconventional Natural Gas Supplies

Estimates of domestic natural gas reserves have increased sharply in recent years. In a biennial report released earlier this year, the Potential Gas Committee, a group of academics and industry experts supported by the Colorado School of Mines, raised its assessment of proven and potential U.S. natural gas reserves by 35%. The group attributed this substantial jump to the

2

increased accessibility of shale gas.[1] The consulting firm PFC Energy reports that shale gas production has expanded from 1% of U.S. natural gas production in 2000 to approximately 10% today.[2] And experts expect a sustained swell in exploration of unconventional sources. The Energy Information Administration (EIA) within the Department of Energy predicts that unconventional gas exploration will be the largest contributor to increases in domestic natural gas production over the next two decades, with its share of domestic production growing to 56% in 2030.[3] While EIA foresees tight sand formations as the largest source of unconventional natural gas, it notes that shale is the fastest growing source and predicts that accelerated shale gas production will continue.[4]

Formations with shale gas potential stretch across much of the United States. Exploration of these formations in Texas, Arkansas, and Louisiana has been underway for years, and exploration in the Marcellus Shale that spans New York, Pennsylvania, and West Virginia is intensifying. Experts at Pennsylvania State University believe that the Marcellus Shale alone could hold enough gas to meet U.S. demand for 14 or more years.[5]

New natural gas supplies could enhance the stability and environmental sustainability of U.S. energy use. Unconventional sources of natural gas would reduce disruptions to supply from Gulf Coast hurricanes and limit the nation's reliance on natural gas imports. In addition, increased use of natural gas to power vehicles could reduce domestic imports of petroleum. Natural gas emits only about half as much carbon as coal, making it an attractive source of electricity generation as the nation seeks to reduce its production of greenhouse gases. Unlike coal-burning and nuclear power plants, natural gas plants can cut on and off quickly and could supplement energy from wind and solar power.[6] For these reasons, many experts, including U.N. Foundation leader and former Colorado Senator Timothy Wirth, believe that "natural gas can serve as a bridge fuel to a low-carbon, sustainable energy future."[7]

---

[1] Potential Gas Committee, *Potential Gas Committee reports unprecedented increase in magnitude of U.S. natural gas resource base* (June 18, 2009).

[2] *An Energy Answer in the Shale Below? New Technology Opens Vast Stores of Natural Gas, and the Land Rush Is On,* Washington Post (Dec. 3, 2009).

[3] U.S. Department of Energy, Energy Information Administration, *Annual Energy Outlook 2009,* at 77 (online at http://www.eia.doe.gov/oiaf/aeo/pdf/trend_4.pdf) (accessed Feb. 2, 2010).

[4] *Id.*

[5] *An Energy Answer in the Shale Below? New Technology Opens Vast Stores of Natural Gas, and the Land Rush Is On,* Washington Post (Dec. 3, 2009).

[6] *Id.*

[7] *Id.*

3

B.   Concerns about Hydraulic Fracturing

According to the Department of Energy, advances in hydraulic fracturing technology, as well as a rise in the price of natural gas, have made it possible for oil and gas companies to extract gas resources once thought unattainable.[8] In hydraulic fracturing, the companies force fracturing fluids and propping agents into existing oil and gas production wells at extremely high pressure, which cracks the oil or gas seams and allows trapped natural gas and oil to escape. Without hydraulic fracturing and improvements in horizontal drilling, oil and gas companies likely would not be able to access unconventional sources of oil and natural gas in an economical manner.

Hydraulic fracturing is not without controversy and concern. Oil and gas companies use a variety of additives and chemicals in their fracturing fluids with the goal of widening and extending the length of the fractures and transporting large amounts of material to "prop open" the fractures. While some of these additives are harmless, such as sand used as a proppant, others may contain constituents of potential concern to human health and the environment.[9] Several communities have raised concerns about this practice's potential impact on drinking water, with some alleging that hydraulic fracturing is to blame for the contamination of local wells.[10]

Federal regulators currently do not have access to a full accounting of the types and quantities of chemicals used in hydraulic fracturing fluids, although some states require disclosure. Under the Emergency Planning and Community Right to Know Act, approximately 22,000 industrial and federal facilities must report to EPA the quantity of toxic chemicals they release, store, or transfer, which is then made public in the annual Toxics Release Inventory (TRI). Oil and gas exploration and production facilities are exempt from this reporting requirement.[11] EPA also does not have authority under the Safe Drinking Water Act (SDWA) to require disclosure of the chemicals injected in hydraulic fracturing operations.

---

[8] U.S. Department of Energy, *Modern Shale Gas Development in the United States: A Primer* (Apr. 2009) at 9.

[9] Environmental Protection Agency, *Evaluation of Impacts to Underground Sources of Drinking Water by Hydraulic Fracturing of Coalbed Methane Reservoirs* (June 2004) (EPA 816-R-04-003) at 4-3.

[10] *See, e.g., With Natural Gas Drilling Boom, Pennsylvania Faces an Onslaught of Wastewater*, ProPublica (Oct. 4, 2009); *Dirty Well Water Raises Stink Near Drilling Sites; Residents Cite Gas Firm for Poor Quality*, Arkansas Democrat-Gazette (July 5, 2009); *Debate Shows Merits, Dangers of Drilling Technique*, Associated Press (Dec. 23, 2008); *Controversial Path to Possible Glut of Natural Gas*, Christian Science Monitor (Sept. 18, 2008).

[11] 40 C.F.R. § 372.23.

4

EPA has raised particular concerns about diesel fuel, noting that the "use of diesel fuel in fracturing fluids poses the greatest threat" to underground sources of drinking water.[12] Diesel contains constituents regulated under SDWA because of their toxicity, including benzene, toluene, ethylbenzene, and xylenes (BTEX chemicals).[13] The Department of Health and Human Services, the International Agency for Research on Cancer, and EPA have determined that benzene is a human carcinogen.[14] Chronic exposure to toluene, ethylbenzene, or xylenes can damage the central nervous system, liver, and kidneys.[15]

In December 2003, EPA entered into a voluntary memorandum of agreement with the three largest hydraulic fracturing companies, Halliburton, BJ Services, and Schlumberger, to "eliminate diesel fuel in hydraulic fracturing fluids injected into coalbed methane production wells in underground sources of drinking water."[16] The MOA focused on coalbed methane wells, as these wells tend to be shallower and closer to underground sources of drinking water than conventional oil and gas production wells. The MOA does not contain any enforcement provisions nor does it confer immunity in an action to enforce the SDWA or EPA's regulations on underground injection.[17]

In 2005, Congress exempted hydraulic fracturing from regulation under the SDWA as part of the Energy Policy Act.[18] Many dubbed this provision the "Halliburton loophole" because of Halliburton's ties to then-Vice President Cheney and its role as one of the largest providers of hydraulic fracturing services.[19] Specifically, Congress modified the definition of "underground injection" to exclude "the underground injection of fluids or propping agents (other than diesel fuels) pursuant to hydraulic fracturing operations related to oil, gas, or geothermal production

---

[12] U.S. Environmental Protection Agency, *Evaluation of Impacts to Underground Sources of Drinking Water by Hydraulic Fracturing of Coalbed Methane Reservoirs* (June 2004) (EPA 816-R-04-003) at 4-11.

[13] *Id.*

[14] U.S. Department of Health and Human Services, Agency for Toxic Substances and Disease Registry, *Public Health Statement for Benzene* (Aug. 2007).

[15] U.S. Environmental Protection Agency, *Basic Information about Toluene in Drinking Water* (online at www.epa.gov/safewater/contaminants/basicinformation/toluene.html), *Basic Information about Ethylbenzene in Drinking Water* (online at www.epa.gov/safewater/contaminants/basicinformation/ethylbenzene.html) and *Basic Information about Xylenes in Drinking Water* (online at www.epa.gov/safewater/contaminants/basicinformation/xylenes.html) (accessed Feb. 2, 2010).

[16] Memorandum of Agreement between the U.S. Environmental Protection Agency and BJ Services Company, Halliburton Energy Services, Inc., and Schlumberger Technology Corporation (Dec. 12, 2003).

[17] *Id.*

[18] Pub. L. No. 109-58 (2005).

[19] *The Halliburton Loophole*, New York Times (Nov. 9. 2009).

5

activities."[20] As a result of this exemption, EPA cannot use the SDWA to regulate hydraulic fracturing unless it can show the use of diesel fuels.

Environmental groups, public health officials, and communities across the country have raised other concerns about hydraulic fracturing, beyond potential impacts on drinking water. In Texas, state regulators are responding to tests showing high levels of benzene in the air near wells in the Barnett Shale gas fields.[21] In Pennsylvania, state regulators are facing a new challenge of how to ensure proper disposal of the millions of gallons of wastewater generated from natural gas development in the Marcellus Shale.[22] In New York, the state Department of Environmental Conservation analyzed wastewater extracted from wells and found levels of radium-226 as high as 267 times the limit safe for discharge into the environment and thousands of times the limit safe for people to drink.[23] Others have raised concerns about water scarcity, since the drilling and hydraulic fracturing of a horizontal shale gas well may require 2 to 4 million gallons of water.[24]

C. EPA's Recent Work on Hydraulic Fracturing

In May 2009, EPA Administrator Lisa Jackson said that she found allegations of drinking water contamination linked to hydraulic fracturing "startling" and told members of Congress that it may be time to take another look at the safety of the hydraulic fracturing process.[25] EPA hired a consulting firm to survey media reports and publicly available documents describing several cases of drinking water contamination allegedly linked to hydraulic fracturing. Based on this review of available literature, the firm concluded that 12 of the contaminant cases examined "may have a possible link to hydraulic fracturing, but, to date, EPA has insufficient information on which to make a definitive decision."[26]

In Pavillion, Wyoming, EPA, using its authority under the Superfund program, has been testing residential and municipal wells, in response to community concerns about declining drinking water quality. The first phase of testing found hydrocarbons and 2-butoxyethanol, a

---

[20] 42 U.S.C. § 300h(d).

[21] *State worried about air pollution near Barnett Shale wells*, Star-Telegram (Nov. 22, 2009); *Agency finds high benzene levels on Barnett Shale*, Associated Press (Jan. 27, 2010).

[22] *What can be done with wastewater?*, Pittsburgh Post-Gazette (Oct. 4, 2009).

[23] *Is New York's Marcellus Shale Too Hot to Handle?*, ProPublica (Nov. 9, 2009).

[24] Department of Energy, *Modern Shale Gas Development in the United States: A Primer* (Apr. 2009) at 64.

[25] House Committee on Appropriations, Subcommittee on Interior, Environment, and Related Agencies, Testimony of the Honorable Lisa Jackson, Administrator, U.S. Environmental Protection Agency, *Hearing on the Environmental Protection Agency,* 111th Cong. (May 19, 2009).

[26] Cadmus Group, *Hydraulic Fracturing: Preliminary Analysis of Recently Reported Contamination* (Sept. 2009).

6

foaming agent used in hydraulic fracturing fluids, in several wells. While EPA has been unable to "pinpoint any specific source at this time," the agency acknowledged a potential connection between this contamination and nearby oil and gas production activities.[27]

The conference report for the Department of the Interior, Environment, and Related Agencies Appropriations Act for Fiscal Year 2010, signed into law on October 30, 2009, requested that EPA conduct a new scientific study of the hydraulic fracturing process. Specifically, the report states that EPA is to "carry out a study of the relationship between hydraulic fracturing and drinking water, using a credible approach that relies on the best available science, as well as independent sources of information."[28]

II.   The Oversight Committee Investigation

As Chairman of the House Committee on Oversight and Government Reform, Chairman Waxman wrote to the CEOs of Halliburton, BJ Services, and Schlumberger and requested data on the types and volume of chemicals used in their hydraulic fracturing fluids between 2005 and 2007.[29] The information provided shows that at least two of these companies continued to use diesel fuel in their fracturing fluids after signing the 2003 agreement with EPA. It also shows that they use other chemicals in their fluids that could be a cause for concern if they entered drinking water supplies.

A.   Halliburton

Halliburton provided data to the Oversight Committee revealing that it continued to use diesel and BTEX chemicals in the company's fracturing fluids after signing the MOA:

- Halliburton reported using fluids containing diesel fuel in 2005, 2006, and 2007 to fracture oil and gas wells in 15 states. Specifically, Halliburton reported using more than 807,000 gallons of seven diesel-based fluids over the three year period.[30]

---

[27] U.S. Environmental Protection Agency, *Pavillion Groundwater Investigation, Pavillion, Wyoming: Phase I Sampling Results* (Aug. 11, 2009).

[28] Conference Report for the Department of the Interior, Environment, and Related Agencies Appropriations Act, 2010, 111th Cong. (2009) (Rept. 111-316).

[29] Letter from Henry A. Waxman, Chairman, Committee on Oversight and Government Reform, to David Lesar, Chairman, President, and CEO, Halliburton (Nov. 26, 2007); Letter from Henry A. Waxman, Chairman, Committee on Oversight and Government Reform, to Andrew Gould, Chairman and CEO, Schlumberger (Nov. 26, 2007); Letter from Henry A. Waxman, Chairman, Committee on Oversight and Government Reform, to J.W. Stewart, Chairman, President, and CEO, BJ Services (Nov. 26, 2007).

[30] Halliburton Material Safety Data Sheet (MSDS), *BC-200* (Jan. 2009); Halliburton MSDS, *CL-22M Crosslinker* (Jan. 2009); Halliburton MSDS, *Diesel Fuel* (Jan. 2008); Halliburton MSDS, *LGC-8* (Jan. 2009); Halliburton MSDS, *LGC-35* (Jan. 2009); Halliburton MSDS, *LGC-V* (Jan. 2007); Halliburton MSDS, *LGC-VI* (Jan. 2009).

7

- Halliburton also reported using fracturing fluids containing BTEX chemicals in 2005, 2006, and 2007 to fracture oil and gas wells in 14 states. Specifically, Halliburton reported using nearly 235,000 gallons of six fracturing fluids containing BTEX chemicals over the three year period.[31]

Halliburton's data did not distinguish between fracturing fluids used in oil wells versus natural gas wells and did not specify whether the company used fracturing fluids containing diesel in coalbed methane wells located within underground sources of drinking water, as prohibited by the MOA.

B.   BJ Services

BJ Services provided data to the Oversight Committee revealing that it continued to use diesel and BTEX chemicals in the company's fracturing fluids in coalbed methane wells after signing the MOA:

- BJ Services reported using 1,706 gallons of diesel-based slurry in two dozen coalbed methane fracturing jobs in Arkansas and Oklahoma in 2005, 2006, and 2007.[32] In a letter to the Oversight Committee, counsel for BJ Services acknowledged that these events "were in violation of the MOA" and expressed a commitment to uncovering how they occurred. The company's counsel also noted that BJ Services subsequently sent a reminder to "all employees who design or perform fracturing operations about the requirements of the MOA."[33]

- In addition to the diesel-based slurries, BJ Services reported using 833 gallons of other fluids containing diesel fuel to fracture coalbed methane wells in Arkansas and Oklahoma in 2005, 2006, and 2007.[34] Counsel for BJ Services also reported that the company uses "biodegradable balls (typically about an inch in diameter) that are pumped into the wellbore to seal the perforation openings; they ultimately break apart, fall to the bottom of the wellbore, and dissolve, never actually entering the oil/gas reservoir."[35] These

---

[31] Halliburton MSDS, *Aromatic 100* (Jan. 2008); Halliburton MSDS, *Barsol D-100* (Jan. 2007); Halliburton MSDS, *Parachek 160 Paraffin Inhibitor* (June 2007); Halliburton MSDS, *Parasperse Cleaner* (June 2007); Halliburton MSDS, *Xylene* (June 2007); Halliburton MSDS, *Xylene Bottoms* (Jan. 2007).

[32] BJ Services Company MSDS, *XLFC-1* (Nov. 2006); BJ Services Company MSDS, *XLFC-5* (Nov. 2006).

[33] Letter from Counsel to Henry A. Waxman, Chairman, Committee on Oversight and Government Reform (Jan. 24, 2008).

[34] BJ Services Company MSDS, *FLC-42L* (Oct. 2006); BJ Services Company MSDS, *GW-3L* (Oct. 2006).

[35] Letter from Counsel to Henry A. Waxman, Chairman, Committee on Oversight and Government Reform (Jan. 24, 2008).

8

biodegradable balls contain diesel fuel, according to company documents.[36] The company did not say explicitly whether it used these fracturing fluids and materials in violation of the MOA.

- BJ Services also reported using 217 gallons of a fluid containing xylene, one of the toxic BTEX chemicals, to fracture coalbed methane wells in three states in 2005, 2006, and 2007.[37]

BJ Services provided data only on fluids used to fracture coalbed methane wells. The Oversight Committee did not receive data on whether BJ Services used diesel-based fluids in other types of fracturing jobs between 2005 and 2007.

C.   Schlumberger

Based on the data Schlumberger provided to the Oversight Committee, we have no evidence that the company used diesel-based fluids to fracture coalbed methane wells between 2005 and 2007. Schlumberger did report using 170 gallons of two corrosion inhibitors that contain nonspecific "aromatic hydrocarbons."[38] This is a category of chemicals that can include benzene and other BTEX chemicals.[39] Schlumberger did not provide data on its fracturing activities in other types of wells.

III.   The Need for Additional Investigation

The information provided by the companies raises several questions. First, the use of diesel fuel in fracturing fluids by Halliburton and BJ Services raises questions about the effectiveness of the 2003 MOA and whether the companies violated the Safe Drinking Water Act when they used these fluids.

Second, the companies provided data on which chemicals they used in their hydraulic fracturing fluids, but they did not specify whether they injected these fluids in wells located in, near, or below underground sources of drinking water. This information is needed to assess whether the use of the chemicals posed a threat to drinking water supplies.

Third, the responses indicated that the companies used other potentially dangerous chemicals besides diesel fuel in hydraulic fracturing fluids. Halliburton and BJ Services, for example, both reported using some BTEX chemicals in their fluids. According to the New York

---

[36] BJ Services Company MSDS, *BioSealers* (Oct. 2006).

[37] BJ Services Company MSDS, *NE-118* (Oct. 2006).

[38] Schlumberger MSDS, *Corrosion Inhibitor A261* (Feb. 2005); Schlumberger MSDS, *Corrosion Inhibitor A262* (Apr. 2005).

[39] *See* New York Department of Environmental Conservation, *Draft Supplemental Generic Environmental Impact Statement Well Permit Issuance for Horizontal Drilling And High-Volume Hydraulic Fracturing to Develop the Marcellus Shale and Other Low-Permeability Gas Reservoirs* (Sept. 2009) at 5-53.

9

State Department of Environmental Conservation, oil and gas companies have proposed using hundreds of chemicals in hydraulic fracturing fluids in the Marcellus Shale formation in New York, including more than a dozen different petroleum distillates.[40] More information about these chemicals and their use is required to assess their potential environmental impact.

Another set of questions involves the practices of smaller companies. When Halliburton, BJ Services, and Schlumberger signed the diesel MOA in 2003, the three companies performed 95% of the hydraulic fracturing jobs in the United States each year.[41] Since that time, smaller companies have increased their market share. Frac Tech, for example, describes itself as "one of the largest and fastest growing land stimulation companies."[42] Superior Well Services says it is a "growing oilfield services company operating in many of the major oil and natural gas producing regions of the United States."[43] Little is known about the practices of these and other small and medium sized companies that provide fracturing services across the country.

Finally, many have raised concerns about how oil and gas companies dispose of fracturing fluids and other produced water after it is extracted from the well. The Oversight Committee did not request any information on wastewater produced from hydraulic fracturing operations. More information is needed to assess the chemical contents of this waste and determine how companies can dispose of it in an environmentally safe manner.

IV.   The Committee's Letters

To help answer these questions, the Subcommittee on Energy and Environment is sending a new request to eight companies engaged in hydraulic fracturing in the United States: Halliburton, BJ Services, and Schlumberger, as well as Frac Tech Services, Superior Well Services, Universal Well Services, Sanjel Corporation, and Calfrac Well Services, five smaller companies that comprise a growing share of the market. The Committee is requesting the most recent data on the types and quantities of chemicals used in hydraulic fracturing fluids with additional information on whether the companies injected these fluids in, near, or below an underground source of drinking water. The Committee also is requesting documents related to any allegations that the hydraulic fracturing caused harm to human health or the environment. In

---

[40] New York City Council Committee on Environmental Protection, Testimony of Dusty Horwitt, Senior Counsel, Environmental Working Group, (Oct. 23, 2009), citing New York Department of Environmental Conservation, *Draft Supplemental Generic Environmental Impact Statement Well Permit Issuance for Horizontal Drilling And High-Volume Hydraulic Fracturing to Develop the Marcellus Shale and Other Low-Permeability Gas Reservoirs* (Sept. 2009) at 5-45-5-51, 5-53.

[41] Environmental Protection Agency, *Evaluation of Impacts to Underground Sources of Drinking Water by Hydraulic Fracturing of Coalbed Methane Reservoirs* (June 2004) (EPA 816-R-04-003) at 4-19.

[42] Frac Tech Services Home Page (online at www.fractech.net/about/index.htm) (accessed Feb. 1, 2010).

[43] Superior Well Services Home Page (online at www.superiorwells.com/index.php) (accessed Feb. 1, 2010).

10

addition, the Committee is requesting information on the chemical contents of water produced from hydraulic fracturing operations and how the companies dispose of this waste.

Hydraulic fracturing and other new technologies for unlocking unconventional natural gas supplies have tremendous potential. These technologies have created a natural gas boom in parts of the country that can contribute to the nation's energy independence and reduce carbon emissions. But as the use of these technologies expands, there needs to be oversight to ensure that their use does not threaten the public health of nearby communities. The goal of this investigation is to provide the Committee with a fuller understanding of the promise and the potential risks posed by the use of hydraulic fracturing to produce oil and natural gas from unconventional sources.

For additional information, please contact Alison Cassady or Stacia Cardille of the Committee staff at (202) 226-2424.

11

Natural Gas Processing: The Crucial Link Between Natural Gas Production and Its Transportation to Market

This special report examines the processing plant segment of the natural gas industry, providing a discussion and an analysis of how the gas processing segment has changed following the restructuring of the natural gas industry in the 1990s and the trends that have developed during that time. It focuses upon the natural gas industry and its capability to take wellhead quality production, separate it into its constituent parts, and deliver pipeline-quality natural gas (methane) into the nation's natural gas transportation network. Questions or comments on the contents of this article may be directed to James Tobin at James.Tobin@eia.doe.gov or (202) 586-4835, Phil Shambaugh at Phil.Shambaugh@eia.doe.gov or 202-586-4833, or Erin Mastrangelo at Erin.Mastrangelo@eia.doe.gov or (202)-586-6201.

The natural gas product fed into the mainline gas transportation system in the United States must meet specific quality measures in order for the pipeline grid to operate properly. Consequently, natural gas produced at the wellhead, which in most cases contains contaminants[1] and natural gas liquids,[2] must be processed, i.e., cleaned, before it can be safely delivered to the high-pressure, long-distance pipelines that transport the product to the consuming public. Natural gas that is not within certain specific gravities, pressures, Btu content range, or water content levels will cause operational problems, pipeline deterioration, or can even cause pipeline rupture (see Box, "Pipeline-Quality Natural Gas").[3]

Although the processing/treatment segment of the natural gas industry rarely receives much public attention, its overall importance to the natural gas industry became readily apparent in the aftermath of Hurricanes Katrina and Rita in September 2005. Heavy damage to a number of natural gas processing plants along the U.S. Gulf Coast, as well as to offshore production platforms and gathering lines, caused pipelines that feed into these facilities to suspend natural gas flows while the plants attempted to recover.[4] While several processing plants in southern Mississippi and Alabama were out of commission for only a brief period following Katrina, 16 processing plants in Louisiana and Texas with a total capacity of 9.71 billion cubic feet per day (Bcf/d) and a pre-hurricane flow volume of 5.45 Bcf/d were still offline 1 month following the two storms.[5] Consequently, a significant portion of the usual daily output that flowed into the interstate pipeline network from the tailgates of these plants was disrupted, in some cases indefinitely.

---

[1] Includes non-hydrocarbon gases such as water vapor, carbon dioxide, hydrogen sulfide, nitrogen, oxygen, and helium.

[2] Ethane, propane, and butane are the primary heavy hydrocarbons (liquids) extracted at a natural gas processing plant, but other petroleum gases, such as isobutane, pentanes, and normal gasoline, also may be processed.

[3] For a detailed examination of the subject see Joseph Wardzinski, et al., "Interstate Natural Gas – Quality Specifications & Interchangeability," Center for Energy Economics, Bureau of Economic Geology, The University of Texas at Austin (Houston, Texas, December 2004). http://www.beg.utexas.edu/energyecon/lng/

[4] Some of these feeder pipelines also had to suspend operations because they themselves suffered damage, the production platforms that they serviced were damaged, or the connecting pipelines were damaged.

[5] Department of Energy, "DOE's Hurricane Response Chronology" provided by Secretary Samuel Bodman at Senate Energy and Natural Resources Committee Hearing, October 27, 2005.

Pipeline-Quality Natural Gas

The natural gas received and transported by the major intrastate and interstate mainline transmission systems must meet the quality standards specified by pipeline companies in the "General Terms and Conditions (GTC)" section of their tariffs. These quality standards vary from pipeline to pipeline and are usually a function of a pipeline system's design, its downstream interconnecting pipelines, and its customer base. In general, these standards specify that the natural gas:

- Be within a specific Btu content range (1,035 Btu per cubic feet, +/- 50 Btu)

- Be delivered at a specified hydrocarbon dew point temperature level (below which any vaporized gas liquid in the mix will tend to condense at pipeline pressure)

- Contain no more than trace amounts of elements such as hydrogen sulfide, carbon dioxide, nitrogen, water vapor, and oxygen

- Be free of particulate solids and liquid water that could be detrimental to the pipeline or its ancillary operating equipment.

Gas processing equipment, whether in the field or at processing/treatment plants, assures that these tariff requirements can be met. While in most cases processing facilities extract contaminants and heavy hydrocarbons from the gas stream, in some cases they instead blend some heavy hydrocarbons into the gas stream in order to bring it within acceptable Btu levels. For instance, in some areas coalbed methane production falls below the pipeline's Btu standard, in which case a blend of higher btu-content natural gas or a propane-air mixture is injected to enrich its heat content (Btu) prior for delivery to the pipeline. In other instances, such as at LNG import facilities where the heat content of the regasified gas may be too high for pipeline receipt, vaporized nitrogen may be injected into the natural gas stream to lower its Btu content.

In recent years, as natural gas pricing has transitioned from a volume basis (per thousand cubic feet) to a heat-content basis (per million Btu), producers have tended, for economic reasons, to increase the Btu content of the gas delivered into the pipeline grid while decreasing the amount of natural gas liquids extracted from the natural gas stream. Consequently, interstate pipeline companies have had to monitor and enforce their hydrocarbon dew point temperature level restrictions more frequently to avoid any potential liquid formation within the pipes that may occur as a result of producers maximizing Btu content.

Energy Information Administration, Office of Oil and Gas, January 2006
1

Figure 1. Generalized Natural Gas Processing Schematic

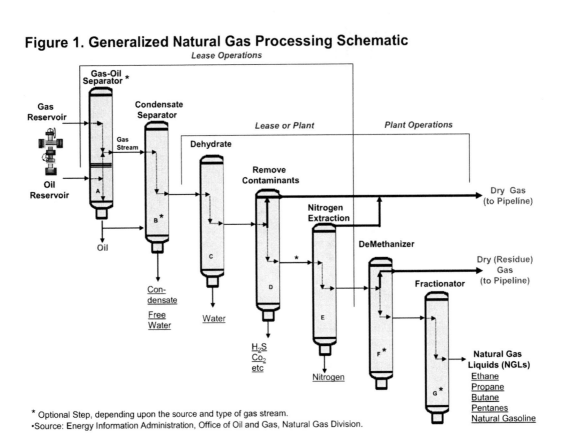

*Optional Step, depending upon the source and type of gas stream.
•Source: Energy Information Administration, Office of Oil and Gas, Natural Gas Division.

In 2004, approximately 24.2 trillion cubic feet (Tcf) of raw natural gas was produced at the wellhead.[6] A small portion of that, 0.1 Tcf, was vented or flared, while a larger portion, 3.7 Tcf, was re-injected into reservoirs (mostly in Alaska) to maintain pressure. The remaining 20.4 Tcf of "wet"[7] natural gas was converted into the 18.9 Tcf of dry natural gas that was put into the pipeline system. This conversion of wet natural gas into dry pipeline-quality natural gas, and the portion of the natural gas industry that performs that conversion, is the subject of this report.

Background

Natural gas processing begins at the wellhead (Figure 1). The composition of the raw natural gas extracted from producing wells depends on the type, depth, and location of the underground deposit and the geology of the area. Oil and natural gas are often found together in the same reservoir. The natural gas produced from oil wells is generally classified as "associated-dissolved," meaning that the natural gas is associated with or dissolved in crude oil. Natural gas production absent any association with crude oil is classified as "non-associated." In 2004, 75 percent of U.S. wellhead production of natural gas was non-associated.

Most natural gas production contains, to varying degrees, small (two to eight carbons) hydrocarbon molecules in addition to methane. Although they exist in a gaseous state at underground pressures, these molecules will become liquid (condense) at normal atmospheric pressure. Collectively, they are called condensates or natural gas liquids (NGLs). The natural gas extracted from coal reservoirs and mines (coalbed methane) is the primary exception, being essentially a mix of mostly methane and carbon dioxide (about 10 percent).[8]

---

[6]Energy Information Administration, *Natural Gas Annual 2004* (December 2005), Table 1. http://www.eia.doe.gov/oil_gas/natural_gas/data_publications/natural_gas_annual/nga.html.

[7]Wet gas is defined as the volume of natural gas remaining after removal of condensate and uneconomic nonhydrocarbon gases at lease/field separation facilities and less any gas used for repressurization.

[8]The Energy Information Administration estimates that about 9 percent of 2004 U.S. dry natural gas production, or about 1.7 Tcf, came from coalbed methane sources, which do not contain any natural gas liquids. *U.S. Crude Oil and Natural Gas, and Natural Gas Liquids Reserves: 2004 Annual Report.* http://www.eia.doe.gov/oil_gas/natural_gas/data_publications/

Natural gas production from the deepwater Gulf of Mexico and conventional natural gas sources of the Rocky Mountain area is generally rich in NGLs and typically must be processed to meet pipeline-quality specifications. Deepwater natural gas production can contain in excess of 4 gallons of NGLs per thousand cubic feet (Mcf) of natural gas compared with 1 to 1.5 gallons of NGLs per Mcf of natural gas produced from the continental shelf areas of the Gulf of Mexico. Natural gas produced along the Texas Gulf Coast typically contains 2 to 3 gallons of NGLs per Mcf.[9]

The processing of wellhead natural gas into pipeline-quality dry natural gas can be quite complex and usually involves several processes to remove: (1) oil; (2) water; (3) elements such as sulfur, helium, and carbon dioxide; and (4) natural gas liquids (see Box, "Stages in the Production of Pipeline-Quality Natural Gas and NGLs"). In addition to those four processes, it is often necessary to install scrubbers and heaters at or near the wellhead. The scrubbers serve primarily to remove sand and other large-particle impurities. The heaters ensure that the temperature of the natural gas does not drop too low and form a hydrate with the water vapor content of the gas stream. These natural gas hydrates are crystalline ice-like solids or semi-solids that can impede the passage of natural gas through valves and pipes.

The wells on a lease or in a field are connected to downstream facilities via a process called gathering, wherein small-diameter pipes connect the wells to initial processing/treating facilities. Beyond the fact that a producing area can occupy many square miles and involve a hundred or more wells, each with its own production characteristics, there may be a need for intermediate compression, heating, and scrubbing facilities, as well as treatment plants to remove carbon dioxide and sulfur compounds, prior to the processing plant (see Box "Other Key Byproducts of Natural Gas Processing"). All of these factors make gathering system design a complex engineering problem.

In those few cases where pipeline-quality natural gas is actually produced at the wellhead or field facility, the natural gas is moved directly to receipt points on the pipeline grid. In other instances, especially in the production of non-associated natural gas, field or lease facilities referred to as "skid-mount plants" are installed nearby to dehydrate and decontaminate raw natural gas into acceptable pipeline-quality gas for direct delivery to the pipeline grid. These compact "skids" are often specifically customized to process the type of natural gas produced in the area and are a relatively inexpensive alternative to transporting the natural gas to distant large-scale plants for processing.

Natural gas pipeline compressor stations,[10] especially those located in production areas, may also serve as field level processing facilities. They often include additional facilities for dewatering natural gas and for removal of many hydrocarbon liquids. Some pipeline compressor stations located along the coast of the Gulf of Mexico, for instance, are set up to process offshore production to a degree permitting delivery of a portion of its natural gas throughput directly into the pipeline grid. The remaining portion is forwarded to a natural gas processing plant for further processing and extraction of heavy liquids.

Non-pipeline-quality production is piped to natural gas processing plants for liquids extraction and eventual delivery of pipeline-quality natural gas at the plant tailgate. A natural gas processing plant typically receives gas from a gathering system and sends out processed gas via an output (tailgate) lateral that is interconnected to one or more major intra- and inter-state pipeline networks. Liquids removed at the processing plant usually will be taken away by pipeline to petrochemical plants, refineries, and other gas liquids customers. Some of the heavier liquids are often temporarily stored in tanks on site and then trucked to customers.

Various types of processing plants have been utilized since the mid-1850s to extract liquids, such as natural gasoline, from produced crude oil. However, for many years, natural gas was not a sought after fuel. Prior to the early 20th century, most of it was flared or simply vented into the atmosphere, primarily because the available pipeline technology permitted only very short-distance transmission.[11]

It was not until the early 1920s, when reliable pipe welding techniques were developed, that a need for natural gas processing arose. Yet, while a rudimentary network of relatively long-distance natural gas pipelines was in place by 1932, and some natural gas processing plants were installed upstream in major production areas,[12] the depression of the 1930s and the duration of World War II slowed the growth of natural gas demand and the need for more processing plants.[13]

After World War II, particularly during the 1950s, the development of plastics and other new products that required natural gas and petroleum as a production component

---

[9] Enterprise Products Partners LP, Annual SEC 10K filing, 2004, p. 18.

[10] All compressor stations contain some type of separation facilities which are designed to filter out, before compression, any water and/or hydrocarbons that may form in the gas stream during transport.

[11] William L. Leffler, "The Technology and Economic Behavior of the U.S. Propane Industry" (Tulsa, Oklahoma, 1973, The Petroleum Publishing Company), Chapter 1.

[12] Most of these pipelines extended from the Texas Panhandle and Louisiana to the Midwestern United States. Gas processing plants for these systems were located primarily in the Houghton Basin of northern Texas/Oklahoma/Kansas and the Katy area of eastern Texas.

[13] Arlon R. Tusing & Bob Tippee, "The Natural Gas Industry: Evolution, Structure, and Economics" (Tulsa, Oklahoma, 1995, Pennwell Publishing Company).

Energy Information Administration, Office of Oil and Gas, January 2006   **3**

Stages in the Production of Pipeline-Quality Natural Gas and NGLs

The number of steps and the type of techniques used in the process of creating pipeline-quality natural gas most often depends upon the source and makeup of the wellhead production stream. In some cases, several of the steps shown in Figure 1 may be integrated into one unit or operation, performed in a different order or at alternative locations (lease/plant), or not required at all. Among the several stages (as lettered in Figure 1) of gas processing/treatment are:

A) **Gas-Oil Separators**: In many instances pressure relief at the wellhead will cause a natural separation of gas from oil (using a conventional closed tank, where gravity separates the gas hydrocarbons from the heavier oil). In some cases, however, a multi-stage gas-oil separation process is needed to separate the gas stream from the crude oil. These gas-oil separators are commonly closed cylindrical shells, horizontally mounted with inlets at one end, an outlet at the top for removal of gas, and an outlet at the bottom for removal of oil. Separation is accomplished by alternately heating and cooling (by compression) the flow stream through multiple steps. Some water and condensate, if present, will also be extracted as the process proceeds.

B) **Condensate Separator:** Condensates are most often removed from the gas stream at the wellhead through the use of mechanical separators. In most instances, the gas flow into the separator comes directly from the wellhead, since the gas-oil separation process is not needed. The gas stream enters the processing plant at high pressure (600 pounds per square inch gauge (psig) or greater) through an inlet slug catcher where free water is removed from the gas, after which it is directed to a condensate separator. Extracted condensate is routed to on-site storage tanks.

C) **Dehydration:** A dehydration process is needed to eliminate water which may cause the formation of hydrates. Hydrates form when a gas or liquid containing free water experiences specific temperature/pressure conditions. Dehydration is the removal of this water from the produced natural gas and is accomplished by several methods. Among these is the use of ethylene glycol (glycol injection) systems as an absorption* mechanism to remove water and other solids from the gas stream. Alternatively, adsorption* dehydration may be used, utilizing dry-bed dehydrators towers, which contain desiccants such as silica gel and activated alumina, to perform the extraction.

D) **Contaminant Removal**: Removal of contaminates includes the elimination of hydrogen sulfide, carbon dioxide, water vapor, helium, and oxygen. The most commonly used technique is to first direct the flow though a tower containing an amine solution. Amines absorb sulfur compounds from natural gas and can be reused repeatedly. After desulphurization, the gas flow is directed to the next section, which contains a series of filter tubes. As the velocity of the stream reduces in the unit, primary separation of remaining contaminants occurs due to gravity. Separation of smaller particles occurs as gas flows through the tubes, where they combine into larger particles which flow to the lower section of the unit. Further, as the gas stream continues through the series of tubes, a centrifugal force is generated which further removes any remaining water and small solid particulate matter.

E) **Nitrogen Extraction:** Once the hydrogen sulfide and carbon dioxide are processed to acceptable levels, the stream is routed to a Nitrogen Rejection Unit (NRU), where it is further dehydrated using molecular sieve beds. In the NRU, the gas stream is routed through a series of passes through a column and a brazed aluminum plate fin heat exchanger. Using thermodynamics, the nitrogen is cryogenically separated and vented. Another type of NRU unit separates methane and heavier hydrocarbons from nitrogen using an absorbent* solvent. The absorbed methane and heavier hydrocarbons are flashed off from the solvent by reducing the pressure on the processing stream in multiple gas decompression steps. The liquid from the flash regeneration step is returned to the top of the methane absorber as lean solvent. Helium, if any, can be extracted from the gas stream through membrane diffusion in a Pressure Swing Adsorption (PSA) unit.

F) **Methane Separation:** The process of demethanizing the gas stream can occur as a separate operation in the gas plant or as part of the NRU operation. Cryogenic processing and absorption methods are some of the ways to separate methane from NGLs. The cryogenic method is better at extraction of the lighter liquids, such as ethane, than is the alternative absorption method. Essentially, cryogenic processing consists of lowering the temperature of the gas stream to around -120 degrees Fahrenheit. While there are several ways to perform this function the turbo expander process is most effective, using external refrigerants to chill the gas stream. The quick drop in temperature that the expander is capable of producing condenses the hydrocarbons in the gas stream, but maintains methane in its gaseous form. The absorption* method, on the other hand, uses a "lean" absorbing oil to separate the methane from the NGLs. While the gas stream is passed through an absorption tower, the absorption oil soaks up a large amount of the NGLs. The "enriched" absorption oil, now containing NGLs, exits the tower at the bottom. The enriched oil is fed into distillers where the blend is heated to above the boiling point of the NGLs, while the oil remains fluid. The oil is recycled while the NGLs are cooled and directed to a fractionator tower. Another absorption method that is often used is the refrigerated oil absorption method where the lean oil is chilled rather than heated, a feature that enhances recovery rates somewhat.

G) **Fractionation**: Fractionation, the process of separating the various NGLs present in the remaining gas stream, uses the varying boiling points of the individual hydrocarbons in the stream, by now virtually all NGLs, to achieve the task. The process occurs in stages as the gas stream rises through several towers where heating units raise the temperature of the stream, causing the various liquids to separate and exit into specific holding tanks.

* Adsorption is the binding of molecules or particles to the surface of a material, while absorption is the filling of the pores in a solid. The binding to the surface is usually weak with adsorption, and therefore, usually easily reversible.

Sources: Compiled from information available at the following Internet web sites: American Gas Association (http://www.naturalgas.org/ naturalgas/naturalgas.asp), Environmental Protection Agency (http://www.epa.gov/ttn/chief/ap42/ch05/final/c05s03.pdf), Cooper Cameron Inc. (http://www.coopercameron.com/cgi-bin/petreco/products/products.cfm?pageid=gastreatment), AdvancedExtractionTechnologies, Inc. (http://www.act.com/gtip1.htm#refriglean), SPM-3000 Gas Oil Separation Processing (GOSP) (http://www.simtronics.com/ catalog/spm/spm 3000.htm), and Membrane Technology and Research, Inc. (http://www.mtrinc.com/Pages/NaturalGas/ng.html#).

Energy Information Administration, Office of Oil and Gas, January 2006

4

336 703-739-3790 TCNNaturalGas.com

Other Key Byproducts of Natural Gas Processing

While natural gas liquids, such as propane and butane, are the byproducts most often related to the natural gas recovery process, several other products are also extracted from natural gas at field or gas treatment facilities.

Helium (He)

The world's supply of helium comes exclusively from natural gas production. The single largest source of helium is the United States, which produces about 80 percent of the annual world production of 3.0 billion cubic feet (Bcf). In 2003, U.S. production of helium was 2.4 Bcf, about two-thirds of which came from the Hugoton Basin in north Texas, Oklahoma, and Kansas (Figure 2). The rest mostly comes from the LaBarge field located in the Green River Basin in western Wyoming, with small amounts also produced in Utah and Colorado. According to the National Research Council, the consumption of helium in the United States doubled between 1985 and 1996, although its use has leveled off in recent years. It is used in such applications as magnetic resonance imaging, semiconductor processing, and in the pressurizing and purging of rocket engines by the National Aeronautics and Space Administration.

Twenty-two natural gas treatment plants in the United States currently produce helium as a major byproduct of natural gas processing. Twenty of these plants, located in the Hugoton-Panhandle Basin, produce marketable helium which is sold in the open market when profitable, while transporting the remaining unrefined helium to the Federal Helium Reserve (FHR). The FHR was created in the 1950s in the Bush salt dome, underlying the Cliffside field, located near Amarillo, Texas. Sales of unrefined helium in the United States for the most part, come from the FHR.

Carbon Dioxide (CO$_2$)

While most carbon dioxide is produced as a byproduct of processes other than natural gas treatment, a significant amount is also produced during natural gas processing in the Permian Basin of western Texas and eastern New Mexico. A limited amount is also produced in western Wyoming. In 2004 about 6.2 Bcf of carbon dioxide was produced in seven plants in the United States.

The carbon dioxide produced at these natural gas treatment plants is used primarily for re-injection in support of tertiary enhanced oil recovery efforts in the local production area. The smaller, uneconomic, amounts of carbon dioxide that are normally removed during the natural gas processing and treatment in the United States are vented to the atmosphere.

Hydrogen Sulfide (H$_2$S)

Almost all the elemental sulfur today is sulfur recovered from the desulfurization of oil products and natural gas. Hydrogen sulfide is extracted from a natural gas stream, or condensate, that is referred to as "sour." It is passed through a chemical solution that removes hydrogen sulfide and carbon dioxide, which are then fed to plants where the hydrogen sulfide is converted to elemental sulfur. The small quantities of non-sulfur components are incinerated and vented into the atmosphere. "Sour" condensate from plant inlet separators is fed to a condensate stabilizer where hydrogen sulfide and lighter hydrocarbons are removed, compressed, and then cycled to sulfur plants.

---

coincided with improvements in pipeline welding and pipeline manufacturing techniques. The increased demand for natural gas as an industrial feedstock and industrial fuel supported the growth of major natural gas transportation systems, which in turn improved the marketability and availability of natural gas for residential and commercial use.

Consequently, as the natural gas pipeline network itself became more efficient and regulated, the need for more and better natural gas processing increased both the number and operational efficiencies of natural gas processing plants.

National Overview

More than 500 natural gas processing plants currently operate in the United States (Table 1). Most are located in proximity to the major gas/oil producing areas of the Southwest and the Rocky Mountain States (Figure 2).[14] Not surprisingly, more than half of the current natural gas processing plant capacity in the United States is located convenient to the Federal offshore, Texas, and Louisiana. Four of the largest capacity natural gas processing/treatment plants are found in Louisiana while the greatest number of individual natural gas plants is located in Texas.

Although Texas and Louisiana still account for the larger portion of U.S. natural gas plant processing capability, other States have moved up in the rankings somewhat during the past 10 years as new trends in natural gas production and processing have come into play. For instance:

---

[14] The largest gas producing areas and States in 2004 were Texas onshore, the Federal offshore (waters off Texas, Louisiana, Alabama, and Mississippi), Oklahoma, New Mexico, Wyoming, Louisiana onshore, Colorado, and Kansas.

Table 1. Natural Gas Processing Plant Capacity in the Lower 48 States, 1995 and 2004

State	Natural Gas Processing Capacity (Million cubic feet per day)				Number of Natural Gas Processing/Treatment Plants				Percentage Change 1995 to 2004	
	In 2004	Percent of Total U.S.	In 1995	Percent of Total U.S.	In 2004	Percent of Total U.S.	In 1995	Percent of Total U.S.	In Capacity	In Number
Louisiana	16,512	27.3	15,569	28.0	61	11.5	87	12.0	6.1	-29.9
Texas	15,825	26.1	18,259	32.9	166	31.3	278	38.2	-13.3	-40.3
Wyoming	6,920	11.4	4,730	8.5	45	8.5	53	7.3	46.3	-15.1
Kansas	3,533	5.8	3,424	6.2	10	1.9	11	1.5	3.2	-9.1
New Mexico	3,427	5.7	3,697	6.7	25	4.7	34	4.7	-7.3	-26.5
Oklahoma	3,438	5.7	4,220	7.6	59	11.1	100	13.8	-18.5	-41.0
Illinois	2,202	3.6	2	--	2	0.4	1	0.1	--	100.0
Colorado	2,093	3.5	1,490	2.7	43	8.1	40	5.5	40.5	7.5
Mississippi	1,572	2.6	40	0.1	6	1.1	5	0.7	--	20.0
Alabama	1,310	2.2	468	0.8	15	2.8	12	1.7	179.9	25.0
California	1,037	1.7	925	1.7	24	4.5	31	4.3	12.1	-22.6
Utah	970	1.6	779	1.4	16	3.0	13	1.8	24.5	23.1
Michigan	483	0.8	524	0.9	16	3.0	19	2.6	-7.8	-15.8
West Virginia	460	0.8	421	0.8	8	1.5	7	1.0	9.3	14.3
North Dakota	222	0.4	241	0.4	8	1.5	9	1.2	-7.9	-11.1
Kentucky	154	0.3	178	0.3	3	0.6	5	0.7	-13.5	-40.0
Montana	133	0.2	115	0.2	3	0.6	8	1.1	15.7	-62.5
Florida	90	0.1	361	0.6	1	0.2	2	0.3	-75.1	-50.0
Arkansas	67	--	70	0.1	7	1.3	6	0.8	-4.3	16.7
Pennsylvania	62	0.1	20	--	9	1.7	2	0.3	210.0	350.0
Ohio	23	--	23	--	3	0.6	3	0.4	--	0.0
Nebraska	0	--	10	--	0	0.0	1	0.1	NA	NA
Total Lower 48 States	60,533	100.0	55,566	100.0	530	100.0	727	100.0	8.9	-27.1

Note: -- = less than .05 or greater than 999.99 percent. Although more than 8 billion cubic feet per day of gas processing capacity exists in the State of Alaska, almost all of the natural gas that is extracted does not enter any transmission system. Rather, it is re-injected into reservoirs.

Source: Energy Information Administration, Gas Transportation Information System, Natural Gas Processing Plant Database (Compiled from data available from the Form EIA-64A, Form EIA-816, PentaSul Inc's *LPG Almanac*, and Internet sources.)

- **The Aux Sable natural gas plant, one of the largest natural gas processing plants in the Lower 48 States with an initial design capacity of 2.2 Bcf/d, was built in 2000 in Illinois, a State that has little or no natural gas production of its own.** Located at the receiving end of the Alliance Pipeline, which was built specifically to transport "wet" natural gas from British Columbia and Alberta, Canada, to Aux Sable, the plant currently processes about 1.5 Bcf daily, separating methane from natural gas liquids. The plant's northern Illinois location was selected to take economic advantage of extracting natural gas liquids in the Chicago (hub) area with its easy access to several hydrocarbon products pipelines, while delivering "dry" natural gas to the interstate pipeline system via the Chicago Hub. Four interstate, and two intrastate, pipelines receive natural gas at the Aux Sable plant tailgate.

- **Since 1995, average daily natural gas plant processing capacity in the United States increased by 49 percent as new and larger capacity plants were installed and a number of existing ones were expanded.** Over the past 10 years, average plant

capacity increased from 76 million cubic feet per day (MMcf/d) to 114 MMcf/d and decreased in only 4 of the 22 States with natural gas processing plant capacity (Table 1). In Texas, although the number of plants and overall processing capacity decreased, the average capacity per plant increased from 66 MMcf/d to 95 MMcf/d as newer plants were added and old, less efficient plants were idled. In Alabama, Mississippi, and the eastern portion of South Louisiana, new larger plants and plant expansions built to serve new offshore production increased the average plant capacity significantly in those areas.

- **Expanding natural gas production in Wyoming in recent years led to the installation of seven new gas processing plants and the expansion of several more.** Since 1995, Wyoming's natural gas plant processing capacity increased by almost 46 percent, adding more than 2.2 Bcf/d (Table 1). Much of the activity has been focused in the southwestern area of Wyoming's Green River Basin where one of the nation's largest gas plants, the Williams Company's 1.1 Bcf/d Opal facility, is located. Increased natural gas development behind the plant and a significant expansion of pipeline capacity at

Energy Information Administration, Office of Oil and Gas, January 2006

6

338 703-739-3790 TCNNaturalGas.com

Figure 2. Concentrations of Natural Gas Processing Plants, 2004

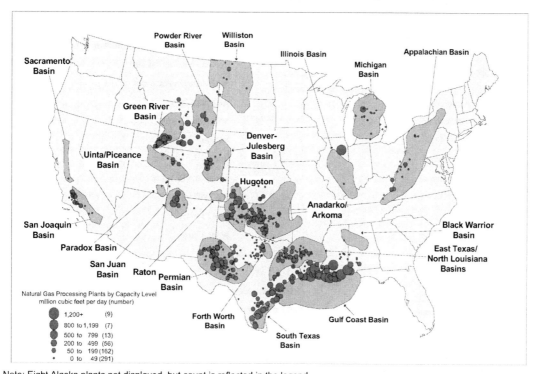

Note: Eight Alaska plants not displayed, but count is reflected in the legend.
Source: Energy Information Administration, Gas Transportation Information System, Natural Gas Processing Plant Database.

the plant tailgate (Kern River Transmission and Northwest Pipeline systems) necessitated two significant plant expansions at Opal since 2000, the last being a 350-MMcf/d increase in early 2004.

• **Successful exploration and development in the Piceance Basin in western Colorado and increased natural gas production in the San Juan Basin in southern Colorado have contributed to the installation of 13 new or replacement plants in the State and the expansion of several existing facilities.** In part, these increases have supported the installation of new pipeline systems in the region such as the TransColorado Gas Transmission system built in 1999, which can transport up to 650 MMcf/d of Piceance and San Juan basin production to interstate pipeline connections with western markets.

Over the next several years, additional new natural gas processing plants and capacity can be expected to be installed in Wyoming and Colorado as exploration and development efforts in those States continue, especially if the prices of natural gas and natural gas liquids remain high. Increased

exploration and development has increased the level of proved natural gas reserves in these two States by more than 45 percent, or 18.6 trillion cubic feet, since 1995 (Figure 3).

Moreover, it can be expected that new plant capacity will be needed in other areas currently undergoing increased exploration and development, such as the Fort Worth Basin in northeast Texas (gas shale), the Texas panhandle, and the east Texas area. Since 1995, growth in the level of proved natural gas reserves in these areas has been significant.

Shift in Installation Patterns

While a number of market factors can influence the location and level of gas processing capacity in the United States, shifts in exploration and development activity and subsequent changes in natural gas production levels have had the greatest impact during the past 10 years. The level of overall natural gas plant processing capacity in an area follows the development of new oil and gas fields (rise in supply) and the decline of older fields (fall in supply).

Energy Information Administration, Office of Oil and Gas, January 2006

7

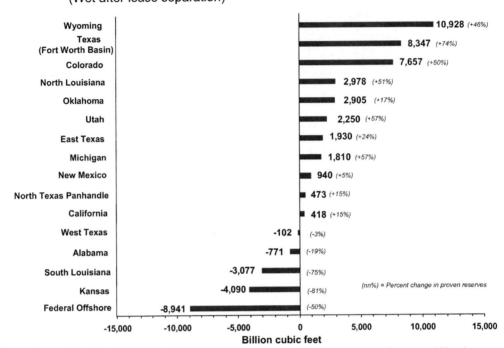

Figure 3. Major Changes in Proved Natural Gas Reserves, 1995 to 2004
(Wet after lease separation)

Source: Energy Information Administration, *U.S. Crude Oil and Natural Gas, and Natural Gas Liquids Reserves, 1995 and 2004 Annual Reports*: Table 9.

As natural gas production (Table 2) and annual added proved reserves (Figure 3) decreased significantly in southern Louisiana and the Gulf of Mexico (GOM) between 1995 and 2004,[15] several natural gas processing plants in the region were idled, especially in the western portion of the region where older production fields are predominate. However, in the deepwater and eastern portion of the Gulf several substantial new natural gas deposits were developed and began producing during the period. Subsequently, new natural gas production facilities and new gathering pipelines were built to deliver this natural gas onshore. To accommodate these new natural gas flows, eight natural gas plants located in southern Louisiana were expanded. These expansions helped increase Louisiana's overall natural gas plant capability by 6 percent between 1995 and 2004, despite declining overall natural gas production both onshore and off.

Increased deepwater natural gas development also affected the number and capacity of natural gas processing facilities in Alabama and Mississippi. In Alabama, two of the seven new processing plants installed after 1995 were principally dedicated to processing offshore production delivered via the Dauphin Island Gathering System and Transco's Mobile Bay lateral. Both were large 600-MMcf/d facilities located along Mobile Bay.[16] In Mississippi, a new 500-MMcf/d plant was developed in the mid-1990s at Pascagoula, primarily to serve onshore production. The plant's capacity was doubled in 2000 in order to accept natural gas from the offshore via the new Destin Pipeline. Growth in natural gas processing demand owing to new offshore production brought Mississippi and Alabama, from a ranking (by overall capacity) of 18th and 11th, respectively, in 1995, to 9th and 10th in 2004.

The Rocky Mountain States have seen expanding development of coalbed methane resources as well as steadily increasing exploration/development efforts and

---

[15]In 1995, proved gas reserve additions from new fields and new reservoir discoveries in old fields in southern Louisiana and the Gulf of Mexico amounted to 3,174 Bcf (wet basis) with gas production at 5,827 Bcf, while the corresponding figures in 2004 were 991 Bcf and 4,866 Bcf, respectively. Energy Information Administration, *U.S. Crude Oil, Natural Gas and Natural Gas Liquids Reserves*, 1995 and 2004 Annual Reports, Table 9.

[16]In 2004, a co-owner of one of the facilities removed one processing train (300 MMcf/d) from the plant and moved it to Louisiana.

Energy Information Administration, Office of Oil and Gas, January 2006

8

Table 2. Major Lower 48 Natural Gas Producing States and Federal Offshore

(Volumes in Trillion Cubic Feet)

State	Wet Gas Production		Percentage Change	Processed Volume (Gas to Liquids)		Percent Processed	
	1995	2004	1995-2004	1995	2004	1995	2004
Texas	5.11	5.66	10.8	0.39	0.35	7.6	6.2
Federal Offshore	4.67	4.01	-14.0	0.04	0.09	0.9	2.3
Oklahoma	1.66	1.66	-0.2	0.10	0.10	6.0	5.8
New Mexico	1.48	1.62	9.7	0.08	0.09	5.4	5.7
Wyoming	0.84	1.59	89.4	0.03	0.07	3.6	4.5
Louisiana	1.50	1.36	-9.5	0.10	0.04	6.7	2.8
Colorado	0.54	1.09	101.1	0.03	0.04	5.6	3.3
Kansas	0.71	0.40	-43.1	0.08	0.02	11.3	5.9
Total	16.51	17.39	5.3	0.85	0.80	5.1	4.6

Source: Energy Information Administration, *U.S. Crude Oil and Natural Gas, and Natural Gas Liquids Reserves: 1995 and 2004 Annual Reports.*

growing production from tight-sands and conventional natural gas sources. As a result, significant increases in natural gas plant processing capacity in Wyoming, Colorado, and Utah have occurred. While Montana has much less overall natural gas processing capacity than the other Rocky Mountain States, it too experienced an increase in processing capacity (Table 1) as natural gas production in the State rose by 16 percent and proved reserves grew by 27 percent during the past decade.

As mentioned earlier, the number of plants and the level of natural gas processing capacity in Texas decreased by 40 and 13 percent, respectively, between 1995 and 2004. While natural gas production within Texas increased overall during that time period, several areas such as the Permian Basin in the western part of the State experienced decreases. A number of natural gas plants in that area were idled while new processing plants were built in developing areas such as the Fort Worth Basin area in northeast Texas.

In most of the country, the increases and decreases in installed natural gas processing capacity have closely tracked the changes in proved natural gas reserves since 1995. Moreover, where significant new proved reserves have been added, the expectation is that eventually new natural gas production will follow, and new natural gas processing plants will need to be installed accordingly (Figure 3).

Impact of Restructuring

As the FERC-mandated restructuring of the natural gas industry[17] took effect during the 1990s, changes also occurred in the economics of natural gas processing plant ownership. Before restructuring, many natural gas processing plants were owned and operated by natural gas and oil producers as part of their overall energy production and

marketing business. With restructuring, many of these producers sold their natural gas processing facilities in order to focus on exploration and development activities.

Before restructuring, more than 310 individual companies owned and/or operated natural gas processing plants. By 1995 there were 270 companies, and by 2004 the number had dropped to 209. Yet, the amount of new processing capacity rose by 8.9 percent during the same 9-year period (Table 1). As competition increased and the economics of production and processing changed under restructuring, consolidation of plant ownership significantly increased. In 2004, for instance, the top 10 natural gas plant owner/operators had access to or owned about 74 percent (44.5 Bcf/d) of the total natural gas plant capacity in the United States. This compares with about half that much in 1995, although the percentage of plants owned/operated remained at about 36 percent.

Between 1995 and 2004, the type of companies owning/operating processing plants shifted from primarily oil/gas producers to what are now referred to as "midstream" companies or operating divisions. These entities focus their efforts on the natural gas gathering, natural gas processing, and natural gas storage operations segments of the industry. In 1995 production companies such as Shell Western E&P, Texaco Production, Exxon Co USA, and Warren Petroleum controlled the largest share of natural gas plant processing capacity. In 2004, however, midstream operating companies such as Duke Energy Field Services (54 plants, 7.5 Bcf/d capacity), Enterprise Products Operating LP (26, 6.3 Bcf/d), Targa Resources[18] (21, 3.4 Bcf/d), and BP PLC (13, 5.6 Bcf/d), predominate.[19]

Natural Gas Processing Cost Recovery

The primary role of a natural gas processing plant in today's marketplace is to produce pipeline-quality natural gas. The production of natural gas liquids and other products from the natural gas stream is secondary. The quantity and quality of the byproducts actually produced during a particular time period is, in many instances, a function of their current market prices. If the market value of a byproduct falls below the current production cost, a natural gas plant owner/operator may suspend its production temporarily. In some instances, a plant operator may increase the Btu content of its plant residue (plant tailgate) gas stream, as long as it remains within pipeline tolerances, in order to absorb some of the byproducts. In other cases the raw liquid stream (minus methane) is stored on-site temporarily or sold off.

---

[17] FERC Order 636, issued in 1993, primarily dealt with revising how interstate pipeline companies did business. Order 636 required interstate pipeline companies to change from buying and selling the natural gas they transported to selling the transportation service only.

[18] In late 2005, Targa Resources, Inc., acquired the gas processing plant interests of Dynegy Midstream Services LP in Louisiana, Texas, and New Mexico. In combination with its existing gas plant assets, the acquisition moved Targa Resources significantly higher in the rankings of midstream companies.

[19] In those cases where a gas plant is not fully owned by the party, a percentage of the total capacity of the plant equal to the ownership percentage was included in the Bcf/d capacity item.

As noted earlier, before restructuring of the natural gas industry in the 1990s, most natural gas processing was performed by an affiliate of the production company. The processor was reimbursed through what is commonly referred to as a keepwhole contract.[20] Under such a contract the NGLs recovered at the facility are retained by the processor as payment, while the other party's delivery is "kept whole" by returning an amount of residue (plant tailgate) natural gas (equal on a Btu basis to the natural gas received at the plant inlet) at the tailgate of the plant.

In today's more competitive restructured marketplace, where supply/demand fluctuations are more commonplace, natural gas prices are more variable, and price levels are relatively high compared with other forms of energy, including NGLs, "keepwhole" arrangements tend to create income uncertainty for processors. Such arrangements are profitable when the value of the NGLs is greater as a separated liquid than as a portion of the residue natural gas stream; they are less profitable when the value of the NGLs is lower as a liquid than as a portion of the residue natural gas stream.

As a result, participants in the natural gas processing industry have been replacing keepwhole contracts with alternative arrangements as the contracts come up for renewal. Several unique types of natural gas processing arrangements are being offered in their place. Among them are: percent-of-liquids contracts, percent-of-index contracts, margin-band contracts, fee-based contracts, and hybrid contracts. In broad terms, they function as follows:

- *Percent-of-liquids or percent-of-proceeds.* With this type of contract the processor takes ownership of a percentage of the NGL mix extracted from a producer's natural gas stream. The producer either retains title to, or receives the value associated with, the remaining percentage of the NGL mix. The producer reimburses the processor for the costs involved in the liquids extraction operation.

- *Percent-of-index contracts.* Under this type of contract the processor generally purchases its natural gas at either a percentage discount to a specified index price, a specified index price less a fixed amount, or a percentage discount to a specified index price less an additional fixed amount. The processor then resells the natural gas at the index price or at a different percentage discount to the index price.

- *Margin-band contracts.* Under this type of arrangement the processor takes ownership of NGLs extracted from the natural gas stream delivered by the producer, while the producer is paid a return based on the energy value of the NGL mix that was extracted from the natural gas

stream less the fuel consumed in the extraction process. Both parties accept specified floor and ceiling return levels which are intended to provide an acceptable return to each party when natural gas processing economics tend to become negative or the economic gains become excessive.

- *Fee-based contracts.* In these contracts a set fee is negotiated based on the anticipated volume of natural gas to be processed. The producer either retains title to, or receives the value associated with, any NGLs extracted and is responsible for all energy costs of processing.

- *Hybrid contracts.* Such arrangements usually provide processing services to a producer under a monthly percent-of-liquids arrangement initially, with the producer having the option of switching to either a fee-based arrangement or in certain cases to a keepwhole basis. The intent is to give both producer and processor the incentive to maintain operations during periods of natural gas price swings, especially during those periods when the price of natural gas is high relative to the economic value of NGLs.

Contracts for natural gas processing have terms ranging from month-to-month to the life of the producing lease. Intermediate terms of 1 to 10 years are also common.

Outlook and Potential

Since 1995, natural gas plant processing capacity has increased by almost 9 percent (Table 1), with most of this growth following new production field development. Based upon trends that have developed over the past several years, especially in the finding of newly proved reserves (Figure 3), or lack thereof, two areas of the country in particular could experience sizable shifts in natural gas processing plant resources, with increases expected in the Rocky Mountain area and decreases expected along the Gulf Coast.

Continuing a trend begun in the late 1990s, ongoing expansion of natural gas exploration and development in Colorado, Utah, and Wyoming could add to natural gas plant processing requirements over the next several years.[21] Each of these States experienced a 25 percent or greater increase in installed natural gas processing plant capacity over the past decade. It is generally anticipated that the Unita Basin of eastern Utah and the Piceance Basin of western Colorado will become more actively developed over the next decade, with several new large-scale capacity natural gas pipelines scheduled to be installed to transport the produced natural gas

---

[20] Much of the background material used in this section is based on information and discussions of gas processing contracts found in the 2004 SEC 10K filings of Enterprise Products Partners LP and MarkWest Energy Partners LP.

[21] On November 30, 2005, EnCana Ltd announced that it has begun construction of a new 650 MMcf/d natural gas processing plant in northwestern Colorado to accommodate increasing natural gas production in the Piceance Basin. The plant is scheduled to be in service in early 2007. Platts Inc., *Gas Daily*, December 1, 2005, p. 4.

to western and midwestern markets.[22] These new pipelines will also need new processing plants to be installed to treat this natural gas prior to receipt.

New natural gas processing capacity will perhaps be needed in Texas as well. Despite a net decrease in natural gas plant capacity in the State of about 13 percent between 1995 and 2004 (Table 1), several new plants were added and others are planned as a result of increased development in the Barnett Shale Formation of the Fort Worth Basin in northeast Texas. The gas shales located in this area, which encompasses several counties north and west of Dallas, Texas, were once considered uneconomical to develop, but the advent of new technologies has greatly improved its potential and, thus, its attraction to natural gas producers.

In southern Louisiana and the Gulf of Mexico, on the other hand, decreasing natural gas production and a significant drop in the volume of new proved natural gas reserves found in the region during the past decade likely will slow growth of natural gas processing capacity along the Gulf Coast over the next several years. However, since the Gulf of Mexico and southern Louisiana will remain the largest natural gas producing area in the country for years to come, most existing natural gas processing plants in the region should remain active, although perhaps processing at lower daily flow rates.

The potential remains, nevertheless, for the discovery of some major natural gas finds in the deepwater regions of the Gulf, which could lead to expansion of some existing plants or even installation of an occasional new one. However, in the short term, this seems unlikely. No new offshore-to-onshore pipelines are scheduled for development through 2008, except for those related to LNG imports through the Gulf States.[23] The lack of proposals for pipeline development would tend to indicate that existing plant capacity serving the Gulf of Mexico is adequate for the foreseeable future.

Although gross natural gas production in the United States has remained relatively level since 2000,[24] rising natural gas wellhead prices can be expected to lead to increases in natural gas exploration and development efforts. Some increases in production could occur in the older production fields, but much of the additional natural gas production will probably come from newly developed reserves found in the areas mentioned above. Consequently, as new sources of production are developed, new processing facilities, or greater use of now-underutilized plant capacity, will follow suit, while some older facilities, particularly those taking gas from depleting areas, will be closed or relocated.

---

[22] Energy Information Administration, Gas Transportation Information System, Natural Gas Pipeline Projects Database, as of December 2005.

[23] Imported LNG supplies often have higher Btu content than domestic natural gas supplies and may need to be processed to meet U.S pipeline quality specifications. The introduction of additional LNG volumes into the Gulf area may increase processing plant utilization beyond what is required for domestic natural gas production. However, this need is uncertain and depends on the construction of new facilities and the quality of the future LNG imports.

[24] See Energy Information Administration, *Natural Gas Annual 2004*, (Washington, D.C. December 2005), Table 1. http://www.eia.doe.gov/oil_gas/natural_gas/data_publications/natural_gas_annual/nga.html

Order Code RL33716

CRS Report for Congress

Alaska Natural Gas Pipelines:
Interaction of the Natural Gas and Steel Markets

Updated March 28, 2007

Stephen Cooney
Industry Specialist
Resources, Science, and Industry Division

Robert Pirog
Specialist in Energy Economics and Policy
Resources, Science, and Industry Division

Congressional
Research
Service

**Prepared for Members and
Committees of Congress**

Alaska Natural Gas Pipelines:
Interaction of the Natural Gas and Steel Markets

Summary

In 1976 Congress approved legislation to establish the regulatory framework for building a pipeline to bring natural gas from the Alaska North Slope to the lower 48 states (Alaska Natural Gas Transportation Act, 15 U.S.C. § 719 *et seq*.). Despite the rich deposits of natural gas and the success of the Alaska oil pipeline, the Alaska segment of a gas pipeline has never been started. To encourage its development, Congress passed in 2004 and the President signed into law the Alaska Natural Gas Pipeline Act (Division C of P.L. 108-324), which includes a federal loan guarantee of as much as $18 billion. Since then, North Slope producers, other potential pipeline developers, and the state of Alaska have been in extensive discussions on building a gas pipeline. Under a provision of the 2004 law, as no application for a certificate of public convenience and necessity for the pipeline had been received 18 months after passage of the law, the Department of Energy on April 13, 2006, began a study on alternative approaches to the construction and operation of an Alaska natural gas transportation system.

Two major issues or uncertainties may serve as economic constraints on such a major capital investment undertaking. The first is whether the price of natural gas over the long term will repay investment in a project now estimated to cost $25 billion or more, and which would not deliver gas to the major U.S. markets before 2017. Natural gas prices in the North American market are high, but volatile. Spot prices rose to more than $13 per million BTUs in 2005, then fell to less than $6 by late summer 2006. The natural gas spot price reached $9 per million BTUs in only one week during the winter 2006-07 heating season. Developments of liquefied natural gas technology and of advanced drilling technologies portend new sources of supply. At the same time, the Department of Energy's Energy Information Administration reports that the only significant increase in U.S. demand for natural gas over the past 10 years has been for electricity generation.

Secondly, the price of steel, the material to be used in building a pipeline, has more than doubled since 2003, and may account for a significant share of increased cost estimates. Earlier, the pipeline project was viewed by some observers as a possible way to boost domestic steel demand, at a time when prices were low, many major North American producers had gone into bankruptcy, and trade safeguards were in place. But the steel industry has recovered and restructured. Moreover, because of the conditions under which the pipeline would be built and operated, the gas producers' pipeline consortium has specified a grade of steel that is not yet produced anywhere commercially. The American Iron and Steel Institute (AISI) estimates that 3 to 5 million tons of steel could be required, but states that sufficient capacity can be readily developed in North America for manufacturing the necessary steel pipe. P.L. 108-324 contains a "sense of Congress" resolution that North American steel should be used in the project. ExxonMobil Corporation, one of the three developers of Alaska North Slope oil and gas, has, however, announced an agreement with two Japanese companies to commercialize a new type of high-strength steel that could reduce Alaska pipeline costs.

Contents

List of Figures

List of Tables

Alaska Natural Gas Pipelines: Interaction of the Natural Gas and Steel Markets

Introduction

In 1976, Congress approved legislation to establish the regulatory framework for building a pipeline to bring natural gas from the Alaska North Slope to the lower 48 states. Despite the rich deposits of natural gas in Alaska and the success of the Alaska oil pipeline, the Alaska segment of a gas pipeline has never been started. To encourage development of the gas pipeline, Congress passed further legislation in 2004, including a federal loan guarantee of as much as $18 billion. Since then, the North Slope producers, other potential pipeline developers, and the state government of Alaska have been engaged in extensive discussions on building a gas pipeline.

This report focuses on two major issues or uncertainties that may serve as economic constraints on a capital investment undertaking of this major scale:

- Natural gas prices in the North American market are high, but volatile. With Gulf of Mexico production shutdowns occasioned by major hurricanes in 2004 and 2005, spot prices rose to more than $13 per million BTUs. Prices fell to less than $6 by late summer 2006. They increased again in the winter 2006-07 heating season, but only once exceeded $9 per million BTUs. Advances in liquefied natural gas technology and transportation, and in drilling technologies in difficult operating environments, portend new sources of supply for the domestic market. It is not clear if the fundamental demand-supply balance in the market will sustain a high enough price over the long term to make building an Alaska gas pipeline a profitable venture.

- The price of steel, the major construction material to be used in building a pipeline, has more than doubled since 2003. Earlier, the pipeline project was viewed by some observers as a possible way to boost domestic steel demand, at a time when prices were low, global capacity was ample, the domestic industry was being protected by extensive trade safeguards, and many major North American producers had gone into bankruptcy. But the steel industry has recovered and restructured. Higher prices for steel have contributed to an estimated increase in the cost estimates for the Alaska gas pipeline from less than $20 billion to at least $25 billion. Moreover, because of the conditions under which the pipeline will be built and

CRS-2

operated, the gas producers have specified a grade of steel that is not yet produced anywhere commercially.

Northern Natural Gas Pipelines: Issues and Alternatives[1]

Bringing North Slope Gas to Market

An Untapped Resource. Alaskan natural gas is a largely untapped U.S. energy resource. The Alaska Department of Natural Resources (DNR) estimates gas reserves in the North Slope at 35.4 trillion cubic feet (tcf), which is the energy equivalent of about 6.3 billion barrels of oil.[2] For comparison, the entire annual U.S. consumption of natural gas is approximately 20 tcf. But most of the gas produced on Alaska's North Slope, 80% of the eight to nine billion cubic feet produced annually, has been reinjected into the ground.[3] Only a small amount has been used for operations in conjunction with oil production and transportation, such as powering oil through pipelines, and other local uses.

Alaskan natural gas resources have not been developed because of a lack of cost-effective transportation to major consuming markets. Using a more stringent definition than the state, the Energy Information Administration (EIA) of the federal Department of Energy estimated that proved natural gas reserves in the entire state of Alaska were 8.2 tcf at the end of 2005. Because of the lack of a pipeline, or near-term prospects for a pipeline, the remainder of Alaska's gas reserves is commercially unrecoverable.[4]

Congressional Support for an Alaskan Gas Pipeline. Congress has established a statutory framework for an Alaska natural gas pipeline. The legislative authority for designation of an Alaska natural gas pipeline route, and for the U.S. role in the approval, construction and operation of such a pipeline, was established in the Alaska Natural Gas Transportation Act of 1976 (15 U.S.C. § 719 *et seq.*), which remains in effect. Acting under that framework, a private sector consortium planned a natural gas pipeline that would parallel the existing Alaska oil pipeline (Trans Alaska Pipeline System) from the North Slope to Fairbanks, and then head southeastward along the Alaska Highway and into Canada via the Yukon Territory, British Columbia, and Alberta. This is the proposed Alaska Natural Gas

---

[1] This section of the report was written by Stephen Cooney.

[2] Alaska Dept. of Natural Resources, Div. of Oil and Gas. *Alaska Oil and Gas Report* (May 2006), p. 3-2.

[3] Natural gas pumped back into the ground enhances the flow of oil.

[4] U.S. Dept. of Energy. Energy Information Administration. *U.S. Crude Oil, Natural Gas, and Natural Gas Liquid Reserves: 2005 Annual Report* (advance summary), Table 3. EIA adheres to the standard definition that proved reserves are recoverable in today's economic conditions with today's technology. The Alaska DNR's *stated* definition substantially is the same: "Remaining reserves are oil and gas that are economically and technologically feasible to produce and are expected to produce revenue in the foreseeable future." *Alaska Oil and Gas Report* (May 2006), p. 3-1.

CRS-3

Transportation System (ANGTS), which was approved by the U.S. and Canadian governments in the 1970s.[5]

In 2004, Congress approved, and the President signed into law on October 13, 2004, legislation that amended and extended the original act (Alaska Natural Gas Pipeline Act of 2004, Division C of P.L. 108-324).[6] This law amends the 1976 act and expands it by adding several important new provisions, including a federal loan guarantee for the project. Details of this law are discussed below.

No Gas Pipeline Is Started in Alaska. Phase I ("prebuild") of the ANGTS pipeline was actually completed in the early 1980s and is in operation. Its two legs stretch from a central collecting point in Alberta in the direction of the U.S. West Coast and the Midwest. They deliver one-third of Canada's total annual natural gas exports to the United States.[7]

But the crucial third leg, connecting the "prebuilt" network to the North Slope, has never been started. It would run for 2,140 miles, from Prudhoe Bay to Edmonton, Alberta.[8] Proposed pipeline capacity enhancements from Canada to the Midwest would increase the total length to 3,500 miles.[9] The planned ANGTS pipeline along the Alaska Highway route and the completed lower legs of the pipeline into the United States are shown in **Figure 1**.

---

[5] *Ibid.*, pp. 45-46.

[6] Codified at 15 U.S.C. § 720 *et seq.*

[7] The "prebuild" section of the Alaska Natural Gas Pipeline in Alberta was completed by the Foothills Pipe Lines consortium. In 2003, TransCanada Corp., the major partner in the consortium, acquired 100% ownership of Foothills' interests; TransCanada Corp. website, "Alaska Highway Pipeline Project," and "Setting the Record Straight: Alaska Highway Pipeline," presentation by CEO Hal Kvisle (Apr. 7, 2005), p. 9. Also, information on the prebuilt pipeline from the former website of Foothills Pipe Lines Ltd., 2003.

[8] The length of 2,140 miles is from a chart in Arctic Resources Corporation (ARC), *The Right Solution to Tap Arctic Gas* (Nov. 12, 2002), Fig. 2. It was confirmed to the author in a CRS interview with EIA on Nov. 19, 2003.

[9] Sen. Lisa Murkowski. "Murkowski Says Gas Loan Guarantee Designed to Help Get Alaska Natural Gas to Market, Regardless of Final Project," press release, Dec. 2, 2003.

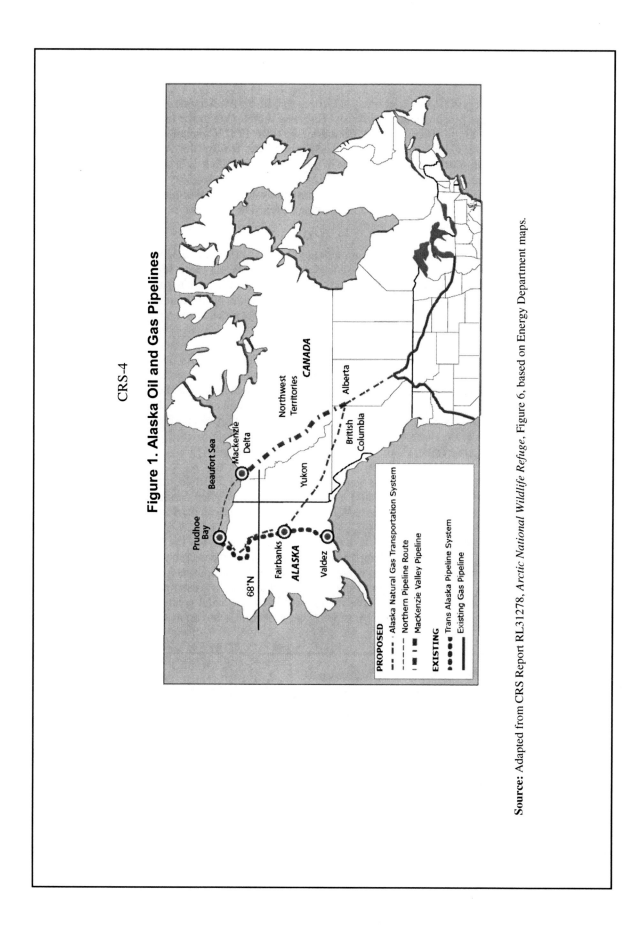

CRS-4

Figure 1. Alaska Oil and Gas Pipelines

Source: Adapted from CRS Report RL31278, *Arctic National Wildlife Refuge*, Figure 6, based on Energy Department maps.

CRS-5

In January 2004, two consortia filed proposals with the Alaska state government to build a gas pipeline along the Alaska Highway route. One group included the three North Slope oil and natural gas producers – BP PLC, ConocoPhillips, and Exxon Mobil Corporation.[10] The other group was led by the Alaska Gas Transmission Company, a subsidiary of MidAmerican, which is a major U.S. pipeline operator. But in March 2004, MidAmerican cited "the inability of the state of Alaska to complete a contract that would have allowed [our consortium] to move forward on an accelerated schedule with an exclusive five-year period," and withdrew its proposal.[11]

In June 2004, TransCanada Corporation, a Canadian pipeline company, filed its own separate application to build the complete pipeline. While Frank Murkowski, then Governor of Alaska, negotiated primarily with the producers' group, TransCanada has continued to seek a role in constructing the pipeline, emphasizing that it alone holds the right to build the segment that will cross Canadian territory.[12]

The Northern Route and Mackenzie Delta Gas. A different route to the Alaska Highway pipeline was proposed by a separate group, the Arctic Resources Consortium (ARC), based in Canada. This was the Northern Route Gas Pipeline Project. It was designed to access the Prudhoe Bay gas field in Alaska, then to swing offshore across the top of the state, under the Beaufort Sea, and to join the existing Alberta pipeline connection via the Mackenzie River (see **Figure 1**). This route also could deliver to the North American market the more recently discovered gas reserves of the Mackenzie Delta, as well as the Alaska North Slope gas.

A Mackenzie River pipeline would require a separate 1,350 mile project. ARC claimed that it could feasibly build a single 1,665-mile pipeline connecting both Alaska North Slope and Mackenzie Delta gas to North American markets.[13]

However, the northern route was opposed in both Congress and the Alaska state legislature. The Alaska legislature enacted a law that bans construction of a gas pipeline in northern state waters, while strongly supporting proposals for a pipeline to the south. It has been suggested that "... State officials see a greater gain through the income multiplier effect of construction within the state and greater access by Alaskan communities to the new gas supplies. Also at issue is the fact that a Canadian

---

[10] "Exxon," *Petroleum News* (Feb. 8, 2004), p. 10.

[11] Mid American Energy Holding Co., "Application Filed to Build Alaska Pipeline," press releases, Jan. 22 and Mar. 25, 2004

[12] TransCanada, "Alaska Highway Pipeline Project," and "Setting the Record Straight," esp. p. 6; and, AP, "TransCanada Presents Murkowski with a Proposal," *Anchorage Daily News* (Jul. 15, 2006). According to the Federal Energy Regulatory Commission (FERC), the TransCanada proposal was made under the original 1976 U.S. law, Canada's 1978 Northern Pipeline Act, and a 1977 bilateral U.S.-Canadian agreement. The North Slope producers' proposal is pursuant to the 2004 Act and other provisions of U.S. law. FERC, *Second and Third Reports to Congress on Progress Made in Licensing and Constructing the Alaska Natural Gas Pipeline* (Jul. 10, 2006, and Jan. 31, 2007), pp. 1-2 in both reports.

[13] ARC, *Right Solution*, Fig. 2 and p. 7.

352 703-739-3790 TCNNaturalGas.com

CRS-6

route would likely serve new Canadian gas fields, which would then compete with Alaska in U.S. markets."[14]

The Senate-passed version of the energy bill in the 107th Congress agreed with the Alaskan position (H.R. 4, approved on April 25, 2002). It provided that no pipeline could be constructed for Prudhoe Bay gas that traverses the submerged lands of the Beaufort Sea, as well as its adjacent shoreline, and that enters Canada "at any point north of 68°N latitude." In a March 2003 article, Peter Behr of the *Washington Post* reported that the route along the Alaska Highway was "mandated by the Senate ... to secure the greatest number of construction jobs for Alaskans."[15]

In the 108th Congress, the House on April 11, 2003, passed a version of its energy bill, which included the same provision as the Senate on the location of the natural gas pipeline. The same provision was passed again by the Senate in the 109th Congress and became law as Section 103(d) of the 2004 Alaska Natural Gas Pipeline Act.[16] But the law also includes a "sense of Congress" provision (Sec. 114) that, as North American gas demand will continue to increase "dramatically," it will be necessary to complete a separate Mackenzie Delta natural gas project, and that "Federal and State officials should work together with officials in Canada to ensure both projects can move forward in a mutually beneficial fashion." This section further stated that, "Federal and state officials should acknowledge that the smaller scope, fewer permitting requirements and lower cost of the Mackenzie Delta project means it will most likely be completed before the Alaska Natural Gas Pipeline."[17]

The Liquefied Natural Gas Option. High prices for natural gas since 2000 have revived interest in the United States and abroad in developing liquefied natural gas (LNG) technology. LNG is gas that has been liquefied by cryogenic technology, transported in special-purpose carriers, then regasified for normal commercial use. All four LNG plants that were built in the United States in the 1970s have been reopened, and more are currently being considered, including on the U.S. West Coast.[18]

Thus, another possibility that has emerged is a new natural gas pipeline wholly within Alaska to feed an LNG operation. From there, the LNG could be transshipped by special-purpose maritime carriers to domestic or foreign markets. Alaska voters in a November 2002 referendum by 61% authorized a new state authority to build a gas pipeline to parallel the existing oil pipeline from Prudhoe Bay to Valdez, and to build a new LNG plant there. This project was promoted by the Alaska Gas Port

---

[14] CRS Report RL31278. *Arctic National Wildlife Refuge: Background and Issues*, by M. Lynne Corn.

[15] *Washington Post.* "Natural Gas Line Proposed in Alaska," by Peter Behr (Mar. 26, 2003).

[16] 15 U.S.C. § 720a(d).

[17] 15 U.S.C. § 720*l*.

[18] Dept. of Energy. EIA. *The Global Liquefied Natural Gas Market: Status & Outlook* (DOE/EIA-0637), December 2003. For details on the emerging LNG industry see CRS Report RL32445, *Liquefied Natural Gas Markets in Transition*, by Robert Pirog.

CRS-7

Authority.[19] But ConocoPhillips Alaska representatives in July 2003 reportedly shared with state officials the results of an extensive multi-company industry study, which concluded that an Alaska North Slope LNG project was not commercially competitive with other LNG projects.[20]

Financing the Pipeline under Federal Legislation

A key question on approaches to building a pipeline is government financial support. The three major North Slope oil and gas development companies, ExxonMobil, ConocoPhillips and BP, undertook a joint study of the costs of a natural gas pipeline, especially in view of a rise in the North American price of natural gas. The study, completed in April 2002, estimated the cost of a new pipeline as $19.4 billion if the ANGTS route were used, and $18.6 billion if it followed the northern route, via the Beaufort Sea and the Mackenzie Delta. Either way, the companies concluded that the cost was prohibitive for natural gas to be commercially delivered to the U.S. market, even at relatively high natural gas price levels.[21] Subsequently, the rise in the price of steel and other factors have increased cost estimates for a pipeline along the Alaska Highway to $25 billion.[22]

In response to this question of cost, Congress has considered a number of financial measures to support construction of an Alaska pipeline. In 2002, the Senate included a $10 billion loan guarantee for private sector parties that would undertake the project (Sec. 710 of H.R. 4, as approved in April 2002), and a price floor mechanism that would guarantee a minimum price for Alaskan natural gas through tax credits (Sec. 2503 of the same bill). In the 108th Congress, the Senate Energy and Natural Resources Committee increased the Alaska natural gas pipeline loan guarantee to $18 billion (S. 14 § 144). The price floor provision was included as Section 511 of the revised Energy Tax Incentives Act (S. 1149) reported by the Senate Finance Committee.[23] The stated intention of the Energy Committee was to amend the Energy Tax Incentives Act "into S. 14 during floor action."[24]

---

[19] Ben Spiess, "Ulmer Authorizes Gas Pipeline Referendum for November 5 Ballot," *Anchorage Daily News* (Mar. 13, 2002), p. F4; Tim Bradner, "Voters Approve Gas Authority; Now What?" *Alaska Journal of Commerce* (Nov. 17, 2002), p. B1; FERC, *Second Report*, p. 2. San Diego-based Sempra Energy is building an LNG terminal in Baja California, Mexico, and another LNG terminal, aimed largely at the U.S. market, is being developed in Kitimat, British Columbia; see *Oil Daily*, "British Columbia's Kitimat Terminal Still Lacks Supply Deal" (Aug. 15, 2006), p. 5.

[20] Kristen Nelson, "LNG Not Cost Competitive for ConocoPhillips," *Petroleum News* (July 13, 2003), p. 2. The FERC *Third Report* still lists this option, p. 1.

[21] CRS interview with ExxonMobil spokesman Robert H. Davis, April 25, 2003. The study assumed that the pipeline would be completed to Chicago, so it could be possible to effect some savings if capacity could be shared with the existing ANGTS "prebuilt" pipeline to the Midwest.

[22] FERC, *Second Report*, p. 15.

[23] See S.Rept. 108-54, part J.

[24] Senate Committee on Energy and Natural Resources. "Highlights of the Energy Policy Act
(continued...)

CRS-8

The Bush Administration in 2002 indicated its opposition to the "price-floor subsidy provision ... and any similar provision because it would distort markets, could cost over $1 billion in annual lost revenue, and would likely undermine Canada's support for construction of the pipeline and thus set back broader bilateral energy integration."[25] The Statement of Administration Policy of May 8, 2003, on Senate energy legislation reiterated opposition to "the price-floor tax subsidy provision in the Senate Finance Committee bill, because it could distort markets and could be very costly."[26] In response, Senators John Breaux, Jeff Bingaman and Tom Daschle wrote President Bush on May 21, 2003, asking him to "reconsider" this position. The three Senators argued that, "Given the inevitable volatility of gas prices over the 50 year life of this project, this Administration position effectively means that no pipeline will be built ..."[27]

The Canadian government position has been one of declared official neutrality between the two (or more) potential routes, but opposition to any mandated, unilateral selection of routes by the U.S. government, particularly if this is included in a policy utilizing price support mechanisms for Alaskan gas, which Canada strenuously opposes.[28] Price supports and any other mechanisms that favor Alaskan gas over imports from Canada also may raise questions under World Trade Organization agreements.

The conference report of November 18, 2003, on H.R. 6 (H.Rept. 108-375) included the loan guarantee provision as approved in the Senate Energy Committee, but did not include the price floor/tax credit mechanism to reduce the risk of low natural gas prices. The loan guarantee provision was incorporated into the final 2004 Alaska Natural Gas Pipeline Act. It would authorize the Secretary of Energy to issue a guarantee within two years after a "final certificate of public convenience and necessity (including any Canadian certificates of public convenience and necessity) is issued for the project." The guarantee "shall not exceed" 80% of the total cost of a "qualified" project, up to $18 billion.[29]

According to a press report, ConocoPhillips publicly confirmed that it would not participate in the pipeline project without a price floor mechanism. An Alaska executive of the company informed a conference in Anchorage on November 20, 2003, that, "We're not going to be able to advance the project without the risk mitigation." The same press source stated that BP was still "interested" in moving

---

[24] (...continued)
of 2003 and the Energy Tax Incentives Act of 2003," press release, May 1, 2003.

[25] Secretary of Energy Spencer Abraham. Letter to Rep. W.J. Tauzin, June 27, 2002.

[26] Office of Management and Budget. "Statement of Administration Policy: S. 14 — Energy Policy Act of 2003" (May 8, 2003), p. 2.

[27] Sens. Breaux, Bingaman and Daschle. Letter to President George W. Bush, May 21, 2003.

[28] Ambassador of Canada Michael Kergin. "Trust the Market (and Canada)," article in *Wall Street Journal*, May 15, 2002; letter to U.S. Under Secretary of State for Economic Affairs Alan P. Larson, Sept. 17, 2002. This position was confirmed in a CRS interview with Paul Connors, Energy Counsellor to the Canadian Embassy (Aug. 3, 2006).

[29] 15 U.S.C. § 720n(c)(2).

CRS-9

forward with the project, though it would find the risk-mitigation tax credit "helpful."[30] Despite the stance, negotiations on building the pipeline continued between the state of Alaska and the North Slope producers.

In addition to the basic loan guarantee and to enhance the prospects for the LNG alternative, Senator Lisa Murkowski sought to "provide equal financial incentives" for federal support in transporting Alaska natural gas to U.S. markets, "whether that gas moves by pipeline through Canada or by tanker from Alaska's south coast."[31] She succeeded in adding to earlier legislation a provision to permit the consideration of an option providing a loan guarantee for an LNG transportation project in Alaska.[32] This language was incorporated in the 2004 Act. The portion of the Alaska gas pipeline $18 billion federal loan guarantee that could be used to cover an LNG project is limited to $2 billion. The cost of building LNG tankers could be included.[33]

Pursuit of the LNG option would entail a much shorter pipeline (the Trans Alaska oil pipeline is about 800 miles long) and, therefore, would imply use of a much smaller amount of steel. Of course, if the federal guarantee is used, an additional amount of domestic steel may be required for building Jones Act-qualified LNG tankers. The companies that own the gas remain less interested in an LNG project. During the administration of Alaska Governor Frank Murkowski, they focused on the Alaska Highway pipeline.[34]

State-Level Pipeline Negotiations in Alaska: A New Governor and a New Approach

Essentially rejecting both the TransCanada and LNG project proposals, Gov. Murkowski pursued an agreement with the three North Slope producers. His goal, and theirs, was to assure fiscally stable conditions under which the pipeline can be built. This has meant seeking both a long-term fiscal contract between producers and the state under the Alaska Stranded Gas Development Act, as well as changes to the state's oil and gas tax and royalty laws. A draft contract was reached in early 2006 with the producers, which provided a 20% ownership share for the state of Alaska in

---

[30] Tim Bradner, "ConocoPhillips Out of Gas Line," *Alaska Journal of Commerce* (Nov. 30, 2003).

[31] Sen. Lisa Murkowski, "Murkowski Says Gas Loan Guarantee Designed to Help Get Alaska Natural Gas to Market ..." press release (Dec. 2, 2003).

[32] Description quoted from H.Rept. 108-401, p. 1180. See account in Larry Persily, "Federal Loan Guarantee Extended to LNG," *Petroleum News* (Dec. 7, 2003), p. 13.

[33] Inclusion of the cost of building LNG tankers is justified on grounds that they would have to be U.S.-built and -manned under the Jones Act, and therefore the price of construction may be "two to three times as much as foreign-built ships;" Sen. Murkowski press statement (Dec. 2, 2003). See 15 U.S.C. § 720n(a)(1), (c)(2), and (g)(4) on LNG project coverage.

[34] Christian Schmollinger, "Pork Barrel Language No Guarantee for Alaska LNG Project," *Oil Daily* ((Dec. 4, 2003);Associated Press, "Governor Pushes Alaska Highway Pipeline Route ..." *Anchorage Daily News* (Dec. 2, 2003), p. F2; Tim Bradner, "Pipeline Firms Eye Highway Line," *Alaska Journal of Commerce* (Dec. 14, 2003), p. B1.

CRS-10

the primary project elements, plus royalties to be paid in gas, rather than cash. In return, the companies would have received a guarantee of a long-term stable tax rate.[35]

In August 2006, a special session of the legislature approved a new Petroleum Production Tax (PPT) regime for oil and gas producers, according to press reports. The new plan fundamentally shifted the basis of taxation, as sought by the governor and producers, from a tax on production to a tax on net profits. The new law also allowed for deductions and tax credits for new investments. Though it did not allow a deduction for building a gas pipeline, it did allow companies to deduct the cost of gas treatment plants and other infrastructure. The final law raised the tax on profits from 20%, as originally proposed, to 22.5%. It also added a surtax at any time when the price of oil is higher than $55 per barrel, and set a floor to the tax rate at 4% of gross revenues when the price of oil is low.[36]

The legislature refused to approve the draft contract in two separate special sessions in summer 2006. The oil companies' refusal so far to develop the North Slope gas fields is controversial in Alaska. For example, it is reported that ExxonMobil and its predecessor, Exxon Corporation, "which operates ... the state's largest untapped gas field ... has put off developing the field for 30 years and recently fended off a state order to submit a new development plan or face losing its leases." The producers reportedly were concerned with the amendments to the state tax regime as finally approved, and determined to secure contract provisions as favorable as possible.[37] Governor Murkowski lost his bid for re-election in the Republican primary on August 22, 2006. The natural gas pipeline contract provisions were an issue in the campaign. Even before his successor, Governor Sarah Palin, took office, the outgoing administration cancelled on grounds of non-development a major oil and gas lease held by ExxonMobil.[38]

Gov. Palin announced a new approach to achieving a privately built pipeline. She proposed in March 2007 the "Alaska Gasline Inducement Act," designed to replace the Alaska Stranded Gas Act. Her approach would establish a new competition under which all applicants willing to accept conditions of the law would be invited to submit their plans for the pipeline. Requirements include acceptance of a three-year "open season," in which the pipeline licensee would solicit firm commitments from all parties to ship gas on the pipeline. Applicants must also commit to a firm date by which they would apply for a final certificate authorizing the pipeline. Under AGIA, the state would match the licensee's costs in seeking certification up to a level of $500 million. After the first gas is shipped through the pipeline, the state would also promise a ten-year tax holiday for the pipeline operator

---

[35] FERC, *Second Report*, p. 2.

[36] *Oil Daily*, "Alaska Legislature Approves New Tax Regime for Oil Producers" (Aug. 15, 2006), p. 5.

[37] *Ibid.,* and "Alaska, Exxon Headed for Showdown on Point Thomson" (Oct. 6, 2006), p. 5; "Candidate Knowles calls for caution on Point Thomson Standoff" (Oct. 11, 2006), p. 5.

[38] FERC, *Third Report*, p. 4. This action may be legally challenged.

CRS-11

under the AGIA. The state PPT would remain in effect under Gov. Palin's plan, but subject to future review.[39]

As stated by FERC in its *Second Report*, "When the commercial project emerges [from negotiations between the state of Alaska and producers, and from the fiscal framework legislated by the state], DOE will proceed with structuring the loan guarantee."[40] FERC further estimated that it would be at least 10 years after any contract is approved before gas would flow from Alaska to the lower 48 states.[41] Moreover, in its *Third Report*, FERC concluded in January 2007 that:

> ... [N]o pipeline application has been developed, and the prospects of an application are more remote than a year ago. Over the past year the schedule for an Alaska gas pipeline has slipped considerably. The main obstacle to progress is the failure to resolve state issues necessary before a project sponsor will commit to go forward. The fresh competitive approach announced by the new governor must be successful if Alaska gas is to be part of the nation's energy supply solution anytime in the coming years.[42]

The Department of Energy on April 13, 2006, started a study of alternative approaches to the construction and operation of an Alaska natural gas transportation system. Such a study was required under Section 109 of the 2004 Alaska Natural Gas Pipeline Act, if no application for a certificate of public convenience and necessity for the pipeline had been received 18 months after passage of the law in October 2004.[43] The study includes consultations with the Army Corps of Engineers and the Treasury Department. The study, reported in September 2006 to be in a "pre-scoping" phase, may include consideration of establishment of a federal corporation to construct the pipeline project. The results of the study and any recommendations, including proposals for legislation, are to be submitted to Congress.[44]

Progress on Canada's Mackenzie Pipeline Project

As noted above, Congress, when approving the 2004 Alaska pipeline law, found that there was ample demand in North America for gas from both Alaska and the

---

[39] Gov. Palin's bill is described and defended in various release from her office: "Gov. Palin Unveils the AGIA" (news release 07-045), Mar. 2, 2007; "Weekly Gasline Briefing #4" (Mar. 2, 2007) and #5 (Mar. 8, 2007); "Executive Summary of AGIA" (Mar. 5, 2007); Gov. Sarah Palin, "Gasline Inducement Act Is Ready to Go," *Fairbanks Daily News-Miner* (Mar. 4, 2007). For a press analysis, see "Palin Bets Her Image on Gas Line," *Juneau Empire* (Mar. 11, 2007). Note that federal regulations for the "open season," as established by FERC have been legally challenged by the North Slope producers on some specific points; FERC, *Third Report*, pp. 5-6.

[40] FERC, *Second Report*, p. 7.

[41] *Ibid.*, pp. 11-12.

[42] FERC, *Third Report*, p. 7.

[43] 15 U.S.C. § 720g.

[44] FERC, *Second Report*, p. 7; *Petroleum News*, "Federal Regulators Move on Gas Line" (Sept. 24, 2006), p. 4.

CRS-12

Mackenzie River Delta of Canada, and that both projects should go forward. Moreover, gas from the Mackenzie Delta may be used as fuel for the major oil sands project in Alberta, rather than for consumption elsewhere in North America. However, there is some possibility that moving forward simultaneously with the Mackenzie and Alaska pipelines could create a competition for both steel and labor, and thereby drive up the costs and create delays for both projects.

As currently planned, the Mackenzie pipeline would be about 800 miles long, and would consist of 30-inch-diameter pipe of a grade that is presently available commercially. The pipe would be mostly above ground, because of the difficulties in constructing and maintaining a pipeline built through permafrost. The anticipated delivery rate of the pipeline would be 1.2 billion cubic feet per day (bcf/d), if built under current plans, compared to total current production in Canada of 17 bcf/d. If more gas is found than currently anticipated in the Mackenzie Delta region, plans are that the pipeline could be looped along the same route.[45]

Current plans are that all of the Mackenzie gas would be devoted to the Alberta oil sands project. Natural gas is the primary fuel for that project. Current usage by that project is only about a half-million bcf/d, but when the project is built out to planned full capacity by 2015, the natural gas requirement would be 2.1 million bcf/d, or more than the anticipated throughput of the Mackenzie pipeline. At that time, total nominal capacity of the oil sands projects would be 4.4 million barrels of oil per day (mbd), though official projections by the Canadian National Energy Board are for an average peak output of 3.0 mbd. The oil sands project is calculated to achieve a required return of 10% on the projected capital investment, as long as the price of oil is at least in the range of $30-35 per barrel.[46]

FERC found that development of the Mackenzie pipeline "poses certain problems and risks to an Alaskan project." This not because direct competition in the gas market, but because of a lack of sufficient pipeline grade steel and a shortage of skilled labor required to build two technically challenging Arctic projects of such magnitude at the same time.[47] Both FERC and the Canadian government emphasize that the project has been expedited by creation under Canadian law of a "Joint Review Panel," which is considering all environmental and social aspects of the project, and plans to produce a final report to the National Energy Board (NEB) in 2007. One potentially contentious issue that remains unresolved is provision of an acceptable level of access to and benefits from the project for aboriginal peoples who live in and near the Mackenzie Valley.[48] If all these issues could have been resolved along the time line projected by the Canadian government, the Mackenzie pipeline could be

---

[45] Connors interview, Canadian Embassy; FERC, *Second Report*, p. 9.

[46] Govt. of Canada. National Energy Board (NEB). *Canada's Oil Sands: Opportunities and Challenges to 2015 — An Update* (June 2006), pp. 5, 12-13, 16-18. However, the report notes an 88% increase in the estimated cost of natural gas used in the project in less than two years since the first report issued by the Board, and the consequent intensification of efforts to develop alternate energy sources.

[47] FERC, *Second Report*, p. 9.

[48] Canadian Embassy interview.

CRS-13

finished by 2012, before the peak of construction activity projected for an Alaska pipeline.[49]

But concerns about rising costs may contribute to further delays in approval of the Mackenzie gas project. It has been reported that the Joint Review Panel process has already led to a delay of one construction season in the project, and that cost estimates for the pipeline will increase from $C7.5 billion to $C10 billion in detailed project estimates being prepared by Imperial Oil of Canada, an ExxonMobil affiliate active in both the oil sands and Mackenzie gas projects. A private sector analyst, quoted in the same article, estimated that development of Mackenzie Delta gas is only economic if crude oil is in the range of $60-70 per barrel and natural gas is $7-9 per million BTUs.[50]

In keeping with the expected rise in pipeline costs, recent estimates presented by Imperial Oil with respect to the budget and time line for the overall Mackenzie gas project indicate that:

- The Mackenzie Pipeline will not receive a permit before 2008;
- Construction will not begin before 2010;
- Construction would require four years, and not be completed before 2014;
- There is presently not enough gas expected to be recovered from the mackenzie fields to fill the pipeline, and additional supply would need to be committed from other fields that may be nearby.[51]

If the Mackenzie pipeline project does not go ahead, there should be no impact on the Alaska project. But if the Mackenzie project is further delayed before proceeding, it may lead to increased costs and delays in keeping with FERC's concerns, should the Alaska project be constructed simultaneously.

Evaluating an Alaskan Pipeline Investment Project[52]

Large scale capital investment projects, such as an Alaskan natural gas pipeline, typically require substantial financial commitments at the inception of, and in the early years of, the project and promise to provide net profits to investors for many years into the future. For this reason, before undertaking such projects, investors use financial tests such as net present value analysis, that seek to determine whether, for any particular project, the value today of the proposed investment funds, are less than, or

---

[49] Ibid., pp. 9-10; NEB, esp. fig. 6.2; Canadian Embassy interview.

[50] *Petroleum News*, "Costs Pose Threat" (Sept. 3, 2006), p. 1.

[51] *Ibid.*, "Make-or-Break Mac Budget" (Mar. 18, 2007).

[52] This section was written by Robert Pirog. The purpose of this section is not to carry out an analysis of the economic viability of an Alaskan natural gas pipeline project. The purpose is to highlight those factors which might influence the viability of the project, and to tie them to understanding developments in the natural gas and steel industries and markets.

CRS-14

greater than, the discounted future profit stream. The principal financial advantage to having funds currently available is that they can be invested in financial assets and earn a market rate of return.[53] A key factor in evaluating capital investment project decisions is whether this financial return, which is given up, or traded off, is compensated by the potential earnings of the real capital investment.[54]

Because of the nature of the net present value investment test, any factor that affects the revenue the project might earn, or the costs that the project might accrue, is likely to affect the determination of whether the project is profitable and likely to be implemented. In the case of an Alaskan natural gas pipeline, the key market factors are likely to be natural gas prices and consumption levels, which will largely determine the revenue derived from the pipeline, and the price and availability of steel required to construct the pipeline, which is a major part of projected costs.[55] As a result, analyses of the natural gas and steel industries and markets carried out in this report can contribute to understanding the nature of the debate concerning the need for, and economic viability of an Alaska natural gas pipeline. Additionally, these analyses can identify the factors that determine the risk of the project. In a large scale project that could have economy-wide implications, such as an Alaskan natural gas pipeline, risk sharing may be one approach for government policy concerning the project.

Pipeline Returns

An Alaskan natural gas pipeline's main purpose is to deliver natural gas supplies from fields at the North Slope of Alaska to consuming markets in the lower 48 states. This natural gas is now "stranded" in the sense that it can be physically produced, but cannot be delivered to consumers because of the lack of a transportation system. Currently, the gas is not wasted: it is re-injected into oil wells operating in the area, increasing the productivity of those wells.

The key factors determining the returns, or revenues, that might be earned by an Alaskan natural gas pipeline are the expected price of natural gas over the life of the pipeline, the quantity of natural gas that might be delivered through the pipeline each year, and the number of years that the pipeline, and the producing fields that feed natural gas into it, will be operational. These factors are all related to the current, and future, projected conditions of the natural gas market. An analysis of the natural gas market is carried out later in the report.

---

[53] This rate of return may vary depending on the class of financial asset chosen for investment. However, the financial rate of return is generically referred to as the rate of interest.

[54] The most common investment test is net present value analysis. This technique compares the inflation adjusted net discounted profits of the project over time to the initial investment. If the net present value of the project is greater than zero, *ie.* discounted profits are greater than the initial investment, the project qualifies for implementation.

[55] An additional factor is the availability of skilled labor to construct and operate the pipeline, a factor not specifically analyzed in this report.

CRS-15

Pipeline Costs

The costs of an Alaskan natural gas pipeline fall into two categories: investment, or capital costs, and operating costs. A large number of factors enter into the determination of either class of costs. In a subsequent section, this report focuses on one of the main capital costs of the project: the cost and timely availability of steel pipe that would be used in construction of the pipeline. The report focuses on that cost factor because of its potential significance to the North American steel industry.

Risk Factors

In financial analysis, the riskiness of a given factor is taken to be equivalent to its variability.[56] If the value of a factor is taken to be constant, this implies that the factor is risk free. If its volatility is low, its riskiness is low, and if the factor's value demonstrates high volatility, this is associated with high levels of risk.[57] Generally, higher levels of risk associated with a capital investment project must be compensated with higher levels of expected return if the project is to be approved for implementation through application of the net present value criterion.

In relation to an Alaskan natural gas pipeline, several of the key market factors that will determine the expected revenues and costs are likely to exhibit considerable risk. These factors include the price of steel to be used in the construction of the pipeline, the near and long term price of natural gas, and the price of labor, both for construction and operation of the pipeline. The demand for natural gas has been projected by many analysts to be relatively assured, but available historical and current market data suggests that it too might better be considered as subject to risk.

The relationship between risk factors and the viability of an investment decision may be of importance when evaluating whether public policy measures to encourage carrying out of the project are appropriate. If the benefits of a project are captured in their entirety by the investors, there is little reason for active public support. However, if the completion of the project is judged to include significant public benefits, then there may be a case made for active support of the project through public support.

Public support for an investment project might occur through loan guarantees, direct investment participation, price and regulatory guarantees, policies which encourage demand for the delivered product, and the discouragement of substitute products or services. However, critics argue that if the market will not support the economic viability of the project, neither should the government. Some of these policy options were discussed in an earlier section of this report.

---

[56] Gitman, Lawrence J., *Principles of Managerial Finance,* 8th ed., Addison-Wesley, 1997, p.228.

[57] The volatility based definition of risk includes favorable as well as unfavorable movements of the factor. For example, the market price of natural gas might decrease, or increase, by 10% in a month. Either movement in the price would be consistent with identifying the price of natural gas as a risk factor.

362 703-739-3790 TCNNaturalGas.com

CRS-16

Market Conditions in the Natural Gas Markets[58]

An Alaskan natural gas pipeline is unlikely to come online before 2016, and from that point, its throughput is likely to be a part of U.S. natural gas supply through the middle of the century. As a result of this long time frame, analyzing the likely values for risk factors associated with the project may come from both future projections of market behavior as well as historical trends.

Long Run Natural Gas Markets: EIA's Projections

A widely used long run projection of energy markets is the EIA's *Annual Energy Outlook 2006* (AEO), which provides market projections and analysis out to 2030.[59] The AEO reference case projects aggregate U.S. natural gas demand to rise by about 20% from 2004 to 2030, from 22.4 trillion cubic feet (tcf) to 26.9 tcf in 2030.[60] Almost all of the gains in demand, approximately 18%, are projected to take place by 2017, with less than 2% growth, relative to 2004, taking place from 2018 through 2030. The AEO projects this growth in demand to be led by electricity generators demand growth through 2019, with more limited growth in the residential, commercial, and industrial sectors, due to the effect of higher projected prices. The AEO's 4.5 tcf projected demand increase provides the demand-side basis for the construction of an Alaskan natural gas pipeline, which itself would deliver approximately 1.5 tcf per year.

The AEO projects a changing mix of supply sources which might meet U.S. demand. Conventional onshore production of natural gas in the lower 48 states is projected to decline by about 10% from 2004 to 2030 to 4.2 tcf. Production from the shallow waters of the Gulf of Mexico is also projected to decline, by about 25% from 2004 to 2030, to 1.8 tcf. Onshore production from unconventional sources in the lower 48 states is projected to increase by about 27% from 2004 to 2030, to 9.5 tcf while deepwater production from the Gulf of Mexico is expected to increase by about 78% from 2004 to 2014, and then decline by about 35% from 2015 to 2030.[61] Over the period 2004 to 2030, deepwater Gulf of Mexico production is expected to increase by about 17% to 2.1 tcf. In 2030, Alaskan natural gas production is projected to total about 2.1 tcf. This mixture of decreasing and increasing supply sources provides the supply-side basis for the construction of an Alaskan natural gas pipeline.

Imports of natural gas by pipeline from Canada are projected to decline by about 44% from 2004 and 2030, to 1.8 tcf. Net imports of LNG are projected to increase by

---

[58] This section was written by Robert Pirog.

[59] The *Annual Energy Outlook 2006* is not a forecast, it is a projection. It is in the form of a baseline; a projection of what might occur if current conditions and policies remain in place and no new policies, or new extraneous conditions affect the market.

[60] In addition to the reference case, the AEO includes high and low economic growth and high and low price cases. These differing assumptions affect the natural gas values cited in this report.

[61] Unconventional sources of natural gas include coalbed methane, tight sandstones, and gas shale.

CRS-17

about 42% from 2004 to 2030, to 4.4 tcf. In the AEO reference case, both the Alaskan natural gas production and the LNG totals are dependent on major capital investments taking place over the next ten years: a pipeline in the case of Alaska and receiving terminals in the case of LNG.

While a variety of factors, including personal income levels, industrial structure, technology, and environmental considerations are likely to affect the demand and supply of natural gas in U.S. markets in the future, the key element is price. The AEO projects the price of natural gas to decline from the 2004 levels to an average of $4.46 per thousand cubic feet (mcf) by 2016, rising to $5.92 per mcf by 2030.[62] Prices at these projected levels are likely to encourage the construction of an adequate number of new LNG terminals in the United States, as well as providing incentive to build an Alaskan natural gas pipeline, according to the AEO.

Recent History of Natural Gas Markets

Since 1998, at the aggregate level, the U.S. natural gas market has maintained the appearance of balance and stability with respect to demand, supply, and reserves. As shown in **Table 1**, consumption, production, and proved reserves have been quite stable since the late 1990s. Only the wellhead price of natural gas has shown high volatility, which might be associated with an unsettled market.

Table 1: Overview of U.S. Natural Gas Market
(Volumes in trillion cubic feet; price in dollars per thousand cubic feet)

Year	1998	1999	2000	2001	2002	2003	2004	2005	2006
Consumption	22.4	22.4	23.3	22.2	23.0	22.3	22.4	22.2	21.8
Production	19.0	18.8	19.1	19.6	18.9	19.1	18.6	18.1	18.5
Proved Reserves	164	167	177	183	187	189	192	204	N/A
Wellhead Price	1.96	2.19	3.68	4.00	2.95	4.88	5.46	7.33	6.42

Source: Energy Information Administration, available at [http://www.eia.doe.gov].

Consumption. The sectoral demand data, which underlie the aggregate data of **Table 1**, show that important shifts have taken place in the composition of demand, even though the aggregate totals have not changed greatly.

---

[62] In the AEO, prices are expressed in base year, here 2004, levels. Actual, nominal, prices in the future will likely be higher reflecting the average rate of inflation over the period. However, it is not definite that the future price will merely capture inflation. Actual, observed, future prices might be higher or lower than the AEO projections, depending on relative demand and supply conditions.

CRS-18

Consumers of natural gas fall into four major groups: residential, commercial, industrial, and electric power generators.[63] While the aggregate demand for natural gas is frequently estimated to be relatively inelastic, or unresponsive to changes in price, this may not be equally true for all sectors and may have contributed to sectoral shifts.

Residential consumer demand has declined since 1998 by about 3%, probably in response to residential gas prices that were over twice as high in 2006 as in 1998.[64] The effect of higher prices was likely offset by the trend toward more and larger homes, as well as higher consumer incomes. Residential consumers may not have tied home heating decisions to the cost of natural gas due to the lack of real-time metering and this might also have supported demand.

Commercial demand has decreased since 1998 by about 5%, in response to commercial gas prices that also were more than twice as high in 2006 as in 1998. Industrial demand for natural gas has declined by 23% since 1998 in response to increases in industrial prices for natural gas since 1998. Industrial consumption of natural gas, either for production process heating, or as a raw material, may be more price responsive than that of the other consuming sectors. Cost increases might be passed on to consumers, or they might be absorbed as lower profits, depending on the nature of the market for the industries' products. For example, an industry that is a large consumer of natural gas as a raw material and has no suitable substitute, is nitrogenous fertilizer manufacturing.[65] Also, the U.S. fertilizer industry is open to foreign competition, which prevents an easy pass-through of cost increases to consumers. It is capable of moving production overseas where natural gas prices are generally lower, likely accounting for part of the reduced demand from the industrial sector.[66]

The demand for natural gas by electric power generators has increased by about 36% from 1998 to 2006. Since the early 1990's, technology, emissions performance, the availability of long term contracts, and low prices for part of the period have favored natural gas as the fuel of choice for new generating capacity. Household and commercial demand for electricity is relatively price inelastic because of the nature of its use in the home, and in businesses, as well as the lack of real time metering to allow users to determine the true cost of their electricity use decisions.

---

[63] Each of these consumer groups pay a different price per unit for natural gas. Generally, large scale consumers pay less per unit than smaller consumers. For example, the EIA reported that in June 2006 residential consumers paid $14.95 per mcf while industrial consumers paid $6.87 per mcf.

[64] The residential price of natural gas was $6.82 in 1998, and $13.76 in 2006.

[65] See *Domestic Nitrogen Fertilizer Production Depends on Natural Gas Availability and Prices*, GAO-03-1148, September 2003, for a further discussion of the effect of natural gas prices on the nitrogen fertilizer industry.

[66] Imports of fertilizer by the United States have increased from an annual rate of $3.2 billion in 1997 to $8.2 billion in 2006 and the United States has shifted from a net exporter to a net importer.

CRS-19

An important question in the evaluation of an Alaskan natural gas pipeline is whether its role will be to allow demand growth for all, or part, of the 26.9 tcf projected demand in 2030, or whether its role will be to replace diminished production from currently existing sources, or both. One scenario could begin with the assumption that demand patterns observed over the past nine years will continue in the future. This approach would have residential and commercial demand nearly flat, electric power demand increasing, and industrial demand decreasing. Industrial demand decreases have been large enough to offset growth in electric power generation because, among the sectors, industry is the largest user of natural gas. Another scenario might be that those uses of natural gas in the industrial sector that are price responsive will be exhausted at some level, and after that usage level is attained, industrial demand would not decline as rapidly in response to price as in the past. Thus, demand would rise over the next decades. On balance, reviewing the period since 1998, it is not clear whether aggregate U.S. demand growth could provide the major justification for an Alaskan pipeline.

Production and Imports. Production data for U.S. natural gas production shown in **Table 1** indicates that although year-to-year variations exist, there does not appear to be a clear upward or downward trend. U.S. production decreased by about 5% between 2000 and 2005, but by only by 2.6% over the period 1998 to 2006. Peak U.S. production levels were attained in 2001, near the beginning of the period of volatile, escalated prices. Production is likely related to price, but technology and the geological characteristics of the gas fields also play an important role in determining output.

The difference between U.S. production and U.S. consumption is made up by imports, mostly by pipeline from Canada. The natural gas market, unlike the crude oil market, is regional rather than global in scope, extending along pipeline systems. It is possible that the geographic scope of the U.S. natural gas market may expand in the coming decades through the expansion and maturation of the LNG market.

Imports from Canada increased by approximately 18% over the period 1998 to 2006. Imports of LNG increased by about 585% over the period 1998 to 2006, but still accounted for less than 3% of U.S. consumption in 2006. Imports from Canada are expected to decline in the coming decades as Canadian domestic consumption increases, more natural gas is used in the production of oil from oil sands, and Canadian fields continue to deplete. These trends could be moderated by the opening of new supplies, especially those delivered through the proposed construction of the Mackenzie River natural gas pipeline, or through technological improvements.

The United States currently has four operational LNG receiving facilities. Plans for expansion at existing facilities, coupled with the construction of new facilities could increase the U.S. consumption of LNG considerably. However, the spot market for LNG has been slow to develop on the production side, and other competing uses

366 703-739-3790 TCNNaturalGas.com

CRS-20

are vying with LNG for available natural gas feedstock supplies.[67] The market for LNG remains largely a long-term contract market.[68]

Natural Gas Reserves. Proved reserves are those reserves that are recoverable using currently available technology under existing economic conditions, including price. These reserves provide the basis for current and future production. Current production draws down the level of proved reserves, and new discoveries increase, or maintain, the level of proved reserves.

Data in **Table 1** show that the level of U.S. proved reserves of natural gas has increased by approximately 24% over the period 1998 to 2005. Another key measure of the production base is the reserve-to-production ratio. In 1998 this ratio was 8.6, implying that at then-current production rates the reserve base could sustain production for 8.6 years. By 2005, the reserve-to-production ratio had increased to 11.2, implying that the reserve base could sustain U.S. production levels longer than in 1998.[69] This increase came after the production of over 133 tcf from the U.S. reserve base during the period 1998 to 2004. Natural gas discoveries have more than replaced production draws during this period.

As noted by the EIA in the AEO, the sources of U.S. gas production are moving away from conventional, onshore to more costly unconventional and deep offshore supplies, which may imply an upward trend in the price of natural gas, but also suggests that availability is not likely to be sharply reduced relative to current levels.

Natural Gas Prices. The wellhead price data presented in **Table 1** suggests that prices have generally been rising since 1998, with a good deal of volatility. Notable was the decline in prices in 2002, consistent with the downturn in U.S. production that year, but seemingly at odds with the increased consumption that year. Since 2003, the price trend has been upward and volatile, with wellhead prices peaking above $10 per tcf in both October and December 2005, before moderating in 2006.[70]

The wellhead price of natural gas has risen by about 225% over the period 1998 to 2006. Price increases of this magnitude might ordinarily be associated with a major change in the underlying market fundamentals. If consumption demand had increased markedly, or production had diminished, or even if the reserve base upon which consumption and production are based had been reduced, sharply affecting

---

[67] See CRS Report RL32666, *The Gas to Liquids Industry and Natural Gas Markets.*

[68] See CRS Report RL32445, *Liquified Natural Gas (LNG) Markets in Transition: Implications for U.S. Supply and Price*, by Robert Pirog.

[69] In recent years, the overall industry reserve-to-production ratio has been about nine years.

[70] Monthly natural gas price data is affected by a wide variety of short run forces which affect the market. Weather, a highly variable factor, can affect monthly prices by creating unexpected changes in the average draw from, or injection into storage, as well as consumption. Extreme weather conditions, such as hurricane Katrina, have also been shown to be able to affect natural gas production adding more volatility to price.

CRS-21

expectations for the future, then the change in price could be explained in terms of normal market demand and supply adjustment.[71] However, the data presented in **Figure 2** is seemingly more consistent with market stability than upheaval.

Figure 2: U.S. Natural Gas Price, Consumption and Production Indexes

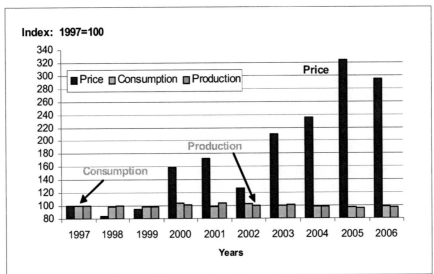

Source: Energy Information Administration, available at [http://www.eia.doe.gov]. Index computed by CRS.
Note: 2006 indexes estimated from data for January-June 2006.

Other explanations for the pattern of natural gas price movements since 1997 include the effects of financial trading of natural gas futures contracts. One approach suggests that the increased interest in natural gas markets by financial traders in itself has caused prices to rise. Another approach claims that speculators have used illegal strategies to create artificial prices in the natural gas market.

In a recent study, Mark N. Cooper investigated the case for influence by financial traders on natural gas prices.[72] Cooper identifies what he sees as a pattern of increased interest in natural gas trading by financial investors and movements in the wellhead

---

[71] The prices of crude oil and natural gas usually stand in a 6:1 ratio based on energy content. That is, the price of a barrel of crude oil is six times the price of 1 mcf of gas. During 2006, the ratio has been over 10:1, although this is likely due to the price of crude oil rising to reflect geopolitical uncertainties and the tight demand/supply balance in the world oil market.

[72] Mark N. Cooper, *The Role of Supply, Demand and Financial Commodity Markets in the Natural Gas Price Spiral,* prepared for the Midwest Attorneys General Natural Gas Working Group, May 2006.

CRS-22

price of natural gas. For example, Cooper notes that while the price of natural gas was relatively stable in the 1990s, it began to increase in the spring of 2000, a period coincident with the expansion of natural gas trading on the Enron Online trading platform.[73] Cooper also notes that after Enron's departure from the market in December 2001, the wellhead price of natural gas declined in early 2002.[74]

While Cooper's study presents examples of possible correlation between movements of natural gas prices and financial trading patterns, he does not carry out statistical analysis that might demonstrate more conclusively causal links between the two sets of data. Irrespective of the effect on price, the trading of natural gas futures contracts does allow consumers and producers of natural gas to re-distribute the price risk they face to speculators who are more willing to bear that risk.

Studies undertaken by the New York Mercantile Exchange (NYMEX) and the Commodity Futures Trading Commission (CFTC) present conclusions different from Cooper. Both studies are limited to the regulated, standard contract part of the futures and derivative market. The over-the-counter segment of the futures and derivatives market is exempt from regulatory oversight. The NYMEX study found that hedge funds comprised only a modest share of trading in natural gas futures contracts and their activities were not a likely source of excess volatility in the market.[75] The CFTC study found that hedge fund trading on energy futures and derivatives markets and commodity prices were not linked, and that price volatility was not increased by their trading activities.[76] Unlike the Cooper study, the NYMEX and CFTC studies are based on extensive statistical analysis of price and other market data.

Uncertainties

Comparison of the AEO projection of natural gas market conditions to the actual performance of the market over the past nine years yields differing pictures of the market itself, as well as conditions for an Alaskan natural gas pipeline.

This report has identified the future natural gas price, the quantity demanded, and the output levels of existing gas production sources as key risk factors in evaluating the economic feasibility of an Alaskan natural gas pipeline. These factors are interrelated in the sense that they each help determine the other's value. If an Alaskan natural gas pipeline is constructed, and either new demand is not created, or existing production sources do not decline, or are replaced with gas from other more technically or economically viable sources, the 4.5 billion cubic feet of gas per day the pipeline will be capable of delivering could depress the market price. In this scenario,

---

[73] The growth of the Enron Online trading platform led to both an increase in financial trading as well as being associated with the illegal activities that led to Enron's bankruptcy.

[74] Cooper, p. 8.

[75] New York Mercantile Exchange, *A Review of Recent Hedge Fund Participation in NYMEX Natural Gas and Crude Oil Futures Markets,* March 1, 2005, p.3.

[76] U.S. Commodity Futures Trading Commission, *Price Dynamics, Price Discovery and Large Futures Trader Interactions in the Energy Complex,* April 28, 2005, p.24.

CRS-23

the economic viability of the pipeline would be in danger as well as that of other relatively high cost sources of gas.

LNG imports also have the potential to change the economics of an Alaskan natural gas pipeline. While the United States currently uses LNG for less than 4% of its total consumption needs, plans exist to expand currently available offloading facilities and to construct many new facilities. These facilities, are capital intensive, although for comparable capacity they may cost a fraction of the cost of a pipeline. If they are built, and gas begins to flow through them, they could be viewed as competing for the same increase in demand that the AEO projects for the future.

Over-capacity might be a concern to the natural gas market. Residential demand growth depends on the extent of new home construction, which is just coming out of a major growth phase and slowing down. Commercial demand is relatively flat, while industrial demand is declining. To the extent that permanent demand destruction has occurred in the industrial sector, it may be unrealistic to assume any growth over the near term. Electricity generation by natural-gas-fired generators, however, is projected to continue to experience growth and provide support for the growth in natural gas demand.[77]

Short Term Market Conditions

Current, and near-term, natural gas market indicators are of limited use when planning long term capital projects in the industry. The market-fundamental-based value of natural gas in the short term is determined by the interaction of consumption, production, and stored quantities. Since production is relatively constant during any year, and consumption tends to be seasonal, stored quantities of natural gas balance the market. The primary short term direct determinant of consumption, and indirect determinant of stored quantities, is the weather. Exceptionally cold weather during the winter heating season can cause demand to surge. Exceptionally warm weather during the summer season can cause electricity demand, much of which on the margin is natural gas generated, to surge. Storage injections typically occur during the spring and summer. Storage draws typically occur during the winter heating season. If a cold winter (large withdrawals from storage) is followed by a very warm summer (below expected injections into storage), it is likely that the price of natural gas will experience upward volatility. However, this upward price movement may not be permanent, or even indicative of long term trends. A cold winter might be followed by more temperate conditions, reversing the natural gas price pressure.

Long-term economic decisions, such as the construction of an Alaska natural gas pipeline, are usually based on expected outcomes over a time period commensurate with the economic life of the project. Favorable, or unfavorable, short run conditions on the commodity market are often discounted.

---

[77] Many factors are likely to contribute to the potential growth in electricity demand. For example, high prices for natural gas could make coal fired powerplants competitive. Climate change legislation, if enacted, could influence the growth of electricity demand and the mix of fuels used in electricity generation.

CRS-24

The Impact of Steel Prices and Availability[78]

The Reversal in Steel Prices

The Alaska natural gas pipeline project was supported by the North American steel industry in a period of low prices and company bankruptcies, because it could provide a boost to employment and revenues. For example, the American Iron and Steel Institute (AISI) estimated that the project could generate "up to 10,000 work years of direct employment from North American steel supply.[79] In addition almost 4,000 additional work years would be used to manufacture pipe from steel." This estimate was based on the use of three to five million tons of steel. By comparison, AISI noted that in 1999-2000, "three North American steel pipe producers supplied over 1,000,000 tons of steel for the 2,000 mile Alliance Pipeline running from Northern British Columbia to Chicago," which AISI stated was "the most technologically advanced and largest pipeline construction project ever in North America."[80]

Figure 3. Prices for Large-Diameter Steel Pipe and Plate

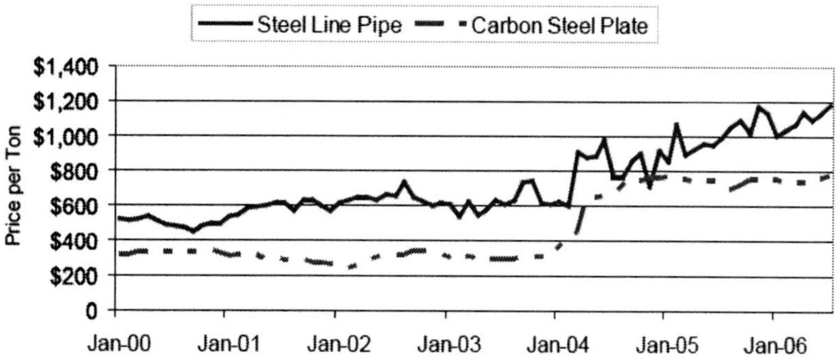

Sources: *Preston Pipe & Tube Report*; Global Insight, steel plate data reported from *Purchasing* magazine.
Note: Pipe prices represent average transaction price (by weighted average value) for double-submerged arc-welded pipe > 24" diameter , combining both domestic and import shipments. Plate prices are for coiled plate.

---

[78] This section was written by Stephen Cooney.

[79] The phrase "North American steel" is used throughout this report and most AISI documents, instead of "U.S." steel. U.S. and Canadian steelmakers compete within the same free trade area, and the same industry union, the United Steelworkers, operates on both sides of the border. Moreover, if the pipeline were to run through Canada, participation by Canadian steelmakers in any competitive bidding process would presumably be required.

[80] Quotations from Andrew G. Sharkey, III, AISI. Letter to Sen. Frank Murkowski (April 17, 2002), with attached statement. Estimates of total amounts of steel from CRS interviews with Chip Foley, AISI, April 22 and 24, 2003. The total production of steel in the United States has recently been about 100-110 million tons per year, with imports adding roughly 30-40 million tons annually to U.S. supply; AISI, *Annual Statistical Report* (2005), figs. in frontispiece, "U.S. Steel Shipments" and p. 46, "Imports of Steel Mill Products."

CRS-25

The situation now, just a few years later, is almost totally reversed. The North American steel industry has restructured, and recovered profitability because of strong domestic and worldwide demand.[81] Now, higher prices resulting from both strong demand and increased production costs for carbon steel plate, used in making large-diameter steel pipe, may alter the basic economics of an Alaska natural gas pipeline project.

As illustrated in **Figure 3**, data reported by the consulting firm Global Insight (formerly known as DRI-WEFA) indicate that the price of carbon plate has more than doubled during the past five years.[82] As of late 2001, DRI-WEFA reported that spot prices for plate were between $250 and $300 per ton. This was consonant with an overall depression in steel prices. DRI-WEFA at the time stated that the "... composite of eight carbon spot prices sets a new low almost every month, and in the past seven years has fallen 44%."[83] Carbon steel plate was one of many steel mill products protected from imports by special tariffs, known as safeguard remedies, between March 2002 and December 2003, when they were terminated by President Bush. During 2003, steel prices began to strengthen, and carbon plate averaged $303 per ton for the year. After the the safeguards ended, steel prices escalated instead of falling, as one might expect, because of a global recovery in demand. The carbon plate price average doubled to $633 per ton in 2004. For 2005, the average price was even higher at $744, and it was still at a similar level in mid-2006. Global Insight forecasts carbon plate prices to decline over the next two years, but only gradually, and to a level still more than double the price early in the decade.[84] While the price of flat-rolled steel is expected to fall because of reduced light vehicle output by the major U.S. domestic producers, Global Insight analyst John Anton has also stated that, "Not all products will decline, as markets for structurals and plate are still tight ..."[85]

Figure 3 illustrates the parallel increase in large-diameter pipe prices consonant with the underlying increase in price of steel plate. As of late 2001 and early 2002, the price of large-diameter pipe was generally around $600 per ton. As shown in **Figure 3**, the price of coiled plate was less than half that level. By late 2005, the average reported price of large-diameter pipe was more than $1,000 per ton, with plate, now more than $750 per ton, accounting for the increase. By mid-2006, the price of pipe was approaching $1,200 per ton, with the cost of coiled plate close to

---

[81] See CRS Report RL32333, *Steel: Price and Policy Issues*, by Stephen Cooney, for details.

[82] Figure 3 uses a price series for coiled plate. This is the steel used for the highest grade steel pipe of the largest diameter, which is now spiral-welded. Much large diameter pipe is also made from "cut-to-length" plate. The prices of the two types of plate are close and generally move in tandem.

[83] Based on data from *Purchasing* magazine. DRI-WEFA. *Steel Industry Review* (4th Qtr. 2001), p. 18 and table 16.

[84] Global Insight. *Steel Industry Review* (2nd Qtr. 2006), tabs. 1.11-1.12. Even higher prices of $840-880 per ton were quoted on the West Coast, from which plate could be provided for mills to manufacture large-diameter pipe to be used in Alaska; *American Metal Market* (*AMM*), "West Sees More Steel Plate But Prices Holding Ground" (Aug. 31, 2006).

[85] Global Insight. *Steel Monthly Report* (Sept. 2006), p. 2.

372

CRS-26

$800. Moreover, availability of plate for outside-diameter pipe wider than 36" is limited in the U.S. market to one integrated mill, or possibly only to import sources. This has resulted in 2006 price quotes above $1,050 per ton, or three times the price quoted for similar product in 2003.[86]

The increased cost of steel could account for a substantial share of the increase in cost estimates for the Alaska natural gas pipeline. Actual prices for large quantities of steel pipe for major projects are negotiated by the steel supplier and seller, and are not made publicly available. But average monthly transaction prices are reported in *Preston Pipe & Tube Report*, the only data source for large-diameter steel pipe prices. In a previous section of the report, it was noted that a producers' study in 2002-2003 estimated a total pipeline cost of $18 billion to $19.6 billion for the Alaska Highway route, and that more recent estimates were at least $25 billion. An informed 2006 estimate for the tonnage of pipe needed is at least four million tons (which is also the midpoint of the estimate quoted earlier by AISI).[87] The data in **Figure 3** show an increase in the average price of steel from about $300 to about $750 per ton, and for large-diameter pipe from around $600 to about $1,100 per ton. But pipe for use in Arctic conditions would probably require the highest grade of steel available (see below), so the increase in price since the earlier project estimates were produced may be on the order of at least $500-600 per ton. That would imply an increased cost of steel pipe for the project of about $2.0-2.5 billion, which alone could account for half or more of the increase in overall project cost estimates.

North American Large Pipe Production Capacity

Section 111 of the 2004 Alaska Natural Gas Pipeline Act expresses the sense of Congress that, as "an Alaska natural gas transportation project would provide specific significant economic benefits to the United States and Canada ..." its sponsors "should make every effort to ... use steel that is manufactured in North America ..."[88] The relative capabilities of U.S. and Canadian industries to supply steel for the project would depend on a number of variables, including the time frame for completing the project, the final route chosen, and the pipeline specifications. The North Slope natural gas producers have indicated that they would require a pipe of maximum capacity, to ensure the ability to transport a high enough volume of gas to earn an adequate return on a privately financed system. When the 800-mile Trans Alaska oil pipeline was built in the 1970s, it used 500,000 tons of special cold-weather steel 48-inch diameter pipe imported from Japan.[89] There are a number of questions today about the capacities of the North American industry to supply the steel that might be required to construct an Alaska natural gas pipeline.

The increase in oil and gas prices in 2005-06 has encouraged North American drilling activity and increased demand for all steel products used in the oil and gas

---

[86] Interview with David Delie, Berg Steel Pipe (Feb. 15, 2007).

[87] Ipsco Inc. *Northern Pipelines* (presentation to U.S. federal agencies, Apr. 2006), p. 22.

[88] 15 U.S.C. § 720i.

[89] U.S. Dept. of the Interior, with Argonne National Laboratory. "TAPS History," in *TAPS Renewal Environmental Impact Statement*, [http://tapseis.anl.gov].

CRS-27

industry, including large-diameter pipe for long-distance gas transmission. But there are currently only a few large-diameter pipe producers active in North America:[90]

- Ipsco, Inc., originally a Canadian company, which now has more of its assets in U.S. mills and its operational headquarters in Illinois, is the largest North American producer of large-diameter pipe. It operates a pipe mill in Regina, Saskatchewan, with an annual capacity of 350,000 tons, and a capability to make pipe up to 80 inches wide. Plate is supplied from a mill there, and from mills in Iowa and Alabama. The company is also building a new R&D facility in Regina devoted to pipe technology. Ipsco recently announced a deal to acquire NS Group, a Kentucky-based pipe and tube manufacturer, but that company specializes in smaller diameter oil country tubular goods (OCTG) products, not large-diameter pipe.

- Oregon Steel Mills, a U.S.-based steel minimill company, currently operates a large-diameter pipe mill in Camrose, Alberta. Originally this was a joint venture with the Canadian steelmaker, Stelco. Oregon Steel acquired full control of the facility, which has an annual capacity of 180,000 tons of pipe ranging from 20 to 42 inches in diameter. Oregon Steel is also opening in late 2006 a new large-diameter pipe mill complex in Portland, Oregon. It will have an annual capacity of 175,000-200,000 tons of 24 to 60 inch diameter pipe. In January 2007, Oregon Steel was acquired by a Russian company, Evraz Steel.[91]

- Berg Steel Pipe, a subsidiary of Europipe, jointly owned by German and French steel interests, manufactures pipe in Panama City, Florida. Berg buys domestic or imported plate for manufacturing pipe with a diameter from 24 to 72 inches. It recently announced plans to expand with a second mill along the Gulf Coast, but this would be for pipe of lesser diameter.

Ipsco and Oregon both operate minimills that supply plate for making pipe. Nucor, the largest operator of minimills in North America, makes plate at two mills in North Carolina and Alabama, and also can supply plate to customers for pipemaking operations.[92] Among the large integrated companies, both U.S. Steel and Bethlehem Steel have closed some steel pipemaking operations in recent years,

---

[90] Data for the following list based on Ipsco, *Northern Pipelines*, table on p. 25; Oregon Steel Mills corporate website; and, *AMM*, "A Big Backlog and Even Bigger Potential in Large-Diameter Pipe" (Sept. 11, 2006 print ed.), pp. 6-7. On the Ipsco-NS deal, see *Wall St. Journal*, "Ipsco to Buy NS for $1.46 Billion in Steel-Tube Push" (Sept. 11, 2006), p. A2; *AMM*, "Ipsco's $1.5B Buy of NS Shores Up OCTG Stance" (Sept. 12, 2006).

[91] *Ibid.*, "Evraz Given 'Go' to Pursue $2.3B Buy of Oregon Steel" (Jan. 11, 2007); and, "Oregon Steel Purchase Completed" (Jan. 25, 2007), p. 6.

[92] See "Nucor Steel — Hertford" and "Nucor Steel Tuscaloosa, Inc." on Nucor Corp. website. AISI confirmed that Nucor does supply plate for OCTG pipe applications.

374 703-739-3790 TCNNaturalGas.com

CRS-28

though U.S. Steel makes smaller diameter pipe and tubing for OCTG applications.[93] U.S. Steel has not in recent years been a major market force in plate. In 2003, it agreed to trade its plate operation at Gary, Indiana, to Bethlehem's successor, Mittal Steel, for a different type of operation in the same vicinity.[94] According to its corporate website, Mittal produces plate at its large integrated mill in Burns Harbor, Indiana, as well as rolling plate at two plants in Pennsylvania, some of which may be supplied to makers of larger diameter pipe.[95] Both minimills and integrated steel mills since 2003 have faced much higher input costs, which have driven the price of plate higher along with increased industrial demand.[96]

These data portend a limited North American capacity in the face of a dramatic recent increase in demand for steel in pipelines. James Declusin, then CEO of Oregon Steel, stated that when his company decided to proceed with the new large-diameter pipe mill, it projected total ongoing demand for about 2.5 million tons per year — and, "Since then there have been even more projects on the drawing board." His large-diameter pipe facilities are "booked through mid-2008," and there are reports of demand remaining at a high level through 2009-10.[97] John Tulloch, a senior executive at Ipsco, noted that large-diameter pipe historically accounts for 10-20% of U.S. steel plate usage. Though "we had been at 10% or lower for a while there, now we are at the higher end of that range, much closer to 20%."[98]

The potential shortage of large-diameter pipe has led to a number of projects to expand capacity. In addition to the Oregon Steel and Berg Pipe projects mentioned above, plans have been announced by Lone Star Technologies of Texas and Welspun Group of India to build a joint venture project somewhere in the South. Two Korean companies, POSCO, which already operates a joint-venture rolling mill with U.S. Steel in California, and SeAH Steel have announced plans for a large-diameter pipe mill with a capacity of more than 300,000 tons, probably somewhere on the West Coast. Overall, it is reported that EIA estimates that by 2008 U.S. large-diameter

---

[93] The Bethlehem pipemaking operation in Steelton, PA, was acquired by Dura-Bond Industries, a pipe coatings specialist, and is now operated by them. It manufactures line pipe of up to 42" in diameter. The Dura-Bond website did not report any long-distance oil or gas pipeline projects completed, nor was this facility included in the report compiled by Ipsco. The Ipsco list also did not refer to the Baytown, Texas, large-diameter pipe mill originally built by U.S. steel and acquired in the 1990s by Jindal Steel of India. Only limited information has been found on large-diameter pipe output of this mill, known as Jindal SAW Pipe.

[94] CRS Report RL31748, *The American Steel Industry: A Changing Profile*, by Stephen Cooney.

[95] See "Plate" listing under "Flat Products" at Mittal Steel USA website.

[96] CRS Report RL32333, *Steel: Price and Policy Issues*, by Stephen Cooney.

[97] *AMM*, "Big Backlog," p. 6. *AMM* also reports European pipe mills, including Berg's parent companies, booked up through 2007 or 2008; "Salzgitter Plant Sold Out of Pipe until 2008" (Oct. 5, 2006), p. 6.

[98] *Ibid.*, "Rigged for Profits," p. 5.

CRS-29

pipemaking capacity could total 56% more than in 2007.[99] These additional mills will all use spiral-weld technology, which is newer and more efficient than straight-seam welding of large pipes, but which also may not be suitable for the special requirements being contemplated for an Alaska natural gas pipeline.

Globally, the Ipsco report also counts about three million tons of annual capacity in large-diameter steel pipe outside North America. This is divided roughly equally between the Europipe consortium in Germany (Berg's parent company) at 1.6 million tons, and three major Japanese steelmakers (Nippon Steel, Sumitomo and JFE) at about a half-million tons each.[100]

Steel industry sources emphasize that the capability of the industry to supply pipe for the Alaska natural gas project will also depend on the timing and specifications for the pipe. The maximum diameter being considered is 52 inches, capable of delivering 6.0 billion cubic feet of gas per day (bcf/d), as indicated in data provided by AISI. But 52-inch pipe has only been produced in very limited amounts in North America (or anywhere else). Moreover, the Alaska natural gas producers in the pipeline consortium have indicated that they want to specify a measure of strength, X100 or X120 grade pipe, that is beyond the X80 grade — currently the highest available.

In its report, Ipsco flatly stated that, "No North American producer can currently supply the pipe proposed for the Alaska pipeline ... no pipeline operating uses these specifications ... if the line is as specified today (48"-52" [diameter] x 0.80" [thickness] x X100), we are not able to supply the pipe without major capital expenditures and lead time." The company added that it was "proceeding with X100 trials," but that the specifications would require "designing out of market capability." Moreover, "due to extremely large volume [it is] very unlikely [that] it will be supplied by one supplier ... [and the] proposed gauge and grade requirements will necessitate capital investment by any potential supplier throughout the world."[101]

Use of this size and grade of pipe would create logistical complexities in pipeline construction and operation, requiring, for example, 48 compressor stations along the Alaska route. Using a 48-inch pipe might reduce operational and construction difficulties somewhat, and it could be made from X80-rated steel, but would reduce capacity to 4.0 bcf/d. Downsizing to a 42-inch pipe would substantially reduce pipe manufacturers' retooling costs, but would also reduce capacity to 2.0 bcf/d.[102] By comparison, construction and operational difficulties

---

[99] Ibid., "Strong Demand Spurs Flood of Large-Diameter Pipe Projects" (Feb. 12, 2007), p. 4.

[100] Ipsco, Northern Pipelines, pp. 24-25.

[101] Ipsco, Northern Pipelines, pp. 14-15, 22-23. In an interview with CRS, an Ipsco representative pointed out that the 4 million ton figure was based on the full projected pipeline length to the U.S. Midwest, and that the highest Arctic grade of steel would not be required for the more southern sections of the pipeline.

[102] Estimates and data from 2002 analyses supplied by member companies to AISI task force

(continued...)

CRS-30

would be much less along the Mackenzie River route. Only 10 compressor stations would be required along the river valley route, and a total of only 465,000 tons of 30-inch mainline pipe, which, for example, Ipsco states it could now provide commercially. Ipsco was also the largest supplier of pipe for the Alliance pipeline cited by AISI, and delivered 716 miles of 36-inch, X70 pipe.[103]

U.S. steel industry sources expect that North American steel companies can and would make the investment, and provide the expertise necessary, to supply steel for an Alaska natural gas pipeline. President Andrew Sharkey of AISI stated in the letter cited earlier to then-Senator Frank Murkowski that "North American steel and pipe industries stand ready to work with all other interested parties to arrive at the best pipeline design necessary to accomplish the objective." He further advocated that North American steel suppliers be fully included in the design of pipeline and be given an opportunity to compete for steel procurement.[104]

The ExxonMobil High-Strength Pipeline Steel Project

An alternative type of pipe to that supplied from currently available sources has been advanced by one of the three producers of Alaska oil and gas, the ExxonMobil Corporation. It hopes to achieve substantial cost reductions by using innovative technology in building the pipeline.

In seeking to achieve such a technology breakthrough, ExxonMobil representatives on April 22, 2003, signed a letter of intent with two Japanese companies, Nippon Steel Corporation (NSC) and Mitsui & Co. Ltd., "to commercialize a jointly developed new steel, which is 20-50% stronger than alternative pipeline steels in use today. The agreement includes possible upgrades to an NSC pipe mill." The announcement also noted that the formulation for the steel had first been developed in ExxonMobil Upstream Research laboratories, and that further work to make commercial production viable has already occurred jointly with Nippon Steel.[105] The technical announcement indicated that the new steel would be rated X100 and X120, grades that hitherto have not been manufactured anywhere.[106] Press commentary on the ExxonMobil announcement stated that pipe made from the new grade of steel would be lighter in weight, and therefore easier to handle — meaning significant potential reductions in construction costs. In addition to production and long-distance pipeline interests in Alaska and the Mackenzie Delta, ExxonMobil also has interests in a Sakhalin-to-Japan gas pipeline project and the

---

[102] (...continued)
established on the Alaska Natural Gas Pipeline (provided to CRS on April 22, 2003).

[103] Ipsco, *Northern Pipelines*, pp. 12, 21.

[104] AISI letter and statement to Sen. Murkowski, April 17, 2002.

[105] ExxonMobil. "ExxonMobil Signs Letter of Intent with Nippon Steel and Mitsui & Co. Ltd. to Commercialize Advanced High Strength Steel," press release, April 22, 2003.

[106] Technical details are presented in *Proceedings of the Thirteenth (2003) International Offshore and Polar Engineering Conference*, vol. IV (2003), "Steel Development," at [http://www.isope.org].

CRS-31

west-east pipeline project being considered to bring gas from Central Asia to China.[107]

CRS contacted ExxonMobil in August 2006 regarding further progress on the high-strength steel project. In response, a company representative replied, "Technical and developmental aspects of the X120 high-strength steel pipeline continue to be studied by ExxonMobil, and there is no new information that we can convey at this time regarding its applicability to specific projects or the timing of its commercial availability."[108]

The ExxonMobil proposal for a technologically innovative grade of steel for pipeline construction would not rely on U.S. (or Canadian) steel industry technology. The new grade of steel could be produced under license, although tooling and set-up costs would be substantial for multiple manufacturers working in different locations. But the required order for an Alaska natural gas pipeline may be so large as to require sharing of the work by multiple mills anyway.

Conclusion[109]

The Alaska natural gas pipeline would be a major capital investment. If, or when, it is built, the investment decision will depend on a complex set of factors that will determine its potential profitability. Those factors, on the expected revenue and cost sides, are linked to conditions in two markets: natural gas and steel. If a pipeline is to be constructed, estimates provided in this report suggest that its throughput of natural gas might equal about one third of potential U.S. future demand growth for natural gas. LNG terminals will be the primary competition for the pipeline in filling this potential demand. Should the expected demand growth fall short of projections, natural gas prices will likely decline affecting the potential profitability of both the pipeline and the LNG terminals.

On the cost side, the pipeline could generate a major steel order for the North American industry. However, the size of the pipe, as well as other required specifications, suggest that it will be expensive. Steel prices have been rising over the past several years, resulting in substantial increases in the estimated materials cost of the pipeline. Additionally, innovative production capacity to produce the required pipe might have to be constructed first particularly since no one anywhere has yet produced pipe with the dimensions and grade specified to date, further affecting the economics of the project.

---

[107] *Oil Daily*, "Exxon Steel Deal Boosts ANS Gas Prospects," April 23, 2003. But there has also been speculation about the future of ExxonMobil's Sakhalin project, in view of actions taken in 2006 by the Russian government against foreign-owned operators of energy projects in the Far East region; Andrew Neff, "Death by a Thousand Cuts – Rising Resource Nationalism in Russia," presented at Global Insight World Economic Conference (Oct. 26, 2006).

[108] Email from Robert H. Davis, media adviser, ExxonMobil Corp., Aug. 18, 2006.

[109] Written by Robert Pirog and Stephen Cooney.

CRS-32

The joint venture between ExxonMobil and the two Japanese steel companies appears to present an option that could spur a debate with respect to whose technology, and whose steel, would be used in this major investment project.

Order Code RL34671

CRS Report for Congress

The Alaska Natural Gas Pipeline: Status and Current Policy Issues

September 12, 2008

William F. Hederman
Specialist in Energy Policy
Resources, Science, and Industry Division

Congressional
Research
Service

**Prepared for Members and
Committees of Congress**

The Alaska Natural Gas Pipeline:
Status and Current Policy Issues

Summary

On August 27, 2008, the governor of Alaska signed legislation awarding a license to TransCanada Alaska (TransCanada) to permit, develop, and build a natural gas pipeline from Prudhoe Bay, Alaska, to the gas market hub in Alberta, Canada, with $500 million of state support. Since the discovery of significant oil and gas reserves in Prudhoe Bay in 1968, Alaska state and federal policymakers have sought to accelerate bringing these important energy resources to market, especially to market in the lower-48 states. The Trans Alaska Pipeline System (TAPS) began shipping crude oil from Prudhoe Bay in 1978. Efforts to build a gas pipeline still have achieved little progress 30 years later.

This report provides a brief review of efforts to develop and construct a natural gas pipeline from Prudhoe Bay, a status report on recent efforts to proceed, and an analysis of major relevant policy issues.

In 1976, Congress passed the Alaska Natural Gas Transportation Act (ANGTA) as one element of a multi-pronged effort to respond to the natural gas supply problems caused by earlier wellhead price controls. Engineering work was underway on the pipeline when, in the early 1980s, the natural gas market in North America entered a prolonged period of relatively low prices for natural gas because domestic producers had responded vigorously to high prices during the phased decontrol of wellhead prices through the Natural Gas Policy Act of 1978 (NGPA). Interest in developing the pipeline waned because of the poor market prospects.

In 1997, the United States became a net importer of liquefied natural gas (LNG) for the first time. In retrospect, this was a leading indicator of a tightening natural gas supply for the North American market. Congress again promoted development of the pipeline in the Alaska Natural Gas Pipeline Act (ANGPA) in 2004 and with related amendments in the Energy Policy Act of 2005 (EPAct 2005).

The State of Alaska has pursued the natural gas pipeline development with a sense of urgency for several years. In 2001, Alaska established an interagency task force to move forward with a pipeline. The administration immediately preceding the current governor reached a controversial agreement with the Prudhoe Bay producers (ExxonMobil, BP, ConocoPhillips). The current governor proceeded with a new initiative, the Alaska Gasline Inducement Act (AGIA) that has led to the August 27 signing mentioned earlier.

Two producers, ConocoPhillips and BP, have formed Denali Pipeline to develop a Prudhoe Bay-to-market pipeline without AGIA support. The third, and largest, producer, ExxonMobil, has not supported any currently active pipeline development initiative.

Many challenges remain at this time. The key parties, however, appear constructively engaged in the effort to make available this significant energy supply option.

Contents

List of Figures

List of Tables

The Alaska Natural Gas Pipeline:
Status and Current Policy Issues

Introduction

Forty years ago, major oil and natural gas resources were discovered at Prudhoe Bay, Alaska. Since 1976, Congress has acted to promote the successful development of a natural gas pipeline from the Alaska North Slope (ANS) to the lower-48 states.[1] In the Alaska Natural Gas Pipeline Act of 2004 Congress established a statutory finding of public need for this project, stating in Section 103(b)(2) that:

(A) a public need exists to construct and operate the proposed Alaska natural gas transportation project; and

(B) sufficient downstream capacity will exist to transport the Alaska natural gas moving through the project to markets in the contiguous United States.

On August 27, 2008, Alaska's governor signed legislation into law that officially awarded to TransCanada Corporation (TransCanada) a license to permit, develop, and build an Alaska natural gas pipeline from Prudhoe Bay, Alaska, to the lower-48 states with $500 million from the state. At full initial capacity of 4.5 billion cubic feet per day, this pipeline could initially supply an amount equal to about 7% of U.S. natural gas consumption in 2007.[2]

This report provides a brief review of the history of efforts to develop this project, a report on recent developments and project status, and a summary of remaining policy issues and the project outlook at this time.[3]

Historical Overview

Since the discovery of the major natural gas and oil reserves on the Alaska North Slope in 1968, Congress has passed several measures to encourage the development of the natural gas resources there. **Table 1** presents several highlights of this process.

---

[1] Alaska Natural Gas Transportation Act of 1976 (15 U.S.C. Sec. 719 *et seq.*).

[2] U.S. Energy Information Administration, *Natural Gas Monthly*, April 2008, Table 2.

[3] CRS reports on this subject include CRS Report, *Major Alaska Gas Pipeline Issues — A Perspective*, by Alvin Kaufman, Gary Pagliano, Joseph Riva, and Susan Bodilly, October 17, 1979 and CRS Report RL33716, *Alaska Natural Gas Pipelines: Interaction of the Natural Gas and Steel Markets*, by Stephen Cooney and Robert Pirog, updated March 28, 2007.

CRS-2

In 1976, Congress passed the Alaska Natural Gas Transportation Act (ANGTA). The purpose of that legislation was to provide for sound decision-making on the natural gas transportation system that provided for Congressional and presidential participation in the process and to expedite construction and the start of operations. Briefly, the policy steps of the process moved expeditiously, all completed in 1977. In step one, the Federal Power Commission transmitted a recommendation of one of three transportation system options (May 1977), the land-based pipeline route along the Alaska Highway.[4] Two alternatives were land-based pipeline systems and one was a combination pipeline across Alaska and an LNG export terminal in Valdez. In step two, the president recommended the same Alaska Highway alternative (September 1977). In step three, Congress approved the president's decision through a joint resolution. That may have been the last time this project proceeded according to the original plan.

In the winter of 1977-1978, the nation experienced serious problems with natural gas deliveries through the interstate market because of the distortions of wellhead natural gas price controls. These price controls had been driven by a Supreme Court decision in 1954 (Phillips Petroleum Co. v. Wisconsin, 347 U.S. 672). In response to these delivery problems, Congress passed the Natural Gas Policy Act of 1978 (NGPA) and the Powerplant and Industrial Fuel Use Act of 1978 (PIFUA).

As natural gas supply and demand began to respond favorably to the energy policy legislation of 1978, the desirability of the Alaska natural gas transportation system declined.[5] Moreover, in an often repeated pattern for major U.S. energy supply projects, cost estimates for this transport system increased. Natural gas prices softened significantly as a natural gas supply "bubble" developed, and persisted for years, in response to wellhead price decontrol.[6] Commercial attention to the Alaska gas pipe initiative essentially disappeared during the 1980s.

Although the full pipeline project made no progress, as Canadian natural gas supplies from the Western Canadian sedimentary basin increased in the late 1970s and early 1980s, producers from the province of Alberta, Canadian authorities, and U.S. and Canadian pipeline companies worked to pre-build the downstream legs of the Alaska Natural Gas Transportation System (ANGTS) from Alberta to California and to the Midwest. The concept was that Canadian producers would loan the gas to the U.S. consumers and be repaid in kind when the Alaska North Slope supplies arrived. This concept led to tight provincial regulatory scrutiny of reserves-to-production ratios as Canadian producers sought export approvals from Alberta regulators.

---

[4] The Federal Power Commission (FPC) was the predecessor of the Federal Energy Regulatory Commission (FERC).

[5] See discussion in D. Fried and W. Hederman, "The Benefits of an Alaska Natural Gas Pipeline," *The Energy Journal*, Vol. 2, No. 1, January 1981, p.22.

[6] A natural gas supply "bubble" is a temporary oversupply of capacity to produce natural gas.

CRS-3

The Western leg of ANGTS was Pacific Gas Transmission, and it went into service from Alberta to California in 1981. The eastern leg of ANGTS (Northern Border Pipeline) went into service in 1982.

Table 1. Selected Dates from Alaska Natural Gas Development

1968	Prudhoe Bay oil and gas discovered
1971	United States begins export of LNG to Japan from south central Alaska (Cook Inlet)
1976	Alaska Natural Gas Transportation Act (ANGTA) passed, P.L. 94-586
1977	Presidential Decision and FPC Report to Congress on ANGTS
1977	FERC (successor to FPC) issues conditional certificate for pipeline
1978	TAPS oil pipeline into service (ANS natural gas re-injected)
1979	Office of Federal Inspector (OFI) established
1981	"Western leg" of Alaska gas pipeline (Pacific Gas Transmission) pre-build into service
1982	"Eastern leg" (Northern Border Pipeline) pre-build into service
1983	Maritime Administration study of alternatives to pipeline released
1992	OFI eliminated
1997	United States becomes net importer of LNG for the first time
2001	Alaska Natural Gas Interagency Task Force established (State Dept., Dept. of Interior (including MMS and BLM), Dept. of Transportation, Dept. of Energy (including FERC))
2004	Alaska Natural Gas Pipeline Act passed, Division C, P.L. 108-324
2006	New governor announces Alaska Gasline Inducement Act (AGIA) initiative
2007	Five proposals submitted for AGIA consideration
2008	Governor determines one AGIA proposal meets AGIA criteria
2008	Conoco Phillips and BP announce the Denali Project as an alternative to an AGIA project
2008 (August)	Alaska legislature approves governor's AGIA recommendation and it becomes law

In response to the lack of progress on the land-based pipeline system, the U.S. Maritime Administration authorized a study of marine system options in the 1980s to determine whether there might be commercial opportunities for the U.S. shipbuilding industry. The results indicated roughly comparable economics for the pipeline and LNG options to the U.S. west coast. LNG sales to the Pacific Rim

CRS-4

generally had greater economic potential, but were not politically viable in terms of the large energy exports that such options could entail.[7]

In 1992, approximately 13 years after the Office of the Federal Inspector had been established to expedite the Alaska natural gas pipeline project, it shut down.

In 1997, U.S. imports of LNG began using the lower-48 receiving and regasification facilities built during the 1970s. The United States imported enough LNG that, for the first time, imports exceeded the approximately 60 billion cubic feet per year exported from the Cook Inlet/Kenai Peninsula of South Central Alaska. This milestone proved to be an early indicator of a tightening supply situation in the lower-48.

Serious reconsideration of the construction of a natural gas pipeline from the Alaska North Slope began around 2000. One important sign of the renewed interest was the inclusion in the 2001 National Energy Plan of the recommendation to expedite construction of a natural gas pipeline from the Alaska North Slope to make deliveries to the lower-48. Also in 2001, the Alaska natural gas interagency task force formed. This task force included the State Department, the Department of the Interior (including Bureau of Land Management and the Minerals Management Service), the Department of Transportation, and the Department of Energy (including the Federal Energy Regulatory Commission).

In 2004, Congress passed the Alaska Natural Gas Pipeline Act. Among its provisions, it:

- clarified that the Federal Energy Regulatory Commission could consider any application under the Natural Gas Act or the Alaska Natural Gas Transportation Act;
- created an Office of the Federal Coordinator (OFC);
- provided for a loan guarantee of as much as $18 billion;
- provided for accelerated tax depreciation (7 years versus 15 years);
- provided for an enhanced oil recovery tax credit for the cost of a gas treatment plant on the Alaska North Slope; and
- established guidance to ensure the Federal Energy Regulatory Commission would regulate the open season capacity bidding procedures so that access to pipeline capacity would become available to parties beyond the three major Alaska North Slope producers to promote competition in Alaska North Slope development of natural gas.[8]

The Federal Energy Regulatory Commission issued a final rule on the open season matter on February 9, 2005 (FERC Order No. 2005).

---

[7] W. F. Hederman, "A Review of Marine Systems Use in Developing Alaska Natural Gas," SPE 11294, *SPE Hydrocarbon Economics and Evaluation Symposium*, March 2, 1983, Dallas, TX.

[8] Division C, Public Law 108-324.

CRS-5

The Energy Policy Act of 2005 (EPAct 2005), also addressed the Alaska natural gas pipeline. In Section 1810, Congress required that the FERC submit to Congress, on a semi-annual basis, reports describing the progress made regarding licensing and building the pipeline.[9]

Recent Developments

There are four projects that are being actively promoted at this time. Two are mutually exclusive to transport Alaska North Slope natural gas to the lower-48 states, the TransCanada project and the Denali project. Two smaller projects focus on intra-Alaska issues: the "bullet line" to South Central Alaska and an LNG project with a pipeline to Valdez that could proceed with varying levels of supply.

In January TransCanada submitted the only proposal to the Alaska Gasline Inducement Act (AGIA) process that the governor judged complete. This proposal resembles the original Alaska Natural Gas Transportation System (ANGTS). TransCanada has stated that it will not be responsible for natural gas treatment into the pipeline and will only accept pipeline quality gas into the pipe. It also stated a willingness to develop the gas treatment facilities if necessary.

The pipeline would follow the Trans-Alaska Pipeline system (TAPS) past Fairbanks to Delta Junction then follow the Alaska Highway to Alberta, Canada. The natural gas would move through Alberta via TransCanada's existing pipeline network. The natural gas would continue to the lower-48 states via the ANGTS pre-build lines and other existing pipeline capacity. Through AGIA, TransCanada would receive $500 million from the state of Alaska to support its expenses to prepare cost estimates, environmental work, etc., for an open season for potential shippers and for applying to the FERC for a certificate and tariff.[10] The original capacity of this pipeline would be between 4.5 to 5 billion cubic feet per day (Bcf/d). According to FERC staff, it would be expandable to 5.9 Bcf/d with compression only,[11] which means expansion to this level would be relatively low cost.

Conoco Philips and BP, two of the three major Prudhoe Bay natural gas producers, have made a proposal outside of the AGIA process to build a pipeline. This BP Conoco Philips Denali Project (BPCPDP) would follow a similar right of way (ROW) to the TransCanada project. BPCPDP would include a gas treatment facility and would consider the option of new pipelines through Alberta and to the lower-48 states if deemed necessary.

---

[9] P.L. 109-58, 119 Stat. 594(2005), 42 U.S.C. Section 15801 *et seq.*

[10] In an "open season" process, all parties wishing to become shippers can compete for available capacity on a pipeline. There are no special rights for existing shippers or other parties.

[11] FERC, *Sixth Report to Congress on Progress Made in Licensing and Constructing the Alaska Gas Pipeline*, August 29, 2008, p. 8.

CRS-6

Figure 1. Alaska Oil and Gas Pipelines

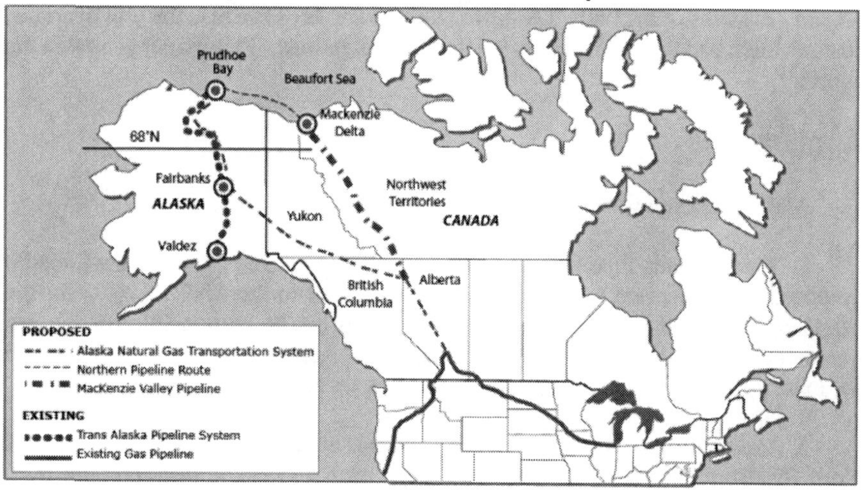

Source: Adapted from CRS Report RL31278, *Arctic National Wildlife Refuge*, Figure 6, based on Energy Department maps.

The other two proposals are of more local interest than national interest. An in-state plan for a new pipeline linking Anchorage and other parts of south central Alaska, as proposed by Enstar, Inc. and the Alaska Natural Gas Development Authority (ANGDA), recently gained approval from the governor of Alaska. This pipeline would initially run about 450 miles from Cook Inlet to Fairbanks (in central Alaska). If necessary (for instance, if a large pipeline is not operational when needed for in-state Alaska demand) then a small diameter "bullet line" may extend to the Brooks Range (north Alaska) to bring natural gas south to Fairbanks, Anchorage, and other Alaska markets. This pipeline would have an in-service target date of 2013 and deliver 460 million cubic feet per day for a cost of approximately $3 billion.

Finally, a project option that began with all-Alaska project proposals would involve an extension to Valdez on the southern coast of Alaska of the main line natural gas pipeline to the lower-48. This line would deliver an unspecified volume of natural gas to be liquefied for export as LNG either to North American or other markets. The intent would be for Alaska to participate in some value-addition economic activity. With the announcement of state support of the other projects, the prospects for the LNG option appear less likely.

Alaska's Selection Process

When Alaska's new governor took office in December 2006, she reiterated her commitment to make progress on an Alaska gas pipeline a priority for the state. In 2007, Alaska passed the Alaska Gasline Inducement Act (AGIA), proceeded with a Request for applications (RFA), and determined that one application was complete.

CRS-7

In a related development, the state of Alaska announced it was taking back the oil and gas leases of the Point Thompson unit on the ANS because the unit operator, ExxonMobil, had failed to meet development obligations. This matter is now in the courts.[12]

Applications

Alaska received five applications through the AGIA process:

1. TransCanada Pipelines Ltd. and Foothills Pipe Lines, Ltd. (TransCanada) proposed a pipeline that would follow a route similar to the ANGTS route for the originally approved project. TransCanada would not be responsible for the gas treatment plant on the ANS and the pipeline would stop at Alberta and connect with the existing TransCanada Alberta network (Alberta hub).

2. Alaska Gasline Port Authority, a municipal entity (City of Valdez, Fairbanks North Star Borough, and North Slope Borough), proposed a natural gas pipeline from the ANS to Valdez, where the gas would be liquefied and exported, providing added value within Alaska.

3. Alaska Natural Gasline Development Authority (ANGDA) proposed a smaller capacity lateral line to link from whatever major line was selected to move gas to South Central Alaska (Anchorage and other locations) to make up for declining production there.

4. Little Susitna Construction Company and a subsidiary of China Petroleum and Chemical Corporation (Sinopec) proposed a pipeline from the ANS to Valdez in the south where the gas would be liquefied and exported to the Pacific Rim.

5. AEnergia LLC, a startup formed by persons with large engineering project experience, proposed an ANS to Alberta pipeline that would be jointly owned by the producers (74%), the State of Alaska (25%), and AEnergia (1%).

The state determined that one application, TransCanada's, was complete. That is the only project that advanced to the evaluation step. Alaska awarded TransCanada the AGIA license on August 27, 2008.

During the state AGIA process, Conoco Phillips sought out-of-time consideration for a project that did not meet the AGIA requirements. This proposal was quickly rejected. In April, Conoco Phillips and BP announced a joint proposal, the Denali Project. ExxonMobil, a major player in any successful development, has expressed both objections and support (for no project in particular) for developments so far.

---

[12] Bradner, Tim, "Exxon continues work at Point Thompson site," *Alaska Journal of Commerce*, September 7, 2008; story available at [http://www.alaskajournal.com/stories/090708/hom_20080907023.shtml]

CRS-8

The governor dismissed the BP Conoco Phillips Denali Project proposal. Other state and federal energy policy makers have welcomed the Denali proposal.

Recent Reports

The results of recent reports prepared for the state of Alaska were presented at recent legislative hearings in the AGIA process.[13] A project cost/schedule and tariffs analysis appears to provide input for the overall net present value (NPV) analysis. This cost/schedule analysis presents a range of cost estimates.[14] The range, however, appears rather narrow in light of the recent general cost escalation on energy products and services and the specific costs escalation announced for another North American Arctic gas development project, the Mackenzie Valley project (now above $16 billion (Canadian)) for this 760 mile pipeline.[15]

The net present value analysis prepared for the State calls the TransCanada project economics "robust" and finds benefits for all stakeholders across a "wide range of project cost outcomes,"[16] but there is not adequate information in the presentation posted on the AGIA website to assess these results independently.[17]

Current Status of AGIA

The Alaska Legislature held special sessions called by the governor to consider the AGIA proposal. Legislative meetings occurred in multiple locations around Alaska. The recent approval means that TransCanada will get $500 million from the state to support TransCanada's next steps in the project approval process. In particular, TransCanada must proceed to an open season and to apply for a certificate from the FERC. The state funds will help pay for these steps.

Policy Issues

Policy issues related to the construction and operation of an Alaska natural gas pipeline include:

- national energy supply,
- open access to the pipeline,
- project risk management and sharing,
- diligent development of the resources,

---

[13] The AGIA website is located at [http://gov.state.ak.us/agia/].

[14] AGIA Analysis Technical Team, B. Sparger and E. Briel, "Analysis of Project Costs/Schedules & Tariffs," Alaska Gasline Inducement Act Legislative License Hearings, Juneau, ALASKA, June 6-10, 2008.

[15] [http://www.mackenziegasproject.com]

[16] "Net Present Value (NPV) analysis," State of Alaska - Anchorage Special Session, June 18, 2008.

[17] AGIA website: [http://gov.state.ak.us/agia/].

CRS-9

- international issues,
- Alaska economic development, and
- environment.

Energy Supply

Prudhoe Bay on the north slope of Alaska is the largest oil accumulation in North America. The production of the associated and dissolved natural gas has implications for oil production. Early in the efforts to proceed with the natural gas pipeline, some expressed concern that continued reinjection of the co-produced natural gas could damage the structure of the reservoirs and harm oil production. Reservoir simulation modeling and actual results ultimately proved this concern to be unfounded.

Advanced enhanced oil recovery techniques now use the natural gas and condensates to maintain oil production at levels above those that would result from natural decline rates. The Alaska Oil and Gas Conservation Commission must approve natural gas production rates after reviewing potential effects on oil production. The potential natural gas reserves on the ANS exceed 100 trillion cubic feet.[18]

In 1995, the U.S. Geological Survey (USGS) estimated that the ANS may contain as much as 590 trillion cubic feet of in-place gas in the form of hydrates.[19] This immense resource base remains unavailable at this time because there are no commercially viable technologies to produce methane from hydrates.

In 2008, the USGS completed an assessment of undiscovered conventional oil and gas resources in all areas north of the Arctic Circle that applied a geology-based probabilistic technique. The results indicate that more than 1,600 trillion cubic feet of natural gas, 44 billion barrels of natural gas liquids, and 90 billion barrels of oil remain to be found in the Arctic. The extent to which these resources are under United States territory or other Arctic nations has not yet been determined.[20]

The vast resources proven and expected from Arctic Alaska have provided strong reasons to get a natural gas pipeline in operation.

The ANGPA found that an Alaska natural gas transportation project would provide specific significant economic benefits to the United Sates and Canada. Recent independent gas producer assertions, however, suggest that technology advances for gas shales in the last two to three years may assure strong lower-48

---

[18] USGS Open File Report 2004-1440, *Conventional Natural Gas Resource Potential, Alaska North Slope*, by David W. Houseknecht, December 13, 2004.

[19] USGS Open File Report 2004-1452, *Alaska North Slope Gas Hydrate Energy Resources*, by Timothy S. Collett, no date.

[20] Available at [http://geology.com/usgs/arctic-oil-and-gas-report.shtml].

392 703-739-3790 TCNNaturalGas.com

CRS-10

domestic natural gas supplies for the foreseeable future.[21] Whether these new assertions affect pipeline project financing for the Alaska project remains to be determined.

Open Access to the Pipeline

An important policy concern regarding development of this pipeline is that it provide a means for all potential natural gas producers on the ANS to transport gas to market through it. If the three Prudhoe Bay producers were to build a private pipeline with no capacity for others, it would not provide an incentive for additional exploration and production from others on the ANS. The FERC has required open access on this pipeline.[22]

Project Risk Management and Sharing

This pipeline project would be the largest civilian construction project in the history of North America. Current cost estimates range from $26 billion to $40 billion. It would likely take at least ten years from approval to completion/operation. Its developers and their financial backers would face immense execution, financial, market, and political risk. Congress has acknowledged the magnitude of these risks and authorized up to $18 billion of loan guarantees to help address the risk challenge (ANGPA 2004, P.L. 108-324). The congressionally approved $18 billion loan guarantee relates to the risks associated with a potential drop in delivered natural gas values compared to current forecasts. Although current prices and forecast prices are high, natural gas prices and the outlook for future prices can change.

Currently, it appears that an Alaska natural gas pipeline would operate under tariffs approved by the Federal Energy Regulatory Commission (FERC) for the United States and by the National Energy Board (NEB) for Canada. The pipeline operators would have contractual commitments from shippers for transporting gas through the pipeline.

Producers and the state of Alaska might face financial risk on the price of the natural gas produced. The value of the natural gas on the Alaska North Slope would be the market value where the pipeline delivered the gas minus the tariff payment to deliver the natural gas to market. As currently envisioned, the Alaska North Slope producers would be the shippers. Local gas distribution companies (LDCs) or other natural gas consumers or marketers could also commit to transport contracts with the pipeline. In the case of LDCs, it appears that most state regulators would not approve the necessary long-term contracts at this time.

---

[21] See, for example, Navigant Consulting, Inc., *North American Natural Gas Supply Assessment*, July 4, 2008.

[22] Regulations Governing the Conduct of Open Seasons for Alaska Natural Gas Transportation Projects, FERC Stats. & Regs., Regs. Preambles ¶ 31,174 (February 9, 2005); 70 Fed. Reg. 8,269 (February 18, 2005) (Order No. 2005) and Regulations Governing the Conduct of Open Seasons for Alaska Natural Gas Transportation Projects, FERC Stats. & Regs., Regs. Preambles ¶ 31,187 (June 1, 2005); 70 Fed. Reg. 35,011 (June 16, 2005) (Order No. 2005-A).

CRS-11

Federal policymakers may want to make sure that all participants in this project accept a fair share of the risks so that they will take responsibility and be accountable for successful implementation. For example,

- Supply risk appears minor but the Point Thompson natural gas may be necessary to realize the economies of scale on the pipeline. The state of Alaska and ExxonMobil continue to dispute the pace of development there. This dispute could endanger the timely availability of these natural gas volumes and harm project economics.

- Construction risk appears serious with regard to cost overruns. Given the recent cost escalation experienced in energy projects generally, the potential for this project to cost more than the $26 billion (U.S. dollars)[23] initial estimate appears likely and to exceed the highest estimates heard to date, $40 billion, remains possible.

- Engineering completion risk appears small. All the potential project developers (BP, Conoco Philips, ExxonMobil, and TransCanada) have relevant and appropriate scale pipeline system engineering experience.

- Market risk appears moderate in terms of the potential market value at time of delivery. The Canadian Energy Research Institute (CERI) has reportedly estimated that market value for the natural gas would need to exceed $10 (Canadian) per million Btu for the project to be viable.[24] Because it appears producers must deliver the natural gas to Alberta or the lower-48 states, the market risks fall on them. This explains the importance to them of control over project costs, which affect the netback value at Prudhoe Bay. Alternatively, gas distribution companies or other natural gas purchasers could also purchase pipeline capacity and assume some market risk. Current state regulatory practice does not appear to encourage such long term commitments. This is a policy area that would benefit from additional analysis but is a state-level issue.

- The three Prudhoe Bay producers have sought guarantees on Alaska tax and royalty policy that the state has viewed as unreasonable. On long-term, multi-decade agreements, flexibility from all parties is often a key to successful agreements. Rather than locking all factors down permanently up front, agreeing to the timing of renegotiation and the range of acceptable variations might provide a faster path to agreement.

---

[23] Unless specifically mentioned otherwise, all dollars are in current U.S. dollars.

[24] P. Howard, D. McColl, D. Mutysheva, and P. Kralovic, *Ensuring Market Access: The Capacity of Western Canada's Natural Gas Pipeline System*, Canadian Energy Research Institute, Study No. 113, 2008.

394

CRS-12

- TransCanada, in its AGIA application, also proposed another measure to mitigate financial risks. This proposal, known as the Bridge Shipper proposal, would have the United States federal government take the risk for unused capacity were the pipeline finished and there were not adequate natural gas flowing to use the capacity. TransCanada points out that it is prepared to proceed with the pipeline without such Bridge Shipper support and provided it as an "outside the box" idea invited by Alaska in the AGIA invitation. If the pipeline were built with 4.5 billion cubic feet per day (Bcf/d) capacity and no natural gas producers or customers signed on for capacity, the levelized annual bridge shipper contingent liability for all capacity could be as high as approximately $3 billion (nominal) per year for 25 years.[25] The primary purposes of this proposal appear to be (1) to buttress the attractiveness for those who might finance the project and (2) to allow the project to proceed without Prudhoe Bay producer commitments so that it will be easier to make the case later on that these producers are not working diligently to develop the resource.

The magnitude and complexity of the risks for this project have always presented challenges for success — and for project start-up. There is little reason to expect these challenges to diminish significantly.

Diligent Development

The slow pace of development on the Alaska natural gas pipeline has led some pipeline proponents to conclude that the Prudhoe Bay producers would prefer not to develop these resources at this time. This controversy has expanded on the ANS when, in April 2008, the Alaska State Department of Natural Resources terminated ExxonMobil's lease in the Point Thompson unit east of Prudhoe Bay. ExxonMobil disputes the termination and this matter will likely end up in the court system for many years if there is no settlement.

Recent announcements by ExxonMobil indicate they intend to proceed with Point Thompson development activity. They have also indicated a willingness to move forward on a Prudhoe Bay to lower-48 pipeline.[26] Progress on the pipeline may require progress on Point Thompson, as well.

International Issues

Any onshore pipeline from Alaska to the lower-48 states must go through Canada. Canada has cooperated with the United States for decades on a variety of matters related to this pipeline (e.g., the pre-build segments in the early 1980s).

---

[25] $1.96/MMBtu x 1.067 MMBtu/1 mcf x 4.5 million mcf/day x 365 day/year = $3.4 billion/year

[26] See, for example, Dow Jones news service, "Exxon: Set to work with TransCanada, Conoco, BP on Alaska Pipeline," August 7, 2008, 2:40 PM EST.

CRS-13

Canadian matters that could affect an Alaska natural gas pipeline include the Mackenzie Valley pipeline; TransCanada's certification; the Alberta pipeline network status; oil sands development (which could consume significant quantities of natural gas as fuel); and Alberta natural gas production.

The Mackenzie Valley in the Canadian Arctic contains an estimated 6 trillion cubic feet of natural gas. It was discovered at approximately the same time as the Alaska North Slope gas at Prudhoe Bay. At one time, development of Mackenzie Valley gas appeared likely to be through a spur line connecting to the pipeline from Alaska. That configuration appears less likely today and Canadian interests hope to proceed with a Mackenzie Valley pipeline before the Alaska pipeline project begins.[27]

Mackenzie Valley gas, if developed, may go to the oil sands of northern Alberta to provide fuel for the steam generation required to produce crude oil there. The demand for steel and pipe for a Mackenzie Valley project are significant, and it is not clear that there is adequate, large diameter pipe reduction capacity in the entire world to serve both Alaska and Mackenzie Valley projects at the same time. Supporters of the Mackenzie Valley pipeline intend to precede the Alaska project. Mackenzie Valley pipeline supporters fear that if the Alaska line is completed first, then the economics for their pipeline may not remain viable.

TransCanada's ownership of Foothills Pipe Lines, Ltd., which was certificated for the section of the Alaska pipeline through Canada in Canada's Northern Pipeline Act (NPA, section 21), with the right-of-way approved (pursuant to section 37 of the NPA), has been an important consideration throughout Alaska pipeline discussions.

At this time, there appears to be the expectation that in ten years, when Alaska natural gas could start to flow through Alberta, there will be spare capacity in the Alberta pipeline grid. The treaty provisions included in the NPA appear to commit to providing sufficient capacity without specifying a capacity figure, and there is no sunset date in the legislation.

Oil sands development has accelerated in northern Alberta and costs have increased as pressure mounts for the available labor and other input requirements. Much of the Mackenzie natural gas is expected to serve the growing oil sands load.

Alberta gas production has been declining. There is the potential that unconventional gas production could reverse this trend but there is no concrete evidence of a turn-around at this time.

Another potentially important policy matter relates to the quantities of natural gas reaching the lower-48. The proposal to end an Alaska natural gas pipeline at the Alberta border and use the Alberta pipeline grid, the Alaska natural gas transportation system pre-build lines to California and the Midwest, as well as other pipelines downstream of Alberta into the lower-48 is possible because Alberta natural gas

---

[27] Mackenzie Natural Gas Pipeline Group, "Scope of Applications," at [http://www.mackenziegasproject.com].

CRS-14

production is declining. This decline has left spare capacity that could be used by the Alaska natural gas traversing Canada. Given that the rationale for federal support of the Alaska natural gas pipeline is to increase lower-48 natural gas supplies, there is the potential for misunderstanding if Canadian exports to the United States decrease as Alaska natural gas arrives. This matter may require some attention before the phenomenon occurs.

Finally, on the international dimension, other nations have expressed interest in a role in ANS natural gas pipeline development. China's Sinopec participated in the AGIA process as a partner with Little Susitna Corporation in an application judged incomplete. More recently, the chairman of GazProm has expressed an interest in participating in the BP and Conoco Philips Denali Project.[28]

Alaska Economic Development

The Alaska natural gas pipeline project has important implications for the state's economic health through construction job creation and revenue generation from production royalties. In addition, the presence of a major interstate pipeline from the ANS to the lower-48 would change the economics for many local energy markets within Alaska. For example, both TransCanada and Denali have agreed to provide up to five delivery points within Alaska. This can allow local communities without natural gas service to gain service if they are near the pipe right-of-way.

Presumably one of the delivery points would link with the Anchorage-Fairbanks gas bullet line. This would allow ANS natural gas to flow south to Anchorage and other South Central Alaska markets when Cook Inlet production declines. There might also be a development opportunity for a relatively small pipeline to South Alaska for LNG exportation. This would be another local value-add and job generator. TransCanada has also assured the State that if shippers preferred to go to South Alaska for an LNG system, they would accommodate that.

Environmental Effects

The addition of the significant natural gas supplies from Alaska's north slope to the lower 48 fuel supplies is generally considered a positive development in terms of the environment. The immensity of the roughly 1,750-mile construction project has caused some concern about potential environmental effects to the land and wildlife near the construction area.

Congress has addressed this issue by delegating the Federal Energy Regulatory Commission as the lead federal agency to assure all environmental regulations of the national environmental policy act (and EPA) are met and that relevant agencies worked to meet environmental impacts statement deadlines established by the commission. In recognition of the complexity of this particular project, Congress created an Office of the Federal Coordinator (OFC) to enhance coordination and progress. Canadian regulators also coordinate with the OFC.

---

[28] Charles Ganske, "Gazprom may bid on Alaska Pipeline," *WorldPoliticsReview* blog, June 8, 2008.

CRS-15

Conclusion

A concerted effort by the State of Alaska and other interested parties has resulted in new momentum to proceed with an Alaska natural gas pipeline from Prudhoe Bay to the lower-48 states. Many challenges remain at this time. The key parties, however, appear constructively engaged in the effort to make available this significant energy supply option.

Expansion of the U.S. Natural Gas Pipeline Network:
Additions in 2008 and Projects through 2011

This report examines new natural gas pipeline capacity added to the U.S. natural gas pipeline system during 2008. In addition, it discusses and analyzes proposed natural gas pipeline projects that may be developed between 2009 and 2011, and the market factors supporting these initiatives. Questions or comments on this article should be directed to Damien Gaul at damien.gaul@eia.doe.gov or (202) 586-2073.

Robust construction of natural gas infrastructure in 2008 resulted in the completion of 84 pipeline projects in the lower 48 States, adding close to 4,000 miles of natural gas pipeline. These completions of new natural gas pipelines and expansions of existing pipelines in the United States represented the greatest amount of pipeline construction activity in more than 10 years.

Increased access to growing supplies continued to drive the high level of pipeline construction during the year. The push for access to new supply sources has led to rapid infrastructure growth in relatively undeveloped production regions such as the Rocky Mountains, as well as additions to well-established natural gas transportation corridors such as in Northeast Texas, where industry is exploiting unconventional resources. Furthermore, infrastructure additions related to imports of natural gas, including liquefied natural gas (LNG), were substantial in 2008.

Pipeline construction activity tends to mirror long-term trends in the natural gas industry because of a lengthy regulatory approval process and the need for substantial capital investment. In fact, the substantial pipeline construction activity recorded in 2008 reflects the natural gas business climate earlier this decade, when domestic production was declining and industry began searching for and investing in alternatives to the then-current conventional production base.

The impact of this year's slate of completed transportation projects on natural gas production and proved reserves has been dramatic. Between 1998 and 2007, natural gas production in the most rapidly expanding production areas of the Nation (northeast Texas, Wyoming, Colorado, and Utah (Figure 1)) increased by 129 percent overall, while proved natural gas reserves grew by 188 percent.[1] These areas contributed to a 4-percent increase in production and a 45-percent increase in proved reserves for the nation.

The number of proposed pipeline projects suggests that construction activity will remain strong over the next several years. For example, the 78 proposed projects scheduled for completion in 2009 indicate that the second-highest level of capacity additions in the last decade could be completed during the year.[2] However, the on-schedule completion of all currently anticipated projects as designed is very unlikely. The current economic downturn has

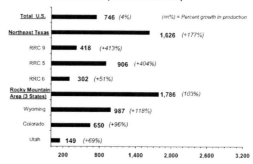

Figure 1. Natural Gas Production Growth, 1998 to 2007 (Billion cubic feet)

Total U.S.	746	(4%)
Northeast Texas	1,626	(+177%)
RRC 9	418	(+413%)
RRC 5	906	(+404%)
RRC 6	302	(+51%)
Rocky Mountain Area (3 States)	1,786	(103%)
Wyoming	987	(+118%)
Colorado	650	(+96%)
Utah	149	(+69%)

(nn%) = Percent growth in production

Note: RRC = Texas Railroad Commission District.
Source: Energy Information Administration, U.S. Crude Oil and Natural Gas, and Natural Gas Liquids Reserves: 1998 and 2007 Annual Reports.

limited financing options for projects and contributed to a significant decline in natural gas spot prices. Nonetheless, the fundamental conditions for the build-out of the pipeline system remain intact, given the need to access and exploit unconventional resources such as tight gas, coal-bed methane, and natural gas from shale formations.

The Energy Information Administration projects that natural gas production from unconventional resources in the United States will increase 35 percent, or 3.2 trillion cubic feet (Tcf), between 2007 and 2030.[3] The largest increase in unconventional production is expected to come from the development of shale formations in the lower 48 States. Shale production is occurring primarily in four fields in the Southwest (Barnett, Woodford, Fayetteville, and Haynesville formations in Texas, Oklahoma, Arkansas, and Louisiana, respectively) and one field in the Northeast (Marcellus, located primarily in Pennsylvania and New York). In 2008, industry continued to achieve substantial success producing from these shale formations, leading to a massive increase in EIA's estimate of an unproved shale resource base of 267 Tcf.[4]

Highlights

In 2008, 84 completed pipeline projects added 44.6 billion cubic feet (Bcf) per day of capacity to the pipeline grid (Figure 2). The additions, which cost an estimated $11.4

[1]Based on data from the Energy Information Administration, *U.S. Crude Oil, Natural Gas, and Natural Gas Liquids Reserves Annual Report* 2007 and 1998, Table 8 (November 2008) and (November 1999), http://www.eia.doe.gov/oil_gas/natural_gas/data_publications/crude_oil_natural_gas_reserves/reserves_historical.html.

[2]Energy Information Administration, GasTran Natural Gas Transportation Information System, Natural Gas Pipeline Projects Database, 2009.

[3]Energy Information Administration, *Updated Annual Energy Outlook 2009 (Reference Case Service Report)*, Table 14, (Washington DC, April 2009), http://www.eia.doe.gov/oiaf/servicerpt/stimulus/index.html.

[4]Energy Information Administration, *Assumptions to the Annual Energy Outlook 2009* (Washington DC, March 2009), http://www.eia.doe.gov/oiaf/aeo/assumption/oil_gas.html.

Figure 2. Natural Gas Pipeline Capacity Additions, 1998-2011

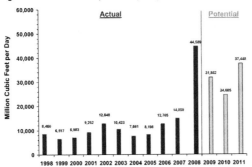

Figure 3. Additions to Pipeline Mileage, 1998-2011

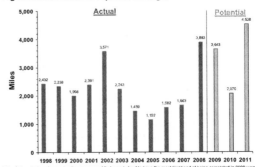

billion, included both long-haul pipeline additions and shorter, though large-diameter, extensions to access three new LNG terminals and several underground storage fields. These figures represent a nearly three-fold increase over 2007, when $4.3 billion was spent to complete 50 projects that added 14.9 Bcf per day of capacity to the network.

The scale of the natural gas pipeline projects completed in 2008 was exceptional. The added capacity for each of the top 15 projects exceeded 1 Bcf per day, the largest being 2.6 Bcf per day. The average added capacity per project overall was 522 million cubic feet (MMcf) per day, compared with only 290 MMcf per day in 2007, which was the second largest construction year in the last 10 years.

Construction activity between market regions in the lower 48 States was particularly vigorous, with 3,893 miles of new pipeline added in 2008, more than double the 1,663 miles of pipeline added in 2007 (Figure 3). The average added miles of pipeline laid per project (for projects with greater than 5 miles of new pipeline) was 69 miles compared with only 47 miles in 2007.

Many individual projects that were completed in 2008 had industry-wide implications because of their size and scope. This article will highlight these projects, as well as others that are indicative of significant trends in the natural gas industry. For instance:

- In February 2008, Cheniere Energy Inc. completed its Sabine Pass LNG Line with a capacity of 2.6 Bcf per day leading from the Sabine Pass LNG terminal on the Gulf Coast in Cameron Parish, Louisiana, to Southwest Louisiana. The 92-mile pipeline, with interconnections with six interstate pipelines, allows for flexibility in marketing LNG supplies delivered to the region.[5] The Sabine Pass LNG Line was one of

three natural gas pipeline construction projects completed in 2008 that connected LNG terminals to the pipeline grid and underground storage fields.

- In terms of added miles, the largest natural gas pipeline project completed in 2008 was the 718-mile, Rockies Express West (REX-West) Pipeline system. Commencing at the Cheyenne Hub in northeastern Colorado and terminating in eastern Missouri, this pipeline links expanding natural gas production from Wyoming and western Colorado to the Midwest region. REX-West represents only a portion of the entire Rockies Express Pipeline project, which will eventually connect Rockies producing fields with markets in the northeastern United States.

- The Southeast Supply Header System began transporting supplies from the Perryville Hub in Delhi, Louisiana, to Florida Gas Transmission's interconnect at Lucedale, Mississippi. in September 2008. The 270-mile, 42-inch diameter pipeline has the capacity to transport 1 Bcf per day of natural gas from northern Louisiana to premium Southeast markets. The project was originally conceived as an alternative source of supply during hurricane-related disruptions in the Gulf of Mexico, but it has since also become an important outlet for growing unconventional supplies into the Perryville Hub from the Barnett Shale and other shale formations.

These construction projects, as well as other transportation additions out of the North Texas and Rockies producing regions and additions related to LNG projects, have already had an impact on regional pricing dynamics. For example, REX-West has allowed for greater integration of the Rockies and Midcontinent markets, such that prices in the two regions appear to trade in sync, with only

---

[5]As often occurs with pipeline projects, this project involves numerous phases. For the purposes of accounting of yearly mileage additions in this

article, only 16 miles of this pipeline is represented in 2008 (See Table 7). The remaining 69 miles of this pipeline is accounted for as part of a larger project that is expected to be completed in 2009.

Energy Information Administration, Office of Oil and Gas, September 2009   2

transportation costs separating price quotes on average. In fact, the transportation improvements discussed in this report will likely enhance continent-wide competition among supply basins, possibly causing relative prices among regional markets in the lower 48 States to adjust.[6]

National Overview

Overall, the interstate natural gas pipeline grid consists of about 183 Bcf per day of capacity and approximately 217,000 miles of pipeline (Table 1). The Federal Energy Regulatory Commission (FERC) regulates interstate pipeline companies as common carriers, or transportation-service companies. Additionally, State authorities regulate substantial pipeline capacity considered "intrastate" that exist in individual States for economic regulatory purposes. Unlike FERC-regulated entities, intrastate pipeline operators often own supplies transported on their systems and act as natural gas merchants. EIA estimates that intrastate capacity exceeds 32 Bcf per day and intrastate pipeline systems extend over 76,000 miles.[7]

Most Additions Occurred On The Interstate Grid. In 2008, 65 of the 84 completed projects involved expansion of the interstate natural gas pipeline network, adding 35.2 Bcf per day of new capacity to the grid. The remaining 19 projects, representing 9.4 Bcf per day of capacity, improved capacity and transportation service on intrastate pipelines.

More than one-third of the pipeline projects in 2008 addressed a growing need for additional natural gas pipeline capacity to support transportation of new natural gas production to regional markets, adding 16.3 Bcf per day of pipeline capacity overall. Such projects were concentrated in the expanding natural gas production areas of Wyoming, western Colorado, and the Barnett shale formation in northeast Texas. About 10 percent of all newly added natural gas pipeline capacity for 2008, or 4.6 Bcf per day, was attributable to new intrastate pipelines built to transport expanding Barnett shale production specifically. This layer of infrastructure primarily provided access to local markets and interconnections with the interstate natural gas pipeline network.

Several major interstate pipeline projects were constructed to continue the flow of natural gas from the Barnett Shale beyond east Texas to interstate pipeline interconnections in Louisiana, Mississippi, and Alabama. These included the new Southeast Supply Header Pipeline (Louisiana to Mississippi), the new Gulf South Southeast Extension (Mississippi to Alabama), and the Gulf South Texas to Mississippi Expansion. These projects added more than 4.1 Bcf per day to capacity in the Gulf Coast region.

---

[6] See, for example, Bentek Energy, LLC, *Catch the Wave*, Consultant Report (February 2009). Portions available on the Internet at: http://www.bentekenergy.com/Bentek/CatchTheWave.aspx.

[7] Energy Information Administration, GasTran Natural Gas Transportation Information System.

The major natural gas pipeline additions of 2008 included several large-capacity pipelines, linking the interstate natural gas pipeline network to several LNG import terminals that were newly commissioned or expanded during the year. Such projects accounted for 10.9 Bcf per day of new natural gas pipeline capacity, or about 24 percent of total new capacity. Nine major bidirectional header systems built to support new natural gas underground storage facilities accounted for another 8.5 Bcf per day, or 19 percent of new pipeline capacity.

Regional Dynamics Changed With Additions. The network of connecting natural gas pipelines now links most production regions across North America, including those in Canada, to multiple market centers and associated consuming regions. The transportation of natural gas through the U.S. pipeline grid generally occurs along several major corridors, such as from the Gulf of Mexico region to the Northeast or from the Rockies to the U.S. West Coast. Corridors from the Southwest to the Northeast and from the Southwest to Midwest have been the major paths for natural gas flows since the construction boom in the years following World War II.

In 2008, the vast majority of expansions and capacity additions were built to expand transportation capability in established corridors (Figure 4). However, industry completed a new corridor from the Rocky Mountain region to the Midwest that will be extended in the Northeast in 2009. The construction of the Rockies Express Pipeline (REX) is occurring in three stages, two of which are now complete. The first stage, often referred to as the Entrega Pipeline, was completed in 2007, providing local infrastructure enhancements within the Rockies producing region. In 2008, REX began initial flows for the interstate portion of the project with the completion of REX-West, providing service from the Cheyenne Hub in Colorado to Aubrain, Missouri. This new pipeline allows Rockies supplies to compete directly with Midcontinent supplies. Eventually, REX will transport Rockies-area supplies east of the Mississippi River, possibly as far as Pennsylvania.

EIA's Natural Gas Pipeline Capacity Database divides the lower 48 States into six regions: Northeast, Southeast, Midwest, Southwest, Central, and West (Figure 5). Each of the market regions has distinct characteristics, such as the very large population centers in the Northeast or the vast production capability in the Southwest. Understanding the supply and demand of the separate regions provides insight regarding future transportation requirements. In 2008, only 7 of the 84 completed projects crossed regional boundaries, slightly more than in recent years, but nonetheless reflecting an emphasis on localized expansions or upgrades. Additions to interregional capacity during the year totaled 3.6 Bcf per day overall, significantly more than the 2007 level of just 1.1 Bcf per day.

Table 1. Thirty Largest U.S. Interstate Natural Gas Pipeline Systems, 2008

(Ranked by system capacity, million cubic feet per day (MMcf/d))

Pipeline Name	Market Regions Served	Primary Supply Regions	States in Which Pipeline Operates	Transported in 2007 (million decatherm) [1]	System Capacity (MMcf/d) [2]	System Mileage
Columbia Gas Transmission Co.	Northeast	Southwest, Appalachia	DE, PA, MD, KY, NC, NJ, NY, OH, VA, WV	1,849	9,350	10,365
Transcontinental Gas Pipeline Co.	Northeast, Southeast	Southwest	AL, GA, LA, MD, MS, NC, NY, SC, TX, VA, GM	2,670	8,466	10,450
Northern Natural Gas Co.	Central, Midwest	Southwest	IA, IL, KS, NE, NM, OK, SD, TX, WI, GM	1,055	7,442	15,874
Texas Eastern Transmission Corp.	Northeast	Southwest	AL, AR, IL, IN, KS, KY, LA, MI, MO, MS, NJ, NY, OH, OK, PA, TX, WV, GM	1,438	7,332	9,212
ANR Pipeline Co.	Midwest	Southwest	AR, IA, IL, IN, KS, KY, LA, MI, MO, MS, NE, OH, OK, WI, GM	2,044	7,129	10,600
Tennessee Gas Pipeline Co.	Northeast, Midwest	Southwest, Canada	AR, KY, LA, MA, NY, OH, PA, TN, TX, WV, GM	1,801	6,686	14,463
Dominion Transmission Co.	Northeast	Southwest, Appalachia	PA, MD, NY, OH, VA, WV	621	6,655	3,505
Gulf South Pipeline Co.	Southeast, Southwest	Southwest	AL, FL, LA, MS, TX, GM	676	6,260	6,886
El Paso Natural Gas Co.	Western, Southwest	Southwest	AZ, CO, NM, TX	1,638	6,182	10,302
Centerpoint Gas Transmission Co.	Southwest	Southwest	AR, KS, LA, OK, TX	960	5,385	6,374
Northwest Pipeline Corp.	Western	Canada, Central	CO, ID, OR, UT, WA, WY	812	4,950	3,880
Natural Gas Pipeline Co. of America	Midwest	Southwest	AR, IA, IL, KS, LA, MO, NE, OK, TX, GM	1,783	4,848	9,306
Colorado Interstate Gas Co.	Central	Central, Southwest	CO, KS, OK, TX, WY	854	4,099	4,143
Texas Gas Transmission Corp.	Midwest	Southwest	AR, IN, KY, LA, MS, OH, TN	784	4,065	5,671
Southern Natural Gas Co.	Southeast	Southwest	AL, GA, LA, MS, SC, TN, TX, GM	867	3,967	7,635
Algonquin Gas Transmission Co.	Northeast	Southwest	CT, MA, NJ, NY, RI	366	3,347	1,128
Questar Pipeline Co.	Central	Central	CO, UT, WY	408	3,192	1,858
Trunkline Gas Co.	Midwest, Southeast	Southwest	AR, IL, IN, KY, LA, MS, TN, TX, GM	646	3,025	4,202
Great Lakes Gas Transmission Co.	Midwest	Canada	MI, MN, WI	833	2,958	2,115
Panhandle Eastern Pipeline Co.	Midwest	Southwest	IL, IN, KS, MI, MO, OH, OK, TX	662	2,840	6,445
Southern Star Central Pipeline Co.	Central	Central	CO, KS, MO, NE, OK, TX, WY	318	2,801	5,803
Wyoming Interstate Gas Co.	Central	Central	CO, WY	756	2,736	848
Gas Transmission Northwest Corp.	Western	Canada	ID, OR, WA	838	2,636	1,356
Northern Border Pipeline Co.	Midwest, Central	Canada	IA, IL, IN, MN, MT, ND, SD	886	2,626	1,400
Transwestern Gas Co.	Western	Southwest, Central	AZ, CO, NM, TX	645	2,439	2,387
Columbia Gulf Transmission Co.	Southeast, Northeast	Southwest	KY, LA, MS, TN, GM	1,113	2,386	4,124
National Fuel Gas Supply Co.	Northeast	Canada, Appalachia	NY, PA	307	2,312	1,481
Florida Gas Transmission Co.	Southeast	Southwest	AL, FL, LA, MS, TX, GM	750	2,217	4,889
Alliance Pipeline Co. (US)	Midwest	Canada	ND, MN, IA, IL	632	2,053	888
Kern River Gas Transmission Co.	Western	Central	CA, NV, UT, WY	826	1,833	1,680
Sub-total				29,838	132,217	169,270
Other Interstate Systems	--	--	--	6,868	50,673	48,036
Total				36,706	182,890	217,306

[1] This figure, found on Line 19 of Gas Accounts in FERC Form 2, Page 520, represents throughput "transported for others" only. It does not include natural gas transported in association with gathering, distribution, or storage operations.

[2] Capacity levels are reported to FERC in Btu, decatherms, or volumetric units. For this presentation, reported capacity figures are presented as volumetric (MMcf/d = million cubic feet per day) assuming a conversion factor of 1 MMcf/d = 1 MDth/d (thousand decatherms per day) = 1 Bbtu/d (billion btus per day).

Note: GM = Gulf of Mexico.

Source: Federal Energy Regulatory Commission (FERC), Capacity: FERC Annual Peak Day Capacity Report Section 284.13(d); Mileage & Transport: FERC Form 2 & 2A "Major and Non-major Natural Gas Pipeline Annual Report," 2007, adjusted for natural gas pipeline projects completed in 2008, as found in the Energy Information Administration, Natural Gas Transportation Information System, Natural Gas Pipeline Projects Database, as of December 31, 2008.

Energy Information Administration, Office of Oil and Gas, September 2009   4

Figure 4. **General Locations of Natural Gas Pipeline Construction Projects Completed in 2008, With Capacity of 500 Million Cubic Feet per Day and Larger**

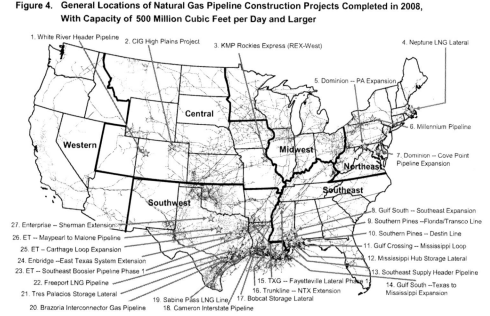

Notes: Map keyed to Tables 3 through 8. **Security:** EIA has determined that publication of this figure does not raise security concerns, based on the application of Federal Geographic Data Committee's *Guidelines for Providing Appropriate Access to Geospatial Data in Response to Security Concerns;* **Regions:** The six U.S. regions shown in this figure are based in whole or in part upon the 10 Federal regions as defined by the U.S. Department of Labor's Bureau of Labor Statistics. ET = Energy Transfer LP, CIG = Colorado Interstate Pipeline Co., KMP = Kinder Morgan Partners.
Source: Energy Information Administration, GasTran Natural Gas Transportation Information System, Natural Gas Pipeline Projects Database.

Figure 5. Natural Gas Pipeline Capacity Between Regions, 2009
(Volumes shown are in million cubic feet per day (MMcf/d))

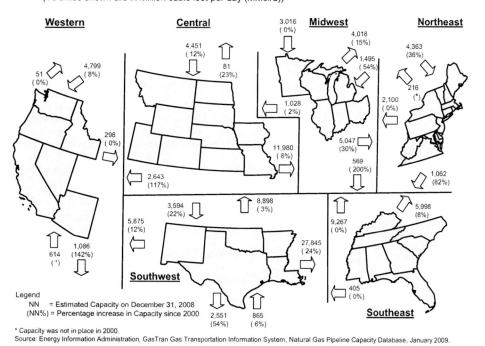

Legend
NN = Estimated Capacity on December 31, 2008
(NN%) = Percentage increase in Capacity since 2000

* Capacity was not in place in 2000.
Source: Energy Information Administration, GasTran Gas Transportation Information System, Natural Gas Pipeline Capacity Database, January 2009.

Energy Information Administration, Office of Oil and Gas, September 2009 5

Table 2. Recent and Proposed Regional Natural Gas Pipeline Additions and Expansions, 2009 - 2011

Region (within or into)	Completed in 2007			Completed in 2008			Scheduled/Proposed for 2009[1]			Proposed for 2010[1]			Proposed for 2011[1]		
	Added Capacity (MMcf/d)[2]	Estimated Cost (Million Dollars)	Miles	Added Capacity (MMcf/d)[2]	Estimated Cost (Million Dollars)	Miles	Added Capacity (MMcf/d)[2]	Estimated Cost (Million Dollars)	Miles	Added Capacity (MMcf/d)[2]	Estimated Cost (Million Dollars)	Miles	Added Capacity (MMcf/d)[2]	Estimated Cost (Million Dollars)	Miles
Central	4,280	1,607	619	6,515	2,452	1,088	2,558	470	243	3,655	1,820	871	1,528	491	290
Midwest	460	27	13	311	102	42	3,049	3,694	606	0	0	0	2,067	1,416	254
Northeast	1,749	784	134	4,987	1,952	491	2,382	1,194	112	2,491	1,276	249	4,318	2,465	569
Southeast	430	304	184	10,092	3,497	891	3,403	845	260	9,911	2,006	601	9,364	3,748	1,000
Southwest	6,971	1,471	700	22,553	3,307	1,382	19,684	4,855	2,113	6,283	577	293	13,915	2,162	688
Western	723	39	13	70	41	0	671	821	309	345	107	27	5,276	5,377	1,686
Mexico/Canada	245	70	0	60	1	0	105	37	0	1,920	NA	29	980	49	41
U.S. Total	14,859	4,302	1,663	44,589	11,352	3,893	31,852	11,916	3,643	24,605	5,786	2,070	37,448	15,707	4,528

[1] Only projects that were approved or under construction prior to May 1, 2009, and which have a proposed completion date in 2009 are included under "Scheduled for 2009." All other projects that have a proposed completion date in 2010 through 2011, other than those canceled or on-hold, are included under 2010 or 2011.

[2] When announcing the design capacity for a proposed project or expansion, a pipeline company may provide either a volumetric (per cubic feet) or energy content (btus/therms) value. In this table, reported capacity figures are presented as volumetric (MMcf/d = million cubic feet per day) assuming a conversion factor of 1 MMcf/d = 1 MDth/d ((thousand decatherms per day) = 1 Bbtu/d (billion btus per day).

Notes: A project that crosses interregional boundaries is included in the region in which it terminates. Offshore Gulf of Mexico projects are included in the Southwest region.

Source: Energy Information Administration, GasTran Natural Gas Transportation Information System, Natural Gas Pipeline Projects Database, as of May, 2009.

Pipeline companies often operate as individual entities, but larger corporations own many "families" of pipelines. For example, El Paso Corporation currently owns the largest family, consisting of 43,000 miles of pipeline. El Paso owns Tennessee Gas Pipeline, Colorado Interstate Gas (CIG), Wyoming Interstate Gas, and El Paso Natural Gas. Kinder Morgan Incorporated, one of the developers of Rockies Express, also owns a variety of interstate and intrastate pipelines, such as Natural Gas Pipeline of America (NGPL) and KM Interstate Transmission. Williams Companies owns Transcontinental Gas Pipeline Company and Northwest Pipeline Corporation.

The pipeline with the greatest deliverability, or potential volume that can be delivered to customers at full operation, is the Columbia Gas Transmission system, which has 10,365 miles of pipeline and can transport up to 9.4 Bcf per day. Columbia Gas, which Indiana-based NiSource Inc owns, transports supplies to customers in the Northeast from production fields in the Appalachian Basin, as well as from the Gulf of Mexico region through a connection with affiliate Columbia Gulf Transmission at Leach, Kentucky.

The number of proposed natural gas pipeline expansion projects indicates that pipeline construction activity in the United States is expected to continue at an elevated pace through 2011 and will involve the largest transportation providers in the country. Approximately 180 projects, representing a potential 10,200 miles of new large pipeline and approximately 94 Bcf per day of capacity, already are being planned or have been approved by U.S. regulatory authorities (Table 2). However, competition among projects for markets results in the rejection of some project proposals. The current slate of proposed projects would provide about 3.5 percent more pipeline miles to the national pipeline grid. Current estimates for the cost of this total effort are close to $33 billion, but costs can vary considerably under different economic conditions.

Regional Overview

Central Region

The natural gas industry completed 15 projects in the Central region in 2008, adding 6.5 Bcf per day of capacity Table 3). This capacity addition was the region's largest in EIA's 11-year database of pipeline additions. It also continues a trend of significant growth in pipeline infrastructure in the region as producers have increased supplies, including unconventional production in the form of coalbed methane and natural gas from tight-gas formations. Between 1998 and 2008, 24.8 Bcf per day of capacity was added to the Central region's grid.

Infrastructure expansion out of the region has been critical for producers in recent years because demand growth in the region is significantly lower than the growth in available supplies. This imbalance has resulted in numerous new pipeline projects, such as the expansion of the Kern River Pipeline to the west and the Cheyenne Plains Pipeline to the east. In 2008, a portion of the REX project, the newest pipeline further integrating Rockies supplies with markets outside the region, came on-line. A joint venture of Kinder Morgan Energy Partners, Sempra Energy, and Conoco, Inc. completed the 718-mile western portion of REX, which was the largest factor in overall pipeline mileage additions reaching 1,088 miles.

Other significant infrastructure projects during 2008 included the creation of the White River Hub, a new market center in Colorado, and several compression upgrades boosting capacity at existing pipelines. Altogether, the infrastructure improvements in the Central region in 2008 cost more than an estimated $2.4 billion, compared with overall expenditures of $1.6 billion in 2007. Eleven of the 15 projects completed improved interstate pipeline infrastructure, with the remaining 4 projects improving intrastate infrastructure.

REX-West Expands Corridor To The Midcontinent. Most receipt and delivery points on REX-West became operational on January 8, 2008, providing a direct connection between the Rockies supply region and the Midcontinent. However, the completion of the entire REX-West from Rio Blanco Country, Colorado, to Audrain, Missouri, occurred in May 2008 with the completion of an interconnection with Panhandle Eastern Pipe Line. The construction of REX-West cost $1.9 billion. Although REX-West started operations at a capacity of 1.5 Bcf per day, available capacity will eventually increase to 1.8 Bcf per day when the entire REX project is complete. This producer-led pipeline project had an immediate impact on upstream prices and transportation routes in long-established market regions in the lower 48 States. As a result, direct price competition between Rockies supplies and supplies from basins ranging from the Midcontinent to West Texas and Canada has emerged.

After flows on REX increased rapidly in the spring of 2008, the pipeline generally operated near targeted capacity levels with the exception of a maintenance-related capacity reduction in September. As the lowest-priced supply in the lower 48 States, the steady flow of Rockies production into the Midcontinent region through REX has resulted in a relative decline in prices in the Midcontinent region. Direct price competition has also displaced some traditional flows in the Midcontinent to other parts of the pipeline network, in part because interstate pipelines with which REX-West has interconnections formally were transporting supplies at near capacity for deliveries into the Midwest.

The completion of REX-East, the third phase of the REX project, is expected by the end of 2009, extending the

pipeline an additional 639 miles eastward. The pipeline's terminus will be located in Clarington, Ohio, near the border with West Virginia, where REX will interconnect with several interstate pipelines. The completion of REX-East will allow Rockies production to compete with existing sources of supplies in the U.S. Northeast. However, as with REX-West, the REX-East segment will begin service in stages. The first major milestone in the construction process was completed in June 2009, providing transportation service through Lebanon, Ohio.

The completion of REX-East, the final leg of the massive REX project, will provide Rockies producers direct access to eastern markets for the first time. As with REX interconnections with other pipelines in the Midcontinent, REX supplies will compete directly with established supply routes, possibly displacing existing supplies with a lower-cost alternative. In total, REX will interconnect with more than 25 intrastate and interstate pipelines transporting natural gas from the Gulf region as well as from the Midcontinent.

Intraregional Additions Create New Hub. During 2008, Questar Corporation completed its $58-million White River Header Pipeline project, a 6-mile pipeline segment with a very large capacity of more than 2.5 Bcf per day. The lateral connects several major interstate pipelines in the Rockies, including Wyoming Interstate, Questar Pipeline, and Northwest Pipeline, allowing for greater flexibility for shippers to market supplies outside the region. In fact, the new lateral was part of several infrastructure enhancements in the area, creating a new major trading hub called the White River Hub. As a result, Enterprise Product Partners LP doubled its capacity at its Meeker processing plant to 1.5 Bcf per day to process increased flows from the Piceance Basin. In addition,

Table 3. Natural Gas Pipeline Construction Projects Completed in 2008, Central Region
(Map Key references Figure 4)

Ending Region & State	Begins in State -- Region		Map Key	Pipeline - Project Name	FERC Docket Number (Interstate Projects)	Type of Project	In Service Date	Estimated Cost (Million Dollars)	Miles	Additional Capacity (MMcf/d)
Central										
CO	CO	Central	1	Questar – 'White River Header Pipeline	CP08-398	Lateral	15-Nov-08	58	6	2,565
CO	CO	Central	2	CIG – High Plains Project	CP07-207	New line	15-Nov-08	216	164	900
CO	CO	Central	–	EnCana -- East Dry Hollow Loop Pipeline	Not applicable	Gathering Lateral	1-Nov-08	12	7	250
CO	CO	Central	–	Kinder Morgan -- Colorado Lateral Project	CP07-430	Lateral	1-Dec-08	30	41	74
CO	UT	Central	–	Questar – Greasewood/Meeker Expansion	Not applicable	Compression	15-Jan-08	12	0	75
CO	WY	Central	–	WIG – Medicine Bow 08 Expansion	CP07-395	Compression	29-Oct-08	32	0	330
IA	IA	Central	–	Northern Natural – East Leg I Expansion	CP08-95	Looping	1-Nov-08	7	8	13
KS	CO	Central	–	Cheyenne Plains Kirk Compressor Station	CP07-128	Compression	15-Aug-08	20	0	90
MO	CO	Central	3	Rockies Express (REX-West)	CP06-354	New Pipeline	15-Apr-08	1,930	718	1,500
ND	WY	Central	–	WB East/West Mondak Subsystem Expansion	CP08-154	Compression	1-Nov-08	7	0	41
NE	NE	Central	–	Kinder Morgan -- Grand Island Expansion	Blanket Certif	Looping/Compression	7-Nov-08	23	26	22
NE	NE	Central	–	Northern Natural – West Leg II Expansion	CP08-97	Looping	1-Nov-08	9	12	11
WY	WY	Central	–	Fort Union -- Gathering Header Expansion	Not applicable	Gathering Header	15-May-08	69	106	450
WY	WY	Central	–	WIG – Mainline Expansion	CP07-14	Compression	5-Feb-08	22	0	150
WY	WY	Central	–	MIGC -- Southern (Python) Expansion	CP07-178	Compression	15-Feb-08	4	0	45
							Total	2,452	1,088	6,515

Notes: Totals may not sum due to independent rounding. See final page for a discussion of naming conventions used in this table.

Source: Energy Information Administration, GasTran Natural Gas Transportation Information System, Natural Gas Pipeline Projects Database.

Energy Information Administration, Office of Oil and Gas, September 2009   **7**

Questar Pipeline increased capacity by 75 MMcf per day through new compression at a cost of $12 million.

Also in the Central region, Colorado Interstate Gas Company (CIG) completed its High Plains Project, laying about 164 miles of 24-inch and 30-inch pipeline and associated compressor facilities in Weld, Adams, and Morgan counties in Colorado. The expansion increased CIG's capacity by 900 MMcf per day to meet growing demand in the Denver metropolitan area. A joint venture of CIG and Xcel Energy called WYCO Development funded the $216-million project.

Activity Will Remain Elevated. Infrastructure growth in the Central region is likely to stay elevated over the next several years. Industry has scheduled projects representing about 2.6 Bcf per day of added capacity over the next 3 years at a combined estimated cost of $2.8 billion. These projects include Questar Pipeline's plans for a large looping project for its mainline in Utah, as well as the REX owners' plans to build further capacity out of the Rockies to the Chicago area in the form of a new pipeline, Chicago Express. In addition, El Paso is currently navigating FERC's regulatory process in order to construct Ruby Pipeline, a 1.5-Bcf-per-day pipeline from Wyoming to the California-Oregon border.[8]

Wyoming Interstate Company (WIC) is progressing with an expansion of its system in the Piceance Basin. WIC is adding compression at its Greasewood Station in Rio Blanco County, Colorado, to boost capacity by 50 MMcf per day. After the completion of this upgrade, the construction of a new Snake River Compressor Station in Moffat County, Colorado, will commence, providing the system an additional 180 MMcf per day of capacity.

Midwest Region

Only three pipeline projects were completed in the Midwest region in 2008, accounting for just 311 MMcf per day of new capacity. The Midwest was one of only two regions in which pipeline capacity additions in 2008 were lower than in 2007. However, expenditures related to infrastructure development were considerably higher ($102 million in 2008 in comparison to just $27 million in 2007). The higher expenditures related to more pipeline mileage additions. Approximately, 42 miles of new pipeline was added to the region in 2008, compared to 13 miles in 2007 (Table 4).

In terms of cost and added capacity, the largest project in the Midwest region was Michigan Consolidated Gas Company's 16-mile pipeline lateral in western Michigan.. The project, which cost $80 million, added capacity of 120 MMcf per day for greater service reliability to the southern Grand Rapids region. Secondly, We Energies, Inc., a local utility in eastern Wisconsin, constructed a new 13-mile lateral from the interstate Guardian Pipeline, in the Green Bay area, to enhance service to the city at a cost of $15 million. Finally, Greater Minnesota Transmission, LLC completed a 13-mile lateral in Dakota County, Minnesota, with a capacity of 91 MMcf per day.

Infrastructure Additions Are Expected to Grow. Although relatively modest over the past several years, infrastructure activity in the Midwest region is expected to increase significantly in the coming years, particularly with the completion of the eastern portion of Rockies Express. A portion of REX-East was completed in June 2009, bringing an additional 1.5 Bcf per day of capacity into the Midwest to areas south of Chicago. By the end of 2009, REX-East will reach its terminus at Clarington Hub in Ohio.

Over the next couple of years, significant capacity additions in the Midwest region may occur with expansions of NGPL and Rockies Express into the Chicago area. The two pipeline companies, owned in part by Kinder Morgan, will expand their respective systems and construct a joint pipeline, with first operations expected in 2010. The system improvement will provide up to 1 Bcf per day of incremental capacity from production areas in the Rockies through Iowa, but the pipeline will eventually provide

Table 4. Natural Gas Pipeline Construction Projects Completed in 2008, Midwest Region

(Map Key references Figure 4)

Ending Region & State	Begins in State -- Region		Map Key	Pipeline - Project Name	FERC Docket Number (Interstate Projects)	Type of Project	In Service Date	Estimated Cost (Million Dollars)	Miles	Additional Capacity (MMcf/d)
Midwest										
MI	MI	Midwest	–	MichCon – Jamestown Pipeline	Not applicable	Lateral	1-Sep-08	80	16	120
MN	MN	Midwest	–	Greater Minnesota – Cannon Falls Pipeline	Not applicable	Lateral	15-Apr-08	7	13	91
WI	WI	Midwest	–	We – Fox Valley Lateral	Not applicable	Lateral	20-Nov-08	15	13	100
							Total	102	42	311

Notes: Totals may not sum due to independent rounding. See final page for a discussion of naming conventions used in this table.

Source: Energy Information Administration, GasTran Natural Gas Transportation Information System, Natural Gas Pipeline Projects Database.

---

[8] For the purposes of this report, the capacity addition from the Ruby Pipeline is calculated as occurring in the Western region. Infrastructure additions that cross regional boundaries are tabulated only according to their ending region in order to avoid double-counting.

Table 5. Natural Gas Pipeline Construction Projects Completed in 2008, Northeast Region
(Map Key references Figure 4)

Ending Region & State	Begins in State – Region		Map Key	Pipeline - Project Name	FERC Docket Number (Interstate Projects)	Type of Project	In Service Date	Estimated Cost (Million Dollars)	Miles	Additional Capacity (MMcf/d)
Northeast										
CT	NJ	Northeast	–	Algonquin – Ramapco Expansion	CP06-76	Compression/Line upgrade	1-Nov-08	192	5	325
CT	NY	Northeast	–	Iroquois – 08/09 Expn Phase 1	CP07-457	Looping	15-Nov-08	58	9	95
DE	PA	Northeast	–	Eastern Shore -- Expansion	CP06-53	Looping/Compression	15-Nov-08	8	9	11
MA	MA	Northeast	4	Neptune -- LNG Lateral	Coast Guard	Lateral	15-Oct-08	23	13	750
MA	**NB**	**Canada**	–	**Maritimes & Northeast Phase IV LNG**	**CP06-335**	**Looping/Compression**	**15-Dec-08**	**321**	**2**	**420**
MD	PA	Northeast	5	Dominion -- PA Expansion	CP05-131	Looping/Extension	1-Nov-08	175	113	700
NJ	**OH**	**Midwest**	–	**TETCO -- TIME II Expansion Phase 2**	**CP06-115**	**Looping/Compression**	**1-Nov-08**	**54**	**10**	**150**
NJ	PA	Northeast	–	Transco -- Sentinel Expansion Phase I	CP08-31	Looping/Compression	15-Dec-08	33	4	40
NY	CT	Northeast	–	Iroquois – MarketAccess Project	CP02-31	Compression	5-Nov-08	42	0	100
NY	NY	Northeast	6	Millennium Pipeline	CP98-150	New Pipeline	22-Dec-08	664	182	525
NY	NY	Northeast	–	Wycott -- Greyhawk North Lateral	CP03-33	Lateral	1-Aug-08	5	4	400
NY	NY	Northeast	–	Central New York -- Stagecoach Lateral	CP06-64	Lateral	1-Dec-08	16	9	400
NY	NY	Northeast	–	Empire/Millennium Expansion	CP06-5/6/7	Compression/Extension	15-Dec-08	187	78	250
VA	MD	Northeast	7	Dominion -- Cove Point Expansion	CP05-132	Looping/Compression	15-Dec-08	160	48	800
WV	WV	Northeast	--	Dominion -- TL-263 Expansion Project	CP07-10	Looping/Compression	1-Nov-08	15	6	21
							Total	1,952	491	4,987

Notes: Interregional project is in **bold print**. In the table, a project that crosses interregional boundaries is included in the region in which it terminates. Totals may not sum due to independent rounding. See final page for a discussion of naming conventions used in this table.

Source: Energy Information Administration, GasTran Natural Gas Transportation Information System, Natural Gas Pipeline Projects Database.

greater capacity through the Midwest to Michigan. Supplies for this project would likely come from the Rockies producing fields. As a result, the viability of the proposed project will depend on growth in Rockies production, as well as competition from other companies that have proposed new outlets for Rockies production.

In 2009, Guardian Pipeline LLC, which commenced operations in 2002, will provide service to Green Bay, Wisconsin, for the first time, through the completion of a 119-mile extension from Guardian's current terminus near Ionia, Wisconsin. The expansion would add about 550 MMcf per day of capacity into the Green Bay area at a cost of between $200 and $250 million. As noted above, We Energies, a local utility in the Green Bay area, has completed construction of infrastructure to receive shipments from Guardian's expansion.

Northeast Region

Fifteen pipeline projects were completed in the Northeast region in 2008, representing 5.0 Bcf per day of additional capacity and 491 miles of new pipeline (Table 5). As was the case with several of the regions in 2008, these new mileage and capacity additions were at least double the level of the previous year and were the highest for this region in EIA's 11-year database of pipeline construction activity. Based on current construction and announced projects, EIA anticipates growing construction activity in the Northeast through 2011 and beyond, even if some planned projects are not completed.

LNG-Related Projects Begin Operations. The largest projects completed in the Northeast during 2008 in terms of capacity were related to bringing regasified natural gas to market from LNG import terminals. Dominion Corporation completed an integrated pipeline project that increased pipeline capacity from the Cove Point LNG terminal in Southern Maryland (which also was upgraded during the

year). At a cost of $160 million, Dominion constructed 48 miles of new pipeline from the LNG terminal to interstate pipeline connections in Virginia that will allow the gas to reach the Perulack Compressor Station in Juniata County, Pennsylvania. Secondly, the company added 113 miles of pipeline facilities extending northward from the Perulak station to Dominion's Leidy Hub complex in Clinton County, Pennsylvania. Dominion Cove Point Pipeline now has a capacity to transport 1.8 Bcf per day, an increase of 800 MMcf per day.

Suez LNG North America, Inc. completed a pipeline project to support its Neptune LNG offshore port, which will be located about 10 miles offshore Gloucester, Massachusetts. Similar to other offshore ports currently active in the United States and the United Kingdom, the facility does not have storage capacity. In fact, the port more closely resembles a buoy than a full-scale LNG terminal complex. Nonetheless, Neptune LNG will have the capacity to send out 750 MMcf per day of natural gas to the pipeline grid. The $23-million pipeline project included the installation of a 13-mile sub-sea pipeline that connects the Neptune LNG facility with the existing Spectra Energy HubLine.

Intraregional Projects Dominate Activity. Notwithstanding these LNG-related projects, pipeline expansions in the Northeast region in 2008 served primarily to improve service within the region itself. In the past few years, building long-haul capacity into the region has proved difficult, in part because of opposition from local communities and environmental organizations. While all of the projects completed in 2008 connected with to interstate pipelines, they did not extend beyond the Northeast region.

The Millennium Pipeline, a 182-mile, 30-inch line across southern New York, was completed after many years in the planning process. The pipeline serves markets along its route through the lower Hudson Valley and provides service to New York City markets through interconnections with other interstate pipelines. Millennium, which NiSource, Inc., KeySpan Corporation, and DTE Energy Company own, can transport up to 525 MMcf per day.

In association with the opening of Millennium, two current pipeline operators in the Northeast expanded their facilities in order to receive increased flows on their systems from interconnections with the new pipeline. Algonquin Gas Transmission Company completed its $192-million Ramapo system expansion, which included a new compressor station in Oxford, Connecticut; upgrades to existing compressor stations; and the replacement of pipeline facilities near Ramapo, New York. Secondly, Empire Pipeline, which originates at the United States-Canadian border near Buffalo, New York, began service on an 78-mile, 24-inch pipeline called the Empire Connector. This pipeline extends from near Rochester, New York, south to Corning, where it connects with Millennium Pipeline. The $187 million project has a capacity of 250 MMcf per day.

Transcontinental Gas Pipeline Corp. (Transco) in 2008 began a major system expansion involving additional compression and replacement of existing pipeline in the Mid-Atlantic. Transco's Sentinel Expansion Project will provide an additional transportation capacity of 142 MMcf per day from Transco's existing point of interconnection in Fairfax County, Virginia, to delivery points in Pennsylvania, Delaware, New Jersey, and New York. In 2008, Transco completed the first phase of the expansion, adding 40 MMcf per day in capacity. The second phase of the project will be completed in 2009, adding 102 MMcf per day in capacity. The estimated total cost for the Sentinel Expansion is $155 million.

Expansion Of Grid Poised To Continue. The level of pipeline construction in the Northeast is likely to increase in the next few years as long-planned system expansions take place and flows from new LNG facilities and existing LNG facility expansions commence. Thirty-two pipeline projects, totaling as much as 8.5 Bcf per day of new capacity, have been announced, submitted for regulatory review, or approved for development between 2009 and 2011. However, the completion of many of these projects is far from certain, especially those that have yet to be filed with FERC.

The development of the Marcellus Shale in New York and Pennsylvania is spurring the construction of pipeline infrastructure in the region, particularly large-scale expansions of existing pipelines. Much of the region's existing pipeline grid was built to transport flows from the Gulf of Mexico. The Marcellus shale encompasses more than 10,500 square miles and contains significant undeveloped resources, necessitating a re-orientation of the region's existing pipeline grid as well as new gathering pipelines. For example, El Paso's Tennessee Gas Pipeline plans to construct approximately 125 miles of 30-inch pipeline and add approximately 46,000 horsepower of compression facilities in its existing pipeline corridor in Pennsylvania to transport

growing Appalachian production to Northeast markets. The project will add capacity of 200 MMcf per day.

Numerous proposals to expand existing infrastructure to provide an outlet for increased supplies from the Rockies are also under consideration. Once the REX-East is complete, Rockies supplies will have access to many interstate pipelines from the pipeline's terminus in Clarington, Ohio. However, expansion of existing interstate pipelines in the region is required to transport increased supplies. For example, Texas Eastern Transmission, LP, has an application pending at FERC seeking a certificate to expand the capacity of its system by 395 MMcf per day from a supply point in Clarington, Ohio, and by 60 MMcf per day from the Oakford storage facility in Westmoreland County, Pennsylvania.

National Fuel Gas Company has proposed a 324-mile pipeline to deliver Rockies gas from Ohio to Corning, New York. In addition, Williams Companies' proposed Rockies Connector Pipeline would extend approximately 250 miles, connecting its Transco Station 195 in York County, Pennsylvania, to the eastern terminus of the REX-East in Ohio. The owners of REX have also proposed extending the pipeline further east to Linden, New Jersey, by 2011.

Southeast

After several years of minimal capacity additions, numerous large-scale pipelines were completed in the Southeast region in 2008. The capacity additions related to several market trends developing in both the Southeast region specifically and the country as a whole. Capacity into the Southeast region grew in part because of the need to build pipeline capacity out of the adjacent Southwest region, where supply growth from new unconventional resource development in northeastern Texas (Barnett Shale) and parts of Oklahoma and Arkansas (Fayetteville and Woodford Shales) has been significant. Capacity into the Florida market increased and several underground storage fields began operations, requiring related large-diameter pipeline infrastructure.

Nineteen pipeline expansions were completed in the Southeast region in 2008, representing 10.1 Bcf per day of additional capacity and 891 miles of new pipeline (Table 6). The added capacity, which cost an estimated $3.5 billion, was greater than that of any year in the last decade. Although pipeline construction activity has been relatively limited in recent years compared with other regions, the increased activity in 2008 is expected to continue through 2011 and beyond, even if some planned projects are not completed.

New Capacity Provides Outlet For Supplies. Among the completed pipeline projects providing new access to growing unconventional supplies from the west was Southeast Supply Header Pipeline (SESH), a new $842-million interstate pipeline constructed by a joint venture of Spectra Energy and CenterPoint Energy Gas Transmission. SESH began full service in October 2008, providing 1.1 Bcf per day of

Table 6. Natural Gas Pipeline Construction Projects Completed in 2008, Southeast Region
(Map Key references Figure 4)

Ending Region & State	Begins in Region	State – Region	Map Key	Pipeline - Project Name	FERC Docket Number (Interstate Projects)	Type of Project	In Service Date	Estimated Cost (Million Dollars)	Miles	Additional Capacity (MMcf/d)
Southeast										
AL	AL	Southeast	--	Gulf South – Mobile Compressor Expansion	CP07-396	Compression	31-Aug-08	23	0	250
AL	MS	Southeast	8	Gulf South – Southeast Expansion	CP07-32	Extension	1-Jun-08	1,296	111	1,272
AL	MS	Southeast	9	Southern Pines -- Florida/Transco Header	CP02-229	New Pipeline	15-Nov-08	52	26	1,000
AL	**LA**	**Southwest**	**13**	**Southeast Supply Header Pipeline**	**CP07-44**	**New Pipeline**	**5-Oct-08**	**842**	**270**	**1,140**
FL	AL	Southeast	--	Gulfstream -- Phase 4 (Bartow)	CP07-51	New pipeline	1-Dec-08	117	18	155
FL	FL	Southeast	--	Gulfstream -- Bayside Lateral	Not applicable	Lateral	1-Dec-08	30	28	200
FL	FL	Southeast	--	Gulfstream -- Phase 3a Expansion	CP00-06-014	Extension	1-Sep-08	129	34	185
FL	FL	Southeast	--	Florida Gas -- East Leg Expansion	CP07-82	Looping	1-Jul-08	16	7	10
GA	GA	Southeast	--	SONAT – Cypress Phase 2	CP05-388	Compression	1-Apr-08	21	0	100
KY	KY	Southeast	--	Equitrans – Big Sandy Pipeline Phase I	CP06-275	New Pipeline	1-Apr-08	60	68	70
KY	KY	Southeast	--	Equitrans - Big Sandy Pipeline Phase II	CP06-275	Compression	1-Apr-08	20	0	60
MS	MS	Southeast	10	Southern Pines -- Destin Line	CP02-229	New Pipeline	15-Nov-08	6	3	1,000
MS	MS	Southeast	11	Gulf Crossing -- Mississippi Loop	CP07-401	Looping/Compression	18-Dec-08	25	18	1,000
MS	MS	Southeast	12	Mississippi Hub -- Storage Lateral	CP07-4	Lateral	15-Dec-08	0	11	1,200
MS	MS	Southeast	--	Monroe Storage Field -- TETCO Lateral	CP07-406	Lateral	15-Dec-08	42	23	465
MS	**TX**	**Southwest**	**14**	**Gulf South – Texas to Mississippi Exp.**	**CP06-446**	**New pipeline**	**31-Jan-08**	**767**	**243**	**1,700**
NC	**VA**	**Northeast**	--	**East Tennessee – CNX Increase**	**CP08-35**	**Compression**	**1-Sep-08**	**5**	**0**	**90**
NC	**VA**	**Northeast**	--	**East Tennessee – Patriot Extension III**	**CP01-415**	**Compression**	**15-Oct-08**	**20**	**0**	**75**
TN	TN	Southeast	--	Midwestern -- Eastern Extension Project	CP05-372	Extension	15-Apr-08	26	31	120
							Total	3,497	891	10,092

Notes: Interregional project is in **bold print**. In the table, a project that crosses interregional boundaries is included in the region in which it terminates. See final page for a discussion of naming conventions used in this table.

Source: Energy Information Administration, GasTran Natural Gas Transportation Information System, Natural Gas Pipeline Projects Database.

capacity from CenterPoint's Perryville Hub in northeast Louisiana to interconnections with Florida Gas Transmission (FGT) in Mississippi and the Gulfstream Natural Gas System in Coden, Alabama. SESH interconnects with several interstate natural gas pipelines along its 270-mile route, providing opportunities for unconventional supplies to reach Southeast and Northeast markets as well as several storage facilities. SESH capacity has also been marketed to Florida utilities as a valuable alternative to offshore Gulf of Mexico supply, which has experienced intermittent disruptions in recent years during hurricane season.

At a cost of $767 million, Gulf South Pipeline Company LLP completed a large-scale expansion of its system in the region to provide a similar outlet for Southwestern supplies. Gulf South's Texas-to-Mississippi expansion, including about 243 miles of high-pressure pipeline, came online in January 2008. The expansion connects the company's existing system in DeSoto Parish in northwest Louisiana to its 30-inch diameter pipeline in Simpson County, Mississippi. With the addition of 110,604 horsepower of compression as well as the pipeline facilities, the project is capable of transporting up to 1.7 Bcf per day from the pipeline-constrained production areas in Texas to interconnections with other interstate pipelines along its path for eventual delivery to the Midwest, Northeast, and Southeast.

Additionally, significant pipeline capacity was added in the Southeast region in 2008 in conjunction with the completion of new underground storage capacity. Near Jackson, Mississippi, EnergySouth, Inc. completed the Mississippi Hub, a large, new underground salt-dome storage complex that will eventually be able to hold 30 Bcf. Related to this development, the owners of the complex constructed a 11-mile pipeline lateral with a capacity of 1.2 Bcf per day. Additionally, SG Resources Mississippi, LLC constructed the Southern Pines Energy Center in Greene County,

Mississippi. The new complex includes 29 miles of dual 24-inch bidirectional natural gas pipelines and associated facilities connecting with the FGT system and Transco.

Capacity additions in the Southeast in 2008 were also related to the ongoing expansion of the El Paso Corp.-owned Southern LNG terminal located on Elba Island, Georgia. Southern Natural Gas Company (SNG), which owns the interstate pipeline network that connects to the LNG terminal, completed a second phase of the new 167-mile Cypress Pipeline. This pipeline extends from the SNG system into southern Georgia and northern Florida, interconnecting with FGT near Jacksonville, Florida. The construction activity in 2008 added 100 MMcf per day of capacity to the new line. The third phase of the project is intended to boost Cypress Pipeline's capacity through the installation of additional compressor units, resulting in more than 250 MMcf per day of incremental transportation capability.

New Projects Are On The Horizon. Construction activity in the Southeast is likely to remain elevated in the near-term as industry continues to seek market outlets in the Southwest forgrowing unconventional supplies. For example, Texas Gas Transmission (TGT), which is a 5,900-mile pipeline that Boardwalk Pipeline Partners owns, intends to increase the capacity of its proposed Fayetteville and Greenville laterals to 1.7 Bcf per day from the initial design capacity for each project of 800 MMcf per day. The lateral projects, which were placed into service in early 2009, provide takeaway capacity for natural gas from the Fayetteville Shale area in north-central Arkansas. The Fayetteville lateral is a 100-mile, 36-inch pipeline traversing several counties in Arkansas and interconnecting with TGT's mainline in Coahoma County, Mississippi. The Greenville lateral is a 96-mile pipeline extending from TGT's mainline near Greenville, Mississippi, east to Kosciusko, Mississippi.

In total, EIA is tracking 39 proposed infrastructure projects for the region over the next 3 years. If all were to be completed, the increase in the region's capacity would be 22.7 Bcf per day, while 1,860 miles would be added to the pipeline grid. The estimated cost of these additions is $6.6 billion.

Southwest and the Gulf of Mexico

In the Southwest, infrastructure additions were massive in 2008, as the industry responded to the need for more capacity following increases in regional production, particularly in the Barnett Shale in Northeast Texas, as well as potential increased volumes of regasified natural gas from newly constructed LNG terminals in the region. Pipeline construction activity resulted in 30 pipeline completions, which together amounted to the largest-scale infrastructure addition in any region in the 11-year history of EIA's data of construction activity (Table 7).

In 2008, capacity additions of 22.6 Bcf per day were three times the level of the previous year, while the 1,382 miles of new pipeline was nearly double the previous year's addition of 700 miles of pipeline. The estimated cost of the infrastructure additions was $3.3 billion, compared with the 2007 total of $1.5 billion. Of the 30 pipeline projects constructed in the Southwest, 13 were related to new pipelines or expansions in the northeast Texas area or to new flows from development of supplies from the Barnett, Woodford, or Fayetteville Shale formations. These expansions accounted for approximately 72 percent (1,001 miles) of the added pipeline mileage in the region and 30 percent (6.7 Bcf per day) of the added capacity in the region.

Projects Enhanced Takeaway Capacity. Completed projects in 2008 included several enhancements to the interstate grid and new connections between market centers. The most significant projects took place on intrastate systems that Enterprise Product Partners and Energy Transfer Partners, LP own.

Table 7. Natural Gas Pipeline Construction Projects Completed in 2008, Southwest Region
(Map Key references Figure 4)

Ending Region & State	Begins in State – Region		Map Key	Pipeline - Project Name	FERC Docket Number (Interstate Projects)	Type of Project	In Service Date	Estimated Cost (Million Dollars)	Miles	Additional Capacity (MMcf/d)
Southwest										
AR	AR	Southwest	15	TXG – Fayetteville Lateral Phase 1	CP07-417	New Pipeline	15-Sep-08	205	66	967
AR	AR	Southwest	–	Centerpoint -- Cove Compressor Station	CP07-437	Compression	1-Nov-08	26	0	200
AR	AR	Southwest	–	Ozark – Standing Rock Compressor	CP08-20	Compression	15-Nov-08	19	0	100
GM	GM	Offshore	–	Enbridge --Neptune Deepwater Project	Not applicable	Gathering Lateral	15-Feb-08	50	29	200
GM	GM	Offshore	–	Williams – Blind Faith Extension	Not applicable	Gathering	1-Nov-08	255	71	200
LA	LA	Southwest	16	Port Barre – Bobcat Storage Lateral	CP06-66/67/68	Laterals	15-Oct-08	30	20	1,200
LA	LA	Southwest	17	Trunkline -- NTX Extension	CP06-452	Extension	1-Feb-08	20	14	625
LA	LA	Southwest	18	Sempra --Cameron Interstate Pipeline	CP05-119	Lateral	1-Sep-08	115	36	2,350
LA	LA	Southwest	19	Cheniere -- Sabine Pass LNG Line	CP07-426	Lateral	15-Feb-08	350	16	2,600
LA	LA	Southwest	–	PetroLogistics --Choctaw II Storage Lateral	CP07-427	Lateral	15-Oct-08	15	10	300
LA	LA	Southwest	–	Columbia Gulf – Henry Hub Expansion	Not applicable	Compression	15-Mar-08	25		230
LA	TX	Southwest	–	Centerpoint Perryville Expansion Phase 3	CP07-41	Compression	2-May-08	41	0	316
LA	TX	Southwest	–	NGPL -- Louisiana/Gulf Coast Line Expansion	CP07-03	Looping/Compression	14-Feb-08	69	5	200
NM	NM	Southwest	–	TW San Juan Lateral Expansion	CP06-459	Looping	22-Jul-08	72	25	375
NM	NM	Southwest	–	MarkWest -- Lea County Expansion	CP08-01	Looping	15-Sep-08	3	3	110
OK	OK	Southwest	–	Enogex --Woodford Shale Gathering Header	Not applicable	Lateral	1-May-08	50	30	350
TX	TX	Southwest	20	Freeport LNG – Brazoria Interconnector	Not applicable	Lateral	1-Apr-08	56	30	2,600
TX	TX	Southwest	21	NGS – Tres Palacios Storage Lateral	CP07-90	Lateral	1-Oct-08	60	42	2,500
TX	TX	Southwest	22	Freeport LNG Pipeline	CP03-75	Lateral	1-Apr-08	18	10	1,750
TX	TX	Southwest	23	Energy Transfer -- SE Boosier Pipeline Phase 1	Not applicable	New Pipeline	28-Apr-08	360	165	900
TX	TX	Southwest	24	Enbridge -- East Texas System Extension	Not applicable	Extension	15-Apr-08	465	190	700
TX	TX	Southwest	25	Energy Transfer -- Carthage Loop Expansion	Not applicable	Looping/Compression	10-Sep-08	94	32	500
TX	TX	Southwest	26	Energy Transfer -- Maypearl to Malone	Not applicable	New Pipeline	1-Aug-08	50	25	600
TX	TX	Southwest	27	Enterprise Products -- Sherman Extension	Not applicable	Extension	15-Dec-08	400	178	1,100
TX	TX	Southwest	–	Energy Transfer -- SE Boosier Pipeline Phase 2	Not applicable	Compression	1-Nov-08	70	165	400
TX	TX	Southwest	–	TETCO Cedar Bayou Lateral Project	CP07-411	Lateral	28-May-08	17	4	360
TX	TX	Southwest	–	Energy Transfer -- Northside to Paris Loop	Not applicable	Expansion	1-Aug-08	260	145	350
TX	TX	Southwest	–	Kinder Morgan -- Tejas/Texas Pipeline Link	Not applicable	New line	15-Sep-08	72	58	225
TX	TX	Southwest	–	El Paso -- Hobbs Lateral	CP08-14	Lateral	26-Nov-08	17	7	150
TX	TX	Southwest	–	Trunkline -- Field Zone Expansion II	CP08-99	Lateral	15-Nov-08	23	7	95
							Total	3,307	1,382	22,553
Mexico										
MX	TX	Southwest	–	Encinal -- 'Petrolero Project	CP07-418	Border Crossing	30-Jun-08	1	0	60
							Total	1	0	60

Notes: Interregional project is in **bold print**. In the table, a project that crosses interregional boundaries is included in the region in which it terminates. See final page for a discussion of naming conventions used in this table.

Source: Energy Information Administration, GasTran Natural Gas Transportation Information System, Natural Gas Pipeline Projects Database

Enterprise Product Partners completed a portion of its Sherman Extension project, which in total is one of the larger infrastructure projects slated for northeast Texas in recent years. The 178-mile pipeline extends Enterprise's Texas intrastate system from Barnett production sites in Erath County, Texas, to Grayson County, Texas, where there will be access to points eastward through an interconnection with the Gulf Crossing interstate pipeline. The $400-million project provides Barnett producers access to markets in the Southeast, Midwest, and Northeast. By the end of 2009, Enterprise intends to build a 40-mile supply lateral that would extend from the Sherman Extension to the Trinity River Basin north of Arlington, Texas. The lateral would provide up to 1 Bcf per day of gas takeaway capacity for producers in Tarrant and Denton counties, according to the company.

Energy Transfer Partners, LP, was also one of the more active companies adding infrastructure to the Southwest region during the year, completing 532 miles of new pipeline with a combined capacity of 2.8 Bcf per day. Among other projects, the company's completions during the year included the 165-mile Bossier Pipeline with a capacity of 900 MMcf per day; the 145-mile Paris Loop expansion with a capacity of 350 MMcf per day; and the 32-mile Carthage Loop Expansion with a capacity of 500 MMcf per day. These pipelines are located in Central and Northeast Texas.

LNG-Related Projects Were Completed. Capacity additions in the Southwest region resulting from increased investment in LNG infrastructure were significant in 2008. Two new LNG terminals opened during 2008 and a third has opened in 2009. Related pipeline infrastructure completed during the course of 2008 represented an investment of $539 million. Although the pipeline infrastructure related to LNG terminals was quite short in terms of added mileage at a combined 130 miles, the infrastructure additions generally involved 42-inch pipeline with very large capacities in order to transport the massive send-out potential from LNG terminals. During 2008, approximately 9.3 Bcf per day of capacity additions were completed relating to LNG terminals in the region.

Related to the Sabine Pass LNG terminal in Cameron Parrish, Louisiana is the $572-million Creole Trail Pipeline, which

Cheniere Energy owns and operates. This new pipeline connects the Sabine Pass LNG and Creole Trail LNG facilities, both of which Cheniere owns, and then connects to multiple interstate pipelines in southern Louisiana. The total length of the line is just 16 miles, but it adds capacity of 2.6 Bcf per day to the network. Another LNG-related infrastructure enhancement involved Freeport LNG. In early 2008, Freeport LNG completed a 10-mile pipeline associated with its sendout of regasified LNG. With a capacity of 1.8 Bcf per day, the Freeport LNG Pipeline can transport natural gas to Stratton Ridge, Texas, where the pipeline interconnects with several intrastate systems.

The level of pipeline construction in the Southwest is likely to remain elevated in the next few years as long-planned system expansions take place and flows from new LNG facilities and existing facility expansions commence. Forty-seven projects, totaling as much as 40 Bcf per day of new capacity, have been announced, submitted for regulatory review, or approved for development between 2009 and 2011. If all were to be completed, the increase in the region's capacity would be 40 Bcf per day, while 3,100 miles would be added to the pipeline grid. The estimated cost of these additions would be $7.6 billion. However, the completion of many of these projects is far from certain, especially those that have yet to be filed with the FERC.

West

Very little capacity was added to the West region infrastructure in 2008. Only two natural gas pipeline projects, together adding 70 MMcf per day of capacity at a combined cost of $41 million, were completed in the region during the year (Table 8). This was the fourth consecutive year in which there was little activity in the West region, which is primarily characterized as a consuming region with extensive demand in the electric power sector.

Both infrastructure projects added compression to existing pipelines in the region. El Paso Natural Gas Company upgraded its system in Pinal County, Arizona, adding 30 MMcf per day of capacity to its Phoenix Lateral. The compression project cost $24 million. According to the company, the project was undertaken because of significant growth in demand for natural gas service in the western areas

Table 8. Natural Gas Pipeline Construction Projects Completed in 2008, Western Region
(Map Key references Figure 4)

Ending Region & State	Begins in State – Region	Map Key	Pipeline - Project Name	FERC Docket Number (Interstate Projects)	Type of Project	In Service Date	Estimated Cost (Million Dollars)	Miles	Additional Capacity (MMcf/d)
Western									
AZ	AZ Western	–	El Paso -- Picacho Compressor Station	CP07-448	Compression	1-Dec-08	24	0	30
NV	NV Western	–	Tuscarora -- System Expansion	CP07-27	Compression	1-Apr-08	17	0	40
						Total	41	0	70

Notes: Totals may not sum due to independent rounding. See final page for a discussion of naming conventions used in this table.

Source: Energy Information Administration, GasTran Natural Gas Transportation Information System, Natural Gas Pipeline Projects Database.

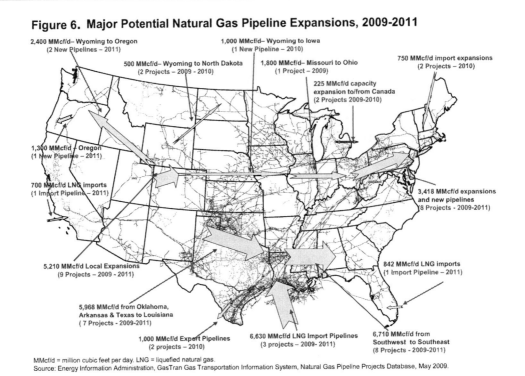

Figure 6. Major Potential Natural Gas Pipeline Expansions, 2009-2011

2,400 MMcf/d– Wyoming to Oregon
(2 New Pipelines – 2011)

500 MMcf/d– Wyoming to North Dakota
(2 Projects – 2009 - 2010)

1,000 MMcf/d– Wyoming to Iowa
(1 New Pipeline – 2010)

1,800 MMcf/d– Missouri to Ohio
(1 Project – 2009)

750 MMcf/d import expansions
(2 Projects – 2010)

225 MMcf/d capacity
expansion to/from Canada
(2 Projects 2009-2010)

1,300 MMcf/d Oregon
(1 New Pipeline – 2011)

700 MMcf/d LNG imports
(1 Import Pipeline – 2011)

3,418 MMcf/d expansions
and new pipelines
(8 Projects - 2009-2011)

5,210 MMcf/d Local Expansions
(9 Projects - 2009 - 2011)

842 MMcf/d LNG imports
(1 Import Pipeline – 2011)

5,968 MMcf/d from Oklahoma,
Arkansas & Texas to Louisiana
(7 Projects - 2009-2011)

1,000 MMcf/d Export Pipelines
(2 projects – 2010)

6,630 MMcf/d LNG Import Pipelines
(3 projects – 2009- 2011)

6,710 MMcf/d from
Southwest to Southeast
(8 Projects - 2009-2011)

MMcf/d = million cubic feet per day. LNG = liquefied natural gas.
Source: Energy Information Administration, GasTran Gas Transportation Information System, Natural Gas Pipeline Projects Database, May 2009.

El Paso serves, particularly in the Phoenix metropolitan area. Tuscarora Gas Transmission Company constructed a new compressor station on its existing interstate pipeline system in Modoc County, California, to provide 40 MMcf per day of capacity to Sierra Pacific Power Company. Sierra Pacific will use the new capacity entitlement to fuel its new 514-megawatt Tracy Combined Cycle Power Plant.

Capacity Increases Needed for Rockies Supplies. Although pipeline construction activity in the West region will likely continue to be limited in the next few years, several significant projects are underway. The largest project currently proposed for the region is El Paso Corporation's Ruby Pipeline, which will transport Rockies natural gas to a terminus near Malin, Oregon. The 680-mile pipeline, which could begin operations as early as 2011, will have an initial capacity of 1.5 Bcf per day, according to El Paso.

A consortium of Williams Gas Pipeline Company LLC, TransCanada Pipeline USA, Ltd., and Sempra Pipelines & Storage Corporation launched a similar proposal to move Rockies supplies to the Northwest region of the country. The proposed Sunstone Pipeline would require construction of approximately 601 miles of 42-inch pipeline extending from Opal, Wyoming, to an interconnect with an existing pipeline near Stanfield, Oregon.

A host of LNG-related projects are also still active in the West region, most of which would involve construction of new pipeline in some form. However, project timelines have

extended beyond 2011. FERC has issued final environmental approval for the LNG import terminal proposed by Jordan Cove Energy Project, LP (Jordan Cove), and the associated send-out natural gas pipeline proposed by Pacific Connector Gas Pipeline, LP (Pacific Connector). Jordan Cove's LNG terminal would be located on the bay side of the North Spit of Coos Bay in southern Oregon. Pacific Connector's proposed 36-inch sendout pipeline would extend from Jordan Cove's LNG terminal about 234 miles southeast across Coos, Douglas, Jackson, and Klamath counties to a terminus near Malin, Oregon, where it would interconnect with several existing interstate pipeline systems.

Observations and Outlook

Pipeline infrastructure expansion activity in the lower 48 States will likely remain elevated in the near-term, with most activity dedicated to increasing capacity from the Rockies and Midcontinent developing production fields to major consuming areas to the east (Figure 6). Natural gas pipeline capacity added during 2008, totaling 45 Bcf per day was substantially higher than the additions of prior years, going back at least to 1998. The current inventory of 180 project proposals for the 3 years ending 2011 would bring an additional 94 Bcf per day of capacity to the grid with average capacity of about 575 MMcf per day for each project.

While only a portion of these scheduled projects are likely to be completed, EIA expects at least several more years of large-scale additions to the pipeline grid. The scheduled projects for the near-term (2009-2011), which account for more than 10,200 miles of potential new natural gas pipeline, will continue to be mostly oriented around the addition and expansion of capacity from new supply sources. A substantial amount of pipeline capacity additions over the next 3 years will come from the intense development activity in the Rockies and the northeast Texas producing areas (Table 9).

EIA also forecasts domestic production, particularly production from unconventional sources, to continue to show gains in the long-term. In the *Annual Energy Outlook*, natural gas in tight sandstone formations is the largest source of unconventional production, accounting for 29 percent of total U.S. production in 2030. Production from shale formations is the fastest growing source, expected to grow over 200 percent to 3.7 Tcf per year.[9] However, the expected growth in natural gas production from shale formations is far from certain, and continued exploration is needed to provide additional information on the resource potential. EIA projects that the expected continued development of domestic resources will require steady additions to the pipeline grid in the long-term.

---

[9] Energy Information Administration, *Updated Annual Energy Outlook 2009 (Reference Case Service Report)*, Table 14, (Washington DC, April 2009).

Table 9. Largest 20 Planned Natural Gas Pipeline Projects for 2009, 2010, and 2011, By Level of Added Capacity

Year Planned	State Begin	State End	Region End	Developer	Project Name	FERC Docket Number	Type of Project	Status (as of May 2009)	Miles	Additional Capacity (MMcf/d)[1]
2009	TX	LA	Southwest	Golden Pass LNG Terminal LP	Golden Pass LNG Laterals	CP04-400	Lateral	Completed	70	2,500
2009	LA	LA	Southwest	Kinder Morgan Louisiana PL Co	Sabine Pass LNG Leg 1	CP06-449	New Pipeline	Construction	135	2,130
2009	LA	LA	Southwest	Cheniere Creole Trail LLP	Creole Trail Pipeline	CP07-426	Lateral	Construction	117	2,000
2009	MO	OH	Midwest	Kinder Morgan Energy Partners	Rockies Express (REX East)	CP07-208	New Pipeline	Construction	439	1,800
2009	OK	OK	Southwest	Gulf Crossing Pipeline Co LLC	Gulf Crossing Pipeline Project	CP07-398	New Pipeline	Completed	356	1,712
2009	LA	LA	Southwest	Spectra Energy Inc (MHP)	Egan Storage Lateral Loop	CP07-88	Looping	Construction	17	1,700
2009	OK	TX	Southwest	Midcontinent Express Pipeline	Midcontinent Express Pipeline System	CP08-06	New Pipeline	Completed	506	1,500
2009	TX	TX	Southwest	Energy Transfer Co	Texas Independence Pipeline	Not applicable	New Pipeline	Construction	160	1,100
2009	LA	LA	Southwest	Kinder Morgan Louisiana PL Co	Sabine Pass LNG Leg 2	CP06-449	Lateral	Construction	1	1,065
2009	TX	TX	Southwest	Enterprise Product Partners LP	Trinity River Supply Lateral	Not applicable	Lateral	Construction	40	1,000
2009	AR	MS	Southeast	Texas Gas Transmission Co	Fayetteville Lateral Phase 2	CP07-417	New Pipeline	Completed	100	967
2009	LA	LA	Southwest	Regency Intrastate Pipeline Co	Elm Grove Bienville Pipeline	CP09-82	Looping/Compression	Construction	121	800
2009	MS	MS	Southeast	Texas Gas Transmission Co	Greenville Lateral	CP07-417	New Pipeline	Completed	96	750
2009	MA	CT	Northeast	Algonquin Gas Trans Co	East-to-West (EW2) Expansion	CP08-420	Looping/Compression	Applied	31	746
2009	CO	CO	Central	Enterprise Product Partners LP	Collbran Valley Pipeline	Not applicable	Gathering Lateral	Construction	22	650
2009	OK	OK	Southwest	MarkWest Pioneer LLC	Arkoma Connector Pipeline Project	CP08-404	Lateral	Completed	50	638
2009	TX	TX	Southwest	Energy Transfer Co	Cleburne to Tolar Extension	Not applicable	Extension	Completed	35	600
2009	TX	TX	Southwest	Energy Transfer Co	Southern Shale	Not applicable	New Pipeline	Completed	31	600
2009	WI	WI	Midwest	Guardian Pipeline Co	GII Expansion	CP07-08	Extension	Construction	119	537
2009	WV	PA	Northeast	Chestnut Ridge Storage LLC	Uniontown Lateral	CP08-36	Lateral	Applied	17	500
2009	--	--	--	--	Others (58 projects)	--	--	--	1,181	8,557
Total									**3,643**	**31,852**
2010	MS	MS	Southeast	NGS Investments LLC	Leaf River Dome Headers	CP08-08	Lateral	Approved	7	2500
2010	AL	AL	Southeast	McMoran Exploration Inc	Coden Onshore Pipeline	CP04-68	New Pipeline	Approved	5	1600
2010	AR	MS	Southeast	Fayetteville Express Pipeline	Fayetteville Express Pipeline	PF09-4	New pipeline	Applied (NEPA)	187	1600
2010	LA	LA	Southwest	DCP Midstream Partners LP	Haynesville Connector	None yet	New Pipeline	Planning	150	1500
2010	GA	GA	Southeast	Southern Natural Gas Co	Elba Express III	CP06-470	Extension	Approved	189	1175
2010	TX	TX	Southwest	Enbridge/Atmos Energy	BIG Pipeline Project	Not applicable	New line	Planning	100	1000
2010	TX	TX	Southwest	ENSTOR Energy	Houston Energy Center Header Line	CP07-390	New Pipeline	Construction	2	1000
2010	LA	LA	Southwest	Liberty Gas Storage LLC	Liberty Storage Pipeline Expansion	CP08-454	Lateral	Applied	5	1000
2010	WY	IA	Central	Kinder Morgan Energy Partners	REX/NGPL Phase 1	None yet	New Line	Planning	175	1000
2010	WY	WY	Central	Questar Overthrust Pipeline Co	Overthrust Wamsutter/Opal	PF09-6	Looping	Applied (NEPA)	43	800
2010	LA	LA	Southwest	Stark Gas Storage LLC	Stark Storage Pipeline	CP05-08	Lateral	Construction	35	800
2010	ME	ME	Northeast	Downeast LNG LLC	Downeast LNG Lateral	CP07-52/55	Lateral	Applied	30	625
2010	MS	MS	Southeast	Southeast Gas Storage LLC	Black Warrior Field Lateral	CP08-418	Lateral	Approved	5	500
2010	TX	MX	Mexico	Sonora Pipeline LLC	Burgos Hub Mission Line (US Portion)	CP07-74	New Border Crossing	Approved	16	500
2010	LA	LA	Southeast	Gulf South Pipeline Co	Haynesville/Perryville Expansion	None yet	Compression	Planning	0	500
2010	ON	CT	Northeast	Iroquois Pipeline Co	MetroExpress Project	None yet	Looping/Compression	Planning	0	500
2010	TX	MX	Mexico	Sonora Pipeline LLC	Northeast Hub Progresso Line (US Portion)	CP07-74	New Border Crossing	Approved	13	500
2010	WY	MT	Central	Bison Pipeline LLC	Bison Pipeline Project	PF08-23	New Pipeline	Applied (NEPA)	289	400
2010	MI	ON	Canada	Great Lakes Gas Trans Co	Dawn Eclipse Pipeline Proeject	None yet	Compression	Planning	0	400
2010	MI	ON	Canada	Spectra Energy Inc	Dawn Gateway Project	None yet	Compression	Planning	0	400
2010	--	--	--	--	Others (35 projects)	--	--	--	819	6,305
Total									**2,070**	**24,605**
2011	LA	LA	Southwest	Henry Gas Storage LLC	Henry Storage Lateral	PF08-28	Lateral	Applied (NEPA)	12	2600
2011	MS	MS	Southeast	NGS Investments LLC	Leaf River East-West Header	CP08-08	Lateral	Approved	37	2500
2011	LA	LA	Southwest	NGS Investments LLC	Gulf Coast Connector	Planning	Lateral	Planning	40	2000
2011	LA	LA	Southwest	Port Barre Investments LLC	Bobcat Storage Expansion	CP09-19	Laterals	Applied	20	1800
2011	LA	LA	Southwest	Atmos Pipeline and Storage LLC	Fort Necessity Storage Lateral	PF08-10	Lateral	Applied (NEPA)	7.5	1500
2011	MS	MS	Southeast	Gulf LNG Pipeline LLC	Gulf Landing Pipeline	CP06-12/13/14	New Pipeline	Construction	5.02	1500
2011	OH	NJ	Northeast	Kinder Morgan Energy Partners	REX Northeast Express Project	None yet	New Pipeline	Planning	415	1500
2011	WY	OR	Western	El Paso/Bear Energy	Ruby Pipeline Project	CP09-54	New Line	Applied	680	1500
2011	OR	OR	Western	Palomar Gas Pipeline LLC	Palomar Gas Transmission Line	CP09-35	New Pipeline	Applied	217	1300
2011	NY	NY	Northeast	Broadwater Energy LLC	Broadwater Energy Pipeline	CP06-54/55/56	New Pipeline	Approved	21.7	1250
2011	TX	LA	Southwest	Energy Transfer Co	Tiger Pipeline	PF09-9	New line	Applied (NEPA)	180	1250
2011	LA	LA	Southwest	Black Bayou Storage LLC	Black Bayou Storage Lateral	CP07-451	Lateral	Applied	7.15	1200
2011	WY	OR	Western	Sunstone Pipeline LLC	Sunstone Pipeline Project	PF09-2	New Pipeline	Applied (NEPA)	601	1200
2011	LA	FL	Southeast	Cheniere Energy Co	Southern Trail LNG Line	CP05-357	New line	Applied	348	1050
2011	OK	OK	Southwest	Enogex LLC	Heartland Crossing	Not applicable	New Pipeline	Announced	0	1000
2011	OH	OH	Midwest	Kinder Morgan Energy Partners	REX Northeast Express Phase	None yet	Compression	Planning	0	1000
2011	TX	LA	Southwest	Enbridge Pipeline Co	LaCrosse Pipeline	None yet	New line	Announced	300	1000
2011	IA	IL	Midwest	Kinder Morgan Energy Partners	REX/NGPL Joint Project Phase 2	None yet	New Line	Planning	240	1000
2011	TX	TX	Southwest	Pivotal Energy Development	Golden Triangle Storage Lateral	CP07-414	Lateral	Construction	9	900
2011	BH	FL	Southeast	AES Ocean Express Pipeline LLP	Ocean Express Offshore Pipeline Project	CP02-90	New Pipeline	Approved	46.1	842
2011	--	--	--	--	Others (27 projects)	--	--	--	1,342	9,556
Total									**4,528**	**37,448**
3-Year Total					180 Projects				**10,242**	**93,905**

[1] When announcing the design capacity for a proposed project or expansion, a pipeline company may provide either a volumetric (per cubic feet) or energy content (btus/therms) value. In this table, reported capacity figures are presented as volumetric (MMcf/d).

MMcf/d = million cubic feet per day. ON = Ontario, Canada, BH = Bahamas.

Source: Energy Information Administration, GasTran Natural Gas Transportation Information System, Natural Gas Pipeline Projects Database, as of May 2009.

Note on Terminology used in the Tables

When announcing the design capacity for a proposed project or expansion, a pipeline company may provide either a volumetric (per cubic feet) or energy content (therms) value. In this table, reported capacity figures are presented as volumetric (MMcf/d = million cubic feet per day) assuming a conversion factor of 1 MMcf/d = 1 MDth/d (thousand decatherms per day) = 1 Bbtu/d (billion btu per day). Projects referred to as compressor projects may include placing additional compressor units at an existing station, the upgrading of existing units, or adding one or more new compressor stations to an existing system. Looping refers to the installation of another segment of pipeline parallel to an existing pipeline segment. Looping is used as a means of quickly increasing overall pipeline capacity and/or increasing line-packing (temporary storage) on a pipeline system. A lateral refers to a new pipeline segment built to interconnect a new customer to a local major pipeline or to a local distribution company (LDC) mainline. An extension refers to the building of a new section of pipeline to a service area beyond the original termination point of the transmission system. Projects referred to as new pipelines are entirely new pipeline entities that are not an extension of, or a lateral off of, an existing pipeline system.

Estimates of Peak Underground Working Gas Storage Capacity in the United States, 2009 Update

The aggregate peak capacity for U.S. underground natural gas storage is estimated to be 3,889 billion cubic feet (Bcf). This estimate, based on demonstrated noncoincident peak working gas storage volumes for individual active gas storage fields[1] reported to EIA over the 60-month period ending in April 2009, represents a 2.6 percent increase over last year's estimate. Working gas design capacity, an alternative, less conservative indicator of gas storage capacity, also rose over the past year. Questions or comments on the contents of this article should be directed to Angelina LaRose at angelina.larose@eia.doe.gov or (202) 586-6135.

Underground natural gas storage is a key component of the natural gas market. Natural gas in storage maintains reliability of gas supplies during periods of high demand (including both winter and summer peak days); it supports load balancing for pipelines; and it provides opportunities for owners of natural gas in storage to synchronize their buying and selling activities more effectively with market needs while minimizing their business costs.

The quantity of gas that storage operators hold is one indicator of whether there will be enough supply to meet future demand.[2] Although current supplies (production and net imports) are relatively constant throughout the year, natural gas demand is highly seasonal. Between April and October, natural gas is injected into storage fields for use in winter periods of high demand. During years like 2009, when storage builds have been historically large, the total amount of gas that operators can store becomes particularly important. As storage fields near their maximum capacity, constraints on storage may cause downward pressure on prices paid for current supplies of gas until the winter demand rebalances supply and demand.

This paper reports two measures of aggregate capacity, one based on demonstrated peak working gas storage, the other on working gas design capacity. Demonstrated peak working gas storage volumes provide a conservative measure of capacity that may understate the amount that could actually be stored. In contrast, working gas design capacity, a measure based on the physical characteristics of the reservoir, installed equipment, and operating procedures particular to the site that is often certified by Federal or State regulators, may overstate the amount of storage capacity that is actually available given operational, logistical, and other practical constraints.

Both demonstrated peak working gas storage capacity and working gas design capacity increased from 2008 to 2009.[3]

---

[1] Salt caverns are included in the term "field".

[2] A more detailed discussion of the uses of underground storage, terminology, and fields and operations is available at the Energy Information Administration report, *The Basics of Underground Storage*, http://www.eia.doe.gov/pub/oil_gas/natural_gas/analysis_publications/storagebasics/storagebasics.html.

[3] *Working gas* is the volume of natural gas in the reservoir that is in addition to the base gas, which is the volume of natural gas intended as permanent inventory in a storage reservoir to maintain adequate pressure

- Demonstrated peak working gas storage capacity as of April 2009 was 3,889 Bcf, an increase of 100 Bcf from April 2008.

- Working gas design capacity as of April 2009 was 4,313 Bcf, an increase of 177 Bcf from April 2008.

The increase in natural gas storage capacity estimates can be attributed to the opening of new facilities, capacity expansion at existing facilities, and, for demonstrated peak capacity, greater use of existing storage facilities during the past year.

EIA's methodology and regional estimates are discussed below.[4]

Methodology

As in last year's report, estimates of demonstrated peak storage capacity are based on aggregation of the noncoincident peak levels of gas in storage at individual storage fields as reported monthly over a 5-year period to EIA on Form EIA-191M, "Monthly Underground Storage Report."[5] This data-driven estimate reflects actual operator experience and serves as a conservative proxy for the possible limits of industry capacity. For example, this data reflects storage levels as of the last day of the report month, and a facility may have reached a higher inventory on a different day of the report month, which would not be recorded on Form EIA-191M.[6] However, the noncoincident peak volumes exceed the largest reported monthly working gas volumes for each of the three regions for which storage data are published because not all fields held their highest volumes at the same time.

Aggregate working gas design capacity provides an alternative measure of the amount of natural gas that can be stored. However, logistical, operational, and practical considerations may preclude attainment of maximum design capacities of storage fields, so that a summation of design capacities is likely to exceed actual available maximum storage capacity.

---

and deliverability rates through the withdrawal season. *Working gas design capacity* is calculated as the difference between total storage design capacity and base gas.

[4] The regions in this report are those used for the Energy Information Administration's *Weekly Natural Gas Storage Report*; see http://www.eia.doe.gov/oil_gas/natural_gas/ngs/notes.html.

[5] Noncoincident means that the months of measurement for the peak storage volumes by field may differ; i.e., the months do not necessarily coincide. As such, the noncoincident peak for any region is at least as big as any monthly volume in the historical record.

[6] Data from Form EIA-191M, "Monthly Underground Storage Report" is collected from storage operators on a field level basis. Operators can report field level data either on a per reservoir basis or on an aggregated reservoir basis. It is possible that if all operators reported on a per reservoir basis that the peak working gas storage capacity would be larger.

Regional and National Estimates of Gas Storage Capacity

Table 1 presents national and regional estimates of demonstrated peak working gas capacity and working gas design capacity. Total U.S. demonstrated peak working gas capacity as of April 2009 is estimated to be 3,889 Bcf, 100 Bcf above the April 2008 level, and equivalent to 90.2 percent of aggregate working gas design capacity.[7] In the West Region, peak storage capacity is only 73.3 percent of working gas design capacity, reflecting several still-active fields that have experienced a shift in their primary role from seasonal storage to other functions, such as pipeline load balancing, and fields that are being drawn down to be taken out of service.

In all three regions, demonstrated peak working gas capacity as a percentage of working gas design capacity decreased from 2008 to 2009. This is because working gas design capacity increased faster than the peak working gas capacity in each region as a result of new facilities coming online and facility expansions.[8] The inclusion of new capacity affects the ratio of estimated peak working gas capacity to working gas design capacity, as the incremental build of working gas in storage is on average lower than the increase that is ultimately expected to occur.

Despite the increase in both measures of gas storage capacity, the record-high level of actual working gas in storage in the lower-48 States at the end of any month remains at 3,565 Bcf, reached at the end of October 2007. However, storage operators appear on pace to set a new all-time level for working gas in storage this fall. For example, according to EIA's *Short-Term Energy Outlook* (August 2009), the end-of-October volume is expected to be 3,801 Bcf, which would be 97.7 percent of demonstrated peak working gas capacity as of April 2009.

---

[7] The April 2008 estimate is from the Energy Information Administration report, *Estimates of Peak Underground Working Gas Storage Capacity in the United States* (October 7, 2008), available at http://www.eia.doe.gov/pub/oil_gas/natural_gas/feature_articles/2008/ngpeakstorage/ngpeakstorage.pdf.

[8] New facilities accounted for the addition of 12 Bcf in the East Region, 41.8 Bcf in the Producing Region, and 19 Bcf in the West Region.

Table 1. Estimates of Natural Gas Storage Capacity and Historical Maximum Storage Volumes April 2008 and April 2009
(Billion cubic feet, unless otherwise noted)

Region	Estimated Peak Working Gas Capacity		Working gas design capacity		Peak Working Gas as Percent of Working gas design capacity		National and Regional Maximum End-of-Month Gas Storage Volumes	
	(as of) Apr-2008	(as of) Apr-2009	(as of) Apr-2008	(as of) Apr-2009	(as of) Apr-2008	(as of) Apr-2009	(as of) Apr-2008	(as of) Apr-2009
East	2,153	2,178	2,225	2,268	96.8%	96.0%	2,032	2,032
Producing	1,146	1,202	1,251	1,351	91.6%	89.0%	1,068	1,068
West	490	509	660	694	74.2%	73.3%	470	470
Lower 48	3,789	3,889	4,136	4,313	91.6%	90.2%	3,565	3,565

Note: The historical maximum volume for the lower-48 States does not equal the sum of the regional volumes because the regional data represent values in different months.
Source: Energy Information Administration (EIA), Natural Gas Division. Working gas design capacity: derived from data in the *Natural Gas Monthly* (DOE/EIA-0130), July 2008 and June 2009, Table 11. Peak gas capacity: derived from data reported on the EIA-191M, "Monthly Underground Gas Storage Report."

Although new records can be set every year, more than 61 percent of the individual storage fields that contribute to the peak gas capacity showed no change in the month of their maximum value of working gas in storage when comparing the May 2004 through April 2009 5-year range used in this analysis to the May 2003 through April 2008 used in the previous peak working gas capacity analysis. Approximately, 17 percent of the individual storage fields showed a decline in their maximum value of working gas in storage, as they reached a maximum value between May 2003 and April 2004, months which were not included in the current 5-year range. Excluding fields with known capacity reductions and shifts in operational conditions, adding back the peak gas in storage volumes reached between May 2003 through April 2004 would increase the peak working gas capacity by approximately 20 Bcf. This would increase the peak working gas as percent of working gas design capacity by 1 percent.

Approximately 20 percent of the fields reached a new peak working gas in storage since EIA's 2008 report on working gas capacity. Peak working gas in storage generally increased less than 5 percent above the previous peak at these fields. A significant number of storage fields attained their highest reported levels in October 2007 (Figure 1). These field-level maxima coincided with the historical maximum volume of 3,565 Bcf for the lower 48 States during the same month, as reported in the *Natural Gas Monthly*. However, some of the peak levels that were established at individual fields in October 2007 were exceeded the following year. Of the fields that had a maximum level of gas in storage in October and November 2007 that reached a new maximum level of storage in the current 5-year range, 20 of them reached their new peak gas in storage in October and

November 2008. Among the reasons that these increases occurred were facility expansions and the ramping up of gas being stored in new facilities.

Figure 1. Aggregate Volume Reported by Storage Fields that Attained their Highest Level of Working Gas in the Months, September 2006 through April 2009

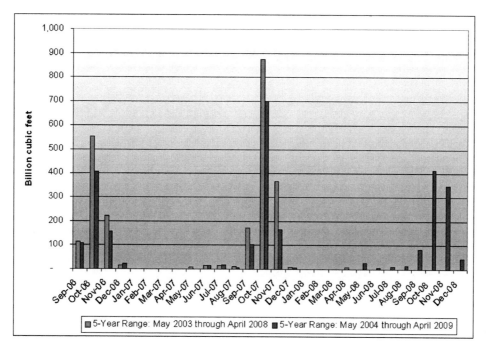

Source: Energy Information Administration (EIA), Natural Gas Division. Volumes derived from data reported on the EIA-191M, "Monthly Underground Gas Storage Report."

Conclusion

The sum of demonstrated monthly peak working gas storage across all active storage fields over a 60-month period, 3,889 Bcf, is a useful, albeit somewhat conservative, measure of aggregate industry capability to store gas. By this measure, storage capacity is 2.6 percent above last year's level. Aggregate working gas design capacity, an upper bound estimate of gas storage capacity, was 4,313 Bcf as of April 2009, 4.3 percent greater than in April 2008.

Order Code RL33212

CRS Report for Congress

Russian Oil and Gas Challenges

Updated June 20, 2007

Robert Pirog
Specialist in Energy Economics and Policy
Resources, Science, and Industry Division

Congressional
Research
Service

**Prepared for Members and
Committees of Congress**

Russian Oil and Gas Challenges

Summary

Russia is a major player in world energy markets. It has more proven natural gas reserves than any other country, is among the top ten in proven oil reserves, is the largest exporter of natural gas, the second largest oil exporter, and the third largest energy consumer. Energy exports have been a major driver of Russia's economic growth over the last five years, as Russian oil production has risen strongly and world oil prices have been very high. This type of growth has made the Russian economy dependent on oil and natural gas exports and vulnerable to fluctuations in oil prices.

The Russian government has moved to take control of the country's energy supplies. It broke up the previously large energy company Yukos and acquired its main oil production subsidiary. The Duma voted to give Gazprom, the state-controlled natural gas monopoly the exclusive right to export natural gas; Russia moved to limit participation by foreign companies in oil and gas production and Gazprom gained majority control of the Sakhalin energy projects. Russia has agreed with Germany to supply Germany and, eventually, the UK by building a natural gas pipeline under the Baltic Sea, bypassing Ukraine and Poland. In late 2006 and early 2007, Russia cut off and/or threatened to cut off gas or oil supplies going to and/or through Ukraine, Moldova, Georgia, and Belarus in the context of price and/or transit negotiations — actions that damaged its reputation as a reliable energy supplier. Russia's ability to maintain and expand its capacity to produce and to export energy faces difficulties. Russia's oil and gas fields are aging. Modern western energy technology has not been fully implemented. There is insufficient export capacity in the crude oil pipeline system controlled by Russia's state-owned pipeline monopoly, Transneft. And, there is insufficient investment capital for improving and expanding Russian oil and gas production and pipeline systems. A number of proposals would build new or expand existing Russian oil and natural gas export pipelines. Some are contentious, and while the Russian government is faced with a perceived need to expand its oil and gas export capacity, it also has limited resources. In mid-May 2007, Russia announced an agreement with Kazakhstan and Turkmenistan to build a natural gas pipeline feeding Central Asian natural gas into Russia's network of pipelines to Europe.

Given that the United States, as well as Russia, is a major energy producer and user, Russian energy trends and policies affect U.S. energy markets and economic welfare in general. An increase in Russia's energy production and its ability to export that energy could ease the supply situation in energy markets in the Atlantic and Pacific Basins. On the other hand, the Russian government's moves to take control of the country's energy supplies may reduce the amount of oil available. Possibly, U.S. suppliers of oil and gas field equipment and services could increase sales and investment in Russia. However, while the investment climate in Russia had been considered to be improving, it arguably is now worsening, as investors complain that it is inhospitable with respect to factors such as poor property rights protection, burdensome tax laws, inefficient government bureaucracy, and a tendency to limit foreign investor participation. This report, which will be updated as events warrant, was originally written by Bernard A. Gelb, CRS Specialist in Industry Economics, retired.

Contents

List of Figures

List of Tables

Russian Oil and Gas Challenges

The Russian Federation is a major player in world energy markets. It has more proven natural gas reserves than any other country and is among the top ten countries in proven oil reserves.[1] It is the world's largest exporter of natural gas, the second largest oil producer and exporter, and the third largest energy consumer. Given that the United States also is a major energy producer and user, Russian energy trends and policies affect U.S. energy markets and U.S. welfare in general.[2]

Oil and Gas Reserves and Production

Most of Russia's 60-74 billion barrels of proven oil reserves (**Table 1**) are located in Western Siberia, between the Ural Mountains and the Central Siberian Plateau. The ample endowment of this region made the Soviet Union a major world oil producer in the 1980s, reaching production of 12.5 million barrels per day (bbl/d) in 1988.[3] However, roughly 25% of Russia's oil reserves and 6% of its gas reserves are on Sakhalin Island in the far eastern region of the country, just north of Japan.

Russian oil production, which had begun to decline before the Soviet Union dissolved in 1991, fell more steeply afterward — to less than six million bbl/d in 1997 and 1998.[4] State-mandated production surges had accelerated depletion of the large Western Siberian fields and the Soviet central planning system collapsed. Russian oil output started to recover in 1999. Many analysts attribute this to privatization of the industry, which clarified incentives and shifted activity to less expensive production. Increases in world oil prices, application of technology that was standard practice in the West, and rejuvenation of old oil fields helped boost output. After-effects of the 1998 financial crisis and subsequent devaluation of the ruble may well have contributed. Russian crude oil production reached 9.0 million bbl/d in 2005 and rose slowly in 2006 to 9.2 million bbl/d.[5]

---

[1] *Oil and Gas Journal*, December 19, 2005. Estimates of proven oil and/or gas reserves by country can differ widely, depending partly on what types of resources are included. Thus, Russia's ranking of reserve holdings may differ among organizations that compile such data.

[2] For broader coverage of Russian political and economic issues, see CRS Report RL33407, *Russian Political, Economic, and Security Issues and U.S. Interests*, by Stuart D. Goldman.

[3] BP. *BP Statistical Review of World Energy*, June 1992. Data for Russia only are not available for 1988.

[4] BP. BP *Statistical Review of World Energy 1997*, June 1997.

[5] Energy Information Administration (EIA), *Country Analysis Briefs, Russia*, April 2007, [http://www.eia.doe.gov/emeu/cabs/Russia/Oil.html] viewed January 8, 2007.

426 703-739-3790 TCNNaturalGas.com

CRS-2

Figure 1. Russia

Source: Energy Information Administration. *Russia Country Analysis Brief*, February 2005 [http://www.eia.doe.gov/emeu/cabs/Region_ni.html], viewed December 3, 2005.

However, Russian crude oil production has been exceeding reserve growth, as "intensive deposit exploitation" combined with old technology is leaving 65% of the oil in the ground, according to the director of the Russian Natural Resources Ministry. Between 1994 and 2005, the increase in Russian oil extraction was about eight billion barrels greater than the increase in reserves. Reserves in Western Siberia, Russia's prime oil producing region, shrank by almost 23 billion barrels between 1993 and 2005.[6]

With about 1,700 trillion cubic feet (tcf), Russia has the world's largest natural gas reserves. In 2005, it was the world's largest natural gas producer and the world's largest exporter. However, production by its natural gas industry has increased very little in recent years, and are projected to continue to increase slowly.[7] Exports only have re-attained their level of the late 1990s.

Growth of Russia's natural gas sector has been impaired by ageing fields, near monopolistic domination over the industry by Gazprom (with substantial government holdings), state regulation, and insufficient export pipelines. Gazprom, Russia's 51%-owned state-run natural gas monopoly, holds more than one-fourth of the world's natural gas reserves, produces nearly 90% of Russia's natural gas, and operates the country's natural gas pipeline network. The company's tax payments account for around 25% of Russian federal tax revenues. Gazprom is heavily regulated, however. By law, it must supply the natural gas used to heat and power Russia's domestic market at government-regulated below-market prices.

---

[6] "Russian Companies Face Crude Crunch," *FSU Oil & Gas Monitor*, April 18, 2007, p. 12.

[7] EIA, *Country Analysis Briefs, Russia,* April 2007 [http://www.eia.doe.gov/emeu/cabs/Russia/Natural Gas.html], viewed May 15, 2007.

CRS-3

Table 1. Oil and Natural Gas Reserves and Production

Country or Region		Proved Reserves (billion bbls of oil/trillion cu. ft. of gas)		Production[a] (mil. bbls/day of oil/ trillion cu. ft. of gas
		BP (End of 2005)	O & G Journal (1/1/07)	BP (2005)
Russian Federation		74/1,688	60/1,680	9.6/21.1
Reference Areas	United States	29/193	22/204	6.8/18.9
	North Sea[b]	n.a./n.a.	13/161	5.9[c]/n.a.
	Saudi Arabia	264/244	260/240	11.0/2.5
	WORLD	1,200/6,348	1,317/6,183	80.0/97.5

Sources: *BP Statistical Review of World Energy June 2006*; Energy Information Administration, *Country Analysis Briefs*, North Sea, "Oil," August 2005 [http://www.eia. doe.gov/emeu/cabs/North_Sea/Oil.html]; Penwell Publishing Company, *Oil & Gas Journal*, December 18, 2006.

n.a. — not available.
a. Includes natural gas liquids.
b. Includes Denmark, Germany, Netherlands, Norway, and United Kingdom.
c. Energy Information Administration estimate.

Potential growth of both oil and natural gas production in Russia is limited by the lack of full introduction of the most modern western oil and gas exploration, development, and production technology. Also, oil companies, whose natural gas is largely flared, and independent gas companies will play an important role by increasing their share of Russian total gas production from 9 percent in 2005 to around 17 percent by 2010, according to the Energy Information Administration.[8] Their success, however, depends largely on gaining access to Gazprom's transmission system.

However, while the investment climate in Russia had been considered to be improving, arguably there are reasons to posit that it is now worsening. As discussed later, a reported proposal to tighten restrictions on the extent to which foreign companies can participate in Russian oil and natural gas production would seem to discourage investment. An unsettled judicial system provides limited and uncertain protection of property rights and rights of minority shareholders. Also, investors complain that the climate is inhospitable with respect to factors such as burdensome tax laws and inefficient government bureaucracy.

---

[8] EIA, *loc. cit.*

CRS-4

Exports

Energy exports have been a major driver of Russia's economic growth over the last five years, as Russian oil production has risen strongly and world oil and gas prices have been relatively high. This type of growth has made the Russian economy very dependent on oil and natural gas exports, and vulnerable to fluctuations in world oil prices. Based upon an International Monetary Fund study, a $1 per barrel increase in the price of Urals blend crude oil for a year results in a $3 billion increase in Russia's nominal Gross Domestic Product.[9]

Petroleum

Almost three fourths of Russian crude oil production is exported; the rest is refined in the country, with some refined products being exported. Of Russia's 6.7 million bbl/d of crude oil exports in 2004, two-thirds went to Belarus, Ukraine, Germany, Poland, and other destinations in Central and Eastern Europe. The remaining 2¼ million bbls/d went to maritime ports and was sold in world markets. Recent high oil prices have enabled as much as 40% of Russia's oil exports to be shipped via railroad and river barge routes — more costly modes than pipelines. Most of Russia's exports of refined petroleum products to Europe are distillate oil used for heating and by trucks.

Russia's capacity to export oil faces difficulties, however. One stems from the fact that crude oil exports via pipeline are under the exclusive jurisdiction of Russia's state-owned pipeline monopoly, Transneft. Bottlenecks in the Transneft system prevent its export capacity from meeting oil producers' export ambitions. Only about four million bbl/d can be transported in major trunk pipelines; the rest is shipped by rail and river routes. Most of what is transported via alternative transport modes is refined petroleum. The rail and river routes could become less economically viable if oil prices fall sufficiently. The Russian government and Transneft are striving to improve the export infrastructure.

Unless significant investment flows into improving the Russian oil pipeline system, non-pipeline transported exports probably will grow. For example, rail routes presently are the only way to transport Russian crude oil to East Asia. Russia is exporting about 200,000 bbl/d via rail to the northeast China cities of Harbin and Daqing and to central China via Mongolia. Since Yukos was the leading Russian exporter of oil to China, there was concern that the breakup of Yukos by the Russian government (see below under "Energy Policy") might affect rail exports to China. However, Lukoil now is the chief supplier of Russian oil to China.

U.S. markets could benefit from a proposed pipeline, which would carry crude oil from Russia's West Siberian Basin and Timan-Pechora basin westward to a

---

[9] Antonio Spilimbergo, *Measuring the Performance of Fiscal Policy in Russia,* IMF Working Paper WP/05/241, International Monetary Fund, December 2005, p. 7. CRS has applied the IMF sensitivity factor to Russia's Gross Domestic Product for 2005 at the official exchange rate, $740.7 billion, as given in *The World Fact Book* of the Central Intelligence Agency [https://www.cia.gov/cia/publications/factbook/geos/rs.html#Econ].

CRS-5

deepwater tanker terminal at Murmansk on the Barents Sea. This could allow for between 1.6 and 2.4 million bbl/d of Russian oil exports to reach the United States via tankers within only nine days, much faster than shipping from the Middle East or Africa. LNG facilities at Murmansk and Arkhangelsk (to the southeast) also have been suggested, possibly allowing for gas exports to American markets.

Oil transportation in the Black Sea region is in flux. Much of Russia's oil is shipped by tankers from the Black Sea to the Mediterranean and to Asia, much of it from the port of Novorossiysk. However, transit through the shallow and congested Bosporus Straits is limited by Turkey for environmental and safety reasons, limiting the effective capacity of pipelines to Novorossiysk.[10] Oil shipped through the Baku-Tbilisi-Ceyhan (BTC) pipeline is from Azerbaijan and potentially from Kazakhstan, posing competition to Russian oil.[11] Azerbaijan oil production has risen steeply in 2007 and, with ample BTC capacity, the Azerbaijan International Operating Company consortium has stopped using the Baku-Novorossiysk pipeline.[12]

Eastward, Russia faces competition for China's oil market from Kazakhstan, which, with China, completed in late 2005 the construction of a pipeline from Atasu in central Kazakhstan to Alaskankou on China's western border. Eventual capacity will be 190,000 bbl/d.[13]

Several consortia have begun producing and exporting oil (mainly to East Asia at present) from Sakhalin island (**Figure 4**). They also plan to export gas to the United States via pipelines to the Siberian mainland and then from liquefied natural gas (LNG) terminals.

Natural Gas

Historically, most of Russia's natural gas exports went to Eastern Europe and to customers in countries that were part of the Soviet Union. But, in the mid-1980s, Russia began trying to diversify its export options. Gazprom has shifted some of its exports to meet the rising demand of European Union countries, Turkey, Japan, and other Asian countries. For Gazprom to attain its long-term goal of increasing its

---

[10] See, for example, Yigal Schleifer, "Russian oil ships stuck in Bosporus strait traffic jam," *Christian Science Monitor*, January 25, 2005. Limited depth, heavy traffic, and environmental considerations have resulted in restrictions by Turkish authorities on travel through the Bosporus. The Baku to Ceyhan pipeline has an advantage in that Ceyhan, a Turkish Mediterranean Sea port, can handle very large carriers, while the Novorossisk and Supsa (in Georgia) ports are restricted to smaller tankers that can transit the Bosporus straits. Ceyhan can remain open all year, whereas Novorossiysk is closed up to two months.

[11] Kazakhstan and Azerbaijan have agreed to allow Kazakh oil to flow through the BTC pipeline. See "Kazakhstan Inks BTC Deal," *The Oil Daily*, June 19, 2006, p. 7.

[12] "AIOC: Oil Production Up, BTC Now Handling All Exports," *FSU Oil & Gas Monitor*, April 25, 2007.

[13] Martin Clark. "Beijing Triumphs with Inauguration of Kazakhstani Crude Pipe," *FSU Oil & Gas Monitor*, December 21, 2005.

CRS-6

European sales, it will have to boost production as well as secure more reliable export routes to the region.

Issues have arisen with the growth of Russia's gas sales to Europe. EU trade representatives have criticized Gazprom's abuse of its dominant market position and two-tiered pricing system, which charged higher prices on exports than on domestic sales. Russia agreed to grant domestic independent natural gas producers access to Gazprom's pipelines, and, in response to calls for fair pricing, the Russian government doubled prices to Russian industrial consumers. But the new price level still is less than half of the prices charged at the German and Ukrainian borders. To correct this, the Russian government has decided increase domestic gas prices gradually over the next few years with the aim of more than doubling them by 2011.[14]

As a major supplier of natural gas to European countries, and the dominant supplier to some, Russia has some ability to set prices.[15] For example, as described later in this report, Gazprom has threatened to cut off natural gas supplies to certain countries if they didn't agree to pay higher prices, and has actually done so. As the only seller of Russia's gas, Gazprom is Russia's largest earner of hard currency.

Russia's natural gas exports to Europe declined markedly in January 2006 as a result of severely cold weather in Russia that greatly increased Russian gas consumption, and also reduced oil exports somewhat. The cold conditions lasted through the month.[16]

As with oil, Russia faces competition for Asian gas markets from Kazakhstan, which, with China, is studying the feasibility of building a pipeline from the former to the latter.[17] Given the proximity of gas producers Turkmenistan and Uzbekistan to Kazakhstan, it is possible that their gas also would go to China via that route.

Energy Policy[18]

The Russian government has moved to take control of the country's energy resources, and to try to use that control to exert influence elsewhere. It is arguable that the push for control was partly the motivation behind the government's prosecution of Mikhail Khodorkovski, CEO of Yukos, who acquired state-owned assets during privatization and adopted open and "transparent" business practices

---

[14] Ed Reed, "Russian Gas Prices to Rise,"*FSU Oil & Gas Monitor*, December 6, 2006, p. 2.

[15] For detailed data on the extent of Europe's dependence on Russian natural gas, see CRS Report RS22562, *Russian Natural Gas: Regional Dependence*, by Bernard A. Gelb.

[16] "Cold spell cuts Russian gas to Europe," *Financial Times*, FT.com, January 18, 2006; "Cold weather cutting Russian gas exports," *Oil & Gas Journal online*, January 23, 2006.

[17] "Kazakhstan, China Consider Gas Pipeline Construction," *FSU Oil & Gas Monitor*, December 7, 2005.

[18] Much of the material in this section is from CRS Report RL33407 and CRS Report RL32466, *Rising Energy Competition and Energy Security in Northeast Asia: Issues for U.S. Policy*, by Emma Chanlett-Avery.

CRS-7

while transforming Yukos into a major global energy company. Yukos is being broken up, with its principal assets being sold off to meet alleged tax debts. Yuganskneftegaz, Yukos' main oil production subsidiary, was sold at a state-run auction to the Baikal Finans Group (previously unheard of), the sole bidder, for $9.4 billion, about half its market value according to western industry specialists. That group soon after sold the unit to Rosneft, the state oil company.[19] Another government takeover followed when Gazprom bought 75% of Sibneft — Russia's fifth largest oil company.[20] Yukos' creditors voted to liquidate the company on July 25, 2006; and the Moscow arbitration court confirmed the vote.[21] Portions of Yukos have been sold off piecemeal since then.

A possible change to a less aggressive policy was hinted at when President Putin announced on January 31, 2006, that Russia will not seek control of more oil companies.[22] However, the Duma voted to give Gazprom the exclusive right to export natural gas,[23] and, as described below, Russia moved to limit participation by foreign companies in oil and gas production and Gazprom gained majority control of the Sakhalin energy projects.

In Eastern Europe, Russian firms with close links to the Russian government have used leverage to buy energy companies to gain control over energy supply. For example, Yukos obtained majority control of a Lithuanian refinery (the only one in the Baltic states) by slowing oil supply to it, and buying it at a reduced price. The Transneft pipeline monopoly diverted the flow of oil shipments to Primorsk, a Russian port, stopping flow to the Latvian port of Ventspils. Some see Transneft's action as a move to obtain control of the firm that operates the Ventspils terminal.[24] Also, Transneft refused to finalize an agreement to transport Kazakhstani oil to Lithuania, undermining Kazakhstan's KazMunaiGaz's attempt to buy the refinery. After several developments, an agreement was reached for Yukos to sell the refinery to a Polish firm.[25]

---

[19] It subsequently was revealed that Baikal Finans was a group of Kremlin insiders headed by Igor Sechin, Deputy Head of the Presidential Administration and close associate of President Putin. Sechin has been Chairman of Rosneft's board of directors since July 2004. The de-facto nationalization of Yuganskneftegaz was declared "the fraud of the year" by Andrei Illarionov, President Putin's chief economic advisor. [http://www.mosnews.com/money/2004//12/28//illarionov.shtml].

[20] "New takeover to make Russia's giant Gazprom one of the world's largest oil and gas companies," *Pravda*, October 1, 2005 [http://english.pravda.ru/russia/economics/01-10-2005/8997-gazprom-0] viewed February 6, 2006.

[21] "Yukos: The Final Curtain," *FSU Oil & Gas Monitor,* 26 July 2006, p. 5; Ben Aris. "Death of Yukos," *FSU Oil & Gas Monitor*, August 2, 2006, p. 4.

[22] "Putin: Private Oil Companies to Remain Private," *FSU Oil & Gas Monitor,* February 1, 2006.

[23] Tobias Buck and Neil Buckley, "Russian Parliament vote Backs Gazprom Export Monopoly," *Financial Times,* June 16, 2006, p. 8.

[24] Ariel Cohen, "Don't Punish Latvia," *Washington Times*, May 5, 2003.

[25] "Poland's PKN Buys Lithuania Refinery for $2.6 Billion," *Reuters*, May 26, 2006.

CRS-8

Another example of Russia's efforts to maintain or increase control over energy supplies is the routing of new and planned export pipelines. For example, Russia has agreed with Germany, with the support of the United Kingdom (UK), to supply Germany and, eventually, the UK directly by building a natural gas pipeline under the Baltic Sea, thus bypassing Ukraine and Poland. In late January 2006, Gazprom was negotiating with Uzbekistan to obtain control of three of that country's gas fields.[26] Russia also is hoping to participate in the venture that is constructing a gas pipeline between Turkey and Greece.[27]

Several actions in recent years by Russia or its economic agents have been characterized by some as perhaps overaggressive. In 2005, Gazprom wanted to raise Ukraine's price, originally a fraction of the world market price in return for its transmission of the gas to the market level. (A large share of Russia's natural gas exports to Western Europe pass through Ukraine and Belarus, which withdraw a certain amount of gas from the pipelines for its own use.) When negotiations failed, Gazprom reduced gas pressure and flow through the Ukrainian network on January 1, 2006. Ukraine compensated by using some gas intended for West Europe. Gazprom restored supply very shortly after, when those countries complained and pointed out that Russia was risking its reputation as a reliable energy supplier.[28] The dispute was resolved temporarily on January 4, 2006. Gazprom would sell gas at its asking price to a trading company that would mix Russian gas with less expensive gas from Central Asia and sell the mixture to Ukraine at the higher price that Ukraine had indicated it was willing to pay, but much lower than Gazprom's price. Gazprom would pay cash instead of gas in kind to Ukraine's pipeline business for increased transit fees.[29] One report stated that Gazprom wanted to gain at least some ownership of Ukraine's pipeline system.[30, 31]

Later in January 2006, through no fault of Russia, the apparent reliability of its natural gas supplies suffered further when severely cold weather raised Russian gas

---

[26] Vladimir Kovalev. "Gazprom Secures Uzbekistan Gas through Politics and Pipelines," *FSU Oil & Gas Monitor*, January 23, 2006.

[27] Kerin Hope. "Russia to discuss Gazprom role in Aegean pipeline," *FT.com*, February 5, 2006. [http://search.ft.com/search/quickSearch_Run.html], viewed February 6, 2006.

[28] "Russia Turns up the Gas," *Guardian Weekly*, December 23, 2005-January 5, 2006, p. 41; Peter Finn. "Russia Reverses Itself on Gas Cuts," *The Washington Post*, January 3, 2006, p. A12; Andrew E. Kramer. "Russia Restores Most of Gas Cut to Ukraine Line," *The New York Times*, January 3, 2006. [http://www.nytimes.com/2006/01/03/international/europe/03ukraine.html?pagewanted=print], viewed January 3, 2006.

[29] Graeme Smith. "Russia, Ukraine settle gas dispute," GlobeandMail.com, January 5, 2006 [http://www.theglobeandmail.com/international], type "Russia" in search box, viewed January 5, 2006; Peter Finn. "Russia and Ukraine Reach Deal on Gas, Ending Dispute," *The Washington Post*, January 5, 2006, p. A12; Mark Smedley and Mitchell Ritchie. "Russia, Ukraine Settle Gas Pricing Dispute", *Oil Daily*, January 5, 2006, p. 1.

[30] *Oil Daily*, January 5, 2006.

[31] For fuller discussion and analysis of the Russia-Ukraine gas dispute, see CRS Report RS22378, *Russia's Cutoff of Natural Gas to Ukraine: Context and Implications*, by Jim Nichol, Steven Woehrel, and Bernard A. Gelb.

CRS-9

for gas and cut exports below contracted volumes. After a few temporary Russia-Ukraine gas price agreements, a deal was reached in October 2006 in which Ukraine pays a moderate price for gas in return for political and other favors.[32]

In other actions, Russia cut off gas to Moldova in an early January 2006 price dispute. The countries reached an interim agreement after Moldova had been without Russian gas for two weeks.[33] In late 2006, Gazprom appeared to be preparing to cut off gas supplies to Belarus and Georgia unless they agreed to pay much higher prices in 2007. Reportedly, Georgia soon "agreed" to a doubling of Gazprom's prices.[34] Belarus and Gazprom signed a five-year contract on January 1, 2007, providing that Belarus will pay increasingly more for gas (starting at more than twice the old price) and Gazprom will purchase 50% of Belarus' gas pipeline network.[35] The next week, Russia shut off the flow of crude oil to and through Belarus following its announcement of an oil export tax and Belarus' (a) imposition of a customs duty on oil transiting Belarus to other export markets, and (b) taking some of the oil flow as payment of the customs duty.[36] Destination countries had adequate inventory to cope in the short run, but criticized the failure to warn that a shut-off was possible.[37] Oil began flowing again late on January 10, 2007, after Belarus' lifting of the transit duty helped the countries reach a tentative agreement.[38]

The Moldova, Georgia, and Belarus incidents have heightened concern about Russia's reliability and encouraged investigations of non-Russian energy sources by several former Soviet Union as well as West European countries to explore non-Russian sources of energy.

Russia initially opposed western investment in Caspian Sea energy projects, insisted that oil from the region be transported through Russian territory to Black Sea ports, and argued for equal sharing of Caspian Sea oil and gas. This attitude partly

---

[32] "Ukraine Secures Gas Supplies for Questionable Political Price," *FSU Oil & Gas Monitor,* November 1, 2006, p. 7. *Gas Monitor,* 5 July 2006.

[33] Neil Buckley and Sarah Laitner. "Moldova reaches gas deal with Gazprom," *FT.com,* January 17, 2006. [http://search.ft.com/search/quickSearch_Run.html] viewed February 6, 2006.

[34] Information Division, OAO Gazprom, "Gazprom Seals Contracts to Supply Gas to Georgia in 2007" (press release), December 22, 2006; "Georgia 'agrees (to) Russia gas bill,'" BBC News, December 22, 2006, at [http://newsvote.bbc.co.uk/mpapps/pagetools/print/news.bbc.co.uk/2/hi/business/6203721.stm], viewed January 11, 2007;

[35] Alan Cullison, "Belarus Yields to Russia," *The Wall Street Journal,* January 2, 2007, p. A4; "Belarus, Russian Firm Sign 5-Year Deal for Gas," *The Washington Post,* January 2, 2007, p. A10.

[36] "Russian Oil Disruption Rattles European Commission, Germany," *Oil Daily,* January 9, 2007, p. 2; Guy Chazen, Gregory L White, and Marc Champion, "Russian Oil Cutoff Rouses Europe's Doubt," *The Wall Street Journal,* January 9, 2007, p. A3.

[37] Gregory L. White and Guy Chazan, "Oil Spat deepens Worry Over Russia's Reliability,"

[38] "Russia, Belarus End Druzhba Spat," *Oil Daily,* January 11, 2007, p. 1; Peter Finn, "Russia-belarus Standoff Over Oil Ends, Clearing Way for Accord," *The Washington Post,* January 11, 2007.

434 703-739-3790 TCNNaturalGas.com

CRS-10

reflected the extensive energy ties between Russia and Central Asian countries stemming from the numerous transportation routes from that area through Russia. But Russia has become more agreeable, and even cooperative with, western projects; and it has signed an agreement with Azerbaijan and Kazakhstan on Caspian seabed borders essentially based upon shore mileage.

In East Asia, China, Japan, and South Korea, are trying to gain access to the largely undeveloped energy resources of eastern Siberia, as those countries strive to meet their increasing energy needs while reducing dependence on the Middle East. China and Japan appear to be engaged in a bidding war over Russian projects and are contesting access to Russian rival oil pipeline routes.

Many observers believe that Russia tried to use potential participation by American firms in development of the large Shtokmanovskoye gas field as leverage in the negotiations to gain entry into the World Trade Organization (WTO).[39] Ultimately, Russia decided to rule out foreign equity participation in developing Shtokmanovskoye, but will allow foreign company involvement as contractors and owners of the operating company.[40, 41] Another recent development, the July 2006 initial public offering (IPO) in which 13-14% of state-owned oil company Rosneft was sold, has been seen by some as an attempt by Russia to attract investments by major oil companies. Presumably, the latter hope that investing in the Rosneft IPO would gain them easier access to participation in Russian oil and gas projects.[42, 43]

Another instance of Russian moves to gain control of its energy resources is Gazprom's takeover of majority interest in the Sakhalin Energy Investment Company (SEIC) on December 21, 2006, from Royal Dutch Shell. SEIC will remain the operator of the Sakhalin II project.[44] The current SEIC partners will each dilute their stakes by 50% Shell will retain a 27.5% stake, with Mitsui and Mitsubishi holding 12.5% and 10% stakes, respectively. In another Sakhalin development, the Russian government effectively rewrote the production sharing agreement for Sakhalin-II,

---

[39] Ed Reed, Shtokmnanovskoye: the Wait Continues," *NewsBase CIS Oil & Gas Special Report,* July 2006; "G8 Adopts Energy Plan; Shtokman Slipping Away from U.S. Firms?" *Oil Daily,* July 18, 2006; "Russian State Interference" and "Test Drilling on Shtokmanovskoye Begins," *FSU Oil & Gas Monitor,* 26 July 2006.

[40] "Shtokmanovskoye: Door Opens," *FSU Oil & Gas Monitor,* December 13, 2006, p. 8.

[41] "Gazprom Rethinks Shtokmanovskoye Involvement," *FSU Oil & Gas Monitor,* April 11, 2007, p. 6.

[42] Steven Mufson, "Russian Oil Firm IPO Ends Early," *The Washington Post,* July 13, 2006, p. D5; Gregory L. White and Alistair MacDonald, "Demand Allows Rosneft to Price IPO at High End," *The Wall Street Journal,* July 14, 2006, p. C1.

[43] Selling was stopped when 13-14% of the stock had been sold, yielding about $10.4 billion. Joanna Chung and Arkady Ostrovsky, "Rosneft IPO fails to attract big players," *Financial Times,* July 15-16, 2006, p. 9.

[44] Sakhalin Energy, "Gazprom, Shell, Mitsui, Mitsubishi Sign Sakhalin II Protocol," at [http://www.sakhalinenergy.com/en/] viewed January 11, 2007; Ed Reed, "Sakhalin Smash and Grab," *FSU Oil & Gas Monitor,* January 10, 2007, p. 2.

CRS-11

providing for a large annual dividend to Russia before the project's shareholders had recovered their capital expenditures as stipulated in the original agreement.[45]

Given foreign companies' technological capabilities and Russia's need for the most modern oil and gas extraction technology, a reported proposal to tighten restrictions on the extent to which foreign oil companies can participate in Russian oil and natural gas production and other ventures is potentially significant and perhaps a move against Russia's own interests. Foreign companies or companies with 50% foreign participation would not be allowed to develop fields with more than 513 million barrels of oil and 1.77 billion cubic feet of natural gas.[46]

Major Proposed New or Expanded Pipelines[47]

Because Russia's export facilities have limitations of location and size, there are a number of proposals to build new or to expand existing Russian oil and natural gas export pipelines and related facilities. Some proposals are contentious and, while the Russian government perceives a need to expand its oil and gas export capacity, it has limited resources. Several selected proposals are discussed below.

With a 1.2-1.4 million bbl/d capacity, the 2,500-mile Druzhba line is the largest of Russia's oil pipelines to Europe. It begins in southern Russia, near Kazakhstan, where it collects oil from the Urals and the Caspian Sea. In Belarus, it forks at Mozyr, from which one branch runs through Belarus, Poland, and Germany; and the other through Belarus, Ukraine, Slovakia, the Czech Republic, and Hungary (**Figure 2**). Work has begun to increase capacity between Belarus and Poland. An extension to Wilhelmshaven (Germany) would reduce Baltic Sea tanker traffic and allow Russia to export oil to the United States via Germany.

---

[45] "Moscow to Receive Sakhalin Dividends Ahead of Schedule," *FSU Oil & Gas Monitor*, May 2, 2007, p. 11.

[46] Arkady Ostrofsky, "Russia may tighten foreign oil groups' access to reserves," Financial Times, June 14, 2006, p. 8.

[47] Much of the discussion of Russian oil and gas pipelines is taken from the *Russia Country Analysis Brief* of February 2005 and April 2007, prepared by the Energy Information Administration.

CRS-12

Figure 2. Druzhba and Adria Oil Pipelines

Source: Energy Information Administration. *Russia Country Analysis Brief.*

The Baltic Pipeline System (BPS) carries crude oil from Russia's West Siberian and Tyumen-Pechora oil provinces westward to the newly completed port of Primorsk on the Russian Gulf of Finland (**Figure 3**). Throughput capacity at Primorsk has been raised to around one million bbl/d, and, pending government approval, will be expanded to 1.2 million bbl/d. The BPS gives Russia a direct outlet to northern European markets, reducing dependence on routes through the Baltic countries. The re-routing of Russian crude through the BPS has incurred considerable cost to those countries. Russian authorities have stated that precedence will be given to sea ports in which Russia has a stake over foreign ones. But the waterways through which tankers leaving from Primorsk and most other Russian export ports must transit limit tanker size, and therefore the price competitiveness of their cargoes.

Figure 3. Selected Northwestern Oil Pipelines

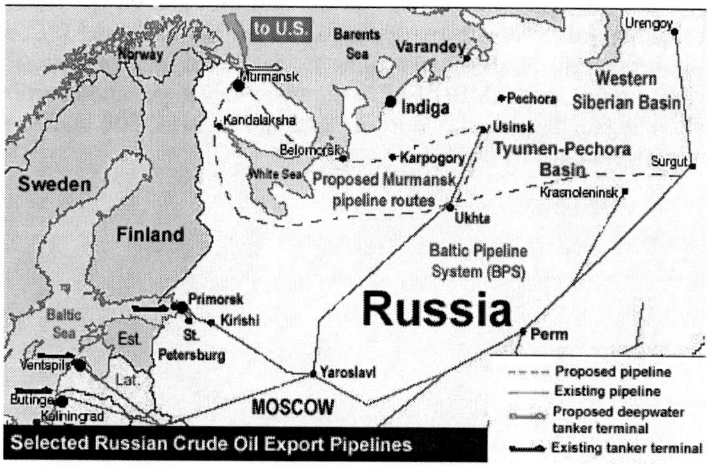

Source: Energy Information Administration. *Russia Country Analysis Brief.*

CRS-13

Proposed lines would carry oil from Russia's West Siberian and Tyumen-Pechora basins west and north to a deepwater terminal at Murmansk or Indiga on the Barents Sea (**Figure 3**). This would enable 1.6-2.4 million bbl/d of Russian oil to reach the United States via tankers in only nine days, much quicker than from the Middle East or Africa. Liquefied natural gas facilities at Murmansk and Arkhangelsk also have been suggested, possibly allowing for gas exports to American markets. The Indiga route would be closer to the Tyumen-Pechora oil fields and shorter; also Transneft's CEO has said that the Murmansk project is not economically feasible. However, in contrast with Murmansk, the port of Indiga ices over during the winter, a disadvantage that may be reduced or eliminated if Arctic ice melting continues.

The Adria oil pipeline runs between Croatia's Adriatic Sea port of Omisalj and Hungary (**Figure 2**). Originally designed to load Middle Eastern oil at Omisalj and pipe it northward to Yugoslavia and then to Hungary, the pipeline's operators and transit states have been considering reversing the flow — a relatively simple step — giving Russia a new export outlet on the Adriatic Sea. Connecting the pipeline to Russia's Southern Druzhba system requires the agreement of Russia, Belarus, Ukraine, Slovakia, Hungary, and Croatia. These countries signed a preliminary agreement on the project in December 2002; however, negotiations over the details (including tariffs and environmental issues) have been slow. Some analysts expect that the Adria pipeline could transport about 100,000 bbl/d of Russian crude oil in the first year of reversal, with an ultimate capacity of about 300,000 bbl/d.

A trans-Balkan Oil Pipeline is being developed as an alternative to bringing oil originating in Southern Russia and the Caspian region to market through the Bosporus. Passage of oil cargoes through the Turkish Straits could be disrupted due to weather or tanker and other cargo congestion. The trans-Balkan pipeline would have a capacity of 750,000 bbl/d. The pipeline would be supplied by oil delivered to the Black Sea through existing pipelines. The oil would then be shipped across the Black Sea by tanker from the Russian ports of Novorossiysk and Tuapse, or the Georgian ports of Supsa and Batumi, to the port of Bourgas in Bulgaria; see **Figure 4**. The oil would then enter the proposed 570-mile pipeline across Bulgaria, Macedonia, and Albania, and terminate at the port of Vlore on the Adriatic Sea, where it could be loaded on tankers for transit to the European and U.S. markets. The governments of all three Balkan nations involved in the proposed pipeline have approved the project, and AMBO LLC, the project developer and coordinator, is seeking financing for the project. Construction could begin in 2008, and the pipeline may become operational by 2011.[48]

---

[48] *Bulgaria Ratifies Trans-Balkan Pipeline*, Boston.com World News, May 31, 2007, available at [http://www.boston.com/news].

CRS-14

Figure 4. Proposed Bosporus Bypass Options

Source: Energy Information Administration, *Russia Country Analysis Brief.*

The prospective large Chinese market for oil has led to serious consideration of building a pipeline from the Russian city of Taishet (northwest of Angarsk) to Nakhodka (near the Sea of Japan) or to Daqing, China (see **Figure 5**). Both routes pass close to Lake Baikal — a site with environment-related obstacles. The Nakhodka route, which is longer, would provide a new Pacific port from which Russian oil could be shipped by tanker to Japan and other Asian markets and possibly to North America. Japan has offered $5 billion to finance construction and $2 billion for oil field development.[49] The Daqing option is favored by China, although China could obtain exports via the Nakhodka route. China has pledged to invest US$12 billion in Russia's infrastructure and energy sector by 2020.[50] From Russia's point of view, the Nakhoda route would offer access to multiple markets, whereas a terminus at Daqing would give China control. However, Russia's environmental

---

[49] Mark Katz. "Don't dismiss China's Daqing oil pipeline," *Asia Times Online*, October 1, 2004.

[50] Sergei Blagov, "China's Russian pipe dream," *Asia Times OnLine*, September 28, 2004.

CRS-15

safety supervisory body rejected the shorter route because it would pass too close to Lake Baikal, a United Nations world heritage site.[51]

Figure 5. Proposed Far East Oil Pipelines

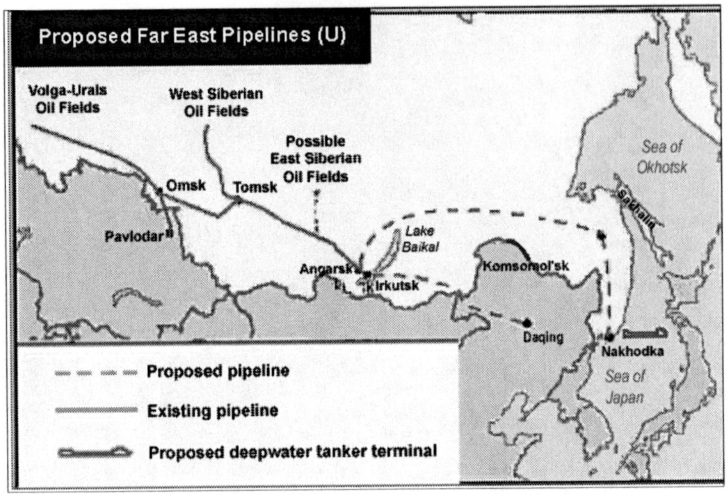

Source: Energy Information Administration, *Russia Country Analysis Brief.*

The 750-mile Blue Stream natural gas pipeline, which has a design capacity of 565 billion cubic feet annually, connects the Russian system to Turkey. Natural gas began flowing through the pipeline, 246 miles of which is underneath the Black Sea, in December 2002. There are discussions In March 2003, Turkey halted deliveries, invoking a contract clause allowing either party to stop deliveries for six months. Turkish leaders reportedly were unhappy with the price structure.[52] Other possible factors include Turkey's commitment to receive more gas than its near term domestic consumption and agreements to transship gas to other countries. An agreement was reached in November 2003 and the flow resumed in December 2003.

The Yamal-Europe I pipeline (unidentified northern route in Russia in **Figure 6**) carries 1 tcf of gas from Russia to Poland and Germany via Belarus. One proposal would expand it by another tcf per year with the addition of a second branch — Yamal-Europe II. However, Poland wants a route entirely through its own country and then to Germany (Yamal-Europe on the map), while Gazprom is seeking a route via southeastern Poland and Slovakia (Yamal II).

---

[51] Eric Watkins. "Russia nixes East Siberia pipeline route," *Oil & Gas Journal Daily Update*, February 6, 2006 [http://ogj.pennet.com/articles/article_display.cfm?article_id= 247386], viewed February 7, 2006.

[52] Mevlut Katik. "Blue Stream's Pipeline's Future in Doubt Amid Russian Turkish Pricing Dispute," Business & Economics, June 2, 2003. Eurasianet.org [http://www.eurasianet.org/ departments/business/articles/eav060203a_pr.shtml], viewed December 18, 2005.

CRS-16

Figure 6. Natural Gas Pipelines to Europe

Existing and Planned Natural Gas Pipelines to Europe

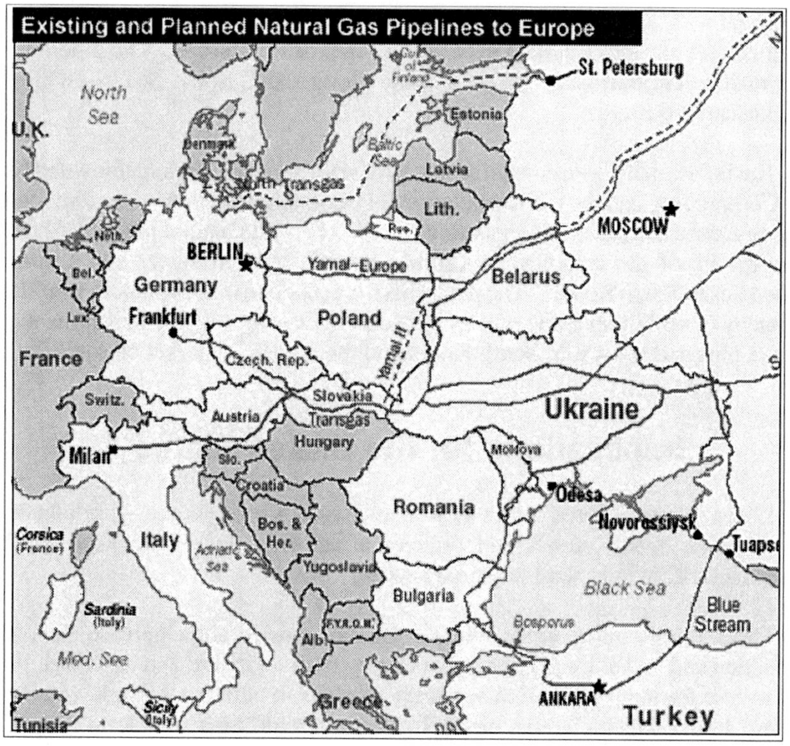

Source: Energy Information Administration, *Russia Country Analysis Brief.*

A North Trans-Gas pipeline, or North European Gas Pipeline (NEGP), extending over 2,000 miles from Russia through the Gulf of Finland to Denmark and, ultimately, to the United Kingdom, via the Baltic and North Seas was proposed in June 2003 by Russia and the United Kingdom.[53] Gazprom and Germany's BASF and E.ON agreed on September 8, 2005, to set up a joint venture to build the pipeline. Originating in the St. Petersburg region, about 700 miles of the pipeline is to pass under the Baltic Sea. The first leg of the pipeline, which is under construction, is scheduled to come on stream in 2010.[54] Russia sees a gain by no longer having to negotiate transit fees with intermediary countries or pay them in natural gas. The pipeline agreement is criticized by some Europeans who object to the fact that it was reached without consultation with them, and see the pipeline as an unfair bypass with political motivation and environmental risk. Perhaps to supplement or substitute for the NEGP, Gazprom is planning to build an LNG plant in the St. Petersburg area.

---

[53] Mark A. Smith. *The Russian, German, and Polish Triangle*, Russian Series 05/61, Conflict Studies Research Centre, October 2005, p. 2.

[54] Ria Novosti. "Factbox: North European Gas Pipeline," December 9, 2005 [http://en.rian.ru/russia/20051209/42408722.html], viewed December 28, 2005. BASF is mainly a chemical manufacturer, but has a subsidiary that explores for and produces oil and natural gas. E.ON is an electric power generator and distributor and a distributor of natural gas.

CRS-17

In a move that threatens to send substantial quantities of Central Asian natural gas through Russia to European markets, Russia announced in mid-May 2007 an agreement with Kazakhstan and Turkmenistan to build a pipeline feeding Central Asian natural gas into Russia's network of pipelines to Europe. The pipeline is to send mainly Turkmenistan gas in a route along the Caspian Sea coast through Kazakhstan into Russia.[55]

Rusia Petroleum — a consortium of TNK-BP, South Korea's state-owned Korea Gas Corporation, and the Chinese National Petroleum Company — has announced plans to construct a pipeline connecting Russia's Kovykta natural gas field (2 trillion cubic meters of gas reserves) to China's northeastern provinces and across the Yellow Sea to South Korea.[56] The plan calls for a pipeline that ultimately would have a capacity of 40 billion cubic meters per year, delivering roughly half of its natural gas to China and the rest to South Korea and the domestic market en route.[57]

Implications for the United States[58]

Given that the United States as well as Russia is a major energy producer and user, Russian energy trends and policies affect U.S. energy markets and U.S. economic welfare in general in a broad sense.

Other things being equal, should Russia considerably increase its energy production and its ability to export that energy both westward and eastward, it may tend to ease the supply situation in energy markets in both the Atlantic and Pacific Basins. In the Atlantic arena, more Russian oil could be available to the United States. In the Pacific area, there would tend to be more supply available to countries trying to assure themselves energy supplies, such as China and Japan. This may ease the global competition for Persian Gulf oil.

On the other hand, the Russian government's moves to take control of the country's energy supplies noted earlier may have the effect of making less oil available on the world market. This could occur if Russia's tendency to limit foreign company involvement in oil and gas development limits the introduction of the most modern technology, or if Russia intentionally limits energy development and production.

Possibly as important as Russian oil and gas industry developments is the associated potential for U.S. suppliers of oil and gas field equipment and services to

---

[55] "Caspian Pipeline Deal Increases Russia's Clout," *The Wall Street Journal*, May 14, 2007, p. A6.

[56] TNK-BP. "Kovykta Project," [http://www.tnk-bp.com/operations/exploration-production/projects/kovykta], viewed December 28, 2005.

[57] Selig S. Harrison. "Gas and Geopolitics in Northeast Asia," *World Policy Journal*, Winter 2002/2003, pp. 22-36.

[58] For more discussion and analysis of U.S.-Russian economic relations, see CRS Report RS21123, *Permanent Normal Trade Relations (PNTR) Status for Russia and U.S.-Russian Economic Ties*, by William H. Cooper.

442 703-739-3790 TCNNaturalGas.com

CRS-18

increase their sales in Russia. As noted above, potential growth of both oil and natural gas production in Russia is limited by the lack of full introduction of the most modern western oil and gas exploration, development, and production technology. Although U.S.-Russian economic relations have expanded since the collapse of the Soviet Union, as successive Russian leaders have been dismantling the central economic planning system, including the liberalization of foreign trade and investment, the flow of trade and investment remains very low. U.S. suppliers of oil and gas field equipment had established a modest beachhead in Russia. However, whereas U.S. exports of oil and gas field machinery and equipment accounted for 14% of U.S. all goods exports to Russia in 2002, they accounted for only 7% in the first 11 months of 2006.

Similar to U.S. trade with Russia, U.S. investments there, especially direct investments, have increased since the dissolution of the Soviet Union, but the levels are far below their expected potential. Even so, as of September 30, 2006, the United States was Russia's third largest source of foreign direct investment, with investments largely concentrated in the transportation, energy, communications, and engineering sectors.[59]

In this context, however, Russian economic policies and regulations have been a source of concerns. The United States and the U.S. business community have asserted that structural problems and inefficient government regulations and policies have been a major cause of the low levels of trade and investment with the United States. While they consider the climate to be improving, potential investors complain that the climate for investment in Russia remains inhospitable. They point to lack of effective intellectual property rights protection, burdensome tax laws, jurisdictional conflicts among Russian federal, regional and local governments, inefficient and corrupt government bureaucracy, and the lack of a market-friendly commercial code as impediments to trade and foreign investments. And, more specifically, the forced breakup of Yukos has clouded prospects for private investment.

In addition, Russian energy trends and policies have possible implications for U.S. energy security. In its oversight role, Congress may have an interest in Russia's large role as a supplier to world energy markets in general, in Russia's role as a possible major exporter of energy to the United States, and in the changed patterns of world energy flows that could result from the completion of new Russian oil and natural gas export pipelines and related facilities or the expansion of existing export pipelines and related facilities.

---

[59] CRS Report RS21123, *Permanent Normal Trade Relations (PNTR) Status for Russia and U.S.-Russian Economic Ties*, by William H. Cooper.

http://tonto.eia.doe.gov/energy_in_brief/liquefied_natural_gas_lng.cfm

Energy Information Administration
Official Energy Statistics from the U.S. Government

Energy in Brief — *What everyone should know about energy*

Last Updated: December 11, 2009

What role does liquefied natural gas (LNG) play as an energy source for the United States?

On an annual basis from 2003 to 2008, the United States imported between 13% and 16% of its natural gas requirements. Most of these imports were in gaseous form delivered by pipeline from Canada. However, natural gas imports have also come in liquid form from overseas. Between 1% and 3% of U.S. demand for natural gas was met by LNG from 2003 to 2008.

U.S. LNG import capacity has increased sharply.

U.S. Capacity to Receive LNG Imports, 2000-2009 (Billion Cubic Feet per Day)

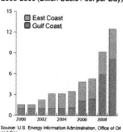

Source: U.S. Energy Information Administration, Office of Oil and Gas

See larger graph on next page.

Trinidad and Tobago provided 75% of U.S. LNG imports in 2008.

Sources of LNG to the United States, 2008 (Percent)

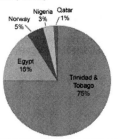

Source: U.S. Energy Information Administration, Office of Oil and Gas, based on data from the Office of Fossil Energy, U.S. Department of Energy.

See larger graph on next page.

What Is LNG?

LNG is natural gas that has been cooled to about minus 260 degrees Fahrenheit for shipment and/or storage as a liquid. The volume of the gas in its liquid state is about 600 times less than in its gaseous form. In this compact form, natural gas can be shipped in special tankers to receiving terminals in the United States and other importing countries. At these terminals, the LNG is returned to a gaseous form and transported by pipeline to distribution companies, industrial consumers, and power plants.

Did You Know?

Even though the United States is primarily an importer of LNG, it is also an exporter. The only LNG export facility, and the oldest active LNG marine terminal in the United States, is located in Kenai, Alaska. The terminal has exported small volumes of LNG to Japan almost continuously since beginning operations in 1969.

Historically, liquefying natural gas provided a means of moving it long distances where pipeline transport was not feasible, allowing access to natural gas from regions with vast production potential that were too distant from end-use markets to be connected by pipeline. Currently, the worldwide LNG industry has grown such that distance is only one of many factors that may influence the development of an LNG project.

U.S. LNG Import Capacity Is Expanding

LNG imports to the United States were generally not viewed as competitive with domestic supplies of natural gas and pipeline imports from Canada through the 1980s and 1990s, resulting in low levels of LNG imports during that time period. That perception began to change by the early 2000s when domestic gas production experienced a period of decline and U.S. natural gas prices rose dramatically. Now, not only have two U.S. LNG import terminals that were idled when gas prices fell in the early 1980s been reopened, but five new terminals have been constructed since 2005.

LNG import capacity is expected to be more than six times greater in 2009 than it was at the beginning of the decade. This increase in LNG receiving capacity provides the potential for growing U.S. LNG imports in coming years. Annual U.S. LNG imports are projected to exceed 1 trillion cubic feet by 2015.[1] However, LNG imports still currently account for a small portion of natural gas requirements in the United States, at just 1.5% in 2008.

Growth in LNG imports to the United States has been uneven in recent years, with substantial changes in year-over-year imports as a result of suppliers' decisions to either bring spare cargos to the United States or to divert cargos to countries where prices may be higher. In 2007, low natural gas prices in several key LNG-consuming countries outside of North America resulted in a surplus in world supplies of LNG and an influx of cargos to the North American market, which is by far the largest regional natural gas market in the world. When prices outside of North America increased in 2008, U.S. LNG imports declined 54% from the 2007 high of 771 billion cubic feet to 352 billion cubic feet (Bcf).

During periods of high global demand for LNG, U.S. prices are generally not competitive with prices offered by buyers in other countries. This is because countries like Japan and South Korea, the two largest LNG-consuming countries in the world, are almost entirely dependent on LNG to meet their substantial natural gas demand. These countries often link LNG prices directly to the price of crude oil, which on an energy-equivalent basis has recently been significantly more expensive than natural gas in North America. The final destination for LNG supplies directed toward the United States and Europe (often referred to as Atlantic Basin trade) is largely determined by the price of natural gas in those competing markets. However, other factors such as existing contracts (some with prices linked to oil prices), available regasification capacity, and available storage also play a role.

Where Do U.S. LNG Imports Come From?

Deliveries of LNG from Trinidad and Tobago, in the southern Caribbean Sea, account for the majority of LNG imports to the United States. The Atlantic LNG facility located in Point Fortin, Trinidad and Tobago, now produces nearly 700 Bcf a year. In recent years, several African countries, including Egypt, Equatorial Guinea, and Nigeria, have also supplied LNG to the United States. Algeria, the African country that until 1995 was the sole supplier of LNG to the United States, has also shipped LNG to the United States in recent years, but on an infrequent basis.

Supplies also have started to arrive from the Snohvit LNG project in Norway. The Snohvit project is the first LNG export project in Western Europe. In the Middle East, Qatar, the largest LNG exporter in the world, has infrequently delivered LNG to the United States. As Qatar continues to expand its production capacity in the next couple of years, regular deliveries to the United States are expected to occur. In 2009, Russia and Yemen for the first time will become LNG exporters. However, supplies from these countries are not expected to reach the United States on a regular basis.

Learn More

※ U.S. LNG Markets and Uses
※ The Global LNG Market
※ LNG Projections to 2030
※ Natural Gas Monthly

🖨 Printer-friendly page

✉ Email this page

🔗 Share this page

[1]However, EIA projects a gradual decline in LNG imports after 2015. Additional details are available in the EIA report, *Updated Annual Energy Outlook 2009 (Reference Case Service Report) SR/OIAF/2009-03*, (Washington, DC, April 2009), Table 13.

U.S. Capacity to Receive LNG Imports, 2000-2009 (Billion Cubic Feet per Day)

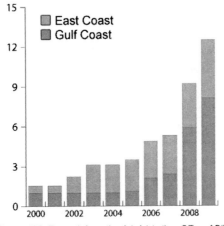

Source: U.S. Energy Information Administration, Office of Oil and Gas

Sources of LNG to the United States, 2008 (Percent)

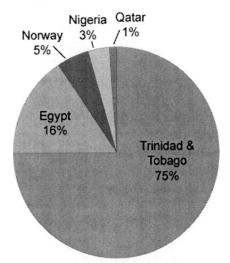

Source: U.S. Energy Information Administration, Office of Oil and Gas, based on data from the Office of Fossil Energy, U.S. Department of Energy.

Order Code RL32073

CRS Report for Congress

Liquefied Natural Gas (LNG) Infrastructure Security: Issues for Congress

Updated May 13, 2008

Paul W. Parfomak
Specialist in Energy and Infrastructure
Resources, Science, and Industry Division

Congressional
Research
Service

**Prepared for Members and
Committees of Congress**

Liquefied Natural Gas (LNG) Infrastructure Security: Issues for Congress

Summary

Liquefied natural gas (LNG) is a hazardous fuel shipped in large tankers from overseas to U.S. ports. Because LNG infrastructure is highly visible and easily identified, it can be vulnerable to terrorist attack. Since September 11, 2001, the U.S. LNG industry and federal agencies have put new measures in place to respond to the possibility of terrorism. Nonetheless, public concerns about LNG risks continue to raise questions about LNG security. Faced with a perceived national need for greater LNG imports, and persistent public concerns about LNG risks, some in Congress are examining the adequacy of security provisions in federal LNG regulation.

LNG infrastructure consists primarily of tankers, import terminals, and inland storage plants. There are nine active U.S. terminals and proposals for many others. Although potentially catastrophic events could arise from a serious accident or attack on such facilities, LNG has a record of relative safety for the last 40 years, and no LNG tanker or land-based facility has been attacked by terrorists. The likelihood and possible impacts from LNG attacks continue to be debated among experts.

Several federal agencies oversee LNG infrastructure security. The Coast Guard has lead responsibility for LNG shipping and marine terminal security under the Maritime Transportation Security Act of 2002 (P.L. 107-295) and the Security and Accountability for Every Port Act of 2006 (P.L. 109-347). The Office of Pipeline Safety (OPS) and the Transportation Security Administration (TSA) both have security authority for LNG storage plants within gas utilities, as well as some security authority for LNG marine terminals. The Federal Energy Regulatory Commission (FERC) approves the siting, with some security oversight, of on-shore LNG marine terminals and certain utility LNG plants. The Coast Guard, OPS and FERC cooperate in the siting approval of new LNG facilities, inspection and operational review of existing facilities, informal communication, and dispute resolution.

Federal initiatives to secure LNG are still evolving, but a variety of industry and agency representatives suggest they are reducing the vulnerability of LNG to terrorism. S. 1594 would strengthen federal protection of vessels and infrastructure handling LNG and other especially hazardous cargoes through new international standards, new training requirements, vessel security cost-sharing, incident response and recovery plans, and other provisions. H.R. 2830, which passed in the House of Representatives on April 24, 2008, but which President Bush has threatened to veto, would require the Coast Guard to secure LNG tankers, and would limit the agency's reliance on state and local resources in doing so, among other provisions. As Congress continues its oversight of LNG, it may consider whether future LNG security requirements will be appropriately funded, whether these requirements will be balanced against evolving risks, and whether the LNG industry is carrying its fair share of the security burden. Congress may also act to improve its understanding of LNG security risks. Finally, Congress may initiate action to better understand the security and trade implications of efforts to promote U.S.-flagged LNG tankers and U.S. crews.

Contents

List of Figures

449

Liquefied Natural Gas (LNG) Infrastructure Security: Issues for Congress

Introduction

Liquefied natural gas (LNG) facilities are receiving a great deal of public attention due to their increasingly important role in the nation's energy infrastructure and their potential vulnerability to terrorist attack. LNG has long been important to U.S. natural gas markets, although energy economics and public perceptions about LNG risks have limited the industry's growth. Concerns about rising natural gas prices and the possibility of domestic gas shortages have been driving up demand for LNG imports. But LNG is a hazardous[1] liquid transported and stored in large quantities. Consequently, LNG infrastructure may directly impact the security of communities where this infrastructure is located. Faced with the widely perceived national need for greater LNG imports, and persistent public concerns about LNG risks, some in Congress are examining the adequacy of security provisions in federal LNG regulation.[2]

S. 1594, which was introduced by Senator Frank Lautenberg and three cosponsors and referred to the Senate Committee on Commerce, Science, and Transportation on June 12, 2007, would strengthen federal protection of vessels and infrastructure handling LNG and other especially hazardous cargoes. H.R. 2830, which passed in the House of Representatives on April 24, 2008, would require the Coast Guard to enforce security zones around LNG tankers, would limit reliance on state and local government resources to provide LNG security, and would require the Coast Guard to certify it has adequate resources for LNG security before approving an LNG facility's security plan. H.R. 2830 would further require a comparative risk assessment of vessel-based and facility-based LNG regasification processes and a report on state and local augmentation of Coast Guard security resources, among other provisions.

This report provides an overview of industry and federal activities related to LNG security. The report describes U.S. LNG infrastructure, the industry's safety record and security risks, and the industry's security initiatives since September 11, 2001. It summarizes recent changes in federal LNG and maritime security law and related changes in the security roles of federal agencies. The report discusses several policy concerns related to federal LNG security efforts: 1) public costs of marine

---

[1] 49 C.F.R. 172.101. *List of Hazardous Materials.* Office of Hazardous Materials Safety, Department of Transportation.

[2] See, for example: U.S. Representative Tim Bishop, "Bishop Calls for Congressional Hearing on Coast Guard's Inability to Protect LNG Tankers," Press release, March 12, 2008.

CRS-2

security, 2) uncertainty regarding LNG terrorism risks, and 3) security implications of promoting U.S.-flagged LNG tankers and U.S. crews.

Scope and Limitations

This report focuses on industry and federal activities in LNG infrastructure security. The report includes some discussion of state and local agency activities as they relate to federal efforts, but does not address the full range of state and local issues of potential interest to policy makers. The report also focuses on shipping, marine terminals and land-based storage facilities within gas utilities; it does not address LNG trucking, special purpose LNG facilities, or LNG-fueled vehicles. The report discusses activities in LNG safety only as they relate to security. For further discussion of LNG terminal safety, including LNG safety-related legislative proposals, see CRS Report RL32205, *Liquefied Natural Gas (LNG) Terminals: Siting, Safety and Regulation*, by Paul Parfomak and Adam Vann.

Background

What is LNG?

When natural gas is cooled to temperatures below minus 260°F it condenses into *liquefied* natural gas, or "LNG."[3] As a liquid, natural gas occupies only 1/600th the volume of its gaseous state, so it is stored more effectively in a limited space and is more readily transported by ship or truck. A single tanker ship, for example, can carry huge quantities of LNG — enough to supply the daily energy needs of over 10 million homes. When LNG is warmed it "regasifies" and can be used for the same purposes as conventional natural gas such as heating, cooking and power generation.

In 2007, LNG imports to the United States originated in Trinidad and Tobago (57.3%), Egypt (15.3%), Nigeria (12.7%), Algeria (9.9%), Qatar (2.4%), and Equatorial Guinea (2.4%).[4] In recent years, some LNG shipments have also come from Malaysia, Oman, Australia, and other countries.[5] Brunei, Indonesia, Libya, and the United Arab Emirates also export LNG, and may be significant U.S. suppliers in the future. In addition to importing LNG to the lower 48 states, the United States exports Alaskan LNG to Japan.

Expectations for U.S. LNG Growth

The United States has used LNG commercially since the1940s. Initially, LNG facilities stored domestically produced natural gas to supplement pipeline supplies

---

[3] Natural gas typically consists of at least 80% methane, although LNG is usually over 90% methane. It may also contain other hydrocarbon gases (e.g., propane) and nitrogen.

[4] U.S. Dept. of Energy, Office of Fossil Energy. "Natural Gas Import/Export Reports." Internal database. January 7, 2008. Excludes December 2007 imports.

[5] Energy Information Administration (EIA). *Natural Gas Year-In-Review 2006*. Washington, DC, March 2007. p. 5.

CRS-3

during times of high gas demand. In the 1970s LNG imports began to supplement domestic production. Due primarily to low domestic gas prices, LNG imports stayed relatively small — accounting for only 1% of total U.S. gas consumption in 2002.[6] In countries with limited domestic gas supplies, however, LNG imports grew dramatically over the same period. Japan, for example, imported 97% of its natural gas supply as LNG in 2002, over 11 times as much LNG as the United States.[7] South Korea, France, Spain, and Taiwan also became heavy LNG importers.

Natural gas demand has accelerated in the United States over the last several years due to environmental concerns about other energy sources, growth in natural gas-fired electricity generation, and historically low gas prices. Supply has not been able to keep up with demand, however, so gas prices have recently become high and volatile. As **Figure 1** shows, average annual gas prices at the wellhead have risen from between $1.50 and $2.50/Mcf ("thousand cubic feet") through most of the 1990s to above $6.00/Mcf since 2005. At the same time, international prices for LNG have fallen because of increased supplies and lower production and transportation costs, making LNG more competitive with domestic natural gas. While cost estimation is speculative, some industry analysts believe that LNG can be economically delivered to U.S. pipelines for between $2.25 to $4.15/Mcf, depending upon the source.[8]

Figure 1. Average U.S. Natural Gas Wellhead Price ($/Mcf)

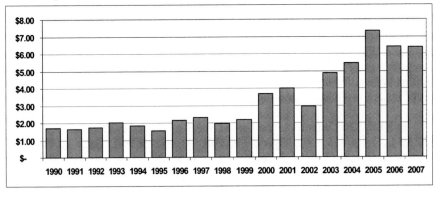

Source: Energy Information Administration. "U.S. Natural Gas Wellhead Price." Internet database. Updated Feb. 29, 2008. [http://tonto.eia.doe.gov/dnav/ng/hist/n9190us3m.htm]

In 2003 testimony before the House Energy and Commerce Committee, the Federal Reserve Chairman, Alan Greenspan, called for a sharp increase in LNG imports to help avert a potential barrier to U.S. economic growth. According to Mr. Greenspan's testimony

---

[6] Energy Information Administration (EIA). *Natural Gas Annual 2005*. Tables 1 and 9. November 16, 2006.

[7] Energy Information Administration (EIA). "World LNG Imports by Origin, 2002." Washington, DC. October 2003.

[8] Donnelly, M. "LNG as Price Taker." *Public Utilities Fortnightly*. November 1, 2006.

452 703-739-3790 TCNNaturalGas.com

CRS-4

... notable cost reductions for both liquefaction and transportation of LNG ... and high gas prices projected in the American distant futures market have made us a potential very large importer.... Access to world natural gas supplies will require a major expansion of LNG terminal import capacity.[9]

If current natural gas trends continue, the Energy Information Administration (EIA) projects U.S. LNG imports to account for 13% of total U.S. gas supply in 2030.[10]

Overview of U.S. LNG Infrastructure

The physical infrastructure of LNG consists of interconnected transportation and storage facilities, each with distinct physical characteristics affecting operational risks and security needs. This overview focuses on the three major elements of this infrastructure: tanker ships, marine terminals, and storage facilities.

LNG Tanker Ships

LNG is transported to the United States in very large, specialized tanker ships. LNG tankers are double hulled, containing several massive tanks, each sealed and insulated to maintain safe LNG temperature and prevent leakage during transit. There are currently 200 tankers in service around the world, with a combined cargo capacity of over 24 million cubic meters of LNG, equivalent to over eight times the average daily U.S. natural gas consumption. More than 200 additional tankers are expected to enter service by 2013.[11] There are no U.S.-flagged LNG tankers.

LNG Marine Terminals

LNG tankers unload their cargo at dedicated marine terminals which store and regasify the LNG for distribution to domestic markets. Onshore terminals typically consist of docks, LNG handling equipment, storage tanks, and interconnections to regional gas pipelines. As discussed later in the report, the siting of onshore LNG import terminals is regulated by the Federal Energy Regulatory Commission (FERC). There are eight active onshore LNG terminals in the United States:

- **Everett, Massachusetts.** The Everett terminal is located across the Mystic River from Boston; tankers must pass through Boston harbor to reach it. The terminal serves gas utilities and electric power

---

[9] Greenspan, Alan, Chairman, U.S. Federal Reserve Board. "Natural Gas Supply and Demand Issues." Testimony before the House Energy and Commerce Comm. June 10, 2003.

[10] Energy Information Administration (EIA). *Annual Energy Outlook 2008* (Revised Early Release). DOE/EIA-0383(2008). Table A13. March 2008. p. 25.

[11] *Lloyd's List.* "US Demand for LNG Puts Pressure on Maritime Manpower." September 11, 2007. p. 10.

CRS-5

producers in New England, receiving approximately 65 LNG shipments annually.[12]

- **Cove Point, Maryland**. Cove Point is located on the Chesapeake Bay 60 miles southeast of Washington, DC. Under federally approved expansion plans, the terminal could be capable of receiving up to 200 shipments per year in 2008.[13]

- **Elba Island, Georgia.** The Elba Island terminal is located on an island five miles down the Savannah River from Savannah, Georgia and ten miles from the Atlantic coast. The terminal completed a major expansion in 2006, allowing it to receive approximately 118 shipments per year.[14]

- **Kenai, Alaska.** Built in 1969, this is the oldest LNG marine terminal in the United States and the only one built for export (to Japan). The Kenai terminal is located in Nikiski near the Cook Inlet gas fields. Since 1969 the terminal has exported an average of approximately 34 LNG shipments each year.[15]

- **Lake Charles, Louisiana.** The Lake Charles terminal is located approximately nine miles southwest of the city of Lake Charles near the Gulf of Mexico. The terminal completed a major expansion in 2006, allowing it to receive up to 175 shipments per year.[16]

- **Peñuelas, Puerto Rico.** The Peñuelas terminal, located on the southern coast of Puerto Rico, is dedicated to fueling an electric generation plant which supplies 20% of Puerto Rico's power.[17] The terminal receives 10 to 15 LNG shipments annually.[18]

- **Quintana Island, Texas.** This terminal is located southeast of the city of Freeport, in Brazoria County. The terminal has the capability

---

[12] Department of Energy, Office of Fossil Energy (OFE). "Imports of Liquefied Natural Gas (LNG)." Unpublished data. Washington, D.C. January 11, 2007.

[13] Federal Energy Regulatory Commission (FERC). "Order Issuing Certificates and Granting Section 3 Authority." Issued June 16, 2006. Docket No. CP05-130-000, *et al*. p. 71.

[14] "El Paso Corporation Announces Start of Service From Elba II Expansion." PR Newswire. February 1, 2006; *Federal Register*, vol. 67, no. 181, September 18, 2002, p. 58784.

[15] Marathon Oil Corporation. *2003 Annual Report*. Houston. March 8, 2004. p. 11.

[16] "Second Trunkline LNG Terminal Expansion Up and Running." *Inside F.E.R.C.* July 31, 2006. p. 12; Federal Register, vol. 67, no. 34, February 20, 2002, p. 7684.

[17] "Gas Natural Acquires Enron's 50% Stake in 540-MW Gas Plant in Puerto Rico." *Platt's Global Power Report*. McGraw-Hill. July 10, 2003. p. 11.

[18] OFE. January 11, 2007.

CRS-6

of receiving approximately 200 ships per year.[19] It received it first commercial cargo in April 2008.[20]

- **Sabine Pass, Louisiana.** This terminal is located near the Sabine Pass Channel in Cameron Parish. The terminal has the capability of receiving approximately 300 ships per year.[21] It also received it first commercial cargo in April 2008.[22]

Offshore LNG terminals connect to land only by underwater pipelines. These offshore terminal designs seek to avoid community opposition, permitting, and operating obstacles which have hindered the construction of new on-shore LNG terminal facilities. Because offshore terminals would be located far from land, they also would present fewer security risks than on-shore LNG terminals. Offshore terminals may present environmental concerns, however, if they use seawater for regasification. Such a process cools the waters in a terminal's vicinity with potential impacts on the local ecosystem due to the lower water temperatures.[23] As discussed later in the report, offshore LNG terminals are regulated jointly by the Maritime Administration (MARAD) and the U.S. Coast Guard. There is currently one operating offshore LNG terminal in U.S. waters:

- **Gulf of Mexico, Louisiana.** The Gulf Gateways (Energy Bridge) terminal was completed in 2004 and received its first LNG shipment in March, 2005. The terminal consists of an offshore gas pipeline buoy system and is served by specialized tankers which regasify their LNG cargoes on board. The terminal expects up to be able to serve up to 60 LNG shipments per year.[24]

A second offshore terminal near Boston, Massachusetts, is scheduled to begin operations in 2008.[25]

In addition to these active terminals, some 28 LNG terminal proposals have been approved by regulators across North America to serve the U.S. market (**Figure 2**). A number of these proposals have been withdrawn, however, due to siting

---

[19] Federal Energy Regulatory Commission. "Order Granting Authorization Under Section 3 of the Natural Gas Act." Docket No. CP03-75-000. June 18, 2004. p.2.

[20] Fowler, T. "Freeport Gets 1st LNG Cargo." *Houston Chronicle*. April 16, 2008.

[21] Federal Energy Regulatory Commission. "Order Granting Authority under Section 3 of the Natural Gas Act and Issuing Certificates." Docket No. CP04-47-000. Dec. 21, 2004. p.2.

[22] Gunter, F. "Cheniere Opens Sabine Pass LNG Terminal." Houston Business Journal. April 21, 2008.

[23] O'Driscoll, M. "LNG: Shell's Gulf Landing Offshore Project Gets Green Light." *Greenwire*. E&E Publishing, LLC. Washington, D.C. Feb 18, 2005.

[24] *Natural Gas Intelligence.* "Energy Bridge Terminal Prepares for First 3 Bcf LNG Delivery This Month." Intelligence Press, Inc. March 7, 2005.

[25] "Boston Offshore LNG Port Nears Clearance to Open." Reuter's. January 9, 2008.

CRS-7

problems, financing problems, or other reasons. Developers have proposed another 13 U.S. terminals prior to filing formal siting applications.[26]

Figure 2. Approved LNG Terminals in North America

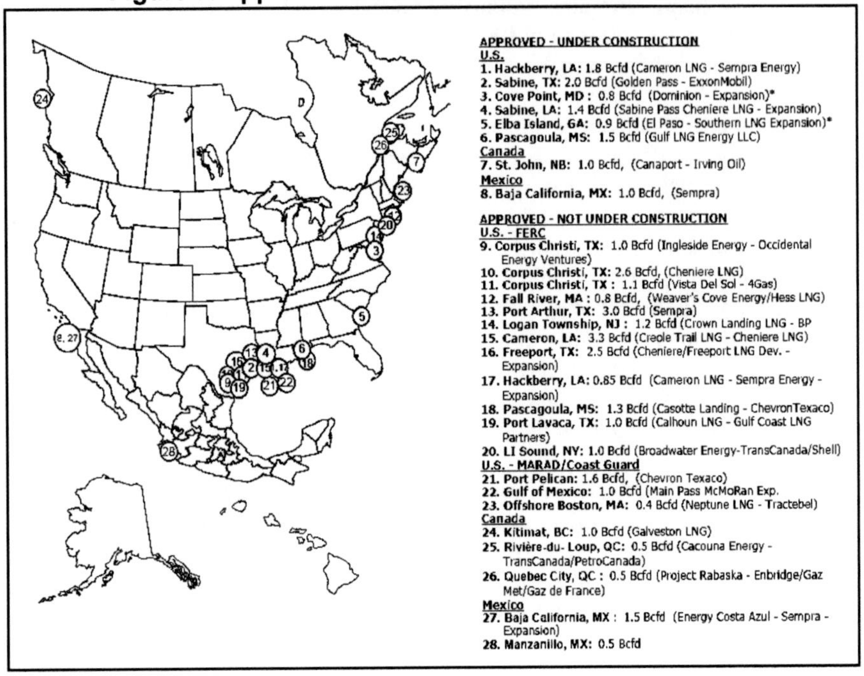

APPROVED - UNDER CONSTRUCTION
U.S.
1. Hackberry, LA: 1.8 Bcfd (Cameron LNG - Sempra Energy)
2. Sabine, TX: 2.0 Bcfd (Golden Pass - ExxonMobil)
3. Cove Point, MD: 0.8 Bcfd (Dominion - Expansion)*
4. Sabine, LA: 1.4 Bcfd (Sabine Pass Cheniere LNG - Expansion)
5. Elba Island, GA: 0.9 Bcfd (El Paso - Southern LNG Expansion)*
6. Pascagoula, MS: 1.5 Bcfd (Gulf LNG Energy LLC)
Canada
7. St. John, NB: 1.0 Bcfd, (Canaport - Irving Oil)
Mexico
8. Baja California, MX: 1.0 Bcfd, (Sempra)

APPROVED - NOT UNDER CONSTRUCTION
U.S. - FERC
9. Corpus Christi, TX: 1.0 Bcfd (Ingleside Energy - Occidental Energy Ventures)
10. Corpus Christi, TX: 2.6 Bcfd, (Cheniere LNG)
11. Corpus Christi, TX : 1.1 Bcfd (Vista Del Sol - 4Gas)
12. Fall River, MA: 0.8 Bcfd, (Weaver's Cove Energy/Hess LNG)
13. Port Arthur, TX: 3.0 Bcfd (Sempra)
14. Logan Township, NJ : 1.2 Bcfd (Crown Landing LNG - BP)
15. Cameron, LA: 3.3 Bcfd (Creole Trail LNG - Cheniere LNG)
16. Freeport, TX: 2.5 Bcfd (Cheniere/Freeport LNG Dev. - Expansion)
17. Hackberry, LA: 0.85 Bcfd (Cameron LNG - Sempra Energy - Expansion)
18. Pascagoula, MS: 1.3 Bcfd (Casotte Landing - ChevronTexaco)
19. Port Lavaca, TX: 1.0 Bcfd (Calhoun LNG - Gulf Coast LNG Partners)
20. LI Sound, NY: 1.0 Bcfd (Broadwater Energy-TransCanada/Shell)
U.S. - MARAD/Coast Guard
21. Port Pelican: 1.6 Bcfd, (Chevron Texaco)
22. Gulf of Mexico: 1.0 Bcfd (Main Pass McMoRan Exp.
23. Offshore Boston, MA: 0.4 Bcfd (Neptune LNG - Tractebel)
Canada
24. Kitimat, BC: 1.0 Bcfd (Galveston LNG)
25. Rivière-du- Loup, QC: 0.5 Bcfd (Cacouna Energy - TransCanada/PetroCanada)
26. Quebec City, QC : 0.5 Bcfd (Project Rabaska - Enbridge/Gaz Met/Gaz de France)
Mexico
27. Baja California, MX : 1.5 Bcfd (Energy Costa Azul - Sempra - Expansion)
28. Manzanillo, MX: 0.5 Bcfd

Source: Federal Energy Regulatory Commission (FERC), "Approved North American LNG Import Terminals," Updated April 21, 2008. [http://www.ferc.gov/industries/lng.asp]

LNG Peak Shaving Plants

Many gas distribution utilities rely on "peak shaving" LNG plants to supplement pipeline gas supplies during periods of peak demand during winter cold snaps. The LNG is stored in large refrigerated tanks integrated with the local gas pipeline network. The largest facilities usually liquefy natural gas drawn directly from the interstate pipeline grid, although many smaller facilities without such liquefaction capabilities receive LNG by truck. LNG tanks are generally surrounded by containment impoundments which limit the spread of an LNG spill and the potential size of a resulting vapor cloud. LNG peak shaving plants are often located near the populations they serve, although many are in remote areas away from people. According to the Pipeline and Hazardous Materials Safety Administration (PHMSA) there are 103 active LNG storage facilities in the United States distributed across 31

---

[26] Federal Energy Regulatory Commission (FERC), "Proposed North American LNG Import Terminals," Updated April 21, 2008. [http://www.ferc.gov/industries/lng.asp]

CRS-8

states.[27] These facilities are mostly in the Northeast where pipeline capacity and underground gas storage have historically been constrained.

LNG Risks and Vulnerabilities

The safety hazards associated with LNG terminals have been debated for decades. A 1944 accident at one of the nation's first LNG facilities killed 128 people and initiated public fears about LNG hazards which persist today.[28] Technology improvements and standards since the 1940s have made LNG facilities much safer, but serious hazards remain since LNG is inherently volatile and is shipped and stored in large quantities. A January 2004 accident at Algeria's Skikda LNG terminal which killed or injured over 100 workers added to the ongoing controversy over LNG facility safety.[29] LNG infrastructure is also potentially vulnerable to terrorist attack.

Physical Hazards of LNG

Natural gas is combustible, so an uncontrolled release of LNG poses a serious hazard of explosion or fire. LNG also poses hazards because it is extremely cold. Experts have identified several potentially catastrophic events that could arise from an LNG release. The likelihood and severity of these events have been the subject of considerable research and analysis. While open questions remain about the impacts of specific hazards in an actual accident, there appears to be consensus as to what the greatest LNG hazards are.

- **Pool fires.** If LNG spills near an ignition source, the evaporating gas in a combustible gas-air concentration will burn above the LNG pool.[30] The resulting "pool fire" would spread as the LNG pool expanded away from its source and continued evaporating. Such pool fires are intense, burning far more hotly and rapidly than oil or gasoline fires.[31] They cannot be extinguished — all the LNG must be consumed before they go out. Because LNG pool fires are so hot, their thermal radiation may injure people and damage property a considerable distance from the fire itself. Many experts agree that a pool fire, especially on water, is the most serious LNG hazard.[32]

---

[27] Pipeline and Hazardous Materials Safety Administration. "Liquefied Natural Gas (LNG) in the U.S." Web page. March 2008. [http://primis.phmsa.dot.gov/comm/LNG.htm]

[28] Bureau of Mines (BOM). *Report on the Investigation of the Fire at the Liquefaction, Storage, and Regasification Plant of the East Ohio Gas Co., Cleveland, Ohio, October 20, 1944.* February 1946.

[29] Junnola, J., et al. "Fatal Explosion Rocks Algeria's Skikda LNG Complex." *Oil Daily.* January 21, 2004. p. 6.

[30] Methane, the main component of LNG, burns in gas-to-air ratios between 5% and 15%.

[31] Havens, J. "Ready to Blow?" *Bulletin of the Atomic Scientists.* July/August 2003. p. 17.

[32] Havens. 2003. p. 17.

CRS-9

- **Flammable vapor clouds**. If LNG spills but does not immediately ignite, the evaporating natural gas will form a vapor cloud that may drift some distance from the spill site. If the cloud subsequently encounters an ignition source, those portions of the cloud with a combustible gas-air concentration will burn. Because only a fraction of such a cloud would have a combustible gas-air concentration, the cloud would not likely explode all at once, but the fire could still cause considerable damage. An LNG vapor cloud fire would gradually burn its way back to the LNG spill where the vapors originated and would continue to burn as a pool fire.[33] If an LNG tank failed due to a collision or terror attack, experts believe the failure event itself would likely ignite the LNG pool before a large vapor cloud could form.[34] Consequently, they conclude that large vapor cloud fires are less likely than instantaneous pool fires.

- **Flameless explosion**. If LNG spills on water, it could theoretically heat up and regasify almost instantly in a "flameless explosion" (also called a "rapid phase transition"). While the effects of tanker-scale spills have not been studied extensively, Shell Corporation experiments with smaller LNG spills in 1980 did not cause flameless explosions. Even if there were a flameless explosion of LNG, experts believe the hazard zones around such an event "would not be as large as either vapor cloud or pool fire hazard zones."[35]

In addition to these catastrophic hazards, an LNG spill poses hazards on a smaller scale. An LNG vapor cloud is not toxic, but could cause asphyxiation by displacing breathable air. Such clouds rise in air as they warm, however, diminishing the threat to people on the ground. Alternatively, extremely cold LNG could injure people or damage equipment through direct contact. The extent of such contact would likely be limited, however, as a major spill would likely result in a more serious fire. The environmental damage associated with an LNG spill would be confined to fire and freezing impacts near the spill since LNG dissipates completely and leaves no residue (as crude oil does).[36]

Safety Record of LNG

The LNG tanker industry claims a record of relative safety over the last 45 years; since international LNG shipping began in 1959, tankers reportedly have carried over 47,000 LNG cargoes without a serious accident at sea or in port.[37] LNG

---

[33] Quillen, D. ChevronTexaco Corp. "LNG Safety Myths and Legends." Presentation to the Natural Gas Technology Conference. Houston, TX. May 14-15, 2002. p. 18.

[34] Havens. 2003. p. 17.

[35] Havens. 2003. p. 17.

[36] Quillen. 2002. p. 28.

[37] Society of International Gas Tanker and Terminal Operators Ltd. (SIGTTO)."Worth Repeating." *SIGTTO News*. Vol. 17. March 2007. p. 10.

CRS-10

tankers have experienced groundings and collisions during this period, but none has resulted in a major spill.[38] The LNG marine safety record is partly due to the double-hulled design of LNG tankers. This design makes them more robust and less prone to accidental spills than single-hulled oil and fuel tankers like the *Exxon Valdez*, which caused a major Alaskan oil spill after grounding in 1989.[39] LNG tankers also carry radar, global positioning systems, automatic distress systems and beacons to signal if they are in trouble. Cargo safety systems include instruments that can shut operations if they deviate from normal as well as gas and fire detection systems.

The safety record of onshore LNG terminals is more mixed. There are more than 40 LNG terminals (and more than 150 other LNG storage facilities) worldwide. Since 1944, there have been approximately 13 serious accidents at these facilities directly related to LNG. Two of these accidents caused single fatalities of facility workers — one in Algeria in 1977, and another at Cove Point, Maryland, in 1979. On January 19, 2004, a fire at the LNG processing facility in Skikda, Algeria killed an estimated 27 workers and injured 74 others. The Skikda fire completely destroyed a processing plant and damaged a marine berth, although it did not damage a second processing plant or three large LNG storage tanks also located at the terminal.[40] The Skikda accident did not injure the rest of the 12,000 workers at the complex, but it was considered the worst petrochemical plant fire in Algeria in over 40 years.[41] According to press reports, the accident resulted from poor maintenance rather than a facility design flaw.[42] Another three accidents at worldwide LNG plants since 1944 have also caused fatalities, but these were construction or maintenance accidents in which LNG was not present.[43]

LNG Security Risks

LNG tankers and land-based facilities may be vulnerable to terrorism. Tankers could be physically attacked to destroy their cargo — or commandeered for use as weapons against coastal targets. Land-based LNG facilities could also be physically attacked with explosives or through other means. Alternatively, computer control systems could be "cyber-attacked," or both physical and cyber attack could happen at the same time. Some LNG facilities could also be indirectly disrupted by other types of terror strikes, such as attacks on regional electricity grids or communications networks, which could in turn affect dependent LNG control and safety systems. Since LNG is fuel for power plants, heating, military bases, and other uses, disruption

---

[38] SIGGTO 2007; CH-IV International. *Safety History of International LNG Operations.* TD-02109. Millersville, MD. July, 2004. pp. 13-18.

[39] Society of International Gas Tanker & Terminal Operators Ltd. (SIGTTO). "Safe Havens for Disabled Gas Carriers." Third Edition. London. February 2003. pp. 1-2.

[40] Junnola, J., et al. January 21, 2004. p. 6.

[41] Hunter, C. "Algerian LNG Plant Explosion Sets Back Industry Development." *World Markets Analysis.* January 21, 2004. p. 1.

[42] Antosh, N. "Vast Site Devastated." *Houston Chronicle.* January 21, 2004. p. B1.

[43] CH-IV International. pp. 6-12.

CRS-11

of LNG shipping or storage poses additional "downstream" risks, especially in more LNG-dependent regions like New England.

LNG Tanker Vulnerability. LNG tankers cause the most concern among security analysts because they are potentially more accessible than fixed terminal facilities, because they may transit nearer to populated areas, and because LNG spills from tankers could be more difficult to control. According to a 2004 report by Sandia National Laboratories, an intentional LNG spill and resulting fire could cause "major" injuries to people and "significant" damage to structures within approximately 500 meters (0.3 mile) of the spill site, more moderate injuries and structural damage up to 1,600 meters (1.0 mile) from the spill site, and lower impacts out to 2,500 meters (1.5 miles).[44] These results are used by federal agencies in reviewing LNG terminal siting applications.

Other LNG hazard studies have reached somewhat different conclusions about LNG tanker vulnerability. A report by the Government Accountability Office (GAO) released in 2007 reviewed six unclassified studies of LNG tanker hazards, including the Sandia study. The GAO report concluded that[45]

> Because there have been no large-scale LNG spills or spill experiments, past studies have developed modeling assumptions based on small-scale spill data. While there is general agreement on the types of effects from an LNG spill, the results of these models have created what appears to be conflicting assessments of the specific consequences of an LNG spill, creating uncertainty for regulators and the public.

Following the GAO report, Members of Congress have expressed continuing concern about the uncertainty associated with LNG tanker vulnerability and hazard analysis.[46] In 2008, Congress appropriated $8 million to fund large-scale LNG fire experiments by the Department of Energy addressing some of the hazard modeling uncertainties identified in the GAO report.[47] It remains to be seen to what degree this research will increase policy makers' confidence in LNG tanker vulnerability analyses.

---

[44] Sandia National Laboratories (SNL). *Guidance on Risk Analysis and Safety Implications of a Large Liquefied Natural Gas (LNG) Spill Over Water*. SAND2004-6258. Albuquerque, NM. December 2004. p. 54.

[45] Government Accountability Office (GAO). *Maritime Security: Public Safety Consequences of a Terrorist Attack on a Tanker Carrying Liquefied Natural Gas Need Clarification*. GAO-07-316. February 2007. p. 22.

[46] See, for example Senator Barbara A. Mikulski, testimony before the House Transportation and Infrastructure Committee, Coast Guard and Maritime Transportation Subcommittee field hearing on the Safety and Security of Liquefied Natural Gas and the Impact on Port Operations. Baltimore, MD. April 23, 2007.

[47] Consolidated Appropriations Act, 2008 (P.L.110-161), Division C — Energy and Water Development and Related Agencies Appropriations Act, 2008, Title III, Explanatory Statement, p. 570.

CRS-12

The *Gaz Fountain* Attack

Although there have been no terrorist attacks on LNG tankers, there is at least one documented case of a gas tanker of similar construction being attacked in wartime. During the Iran-Iraq War in the 1990s, the double-hulled LPG tanker *Gaz Fountain* was fired upon by an Iranian aircraft using three air-to-ground, armor-piercing Maverick missiles. Two of the missiles exploded on or above the ship's deck, causing relatively minor damage. The third missile penetrated the deck and exploded above a butane storage tank, opening a 6 square-meter (65 square-foot) hole in the roof of the tank. The escaping gas ignited, establishing a large fire on deck above the missile entry hole. The fire aboard the *Gaz Fountain* was successfully extinguished by a salvage ship, her remaining cargo was successfully unloaded to another tanker, and she was eventually repaired.[48]

The *Gaz Fountain* attack and salvage provides some evidence as to the robustness of double-hulled gas tankers like those that carry LNG. But the relatively benign outcome in the *Gaz Fountain* attack does not necessarily demonstrate that attacks on LNG tankers would have similarly limited impacts. The *Gaz Fountain* was fortunate that its storage tank was breached only at the top. If missiles had been targeted at the hull of the ship rather than its deck, one might have penetrated the side of a storage tank, causing a major spill on water and an inextinguishable pool fire. Furthermore, if the gas involved had been LNG rather than butane, the *Gaz Fountain* might have been subject to cryogenic damage since LNG is transported at a much lower temperature than butane (-260°F vs. +25°F). According to the Sandia report, such a combination could lead to cascading failure of adjacent storage tanks and, presumably, an even larger fire.[49]

Federal LNG Security Initiatives

Operators of LNG infrastructure had security programs in place prior to September 11, 2001, but these programs mostly focused on personnel safety and preventing vandalism. The terror attacks of September 11 focused attention on the vulnerability of LNG infrastructure to different threats, such as systematic attacks on LNG facilities by foreign terrorists. Consequently, both government and industry have taken new initiatives to secure LNG infrastructure in response to new threats.

Several federal agencies oversee the security of LNG infrastructure. The Coast Guard has lead responsibility for LNG shipping and marine terminal security. The Department of Transportation's Office of Pipeline Safety and the Department of Homeland Security's Transportation Security Administration have security authority for peak-shaving plants within gas utilities, as well as some security authority for LNG marine terminals. FERC has siting approval responsibility, with some security oversight, for land-based LNG marine terminals and certain peak-shaving plants. In

---

[48] Carter, J.A. "Salvage of Cargo from the War-Damaged *Gaz Fountain*." Proceedings of the Gastech 85 LNG/LPG Conference. Nice, France. November 12-15, 1985.

[49] SNL. December 2004. p. 151.

CRS-13

addition to federal agencies, state and local authorities, like police and fire departments, also help to secure LNG.

Security Activities of Federal Maritime Agencies

The two federal agencies with the most significant roles in maritime security as it relates to LNG are the U.S. Coast Guard and the Maritime Administration.

U.S. Coast Guard. The Coast Guard is the lead federal agency for U.S. maritime security, including port security. Among other duties, the Coast Guard tracks, boards, and inspects commercial ships approaching U.S. waters. A senior Coast Guard officer in each port oversees the security and safety of vessels, waterways, and many shore facilities in his geographic area. The Coast Guard derives its security responsibilities under the Ports and Waterways Safety Act of 1972 (P.L. 92-340) and the Maritime Transportation Security Act of 2002 (P.L. 107-295). Maritime security regulations mandated by P.L. 107-295 are discussed below. Under P.L. 107-295 the Coast Guard and the Maritime Administration share siting approval authority for offshore LNG terminals.

Shortly after September 11, 2001, the Coast Guard began to systematically prioritize protection of ships and facilities, including those handling LNG, based on vulnerability assessments and the potential consequences of security incidents. The Coast Guard evaluated the overall susceptibility of marine targets, their use to transport terrorists or terror materials, and their use as potential weapons. In particular, the Coast Guard evaluated the vulnerability of tankers to "a boat loaded with explosives" or "being commandeered and intentionally damaged."[50] While the assessments focused on Coast Guard jurisdictional vessels and facilities, some scenarios involved other vital port infrastructure like bridges, channels, and tunnels.[51] The Coast Guard used these assessments in augmenting security of key maritime assets and in developing the agency's new maritime security standards.

The Coast Guard began increasing LNG tanker and port security immediately after September 11, 2001. For example, the Coast Guard suspended LNG shipments to Everett for several weeks after the terror attacks to conduct a security review and revise security plans.[52] The Coast Guard also worked with state, environmental and police marine units to establish 24-hour patrols in Boston harbor.[53] In July 2002, the Coast Guard imposed a 1,000-yard security zone around the Kenai LNG terminal — and subsequently imposed similar zones around other U.S. LNG terminals.[54] The Coast Guard also reassessed security at the Cove Point terminal before allowing LNG

---

[50] 68*FR*126. July 1, 2003. p. 39244.

[51] Ibid., p. 39246.

[52] McElhenny, J. "Coast Guard Lifts Ban of Natural Gas Tankers in Boston Harbor." Associated Press. October 16, 2001.

[53] Crittenden, J. "Vigilance: Holiday Puts Spotlight on Harbor Security." *Boston Herald.* Boston, MA. June 30, 2002. p. 1.

[54] "LNG Security in Boston to Be Permanent." *Platt's Oilgram News.* New York, NY. August 1, 2002.

CRS-14

shipments to resume there for the first time since 1980.[55] As new LNG terminals have been proposed and approved by federal agencies, the Coast Guard has continued its involvement in LNG security.

The most heavily secured LNG shipments are those bound for the Everett terminal because they pass through Boston harbor. Depending upon the level of alert, the Coast Guard and local law enforcement agencies may put in place numerous security provisions for these shipments, including:

- Inspection of security and tanker loading at the port of origin.
- On-board escort to Boston by Coast Guard "sea marshals."
- 96-hour advanced notice of arrival of an LNG tanker.
- Advance notification of local police, fire, and emergency agencies, as well as the Federal Aviation Administration and the U.S. Navy.
- Boarding LNG tankers for inspection prior to Boston harbor entry.
- Harbor escort by armed patrol boats, cutters, or auxiliary vessels.
- Enforcement of a security zone closed to other vessels two miles ahead and one mile to each side of the LNG tanker.
- Suspension of overflights by commercial aircraft at Logan airport.
- Inspection of adjacent piers for bombs by police divers.
- Posting of sharpshooters on nearby rooftops.
- Additional security measures which cannot be disclosed publicly.[56]

According to the Coast Guard, such security provisions have been in place for the other U.S. LNG terminals as well, depending upon local assessments of security risk and the unique characteristics of each marine area.[57]

On October 22, 2003, the Coast Guard issued final rules to implement the new security requirements mandated by P.L. 107-295. The rules are codified in Title 33 of the Code of Federal Regulations, Chapter 1, Subchapter H. Among other provisions, the rules establish Coast Guard port officers as maritime security coordinators and set requirements for maritime area security plans and committees. The rules require certain owners or operators of marine assets to designate security officers, perform security assessments, develop and implement security plans, and comply with maritime security alert levels. The vessel rules apply to all LNG tankers entering U.S. ports. Facility rules apply to all land-based U.S. LNG terminals or proposed offshore LNG terminals. Finally, the rules require certain vessels, including LNG tankers, to carry an automatic identification system.

---

[55] "Coast Guard, Mikulski Clear Plan to Reactivate Cove Point LNG Plant." *Platt's Inside FERC*. Washington, DC. January 6, 2003. p. 5.

[56] Greenway, H.D.S. "Is it Safe?" *The Boston Globe Magazine*. July, 27, 2003; Lin, J. and Fifield, A. "Risky Business?" *The Philadelphia Enquirer*. February 20, 2005. p. 1.

[57] O'Malley, Mark, Chief, Ports and Facilities Activities, U.S. Coast Guard. Testimony before the House Committee on Transportation and Infrastructure, Subcommittee on Coast Guard and Maritime Transportation hearing on the Safety and Security of Liquid Natural Gas. May 7, 2007; U.S. Coast Guard, Boston, MA, Captain of the Port. Personal communication. March 22, 2007.

CRS-15

The Coast Guard also has authority to review, approve, and verify security plans for marine traffic around proposed LNG marine terminals as part of the overall siting approval process led by FERC. The Coast Guard is responsible for issuing a Letter of Recommendation regarding the suitability of waterways for LNG vessels serving proposed terminals. The Coast Guard acts as a cooperating agency in the evaluation of LNG terminal siting applications.[58]

The Coast Guard also led the International Maritime Organization (IMO) in developing maritime security standards outside U.S. jurisdiction.[59] These standards, the International Ship and Port Facility Security Code (ISPS Code) contain detailed mandatory security requirements for governments, port authorities and shipping companies, as well as recommended guidelines for meeting those requirements. The ISPS Code is intended to provide a standardized, consistent framework for governments to evaluate risk and to "offset changes in threat with changes in vulnerability."[60]

On October 13, 2006, President Bush signed the Security and Accountability for Every Port Act of 2006 (P.L. 109-347). While not addressing LNG security specifically, the act includes general maritime security provisions which could apply to LNG vessels and facilities. These provisions include, among others, requirements relating to maritime facility security plans (Sec. 102); unannounced inspections of maritime facilities (Sec. 103); long-range vessel tracking (Sec. 107); operational centers for port security (Sec. 108); port security grants (Sec. 112); and training and exercise programs (Sec. 112-113). The Coast Guard is the federal agency primarily responsible for implementing these provisions.

Maritime Administration. The Maritime Administration (MARAD) within the Department of Transportation has as its stated mission "to strengthen the U.S. maritime transportation system - including infrastructure, industry and labor - to meet the economic and security needs of the Nation."[61] As noted above, under P.L.107-295, MARAD shares siting approval authority for offshore LNG terminals with the Coast Guard. Among other activities, the agency also administers its Maritime Security Program "to maintain an active, privately owned, U.S.-flag, and U.S.-crewed liner fleet in international trade."[62] Consistent with this mission, Congress passed the Coast Guard and Maritime Transportation Act of 2006 (P. L. 109 — 241) directing

---

[58] U.S. Coast Guard. *U.S. Coast Guard Captain of the Port Long Island Sound Waterways Suitability Report for the Proposed Broadwater Liquefied Natural Gas Facility.* September 21, 2006. p.2. [http://www.uscg.mil/d1/units/seclis/broadwater/wsrrpt/WSR%20Master%20Final.pdf]

[59] 68*FR*126. July 1, 2003. p. 39241.

[60] International Maritime Organization (IMO). "IMO Adopts Comprehensive Maritime Security Measures." Press release. London. December 17, 2002.

[61] Maritime Administration (MARAD). "MARAD Mission, Goals and Vision." Web page. March 16, 2008. [http://www.marad.dot.gov/welcome/mission.html]

[62] Maritime Administration (MARAD). "MARAD Fact Sheet." March 16, 2008. p. 2. [http://www.marad.dot.gov/Headlines/factsheets/PDF%20Versions/Mission%20Fact%20Sheet.pdf]

CRS-16

MARAD to implement a program to promote the transportation of LNG to domestic terminals in U.S. flag vessels (Sec. 304(a)). The act also directs the agency to give top priority to the processing of offshore LNG siting applications that will be supplied by U.S. flag vessels (Sec. 304(b). The act also requires the agency to consider the nation of registry for, and the nationality or citizenship of, officers and crew serving on board LNG tankers when reviewing an LNG terminal siting application (Sec. 304(c)).

Federal Pipeline and Chemical Security Agencies

Office of Pipeline Safety. The Office of Pipeline Safety (OPS) within the Pipeline and Hazardous Materials Safety Administration (PHMSA) of the Department of Transportation has statutory authority to regulate the safety and security of LNG peak-shaving plants. The agency derives this authority under the Natural Gas Pipeline Safety Act of 1968 (P.L. 90-481). The OPS security regulations for LNG peak-shaving facilities are found in 49 C.F.R. 193, *Liquefied Natural Gas Facilities: Federal Safety Standards* (Subpart J-Security). These regulations govern security procedures, protective enclosures, communications, monitoring, lighting, power sources, and warning signs. Federal LNG *safety* regulations (33 C.F.R. 127) and National Fire Protection Association standards for LNG also include provisions addressing security, such as requirements for monitoring facilities and preparing emergency response plans.[63]

On December, 28, 2006, the OPS published in the *Federal Register* a security advisory for LNG facility operators after an August, 2006 security breach at an LNG peak-shaving plant in Lynn, MA.[64] Although not a terrorist incident, the security breach involved the penetration of intruders through several security barriers and alert systems, permitting them to access the main LNG storage tank at the facility. The OPS advisory recommends that LNG facility operators ensure alarms and monitoring devices are functioning; ensure security personnel are properly trained; determine whether security personnel can respond to security breaches in a timely manner; update security procedures to incorporate the most relevant threat information; confirm that personnel properly coordinate their security activities; and independently audit facility security or conduct.[65]

Transportation Security Administration. The Transportation Security Administration (TSA) is the lead federal authority for the security of the interstate gas pipeline network under the Natural Gas Pipeline Safety Act of 1968 (P.L. 90-481). This security authority was transferred to TSA from the Transportation Department's Office of Pipeline Safety (OPS) under the Aviation and Transportation Security Act of 2001(P.L. 107-71). The TSA has asserted its security authority over

---

[63] National Fire Protection Association (NFPA). *Standard for the Production, Storage, and Handling of Liquefied Natural Gas (LNG)*. NFPA 59A. Quincy, MA. 2006.

[64] Pipeline and Hazardous Materials Safety Administration (PHMSA). "Pipeline Safety: Lessons Learned From a Security Breach at a Liquefied Natural Gas Facility." Docket No. PHMSA-04-19856. *Federal Register*. Vol. 71. No. 249. December 28, 2006. p. 78269.

[65] Ibid.

CRS-17

land-based LNG facilities that are considered an integral part of the interstate pipeline network.[66] The TSA exercises its pipeline and LNG security oversight through the Pipeline Security Division (PSD) within the agency's Office of Transportation Sector Network Management.[67] The mission of TSA's Pipeline Security Division currently includes developing security standards; implementing measures to mitigate security risk; building and maintaining stakeholder relations, coordination, education and outreach; and monitoring compliance with security standards, requirements, and regulations.

Since 2003, TSA has put in place a number of initiatives related to pipeline security. These initiatives include the coordination, development, implementation, and monitoring of pipeline security plans; on-site reviews of pipeline operator security; United States and Canadian security assessment and planning for critical cross-border pipelines; regional supply studies for key natural gas markets; and pipelines security training, among other initiatives.[68] As of February 2008, TSA had completed 73 CSR reviews.[69] According to TSA, virtually all of the companies reviewed have developed security plans, identified critical assets, and conducted background checks on new employees. Most have also implemented employee security training programs and raised local community and law enforcement awareness of pipeline security as part of their emergency response obligations.[70] In 2005, TSA issued an overview of recommended security practices for pipeline operators "for informational purposes only ... not intended to replace security measures already implemented by individual companies."[71] The agency released revised guidance on security best practices at the end of 2006 and plans to release a second revision in 2008.[72]

Federal Energy Regulatory Commission (FERC). The FERC is responsible for permitting new land-based LNG facilities, and for ensuring the safe operation of these facilities through subsequent inspections.[73] The initial permitting process requires approval of safety and security provisions in facility design, such as hazard detectors, security cameras, and vapor cloud exclusion zones. Every two years, FERC staff inspect LNG facilities to monitor the condition of the physical

---

[66] TSA, Intermodal Security Program Office. Personal communication. August 18, 2003.

[67] These offices were formerly known as the Pipeline Security Program Office and the Intermodal Security Program Office, respectively.

[68] Transportation Security Administration, *Pipeline Modal Annex*, June 2007, pp. 10-11. [http://www.dhs.gov/xlibrary/assets/Transportation_Pipeline_Modal_Annex_5_21_07.pdf]

[69] TSA, Intermodal Security Program Office, personal communication, February 27, 2008.

[70] Mike Gillenwater, TSA, "Pipeline Security Overview," Presentation to the Alabama Public Service Commission Gas Pipeline Safety Seminar, Montgomery, AL, December 11, 2007; TSA, Pipeline Security Division, personal communication, July 6, 2007.

[71] TSA, Intermodal Security Program Office, *Pipeline Security Best Practices*, October 19, 2005, p. 1.

[72] TSA, February 27, 2008.

[73] U.S. Code of Federal Regulations. 18 C.F.R. 157.

CRS-18

plant and inspect changes from the originally approved facility design or operations.[74] The FERC derives its LNG siting authority under the Natural Gas Act of 1938 (15 U.S.C. 717). The agency has jurisdiction over all on-shore LNG marine terminals and 12 peak-shaving plants involved in interstate gas trade.[75]

In response to public concern about LNG plant security since September 11, 2001, FERC has emphasized the importance of security at LNG facilities. According to the commission, FERC staff played key roles at inter-agency technical conferences regarding security at the Everett and Cove Point LNG terminals. According FERC staff, the commission has added a security chapter to its LNG site inspection manuals which consolidates previous requirements and adds new ones.[76] As part of its biennial inspection program, FERC also inspected 11 jurisdictional LNG sites in 2005 "placing increased emphasis on plant security measures and improvements."[77] FERC's FY2006 annual report states that "the Commission continues to give the highest priority to deciding any requests made for the recovery of extraordinary expenditures to safeguard the reliability and security of the Nation's energy transportation systems and energy supply infrastructure."[78]

Department of Homeland Security. The Department of Homeland Security (DHS) Appropriations Act of 2007 (P.L. 109-295) grants DHS the authority to regulate chemical facilities that "present high levels of security risk" (Sec. 550). In November, 2007, DHS finalized its chemical facility security regulations under the act, requiring that facilities with certain hazardous chemicals, including LNG, at or above screening threshold quantities submit information to DHS through an on-line screening tool. Based on these evaluations, DHS will identify high risk facilities required to conduct a security vulnerability assessments and prepare site security plans to address identified vulnerabilities and meet risk-based performance standards.[79] These regulations may apply to inland LNG peak-shaving plants, although they exempt LNG facilities in ports which are subject to security regulations under the Maritime Transportation Security Act of 2002 (P.L. 107-295), as amended.

---

[74] Foley, R. Federal Energy Regulatory Commission (FERC), Office of Energy Projects. "Liquefied Natural Gas Imports." Slide presentation. January 2003. p. 17.

[75] Robinson, J.M, Federal Energy Regulatory Commission (FERC). Testimony before the Senate Energy and Natural Resources Committee, Subcommittee on Energy. February 15, 2005.

[76] FERC. Personal communication. August 13, 2003.

[77] Federal Energy Regulatory Commission (FERC). 2005 Annual Report. Washington, DC. 2006. p. 18.

[78] Federal Energy Regulatory Commission (FERC). *Federal Energy Regulatory Commission Annual Report FY2006.* 2007. p. 23.

[79] 72 Fed. Reg. 17688. "Chemical Facility Anti-Terrorism Standards." April 9, 2007; 72 Fed. Reg. 65396. "Appendix to Chemical Facility Anti-Terrorism Standards." November 20, 2007.

CRS-19

Federal Interagency Cooperation in LNG Security

The Coast Guard, TSA, and FERC all have potentially overlapping security jurisdiction over certain facilities at onshore LNG terminals. For example, FERC's biennial LNG site visits explicitly include security inspections, and TSA oversees onsite pipeline security — but the Coast Guard asserts lead security authority over the entire terminal in its maritime security regulations. Under current authority, both the Coast Guard and TSA could both require their own facility security assessments for pipelines and LNG storage at LNG marine terminals.

To avoid jurisdictional confusion, the Coast Guard, OPS and FERC have entered into an interagency agreement to ensure that they

> work in a coordinated manner to address issues regarding safety and security at waterfront LNG facilities, including the terminal facilities and tanker operations, to avoid duplication of effort, and to maximize the exchange of relevant information related to the safety and security aspects of LNG facilities and the related marine concerns.[80]

The agreement requires the agencies to cooperate in the siting approval of new LNG facilities, inspection and operational review of existing facilities, informal communication, and dispute resolution.[81] According to FERC, in FY2006, the commission the "performed detailed reviews of [LNG] safety and security issues, in coordination with the U.S. Coast Guard and the U.S. Department of Transportation."[82]

The FERC's security review for new LNG terminal applications is conducted in consultation with the US Coast Guard. Security assessments of individual terminal proposals are conducted by Coast Guard field units through security workshops involving federal, state and local law enforcement officials as well as port stakeholders. FERC engineers provide technical assistance on marine spill issues. FERC and the Coast Guard require LNG terminal applicants to also submit a navigational suitability review under 33 C.F.R. 127, and begin a security assessment of their proposal in accordance with 33 C.F.R. 105. According to FERC, where site-specific security concerns have been raised, the agencies have conducted non-public technical workshops with "all relevant stakeholders and federal, state and local expert agencies" to resolve those security concerns.[83]

---

[80] Federal Energy Regulatory Commission (FERC). "Interagency Agreement Among the Federal Energy Regulatory Commission United States Coast Guard and Research and Special Programs Administration for the Safety and Security Review of Waterfront Import/Export Liquefied Natural Gas Facilities." February 11, 2004. p. 1.

[81] FERC. February 11, 2004. pp. 2-4.

[82] Federal Energy Regulatory Commission (FERC). 2006 Annual Report. Washington, DC. 2007. p. 25.

[83] Robinson, J.M., Federal Energy Regulatory Commission (FERC). Testimony before the Senate Energy and Natural Resources Committee, Subcommittee on Energy. February 15, 2005.

CRS-20

Industry Initiatives for Land-Based LNG Security

After the September 11 attacks, gas infrastructure operators, many with LNG facilities, immediately increased security against the newly perceived terrorist threat. The operators strengthened emergency plans; increased liaison with law enforcement; increased monitoring of visitors and vehicles on utility property; increased employee security awareness; and deployed more security guards.[84] In cooperation with the OPS, the Interstate Natural Gas Association of America (INGAA) formed a task force to develop and oversee industry-wide security standards "for critical onshore and offshore pipelines and related facilities, as well as liquefied natural gas (LNG) facilities."[85] The task force also included representatives from the Department of Energy (DOE), the American Gas Association (AGA), and non-member pipeline operators. With the endorsement of the OPS, the INGAA task force issued security guidelines for natural gas infrastructure, including LNG facilities, in September 2002.[86] The task force also worked with federal agencies, including the Department of Homeland Security, on a common government threat notification system.[87]

Key Policy Issues in LNG Security

Government and industry have taken significant steps to secure the nation's LNG infrastructure. But continued progress in implementing and sustaining LNG infrastructure protection activities may face several challenges. As discussed in detail in the following sections, members of Congress and federal officials are concerned about the growing public costs of LNG security, the uncertainty of terrorist threats against LNG, and security differences between foreign and U.S. LNG vessels and crews.

Public Costs of LNG Marine Security

Some policymakers are concerned about the public cost and sustainability of securing LNG shipments. Overall cost data for LNG security are unavailable, but estimates have been made for Everett shipments. In 2003, the Coast Guard Program Office estimated that it cost the Coast Guard approximately $40,000 to $50,000 to "shepherd" an LNG tanker through a delivery to the Everett terminal, depending on

---

[84] American Gas Association (AGA) *Natural Gas Distribution Industry Critical Infrastructure Security*, 2002, and AGA, *Natural Gas Infrastructure Security — Frequently Asked Questions.* April 30, 2003.

[85] Haener, W.J., CMS Energy Corp. Testimony on behalf of the Interstate Natural Gas Association of America (INGAA) before the House Transportation and Infrastructure Subcommittee on Highways and Transit. February 13, 2002. p. 4.

[86] Interstate Natural Gas Association of America (INGAA) et al., *Security Guidelines Natural Gas Industry Transmission and Distribution.* Washington, DC. September 6, 2002.

[87] Haener. February 13, 2002. p. 4.

CRS-21

the duration of the delivery, the nature of the security escort, and other factors.[88] A 2007 update from the Coast Guard Boston Sector estimates an average direct cost to the Coast Guard of an LNG delivery to Everett of approximately $62,000.[89] State and local authorities also incur costs for overtime police, fire and security personnel overseeing LNG tanker deliveries. The state of Massachusetts and the cities of Boston and Chelsea estimated they spent a combined $37,500 to safeguard the first LNG shipment to Everett after September 11, 2001.[90] Based on these figures, the public cost of security for an LNG tanker shipment to Everett is on the order of $100,000, excluding costs incurred by the terminal owner.

Marine security costs at other active LNG terminals could be lower than for Everett to the extent they are farther from dense populations and face fewer vulnerabilities. But these terminals expect more shipments. Altogether, the nine active onshore U.S. LNG terminals, including Everett, expect to have enough capacity for over 1,100 shipments per year in 2009. Increasing LNG imports to meet 13% of total U.S. gas supply by 2030 as projected by the EIA could require some 2,300 LNG shipments to LNG terminals serving the United States. Assuming an average security cost only half that for Everett, or $50,000 per shipment, annual costs to the public for marine LNG security could exceed $55 million by 2009 if active terminals were operating at full capacity. Security costs could exceed $115 million by 2030 based on the EIA projections.[91] At least over the next several years, however, analysts predict that U.S. LNG terminals will operate well below capacity, so actual marine security costs will likely be lower.[92]

The potential increase in security costs from growing U.S. LNG imports, and the potential diversion of Coast Guard and safety agency resources from other activities have been a persistent concern to policy makers.[93] According to Coast Guard officials, the service's LNG security expenditures are not all incremental, since they are part of the Coast Guard's general mission to protect the nation's waters and coasts. Nonetheless, Coast Guard staff have acknowledged that resources dedicated to securing maritime LNG might be otherwise deployed for boating safety, search and rescue, drug interdiction, or other security missions. LNG security is funded from the Coast Guard's general maritime security budget, so it is not a line

---

[88] U.S. Coast Guard, Program Office. Personal communication. August 12, 2003. This estimate is based on boat, staff and administrative costs for an assumed 20-hour mission.

[89] Cdr. Mark Meservey, House Liaison, U.S. Coast Guard. "Sector Boston LNG Security Approximate Costs." Unpublished memorandum. May 4, 2007.

[90] McElhenny, J. "State Says LNG Tanker Security Cost $20,500." Associated Press. November 2, 2001. p. 1.

[91] Note that security costs associated with any LNG terminals in Canada, Mexico and the Bahamas (built primarily to serve U.S. markets) would not be a direct U.S. responsibility, although such costs might still be priced into LNG supplied from those terminals.

[92] "Liquified Natural Gas Markets in U.S. Emerge in Uncertain Times, Panelists Agree." *Foster Natural Gas Report*. April 11, 2008. p. 5.

[93] See, for example, Representative Peter Defazio, remarks before the House Homeland Security Committee hearing on Securing Liquid Natural Gas Tankers to Protect the Homeland. March 21, 2007.

470 703-739-3790 TCNNaturalGas.com

CRS-22

item in the FY2009 Department of Homeland Security budget request. However, the Coast Guard's FY2006 budget did include an additional $11 million in funding over FY2005 levels for "Increased Port Presence and LNG Transport Security," specifically including "additional boat crews and screening personnel at key LNG hubs."[94]

In a December 2007 report, the GAO recommended that the Coast Guard develop a national resource allocation plan to address growing LNG security requirements.[95] In subsequent testimony before Congress, Coast Guard Commandant Admiral Thad Allen expressed concern about the costs to the Coast Guard of securing dangerous cargoes such as LNG and called for a "national dialogue" on the issue.[96] During questioning, Admiral Allen acknowledged that the Coast Guard did not currently possess sufficient resources to secure future LNG deliveries to a proposed LNG terminal in Long Island Sound which has subsequently been authorized by FERC.[97]

State and local agencies are also seeking more funding to offset the costs of LNG security. Otherwise, they believe that LNG security needs may force them to divert limited local resources from other important public services. Addressing these concerns, the Energy Policy Act of 2005 requires private and public sector cost-sharing for LNG tanker security (Section 311d). In compliance with the act and prior FERC policy, FERC officials require new LNG terminal operators to pay the costs of any additional security or safety needed for their facilities.[98] The FERC has also recommended that LNG terminal operators provide private security staff to supplement Coast Guard and local government security forces.[99]

The public costs of LNG security may decline as federally mandated security systems and plans are implemented. New security technology, more specific threat intelligence, and changing threat assessments may all help to lower LNG security costs in the future. Nonetheless, the potential increase in security costs from growing

---

[94] Department of Homeland Security (DHS). *Budget-in-Brief, Fiscal Year 2006.*

[95] Government Accountability Office. *Maritime Security: Federal Efforts Needed to Address Challenges in Responding to Terrorist Attacks on Energy Commodity Tankers.* GAO-08-141. December 10, 2007. p. 79.

[96] Admiral Thad Allen, Commandant, U.S. Coast Guard. Testimony before the House Committee on Appropriations, Subcommittee on Homeland Security hearing, "Coast Guard Budget: Impact on Maritime Safety, Security, and Environmental Protection." March 5, 2008.

[97] Admiral Thad Allen, March 5, 2008; Federal Energy Regulatory Commission. "Order Granting Authority Under Section 3 of the Natural Gas Act and Issuing Certificates." Docket No. CP06-54-0000. March 20, 2008.

[98] Baldor, L.C. "Federal Agency, R.I. Officials Meet over LNG Terminal." *Associated Press.* March 17, 2005.

[99] Federal Energy Regulatory Commission (FERC). "Response to Senator Jack Reed's 2/1/05 letter regarding the proposed Weaver's Cove LNG Project in Fall River, MA & the proposed KeySpan LNG Facility Upgrade Project in Providence, RI under CP04-293 et al." March 3, 2005. p. 2.

CRS-23

U.S. LNG shipments may warrant a review of these costs and associated recovery mechanisms. S. 1594 would allow the DHS to establish a security cost-sharing plan to assist the USCG in securing LNG tankers and other vessels carrying especially hazardous cargo (Sec. 6). H.R. 2830 would prohibit LNG facility security plans based upon the provision of security by a state or local government unless that government has an LNG security arrangement with the facility operator (Sec. 720 (b)). H.R. 2830 would also require the Coast Guard to enforce LNG tanker security zones (Sec. 720(a)), and would require the Coast Guard to certify that it has adequate security resources in the sector where a terminal would be located before facility security plans for a new LNG terminal are approved (Sec. 720(c)).

The Commandant of the Coast Guard reportedly opposes the requirement in H.R 2830 for the Coast Guard to provide LNG tanker security on the grounds that it undermines "the necessary discretion and flexibility to meet ... mission demands in an often-changing, dangerous operating environment."[100] In prior testimony before Congress, the Commandant stated that such a requirement would not appropriately balance LNG risks against the risks of other dangerous cargoes in marine transportation, and would amount to a subsidy for private LNG companies.[101] The Commandant also reportedly opposes H.R. 2830 because he believes it does not adequately distribute the LNG security burden among the Coast and state and local agencies involved in LNG projects.[102] Echoing the Commandant's objections, President Bush reportedly has threatened to veto H.R. 2830 because of these LNG security provisions.[103] H.R. 2830 passed the House by a margin (395-7) large enough to override a veto, however, and has yet to pass in the Senate, so it remains to be seen whether these provisions will ultimately change in response to the Commandant's or President's objections.

Uncertainty About LNG Threats

The likelihood of a terrorist attack on U.S. LNG infrastructure has been the subject of debate since September 11, 2001. To date, no LNG tanker or land-based LNG facility in the world has been attacked by terrorists. However, similar natural gas and oil facilities have been favored terror targets internationally. For example, since 2001, gas and oil pipelines have been attacked in at least half a dozen countries.[104] In October 2002, the French oil tanker *Limburg* was attacked off the Yemeni coast by a bomb-laden fishing boat.[105] In June 2003, U.S. intelligence

---

[100] Joshi, R. "Allen Slams USCG Funding Bill." *Lloyd's List*. May 1, 2008.

[101] Thad Allen, Commandant, U.S. Coast Guard. Testimony before the House Appropriations Committee, Homeland Security Subcommittee hearing on the Coast Guard Budget: Impact on Maritime Safety, Security, and Environmental Protection. March 5, 2008.

[102] Joshi, R. 2008.

[103] "Bush Warns on LNG Safety Bill." *International Oil Daily*, April 29, 2008.

[104] For specific examples, see CRS Report RL31990, *Pipeline Security: An Overview of Federal Activities and Current Policy Issues*, by Paul Parfomak.

[105] "Ships as Terrorist Targets." *American Shipper*. November, 2002. p. 59.

472 TCNNaturalGas.com

CRS-24

agencies warned about possible Al Qaeda attacks on energy facilities in Texas.[106] The Homeland Security Council included terrorist attacks on "cargo ships" carrying "flammable liquids" among the fifteen hazards scenarios it developed in 2004 as the basis for U.S. homeland security "national preparedness standards."[107]

In addition to warnings of a terrorist threat to energy facilities in general, federal agencies have identified LNG infrastructure in particular as a potential terrorist target. The Department of Homeland Security (DHS) specifically included LNG assets among a list of potential terrorist targets in a security alert late in 2003.[108] The DHS also reported that "in early 2001 there was some suspicion of possible associations between stowaways on Algerian flagged LNG tankers arriving in Boston and persons connected with the so-called 'Millennium Plot'" to bomb targets in the United States. While these suspicions could not be proved, DHS stated that "the risks associated with LNG shipments are real, and they can never be entirely eliminated."[109] The 2004 report by Sandia National Laboratories concluded that potential terrorist attacks on LNG tankers, could be considered "credible and possible."[110] The Sandia report identified LNG tankers as vulnerable to ramming, pre-placed explosives, insider takeover, hijacking, or external terrorist actions (such as a *Limburg*-type, missile or airplane attack).[111] Others further assert that terrorists have demonstrated both the desire and capability to attack such shipping with the intention of harming the general population.[112]

Although they acknowledge the security information put forth by federal agencies, many experts believe that concern about threats to LNG tankers is overstated.[113] In 2003, the head of one university research consortium remarked, for example, "from all the information we have ... we don't see LNG as likely or credible terrorist targets."[114] Industry representatives argue that deliberately causing an LNG catastrophe to injure people might be possible in theory, but would be extremely difficult to accomplish. Likewise, the Federal Energy Regulatory Commission

---

[106] Hedges, M. "Terrorists Possibly Targeting Texas." *Houston Chronicle*. June 24, 2003.

[107] Homeland Security Council. *Planning Scenarios: Executive Summaries*. July 2004. p. 6-1.

[108] Office of Congressman Edward J. Markey. Personal communication with staff. January 5, 2004.

[109] Turner, P.J., Assistant Secretary for Legislative Affairs, Department of Homeland Security (DHS). Letter to U.S. Representative Edward Markey. April 15, 2004. p. 1.

[110] Sandia National Laboratories (SNL). *Guidance on Risk Analysis and Safety Implications of a Large Liquefied Natural Gas (LNG) Spill Over Water*. SAND2004-6258. Albuquerque, NM. December 2004. pp. 49-50.

[111] SNL. December 2004. pp. 61-62.

[112] Clarke, R.A., et al. *LNG Facilities in Urban Areas*. Good Harbor Consulting, LLC. Prepared for the Rhode Island Office of Attorney General. GHC-RI-0505A. May 2005.

[113] McLaughlin, J. "LNG is Nowhere Near as Dangerous as People Are Making it Out to Be." *Lloyd's List*. February 8, 2005. p5.

[114] Behr, Peter. "Higher Gas Price Sets Stage for LNG." *Washington Post*. July 5, 2003. p. D10.

CRS-25

(FERC) and other experts believe that LNG facilities are relatively secure compared to other hazardous chemical infrastructures which receives less public attention. In a 2004 report, the FERC stated that

> for a new LNG terminal proposal ... the perceived threat of a terrorist attack may be considered as highly probable to the local population. However, at the national level, potential terrorist targets are plentiful.... Many of these pose a similar or greater hazard to that of LNG.[115]

The FERC also has remarked, however, that "unlike accidental causes, historical experience provides little guidance in estimating the probability of a terrorist attack on an LNG vessel or onshore storage facility."[116]

Former Director of Central Intelligence, James Woolsey, has stated his belief that a terrorist attack on an LNG tanker in U.S. waters would be unlikely because its potential impacts would not be great enough compared to other potential targets.[117] LNG terminal operators which have conducted proprietary assessments of potential terrorist attacks against LNG tankers, have expressed similar views.[118] In a September 2006 evaluation of a proposed LNG terminal in Long Island Sound, the Coast Guard stated that there were "currently no specific, credible threats against" the proposed LNG facility or tankers serving the facility.[119] The evaluation also noted, however, that the threat environment is dynamic and that some threats may be unknown.[120] Because the probability of a terrorist attack on LNG cannot be known with certainty, policy makers and community leaders must, to some extent, rely on their own judgment to decide whether LNG security measures for a specific facility will adequately protect the public. S. 1594 would increase federal protection of vessels and infrastructure handling LNG through new international standards (Sec. 2); safety and security assistance for foreign ports (Sec. 4-5), incident response and recovery plans (Sec. 7); and other provisions.

---

[115] Federal Energy Regulatory Commission (FERC). *Vista del Sol LNG Terminal Project, Draft Environmental Impact Statement*. FERC/EIS-0176D. December 2004. p. 4-162; For example, based on data from the U.S. Office of Hazardous Materials Safety, 600 LNG tanker shipments would account for less than 1% of total annual U.S. shipments of hazardous marine cargo such as ammonia, crude oil, liquefied petroleum gases, and other volatile chemicals.

[116] FERC. FERC/EIS-0176D. December 2004. p4-162. Notwithstanding this assertion, in its subsequent draft review of the Long Beach LNG terminal proposal, the FERC states that "the historical probability of a successful terrorist event would be less than seven chances in a million per year..." See FERC. October 7, 2005. p. ES-14.

[117] Woolsey, James. Remarks before the National Commission on Energy, LNG Forum, Washington, D.C., June 21, 2006.

[118] Grant, Richard, President, Distrigas. Testimony before the Senate Committee on Energy and Natural Resources, Subcommittee on Energy hearing on "The Future of Liquefied Natural Gas: Siting and Safety." February 15, 2005.

[119] U.S. Coast Guard. *U.S. Coast Guard Captain of the Port Long Island Sound Waterways Suitability Report for the Proposed Broadwater Liquefied Natural Gas Facility*. September 21, 2006. p. 146.

[120] Ibid.

CRS-26

Foreign vs. U.S. LNG Tankers and Crews

There are currently no U.S.-flagged LNG tankers and few, if any, U.S. citizens among LNG tanker crews. Some policy makers are concerned that, compared to U.S. vessels and crews, foreign-flagged LNG tankers may not face the same security requirements or may not face the same level of security oversight and verification.[121] This rationale underlies the provisions in P.L. 109-241 that promote LNG shipping to the United States on U.S.-flagged vessels with U.S. crews. Prompted by these provisions, at least four LNG developers have committed to using U.S. crews in their LNG terminal siting proposals.[122] Some stakeholders have called for similar measures to promote U.S. flags and crews for tankers serving onshore LNG terminals regulated by FERC.

Notwithstanding the LNG tanker provisions in P.L. 109-241, Coast Guard officials have stated that existing security provisions for foreign-flagged LNG tankers and foreign place them on an equal security footing with potential U.S. counterparts.[123]

> Our domestic maritime security regime is closely aligned with the International Ship and Port Facility Security (ISPS) Code.... Under the ISPS Code, vessels in international service, including LNG vessels, must have an International Ship Security Certificate (ISSC). To be issued an ISSC by its flag state, the vessel must develop and implement a threat-scalable security plan that, among other things, establishes access control measures, security measures for cargo handling and delivery of ships stores, surveillance and monitoring, security communications, security incident procedures, and training and drill requirements. The plan must also identify a Ship Security Officer who is responsible for ensuring compliance with the ship's security plan. The Coast Guard rigorously enforces this international requirement by evaluating security compliance as part of our ongoing port state control program.

Others have questioned preferential treatment of U.S. LNG tankers and crews on the grounds that it may impinge on free trade principles by discriminating against foreign LNG tanker operators fully adhering to international standards.[124] Given the potential maritime treaty and trade implications, federal efforts to promote U.S. flags and crews on LNG tankers may require careful consideration of potential benefits and costs.

---

[121] See, for example: Senator Barbara A. Mikulski. Testimony before the House of Transportation and Infrastructure Committee, Coast Guard and Maritime Transportation Subcommittee field hearing on Safety and Security of Liquefied Natural Gas and the Impact on Port Operations. Baltimore, MD. April 23, 2007.

[122] States News Service. "Agreement Means New Jobs for U.S. Mariners on LNG Tankers." February 8, 2008.

[123] O'Malley. May 7, 2007.

[124] "LNG Must Uphold US Free Trade, Warns ICS." *Lloyd's List*. February 21, 2007. p. 3.

475

CRS-27

Conclusions

The U.S. LNG industry is growing quickly. While rising LNG imports may offer economic benefits, they also pose risks. LNG infrastructure is inherently hazardous and it is potentially attractive to terrorists. Both lawmakers and the general public are concerned about these risks, although the LNG industry has a long history of relatively safe operations and has taken steps to secure its assets against terrorist attack. No LNG tanker or land-based facility has been attacked by terrorists, and federal, state and local governments have put in place security measures intended to safeguard LNG against newly perceived terrorist threats. These measures are evolving, but a variety of industry and agency representatives suggest that these federal initiatives are reducing the vulnerability of U.S. LNG to terrorism.

The ongoing debate about LNG infrastructure security in the United States has often been contentious. Local officials and community groups have challenged numerous LNG infrastructure proposals on the grounds that they may represent an unacceptable risk to the public. Heightened public scrutiny of LNG facilities has made it difficult to site new LNG terminals near major gas markets and has increased the cost and complexity of LNG terminal siting approval. Nonetheless, both industry and government officials acknowledge that enough new LNG infrastructure will likely be approved to meet long-term U.S. import requirements. Indeed, federal agencies have approved the construction of a number of new U.S. import terminals, several of them onshore. Numerous additional terminal proposals await federal approval. Together with the expansion of the existing U.S. import terminals and the construction of new LNG terminals in Canada and Mexico, the approved U.S. facilities would provide enough added capacity to meet the bulk of U.S. LNG demand for the next 20 years.

New U.S. LNG terminals may not be ideally located so as to minimize the cost of natural gas, but building them in these locations may be better than not building them at all. Furthermore, because their security has been subject to intense public scrutiny, new LNG terminal and tanker operations may be safer than they might have been without such scrutiny and their siting may be less likely to be challenged at a later time when construction is already underway. The construction and subsequent closure of the Shoreham nuclear power plant in the 1980's due to new public opposition offers an example of the need to resolve safety and security concerns before capital is invested. From a purely economic perspective, therefore, the added costs of building more heavily protected LNG terminals potentially farther from their primary markets may represent the U.S. public's willingness to pay for LNG security. Whether this implicit price of LNG security is reasonable is an open question, but the continued interest of private companies to invest billions of dollars in U.S. LNG terminals suggests that it will not prevent needed LNG development.

As Congress continues its oversight of LNG infrastructure development, it may decide to examine the public costs and resource requirements of LNG security, especially in light of dramatically increasing LNG imports. In particular, Congress may consider whether future LNG security requirements will be appropriately funded, whether these requirements will be balanced against evolving risks, and whether the LNG industry is carrying its fair share of the security burden. Congress

CRS-28

may also act to improve its understanding of LNG security risks. Costly "blanket" investments in LNG security might be avoided if more refined terror threat information were available to focus security spending on a narrower set of infrastructure vulnerabilities. Finally, Congress may initiate action to better understand the security and trade implications of efforts to promote U.S.-flagged LNG tankers.

In addition to these specific issues, Congress might consider how the various elements of U.S. LNG security activity fit together in the nation's overall strategy to protect critical infrastructure. Maintaining high levels of security around LNG tankers, for example, may be of limited benefit if other hazardous marine cargoes are less well-protected. U.S. LNG security also requires coordination among many groups: international treaty organizations, federal agencies, state and local agencies, trade associations and LNG infrastructure operators. Reviewing how these groups work together to achieve common security goals could be an oversight challenge for Congress.

Congressional
Research
Service

Liquefied Natural Gas (LNG) Import Terminals: Siting, Safety, and Regulation

Paul W. Parfomak
Specialist in Energy and Infrastructure Policy

Adam Vann
Legislative Attorney

December 14, 2009

Congressional Research Service

7-5700

www.gov

RL32205

CRS Report for Congress —————————
Prepared for Members and Committees of Congress

Summary

Liquefied natural gas (LNG) is a hazardous fuel shipped in large tankers to U.S. ports from overseas. While LNG has historically made up a small part of U.S. natural gas supplies, rising price volatility, and the possibility of domestic shortages have significantly increased LNG demand. To meet this demand, energy companies have proposed new LNG import terminals throughout the coastal United States. Many of these terminals would be built onshore near populated areas.

The Federal Energy Regulatory Commission (FERC) grants federal approval for the siting of new onshore LNG facilities under the Natural Gas Act of 1938 and the Energy Policy Act of 2005 (P.L. 109-58). This approval process incorporates minimum safety standards for LNG established by the Department of Transportation. Although LNG has had a record of relative safety for the last 45 years, and no LNG tanker or land-based facility has been attacked by terrorists, proposals for new LNG terminal facilities have generated considerable public concern. Some community groups and governments officials fear that LNG terminals may expose nearby residents to unacceptable hazards. Ongoing public concern about LNG safety has focused congressional attention on the exclusivity of FERC's LNG siting authority, proposals for a regional LNG siting process, the lack of "remote" siting requirements in FERC regulations, state permitting requirements under the Clean Water Act and the Coastal Zone Management Act, terrorism attractiveness of LNG, the adequacy of Coast Guard security resources, and other issues.

LNG terminals directly affect the safety of communities in the states and congressional districts where they are sited, and may influence energy costs nationwide. Faced with an uncertain national need for greater LNG imports and persistent public concerns about LNG hazards, some in Congress have proposed changes to safety provisions in federal LNG siting regulation. Legislation proposed in the 110th Congress addressed Coast Guard LNG resources, FERC's exclusive siting authority, state concurrence of federal LNG siting decisions, and agency coordination under the Coastal Zone Management Act, among other proposals. Provisions in the Coast Guard Authorization Act of 2010 (H.R. 3619), passed by the House on October 23, 2009, would require additional waterway suitability notification requirements in LNG siting reviews by FERC (Sec. 1117). The Maritime Hazardous Cargo Security Act (S. 1385), introduced by Senator Lautenberg and three co-sponsors on June 25, 2009, would require a national study to identify measures to improve the security of maritime transportation of liquefied natural gas (Sec. 6).

If Congress concludes that new LNG terminals as currently regulated will pose an unacceptable risk to public safety, Congress may consider additional LNG safety-related legislation, or may exercise its oversight authority in other ways to influence LNG terminal siting approval. Alternatively, Congress may consider other changes in U.S. energy policy legislation to reduce the nation's demand for natural gas or increase supplies of North American natural gas and, thus, the need for new LNG infrastructure.

Congressional Research Service

Liquefied Natural Gas (LNG) Import Terminals: Siting, Safety, and Regulation

Contents

Figures

Congressional Research Service

Liquefied Natural Gas (LNG) Import Terminals: Siting, Safety, and Regulation

Tables

Appendixes

Contacts

Congressional Research Service

Introduction

Liquefied natural gas (LNG) historically has played a minor role in U.S. energy markets, but in reaction to rising natural gas prices, price volatility, and the possibility of domestic shortages, demand for LNG imports has increased significantly in recent years. To meet anticipated growth in LNG demand, new onshore and offshore LNG import terminals have been constructed or approved in United States coastal regions. More have been proposed. Because LNG (like other fossil fuels) is a hazardous[1] liquid transported and stored in enormous quantities—often near populated areas—concerns exist about the federal government's role in addressing LNG safety in the terminal siting process. In addition, various energy policy proposals could impact the need for new LNG terminals by encouraging the development of alternative U.S. energy supplies and promoting conservation and efficiency.

This report provides an overview of recent industry development of new LNG import terminals. The report summarizes LNG hazards and the industry's safety record. It discusses federal laws and regulations related to LNG terminal siting with a focus on the authorities of key federal agencies and safety provisions in the permitting of onshore facilities. The report reviews controversial safety issues in recent LNG siting proceedings, such as safety zones, marine hazards, hazard modeling, and remote siting. The report outlines policy issues related to LNG terminal safety, including the Federal Energy Regulatory Commission's (FERC's) LNG siting authority, regional LNG siting, "remote" siting requirements in federal regulations, state permitting requirements, terrorism, and other issues.

Issues Facing Congress

LNG terminals directly affect the safety of communities in the states and congressional districts where they are sited, and may influence energy costs nationwide. Faced with an uncertain national need for greater LNG imports and persistent public concerns about LNG hazards, some in Congress have proposed changes to safety provisions in federal LNG siting regulation. Legislation proposed in the 110th Congress addressed Coast Guard LNG resources, FERC's exclusive siting authority, state concurrence of federal LNG siting decisions, and agency coordination under the Coastal Zone Management Act, among other proposals.[2] If Congress concludes that new LNG terminals as currently regulated will pose an unacceptable risk to public safety, Congress may consider additional LNG safety-related legislation, or may exercise its oversight authority in other ways to influence LNG terminal siting approval. Alternatively, Congress may consider other changes in U.S. energy policy legislation to reduce the nation's demand for natural gas or increase supplies of North American natural gas and, thus, the need for new LNG infrastructure.

---

[1] 49 C.F.R. § 172.101. *List of Hazardous Materials.* Office of Hazardous Materials Safety, U.S. Department of Transportation.

[2] LNG proposals in the 110th Congress are found in: H.R. 1564, H.R. 2024, H.R. 2830, H.R. 6720, S. 323, S. 1174, S. 1579, S. 2822, S. 3441.

Scope and Limitations

This report focuses broadly on industry and federal activities related to safety in LNG import terminal siting. For a more specific discussion of LNG security, see CRS Report RL32073, *Liquefied Natural Gas (LNG) Infrastructure Security: Issues for Congress*, by Paul W. Parfomak. This report also deals primarily with those parts of LNG terminals which transfer, store, and process LNG prior to injection to natural gas pipelines for transmission off site. For more discussion of general natural gas or pipeline hazards, see CRS Report RL33347, *Pipeline Safety and Security: Federal Programs*, by Paul W. Parfomak. Also, this report discusses mostly onshore facilities and near-shore shipping, since they pose the greatest public hazards. Offshore LNG terminal siting regulations are summarized in the **Appendix**.

Background

What Is LNG and Where Does It Come From?

When natural gas is cooled to temperatures below minus 260° F it condenses into liquefied natural gas, or LNG. As a liquid, natural gas occupies only 1/600th the volume of its gaseous state, so it is stored more effectively in a limited space and is more readily transported. A single tanker ship, for example, can carry huge quantities of LNG—enough to supply a single day's energy needs of over 10 million homes. When LNG is warmed it "regasifies" and can be used for the same purposes as conventional natural gas such as heating, cooking, and power generation.

In 2009, LNG imports to the United States originated in Trinidad (54%), Egypt (34%), Norway (8%), and Nigeria (4%).[3] In recent years, some LNG shipments have also come from Algeria, Qatar, Equatorial Guinea, Malaysia, Oman, Australia, and other countries.[4] Brunei, Indonesia, Libya, and the United Arab Emirates also export LNG, and may be U.S. suppliers in the future. In addition to importing LNG to the lower 48 states, the United States exports Alaskan LNG to Japan.

Expectations for U.S. LNG Import Growth

The United States has used LNG commercially since the 1940s. Initially, LNG facilities stored domestically produced natural gas to supplement pipeline supplies during times of high gas demand. In the 1970s, LNG imports began to supplement domestic production. Primarily because of low domestic gas prices, LNG imports stayed relatively small—accounting for only 1% of total U.S. gas consumption as late as 2002.[5] In countries with limited domestic gas supplies, however, LNG imports grew dramatically over the same period. Japan, for example, imported

---

[3] Energy Information Administration (EIA). *Natural Gas Monthly*. November 2009. p. 9. Data are published only for the first nine months of the year.

[4] Energy Information Administration (EIA). *U.S. Natural Gas Imports by Country*. Online database, November 30, 2009. http://tonto.eia.doe.gov/dnav/ng/ng_move_impc_s1_m.htm.

[5] Energy Information Administration (EIA). *Natural Gas Annual 2005*. Tables 1 and 9. November 16, 2006.

97% of its natural gas supply as LNG in 2002, more than 11 times as much LNG as the United States.[6] South Korea, France, Spain, and Taiwan also became heavy LNG importers.

Natural gas demand growth accelerated in the United States from the mid-1980s through 2000 due to environmental concerns about other energy sources, widespread building of natural gas-fired electricity generation, and low natural gas prices. Domestic gas supplies have not always kept up with growth in demand, however, so prices have become volatile. At the same time, international LNG costs have fallen since the 1970s because of increased supplies and more efficient production and transportation, making LNG more competitive with domestic natural gas.

In 2003 testimony before Congress, the Federal Reserve Chairman called for a sharp increase in LNG imports to help avert a potential barrier to U.S. economic growth. According to the Chairman's testimony: "... high gas prices projected in the American distant futures market have made us a potential very large importer.... Access to world natural gas supplies will require a major expansion of LNG terminal import capacity."[7] Likewise, FERC Commissioner Suedeen Kelly told industry representatives in 2006 that,"while LNG has made a marginal contribution to gas supply over the last 30 years, it is poised to make a major contribution in the future."[8] Because burning natural gas produces only half as much carbon dioxide as burning coal, and also less carbon dioxide than vehicular fuels like gasoline, some also anticipate natural gas demand to grow as the preferred fuel in the near-term for power plants and motor vehicles under a national policy of carbon control.[9] Recent increases in U.S. natural gas production from domestic shale deposits have complicated projections about LNG markets. Nonetheless, many analysts expect continued growth in the U.S. LNG imports over the long term.[10]

Proposed LNG Import Terminals in the United States

LNG tankers unload their cargo at dedicated marine terminals which store and regasify the LNG for distribution to domestic markets. Onshore terminals consist of docks, LNG handling equipment, storage tanks, and interconnections to regional gas transmission pipelines and electric power plants. Offshore terminals regasify and pump the LNG directly into offshore natural gas pipelines or may store LNG for later injection into offshore pipelines.

There are seven active onshore LNG import terminals in the United States: Everett, Massachusetts; Lake Charles, Louisiana; Cove Point, Maryland; Elba Island, Georgia; Peñuelas, Puerto Rico; Freeport, Texas; and Sabine Pass, Louisiana. There are two active offshore import terminals, one located in the Gulf of Mexico and a second near Boston, Massachusetts. (There is also one export terminal in Kenai, Alaska.) In addition to these active terminals, some 25 LNG terminal proposals have been approved by regulators across North America to serve the U.S. market **Figure 1**. A number of these proposals have been withdrawn, however, due to siting

---

[6] Energy Information Administration (EIA). "World LNG Imports by Origin, 2002." Washington, DC. October 2003.

[7] Greenspan, A., Chairman, U.S. Federal Reserve Board. "Natural Gas Supply and Demand Issues." Testimony before the House Energy and Commerce Committee. June 10, 2003.

[8] *Inside F.E.R.C.* "Kelly-LNG Poised for 'Major Contribution' to Energy Supply, to Meet Industrial Demand." April 10, 2006.

[9] See, for example: John D. Podesta and Timothy E. Wirth. *Natural Gas: A Bridge Fuel for the 21st Century.* Center for American Progress. August 10, 2009. http://www.americanprogress.org/issues/2009/08/pdf/naturalgasmemo.pdf.

[10] Rita Tubb. "LNG Imports Projected to Rise." *Pipeline & Gas Journal.* May 1, 2009.

problems, financing problems, or other reasons. Developers have proposed another 8 U.S. terminals prior to filing formal siting applications.[11]

Figure 1. Approved LNG Terminals in North America.

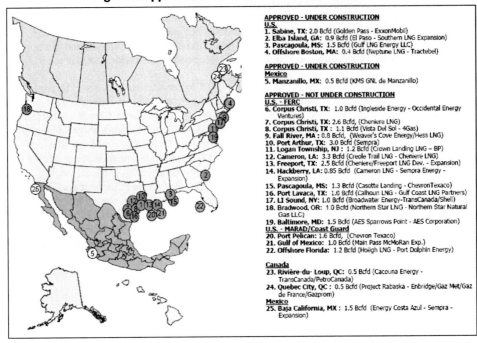

APPROVED - UNDER CONSTRUCTION
U.S.
1. **Sabine, TX:** 2.0 Bcfd (Golden Pass - ExxonMobil)
2. **Elba Island, GA:** 0.9 Bcfd (El Paso - Southern LNG Expansion)
3. **Pascagoula, MS:** 1.5 Bcfd (Gulf LNG Energy LLC)
4. **Offshore Boston, MA:** 0.4 Bcfd (Neptune LNG - Tractebel)

APPROVED - UNDER CONSTRUCTION
Mexico
5. **Manzanillo, MX:** 0.5 Bcfd (KMS GNL de Manzanillo)

APPROVED - NOT UNDER CONSTRUCTION
U.S. - FERC
6. **Corpus Christi, TX:** 1.0 Bcfd (Ingleside Energy - Occidental Energy Ventures)
7. **Corpus Christi, TX:** 2.6 Bcfd, (Cheniere LNG)
8. **Corpus Christi, TX :** 1.1 Bcfd (Vista Del Sol - 4Gas)
9. **Fall River, MA :** 0.8 Bcfd, (Weaver's Cove Energy/Hess LNG)
10. **Port Arthur, TX:** 3.0 Bcfd (Sempra)
11. **Logan Township, NJ :** 1.2 Bcfd (Crown Landing LNG – BP)
12. **Cameron, LA:** 3.3 Bcfd (Creole Trail LNG - Cheniere LNG)
13. **Freeport, TX:** 2.5 Bcfd (Cheniere/Freeport LNG Dev. - Expansion)
14. **Hackberry, LA:** 0.85 Bcfd (Cameron LNG - Sempra Energy - Expansion)
15. **Pascagoula, MS:** 1.3 Bcfd (Casotte Landing - ChevronTexaco)
16. **Port Lavaca, TX:** 1.0 Bcfd (Calhoun LNG - Gulf Coast LNG Partners)
17. **LI Sound, NY:** 1.0 Bcfd (Broadwater Energy-TransCanada/Shell)
18. **Bradwood, OR:** 1.0 Bcfd (Northern Star LNG - Northern Star Natural Gas LLC)
19. **Baltimore, MD:** 1.5 Bcfd (AES Sparrows Point - AES Corporation)
U.S. - MARAD/Coast Guard
20. **Port Pelican:** 1.6 Bcfd, (Chevron Texaco)
21. **Gulf of Mexico:** 1.0 Bcfd (Main Pass McMoRan Exp.)
22. **Offshore Florida:** 1.2 Bcfd (Hoëgh LNG - Port Dolphin Energy)

Canada
23. **Rivière-du- Loup, QC:** 0.5 Bcfd (Cacouna Energy - TransCanada/PetroCanada)
24. **Quebec City, QC :** 0.5 Bcfd (Project Rabaska - Enbridge/Gaz Met/Gaz de France/Gazprom)
Mexico
25. **Baja California, MX :** 1.5 Bcfd (Energy Costa Azul - Sempra - Expansion)

Source: Federal Energy Regulatory Commission (FERC), "Approved North American LNG Import Terminals," updated October 27, 2009. http://ferc.gov/industries/lng/indus-act/terminals/lng-approved.pdf.

Potential Safety Hazards from LNG Terminals

The safety hazards associated with LNG terminals have been debated for decades. A 1944 accident at one of the nation's first LNG facilities killed 128 people and initiated public fears about LNG hazards which persist today.[12] Technology improvements and standards since the 1940s have made LNG facilities much safer, but serious hazards remain since LNG is inherently volatile and is usually shipped and stored in large quantities. A 2004 accident at Algeria's Skikda LNG terminal, which killed or injured over 100 workers, added to the ongoing controversy over LNG facility safety.[13]

---

[11] Federal Energy Regulatory Commission, "Proposed North American LNG Import Terminals," October 27, 2009. http://www.ferc.gov/industries/lng/indus-act/terminals/lng-proposed.pdf.

[12] Bureau of Mines (BOM). *Report on the Investigation of the Fire at the Liquefaction, Storage, and Regasification Plant of the East Ohio Gas Co., Cleveland, Ohio, October 20, 1944.* February 1946.

[13] Junnola, Jill, et al. "Fatal Explosion Rocks Algeria's Skikda LNG Complex." *Oil Daily.* January 21, 2004. p. 6.

Physical Hazards of LNG

Natural gas is combustible, so an uncontrolled release of LNG poses a hazard of fire or, in confined spaces, explosion. LNG also poses hazards because it is so cold. The likelihood and severity of catastrophic LNG events have been the subject of controversy. While questions remain about the credible impacts of specific LNG hazards, there appears to be consensus as to what the most serious hazards are.

Pool Fires

If LNG spills near an ignition source, evaporating gas will burn above the LNG pool.[14] The resulting "pool fire" would spread as the LNG pool expanded away from its source and continued evaporating. A pool fire is intense, burning far more hotly and rapidly than oil or gasoline fires.[15] It cannot be extinguished—all the LNG must be consumed before it goes out. Because an LNG pool fire is so hot, its thermal radiation may injure people and damage property a considerable distance from the fire itself. Many experts agree that a large pool fire, especially on water, is the most serious LNG hazard.[16]

Flammable Vapor Clouds

If LNG spills but does not immediately ignite, the evaporating natural gas will form a vapor cloud that may drift some distance from the spill site. If the cloud subsequently encounters an ignition source, those portions of the cloud with a combustible gas-air concentration will burn. Because only a fraction of such a cloud would have a combustible gas-air concentration, the cloud would not likely ignite all at once, but the fire could still cause considerable damage.[17] An LNG vapor cloud fire would gradually burn its way back to the LNG spill where the vapors originated and would continue to burn as a pool fire.[18]

Other Safety Hazards

LNG spilled on water could (theoretically) regasify almost instantly in a "flameless explosion," although an Idaho National Engineering Laboratory report concluded that "transitions caused by mixing of LNG and water are not violent."[19] LNG vapor clouds are not toxic, but they could cause asphyxiation by displacing breathable air.[20] Such clouds may begin near the ground (or water) when they are still very cold, but rise in air as they warm, diminishing the threat to people. Due to its extremely low temperature, LNG could injure people or damage equipment through

---

[14] Methane, the main component of LNG, burns in gas-to-air ratios between 5% and 15%.

[15] Havens, J. "Ready to Blow?" *Bulletin of the Atomic Scientists.* July/August 2003. p. 17.

[16] Havens. 2003. p. 17.

[17] West, H.H. and Mannan, M.S. "LNG Safety Practices and Regulations." Prepared for the American Institute of Chemical Engineering Conference on Natural Gas Utilization and LNG Transportation. Houston, TX. April 2001. p. 2.

[18] Quillen, D. ChevronTexaco Corp. "LNG Safety Myths and Legends." Presentation to the Natural Gas Technology Conference. Houston, TX. May 14-15, 2002. p. 18.

[19] Siu, Nathan, et al. *Qualitative Risk Assessment for an LNG Refueling Station and Review of Relevant Safety Issues.* Idaho National Engineering Laboratory. INEEL/EXT-97-00827 rev2. Idaho Falls, ID. February 1998. p. 71.

[20] Siu. 1998. p. 62.

---

direct contact.[21] Such contact would likely be limited, however, as a major spill would likely result in a more serious fire. The environmental damage associated with an LNG spill would be confined to fire and freezing impacts near the spill since LNG dissipates completely and leaves no residue.[22]

Terrorism Hazards

LNG tankers and land-based facilities could be vulnerable to terrorism. Tankers might be physically attacked in a variety of ways to release their cargo—or commandeered for use as weapons against coastal targets. LNG terminal facilities might also be physically attacked with explosives or through other means. Some LNG facilities may also be indirectly disrupted by "cyber-attacks" or attacks on regional electricity grids and communications networks which could in turn affect dependent LNG control and safety systems.[23] The potential attractiveness of LNG infrastructure to terrorists as a target is discussed later in this report.

Safety Record of LNG

The LNG tanker industry claims a record of relative safety over the last 50 years; since international LNG shipping began in 1959, tankers have carried over 45,000 LNG cargoes and traveled over 128 million miles without a serious accident at sea or in port.[24] LNG tankers have experienced groundings and collisions during this period, but none has resulted in a major spill.[25] The LNG marine safety record is partly due to the double-hulled design of LNG tankers. This design makes them more robust and less prone to accidental spills than old single-hulled oil and fuel tankers like the *Exxon Valdez*, which caused a major Alaskan oil spill after grounding in 1989.[26] LNG tankers also carry radar, global positioning systems, automatic distress systems and beacons to signal if they are in trouble. Cargo safety systems include instruments that can shut operations if they deviate from normal as well as gas and fire detection systems.[27]

The safety record of onshore LNG terminals is more mixed. There are more than 40 LNG terminals (and more than 150 other LNG storage facilities) worldwide. Since 1944, there have been approximately 13 serious accidents at these facilities directly related to LNG. Two of these accidents caused single fatalities of facility workers—one in Algeria in 1977, and another at Cove Point, Maryland, in 1979. On January 19, 2004, a fire at the LNG processing facility in Skikda, Algeria killed an estimated 27 workers, injured 74 others, destroyed a processing plant, and

---

[21] Siu. 1998. p. 63.

[22] Quillen. 2002. p. 28.

[23] Skolnik, Sam. "Local Sites Potential Targets for Cyberterror." *Seattle Post-Intelligencer*. Seattle, WA. September 2, 2002.

[24] Center for LNG. "LNG Carrier Safety: A Long Record of Safe Operation." Internet page., December 14, 2009. http://www.lngfacts.org/About-LNG/Carrier-Safety.asp; Groupe International des Importateurs de Gaz Naturel Liquéfié, "LNG Ships," Paris, France, 2009, p. 1, http://www.giignl.org/fileadmin/user_upload/pdf/LNG_Safety/3%20-%20LNG%20Ships%208.28.09%20Final%20HQ.pdf.

[25] Foss, 2007; CH-IV International. *Safety History of International LNG Operations*. TD-02109. Millersville, MD. December. pp. 13-18.

[26] Society of International Gas Tanker & Terminal Operators Ltd. (SIGTTO). "Safe Havens for Disabled Gas Carriers." Third Edition. London. February 2003. pp. 1-2.

[27] Petroplus International, N.V. "Energy for Wales: LNG Frequently Asked Questions." Internet home page. Amsterdam, Netherlands. August 4, 2003.

---

damaged a marine berth. (It did not, however, damage a second processing plant or three large LNG storage tanks also located at the terminal, nor did the accident injure the rest of the 12,000 workers at the complex.) [28] It was considered the worst petrochemical plant fire in Algeria in over 40 years.[29] According to press reports, the accident resulted from poor maintenance rather than a facility design flaw.[30] Another three accidents at worldwide LNG plants since 1944 have also caused fatalities, but these were construction or maintenance accidents in which LNG was not present.

LNG Hazard Models

Since the terror attacks of September 11, 2001, a number of technical studies have been commissioned to reevaluate the safety hazards of LNG terminals and associated shipping. The most widely cited of these studies are listed in **Table 1.** These studies have caused controversy because some reach differing conclusions about the potential public hazard of LNG terminal accidents or terror attacks. Consequently, some fear that LNG hazards may be misrepresented by government agencies, or that certain LNG hazards may simply not be understood well enough to support a terminal siting approval.[31]

Hazard analyses for LNG terminals and shipping depend heavily upon computer models to approximate the effects of hypothetical accidents. Federal siting standards specifically require computer modeling of thermal radiation and flammable vapor cloud exclusion zones (49 C.F.R. §§ 193.2057, 2059).[32] Such models are necessary because there have been no major LNG incidents of the type envisioned in LNG safety research and because historical LNG experiments have been limited in scale and scope. But LNG hazards models simulate complex physical phenomena and are inherently uncertain, relying on calculations and input assumptions about which fair-minded analysts may legitimately disagree. Even small differences in an LNG hazard model have led to significantly different conclusions. Referring to previous LNG safety zone studies, for example, FERC noted in 2003 that "distances have been estimated to range from 1,400 feet to more than 4,000 feet for [hazardous] thermal radiation."[33]

---

[28] Junnola, J., et al. January 21, 2004. p. 6.

[29] Hunter, C. "Algerian LNG Plant Explosion Sets Back Industry Development." *World Markets Analysis*. January 21, 2004. p. 1.

[30] Antosh, N. "Vast Site Devastated." *Houston Chronicle*. January 21, 2004. p. B1.

[31] See, for example: Jerry Havens, *Comments Submitted by Jerry Havens on Sparrows Point Final Environmental Impact Statement*, Federal Energy Regulatory Commission, Docket CP07-62-000, January 12, 2009.

[32] Gas Research Institute (GRI). "LNGFIRE: A Thermal Radiation Model for LNG Fires" Version 3. GRI-89/0176. Washington, DC. June 29, 1990; "LNG Vapor Dispersion Prediction with the DEGADIS: Dense Gas Dispersion Model." GRI-89/00242; "Evaluation of Mitigation Methods for Accidental LNG Releases. Vol. 5: Using FEM3A for LNG Accident Consequence Analyses." GRI 96/0396.5. Washington, DC.

[33] FERC. November 2003. p. 4-133.

Liquefied Natural Gas (LNG) Import Terminals: Siting, Safety, and Regulation

Table 1. Recent LNG Hazard Studies

Author	Sponsor	Subject
Lloyd's Register of Shipping[a]	Distrigas (Tractebel)	Focused models of possible terror attacks on LNG ships serving Everett
Quest Consultants Inc.[b]	DOE (lead), FERC, DOT	Models catastrophic breach of an LNG ship tank
James Fay (MIT)[c]	Fair Play for Harpswell	Models fire and vapor hazards of proposed Harpswell LNG terminal
Tobin & Associates[d]	City of Vallejo	Reviews general safety of proposed Mare Island LNG terminal
Lehr and Simecek-Beatty[e]	NOAA staff	Compares hypothetical LNG and fuel oil fires on water
Det Norske Veritas[f]	LNG Industry Companies	Models LNG maximum credible failures
ABSG Consulting[g]	FERC (lead), DOT, USCG	Reviews consequence assessment methods for LNG tanker incidents
Sandia National Laboratories[h]	DOE	Two reports examine effect of large-scale LNG spills on water (additional studies underway)

Source: Congressional Research Service.

a. Waryas, Edward. Lloyd's Register Americas, Inc. "Major Disaster Planning: Understanding and Managing Your Risk." Fourth National Harbor Safety Committee Conference. Galveston, TX. March 4, 2002. Summary excerpts are in this presentation.

b. Juckett, Don. U.S. Department of Energy (DOE). "Properties of LNG." LNG Workshop. Solomons, MD. February 12, 2002. A Quest study summary is in this presentation.

c. Fay, James A. "Public Safety Issues at the Proposed Harpswell LNG Terminal." FairPlay for Harpswell. Harpswell, ME. November 5, 2003.

d. Tobin & Assoc. "Liquefied Natural Gas in Vallejo: Heath and Safety Issues." Report by the LNG Safety Committee of the Disaster Council, Vallejo, CA. January 16, 2003.

e. Lehr, W. and Simecek-Beatty, D. "Comparison of Hypothetical LNG and Fuel Oil Fires on Water." *Journal of Hazardous Materials.* v. 107. 2004. pp. 3-9.

f. Pitblado, R.M., J. Baik, G. J. Hughes, C. Ferro, and S. J. Shaw., Det Norske Veritas. "Consequences of LNG Marine Incidents." Presented at the Center for Chemical Process Safety (CCPS) Conference. Orlando, FL. June 29-July 1, 2004. Available at http://www.dnv.com/press/dnvcompletesstudyonlngmarinereleases.asp.

g. ABSG Consulting. *Consequence Assessment Methods for Incidents Involving Releases from Liquefied Natural Gas Carriers.* GEMS 1288209. Prepared for the Federal Energy Regulatory Commission under contract FERC04C40196. May 13, 2004.

h. Sandia National Laboratories (SNL). Breach and Safety Analysis of Spills Over Water from Large Liquefied Natural Gas Carriers. SAND2008-3153. Albuquerque, NM. May 2008; Sandia National Laboratories (SNL). Guidance on Risk Analysis and Safety Implications of a Large Liquefied Natural Gas (LNG) Spill Over Water. SAND2004-6258. Albuquerque, NM. December 2004.

The LNG hazard studies in **Table 1** have been sponsored by a range of stakeholders and have been performed by individuals with various kinds of expertise. It is beyond the scope of this report to make detailed comparisons of the methodologies and findings of these studies and FERC analysis. Furthermore, each of the available studies (or its application) appears to have significant limitations, or has been questioned by critics. For example, the ABSG Consulting study released by FERC in May 2004, which reviewed existing LNG hazard models, concluded that

- No release models are available that take into account the true structure of an LNG carrier;

- No pool spread models are available that account for wave action or currents; and

- Relatively few experimental data are available for validation of models involving LNG spills on water, and there are no data available for spills as large as the spills considered in this study.[34]

The 2004 Sandia National Laboratories study similarly reported that "there are limitations in existing data and current modeling capabilities for analyzing LNG spills over water."[35] Nonetheless, the Sandia report concluded that "existing [analytic] tools ... can be used to identify and mitigate hazards to protect both public safety and property."[36]

Uncertainty related to LNG hazard modeling continues. A December 2006 study using yet another LNG computer model of a large LNG fire states that "current generation models that are being used to calculate the radiant heat ... from the fire are found to be overly conservative."[37] In February 2007, the Government Accountability Office (GAO) issued a report comparing six recent unclassified studies (including studies in **Table 1**) of the consequences of LNG spills. The GAO report concluded that[38]

> Because there have been no large-scale LNG spills or spill experiments, past studies have developed modeling assumptions based on small-scale spill data. While there is general agreement on the types of effects from an LNG spill, the results of these models have created what appears to be conflicting assessments of the specific consequences of an LNG spill, creating uncertainty for regulators and the public.

Following the GAO report, Members of Congress expressed renewed concern about the uncertainty associated with LNG hazard analysis.[39]

Hazards vs. Risks

In reviewing the various LNG hazard studies, it is important to be clear about the distinction between *hazards* and *risks*. Although theoretical models may try to quantify the effects of "worst-case" hazards, evaluating the risks associated with those hazards requires an estimate of the probability that they will occur. Some argue that a significant *hazard* that is nonetheless highly unlikely does not represent an unacceptable *risk* to the public. In this view, worst-case hazard studies alone do not provide a sufficient basis for evaluating public safety. Unfortunately, few LNG safety studies comprehensively and convincingly address the probability of catastrophic

---

[34] ABSG Consulting. May 13, 2004. p. iii.

[35] SNL. December 2004. p. 14.

[36] SNL. December 2004. p. 14.

[37] Raj, P.K. *Spectrum of Fires in an LNG Facility: Assessments, Models and Consideration in Evaluations*. Prepared for the U.S. Department of Transportation, Pipeline & Hazardous Materials Safety Admin. by Technology & Management Systems, Inc. Burlington, MA. December 5, 2006. p. E-4.

[38] Government Accountability Office (GAO). *Maritime Security: Public Safety Consequences of a Terrorist Attack on a Tanker Carrying Liquefied Natural Gas Need Clarification*. GAO-07-316. February 2007. p. 22.

[39] See, for example Senator Barbara A. Mikulski, testimony before the House Transportation and Infrastructure Committee, Coast Guard and Maritime Transportation Subcommittee field hearing on the Safety and Security of Liquefied Natural Gas and the Impact on Port Operations. Baltimore, MD. April 23, 2007.

---

accidents or attacks actually occurring.[40] In part, this shortcoming arises from a lack of historical LNG incidents and detailed terrorist threat information on which to base such probabilities. Faced with this analytic uncertainty, decision makers are forced to draw the best information they can get and rely upon their own best judgment to reach conclusions about LNG safety.

LNG Terminal Safety in Perspective

Other Hazardous Materials

LNG terminals and tankers have a high profile because of extensive media coverage, although there are few of them relative to all the hazardous chemical plants and ships currently operating near U.S. cities. According to the U.S. Environmental Protection Agency (EPA), for example, more than 500 toxic chemical facilities operate in "urban" areas at which worst-case accidents could affect 100,000 or more people.[41] These include chlorine plants in city water systems and ammonia tanks in agricultural fertilizer production. There are also oil refineries and liquefied petroleum gas (e.g., propane, butane) terminals operating in U.S. ports that pose safety hazards similar to those of LNG. Based on the most recent data available from the U.S. Office of Hazardous Materials Safety, there are over 100,000 annual U.S. shipments of hazardous marine cargo such as ammonia, crude oil, liquefied petroleum gases, and other volatile chemicals.[42] Many of these cargoes pose a hazard similar to LNG and pass through the same harbors serving existing or proposed LNG terminals.

Civil and Criminal Liability

One reason LNG tanker and terminal operators seek to ensure public safety is to avoid civil and criminal liability from an LNG accident; there are no special provisions in U.S. law protecting the fossil fuel industry from such liability. As a result of the 1989 *Exxon Valdez* oil spill, for example, Exxon has been required to pay over $500 million in criminal and civil settlements.[43] In January 2003, the Justice Department announced over $100 million in civil and criminal penalties against Olympic Pipeline and Shell Pipeline resolving claims from a fatal pipeline fire in Bellingham, Washington in 1999.[44] In March 2003, emphasizing the environmental aspects of homeland security, the U.S. Attorney General reportedly announced a crackdown on companies failing to protect against possible terrorist attacks on storage tanks, transportation networks, industrial plants, and pipelines.[45] In 2002, federal safety regulators proposed a $220,000 fine against the

---

[40] One attempt at such a study is: Clarke, R.A., et al. *LNG Facilities in Urban Areas*. Good Harbor Consulting, LLC. Prepared for the Rhode Island Office of Attorney General. GHC-RI-0505A. May 2005.

[41] Based on facilities submitting Risk Management Plans required under Section 112 of the Clean Air Act (42 U.S.C. § 7412) and classified in the December 1, 2003, update of the EPA National Database using EPA's software RMP*Review (v2.1). EPA states that an entire population is highly unlikely to be affected by any single chemical release, even in the worst case. In an actual release, effects on a population would depend on wind direction and many other factors. In addition, these worst-case scenarios do not account for emergency response measures facility operators or others might take to mitigate harm.

[42] Office of Hazardous Materials Safety, Department of Transportation. *Hazardous Materials Shipments*. Washington, DC. October 1998. Table 2. p. 2.

[43] Exxon Shipping Co. et al. v. Baker et al. 554 U.S. (2008) (Supreme Court of the United States of America). June 25, 2008. p. 4.

[44] *Energy Daily*. "Shell, Olympic Socked for Pipeline Accident." January 22, 2003.

[45] Heilprin, John. "Ashcroft Promises Increased Enforcement of Environmental Laws for Homeland Security." (continued...)

Distrigas LNG terminal in Everett, Massachusetts, reportedly for security training violations.[46] Notwithstanding these actions, some observers are skeptical that government scrutiny will ensure LNG infrastructure safety.

Even if no federal or state regulations are violated, LNG companies could still face civil liability for personal injury or wrongful death in the event of an accident. In the Bellingham case, the pipeline owner and associated defendants reportedly agreed to pay a $75 million settlement to the families of two children killed in the accident.[47] In 2002, El Paso Corporation settled wrongful death and personal injury lawsuits stemming from a natural gas pipeline explosion near Carlsbad, New Mexico, which killed 12 campers.[48] Although the terms of those settlements were not disclosed, two additional lawsuits sought a total of $171 million in damages. The impact of these lawsuits on the company's business is unclear, however; El Paso's June 2003 quarterly financial report stated that "our costs and legal exposure ... will be fully covered by insurance."[49]

Regulation of Onshore LNG Siting

The Department of Transportation (DOT) and FERC are the federal agencies primarily responsible for the regulation of onshore LNG facilities. Although federal statutes do not explicitly designate the relative jurisdiction of DOT and FERC, the agencies have clarified their roles through interagency agreement. These roles and their relation to other authorities are summarized below.

Department of Transportation

The DOT sets safety standards for onshore LNG facilities. The DOT's authority originally stemmed from the Natural Gas Pipeline Safety Act of 1968 (P.L. 90-481) and the Hazardous Liquids Pipeline Safety Act of 1979 (P.L. 96-129). These acts were subsequently combined and recodified as the Pipeline Safety Act of 1994 (P.L. 102-508). The acts were further amended by the Pipeline Safety Improvement Act of 2002 (P.L. 107-355) and the Pipeline Safety Improvement Act of 2006 (P.L. 109-468). Under the resulting statutory scheme, DOT is charged with issuing minimum safety standards for the siting, design, construction, and operation of LNG facilities. It does not approve or deny specific siting proposals, because that authority is vested with FERC, as discussed below.

The Pipeline Safety Act, as amended, includes the following provisions concerning LNG facility siting (49 U.S.C. § 60103):

(...continued)

Associated Press. *Washington Dateline*. Washington, DC. March 11, 2003.

[46] "Massachusetts LNG Company Faces RSPA Fines for Security Violations." Bulk Transporter. June 28, 2002; Pipeline and Hazardous Materials Safety Admin. "Summary of Enforcement Actions: Distrigas of Massachusetts Corp." Web page. May 8, 2008. http://primis.phmsa.dot.gov/comm/reports/enforce/Actions_opid_3411.html#_TP_1_tab_1

[47] Business Editors. "Olympic Pipe Line, Others Pay Out Record $75 Million in Pipeline Explosion Wrongful Death Settlement." *Business Wire*. April 10, 2002.

[48] National Transportation Safety Board (NTSB). *Pipeline Accident Report* PAR-03-01. February 11, 2003.

[49] El Paso Corp. *Quarterly Report Pursuant to Section 13 or 15(d) of the Securities Exchange Act of 1934*. Form 10-Q. For the period ending June 30, 2002. Houston, TX.

The Secretary of Transportation shall prescribe minimum safety standards for deciding on the location of a new liquefied natural gas pipeline facility. In prescribing a standard, the Secretary shall consider the—

(1) kind and use of the facility;

(2) existing and projected population and demographic characteristics of the location;

(3) existing and proposed land use near the location;

(4) natural physical aspects of the location;

(5) medical, law enforcement, and fire prevention capabilities near the location that can cope with a risk caused by the facility; and

(6) need to encourage remote siting.

General safety-related regulations may also impact siting decisions and affect the operation of existing facilities. The Secretary is authorized to order corrective action if operating an LNG facility could be hazardous to life, property, or the environment (49 U.S.C. §§ 60112, 60117). DOT's implementing regulations for the Pipeline Safety Act, as amended, are in 49 C.F.R.§§ 190-199. Safety standards, including those on siting, for LNG facilities are in 49 C.F.R. § 193 and are overseen by the Department's Office of Pipeline Safety (OPS) within the Pipeline and Hazardous Materials Safety Administration (PHMSA).

The siting provisions in 49 C.F.R. § 193 incorporate by reference standard 59A from the National Fire Protection Association (NFPA).[50] NFPA 59A requires thermal exclusion zones and flammable vapor-gas dispersion zones around LNG terminals (§§ 193.2057, 193.2059). The DOT regulations also adopt many of NFPA's design and construction guidelines including requirements for LNG facilities to withstand fire, wind, hydraulic forces, and erosion from LNG spills (§§ 193.2067, 193.2155, 193.2301). Other provisions address operations (§§ 193.2501-2521), maintenance (§§ 193.2601-2639), employee qualification (§§ 193.2701-2719), and security (§§ 193.2901-2917).

Federal Energy Regulatory Commission (FERC)

Under the Natural Gas Act of 1938 (NGA), FERC grants federal approval for the siting of new onshore LNG facilities.[51] Section 7 of the NGA authorizes FERC to issue certificates of "public convenience and necessity" for "the construction or extension of any facilities ... for the transportation in interstate commerce of natural gas" (15 U.S.C. § 717f). Section 7 does not expressly mention LNG facilities, however, so recent agency policy has FERC exercising LNG siting regulation under its Section 3 authority, which authorizes FERC to approve the import and

---

[50] National Fire Protection Association (NFPA). *Standard for the Production, Storage, and Handling of Liquefied Natural Gas*, 2001 Edition. NFPA 59A. Quincy, MA. 2001.

[51] Natural Gas Act (NGA) of June 21, 1938, ch. 556, 52 Stat. 812 (codified as amended at 15 U.S.C. §§ 717 et seq.); the Department of Energy Organization Act of 1977 (P.L. 95-91) transferred to the NGA authority to approve siting, construction and operation of onshore LNG facilities to the Secretary of Energy (§ 301b). The Secretary, in turn, delegated this authority to FERC.

export of natural gas (15 U.S.C. § 717b).[52] Specifically, FERC asserts approval authority over the place of entry and exit, siting, construction, and operation of new LNG terminals as well as modifications or extensions of existing LNG terminals.[53]

The Energy Policy Act of 2005 (P.L. 109-58) amends Section 3 of the NGA to give FERC explicit and "exclusive" authority to approve onshore LNG terminal siting applications (§ 311c). The 2005 act requires FERC to promulgate regulations for pre-filing of LNG import terminal siting applications and directs FERC to consult with designated state agencies regarding safety in considering such applications. It permits states to conduct safety inspections of LNG terminals in conformance with federal regulations, although it retains enforcement authority at the federal level. The 2005 act also requires LNG terminal operators to develop emergency response plans, including cost-sharing plans to reimburse state and local governments for safety and security expenditures (§ 311(d)). The 2005 act designates FERC as the "lead agency for the purposes of coordinating all applicable Federal authorizations" and for complying with federal environmental requirements, discussed below (§ 313a). It also establishes FERC's authority to set schedules for federal authorizations and establishes provisions for judicial review of FERC's siting decisions in the U.S. Court of Appeals, among other administrative provisions (§ 313(b)).

FERC implements its authority over onshore LNG terminals through the agency's regulations at 18 C.F.R. § 153. These regulations detail the application process and requirements under Section 3 of the NGA. The process begins with a pre-filing, which must be submitted to FERC at least six months prior to the filing of a formal application. The pre-filing procedures and review processes are set forth at 18 C.F.R. § 157.21. Once the pre-filing stage is completed, a formal application may be filed. FERC's formal application requirements include detailed site engineering and design information, evidence that a facility will safely receive or deliver LNG, and delineation of a facility's proposed location (18 C.F.R. § 153.8). Additional data are required if an LNG facility will be in an area with geological risk (18 C.F.R. § 153.8). The regulations also require LNG facility builders to notify landowners who would be affected by the proposed facility (18 C.F.R. § 157.6d). Facilities to be constructed at the Canadian or Mexican borders for import or export of natural gas also require a Presidential Permit.[54] According to FERC officials, applications under their Section 3-based regulations are also sufficient for Presidential Permit purposes (18 C.F.R. §§ 153.15-153.17).[55]

Under the National Environmental Policy Act of 1969 (P.L. 91-190), FERC must prepare an environmental impact statement during its review of an LNG terminal siting application (18 C.F.R. § 380.6). Applicants must prepare certain environmental reports to aid FERC in its preparation of the environmental impact statement (18 C.F.R. § 380.3(c)(2)(i)). These reports require analysis of, among other things, the socioeconomic impact of the LNG facility, geophysical characteristics of the site, safeguards against seismic risk, facility effects on air and

---

[52] In 1997, FERC reaffirmed its Section 3 authority despite changes to the Natural Gas Act in the Energy Policy Act of 1992 (P.L. 102-486). For details *see* 97 FERC ¶ 61,231 (2001). Also note that FERC's regulatory power regarding LNG importation under section 3 has been held to allow FERC to impose requirements equivalent to any in section 7, so long as FERC finds them necessary or appropriate to the public interest. Distrigas Corp. v. FPC, 495 F.2d 1057, 1066 (D.C. Cir. 1974).

[53] *See* 18 C.F.R. § 153; *see also* Foley, R., Federal Energy Regulatory Commission (FERC), Office of Energy Projects. "Liquefied Natural Gas Imports." Slide presentation. January 2003. p. 10.

[54] Executive Order No. 10,485 requires that FERC obtain a favorable recommendation from the Secretaries of State and Defense prior to issuing a Presidential Permit.

[55] FERC Office of Energy Projects, Personal communication, December 10, 2003.

noise quality, public safety issues in the event of accidents or malfunctions, and facility compliance with reliability standards and relevant safety standards (18 C.F.R. § 380.12). Once these environmental reports are received, the EPA may become involved in the approval process. The EPA often assists in the review of the environmental reports and the issuance of the environmental impact statements.[56]

In an effort to speed the review process for natural gas infrastructure projects (including LNG projects), FERC has approved rules to expand eligibility for "blanket certificates." Blanket certificates are granted by FERC to companies that have previously been granted certificates for construction for public convenience and necessity under Section 7 of the NGA. A company that possesses a blanket certificate may improve or upgrade existing facilities or construct certain new facilities without further case-by-case authorization from FERC. Regulations governing acceptable actions under blanket certificate authority can be found at 18 C.F.R. §§ 157.201-157.218.

FERC also has created a Liquefied Natural Gas Compliance Branch to monitor the safety of operational LNG facilities on an ongoing basis.[57] This branch is responsible for the continued safety inspections and oversight of operating LNG facilities, and it reviews final facility design and engineering compliance with FERC orders. The staff comprises LNG engineers, civil and mechanical engineers, and other experts. The branch coordinates FERC's LNG Engineering Branch, the U.S. Coast Guard (USCG), and DOT to address safety and security at LNG facilities.[58]

FERC-DOT Jurisdictional Issues

Jurisdiction between the two federal agencies with LNG oversight responsibilities historically has been a point of contention.[59] In practice, FERC requires compliance with DOT's siting and safety regulations as a starting point, but can regulate more strictly if it chooses. This working arrangement is not explicitly established under the relevant federal law. Neither do the statutes and regulations clearly define the roles of the agencies vis-a-vis one another. The Pipeline Safety Act, for example, states:

> In a proceeding under section 3 or 7 of the Natural Gas Act (15 U.S.C. § 717b or 717f), each applicant ... shall certify that it will design, install, inspect, test, construct, operate, replace, and maintain a gas pipeline facility under ... section 60108 of this title. The certification is binding on the Secretary of Energy and the Commission... (49 U.S.C. § 60104(d)(2)).[60]

Despite this provision, which might appear to give DOT full control of gas safety regulation (including LNG siting authority), the authors of the House committee report for the revised Pipeline Safety Act indicated their intention to preserve FERC jurisdiction over LNG.[61]

---

[56] In July of 2006 EPA issued a "Liquefied Natural Gas Regulatory Roadmap" in an effort to assist LNG project applicants (both onshore and offshore) in dealing with environmental regulatory requirements. http://www.epa.gov/opei/lng/lngroadmap.pdf

[57] Press Release, Federal Energy Regulatory Commission, "Commission Establishes LNG Compliance Branch," May 2, 2006.

[58] *Id.*

[59] S.Rept. No. 96-182. 1979. p. 4.

[60] 49 U.S.C. § 61018 specifies DOT's requirements for pipeline facility inspection and maintenance.

[61] *See* H.Rept. No. 1390, 1968, *reprinted in* 1968 U.S.C.C.A.N. 3223, 3251. Note, FERC was known as the Federal (continued...)

Congressional Research Service   14

Liquefied Natural Gas (LNG) Import Terminals: Siting, Safety, and Regulation

Accordingly, FERC has held that the Pipeline Safety Act does not remove its jurisdiction under the NGA to regulate LNG safety.[62] In 1985, FERC and DOT executed a Memorandum of Understanding expressly acknowledging "DOT's exclusive authority to promulgate Federal safety standards for LNG facilities" but recognizing FERC's ability to issue more stringent safety requirements for LNG facilities when warranted. This agreement appears to have resolved any jurisdictional conflict between the agencies at that time.[63] In February 2004, FERC streamlined the LNG siting approval process through an agreement with the USCG and DOT to coordinate review of LNG terminal safety and security. The agreement "stipulates that the agencies identify issues early and quickly resolve them."[64]

U.S. Coast Guard

The USCG has authority to review, approve, and verify plans for marine traffic around proposed onshore LNG marine terminals as part of the overall siting approval process led by FERC. The USCG is responsible for issuing a Letter of Recommendation regarding the suitability of waterways for LNG vessels serving proposed terminals. The agency is also responsible for ensuring that full consideration is given in siting application reviews to the safety and security of the port, the LNG terminal, and the vessels transporting LNG. The USCG acts as a cooperating agency in the evaluation of LNG terminal siting applications. The Coast Guard provides guidance to applicants seeking permits for onshore LNG terminals in "Guidance on Assessing the Suitability of a Waterway for Liquefied Natural Gas Marine Traffic" (NVIC 05-05) issued on June 14, 2005.[65] Provisions in the Coast Guard Authorization Act of 2010 (H.R. 3619) would require additional waterway suitability notification requirements in LNG siting reviews by FERC (Sec. 1117).

National Fire Protection Association (NFPA)

As noted above, LNG terminal safety regulations incorporate standards set by the NFPA. The NFPA is an international nonprofit organization which advocates fire prevention and serves as an authority on public safety practices. According to NFPA, its 300 safety codes and standards "influence every building, process, service, design, and installation in the United States."[66] The NFPA LNG Standards Committee includes volunteer experts with diverse representation from industry and government, including FERC, DOT, USCG, and state agencies. The NFPA standards for LNG safety were initially adopted in 1967, with 10 subsequent revisions, most recently in 2009.[67] According to the Society of International Gas Tanker and Terminal Operators (SIGTTO),

---

(...continued)

Power Commission (FPC) at the time.

[62] Chatanooga Gas Co., 51 FPC 1278, 1279 (1974).

[63] See "Notice of Agreement Regarding Liquefied Natural Gas," 31 FERC ¶ 61,232 (1985).

[64] Federal Energy Regulatory Commission (FERC). Press release R-04-3. February 11, 2004.

[65] Available at http://www.uscg.mil/hq/g-m/nvic/NVIC%2005-05.doc.pdf.

[66] National Fire Protection Assoc. (NFPA). *About NFPA*. Web page. Quincy, MA. 2009.

[67] National Fire Protection Association (NFPA). *Standard for the Production, Storage, and Handling of Liquefied Natural Gas*, 2009 Edition. NFPA 59A. Quincy, MA. 2009.

although the NFPA standards originated in the United States, they were the first internationally recognized LNG standards and are widely used throughout the world today.[68]

State Regulatory Roles

While the federal government is primarily responsible for LNG terminal safety and siting regulation, state and local laws, such as environmental, health and safety codes, can affect LNG facilities as well. Under the Pipeline Safety Act, a state also may regulate *intra*state pipeline facilities if the state submits a certification under section 60105(a) or makes an agreement with the DOT under section 60106. Under these provisions, a state "may adopt additional or more stringent safety standards" for LNG facilities so long as they are compatible with DOT regulations (49 U.S.C. 60104(c)). Of course, if a particular LNG facility would otherwise not fall under FERC and DOT jurisdiction, states may regulate without going through the certification or agreement process. Regulation of *inter*state facilities remains the primary responsibility of federal agencies. The Office of Pipeline Safety may, however, delegate authority to *intra*state pipeline safety offices, allowing state offices to act as "agents" administering *inter*state pipeline safety programs (excluding enforcement) for those sections of *inter*state facilities within their boundaries.[69] All 50 states, the District of Columbia, and Puerto Rico are participants in the natural gas pipeline safety program.

State regulation of LNG facility safety and siting runs the gamut from piecemeal to comprehensive. For example, Arizona sets out specific requirements for LNG storage facilities, including "peak shaving" plants used by regional gas utilities, consistent with DOT regulations for construction maintenance and safety standards (Ariz. Admin. Code R14-5-202, R14-5-203, 126-01-001). Colorado and Georgia have comprehensive administrative systems for enforcing the federal standards (see 4 Co. Admin. Code 723-11; Ga. Admin. Code 515-9-3-03).

Apart from state regulation aimed specifically at LNG facilities, generally applicable state and local laws, such as zoning laws and permit requirements for water, electricity, construction, and waste disposal, also may impact the planning and development of LNG facilities. This is discussed in more detail later in this report.

Federal-State Jurisdictional Conflicts

Federal and state government agencies have had jurisdictional disagreements specifically related to the siting of new LNG terminals. In February 2004, for example, the California Public Utilities Commission (CPUC) disputed FERC's jurisdiction over the siting of a proposed LNG terminal at Long Beach because, in the CPUC's opinion, the terminal would not be involved in interstate sales or transportation and therefore would not come under the Natural Gas Act.[70] In March 2004, FERC rejected the CPUC's arguments and asserted exclusive regulatory authority for all LNG import terminal siting and construction.[71] In April 2004, the CPUC voted to assert jurisdiction

---

[68] Society of International Gas Tanker and Terminal Operators (SIGTTO). Personal communication. London, England. December 19, 2003.

[69] 49 U.S.C. § 601. States may recover up to 50% of their costs for these programs from the federal government.

[70] FERC. "Notice of Intervention and Protest of the Public Utilities Commission of the State of California." Docket No. CP04-58-000. February 23, 2004. p. 6.

[71] Lorenzetti, M. "LNG Rules." *Oil & Gas Journal.* April 5, 2004. p. 32.

over the Long Beach terminal and filed a request for FERC to reconsider its March ruling.[72] In June 2004, FERC reasserted its March ruling, prompting a federal court appeal by California regulators. The Energy Policy Act of 2005 effectively codified FERC's jurisdictional rulings, however, leading the CPUC to drop its lawsuit challenging FERC's LNG siting authority in September 2005. Notwithstanding the CPUC case, other state challenges to FERC jurisdiction remain a possibility.

Key Policy Issues

Proposals for new LNG terminal facilities have generated considerable public concern in many communities. Some community groups and government officials fear that LNG terminals may expose nearby residents to unacceptable hazards, and that these hazards may not be appropriately considered in the federal siting approval process. Ongoing public concern about LNG terminal safety has focused congressional attention on the exclusivity of FERC's LNG siting authority, proposals for a regional LNG siting process, the lack of "remote" siting requirements in FERC regulations, state permitting requirements under the Clean Water Act (CWA) and the Coastal Zone Management Act (CZMA), terrorism attractiveness of LNG, the adequacy of Coast Guard security resources, and other issues.

"Exclusive" Federal Siting Authority

As stated earlier in this report, the Energy Policy Act of 2005 (P.L. 109-58) gives FERC the "exclusive" authority to approve onshore LNG terminal siting applications (§ 311(c)). Supporters of this provision argue that it is necessary to prevent federal-state jurisdictional disputes over LNG siting authority, and that it reduces the possibility that state agencies might prevent or unduly delay the development of LNG infrastructure considered essential to the nation's energy supply. They further argue that states retain considerable influence over LNG siting approval through their federally delegated permitting authorities under the Coastal Zone Management Act of 1972 (16 U.S.C. 1451 et seq.), the Clean Air Act (42 U.S.C. 7401 et seq.), and the Federal Water Pollution Control Act (33 U.S.C. 251 et seq.). They maintain that states have a role in siting reviews under provisions in P.L. 109-58 requiring FERC to consult with governor-designated state agencies regarding state and local safety considerations prior to issuing LNG terminal permits (§ 311(d)).

A number of lawmakers at the federal and state levels have suggested that Congress should consider amending or repealing FERC's exclusive authority under P.L. 109-58. Critics of this authority argue that it vests too much power in the federal government at the expense of state agencies, which may have a better understanding of local siting issues and may bear most of the risks or burdens associated with a new LNG facility. They do not believe that FERC adequately seeks state input in its LNG siting reviews, nor adequately addresses state concerns in its siting decisions.[73] Critics question why governors lack the authority to veto onshore LNG terminal proposals as they can offshore terminal proposals under the Deepwater Port Act (33 U.S.C. § 1503(c)(8)). Some in Congress have proposed granting governors similar veto authority over

---

[72] *Gas Daily.* "PUC Seeks Rehearing of FERC's Order on Long Beach LNG Project." April 27, 2004. p. 7.

[73] O'Neill, L. "Senators Drum Up Measure Giving States Authority Over LNG Siting." *Natural Gas Week.* April 14, 2008.

onshore LNG terminal proposals, or other legislation to increase state authority in terminal siting reviews. Several legislative proposals in the 110th Congress would have required state concurrence of federal siting approval decisions for onshore LNG terminals or would have repealed provisions in the Energy Policy Act of 2005 granting FERC exclusive authority to approve LNG terminal siting applications.[74]

Regional Siting Approach

In areas such as the Northeast, where a number of onshore LNG terminal proposals have been particularly controversial, some policy makers have sought to establish a regional approach for identifying suitable sites for such terminals. They argue that FERC's consideration of LNG terminals on a proposal-by-proposal basis does not adequately take into account the regional needs for LNG, public safety concerns, and environmental impacts.[75] They also argue that the proposal-by-proposal approach does not adequately account for the relative merits of multiple LNG and natural gas pipeline facilities proposed in the same region.[76] They assert a regional LNG siting process would be more efficient than FERC's current process because it would focus attention on sites and projects with the highest chances of success rather than having numerous communities and state and local agencies react to individual plans, many of which are unlikely to be approved.[77] One legislative proposal in the 110th Congress would have established a national commission for the placement of natural gas infrastructure, such as LNG terminals, taking regional energy and environmental considerations into account.[78]

FERC officials reportedly have stated in the past that while they are not opposed to regional siting in principle, the commission cannot adopt such a regional approach because it has no land-use authority or responsibility and must let the energy market determine which terminals ultimately are constructed.[79] FERC officials also have reportedly expressed skepticism about the effectiveness of regional siting processes, for example, in finding storage locations for low-level radioactive waste.[80] More recently, however, the acting chairman of FERC reportedly called for more assessment of alternatives to LNG terminals in LNG siting decisions "including full examination of regional gas infrastructure."[81] Whether this statement indicates a future shift in FERC's approach towards LNG siting reviews remains to be determined. As oversight of federal LNG siting activities continues in the 111th Congress, legislators may be asked to consider whether incorporating regional approaches in the LNG siting process could alleviate state concerns about FERC's current process while supporting the nation's needs for new LNG infrastructure.

---

[74] S. 1174, S. 3441, S. 2822, and H.R. 2042

[75] *Foster Natural Gas Report*, "Weaver's Cove Offshore Berth Project Must Be Reviewed From Scratch And By Taking A Regional Approach, Some Parties Insist," July 18, 2008, p. 11.

[76] See, for example: Sickinger, T. "Governor Ups Ante Against LNG Sites." *The Oregonian*. February 15, 2008. p. A1.

[77] *Bangor Daily News*. "Regional Energy." December 8, 2006. p. A10.

[78] H.R. 6720.

[79] *Foster Natural Gas Report*. "Northeast States Need LNG, Especially New England; No Evidence of Regional Planning." December 15, 2006. p. 5.

[80] Howe, P.J. "LNG Supplies, Solutions Lacking." *The Boston Globe*. September 26, 2006. p. C4.

[81] *Foster Natural Gas Report*, "Under FERC's New Acting Chairman, Renewable Energy And Efficiency May Command An Unprecedented Level Of Support," February 17, 2009, p. 12.

"Remote" Siting of LNG Terminals

The LNG safety provisions in the federal pipeline safety law require the Secretary of Transportation to "consider the ... need to encourage remote siting" of new LNG facilities (49 U.S.C. § 60103). Federal regulations contain no clear definition of what constitutes "remote" siting, relying instead on safety exclusion zones to satisfy the remoteness requirements under the Pipeline Safety Act. This regulatory alternative was criticized by the General Accounting Office (GAO) in 1979 testimony to Congress supporting remote siting in the Pipeline Safety Act:

> We believe remote siting is the primary factor in safety. Because of the inevitable uncertainties inherent in large-scale use of new technologies and the vulnerability of the facilities to natural phenomena and sabotage, the public can be best protected by placing these facilities away from densely populated areas.[82]

In 2003, Representative Edward Markey, an original sponsor of the Pipeline Safety Act, reportedly expressed concern that DOT regulations did not go far enough in complying with the congressional intent of the remote siting provisions.[83]

Industry and government officials maintain that exclusion zones do provide adequate public safety based on the current state of knowledge about LNG. They argue that LNG terminals are no longer a new technology and face far fewer operational uncertainties than in 1979. In particular, some experts believe that hazard models in the 1970s were too conservative. They believe that more recent models have led to a better understanding of the physical properties of LNG and, consequently, a better basis for design decisions affecting public safety.[84] They point out that LNG terminals like those in Everett, Massachusetts (1971); Barcelona, Spain (1969); Fezzano, Italy (1969); and Pyongtaek, Korea (1986) have been operating for decades near populated areas without a serious accident affecting the public. Of the 28 existing LNG terminals in Japan, a seismically active country, most are near major cities such as Tokyo and Osaka.[85] While the Algerian terminal accident was serious, experts point out that it did not lead to the catastrophic failure of the main LNG storage tanks and did not cause injuries to the general public. Nonetheless, some policy makers reportedly have called for amendments to federal energy law prohibiting new LNG terminals in urban and densely populated areas.[86]

Other Statutes that May Influence LNG Terminal Siting

The Energy Policy Act of 2005 (§ 311(c)) explicitly preserves states' authorities in LNG siting decisions under the Federal Water Pollution Control Act, the Coastal Zone Management Act of 1972, and other federal laws. Under the Federal Water Pollution Control Act, often referred to as the Clean Water Act (CWA), states have the authority to develop and enforce their own water

---

[82] Peach, J.D. General Accounting Office (GAO), Director, Energy and Minerals Division. Testimony to the Senate Committee on Commerce, Science and Transportation. Washington, DC. April 25, 1979. p. 10. The General Accounting Office is now known as the Government Accountability Office.

[83] Raines, B. "Congress Wanted LNG Plants at 'Remote' Sites." *Mobile Register*. Mobile, AL. November 16, 2003.

[84] Tobin, L.T. Remarks at a meeting of the City of Vallejo Seismic Safety Commission. Meeting minutes. Vallejo, CA. September 11, 2003. p. 5; see also: *Federal Register*. Vol. 62, No. 37. February 25, 1997. pp. 8402-8403.

[85] California Energy Commission (CEC). "Asia Pacific Countries Liquefied Natural Gas (LNG)." January 2008. http://www.energy.ca.gov/lng/worldwide/asia_pacific.html

[86] *Energy Washington Week*. January 10, 2007.

quality standards.[87] Any federal permit applicant for a project that may discharge pollutants into navigable waters must provide the permitting agency with a certification from the state in which the discharge originates or will originate that the discharge is in compliance with the applicable provisions of the CWA, including the state's water quality standards.[88] States potentially could use their certification authority under the Clean Water Act to influence the siting of an LNG project by attaching conditions to the required water quality certificate or by denying certification. This certification authority has become an important tool used by states to protect the integrity of their waters. It is worth noting that the Energy Policy Act of 2005 created one potential avenue of relief for potential developers by providing for expedited review in a federal court of any order or action, or alleged inaction, by a federal or state agency acting under the authority of federal law.[89] Previously, parties seeking to challenge a state's decision regarding a water quality certificate had to do so in state court.[90]

States have been delegated authority under the Coastal Zone Management Act (CZMA, 16 U.S.C. § 1451 et seq.) which also could influence permitting of LNG terminals. Under the CZMA, applicants for federal permits to conduct activity affecting the coastal zone of a state must be certified by that state that the proposed activity is consistent with the state's federally approved coastal program.[91] A state wishing to forestall the licensing of an LNG terminal in its coastal waters could deny the certification required by the CZMA.[92] However, unlike the state-issued water quality certificates required for federal permitting by the Clean Water Act, the CZMA provides an alternative to applicants who are unable to obtain state certification. Under the CZMA, applicants may appeal the state's decision to the Department of Commerce, which may find that the activity is consistent with the objectives of the CZMA, or is otherwise necessary in the interest of national security, and thus override the state's denial of certification.[93] One analyst has suggested that there is a specific set of circumstances in which a state could create a regulatory stalemate pursuant to its CZMA authority by rejecting an application as incomplete (rather than rejecting it as improper or by failing to act). Under these circumstances the statute does not grant the Secretary of Commerce authority to review the decision. Battles between state regulatory agencies and applicants for LNG terminals have played out in this manner on at least two occasions.[94]

The discussion above suggests that authorities under the CWA and CZMA, at a minimum, give states the opportunity to have their concerns addressed when applicants seek federal approval for new LNG terminals. One legal commentator has stated that

---

[87] 33 U.S.C. § 1251(a),(b).

[88] *Id.* at § 1341(a).

[89] EPAct of 2005, P.L. 109-58 at §§ 717r(d)(1)-(2).

[90] For further discussion of the water quality certification process and its impact on LNG siting, see Dweck, J., Wochner, D., and Brooks, M. "Liquefied Natural Gas (LNG) Litigation after the Energy Policy Act of 2005: State Powers in LNG Terminal Siting." *Energy Law Journal,* Vol. 27, No. 45 (2006). p. 482-85.

[91] 16 U.S.C. § 1456(c)(3)(A).

[92] The state must actively state its objection to the applicant's certification; a state's failure to act is presumed to be concurrence with project certification. *Id.*

[93] 16 U.S.C. § 1456(c)(3)(A).

[94] For further discussion, see Ewing, K.A. and E. Petersen. "Significant Environmental Challenges to the Development of LNG Terminals in the United States." *Texas Journal of Oil, Gas and Energy Law.* November 2006. pp. 21-23; Dweck et al., p. 487-90.

> ultimately, while the EPAct of 2005 might have streamlined the federal [LNG siting] review process in some respects and changed the rules under which the review takes place, it has not dramatically changed the balance of power between the federal government and states.[95]

The courts addressed the potential tension between the CZMA and exclusive federal authority over LNG terminal siting in a dispute over a proposed LNG terminal in the Baltimore, MD, area. In AES Sparrows Point LNG, LLC v. Smith,[96] the U.S. District Court for the District of Maryland held that a recent amendment to the Baltimore County Zoning Regulations prohibiting the siting of an LNG facility in a particular "critical area" of the Chesapeake Bay was a part of the state's Coastal Zone Management Plan and thus not preempted by the Natural Gas Act as amended by the Energy Policy Act of 2005. The plaintiffs had claimed that the statutes explicitly gave LNG siting authority to the federal government, and thus the states could not interfere with FERC authority to rule on the plaintiff's LNG facility permit application.[97] However, on appeal the U.S. Court of Appeals for the 4th Circuit reversed the lower court's decision.[98] The appellate court ruled that the Baltimore County zoning regulation in question was not part of the state's Coastal Zone Management Plan because the regulation was never submitted to NOAA for approval.[99] The Supreme Court declined to review this decision in October of 2008.

Another statute that may have an emerging role in the LNG siting process is the Wild and Scenic Rivers Act of 1968 (WSRA).[100] The WSRA was enacted with the intention of preserving certain sections of rivers in the United States "in their free-flowing condition to protect the water quality of such rivers and to fulfill other vital national conservation purposes."[101] Under the WSRA, rivers may be designated as additions to the National Wild and Scenic Rivers system, or as potential additions to the system.[102] Designation of rivers prevents certain future development, including, potentially, projects licensed by FERC.

The WSRA explicitly prohibits FERC from licensing the construction of projects under the Federal Power Act "on or directly affecting any river which is designated ... as a component of the national wild and scenic rivers system."[103] However, projects and developments would be permitted above or below the section of the river designated under WSRA, if that development would not diminish the values present at the time of designation.[104] With regard to rivers that are designated as potential additions to the system, FERC similarly is prohibited from construction of projects along that river and other agencies are prohibited from assisting in such projects for

---

[95] Dweck et al. 2006, p. 475.

[96] 539 F.Supp.2d 788 (D. Md 2007).

[97] The same court had previously overturned a Baltimore County zoning ordinance that prohibited siting of LNG facilities within a certain distance of residential and commercial facilities on those same grounds. See AES Sparrows Point LNG, LLC v. Smith, 470 F.Supp.2d 586 (D.Md. 2007).

[98] AES Sparrows Point LNG, LLC v. Smith, 5237 F.3d 120 (4th Cir. 2008).

[99] Id. at 126-27.

[100] P.L. 90-542, codified at 16 U.S.C. § 1271 et seq. For an examination of the purposes, language and legislative history of this act, and an analysis of its effect on water rights, see CRS Report RL30809, *The Wild and Scenic Rivers Act (WSRA) and Federal Water Rights*, by Cynthia Brougher.

[101] 16 U.S.C. § 1271.

[102] Rivers designated as "potential additions" are those that warrant further study before full extension of the protections of the WSRA. 16 U.S.C. § 1276.

[103] 16 U.S.C. § 1278(a).

[104] Id.

Liquefied Natural Gas (LNG) Import Terminals: Siting, Safety, and Regulation

certain periods of time after the designation to allow for the study and consideration of the river's inclusion in the system.[105]

LNG industry representatives have opined that the WSRA may be used to block LNG facility siting.[106] These representatives cited a legislative proposal in the 110th Congress to designate segments of the Taunton River in Massachusetts as "scenic and recreational" under the WSRA.[107] The industry representatives argue that this provision, if enacted, would be an obstacle towards the construction of the proposed Weaver's Cove LNG Terminal in Massachusetts.[108] The Center for Liquefied Natural Gas described this provision as a "congressional hurdle" and said that it provided a case study of "the gauntlet of things that can be used to oppose a project."[109] As oversight of the federal LNG siting process continues, Congress may consider how federal authorities under the Energy Policy Act of 2005, the CWA, the CZMA, the WSRA, and other federal statutes fit together to achieve their various objectives.

Terror Attractiveness

Potential terrorist attacks on LNG terminals or tankers in the United States have been a key concern of policy makers because such attacks could cause catastrophic fires in ports and nearby populated areas. A 2007 report by the Government Accountability Office states that, "the ship-based supply chain for energy commodities," specifically including LNG, "remains threatened and vulnerable, and appropriate security throughout the chain is essential to ensure safe and efficient delivery."[110] Accordingly, the Coast Guard's FY2006 budget requested funding for "additional boat crews and screening personnel at key LNG hubs."[111] To date, no LNG tanker or land-based LNG facility in the world has been attacked by terrorists. However, similar natural gas and oil assets have been terror targets internationally. The Department of Homeland Security (DHS) included LNG tankers among a list of potential terrorist targets in a security alert late in 2003.[112] The DHS also reported that "in early 2001 there was some suspicion of possible associations between stowaways on Algerian flagged LNG tankers arriving in Boston and persons connected with the so-called 'Millennium Plot'" to bomb targets in the United States. Although these suspicions could not be proved, DHS stated that "the risks associated with LNG shipments are real, and they can never be entirely eliminated."[113] The 2004 report by Sandia National Laboratories concluded that potential terrorist attacks on LNG tankers could be considered "credible and possible."[114] Former Bush Administration counterterrorism advisor Richard Clarke

---

[105] 16 U.S.C. § 1278(b).

[106] Clarke, D., *LNG Sector Fears Use of NewLegislative Tactic to Oppose Facilities*, Energy Washington Week, July 30, 2008.

[107] Ibid.; H.R. 415.

[108] Ibid.

[109] Ibid.

[110] Government Accountability Office (GAO). "Maritime Security: Federal Efforts Needed to Address Challenges in Preventing and Responding to Terrorist Attacks on Energy Commodity Tankers," GAO-08-141, December 10, 2007, p.77.

[111] Department of Homeland Security (DHS). *Budget-in-Brief, Fiscal Year 2006*. https://www.dhs.gov/xlibrary/assets/Budget_BIB-FY2006.pdf.

[112] Office of Congressman Edward J. Markey. Personal communication with staff. January 5, 2004.

[113] Turner, Pamela J., Assistant Secretary for Legislative Affairs, Department of Homeland Security (DHS). Letter to U.S. Representative Edward Markey. April 15, 2004. p. 1.

[114] Sandia National Laboratories (SNL). *Guidance on Risk Analysis and Safety Implications of a Large Liquefied* (continued...)

Congressional Research Service   22

has asserted that terrorists have both the desire and capability to attack LNG shipping with the intention of harming the general population.[115]

Although they acknowledge the security information put forth by federal agencies, some experts believe that concern about threats to LNG infrastructure is overstated.[116] In 2003, the head of one university research consortium reportedly remarked, "from all the information we have ... we don't see LNG as likely or credible terrorist targets."[117] Industry representatives argue that deliberately causing an LNG catastrophe to injure people might be possible in theory, but would be extremely difficult to accomplish. Likewise, FERC and other experts believe that LNG facilities are relatively secure compared with other hazardous chemical infrastructures that receive less public attention. In a December 2004 report, FERC stated that

> for a new LNG terminal proposal ... the perceived threat of a terrorist attack may be considered as highly probable to the local population. However, at the national level, potential terrorist targets are plentiful.... Many of these pose a similar or greater hazard to that of LNG.[118]

FERC also remarked, however, that "unlike accidental causes, historical experience provides little guidance in estimating the probability of a terrorist attack on an LNG vessel or onshore storage facility."[119] Former Director of Central Intelligence James Woolsey has stated his belief that a terrorist attack on an LNG tanker in U.S. waters would be unlikely because its potential impacts would not be great enough compared with other potential targets.[120] LNG terminal operators that have conducted proprietary assessments of potential terrorist attacks against LNG tankers have expressed similar views.[121] In its September 2006 evaluation of a proposed LNG terminal in Long Island Sound, the USCG stated that "there are currently no specific, credible threats against" the proposed LNG facility or tankers serving the facility.[122] The evaluation also noted, however, that the threat environment is dynamic and that some threats may be unknown.[123] Echoing this perspective, a 2008 report by the Institute for the Analysis of Global Security states

> Proponents are correct in that both safety and security measures currently in place make LNG terminals and ships extremely hard targets for terrorists. However, it would be

---

(...continued)

Natural Gas (LNG) Spill Over Water. SAND2004-6258. Albuquerque, NM. December 2004. pp. 49-50.

[115] Clarke, Richard A. et al. *LNG Facilities in Urban Areas.* Good Harbor Consulting, LLC. Prepared for the Rhode Island Office of Attorney General. GHC-RI-0505A. May 2005.

[116] McLaughlin, J. "LNG Is Nowhere Near as Dangerous as People Are Making it Out to Be." *Lloyd's List.* February 8, 2005. p. 5.

[117] Behr, Peter. "Higher Gas Price Sets Stage for LNG." *Washington Post.* July 5, 2003. p. D10.

[118] Federal Energy Regulatory Commission (FERC). *Vista del Sol LNG Terminal Project, Draft Environmental Impact Statement.* FERC/EIS-0176D. December 2004. p. 4-162.

[119] FERC. FERC/EIS-0176D. December 2004. p. 4-162. Notwithstanding this assertion, in its subsequent draft review of the Long Beach LNG terminal proposal, the FERC states that "the historical probability of a successful terrorist event would be less than seven chances in a million per year.... " See FERC. October 7, 2005. p. ES-14.

[120] Woolsey, James. Remarks before the National Commission on Energy LNG Forum, Washington, DC, June 21, 2006.

[121] Grant, Richard, President, Distrigas. Testimony before the Senate Committee on Energy and Natural Resources, Subcommittee on Energy hearing on "The Future of Liquefied Natural Gas: Siting and Safety." February 15, 2005.

[122] U.S. Coast Guard. *U.S. Coast Guard Captain of the Port Long Island Sound Waterways Suitability Report for the Proposed Broadwater Liquefied Natural Gas Facility.* September 21, 2006. p. 146.

[123] Ibid.

---

imprudent to believe that terrorists are either incapable or unwilling to attack such targets. It would be equally imprudent to assume that these targets are impenetrable. If anything, in today's environment, insiders will always remain a potential threat.[124]

Because the probability of a terrorist attack on LNG infrastructure cannot be known, policy makers and community leaders must, to some extent, rely on their own judgment to decide whether LNG security is adequately addressed in FERC siting application reviews. As oversight of the federal role in LNG terminal siting continues, Congress may explore policies to reduce this uncertainty by improving the gathering and sharing of terrorism intelligence related to LNG.

Public Costs of LNG Marine Security

The potential increase in security costs from growing U.S. LNG imports, and the potential diversion of Coast Guard and safety agency resources from other activities have been a persistent concern to policy makers.[125] According to Coast Guard officials, the service's LNG security expenditures are not all incremental, since they are part of the Coast Guard's general mission to protect the nation's waters and coasts. Nonetheless, Coast Guard staff have acknowledged that resources dedicated to securing maritime LNG might be otherwise deployed for boating safety, search and rescue, drug interdiction, or other security missions.

In a December 2007 report, the GAO recommended that the Coast Guard develop a national resource allocation plan to address growing LNG security requirements.[126] In subsequent testimony before Congress, Coast Guard Commandant Admiral Thad Allen expressed concern about the costs to the Coast Guard of securing dangerous cargoes such as LNG and called for a "national dialogue" on the issue.[127] During questioning, Admiral Allen acknowledged that the Coast Guard did not currently possess sufficient resources to secure future LNG deliveries to a proposed LNG terminal in Long Island Sound which has subsequently been authorized by FERC.[128]

State and local agencies also seek more funding to offset the costs of LNG security. Addressing these concerns, the Energy Policy Act of 2005 requires private and public sector cost-sharing for LNG tanker security (§ 311d). In compliance with the act and prior FERC policy, FERC officials require new LNG terminal operators to pay the costs of any additional security or safety needed for their facilities.[129] FERC has also recommended that LNG terminal operators provide private security staff to supplement Coast Guard and local government security forces.[130] A legislative

---

[124] Cindy Hurst. *The Terrorist Threat to Liquefied Natural Gas: Fact or Fiction?* Institute for the Analysis of Global Security. Washington, DC. p. 3.

[125] See, for example, Representative Peter Defazio, remarks before the House Homeland Security Committee hearing on Securing Liquid Natural Gas Tankers to Protect the Homeland. March 21, 2007.

[126] Government Accountability Office. *Maritime Security: Federal Efforts Needed to Address Challenges in Responding to Terrorist Attacks on Energy Commodity Tankers.* GAO-08-141. December 10, 2007. p. 79.

[127] Admiral Thad Allen, Commandant, U.S. Coast Guard. Testimony before the House Committee on Appropriations, Subcommittee on Homeland Security hearing, "Coast Guard Budget: Impact on Maritime Safety, Security, and Environmental Protection." March 5, 2008.

[128] Admiral Thad Allen, March 5, 2008; Federal Energy Regulatory Commission. "Order Granting Authority Under Section 3 of the Natural Gas Act and Issuing Certificates." Docket No. CP06-54-0000. March 20, 2008.

[129] Baldor, L.C. "Federal Agency, R.I. Officials Meet over LNG Terminal." *Associated Press.* March 17, 2005.

[130] Federal Energy Regulatory Commission (FERC). "Response to Senator Jack Reed's 2/1/05 letter regarding the proposed Weaver's Cove LNG Project in Fall River, MA & the proposed KeySpan LNG Facility Upgrade Project in (continued...)

---

proposal in the 110th Congress would have prohibited LNG facility security plans based upon the provision of security by a state or local government lacking an LNG security arrangement with the facility operator, and would have required the Coast Guard to certify that it has adequate security resources in the sector where a terminal would be located before facility security plans for a new LNG terminal could be approved.[131] In the 111th Congress, the public provision of LNG security continues to be an issue. The Maritime Hazardous Cargo Security Act (S. 1385), introduced by Senator Lautenberg and three co-sponsors on June 25, 2009, would require a national study to identify measures to improve the security of maritime transportation of liquefied natural gas, among other provisions (Sec. 6).

Other Issues

Conducting More Safety Research

Analysts have suggested for several years that Congress could call for additional LNG safety research to help reduce uncertainties about specific LNG terminal or shipping hazards.[132] Among the LNG terminal hazard reports issued by federal agencies, LNG developers, and community groups, there appears to be widespread agreement that additional "objective" LNG safety research would be beneficial. The ABSG report states, for example, that "additional research will need to be performed to develop more refined models, and additional large-scale spill tests would be useful for providing better data for validation of models."[133] The 2004 Sandia study similarly concluded that "obtaining experimental data for large LNG spills over water would provide needed validation and help reduce modeling uncertainty."[134] Physical testing (as opposed to computer simulations) of impacts, explosions, and thermal stresses on LNG tanker hulls could also fill important gaps in engineering knowledge about the potential effects of terrorist attacks.

In 2008, Congress appropriated $8 million to fund large-scale LNG fire experiments by the Department of Energy addressing some of the hazard modeling uncertainties identified in the 2007 GAO report.[135] In that report, the GAO stated that DOE's proposed research plan at that time would "address only 3 of the top 10 issues—and not the second-highest ranked issue—that our panel of experts identified as potentially affecting public safety."[136] In response to the GAO's concerns and those of congressional staff, the DOE and Sandia modified their test program to better align with the priorities put forward by the GAO.[137] The DOE's study could, nonetheless, still be subject to the same types of technical limitations and criticisms facing existing analysis, so

---

(...continued)

Providence, RI under CP04-293 et al." March 3, 2005. p. 2.

[131] H.R. 2830.

[132] See, for example: Kytömaa, H. and Gavelli, F. "Studies of LNG Spills Over Water Point Up Need for Improvement." *The Oil and Gas Journal*. May 9, 2005. p. 61.

[133] ABSG Consulting. May 13, 2004. p. iv.

[134] SNL. December 2004. p. 18.

[135] Consolidated Appropriations Act, 2008 (P.L. 110-161), Division C—Energy and Water Development and Related Agencies Appropriations Act, 2008, Title III, Explanatory Statement, p. 570.

[136] GAO. 2007. pp. 22-23.

[137] Anay Luketa, Sandia National Laboratories. *DOE/Sandia National Laboratories Coordinated Approach for LNG Safety and Security Research*. Presentation to the Committee on Gas, NARUC Summer Committee Meetings. Portland, OR. July 22, 2008. Physical testing and model development by Sandia are scheduled to be completed in 2009.

---

while it may reduce key uncertainties, it may not eliminate them altogether. As of December 2009, Sandia had completed two large LNG pool fire experiments, although the test results are not yet available.

Developer Employee Disclosure

Some policy makers have been concerned that LNG terminal developers may engage in non-public community lobbying or other similar activities promoting individual LNG terminals. Concern arises that these activities may limit public information and awareness about proposed terminals and, therefore, may impede the federal LNG siting review process. Accordingly, legislation proposed in the 110th Congress would have required an applicant for siting approval for an LNG terminal to identify each of its employees and agents engaged in activities to persuade communities of the benefits of the terminal.[138] Supporters of such a policy view it as a means of ensuring public transparency in LNG terminal siting. Disclosure requirements of this type might trigger some First Amendment concerns, however. The Supreme Court has recognized that such government disclosure requirements may have a deterrent effect on the exercise of First Amendment rights.[139] In balancing First Amendment interests, for example, against the government's interest preserving the integrity of the legislative process, the Court has generally upheld the constitutionality of disclosure requirements related to "direct" lobbying of members of Congress.[140] It is unclear how the Court would rule on a disclosure law such as S. 323 related to "indirect" lobbying efforts targeting constituents or otherwise taking place at the local level.[141]

Reducing LNG Demand

Some policy makers argue that Congress should try to reduce the need for new LNG terminals by acting to curb growth in domestic LNG demand, or growth in natural gas demand overall. For example, Congress could change public and industrial incentives for conservation and efficiency, switching to other fuels, or developing renewable energy supplies. Conservation and renewable energy provisions in the American Recovery and Reinvestment Act of 2009 (P.L. 111-5), which was signed by President Obama on February 17, 2009, exemplify such policies. Switching to nuclear power or biomass, however, poses its own hazards to communities and the environment, and so may not be preferable to additional LNG infrastructure. Conservation and renewable energy sources are less hazardous, although they face significant technological and cost barriers to public adoption on the scale that would be required.

Another potential way to curb U.S. LNG demand is to encourage greater North American production of natural gas. Provisions in the Energy Policy Act of 2005 promote this objective, as do proposals to encourage construction of an Alaska gas pipeline and to expand natural gas production on the outer continental shelf. An Alaska gas pipeline would take years to build, however, and might not on its own be able to meet anticipated long-term growth in U.S. gas demand.[142] Increased production from natural gas wells in the lower 48 states since 2005, as well

---

[138] S. 323

[139] *Buckley v. Valeo*, 424 U.S. 1, 65 (1976).

[140] *United States v. Harriss*, 347 U.S. 612 (1954).

[141] For further discussion on this topic, see CRS Report RL33794, *Grassroots Lobbying: Constitutionality of Disclosure Requirements*, by Jack Maskell.

[142] For further analysis, see CRS Report R40963, *The Alaska Natural Gas Pipeline: Background, Status, and Issues for* (continued...)

as the recent U.S. economic recession, have reduced possible near-term pressure on natural gas supplies. It is unclear, however, if new domestic gas supplies may offer a sufficient long-term natural gas supply to meet rising gas demand in the future.

Conclusion

Proposals for new U.S. LNG import terminals pose safety challenges. LNG is inherently hazardous and its infrastructure is potentially attractive to terrorists. The 2004 LNG terminal fire in Algeria demonstrates that, despite technological improvements since the 1940s, LNG facilities can still experience serious accidents. Many lawmakers and the general public are concerned about these hazards.

The U.S. LNG industry is subject to more extensive siting and safety regulation than many other similarly hazardous facilities. Federal, state, and local governments have also put in place security measures intended to safeguard LNG against newly perceived terrorist threats. Some community groups and other stakeholders fear that federal siting requirements for LNG facilities are still not stringent enough, but the responsible federal agencies disagree.

The safety issues associated with LNG terminal siting are both important and familiar. Every major energy source poses some hazard to public safety. Similar public concerns have been raised around siting of other types of energy facilities such as nuclear power plants, oil import terminals, pipelines, and electric transmission lines. In evaluating new LNG terminal proposals, therefore, policy makers face a full range of facilities and safety hazards associated with U.S. energy supplies, not only LNG needs and hazards on their own.

Although LNG terminal regulations are extensive, and the global industry has decades of experience operating LNG facilities, many stakeholders question LNG terminal safety. Some of these questions might be resolved through additional research on key LNG topics. LNG siting decisions are already underway, however, so any additional research efforts intended to affect the siting process would probably have to be completed quickly. Revising LNG safety requirements after completion of a facility could be disruptive of energy supplies. Some cite the Shoreham nuclear power plant in the 1980s, which was closed after construction due to new public safety requirements, as an example of the need to resolve safety concerns before capital is invested.

Both industry and government analysts project continued growth in the demand for natural gas. Greater LNG imports represent one way to address this growth in demand, along with increased North American gas production, conservation, fuel-switching, and the development of renewable energy sources. One way or another the fundamental gas supply and demand balance must be maintained. If policy makers encourage LNG imports, then the need to foster the other energy options may be diminished—and vice versa. Thus decisions about LNG infrastructure could have consequences for a broader array of natural gas supply policies.

(...continued)

Congress, by Paul W. Parfomak.

Appendix. Offshore LNG Terminal Regulation

Under the Deepwater Port Act of 1974 (P.L. 93-627) the Secretary of Transportation is directed to "authorize and regulate the location, ownership, construction, and operation of deepwater ports" (33 U.S.C. §§ 1501(a), 1503). The Secretary has delegated this authority to the Maritime Administration (MARAD) within the Department of Transportation, and to the Coast Guard (USCG), within the Department of Homeland Security.[143] Originally, P.L. 93-627 applied only to offshore oil ports and terminals and not LNG facilities. However, the Maritime Transportation Security Act of 2002 (P.L. 107-295) amended P.L. 93-627 to include natural gas facilities, including LNG terminals, developed offshore. As amended, "deepwater ports" are:

> any fixed or floating manmade structure other than a vessel ... located beyond State seaward boundaries ... intended for use as a port or terminal for the transportation, storage, or further handling of oil *or natural gas* for transportation to any State... (33 U.S.C. § 1502(9a))[144]

The Deepwater Port Act sets out a detailed process for offshore facility siting applications. The act also authorizes regulations addressing potential threats to the environment or human welfare posed by development of offshore LNG facilities (33 U.S.C. §§ 1504, 1508; 33 C.F.R. § 148). The act also requires regulations for the designation of safety zones around deepwater ports (33 U.S.C. § 1509(d)). Among the amendments to the act is a provision exempting LNG terminals from the limitation on the number of "deepwater ports" that can be located in a designated "application area," a provision applicable to oil terminals (33 U.S.C. §§ 1504(d)(4), (i)(4)). Additionally, a preexisting provision of the act allows the governor of a state adjacent to a proposed offshore LNG facility to have that facility license conform to state environmental protection, land and water use, or coastal zone management programs (33 U.S.C. § 1508(b)).

The USCG's regulations regarding LNG facilities are codified throughout 33 C.F.R., with major provisions in part 127. These regulations detail the requirements for siting applications, which include information about the proposed location, design, construction, and operation (33 C.F.R. § 148.109). NEPA analysis is often instrumental in siting and safety-related decisions at specific proposed facilities and is facilitated by the Minerals Management Service, the agency responsible for offshore minerals extraction and the Outer Continental Shelf leasing program.[145] Unlike requirements for onshore facilities, the Coast Guard does not appear to require generally applicable exclusion zones for offshore facilities, but relies instead on case-by-case designation of safety zones.[146] Additional USCG regulations include agency oversight of emergency procedures, security, fire protection, and design and construction standards (33 C.F.R. §§ 127.109, 127.701-127.711, 127.601-127.617, 127.1101-127.1113, 149.205).

---

[143] For a recent LNG siting application, MARAD performed financial analysis and USCG evaluated environmental impacts; the agencies cooperated on all other aspects of the review. ("First Offshore Terminal in U.S. is About to Secure Federal License." *Foster Natural Gas Report*. Bethesda, MD. November 20, 2003. p. 21.

[144] The statute defines natural gas to include "liquefied natural gas." 33 U.S.C. § 1502(14).

[145] Sierra B. Weaver, Note, "Local Management of Natural Resources: Should Local Governments Be Able to Keep Oil Out?," 26 *Harv. Envtl. L. Rev.* 231, 246 (2002).

[146] See 33 C.F.R. § 165, Regulated Navigation Areas and Limited Access Areas.

Liquefied Natural Gas (LNG) Import Terminals: Siting, Safety, and Regulation

Author Contact Information

Paul W. Parfomak
Specialist in Energy and Infrastructure Policy
pparfomak@crs.loc.gov, 7-0030

Adam Vann
Legislative Attorney
avann@crs.loc.gov, 7-6978

Order Code RL33763

CRS Report for Congress

Oil and Gas Tax Subsidies:
Current Status and Analysis

Updated February 27, 2007

Salvatore Lazzari
Specialist in Public Finance
Resources, Science, and Industry Division

Congressional Research Service

Prepared for Members and Committees of Congress

Oil and Gas Tax Subsidies:
Current Status and Analysis

Summary

The CLEAN Energy Act of 2007 (H.R. 6) was introduced by the House Democratic leadership to revise certain tax and royalty policies for oil and natural gas and to use the resulting revenue to support a reserve for energy efficiency and renewable energy. Title I proposes to repeal certain oil and natural gas tax subsidies, and use the resulting revenue stream to support the reserve. The Congressional Budget Office (CBO) estimates that Title I would repeal about $7.7 billion in oil and gas tax subsidies over the 10-year period from 2008 through 2017. In House floor debate, opponents argued that the cut in oil and natural gas subsidies would dampen production, cause job losses, and lead to higher prices for gasoline and other fuels. Proponents counterargued that record profits show that the oil and natural gas subsidies were not needed. The bill passed the House on January 18 by a vote of 264-123. This report presents a detailed review of oil and gas tax subsidies, including those targeted for repeal by H.R. 6.

The Energy Policy Act of 2005 (EPACT05, P.L. 109-58) included several oil and gas tax incentives, providing about $2.6 billion of tax cuts for the oil and gas industry. In addition, EPACT05 provided for $2.9 billion of tax increases on the oil and gas industry, for a net tax increase on the industry of nearly $300 million over 11 years. Energy tax increases comprise the oil spill liability tax and the Leaking Underground Storage Tank financing rate, both of which are imposed on oil refineries. If these taxes are subtracted from the tax subsidies, the oil and gas refinery and distribution sector received a net tax increase of $1,356 million ($2,857 million minus $1,501 million).

EPACT05 was approved and signed into law at a time of very high petroleum and natural gas prices and record oil industry profits. The House approved the conference report on July 28, 2005, and the Senate on July 29, 2005, clearing it for the President's signature on August 8 (P.L. 109-58). However, the tax sections originated in the 106th Congress, with its effort in 1999 to help the ailing domestic oil and gas producing industry, particularly small producers, deal with depressed oil prices. Subsequent price spikes prompted concern about insufficient domestic energy production capacity and supply. All the early bills appeared to be weighted more toward stimulating the supply of conventional fuels, including capital investment incentives to stimulate production and transportation of oil and gas.

In addition to the tax subsidies enacted under EPACT05, the U.S. oil and gas industry qualifies for several other targeted tax subsidies (FY2006 revenue loss estimates appear in parenthesis): (1) percentage depletion allowance ($1 billion); (2) expensing of intangible drilling costs for successful wells and non-geological and geophysical costs for dry holes, including the exemption from the passive loss limitation rules that apply to all other industries ($1.1 billion); (3) a tax credit for small refiners of low-sulfur diesel fuel that complies with Environmental Protection Agency (EPA) sulfur regulations ($ 50 million); (4) the enhanced oil recovery tax credit ($0); and (5) marginal oil and gas production tax credits ($0).

Contents

List of Tables

Oil and Gas Tax Subsidies: Current Status and Analysis

Action in the 110ᵗʰ Congress

The CLEAN Energy Act of 2007 (H.R. 6) was introduced by the House Democratic leadership to revise certain tax and royalty policies for oil and natural gas and to use the resulting revenue to support a reserve for energy efficiency and renewable energy. The bill is one of several introduced on behalf of the Democratic leadership in the House as part of its "100 hours" package of legislative initiatives conducted early in the 110ᵗʰ Congress.

Title I proposes to repeal certain oil and natural gas tax subsidies, and use the resulting revenue stream to support the reserve. According to the Congressional Budget Office (CBO), the provisions in Title I would make about $7.7 billion available for the reserve over the 10-year period from 2008 through 2017.[1]

H.R. 6 came to the House floor for debate on January 18, 2007. In the floor debate, opponents argued that the reduction in oil and natural gas incentives would dampen production, cause job losses, and lead to higher prices for gasoline and other fuels. Opponents also complained that the proposal for the Reserve does not identify specific policies and programs that would receive funding. Proponents of the bill counterargued that record profits show that the oil and natural gas incentives were not needed. They also contended that the language that would create the Reserve would allow it to be used to support a variety of research and development (R&D), deployment, tax incentives, and other measures for renewables and energy efficiency, and that the specifics would evolve as legislative proposals come forth to draw resources from the Reserve. The bill passed the House on January 18 by a vote of 264-123.

Background

The Energy Policy Act of 2005 (P.L. 109-58), enacted on August 8, 2005, expanded some of the existing tax subsidies for the oil and gas industry and created several new ones.[2] The oil and gas tax incentives in EPACT05 were added on top

---

[1] U.S. Congress. Congressional Budget Office. H.R. 6, CLEAN Energy Act of 2007. (Letter to Chairman Nick Rahall, Committee on Natural Resources.) Jan. 12, 2007. 4 p. [http://www.cbo.gov/ftpdocs/77xx/doc7728/hr6prelim.pdf]

[2] For a summary and analysis of this law, see CRS Report RL33302, *Energy Policy Act of*
(continued...)

516 TCNNaturalGas.com

CRS-2

of several existing special tax subsidies for oil and gas. The industry also benefits from provisions of current tax law that are not strictly tax subsidies (or tax expenditures) but that nevertheless provide advantages for and reduce effective tax rates of the oil and gas industry.

The remainder of this report discusses these tax provisions in detail. The first section, below, discusses the origin and evolution of the oil and gas tax subsidies that were incorporated into the 2005 act. The second section summarizes each of the oil and gas tax subsidy provisions in the 2005 energy act and reports its corresponding revenue loss estimate. Section three describes other oil and gas tax subsidies, those that existed before EPACT05 and were generally not affected by it. The final section describes several tax provisions that benefit the oil and gas industry; these are not tax subsidies per se — they are not considered to be tax expenditures — but are deemed by some observers to confer excessive (or unfair) benefits for the industry.

Policy Context and Analysis

Tax incentives for oil and gas supply have historically been an integral (if not the primary) component of the nation's energy policy. The domestic oil and gas industry was granted three tax code preferences, or subsidies: (1) expensing of intangible drilling costs (IDCs) and dry hole costs, introduced in 1916; (2) the percentage depletion allowance, first enacted in 1926 (coal was added in 1932); and (3) capital gains treatment of the sale of oil and gas properties.[3] These tax subsidies reduced marginal effective tax rates in the oil and gas industries, reduced production costs, and increased investments in locating reserves (increased exploration). They also led to more profitable production, some acceleration of oil and gas production, and more rapid depletion of energy resources than would otherwise occur. Partially in response to tax incentives, but also due to the low cost of discovering and developing the huge new resource base, there were discoveries during the 1930s of vast reserves in Texas, which led to a period of overproduction of oil and gas and concomitant declines in prices, which led to demand to prorationing under the Texas Railroad Commission.[4]

Beginning in the 1970s and through much of the 1990s, energy tax policy shifted away from fossil fuel supply and moved toward energy conservation through both energy efficiency and the development of alternative and renewable fuels. However, rising and repeated spikes in petroleum prices that began around 2000 and

---

[2] (...continued)
2005: Summary and Analysis of Enacted Provisions. The two-year amortization period was slowed down to five years for integrated producers under 2006 tax legislation, as discussed in the text.

[3] As discussed later, these subsidies were largely eliminated on much of the oil production and assets, but other, less significant subsidies — the special exemption from the passive loss limitation rules and some special tax credits — were added to the tax code.

[4] Glasner, David, *Politics, Prices, and Petroleum: The Political Economy of Energy*, Pacific Institute for Public Policy Research, 1985, pp. 142-144.

CRS-3

were repeated over the next six years (combined with high and spiking natural gas prices, an electricity crisis, and blackouts) caused policymakers to focus on increasing energy production and supply of many diverse energy sources, including oil and gas.

The tax incentives for the oil and gas industry in the EPACT05 originated in the 106th Congress's effort in 1999 to help the ailing domestic oil and gas producing industry, particularly small producers, deal with depressed oil prices. This situation fostered proposals for economic relief through the tax code, particularly for small independent drillers and producers. Proposals focused mainly on production tax credits for marginal or stripper well oil,[5] but they also included carry-back provisions for net operating losses, and other fossil fuel supply provisions.[6] Subsequent comprehensive energy policy legislation, including H.R. 4 in the 107th Congress, proposed an expanded list of oil and gas tax incentives. The energy tax breaks in this bill (the Securing America's Future Energy Act of 2001, as approved by the House on August 1, 2001) were larger in terms of tax revenue loss than any other comprehensive energy policy legislation proposed during this period. They also were larger than those proposed in EPACT05: $33.5 billion of energy tax cuts, compared with the $14.5 billion loss eventually enacted under P.L. 109-58.

Interest in incentives and subsidies was boosted by the belief that much of the crisis was caused by insufficient domestic production capacity and supply. All the early bills appeared to be weighted more toward stimulating the supply of conventional fuels, including capital investment incentives to stimulate production and transportation of oil and gas. These proposals were further repackaged and expanded into the first broadly based energy bills and comprehensive energy policy legislation, such as H.R. 6 in the 109th, that evolved further and ultimately became EPACT05.[7] The House approved the conference report on July 28, 2005, and the Senate on July 29, 2005, clearing it for the President's signature on August 8 (P.L. 109-58).

The 2005 act became law at a time of very high prices for crude oil, petroleum products, and natural gas, and record oil and gas industry profits. This engendered the enmity of the general public and congressional proposals to (1) revoke the incentives enacted under the 2005 act; (2) repeal or pare back the historical, but

---

[5] A stripper well is one that produces small quantities of oil and natural gas. The tax law currently defines this limit as 15 barrels of oil or the equivalent amount of natural gas per day; the oil and gas industry defines it 10 barrels per day or less.

[6] Although no tax bill was passed that reduced taxes on oil and gas, the 106th Congress did enact a package of $500 million in loan guarantees for small independent producers, which became law (P.L. 106-51), in August 1999.

[7] After some existing energy tax incentives expired in 2003, the 108th Congress enacted retroactive extension of several of the provisions as part of the Working Families Tax Relief Act of 2004 (P.L. 108-311). That law, which reduced revenues by about $1.3 billion over 10 years, was enacted on October 4, 2004. About $5 billion in energy tax incentives — both expansion or liberalization of some of the more popular energy tax provisions, as well as some new energy tax incentives — were part of the American Jobs Creation Act of 2004 (P.L. 108-357) enacted on October 22, 2004.

CRS-4

extant, tax subsidies and other tax advantages; and (3) impose sizeable new taxes on the industry such as a windfall profit tax.[8]

Public and congressional outcry did lead to a paring back of one of the tax subsidies liberalized in the 2005 act: two-year amortization, rather than capitalization, of geological and geophysical (G&G) activity costs, including those associated with abandoned wells (dry holes).[9] This exploration subsidy was the largest upstream tax subsidy (as opposed to a "downstream" or a refinery subsidy), in terms of federal revenue loss, enacted under the 2005 act, although it was and still is a relatively small tax subsidy. The Tax Increase Prevention and Reconciliation Act (P.L. 109-222), signed into law in May 2006, reduced the value of the subsidy by raising the amortization period for major integrated oil companies from two years to five years, still faster than the capitalization treatment before the 2005 act, but slower than the treatment under that act. Independent (nonintegrated) oil companies may continue to amortize all G&G costs over two years.

This relatively minor cutback has not muted the calls for rolling back oil and gas tax subsidies, as petroleum prices (and industry profits) remain somewhat high, particularly those of the biggest oil and gas companies. On September 1, 2006, the House Democratic leadership reportedly sent a letter to the House Speaker proposing a rollback of all of the 2005 energy act tax subsidies.[10] On October 25, 2006, then-House Democratic Leader Nancy Pelosi, urged the Congress to repeal those tax breaks.

Many bills were introduced in the 109th Congress to pare back or repeal the oil and gas industry tax subsidies and other loopholes. Many of the bills focused on the oil and gas exploration and development (E&D) subsidy — expensing of intangible drilling costs (IDCs). This subsidy, which has been in existence since the early days of the income tax, is available to integrated and independent oil and gas companies, both large and small alike.[11] It is an exploration and development incentive, which allows the immediate tax write-off of what economically are capital costs, that is, the costs of creating a capital asset (the oil and gas well). On September 18, 2006, Senators Wyden and Bennett introduced a bill (S. 3908) to give consumers a discount on the purchase of more fuel efficient vehicles that would have been paid for by reducing the IDCs deduction for major integrated oil companies. Comprehensive energy legislation (S. 2829) unveiled by Senate Democrats on May 17, 2006, would have not only eliminated expensing of IDCs, but would have also reduced several other tax benefits (or loopholes) to the oil and gas industry (such the foreign tax

---

[8] For an analysis of the windfall profit tax, see CRS Report RL33305, *The Crude Oil Windfall Profits Tax of the 1980s: Implications for Current Energy Policy*, by Salvatore Lazzari.

[9] Prior to the 2005 act, G&G costs for dry holes were expensed in the first year and capitalized for successful wells.

[10] Bureau of National Affairs, Daily Tax Report. *House Democratic Leadership Letter to Speaker Hastert Asking for Rollback of Tax Breaks for Oil Companies*, Sept. 5, 2006.

[11] As discussed below, many of the remaining tax subsidies are available only to independent oil and gas producers, which, however, may be very large.

CRS-5

credits). The latter are not subsidies (or tax expenditures) in the strict sense of special tax measures unavailable generally, but as discussed below, some consider these unnecessary tax benefits nonetheless.[12] H.R. 5234 focused on repealing three of the seven fossil fuel tax provisions in the 2005 act: temporary expensing of equipment costs for crude oil refining, the small refiner exception to percentage depletion, and the amortization of geological and geophysical (G&G) costs. H.R. 5218 would have denied oil and gas companies the new domestic manufacturing deduction under IRC § 199.

There is speculation that in the 110th Congress, the Democratic leadership in both the House and Senate will begin to examine these breaks more closely, particularly because many of their legislative priorities (such as cutting back the increasingly heavy burden of the alternative minimum tax) will have to be paid for.[13]

Oil and Gas Tax Provisions in EPACT05 and their Revenue Effects

EPACT05 included a plethora of spending, tax, and deregulatory incentives to stimulate the production of conventional and unconventional oil and natural gas, such as gas from Alaska, deep water oil and gas in the outer continental shelf, and oil from marginal wells or private and federal lands. These incentives include tax breaks, royalty relief, streamlined permitting procedures, and other measures. The tax incentives include approximately $14.5 billion over 11 years of incentives to both stimulate domestic production and distribution of fossil fuels and reduce the demand for these fuels through energy efficiency and production of alternative and renewable fuels.

Title XIII, subtitle B, of EPACT05 includes the tax incentives for fossil fuel supply — for production, transportation, and distribution — of oil and gas, as well as capital incentives for expanded refinery capacity. The subtitle does not include coal supply incentives, which are subsumed in the electricity infrastructure subtitle. Although many of the oil and gas tax incentives in EPACT05 are production tax credits and other such "upstream" production incentives, some are capital incentives for natural gas infrastructure (accelerated depreciation of natural gas pipelines). In total, the tax incentives alone are worth about $2.6 billion over 11 years to the industry (an average of about $250 million a year in tax breaks).[14]

---

[12] There is an important economic distinction between a subsidy and a tax benefit. As is discussed elsewhere in this report, firms receive a variety of tax benefits that are not necessarily targeted subsidies (or tax expenditures) because they are available generally.

[13] McKinnon, John D. "Are Higher Taxes in the Offing?" *The Wall Street Journal*, Oct. 30, 2006, p. A-6; Bureau of National Affairs, "Menu of Proposals Available to Democrats Looking to Roll Back Oil, Energy Tax Breaks," *Daily Tax Report*, Nov. 14, 2006, p. G-2.

[14] These are CRS compilations based on Joint Committee on Taxation estimates. See U.S. Congress, Joint Committee on Taxation, *Estimated Budget Effects of the Conference Agreement for Title XIII of H.R. 6, The "Energy Tax Incentives Act of 2005,"* July 27, 2005, (continued...)

CRS-6

Subtitle B, thus, applies specifically to the oil and gas industry, including the refinery industry, for increased supply incentives. Tax incentives are provided — again mostly by liberalization of existing tax code provisions. The incentives are both production incentives (i.e., tax benefits are based on quantities of oil and gas) and capital incentives (i.e., tax benefits are based on magnitude of capital investment, such as pipelines). Both unconventional and conventional oil and gas supply are targeted for tax cuts.

Amortization of Geological and Geophysical Expenditures

Firms engaged in the exploration and development (E&D) of oil and gas incur a variety of costs prior to actual extraction. The tax treatment of these "upstream" E&D costs differs depending on the specific type of activity and depending on whether they are incurred by an integrated or nonintegrated (i.e., independent) producer. An independent producer is defined by Internal Revenue Code (IRC) § 613A(d), as described below.

E&D costs may be generally categorized as four types. First, there are the geological and geophysical costs (G&G). These are exploratory costs (such as for seismic surveys) associated with determining the precise location and potential size of a mineral deposit. A second type of cost is the mineral acquisition or lease rights expenses — the costs of buying or leasing the land under which deposits are thought to exist — such as lease bonuses.

If a property is considered prospective for containing economically recoverable deposits of oil or gas, the firm drills exploratory (and, if successful, subsequently development) wells to ascertain the magnitude of the deposits. These activities have associated various types of drilling costs. Tangible drilling costs, the third type of E&D costs, are amounts paid for tangible drilling and nondrilling equipment such as drilling rigs, casings, valves, pipelines, and other tangible machinery and equipment that have a salvage value. Finally, there are intangible drilling costs, or IDCs as they are frequently called. IDCs are amounts paid by the lease operator for fuel, labor, repairs to drilling equipment, materials, hauling, and supplies. They are expenditures incident to and necessary for the drilling of wells and preparing a site for production of oil and gas. For example, roads may have to be constructed to move in derricks and other types of drilling equipment; often a camp may have to be built with residences to house employees. The power for the equipment and the water supplies are also IDCs. IDCs also may include the cost to operators of any exploratory drilling or development work done by contractors under any form of contract, including a turnkey contract.

In general, as noted above, prior to EPACT05, all four types of costs — G&G costs, mineral rights, tangible equipment, and intangible drilling costs — associated with a dry hole were expensable (i.e., deductible in the year in which the well was determined to be dry). Under the 2005 act, both integrated and independent producers were required to amortize the G&G component of the dry hole costs over

---

[14] (...continued)
JCX-59-05.

CRS-7

two years. This reduced the incentive for G&Gs associated with a dry hole but increased the incentive for G&Gs associated with most successful wells. This provision became effective for G&G amounts paid or incurred in taxable years beginning after the date of enactment.

Two-year amortization of G&G costs is still allowed for independent producers, but as a result of a provision in the Tax Increase Prevention and Reconciliation Act (P.L. 109-222, enacted in May 2006), integrated producers must now amortize such costs over five years.[15] Amortization means that the costs are deducted evenly — the same absolute dollars are taken as deductions every year over a specified period of time, in this case two or five years. It is also called straight-line depreciation.[16]

Determination of Independent Producer Status for Purposes of the Oil Depletion Deduction

Firms that extract oil, gas, or other minerals are permitted a deduction to recover their capital investment in a mineral reserve, which depreciates due to physical and economic depletion or exhaustion as the mineral is recovered (IRC § 611). Depletion, like depreciation, is a form of capital recovery: an asset, the mineral reserve itself, is being expended to produce income. Under the income tax, such a loss in value or cost is deductible.

There are two methods of calculating this deduction: cost depletion and percentage depletion. Cost depletion allows for the recovery of the actual capital investment — the costs of discovering, purchasing, and developing a mineral reserve. Each year, and over the period during which the reserve produces income, the taxpayer deducts a portion of the adjusted basis (original capital investment less previous deductions) equal to the fraction of the estimated remaining recoverable reserves that have been extracted and sold. Under this method, the total deductions cannot exceed the original capital investment.

Under percentage depletion, the deduction for recovery of capital investment is a fixed percentage as set by law of the "gross income" (i.e., revenue) from the sale of the mineral. Under this method, total deductions typically exceed, despite the limitations, the capital invested to acquire and develop the reserve.

IRC § 613 states that mineral producers must claim the higher of cost or percentage depletion. The percentage depletion rate for oil and gas is 15% and is limited to average daily production of 1,000 barrels of oil, or its equivalent in gas. For producers of both oil and gas, the limit applies on a combined basis. For example, an oil-producing company with 2006 oil production of 100,000 barrels and natural gas production of 1.2 billion cubic feet (the statutory equivalent of 200,000 barrels of oil) has average daily production of 821.92 barrels (300,000 ÷ 365 days).

---

[15] The 2006 amendment constitutes a reduction in the tax benefits and was part of the compromise for allowing the G&G costs of successful wells to be amortized over two years rather than capitalized.

[16] The term *amortization* is also used in tax parlance as referring to the depreciation of intangible property, such as patents and copyrights.

CRS-8

Percentage depletion is not available to integrated major oil companies; it is available only for independent producers and royalty owners.

Beginning in 1990, the percentage depletion rate was raised on production from marginal wells — oil from stripper wells (those producing no more than 15 barrels per day, on average) and heavy oil. This rate starts at 15% and increases by one percentage point for each whole $1 that the reference price of oil for the previous calendar year is less than $20 per barrel (subject to a maximum rate of 25%). This higher rate is also limited to independent producers and royalty owners, and for up to 1,000 barrels, determined as before on a combined basis (including non-marginal production). Small independents operate nearly 400,000 small stripper wells in about 28 states, about 78% of the nearly 510,000 producing wells in the United States. Output from stripper wells represented about 16% of total domestic production (about 850,000 barrels per day) in the United States in 2004.[17]

The percentage depletion deduction is limited to 65% of the taxable income from all properties for each producer. A second limitation, the 100% net-income limitation, which applied to each individual property rather than to all the properties, was retroactively suspended for oil and gas production from marginal wells by the Working Families Tax Relief Act of 2004 (P.L. 108-311) through December 31, 2005. The 100% net-income limitation also had been suspended from 1998 to 2003. The difference between percentage depletion and cost depletion is considered a subsidy. It was once a tax preference item for purposes of the alternative minimum tax, but this was repealed by the Energy Policy Act of 1992 (P.L. 102-486).

The percentage depletion allowance is available for other types of fuel minerals, at rates ranging from 10% (coal, lignite) to 22% (uranium), and for mined hard rock minerals. The rate for regulated natural gas and gas sold under a fixed contract is 22%; the rate for geo-pressurized methane gas is 10%. Oil shale and geothermal deposits qualify for a 15% allowance. The net-income limitation to percentage depletion for coal and other fuels is 50%, compared with 100% for oil and gas. Under code section 291, percentage depletion on coal mined by corporations is reduced by 20% of the excess of percentage over cost depletion.

For purposes of percentage depletion, before EPACT05, an independent oil producer was one that, on any given day, (1) did not refine more than 50,000 barrels of oil and (2) did not have a retail operation grossing more than $5 million a year (IRC § 613A[d]). EPACT05 raised the 50,000 barrel daily limit to 75,000. In addition, the act changed the refinery limitation from actual daily production to average daily production for the taxable year. Accordingly, the average daily refinery runs for the taxable year may not exceed 75,000 barrels. For this purpose, the taxpayer would calculate average daily refinery runs by dividing total refinery runs for the taxable year by the total number of days in the taxable year. This is effective for taxable years ending after the date of enactment.

---

[17] Both the number of stripper wells and oil output from such wells is reported in American Petroleum Institute, *Basic Petroleum Data Book*, vol. 26, no. 2, (section IV, table 3), August 2006.

CRS-9

Natural Gas Distribution Lines Treated as 15-Year Property

For purposes of determining the depreciation deduction, EPACT05 established a 15-year recovery period for natural gas distribution lines. Prior to this amendment, natural gas distribution lines were assigned a 20-year recovery period. This provisions is effective for property, the original use of which begins with the taxpayer after April 11, 2005, which is placed in service after April 11, 2005, and before January 1, 2011, and does not apply to property subject to a binding contract on or before April 11, 2005.

Temporary Expensing for Equipment Used in Oil Refining

Before the enactment of EPACT05, depreciation rules (the Modified Accelerated Cost Recovery System, MACRS) required oil refinery assets to be depreciated over 10 years using the double declining balance method.[18] Under the 2005 act, refineries are allowed to irrevocably elect to expense 50% of the cost of qualified refinery property, with no limitation on the amount of the deduction. This provision was enacted to increase investments in existing refineries so as to increase petroleum product output and reduce prices.

The expensing deduction is allowed in the taxable year in which the refinery is placed in service. The remaining 50% of the cost remains eligible for regular cost recovery provisions. To qualify for the deduction (1) original use of the property must commence with the taxpayer; (2)(a) construction must be pursuant to a binding construction contract entered into after June 14, 2005, and before January 1, 2008, (b) in the case of self-constructed property, construction began after June 14, 2005, and before January 1, 2008, or (c) the refinery is placed in service before January 1, 2008; (3) the property must be placed in service before January 1, 2012; (4) the property must meet certain production capacity requirements if it is an addition to an existing refinery; and (5) the property must meet all applicable environmental laws when placed in service. Certain types of refineries, including asphalt plants, are not eligible for the deduction, and there is a special rule for sale-leasebacks of qualifying refineries. If the owner of the refinery is a cooperative, it may elect to allocate all or a part of the deduction to the cooperative owners, allocated on the basis of ownership interests. This provision is effective for qualifying refineries placed in service after date of enactment (i.e., it became effective on August 9, 2005).

Arbitrage Rules Not To Apply to Prepayments for Natural Gas

EPACT05 creates a safe harbor exception to the general rule that tax-exempt, bond-financed prepayments violate the tax code's arbitrage restrictions. The term *investment-type property* does not include a prepayment under a qualified natural gas supply contract. The act also provides that such prepayments are not treated as private loans for purposes of the private business tests. Thus, a prepayment financed with tax-exempt bond proceeds for the purpose of obtaining a supply of natural gas

---

[18] Under the double declining balance method of calculating depreciation deductions, the annual deduction is a fixed percentage (200% or double the straight-line rate) of the difference between asset cost and prior year depreciation deductions.

CRS-10

for service area customers of a governmental utility would not be treated as the acquisition of investment-type property. The safe harbor provisions do not apply if the utility engages in intentional acts to render (1) the volume of natural gas covered by the prepayment to be in excess of that needed for retail natural gas consumption and (2) the amount of natural gas that is needed to fuel transportation of the natural gas to the governmental utility. This provision is effective for obligations issued after date of enactment.

Natural Gas Gathering Lines Treated as Seven-Year Property

Under tax law prior to the enactment of EPACT05, the recovery period for natural gas gathering lines could be either 7 or 15 years, depending on whether they were classified as production or transportation equipment. Several court cases reflected the ambiguous tax treatment. Natural gas pipelines had a recovery period of 15 years, whereas natural gas distribution lines had a recovery period of 20 years (which, as noted above, was reduced to 15 years). EPACT05 assigned natural gas gathering lines a seven-year recovery period for MACRS depreciation deductions.

EPACT05 defined a natural gas gathering line as the pipe, equipment, and appurtenances determined to be a gathering line by the Federal Energy Regulatory Commission (FERC) or used to deliver natural gas from the well-head or common point to the point at which the gas first reaches (1) a gas processing plant, (2) an interconnection with an interstate transmission line, (3) an interconnection with an intrastate transmission pipeline, or (4) a direct connection with a local distribution company, a gas storage facility, or an industrial consumer. Also, the act requires that the original use of the property begin with the taxpayer. This provision became effective for property placed in service after April 11, 2005, excluding property with respect to which the taxpayer or related party had a binding acquisition contract on or before April 11, 2005.

Pass Through to Owners of Deduction for Capital Costs Incurred by Small Refiner Cooperatives in Complying with EPA Sulfur Regulations

IRC § 45H allows a small refiner to claim a tax credit for the production of low-sulfur diesel fuel that is in compliance with Environmental Protection Agency (EPA) sulfur regulations (the Highway Diesel Fuel Sulfur Control Requirements). The credit is $2.10 per barrel of low-sulfur diesel fuel produced; it is limited to 25% of the capital costs incurred by the refiner to produce the low-sulfur diesel fuel. The 25% limit is phased out proportionately as a refiner's capacity increases from 155,000 to 205,000 barrels per day.

Section 179B allows a small refiner to also claim a current year tax deduction (i.e., expensing), in lieu of depreciation, for up to 75% of the capital costs incurred in producing low-sulfur diesel fuel that is in compliance with EPA sulfur regulations. This incentive is also prorated for refining capacity between 155,000 and 205,000 barrels per day. The taxpayer's basis in the property that receives the exemption is reduced by the amount of the production tax credit. In the case of a refinery

CRS-11

organized as a cooperative, both the credit and the expensing deduction may be passed through to patrons.

For both incentives, a small business refiner is a taxpayer who (1) is in the business of refining petroleum products, (2) employs not more than 1,500 employees directly in refining, and (3) has less than 205,000 barrels per day (averaged over the year) of total refining capacity. The incentives took effect retroactively beginning on January 1, 2003.

EPACT05 provided that cooperative refineries that qualify for § 179B expensing of capital costs incurred in complying with EPA sulfur regulations could elect to allocate all or part of the deduction to their owners, determined on the basis of their ownership interests. The election is made on an annual basis and is irrevocable once made. The provision became effective as if included in § 338(a) of the American Jobs Creation Act of 2004, which introduced the tax credit.

Modification and Extension of Credit for Producing Fuel from a Nonconventional Source for Facilities Producing Coke or Coke Gas[19]

Section 45K of the Internal Revenue Code (IRC) provides for a production tax credit of $3 per barrel of oil-equivalent (in 1979 dollars) for certain types of liquid, gaseous, and solid fuels produced from selected types of alternative energy sources (so-called "non-conventional fuels") and sold to unrelated parties. The full credit is available if oil prices fall below $23.50 per barrel (in 1979 dollars); the credit is phased out as oil prices rise above $23.50 (in 1979 dollars) over a $6 range (i.e., the inflation-adjusted $23.50 plus $6).

Both the credit and the phase-out ranges are adjusted for inflation (multiplied by an inflation adjustment factor) since 1979. With an inflation adjustment factor of 2.264 (meaning that prices, as measured by the Gross Domestic Product deflator, have more than doubled since 1979), the credit for 2005 production was $6.79 per barrel of oil equivalent, which is the amount of the qualifying fuel that has a British Thermal Unit (Btu) content of 5.8 million. The credit for gaseous fuels was $1.23 per thousand cubic feet (mcf). The credit for tight sands gas is not indexed to inflation; it is fixed at the 1979 level of $3 per barrel of oil equivalent (about $0.50 per mcf). In 2005, the reference price of oil, which was $50.76 per barrel, still below the inflation adjustment phase-out threshold oil price of $53.20 for 2005 ($23.50 multiplied by 2.264), the full credit of $6.56 per barrel of equivalent was available for qualifying fuels.

---

[19] Two of the nine special tax subsidies for oil and gas in EPACT05 were for unconventional gases and synfuels from coal under the § 45K tax credit. These provisions are discussed because the § 45K tax credit has been important to the development of unconventional gases such as coalbed methane and tight sands gas. However, its revenue losses are subsumed under the coal category of **Table 1** largely because in recent years the provision has benefitted primarily the coal industry by increasing the demand for coal.

526 703-739-3790 TCNNaturalGas.com

CRS-12

Qualifying fuels include synthetic fuels (liquid, gaseous, and solid) produced from coal, and gas produced from either geopressurized brine, Devonian shale, tight formations, or biomass. To qualify for the credit, synthetic fuels from coal must undergo a significant chemical transformation, defined as a measurable and reproducible change in the chemical bonding of the initial components. In most cases, producers apply a liquid bonding agent to the coal or coal waste (coal fines), such as diesel fuel emulsions, pine tar, or latex, to produce a solid synthetic fuel. The coke made from coal and used as a feedstock, or raw material, in steel-making operations also qualifies as a synthetic fuel, as does the breeze (small pieces of coke) and the coke gas (produced during the coking process). Depending on the precise Btu content of these synfuels, the § 45K tax credit could be as high as $26 per ton or more, which is a significant fraction of the market price of coal. Qualifying fuels must be produced within the United States. The credit for coke and coke gas is also $3 per barrel of oil equivalent and is also adjusted for inflation, but the credit is set to a base year of 2004, making the nominal unadjusted tax credit less than for other fuels.

The section 45K credit for gas produced from biomass, and synthetic fuels produced from coal or lignite, is available through December 31, 2007, provided that the production facility was placed in service before July 1, 1998, pursuant to a binding contract entered into before January 1, 1997. The credit for coke and coke gas is available through December 31, 2009, for plants placed in service before January 1, 1992, and after June 30, 1998. The section 45K credit used to apply to oil produced from shale or tar sands, and coalbed methane (a colorless and odorless natural gas that permeates coal seams and that is virtually identical to conventional natural gas). However, the credit for these fuels terminated on December 31, 2002 (and the facilities had to have been placed in service, or wells drilled, by December 31, 1992).

The section 45K credit is part of the general business credit. It is not claimed separately; it is added together with several other business credits and is also subject to the limitations of that credit. The section 45K credit is offset (or reduced) by certain other types of government subsidies that a taxpayer may benefit from: government grants, subsidized or tax-exempt financing, energy investment credits, and the enhanced oil recovery tax credit that may be claimed with respect to such projects. Finally, the credit is nonrefundable and cannot be used to offset a taxpayer's alternative minimum tax liability. Any unused section 45K credits generally may not be carried forward or back to another taxable year. (However, under the minimum tax section 53, a taxpayer receives a credit for prior-year minimum tax liability to the extent that a section 45K credit is disallowed as a result of the operation of the alternative minimum tax.)

The Energy Policy Act of 2005 made several amendments to the section 45K tax credit. First, the credit's provisions were moved from § 29 of the tax code to new § 45K. Before this, this credit was commonly known as the "section 29 credit." Second, the credit was made available for qualified facilities that produce coke or coke gas that were placed in service before January 1, 1993, or after June 30, 1998, and before January 1, 2010. Coke and coke gas produced and sold during the period beginning on the later of January 1, 2006, or the date the facility is placed in service, and ending on the date which is four years after such period begins, are eligible for

CRS-13

the production credit, but at a reduced rate and only for a limited quantity of fuel. The tax credit for coke and coke gas is $3.00 per barrel of oil equivalent, but the credit is indexed for inflation starting with a 2004 base year, compared with a 1979 base year for other fuels. A facility producing coke or coke gas and receiving a tax credit under the previous § 29 rules is not eligible to claim the credit under the new section 45K. The new provision also requires that the amount of credit-eligible coke produced not exceed an average barrel-of-oil equivalent of 4,000 barrels per day. Third, the 2005 act provided that with respect to the IRS moratorium on taxpayer-specific guidance concerning the credit, the IRS should consider issuing rulings and guidance on an expedited basis to those taxpayers who had pending ruling requests at the time that the IRS implemented the moratorium. Finally, the 2005 legislation made the general business limitations applicable to the tax credit. Any unused credits can be carried back one year and forward 20 years, except that the credit cannot be carried back to a taxable year ending before January 1, 2006. These new rules were made effective for fuel produced and sold after December 31, 2005, in taxable years ending after that date.

Revenue Effects

Table 1 shows the revenue effects of the tax provisions in EPACT05, organized by type of incentive. These are the original revenue effects estimated for EPACT05, signed into law on August 8, 2005, by the Joint Committee on Taxation (JCT). Because of changes to energy prices, energy markets, and general economic conditions, revenue loss estimates of the same provisions calculated today would most likely differ from those original estimates.

JCT's estimated revenue losses were projected over an 11-year time frame, from FY2005 to FY2015. The total revenue losses are reported in two ways: the absolute dollar value of tax cuts over 11 years, and the percentage distribution of total revenue losses by type of incentive. Each of the seven tax subsidies for the oil and gas industry are shown separately, as well as the aggregate for upstream (exploration, development, and production) operations and downstream operations (refining and transportation/distribution). Also, for perspective, the oil and gas tax revenue losses are compared with those for other industries and with the tax subsidies for energy efficiency and alternative/renewable fuels.

CRS-14

Table 1. Energy Tax Provisions in the Energy Tax Act of 2005 (P.L. 109-58): 11-Year Estimated Revenue Loss, by Type of Incentive

	Amount ($ millions)	Percentage
INCENTIVES FOR FOSSIL FUELS SUPPLY		
(1) Oil & Gas Production:	-1,132	7.8%
a) amortize all G&G costs over 2 years	-974	
b) liberalize the definition of independent producer	-158	
(2) Oil & Gas Refining and Distribution:	-1,501	10.4%
a) gas pipelines treated as 15-year property	-1,019	
b) temporary expensing in refining of liquid fuels	-406	
c) exempt prepayment of natural gas from arbitrage	-53	
d) gas gathering lines treated as 7-year property	-16	
e) expensing for coop refinery of low-sulfur diesel	-7	
(3) Coal	-2,948	20.4%
(4) Subtotal	-5,581	38.6%
ELECTRICITY RESTRUCTURING PROVISIONS		
(5) Nuclear	-1,571	10.9%
(6) Other	-1,549	10.7%
(7) Subtotal	-3,120	21.6%
INCENTIVES FOR EFFICIENCY, RENEWABLES, AND ALTERNATIVE FUELS		
(8) Energy Efficiency	-1,260	8.7%
(9) Renewable Energy & Alternative Fuels	-4,500	31.1%
(10) Subtotal	-5,760	39.8%
(11) Net Energy Tax Cuts	-14,461	100.0%
(12) Non Energy Tax Cuts[a]	-92	
(13) Total Energy and Non-Energy Tax Cuts	-14,553	
(14) Energy Tax Increases[b]	+2,857	
(15) Other Tax Increases	171	
(15) NET TAX CUTS	-11,525	

Source: CRS compilation based on Joint Committee of Taxation estimates.

a. The act includes a provision to expand R&D for all energy activities. This provision is listed as a non energy tax cut to simplify the table.

b. Energy tax increases comprise the oil spill liability tax and the Leaking Underground Storage Tank financing rate, both of which are imposed on oil refineries. If these taxes are subtracted from the tax subsidies (row 2), the oil and gas refinery and distribution sector received a net tax increase of $1,356 ($2,857-$1,501).

CRS-15

The JCT estimates that the 2005 act provides about $2.6 billion in tax cuts for the oil and gas industry as a whole over 11 years, comprising about $1.1 billion for upstream operations and $1.5 billion for downstream, or refining and distribution, operations. For energy conservation and efficiency, the 2005 act provides about $1.3 billion, including a deduction for energy-efficient commercial property, fuel cells, and micro-turbines. Renewables incentives include a two-year extension of the tax code § 45 credit, renewable energy bonds, and business credits for solar. The total renewable tax subsidies in EPACT05 were about $4.5 billion.

Although the above oil and gas tax subsidies may not be justified based on economic theory, and considering the high oil and gas prices over much of the policy period, they are not large when measured relative to the industries' gross product, which measures in the hundreds of billions of dollars.[20] Another misconception is that industry was the beneficiary of many and significant tax breaks before these provisions were enacted. The industry did benefit historically from significant tax subsidies; however, most of these had been either eliminated or pared back since the 1970s.

Tax Increases

Subtitle F of EPACT05 describes the four tax increases or revenue offsets. Two of the tax increases — modification of the § 197 amortization, and an increase in the excise taxes on tires — are negligible, raising taxes by just under an estimated $200 million over 11 years. However, the other two are sizeable tax increases for the oil and gas industry: reinstatement of the Oil Spill Liability Trust Fund and extension of the Leaking Underground Storage Tank (LUST) trust fund rate, which would be expanded to all fuels.

The total oil and gas industry tax increases are roughly $2.8 billion over 11 years, for a net increase in taxes on the industry of about $200 million, according to the JCT estimates. However, because the oil spill liability tax and the Leaking Underground Storage Tank financing taxes are excise taxes on oil and petroleum products, and are imposed on oil refineries, the net effect of the 2005 act on the oil and gas refinery sector was a tax increase of about $1.3 billion over 11 years.

Other Oil and Gas Tax Subsidies

The Energy Policy Act of 2005 expanded some (but not all) of the preexisting tax subsidies for oil and gas and introduced several new ones. Thus, some of the recent proposals to roll back tax subsidies to oil and gas focus on the subsidies that were in effect before the 2005 act, and which continue be in effect.

---

[20] For the economic theory of taxation of exhaustible natural resources, see CRS Report RL30406, *Energy Tax Policy: An Economic Analysis*, by Salvatore Lazzari.

CRS-16

Other Oil and Gas Tax Subsidies

A list of the preexisting federal tax subsidies (incentives) available for the U.S. oil and gas industry — those in effect before EPACT05 and still in effect today — (and their corresponding revenue loss estimates) appears in **Table 2**. The corresponding revenue losses, as estimated by the JCT in its latest tax expenditures compendium, appear in the last column.[21] Note that the table defines tax subsidies or incentives targeted for the oil and gas industry as those that are due to provisions in the tax law that apply only to this industry and not to others.

---

[21] U.S. Congress, Joint Committee Print, *Estimates of Federal Tax Expenditures for Fiscal Years 2006-2010*, prepared for the House Committee on Ways and Means and the Senate Committee on Finance by the Joint Committee on Taxation Staff, Apr. 25, 2006.

CRS-17

Table 2. Special Tax Incentives Targeted for the Oil and Gas Industry and Estimated Revenue Losses, FY2006

Category	Provision	Major Limitations	Original Enacting Legislation/ Regulation	Federal Revenue Losses($ millions) FY2006
Expensing of Intangible Drilling Costs (IDCs) and Amortization of Exploration and Development Expenses	Firms engaged in the exploration and development of oil or gas properties may expense (deduct in the year paid or incurred) rather than capitalize certain types of drilling expenditures. Geological and geophysical expenses paid or incurred in connection with the domestic exploration for, or development of, oil or gas can be amortized ratably (evenly) over five years.	Integrated oil/gas corporations may expense only 70% of IDCs; the remaining 30% must be amortized and all of the excess IDCs over the 10-year amortizable amount are subject to the alternative minimum tax.	1916 Treasury Regulation T.D. 45, article 223	1,100[a]
Percentage Depletion Allowance	Firms that extract oil or gas are permitted to deduct 15% of sales (up to 25% for marginal wells depending on oil prices) to recover their capital investment in a mineral reserve.	Percentage depletion is available only for independent producers (and royalty owners) and only up to 1,000 barrels or equivalent per day; it is limited to 100% of the net income from any individual property and to 65% of the taxable income from all properties for each producer.	Revenue Act of 1926	1,000
Incentives for Small Refiners to Comply with EPA Sulfur Regulations	IRC § 45H allows a small refiner to claim a $2.10 credit per barrel of low-sulfur diesel produced that complies with EPA sulfur regulations. IRC§ 179B allows a small refiner to expense, in lieu of depreciation, up to 75% of the capital costs incurred in producing low-sulfur diesel fuel that is in compliance with EPA sulfur regulations.	Credit limited to 25% of capital costs; expensing phases out for refining capacity of 155,000-205,000 barrels per day.	P.L. 108-357	50[b]

CRS-18

Category	Provision	Major Limitations	Original Enacting Legislation/ Regulation	Federal Revenue Losses FY2006($ millions)
Tax Credits for Enhanced Oil Recovery Costs	IRC § 43 provides for a 15% income tax credit for the costs of recovering domestic oil by qualified "enhanced oil recovery" (EOR) methods, to extract oil that is too viscous to be extracted by conventional primary and secondary water-flooding techniques.	The EOR credit is nonrefundable and is allowable provided that the average wellhead price of crude oil (using West Texas Intermediate as the reference), in the year before credit is claimed, is below the statutorily established threshold price of $28 (as adjusted for inflation since 1990), in the year the credit is claimed. With average wellhead oil prices for 2005 (about $65) well above the reference price (about $38) the EOR credit was not available.	P.L. 101-508	0
Marginal Production Tax Credit	A $3 tax credit is provided per barrel of oil ($0.50/thousand cubic feet [mcf]) of gas from marginal wells, and for heavy oil.	The credit phases out as oil prices rise from $15 to $18 per barrel (and as gas prices rise from $1.67 to $2.00/thousand cubic feet), adjusted for inflation. The credit is limited to 25 barrels per day or equivalent amount of gas and to 1,095 barrels per year or equivalent. Credit may be carried back up to five years. At 2005 oil and gas prices, the marginal production tax credit was not available.	P.L. 108-357	0

Source: Joint Tax Committee estimates and Internal Revenue Service data.

a. The revenue loss estimate excludes the benefit of expensing costs of dry tracts and dry holes, which includes expensing some things that would otherwise be capitalized. This is a normal feature of the tax code but confers special benefits on an industry where the cost of finding producing wells includes spending money on a lot that turn out dry. The revenue loss estimates also include revenue losses associated with the passive loss limitation rule exemption for the oil and gas industry.

b. The JCT reports this revenue loss at less than $50 million but does not report the actual figure.

CRS-19

General Tax Provisions that May Benefit the Oil and Gas Industry

This discussion has so far excluded current-law tax provisions and incentives that may apply to non-oil and gas businesses but that may also confer tax benefits to the oil and gas industry. There are numerous such provisions in the tax code, which some have called loopholes — they are not strictly considered to be tax expenditures. A complete listing of them is beyond the scope of this report; however, four examples, which have been under discussion as possible revenue raisers, follow to illustrate the point.

For example, the current system of depreciation generally allows the writeoff of equipment and structures somewhat faster than would be the case under both general accounting principles and economic theory; the JCT treats the excess of depreciation deductions over the alternative depreciation system as a tax subsidy (or tax expenditure). In FY2006, the JCT estimates that the aggregate economy-wide revenue loss from this accelerated depreciation deduction (including the expensing under IRC § 179) is $6.7 billion. A certain, but unknown, fraction of this revenue loss or tax benefit accrues to the domestic oil and gas industry, but separate estimates are unavailable.

A second example is the deduction for domestic production (or manufacturing) activities under IRC § 199, which, as noted above is the target of H.R. 5218 (109th Congress). Enacted under the American Jobs Creation Act of 2004 (P.L. 108-357, also known as the JOBS bill), the domestic production deduction (IRC § 199) generally allows taxpayers to receive a deduction based on qualified production activities income resulting from domestic production. The deduction is 3% of income for 2006, rising to 6% between 2007 and 2009, and 9% thereafter; it is subject to a limit of 50% of the wages paid that are allocable to domestic production during the taxable year. The revenue impact of this provision is anticipated by the JCT to be a loss of $4.8 billion of federal revenue in FY2007, and $76 billion over the first 10 years of its life. A certain (as yet unknown) fraction of the tax benefits from the deduction will accrue to the domestic oil and gas industry. The deduction applies to oil and gas or any primary product thereof, provided that such product was "manufactured, produced, or extracted in whole or in significant part in the United States." Recently, the JCT estimated the revenues that would be gained by repealing this deduction for the domestic oil and gas industry at about $0.2 billion in FY2007, and about $2 billion from FY2007-FY2012.[22]

A third example concerns the "last-in/first-out" (LIFO) system of inventory accounting under IRC § 472. This method values the goods sold as the most recent inventory purchase. During a period of rising prices, this method of inventory accounting increases production costs and reduces taxable income and tax liabilities. A provision in the Senate version of H.R. 4297 (109th Congress) would have eliminated a portion of the tax benefits from LIFO inventory accounting for major

---

[22] U.S. Congress, Joint Committee on Taxation, *JCT Cost Estimate for McDermott-Kerry Legislation (H.R. 5218, S. 2672) to Eliminate Oil Company Eligibility for JOBS Act Section 199 Tax Breaks*, May 10, 2006.

CRS-20

integrated oil companies with gross receipts in excess of $1 billion. Under threat of presidential veto, this provision, which would have increased taxes on such companies by an estimated $3.5 billion in FY2006, was deleted from the final law, the Tax Increase Prevention and Reconciliation Act of 2006 (P.L. 109-222).[23]

A fourth example is the foreign tax credit, which is a federal tax credit against U.S. tax liabilities for *income* taxes paid to foreign countries. This section of the tax code is intended to prevent the double taxation of foreign source income (income earned abroad by U.S. residents and corporations). However, many countries in which domestic U.S. oil companies conduct business (either through branches or foreign subsidiaries) impose levies that are not strictly considered to be creditable income taxes, which may have the effect of going beyond prevention of double taxation of foreign source income — it may actually lead to a reduction of taxes on domestic source income. A provision in the Senate version of H.R. 4297 (109th Congress) would have denied the foreign tax credit, under certain conditions, for major integrated oil companies with gross receipts in excess of $1 billion. The foreign tax credit would have been denied in the event that the foreign levy was assessed in exchange for an economic benefit provided by the foreign jurisdiction to the domestic oil company and if the foreign jurisdiction did not generally impose an income tax. This provision, which would have increased taxes on such companies by an estimated $0.8 billion over the 10-year period from FY2006 to FY2015, was deleted from the final law, the Tax Increase Prevention and Reconciliation Act of 2006 (P.L. 109-222).[24]

Finally, **Table 2** excludes targeted taxes that impose special tax liabilities on the domestic oil and gas industry — taxes that are not imposed on other industries. These would include taxes such as the motor fuels excise taxes (e.g., the 18.4¢ per gallon tax on gasoline, the 24.4¢ per gallon tax on diesel) and the oil spill liability trust fund excise tax, which imposes a $0.05 per barrel tax on every barrel of crude oil refined domestically.[25] These taxes are imposed on refiners, although under normal (and stable) market conditions they are shifted forward (or passed through the distribution and retailing chain) and largely paid by consumers. The motor fuels excise taxes (including the Leaking Underground Storage Tank Trust Fund Tax) represent a tax liability — the amount of revenues collected by the federal

---

[23] U.S. Congress. Joint Committee on Taxation. *Comparison of Estimated Revenue Effects of the Tax Provisions Contained in H.R. 4297, "The Tax Relief Extension Reconciliation Act of 2005," As Passed by the House, and H.R. 4297, "The Tax Relief Act of 2005," As Passed by the Senate.* February 9, 2006.

[24] U.S. Congress. Joint Committee on Taxation. *Comparison of Estimated Revenue Effects of the Tax Provisions Contained in H.R. 4297, "The Tax Relief Extension Reconciliation Act of 2005," As Passed by the House, and H.R. 4297, "The Tax Relief Act of 2005," As Passed by the Senate.* February 9, 2006.

[25] Moneys are allocated into a fund for cleaning up oil spills.

CRS-21

government — of about $36 billion in FY2006;[26] revenues collected from the oil spill liability excise tax are estimated by the JCT at $0.150 billion.

---

[26] Revenues from motor fuels excise taxes are allocated primarily to the Highway Trust Fund (HTF) and various trust funds, depending on the mode of transportation. The HTF also includes revenue from excise taxes on tires, a heavy vehicle use tax, and retail sales tax on trucks and tractors.

536 703-739-3790 TCNNaturalGas.com

Congressional Research Service

Royalty Relief for U.S. Deepwater Oil and Gas Leases

Marc Humphries
Analyst in Energy Policy

February 4, 2009

Congressional Research Service

7-5700

www.crs.gov

RS22567

CRS Report for Congress ──────────────

Prepared for Members and Committees of Congress

Summary

The most common incentives for offshore oil and gas development include various forms of royalty relief. The Outer Continental Shelf Lands Act (OCSLA) authorizes the Secretary of the Interior to grant royalty relief to promote increased oil and gas production (43 U.S.C. 1337). The Deep Water Royalty Relief Act of 1995 (DWRRA) expanded the Secretary's royalty relief authority in the Gulf of Mexico outer continental shelf (OCS).

As oil and gas prices hit record levels during 2006, allegations arose about missteps at the Minerals Management Service (MMS) regarding the collection of royalties for oil and gas production on the outer continental shelf (OCS). Of particular concern to Congress was that price thresholds for royalty relief in deepwater leases were omitted from deepwater lease sales held in 1998 and 1999. Such thresholds establish a maximum price per barrel of oil or million Btu of natural gas where producers may receive royalty relief; above the threshold price, royalties must be paid. Except for the 1998 and 1999 lease sales, the thresholds are included in all leases eligible (leases issued between 1996-2000) for automatic royalty relief under the Deepwater Royalty Relief Act of 1995 (DWRRA, P.L. 104-58). Without the price thresholds, oil and gas can be produced from a lease up to a specified volume without being subject to royalties, no matter how high the price goes. A recent U.S. District Court decision, however, which was upheld by a 3-member panel in the U.S. Court of Appeals, ruled that the Secretary of the Interior had no authority to impose price thresholds for oil and gas leases held under the DWRRA . Based on the court ruling, the lessees, therefore, should have the right to produce up to the specified volume of oil and gas in the lease, regardless of the price. This ruling could cost the federal treasury as much as $1.8 billion in refunds according to the MMS and between $21-$53 billion over 25 years according to the Government Accountability Office (GAO).

The policy concern for some is not only to amend the 1998 and 1999 leases to include price thresholds but also address the Secretary's authority to impose price thresholds in any of the DWRRA leases issued from 1996-2000.

There are discussions underway in the 111th Congress on how to address the royalty relief issue involving price thresholds and DWRRA leases. In the 110th Congress, the House passed H.R. 6899, the Comprehensive American Energy Security and Consumer Protection Act. Under Title I, this legislation would have, among other things, required the Secretary of the Interior to accept a lessee's request to modify those leases without price thresholds ("covered leases") to include price thresholds. The bill would not have made new oil and gas leases in the Gulf of Mexico available to lessees holding "covered leases" unless current leases included price thresholds or the lessee agreed to pay the proposed "conservation of resources fee." The bill also would have affirmed the Secretary's authority to impose a price threshold in certain leases. The royalty relief provisions were not enacted into law.

Contents

Tables

Contacts

Introduction

As oil and gas prices hit record levels during 2006, allegations arose about missteps at the Minerals Management Service (MMS) regarding the collection of royalties for oil and gas production on the outer continental shelf (OCS). Of particular concern to Congress was that price thresholds for royalty relief in deepwater leases were omitted from deepwater lease sales held in 1998 and 1999. Such thresholds establish a maximum price per barrel of oil or million Btu of natural gas where producers may receive royalty relief; above the threshold price, royalties must be paid. Except for the 1998 and 1999 lease sales, the thresholds are included in all leases eligible (leases issued between 1996-2000) for automatic royalty relief under the Deepwater Royalty Relief Act of 1995 (DWRRA, P.L. 104-58). Without the price thresholds, oil and gas can be produced from a lease up to a specified volume without being subject to royalties, no matter how high the price goes. A recent U.S. District Court decision[1], however, which was upheld by a 3-member panel in the U.S. Court of Appeals, ruled[2] that the Secretary of the Interior had no authority to impose price thresholds for oil and gas leases held under the DWRRA . Based on the court ruling, the lessees, therefore, should have the right to produce up to the specified volume of oil and gas in the lease, regardless of the price. This ruling could cost the federal treasury as much as $1.8 billion in refunds according to the MMS[3] and between $21-$53 billion over 25 years according to the Government Accountability Office (GAO).[4]

OCS Leasing System

The Outer Continental Shelf Lands Act of 1953 (OCSLA), as amended, provides for the leasing of OCS lands in a manner that protects the environment and returns to the federal government revenues in the way of bonus bids, rents, and royalties. Lease sales are conducted through a competitive, sealed bonus-bidding process, and leases are awarded to the highest bidder. Successful bidders make an up-front cash payment, called a bonus bid, to secure a lease. A minimum bonus bid is determined for each tract offered.

Bidding on deepwater tracts in the mid-1990s led to a surge in bonus revenue (e.g., $1.4 billion in FY1997).[5] Bonus bids totaled $9.5 billion in FY2008 up from $902.6 million in FY2007. In addition to the cash bonus bid, a royalty rate of 12.5% or 16.66%, has been imposed on the value of production, with royalties sometimes paid "in-kind."[6] More recently, the MMS imposed an 18.75% royalty rate on its offshore leases. Annual rents range from $5 to $9.50, with lease sizes generally ranging from 2,500 to 5,760 acres. Initial lease terms of 5-10 years are standard, and leases are continued as long as commercial quantities are being produced. The MMS, in the Department of the Interior, administers the offshore leasing program.

---

[1] Kerr-McGee Oil and Gas Corp. v. Allred, No. 2:06-CV-0439 (W.D. La. October 30, 2007).

[2] U.S. Court of Appeals for the 5th Circuit, No. 08-30069. January 12, 2009.

[3] Personal communication with MMS Office of Congressional Affairs, Lyn Herdt, February 4, 2008.

[4] U.S. Government Accountability Office, *Oil and Gas Royalties: Litigation over Royalty Relief Could Cost the Federal Government Billions of Dollars,* June 8. 2008.

[5] Department of the Interior, FY2002 Budget Justifications, p. 63.

[6] A royalty-in-kind payment would be in the form of barrels of oil or cubic feet of natural gas.

Royalty Relief

OCSLA authorizes the Secretary of the Interior to grant royalty relief to promote increased oil and gas production. There are generally four royalty relief categories in the Gulf of Mexico (GOM): Deepwater (more than 200 meters), Shallow Water Deep Gas, End-of-Life, and Special Case. Royalty relief under the End-of-Life and Special Case categories was already in place under OCSLA before the Deep Water Royalty Relief Act of 1995 (DWRRA) and is not involved in the current controversy. DWRRA expanded the Secretary's authority to grant royalty relief to deepwater leases in the Gulf of Mexico OCS. Under DWRRA, the Secretary may reduce royalties if production would otherwise be uneconomic.[7]

In an unresolved matter over price thresholds, the Department of the Interior interprets the DWRRA (P.L. 104-58) to provide the Secretary of the Interior with the authority and discretion to establish thresholds, above which the relief is discontinued. Another interpretation of the law concludes that thresholds are mandatory, not discretionary.[8] In addition, the authority of the Secretary to impose price thresholds has come into question in a lawsuit filed by Kerr-McGee (purchased by Anadarko Petroleum Corporation in 2006).[9] The U.S. District Court, Western District of Louisiana issued a ruling on October 18, 2007, in favor of Kerr-McGee,[10] meaning that the Secretary of the Interior did not have authority to impose price threshold levels in leases issued under DWRRA (1996-2000). The Department of the Interior appealed the District Court ruling. On January 12, 2009, a three-judge panel of the 5th U.S. Circuit Court of Appeals in New Orleans upheld the District Court decision.[11] The ruling could apply to potentially $23-$31 billion in future OCS royalties according to the MMS, but may not affect congressional efforts to impose new fees or establish new lease eligibility criteria discussed below.[12] The GAO estimates the range of royalty revenue loss to the federal treasury at between $30-$53 billion over 25 years. The range of estimated losses are based on a number of assumptions including future prices and production rates. Threshold levels were established in 1995 for eligible deepwater leases and are adjusted annually for inflation.[13] On average, the market price for oil and gas throughout 2008 was above the threshold (with the exception of shallow water deep gas leases), so leases with thresholds were paying royalties on oil production.

---

[7] A description of MMS royalty relief programs is available at http://www.gomr.mms.gov/homepg/offshore/royrelef.html. A more detailed analysis of the royalty relief programs is contained in a Department of the Interior, MMS, report: *Guidelines for the Application, Review, Approval, and Administration of the Deepwater Royalty Relief Program for Pre-Act Leases and Post-2000 Leases*, Appendix 1 to NTL No. 2002-No. 2, February 2002.

[8] Letter to House Committee on Government Reform, by Stephen Lowey of Lowey Dannenberg Bemporad & Selinger, P.C., Re: Gulf of Mexico defective deep water drilling leases, October 31, 2006.

[9] For more details on this case, see CRS Report RL33404, *Offshore Oil and Gas Development: Legal Framework*, by Adam Vann.

[10] Kerr-McGee Oil & Gas Corp. v. Allred.

[11] U.S. Court of Appeals for the 5th Circuit.

[12] See CRS Report RL33974, *Legal Issues Raised by Provision in House Energy Bill (H.R. 6) Creating Incentives for Certain OCS Leaseholders to Accept Price Thresholds*, by Robert Meltz and Adam Vann and CRS General Distribution Memorandum: *Impact of the Kerr-McGee Oil and Gas Corp. v. Allred Ruling on the Proposed Royalty Relief for America Consumers Act of 2007*, by Adam Vann.

[13] Price threshold levels for deepwater oil and gas can be found on the MMS website at http://www.gomr.mms.gov/homepg/offshore/royrelef.html.

DWRRA provides for "fields"[14] with eligible leases to receive royalty suspensions for specific volumes of production at specified depths (**Table 1**). The royalty relief was contingent on the lease being part of a non-producing field before DWRRA was enacted.[15] Eligible leases are those issued in the GOM between 1996 and 2000 at depths greater than 200 meters located wholly west of 87 degrees, 30 minutes West longitude. The lease is offered subject to a lease suspension volume—the amount of oil and gas that can be produced royalty-free. Eligible leases do not require an economic evaluation to be granted royalty relief. Also within the Deepwater category are "Pre-Act" leases (lease sales held before November 1995), Post-2000 leases (lease sales held after November 2000), and leases classified as Expansion Projects, all of which can qualify for royalty relief under DWRRA with an application demonstrating economic need. In addition, "Post 2000" leases or "royalty suspension leases" may be offered with an automatic royalty suspension volume on a "lease," rather than field, basis. The Energy Policy Act of 2005 (EPACT-05, P.L. 109-58) expanded the "post-Act" royalty relief program by providing automatic minimum suspension volumes at specified depths in each lease. For five years after enactment of EPACT-05, the Secretary of the Interior is granted authority to place limits on royalty relief based on the market price of oil and natural gas.

A shallow-water, deep-gas incentive became effective March 1, 2004.[16] The rule suspends the royalty on gas from wells with at least 15,000 feet "true vertical depth" located in waters less than 200 meters deep in the central and western GOM. It also provides a royalty suspension supplement for drilling "certain" unsuccessful deep wells in that region. The gas price threshold for discontinuing this royalty relief was estimated by MMS at $10.37 per million Btu in 2008 for lease sales beyond 2003.[17] The shallow-water, deep-gas incentive was expanded by EPACT-05 to require royalty suspension volumes of at least 35 billion cubic feet of natural gas produced in waters less than 400 meters deep from ultra-deep wells (20,000 feet true vertical depth), leases that have previously produced from wells at 15,000 feet deep, or "sidetrack wells."

Table 1. Minimum Royalty Suspension Volumes Per Lease

DWRRA 1995 (P.L. 104-58)		Energy Policy Act 2005 (P.L. 109-58)	
Depth	Barrels of Oil Equivalent (in millions)	Depth	Barrels of Oil Equivalent (in millions)
200-400 meters	17.5	—	—
400-800 meters	52.5	400-800 meters	5.0
> 800 meters	87.5	800-1,600 meters	9.0
—	—	1,600-2,000 meters	12.0
		> 2,000 meters	16.0

Source: P.L. 104-58 and P.L. 109-58.

---

[14] A *field* is defined as an area consisting of a single reservoir or multiple reservoirs with the same geological structure or stratigraphic trapping condition and may contain more than one lease.

[15] The MMS rule pertaining to royalty relief for each field as opposed to each lease was challenged in district court in Louisiana in 2003. The court ruled in favor of the lessees (and was upheld by the Court of Appeals), allowing royalty relief to apply to individual leases rather than fields (reported at 385 F. 3rd 884, 5th Circuit Court).

[16] 69 *Federal Register* 3492, January 26, 2004.

[17] See the MMS website at http://www.mms.gov/econ/PDFs/currentkick-outsNOV-2008.pdf.

Proponents of these royalty relief measures contend that without incentives, little GOM deepwater or shallow-water, deep-gas drilling would have taken place, because these areas would not have been competitive with foreign offshore prospects (e.g., Brazil and West Africa). Increased GOM drilling enhances U.S. energy security, proponents contend. Critics, during the debate on royalty relief that preceded passage of EPACT-05, charged that the government would forfeit millions of dollars through the subsidy and that drilling costs were already coming down as a result of advances in technology, thus making many deepwater lease tracts economical. According to MMS, deepwater drilling in the Gulf of Mexico has benefitted from a combination of improved technology, higher prices, and royalty reductions.[18]

Deepwater Development

A significant amount of activity is taking place in deepwater GOM. Out of 8,221 active offshore oil and gas leases, about 54% are in deep water Gulf of Mexico. Interest surged after enactment of DWRRA, with 3,000 deepwater leases bid between 1996 and 1999.[19] Annual deepwater oil production rose from 108 million barrels in 1997 (26% of total GOM) to 343 million barrels in 2006 (72% of total GOM). Deepwater natural gas production increased from 382 billion cubic feet in 1997 (7% of total GOM) to 1.1 trillion cubic feet in 2006 (38% of total GOM). Deepwater development, however, is facing major challenges. Currently, about 8% of the DWRRA-eligible leases issued between 1996 and 2000 have been drilled, and only a few are in production (because of rig constraints and large lease inventories). In 2007, of more than 1,600 leases producing in the GOM, 19 were issued in 1998 and 1999 without price thresholds.

MMS maintains that the future of deepwater production looks bright. Proved oil and gas reserve and resource estimates have more than doubled since 2000 (**Table 2**), discoveries are taking place in much deeper waters since 2000, and development time decreased from 10 years in the mid-1990s to seven years in 2006. Although DWRRA spurred a surge of interest in deepwater oil and gas development, major production directly related to the act's incentives has yet to be realized. For leases containing price thresholds, relatively little royalty relief has been granted.

Table 2. Deepwater Proved Reserves and Resources

(in million barrels of oil equivalent)

Year	Proved Reserves	Proved and Unproved Resources and Industry Discoveries
2000	4,015	8,622
2002	4,385	12,871
2004	6,702	15,573
2006	9,435	18,531

Source: DOI, MMS. OCS Report MMS 2006-02.

---

[18] *Deepwater Gulf of Mexico 2006: America's Expanding Frontier*, OCS Report MMS 2006-022, U.S. Department of the Interior, May 2006.

[19] Ibid., Fig. 52.

Congressional Concerns

Controversy over royalty relief had focused on the lack of price thresholds in OCS lease sales held in 1998 and 1999, but because of a recent U.S. District Court ruling, upheld by the Circuit Court of Appeals (discussed above), the authority of the Secretary of the Interior to impose price thresholds may be at issue in all of the DWRRA leases issued from 1996-2000. All lease sales held under the DWRRA (1996-2000) included price thresholds except those held in 1998 and 1999. Without the price thresholds, deepwater producers continue to benefit from royalty relief regardless of the price. The DOI continues to argue that the Secretary of the Interior has the authority and discretion to impose price thresholds in the DWRRA leases and may appeal the ruling further. The MMS and the Government Accountability Office (GAO) estimate that the error in the 1998-99 leases alone could cost the federal government as much as $14.7 billion. The MMS estimated that about $1.2 billion in royalty revenue was foregone through April 2007. In FY2008 the MMS collected about $18 billion in revenues from oil and gas leases on federal lands.

The policy concern for some is not only to amend the 1998 and 1999 leases to include price thresholds but also address the Secretary's authority to impose price thresholds in any of the DWRRA leases issued from 1996-2000.

Some argue that modifications to the leases should be retroactive to capture past as well as future revenues from deepwater oil and gas production. Others in Congress argue that any mandatory modification of the leases might be a breach of contract or unconstitutional, and would be contested in court. MMS has initiated efforts to have lessees voluntarily modify their leases to include price thresholds going forward from October 2006. In December 2006, five companies holding about 25% of the leases have agreed to the MMS initiative.[20] Of the 1,032 deepwater leases issued in 1998 and 1999, 526 are active (under exploration or development) and 19 are currently producing.

Legislative Actions

There are discussions underway in the 111th Congress on how to address the royalty relief issue involving price thresholds and DWRRA leases. In the 110th Congress, the House passed H.R. 6899, the Comprehensive American Energy Security and Consumer Protection Act. Under Title I, this legislation would have, among other things, required the Secretary of the Interior to accept a lessee's request to modify those leases without price thresholds ("covered leases") to include price thresholds. The bill would not have made new oil and gas leases in the Gulf of Mexico available to lessees holding "covered leases" unless current leases included price thresholds or the lessee agreed to pay the proposed "conservation of resources fee."[21] The bill also would have affirmed the Secretary's authority to impose a price threshold in certain leases. The royalty relief provisions were not enacted into law.

---

[20]Companies include BP Plc, ConocoPhillips. Marathon Oil, Royal Dutch Shell, and Walter Oil and Gas Corp.

[21]The fee would be $9/barrel oil and $1.25/million Btu natural gas on covered producing leases and$3.75/acre annually on non-producing leases.

Author Contact Information

Marc Humphries
Analyst in Energy Policy
mhumphries@crs.loc.gov, 7-7264

Congressional Research Service

Natural Gas Passenger Vehicles: Availability, Cost, and Performance

Brent D. Yacobucci
Specialist in Energy and Environmental Policy

February 3, 2010

Congressional Research Service

7-5700

www.crs.gov

RS22971

CRS Report for Congress
Prepared for Members and Committees of Congress

Natural Gas Passenger Vehicles: Availability, Cost, and Performance

Summary

Higher gasoline prices in recent years and concerns over U.S. oil dependence have raised interest in natural gas vehicles (NGVs). Use of NGVs for personal transportation has focused on compressed natural gas (CNG) as an alternative to gasoline. Consumer interest has grown, both for new NGVs as well as for conversions of existing personal vehicles to run on CNG. This report finds that the market for natural gas passenger vehicles will likely remain limited unless the differential between natural gas and gasoline prices remains high in order to offset the higher purchase price for an NGV. Conversions of existing vehicles will also continue to be restricted unless the Clean Air Act (CAA) is amended or if the Environmental Protection Agency (EPA) makes changes to its enforcement of the CAA.

Congressional Research Service

Natural Gas Passenger Vehicles: Availability, Cost, and Performance

Contents

Contacts

Congressional Research Service

549

Introduction

Congressional and consumer interest in natural gas vehicles (NGVs) for personal transportation has grown in recent years, especially in response to higher gasoline prices, concerns over the environmental impact of petroleum consumption for transportation, and policy proposals such as the "Pickens Plan."[1] Although natural gas passenger vehicles have been available for years, they have been used mostly in government and private fleets; very few have been purchased and used by consumers. Larger NGVs—mainly transit buses and delivery trucks—also play a role in the transportation sector, especially due to various federal, state, and local incentives for their use. However, high up-front costs for new NGVs, as well as concerns over vehicle performance and limited fuel infrastructure, have led to only marginal penetration of these vehicles into the personal transportation market.

Current Market

The Energy Information Administration (EIA) estimates that there were roughly 114,000 compressed natural gas (CNG) vehicles in the United States in 2007, and roughly 3,000 liquefied natural gas (LNG) vehicles.[2] Roughly two-thirds of NGVs are light-duty (i.e., passenger) vehicles. This compares to roughly 240 million conventional (mostly gasoline) light-duty vehicles.[3] Further, of the roughly 16.1 million new light-duty vehicles sold in 2007, only about 1,100 (0.01%) were NGVs.[4] For model year (MY) 2010, only one NGV was available from an original equipment manufacturer (OEM) for purchase by consumers—the CNG-fueled Honda Civic GX[5]—although some companies convert vehicles to CNG before they are sold (usually as fleet vehicles).

Life-Cycle Cost Issues

Currently, natural gas vehicles are significantly more expensive than comparable conventional vehicles. For example, the incremental price between a conventional Honda Civic EX and a natural gas-powered Honda Civic GX is nearly $6,000,[6] although some of this difference is made up through a tax credit for the purchase of new alternative fuel vehicles. If a taxpayer qualifies, he or she may claim a credit of up to $4,000 for the purchase of a new Honda Civic GX.[7] This tax

---

[1] On July 8, 2008, T. Boone Pickens announced a plan calling for reduced petroleum imports through the expanded use of natural gas in transportation. For an analysis of this plan, see CRS General Distribution Memoradum, *The T. Boone Pickens Energy Plan: A Preliminary Analysis of Implementation Issues*, by Jeffrey Logan, William F. Hederman, and Brent D. Yacobucci.

[2] U.S. Energy Information Administration (EIA), *Alternatives to Traditional Transportation Fuels 2007*, April 2009. Tables V1 and V4.

[3] Stacy C. Davis, Susan W. Diegel, and Robert G. Boundy, *Transportation Energy Data Book: Edition 27*, 2008. Tables 4.1 and 4.2.

[4] Davis, et al., op. cit. Tables 4.5 and 4.6; EIA, op. cit. Table S1.

[5] For MY2004, there were eight CNG models (from Ford, General Motors, and Honda). This number dropped to five in MY2005, and one in MY2006. U.S. Department of Energy (DOE), *Fueleconomy.gov Website*. Accessed February, 2, 2010.

[6] 2010 Honda Civic EX MSRP: $19,455. 2010 Honda Civic GX MSRP: $25,340. $25,340 -$19,455 = $5,885.

[7] Energy Policy Act (EPAct) of 2005. P.L. 109-58, Sec. 1341.

---

credit is set to terminate at the end of 2010. It should be noted that with higher production, this incremental cost should decrease, but the likely extent of that decrease is unclear.

Since the number of natural gas refueling stations is limited—only about 400 to 500 publicly available nationwide,[8] compared to roughly 120,000 retail gasoline stations[9]—the purchaser of a new NGV might also choose to install a home refueling system. According to *Consumer Reports* and Natural Gas Vehicles for America (NGVAmerica), a FuelMaker Phill system costs between $3,400 and $4,500 plus installation.[10] However, a taxpayer can offset $1,000 of this by claiming a tax credit for installing new alternative fuel refueling infrastructure.[11]

Offsetting the higher up-front costs are likely annual fuel savings in switching from gasoline to natural gas. Using recent average retail gasoline and residential natural gas prices, annual fuel cost savings could be roughly $650.[12] Assuming a 7% discount rate, the current payback period for the CNG vehicle and home refueling system is just over 10 years. Depending on how long a consumer keeps a new vehicle, this payback period may or may not be acceptable to that consumer.

Assuming a smaller differential between natural gas and gasoline prices, or the expiration of the existing tax incentives can significantly increase this payback period; assuming a larger difference in fuel prices, assuming a smaller discount rate, or assuming incremental natural gas vehicle prices decrease in the future, this payback period could be shorter.

Other Potential Benefits and Costs

In addition to the life-cycle cost difference between CNG and conventional vehicles, there are other costs and benefits associated with natural gas vehicles which may not have a defined price tag. For example, any reduction in petroleum dependence (beyond the per-gallon cost savings) is not represented in the above payback period estimate. Some consumers may place a value on displacing petroleum consumption, and thus imports.[13] Further, natural gas vehicles in general

---

[8] Roughly half of the 800 to 1,000 natural gas refueling stations are privately owned or are located at government sites closed to the public (e.g., military bases). Of the public CNG refueling stations, many require a keycard or other prior arrangement with the station operator.

[9] DOE, Alternative Fuels and Advanced Vehicles Data Center (AFDC), *Alternative Fueling Station Locator.* http://www.eere.energy.gov/afdc/fuels/stations_locator.html. Accessed September 16, 2008.

[10] "The natural-gas alternative: The pros & cons of buying a CNG-powered Honda Civic," *Consumer Reports*, April 2008. Stephe Yborra, NGVAmerica, *Frequently Asked Questions About Converting Vehicles to Operate on Natural Gas*, Washington, DC. Accessed October 15, 2008. http://www.ngvc.org/pdfs/FAQs_Converting_to_NGVs.pdf. One potential impediment to this is the fact that in April 2009, FuelMaker declared bankruptcy in Canadian court. In May, Fuel Systems Solutions, Inc., purchased some of FuelMaker's assets, including the Phill brand. Reuters, "Key Developments: Fuel Systems Solutions Inc (FSYS.O)," May 28, 2009, http://www.reuters.com/finance/stocks/keyDevelopments?symbol=FSYS.O&pn=1.

[11] EPAct 2005. P.L. 109-58, Sec. 1342.

[12] Savings based on the following assumptions: 15,000 annual miles traveled (both vehicles); 29 miles per gallon (mpg) fuel economy for gasoline vehicle; 28 mpg equivalent for natural gas vehicle; $2.66 national retail average for regular gasoline; $11.25 per 1,000 cubic feet of residential natural gas; 121.5 cubic feet of natural gas per gasoline gallon equivalent. Therefore, current residential natural gas prices are roughly $1.37 per equivalent gallon. Fuel economy estimates from DOE, *Fueleconomy.gov*. Fuel price estimates are from EIA.

[13] However, it should be noted that a reduction in domestic consumption will likely not lead to a one-to-one reduction in imports, since reducing domestic consumption is also likely to reduce domestic petroleum production.

Natural Gas Passenger Vehicles: Availability, Cost, and Performance

have lower pollutant and greenhouse gas emissions than comparable gasoline vehicles, although this may or may not be true for specific vehicles and pollutants.[14]

A key potential benefit raised by proponents of NGVs is that while the United States imports the majority of the petroleum it uses, most natural gas is domestically produced. Further, domestic output is higher than once thought, likely due to recent growth in unconventional natural gas sources (e.g., coal mine methane, shale gas).[15]

But there are also several potential and measurable drawbacks to natural gas vehicles, many related to vehicle performance and acceptability. For example, CNG engines tend to generate less power for the same size engine than gasoline engines. Thus NGVs tend to have slower acceleration and less power climbing hills.[16] Also, because CNG has a lower energy density than gasoline, CNG vehicles tend to have a shorter range than comparable gasoline vehicles.[17] In addition, for passenger vehicles, the larger natural gas storage tanks often occupy space that would otherwise be used for cargo—generally in the trunk of a sedan and in the bed of a pickup truck.[18] Again, these considerations may or may not play into a individual purchaser's decision, but could affect the overall marketability of the vehicles.

NGV Conversions

A key question raised by those interested in the expansion of natural gas for automobiles is whether existing vehicles can be converted to operate on natural gas. From a technical feasibility standpoint, there are few problems with converting a vehicle to operate on natural gas. Most existing engines can operate on the fuel, and most conversions involve changes to the fuel system, including a new fuel tank, new fuel lines, and modifications to the vehicle's electronic control unit.[19]

However, converting an existing vehicle is more problematic from a practical standpoint. In the United States, NGV conversions—or any other fuel conversion—can potentially run afoul of the Clean Air Act (CAA). All new vehicles (gasoline or otherwise) must pass rigorous tests to prove they will meet emissions standards over the life of the vehicle. These tests tend to be very expensive, although the marginal cost spread over a full product run—thousands to hundreds of thousands of vehicles—is minimal. After a vehicle has been certified by the Environmental

---

[14] DOE, AFDC, *Natural Gas Benefits*. http://www.eere.energy.gov/afdc/fuels/natural_gas_benefits.html. Accessed September 16, 2008.

[15] It should be noted that high natural gas prices may be needed to sustain some of this output. Otherwise, the United States may need to import natural gas to meet growing demand.

[16] The CNG Honda Civic is rated at 113 horsepower (hp), while the gasoline Civic EX is rated at 140 hp (both have 1.8 liter engines). Cars.com vehicle comparison. http://www.cars.com/go/index.jsp. Accessed September 16, 2008.

[17] 170 miles for the Civic GX vs. 345 miles for the gasoline Civic. DOE, *Fueleconomy.gov Website*. Accessed September 16, 2008.

[18] All current natural gas vehicles are modified versions of conventional gasoline vehicles. Presumably, if there were enough consumer demand, a natural gas vehicle designed from the ground up could address the problem of cargo capacity.

[19] NGV Conversion, Inc., *Frequently Asked Questions*. Accessed October 10, 2008. http://ngvus.com/p/index.html.

Natural Gas Passenger Vehicles: Availability, Cost, and Performance

Protection Agency (EPA), any changes to the exhaust, engine, or fuel systems may be considered tampering under the CAA. Section 203(a)(3)(A)[20] states that it is prohibited

> for any person to remove or render inoperative any device or element of design installed on or in a motor vehicle or motor vehicle engine in compliance with regulations under this title prior to its sale and delivery to the ultimate purchaser, or for any person knowingly to remove or render inoperative any such device or element of design after such sale and delivery to the ultimate purchaser.

EPA generally interprets this to mean that any change to a vehicle's engine or fuel systems that leads to higher pollutant emissions constitutes "tampering" under Section 203.

In 1974, EPA issued guidance ("Memorandum 1A") to automaker and auto parts suppliers on what constituted tampering in terms of replacement parts under routine maintenance.[21] The guiding principle EPA has used in enforcing the anti-tampering provisions for alternative fuel conversions is that such changes are allowed as long as the dealer has "reasonable basis" to believe that emissions from the vehicle will not increase after the conversion. Instead of requiring all converted vehicles to undergo testing equivalent to new vehicle testing, EPA allowed vehicle converters flexibility in certifying their emissions.

However, in the 1990s, EPA received data from the National Renewable Energy Lab that many vehicles converted to run on natural gas or liquified petroleum gas (LPG) and certified under the flexibility provisions might be exceeding emissions standards.[22] Therefore, in 1997 EPA issued an addendum to Memorandum 1A tightening the testing standards for these conversions. The original decision required compliance with new testing procedures starting in 1999. Subsequent revisions extended the deadline thorough March 2002.

Currently, certifying vehicle conversions can be very expensive for small producers, since each vehicle must be independently certified. For example, a converter must test the emissions of the conversion of specific "engine families" (e.g., MY2008 4.6L V8 Ford vehicles). Each different engine/emissions system combination must be tested independently (e.g., MY2009 vehicles, or vehicles with different engines). Therefore, the production and use of universal "conversion kits" is effectively prohibited under the EPA enforcement guidance.[23] To allow a market for conversion kits, the CAA would need to be amended to allow for these conversions regardless of vehicle emissions, or EPA would need to conclude that the conversions do not increase emissions. NGVAmerica estimates that it can cost as much as $200,000 to design, manufacture, and certify a conversion for a single engine family.[24]

Some companies have completed the required testing on a limited number of vehicles, and offer conversions. NGVAmerica maintains a list of the companies that currently sell NGV conversion equipment, and the vehicles that have been certified by those companies.[25] In addition to the

---

[20] 42 U.S.C. 7522(a)(3)(A).

[21] EPA, Office of Enforcement and General Counsel, *Mobile Source Enforcement Memorandum 1A*, June 25, 1974.

[22] EPA, Office of Enforcement and Compliance Assistance, *Addendum to Mobile Source Enforcement Memorandum 1A*, September 4, 1997.

[23] To make a conversion kit that would work for all vehicles, a manufacturer would need to certify the emissions of the conversion on every engine family for all model years—an very expensive proposition.

[24] Stephe Yborra, op. cit.

[25] NGVAmerica, *Guide to Available Natural Gas Vehicles and Engines*, Updated November 11, 2009. (continued...)

Civic GX produced by Honda, NGVA lists six companies that convert Ford and General Motors vehicles—mostly light-duty trucks such as pickups and vans. According to EPA requirements, vehicles must be converted by the original manufacturer of the conversion equipment, or by a retrofitter trained and qualified by the conversion manufacturer. NGVAmerica estimates that converting a passenger vehicle can cost over $10,000 (e.g., they estimated $13,500 for a Ford Crown Victoria), although specific costs would be determined by the manufacturer and/or retrofitter.[26] Conversions would be eligible for the $4,000 alternative fuel vehicle tax credit (see "Life-Cycle Cost Issues" above).

Some have questioned whether a vehicle conversion would void the original manufacturer's warranty. However, only those vehicle systems directly modified by the conversion would raise warranty concerns. In those cases, the conversion manufacturer's warranty would warranty the modified systems. For systems not affected by the conversion (e.g., suspension, climate control), the original manufacturer's warranty would still apply.[27]

Legislation

Several bills have been introduced in the 111th Congress that would promote natural gas vehicles and NGV infrastructure. Most notably, the New Alternative Transportation to Give Americans Solutions Act (Nat Gas Act) of 2009 (H.R. 1835 and S. 1408) would provide a wide range of incentives. The Nat Gas Act would significantly expand tax credits for the purchase of NGVs and for the installation of natural gas refueling infrastructure, and extend those credits through 2017 (they are set to expire at the end of 2010). The bill would also provide a tax credit to automakers who produce NGVs, and would authorize grants to those automakers to develop natural gas engines. Finally, the bill would require that 50% of vehicles purchased by federal agencies be NGVs. As of February 2010, both the House and Senate versions of the bill had been referred to committee.

Several other bills would also provide additional tax incentives or government mandates for the purchase of alternative fuel vehicles, including NGVs. Other than the American Clean Energy and Security Act (ACES; H.R. 2454), the House energy and climate change bill, none of these bills has been reported out of committee. ACES would provide many incentives for the use of natural gas over other, more carbon-intensive fuels (i.e., coal and petroleum). ACES would also require a study by EPA on the potential for NGVs to reduce greenhouse gas emissions and criteria pollutants under the CAA.

Conclusion

Higher gasoline prices and concerns about U.S. oil dependence have raised interest in NGVs. Energy policy proposals such as the Pickens Plan have further raised interest in these vehicles. However, currently the number of new passenger vehicles capable of operating on natural gas is

---

(...continued)

http://www.ngvc.org/pdfs/marketplace/MP.Analyses.NGVs-a.pdf.

[26] Stephe Yborra, op. cit.

[27] Ibid.

relatively low, and there are limited opportunities for converting existing gasoline vehicles to run on natural gas.

The market for natural gas vehicles will likely remain limited unless the differential between natural gas and gasoline prices remains high in order to offset the higher purchase price for a natural gas vehicle. Conversions of existing vehicles will also continue to be restricted unless the CAA is amended or if EPA makes changes to its enforcement of the CAA.

Author Contact Information

Brent D. Yacobucci
Specialist in Energy and Environmental Policy
byacobucci@crs.loc.gov, 7-9662

Displacing Coal with Generation from Existing Natural Gas-Fired Power Plants

Stan Mark Kaplan
Specialist in Energy and Environmental Policy

January 19, 2010

Congressional Research Service

7-5700

www.crs.gov

R41027

CRS Report for Congress ————————————————
Prepared for Members and Committees of Congress

Summary

Reducing carbon dioxide emissions from coal plants is a focus of many proposals for cutting greenhouse gas emissions. One option is to replace some coal power with natural gas generation, a relatively low carbon source of electricity, by increasing the power output from currently underutilized natural gas plants.

This report provides an overview of the issues involved in displacing coal-fired generation with electricity from existing natural gas plants. This is a complex subject and the report does not seek to provide definitive answers. The report aims to highlight the key issues that Congress may want to consider in deciding whether to rely on, and encourage, displacement of coal-fired electricity with power from existing natural gas plants.

The report finds that the potential for displacing coal by making greater use of existing gas-fired power plants depends on numerous factors. These include:

- The amount of excess natural gas-fired generating capacity available.

- The current operating patterns of coal and gas plants, and the amount of flexibility power system operators have for changing those patterns.

- Whether or not the transmission grid can deliver power from existing gas power plants to loads currently served by coal plants.

- Whether there is sufficient natural gas supply, and pipeline and gas storage capacity, to deliver large amounts of additional fuel to gas-fired power plants.

There is also the question of the cost of a coal displacement by gas policy, and the impacts of such a policy on the economy, regions, and states.

All of these factors have a time dimension. For example, while existing natural gas power plants may have sufficient excess capacity today to displace a material amount of coal generation, this could change in the future as load grows. Therefore a full analysis of the potential for gas displacement of coal must take into account future conditions, not just a snapshot of the current situation.

As a step toward addressing these questions, Congress may consider chartering a rigorous study of the potential for displacing coal with power from existing gas-fired power plants. Such a study would require sophisticated computer modeling to simulate the operation of the power system to determine whether there is sufficient excess gas fired capacity, and the supporting transmission and other infrastructure, to displace a material volume of coal over the near term. Such a study could help Congress judge whether there is sufficient potential to further explore a policy of replacing coal generation with increased output from existing gas-fired plants.

Congressional Research Service

Displacing Coal with Generation from Existing Natural Gas-Fired Power Plants

Contents

Figures

Tables

Appendixes

Contacts

Introduction

Purpose and Organization

Coal-fired power plants currently account for about 80% of CO_2 emissions from the U.S. electric power industry and about 33% of all U.S. CO_2 emissions.[1] Accordingly, reducing CO_2 emissions from coal plants is a focus of many proposals for cutting greenhouse gas emissions. Options include capturing and sequestering the CO_2 emitted by coal plants, and/or replacing coal-fired generation with low- and zero-carbon sources of electric power, such as wind or nuclear power.

Another option is to replace coal power with increased use of natural gas generation. Natural gas is not a zero-carbon fuel, but gas-fired power using modern generating technology releases less than half of the CO_2 per megawatt-hour (MWh) as a coal plant. Recent large increases in estimates of natural gas reserves and resources, especially from shale formations, have further fed interest in natural gas as a relatively low carbon energy option.

One proposal is that the nation can and should achieve near-term reductions in carbon emissions by making more use of existing natural gas plants. This argument was made at an October 2009 Senate Energy and Natural Resources Committee hearing on *The Role of Natural Gas in Mitigating Climate Change*. An executive for a large natural gas pipeline company stated that "Just as natural gas plays a key role in meeting U.S. energy demands, it can also play a key role in providing meaningful, *immediate*, and verifiable [CO_2] emission reductions."[2] [emphasis added] The witness for Calpine, a large operator of gas-fired power plants, stated that:

> I am here today to tell you that we could, today, simply through the increased use of existing natural-gas fired power plants, meaningfully reduce the CO_2 emissions of the power sector, *immediately* and for the foreseeable future. *In other words, a near- and medium-term solution to our climate change challenge is at hand.* No guesswork. No huge spending programs needed. That power would be reliable—available all day, every day. And if we embrace this solution with the right incentives, American business would continue to invest its own capital in existing proven technologies to build even more natural gas fired plants to dramatically further reduce emissions for the longer term. [emphasis added][3]

Both of these statements emphasize the claimed *immediate* carbon reductions that can result from increased use of natural gas. This would be accomplished by squeezing more electricity from existing gas-fired power plants, so that coal-fired plants can be operated less and CO_2 emissions quickly and substantially reduced.

---

[1] Energy Information Administration (EIA), *Annual Energy Review 2008*, Tables 12.1 and 12.7b, http://www.eia.doe.gov/emeu/aer/envir.html.

[2] Written testimony of Dennis McConaghy, Executive Vice President, TransCanada Pipelines, Ltd., before the Senate Energy and Natural Resources Committee hearing on *The Role of Natural Gas in Mitigating Climate Change*, October 28, 2009, p. 6, http://energy.senate.gov/public/index.cfm?FuseAction=Hearings.Hearing&Hearing_ID=788a1684-b2a2-f5bb-f574-81b9257ba5aa.

[3] Written testimony of Jack Fusco, President and CEO, Calpine Corp., before the Senate Energy and Natural Resources Committee hearing on *The Role of Natural Gas in Mitigating Climate Change*, October 28, 2009, p. 1, http://energy.senate.gov/public/index.cfm?FuseAction=Hearings.Hearing&Hearing_ID=788a1684-b2a2-f5bb-f574-81b9257ba5aa.

This report provides an overview of the issues involved in displacing coal-fired generation with electricity from existing natural gas plants. This is a complex subject and the report does not seek to provide definitive answers. The report aims to highlight the key issues that Congress may consider in deciding whether to rely on, and encourage, displacement of coal-fired electricity with power from existing natural gas plants.

The balance of the report is organized as follows:

- Background on gas-fired generation and capacity.

- Coal displacement feasibility issues.

- Policy considerations.

The report also includes two appendices. **Appendix A**, Background on the Electric Power System, may be of particular value to readers relatively new to the subject. **Appendix B** provides information on the gas-burning combined cycle generating technology discussed in the report.

Issues Not Considered in the Report

Several topics are beyond the scope of this report:

- *What would be the cost of a policy of displacing coal with natural gas?* The cost would depend on a host of uncertain variables, such as future natural gas and coal prices, any need to build additional pipeline and transmission line facilities, and the cost of carbon (if any).

- *Could natural gas be burned on a large scale in existing coal plants?* Assessing this option would require engineering analysis of the plants and determining how many coal plants have access to high capacity natural gas pipelines.

- *How will circumstances change over time?* For example, while existing natural gas plants may have enough excess capacity today to displace a material amount of coal generation, this could change in the future as load grows.

- *What kind of existing natural gas plants could be used to displace coal?* This report focuses on the potential for displacing coal generation with increased use of underutilized "combined cycle" generating plants, the most modern and efficient type of natural gas-fired power plants. Two other types of gas-fired plants have low utilization rates: peaking plants (stand-alone combustion turbines and diesel generators) and old steam-electric natural gas plants. These are not reviewed in the report because they are relatively inefficient and may not be designed or permitted for baseload operation.

Addressing these issues would require computer modeling and engineering analysis beyond the scope of this report. As noted in the concluding section of the report, these issues, if of interest to Congress, could be part of a more comprehensive review of the potential for displacing coal with natural gas.

Background on Gas-Fired Generation and Capacity

The argument for displacing coal with natural gas rests on the fact that the United States has a large base of advanced technology, underutilized, gas-burning power plants. This section of the report describes how this reservoir of underutilized natural gas combined cycle (NGCC) plants came about, and why it may represent an option for reducing the use of coal plants.

Capacity Trends

From the 1990s into this century, gas-fired power plants have constituted the vast majority of new generating capacity built in the United States. This development is illustrated by **Figure 1** for the period 1990 to 2007. Minimal new coal capacity was constructed and the growth in nuclear capacity was limited to uprates to existing plants. Only wind capacity has challenged the pre-eminence of natural gas as the source of new generating capacity, and then only in the latter part of the 2000s when total capacity additions declined sharply.

Figure 1. Net Change in Generating Capacity by Energy Source, 1990 to 2007

Net Summer Capacity

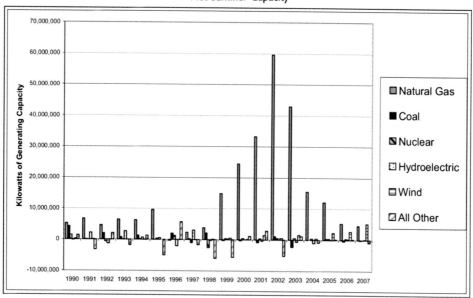

Source: Calculated from data in EIA, *Annual Energy Review 2008*, Table 8.11a, http://www.eia.doe.gov/emeu/aer/elect.html.

Notes: Capacity can decrease when retirements and deratings of units exceed capacity additions and increases. Also, in some cases the primary fuel of a unit may change, such as from wood to coal. The net change is calculated as the year over year change for each type of capacity.

As shown in **Figure 2**, this building boom doubled the natural gas share of total generating capacity between 1989 and 2007. Natural gas-fired capacity is now the largest component of the national generating fleet.

Displacing Coal with Generation from Existing Natural Gas-Fired Power Plants

Figure 2. Shares of Total Generating Capacity by Energy Source, 1989 and 2007

Shares of Total Net Summer Capacity

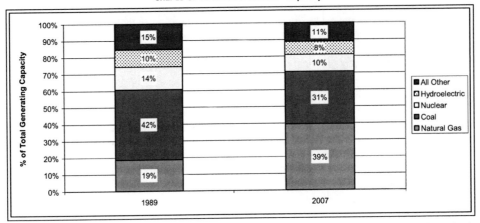

Source: Calculated from data in EIA, *Annual Energy Review 2008*, Table 8.1 1a, http://www.eia.doe.gov/emeu/aer/elect.html.

Although natural gas is the largest source of generating capacity, it trails far behind coal as a source of actual electricity generation.[4] In 2008, coal accounted for 49% of all electricity produced, compared to 21% for natural gas, 20% for nuclear power, and 6% for hydroelectric generation.[5] The remainder of this section will explain why so much new gas-fired generation was built and why it is underutilized.

Factors Supporting the Boom in Gas-Fired Plant Construction

Natural gas was the major source of new capacity in the 1990s and early 2000s in part by default. Nuclear and coal power have been burdened with cost, environmental, and (in the case of nuclear power) safety concerns. Oil-fired generation was essentially ruled out by the costs and supply risks of petroleum supplies. This left natural gas as the energy source for new non-renewable power plants. But in addition to the negatives that surrounded alternatives, gas fired capacity also grew because of favorable technological, cost, environmental, and power market characteristics.

Technology

The new gas-fired plants constructed in the 1990s and subsequently were built around the latest design of combustion turbines—a specialized form of the same kind of technology used in a jet engine, but mounted on the ground and used to rotate a generator. Stand-alone combustion turbines were built to serve as peaking units that would operate only a few hundred hours a year. However, the most important technological development was the application of combustion

---

[4] "Capacity" is a measure of the potential instantaneous electricity output from a power plant, usually measured in megawatts or kilowatts. "Generation" is the actual amount of electricity produced by the plant over a period of time, usually measured in megawatt-hours or kilowatt-hours. For additional information see **Appendix A**.

[5] These four sources accounted for 96% of electricity production in 2008, which is the typical combined share going back to the 1980s. All other sources, such as wind, petroleum, and biomass, account for the remaining 4%.

turbines in modern natural gas combined cycle power plants. (For additional information see **Appendix B**.) These plants were often intended to serve as baseload generators which would operate 70% or more of the time. The NGCC has three important characteristics:

- **The technology is very efficient**, because it makes maximum use of the energy in the fuel through a two-step generating process that captures waste heat that would otherwise be lost.[6]

- **NGCC plants can be built relatively quickly and cheaply**. An NGCC plant costs roughly $1,200 per kilowatt of capacity, about half as much as for a coal-fired plant, and can be built in about two to three years from ground-breaking to operation. This compares to about to five to six years to build a coal plant. Coal plants also tend to have longer pre-construction planning and permitting phases.[7]

- **Combined cycle technology is suitable for relatively small scale and modular construction.** NGCC plants can be economically built at unit sizes of about 100 MW, and larger projects can be constructed by adding units in a building block fashion over time. Coal plants in contrast are generally economical only at a unit size of several hundred megawatts.

For the reasons discussed below, these characteristics made the NGCC an attractive technology option for the independent power producers that dominated the construction of new power plants in the 1990s and after.

Natural Gas Prices

The construction of new gas-fired capacity was also encouraged by relatively low natural gas prices in the 1990s. As illustrated by **Figure 3**, the spot price for natural gas hovered around $2.00 to $3.00 per MMBtu (nominal dollars) through the decade, and a widely held expectation was that gas prices would remain low into the future.[8]

---

[6] By extracting the maximum energy from fuel combustion, modern combined cycles can reportedly achieve heat rates in the range of 6,752 to 6,333 btus per kwh. This compares to 9,200 to 8,740 btus per kwh for steam electric coal technology. (EIA, *Assumptions to the Annual Energy Outlook 2009*, Table 8.2, http://www.eia.doe.gov/oiaf/aeo/assumption/index.html.) This efficiency advantage can make combined cycles very economical to operate.

[7] For more information on power plant cost and construction issues, see CRS Report RL34746, *Power Plants: Characteristics and Costs*, by Stan Mark Kaplan.

[8] Rebecca Smith, "Utilities Question Natural-Gas Forecasting," *The Wall Street Journal*, December 27, 2004.

Displacing Coal with Generation from Existing Natural Gas-Fired Power Plants

Figure 3. Henry Hub Cash Spot Price for Natural Gas
November 1993 to December 2009, Nominal Dollars

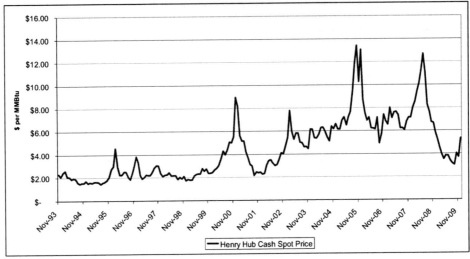

Source: U.S. Federal Reserve Bank of St. Louis FRED database (http://research.stlouisfed.org/fred2/series/GASPRICE?cid=98).

Carbon Dioxide Emissions

The operation of NGCC plants, and natural gas plants generally, produce fewer harmful environmental impacts than coal-fired plants, and have been much easier to site and permit than coal plants. NGCC technology has fewer air emissions than coal plants in part because of the nature of the fuel, and in part because of the greater efficiency of the technology. For example, natural gas when burned inherently emits about half as much carbon dioxide as coal.[9] However, because combined cycle plants are more efficient than typical existing coal plants in converting fuel into electricity, the difference in emissions is greater when measured in terms of CO_2 released per megawatt-hour of electricity produced. By this measure a modern combined cycle emits only about 40% of the CO_2 per MWh as a typical existing coal plant.[10]

Electric Power Industry Restructuring and Overbuilding

Restructuring of the electric power industry (beginning in the late 1970s and accelerating in the 1990s) included federal and state policies that encouraged the separation of power generation and

---

[9] Natural gas emits 117.08 pounds CO_2 per MMBtu burned. The comparable numbers for subbituminous, bituminous, and lignite coal are, respectively, 212.7, 205.3, and 215.4 pounds of CO_2 per MMBtu burned. EIA, *Electric Power Annual 2007*, Table A3, http://www.eia.doe.gov/cneaf/electricity/epa/epa_sum.html.

[10] Other environmental advantages of combined cycle plants include minimal or zero emissions of sulfur dioxides and mercury; no solid wastes, such as ash and scrubber sludge; no coal piles with attendant fugitive dust and runoff problems; and the fuel is delivered by pipeline rather than railroad or truck. A combustion turbine burning natural gas will emit more nitrogen oxides (NOx) per MMBtu of fuel consumed than a coal-fired boiler, and depending on the location of a gas-fired plant it may have to install a low NOx combustion system and a selective catalytic reduction system to capture NOx emissions.

Displacing Coal with Generation from Existing Natural Gas-Fired Power Plants

power plant construction from other utility functions. In the 1990s, new independent power producers (IPPs) bought power plants from utilities and constructed most of the new generating capacity. Because these companies sold power into competitive markets and did not have the security of regulated rates and guaranteed markets, they generally sought to minimize risks by constructing relatively low cost, quick-to-build, power plants.

For these reasons, independent power producers built many NGCC plants, largely to meet baseload demand. As shown in **Table 1**, between 1990 and 2007 over 168,000 MW of NGCC capacity was built at 345 plant sites. This was an enormous building program, equivalent to adding 23% to the entire national generating fleet that existed in 1990. However, the growth in generating capacity did not stop with new combined cycle plants. As also shown in **Table 1**, another 89,843 MW of less efficient stand-alone peaking turbines were constructed, plus another 56,939 MW of other generating technologies. When all of this capacity is added together, generating capacity grew by 43% between 1990 and 2007.

Table 1. Growth in Generating Capacity, 1990 - 2007

	Natural Gas Combined Cycle (NGCC)	Stand-Alone Combustion Turbine (Natural Gas)	All Other Fuel Sources and Technologies	Total
Additions to Generating Capacity, 1990 – 2007 (MW)	168,259	89,843	56,939	315,041
Additions as a Percent of Total 1990 Generating Capacity (734,100 MW)	23%	12%	8%	43%

Source: Calculated from the EIA-860 data file for 2007, http://www.eia.doe.gov/cneaf/electricity/page/eia860.html.

Notes: The capacity shown is net summer capacity. The All Other category contains 2,184 MW of gas-fired capacity, primarily in new internal combustion engines and steam turbines, and 5,432 MW of combined cycle and stand-alone combustion turbine capacity burning fuels other than natural gas (primarily stand-alone combustion turbines using distillate fuel oil).

By the mid-2000s it was apparent that the combined cycle building boom had resulted in excess and underutilized generating capacity. Too many plants were built, in part because of questionable investment decisions by independent developers operating in an immature restructured power market. The capacity glut was compounded by a dramatic increase in gas prices after 2000. (See **Figure 3**.) Even the high efficiency of the combined cycle plants could not compensate for gas prices that at times peaked above $10.00 per MMBtu, compared to $2.00 to $3.00 per MMBtu prices (nominal dollars) in the 1990s.

The consequence of the combined cycle building boom and bust is that the fleet of NGCC plants has a large amount of unused generating capacity, as illustrated in **Table 2** for a "study group" of large combined cycle plants defined for this report.[11] Baseload operation can be reasonably

---

[11] The study group of combined cycle plants consists of plants with the following characteristics: minimum net summer (continued...)

defined as operation at an annual capacity factor of 70% or greater. As shown in **Table 2**, only 13% of combined cycle capacity in the study group operated in this range in 2007. A third of the combined cycle capacity had a utilization rate of less than 30%; that is, the plants were the equivalent of idle more than 70% of the time.

Table 2. Utilization of Study Group NGCC Plants, 2007

Capacity Factor Category	Net Summer Megawatts	Percent of Total NGCC Megawatts	Number of NGCC Plants	Percent of Total NGCC Plants
70% and Greater	22,151	13%	42	13%
Under 70% to 50%	40,103	24%	68	22%
Under 50% to 30%	50,711	30%	90	29%
Under 30%	57,662	34%	114	36%
Total	170,627	100%	314	100%

Source: Calculated from the EIA-860 and EIA-906/920 databases for 2007 (http://www.eia.doe.gov/cneaf/electricity/page/data.html).

Notes: Detail many not add to total due to rounding. For information on the characteristics of the power plants selected for the study group, see footnote 11.

In 2007 the study group of NGCC plants had an average capacity factor of 42%.[12] In contrast, the study group of coal plants had an average capacity factor of 75%.[13] It is this mismatch between combined cycle and coal plant operating patterns—the former, low carbon emitting but underutilized; the latter, high carbon emitting and highly utilized—that creates the interest and perceived opportunity for displacing coal power with gas generation from existing plants.

(...continued)

capacity of 100 MW; the plant operated at some point in time during 2007 and was in operational condition at the end of 2007; the plant's primary fuel was natural gas; and the plant's primary purpose was to sell power to the public. (This last criterion excludes industrial and commercial cogenerators who operate a power plant primarily to provide electricity and steam to a single business establishment.) A total of 314 combined cycle plants with total capacity of 170,627 MW met these criteria. The study group of coal plants had the same criteria except that the capacity floor was 250 MW and the primary fuel had to be coal or waste coal. A total of 298 coal plants with total capacity of 284,646 MW met these criteria. CRS identified the plants and extracted the data from the EIA-860 and EIA-906/920 databases for 2007 (http://www.eia.doe.gov/cneaf/electricity/page/data.html). The 2007 generation from the plants in the combined cycle study group (630.4 million MWh) accounted for 98% of all gas-fired combined cycle generation in the electric power sector in 2007. Similarly, the generation from the coal plants in the study group (1,870.6 million MWh) accounted for 95% of all coal-fired generation in the electric power sector.

[12] Capacity factor is a measure of the actual utilization of a power plant compared to its hypothetical maximum utilization. For additional information see **Appendix A**.

[13] For information on the study group of coal plants see footnote 11. Capacity factors were calculated using the EIA-906/920 generation and EIA-860 generating capacity databases (http://www.eia.doe.gov/cneaf/electricity/page/data.html).

Chapter 24: Displacing Coal with Generation from Existing Natural Gas-Fired Power Plants

Displacing Coal with Generation from Existing Natural Gas-Fired Power Plants

Coal Displacement Feasibility Issues

Estimates of Displaceable Coal-Fired Generation and Emissions

The maximum coal-fired generation and emissions that may be displaceable by existing NGCC plants is estimated in **Table 3** and **Table 4**. As noted above, the plants in the NGCC study group had an average capacity factor of 42% in 2007. As shown in the tables, if the utilization of this capacity could be essentially doubled to 85%, it would generate additional power equivalent to 32% of all coal-fired generation in 2007, and could displace about 19% of the CO_2 emissions associated with coal-fired generation of electricity.

Table 3. Approximation of the Maximum Displaceable Coal-Fired Generation, Based on 2007 Data

(1)	(2)	(3)	(4)	(5)
Actual NGCC Generation, 2007 (MWh)	Hypothetical NGCC Generation at an 85% Capacity Factor (MWh)	Hypothetical Surplus Generation Available for Coal Displacement (MWh) (2) – (1)	Actual Coal-Fired Generation in 2007 (MWh)	Hypothetical Surplus NGCC Generation as a Percentage of Coal Generation (3) / (4)
630,358,373	1,270,487,153	640,128,780	2,016,456,000	32%

Source: CRS estimates based on EIA-906/920 and EIA-860 electric power databases, and EIA, *Electric Power Annual 2007*, Table ES1, http://www.eia.doe.gov/cneaf/electricity/epa/epa_sum.html.

Notes: The generation in column 1 is for the 314 NGCC plants included in the study group defined for this report. For additional information see footnote 11. As discussed in the main body of the report, several factors, such as transmission system limitations, will tend to drive actual displacement below the maximum potential. Also, this estimate is for 2007, and in other years the amount of surplus gas generation and the amount of coal generation will likely vary from 2007 values.

Table 4. Approximation of Maximum Displaceable CO_2 Emitted by Coal-Fired Generators, Based on 2007 Data

(1)	(2)	(3)	(4)	(5)	(6)
Estimated Hypothetical Coal Generation Displaced by Natural Gas (MWh)	Estimated CO_2 Emissions from Displaced Coal Generation (Million Metric Tons)	Estimated CO_2 Emissions From NGCC Generation Used to Displace Coal (Million Metric Tons)	Net Reduction in Emissions of CO_2 by Natural Gas Displacement of Coal (Million Metric Tons) (2) – (3)	Total CO_2 Emissions from Coal for Power Generation, 2007 (Million Metric Tons)	Hypothetical Net Reduction in CO_2 Emissions as a Percentage of 2007 Total Electric Power Coal Emissions of CO_2 (4) / (5)
640,128,780[a]	635.7[b]	253.6[c]	382.1	2,002.4	19%

Source: CRS estimates based on: EIA-906/920 database (http://www.eia.doe.gov/cneaf/electricity/page/eia906_920.html); EIA, *Electric Power Annual 2007*, Table A3, http://www.eia.doe.gov/cneaf/electricity/epa/epa_sum.html; EIA, *Annual Energy Review 2008*, Table 12.7a, http://www.eia.doe.gov/emeu/aer/envir.html.

Congressional Research Service　　　　　　　　　　　　　　　　　　　　　　　　　9

Copyright ©2010 by TheCapitol.Net. All Rights Reserved. No claim made to original U.S. government documents. 703-739-3790 TCNNaturalGas.com **569**

Notes: As discussed in the main body of the report, several factors, such as transmission system limitations, will tend to drive actual displacement below the maximum potential. Also, this estimate is for 2007, and in other years the amount of surplus gas generation and the amount of coal generation will likely vary from 2007 values.

a.   From Table 3, column 3.

b.   In 2007, total coal generation was 2,016,456,000 MWh (Table 3, column 4) and total CO_2 emissions from coal were 2,002.35 million metric tons. This equates to 0.993 metric tons of CO_2 per MWh of coal generation (the comparable value for a modern NGCC plant is about 0.4 metric tons of CO_2 per MWh). Therefore, the estimated CO_2 emissions from the displaced coal is 640,128,780 MWh x 0.993005 metric tons of CO_2 per MWh = 635.651 million metric tons of CO_2.

c.   Actual study group NGCC generation in 2007 was 630,358 MWh (Table 3, column 1). This generation consumed 4,702,226,931 MMBtus of natural gas, or 7.4596 MMBtus of gas per MWh. At this average heat rate, it would take 4,775,104,647 MMBtus of gas to displace 640,128,780 MWh of coal generation. This much gas burn would release 253.6 million metric tons of CO_2, using an emissions factor of 117.08 pounds of CO_2 per MMBtu of natural gas consumed and 2,204.6 pounds per metric ton.

Although these calculations suggest that at most about a third of current (2007) coal-fired generation could be displaced by existing NGCC plants, it is unlikely that this maximum could actually be achieved. This section of the report will discuss issues that relate to the feasibility of actually displacing coal with gas from existing power plants. The issues are:

- Transmission system factors;

- System dispatch factors;

- Natural gas supply and price; and

- Natural gas transportation and storage.

Transmission System Factors

If an NGCC generating unit is located at the same plant site as a coal-fired generating unit, it is probably fair to assume that the NGCC unit can use the same transmission lines as the coal unit and can transmit its power to any load the coal unit is used to meet. However, in most cases coal units and NGCC units are built at separate locations and rely on different transmission paths to move their power. This means that there is no guarantee that the NGCC plant can send its power to the same loads as the coal plant and by doing so displace coal-fired generation.

Even on a regional level, coal and NGCC plants are not necessarily located in the same areas. The maps in **Figure 4** and **Figure 5** show, respectively, the location of large coal and NGCC plants in the conterminous states. The maps show that in some cases coal and NGCC plants are in the same regions, such as east Texas. On the other hand, California has many NGCC plants and no coal plants, while the Ohio River valley has a dense concentration of coal plants and only a handful of NGCC plants.

This section of the report will discuss three types of transmission system constraints that can prevent one power plant from meeting the load currently served by another plant. These limits on the "transmission interchangeability" of coal and NGCC plants are:

- Isolation of the Interconnections;

- Limited long-distance transmission capacity; and

- Transmission system congestion.

Displacing Coal with Generation from Existing Natural Gas-Fired Power Plants

The concluding part of this section presents an analysis of potential coal displacement by gas using the proximity of coal and existing NGCC plants as a proxy for transmission interchangeability.

Figure 4. Location of Large Coal-Fired Power Plants in the Conterminous States

250 Megawatt and Greater Net Summer Capacity

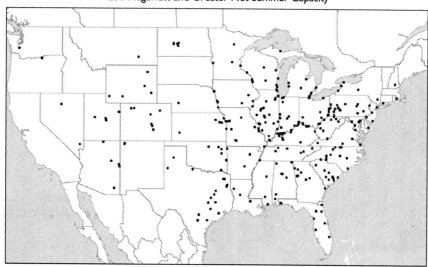

Source: Platts Powermap (fourth quarter 2009 database).

Figure 5. Location of Large NGCC Power Plants in the Conterminous States

100 Megawatt and Greater Net Summer Capacity

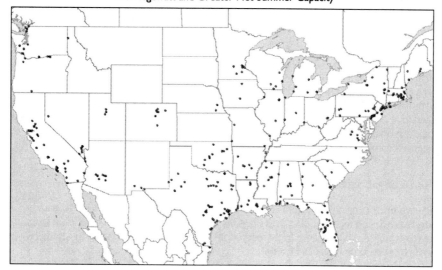

Source: Platts Powermap (fourth quarter 2009 database).

Displacing Coal with Generation from Existing Natural Gas-Fired Power Plants

Isolation of the Interconnections

The electric power grid covering the conterminous states is divided into three "interconnections," Eastern, Western, and the ERCOT Interconnection that covers most of Texas (**Figure 6**). These three interconnections operate in most respects as independent systems. There are only a handful of limited, low capacity links between the interconnections. Consequently, surplus capacity in one interconnection cannot be used to meet load in another interconnection.

Figure 6. United States Power System Interconnections

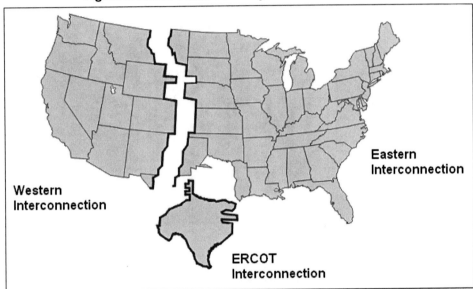

Source: adapted from a map located on the Energy Information Administration website at http://www.eia.doe.gov/cneaf/electricity/page/fact_sheets/transmission.html.

Notes: ERCOT = Electric Reliability Council of Texas.

To illustrate with a hypothetical example, assume 1,000 MW of surplus NGCC capacity in the northern part of the ERCOT Interconnection, and a desired use for that capacity to displace coal in Oklahoma, which is in the Eastern Interconnection. Although the regions are adjacent, from the standpoint of the power grid they are electrically isolated from each other because, with very limited exceptions, the ERCOT and Eastern Interconnections are not linked. Therefore the displacement cannot take place.

Limited Long-Distance Transmission Capacity

Within each interconnection the network of power lines, generating plants, and electricity consumers are linked together. The grid operates in some respects like a single giant machine in which, for example, a disturbance in the operation of the transmission system in Maine is detectible by system monitors in Florida.

Although all generators and loads within an interconnection are linked by the grid, the power grid is not designed to move large amounts of power long distances. The grid was not built in accordance with a "master plan," analogous to the Interstate Highway System. Transmission lines were first built in the early 20th century by single utilities to move electricity to population centers from nearby power plants. As generation and transmission technology advanced, the distances between power plants and loads increased, but the model of a single entity building lines within its service territory to supply its own load still predominated.

Over time the local grids began to interconnect, due to utilities building jointly owned power plants and because power companies began to grasp the economic and reliability benefits of being able to exchange power. Nonetheless, this pattern of development did not emphasize the construction of very long-distance inter-regional lines. Consequently, the capacity to move power long distances within interconnections is limited. For example, while a generator in Maine and a load in Florida are connected by the grid, it is not feasible to send power from Maine to Florida because the transmission lines do not have enough capacity to move the electricity.

Additionally, over distances of hundreds of miles, losses occur with transmission of electricity, making the transfer uneconomic.[14] Power can be moved long distances most efficiently by the highest voltage transmission lines, but only a small portion of the national grid consists of these types of lines.[15] Much of the debate over the proposed increased use of renewable power involves how to build and pay for the new transmission lines that would be needed to move wind and solar power from remote locations to population centers, in part to displace fossil-fueled power plants. Coal displacement by existing gas-fired generators is a similar type of problem. If the existing transmission network does not have sufficient capacity in the right places, then it may not be practical to move gas-powered electricity to loads currently served by coal plants without investing in upgraded or new power lines.

Transmission System Congestion

Even across relatively short distances, options for moving power can be restricted by transmission line congestion. Transmission congestion occurs when use of a power line is limited to prevent overloading that can lead to failure of the line. Congestion can occur throughout a power system:

- Regional congestion: for example, power flows are limited between the eastern and western parts of the PJM power pool (covering much of the Midwest and

---

[14] Line loss is the loss of electrical energy due to the resistance of the length of wire in a circuit. Much of the loss is thermal in nature. (This definition is a composite created from the glossaries at http://www.eia.doe.gov/glossary/glossary_l.htm and http://www.ewh.ieee.org/sb/srisairamec/glossary/k-lglos.htm.)

[15] Most of the transmission grid uses alternating current (AC) technology which is prone to line losses. By using transmission lines with higher kilovolt (kV) ratings, more power can be transported long distances with fewer losses. The highest capacity AC lines currently in use in the United States have a rating of 765 kV, but according to DOE these lines make up less than 2% of the grid. An alternative, direct current (DC) technology, can move large amounts of power long distances with minimal losses. However, DC lines are in only limited use (about 2% of the grid) because they are more difficult and expensive to integrate into the grid than AC lines. Proposals have been made to upgrade the AC network by building more 765 kV lines and lines using even high capacity AC technology (referred to as ultra high voltage transmission), and to build more DC lines. These proposals are generally focused on moving renewable power long distances. For example, see American Electric Power, *Interstate Transmission Vision for Wind Integration*, undated, http://www.aep.com/about/i765project/docs/WindTransmissionVisionWhitePaper.pdf, and the Joint Coordinated System Plan proposal at http://www.jcspstudy.org/. (The transmission line statistics cited in this footnote are from DOE, *National Transmission Grid Study*, May 2002, p. 3, http://www.ferc.gov/industries/electric/indus-act/transmission-grid.pdf.)

Displacing Coal with Generation from Existing Natural Gas-Fired Power Plants

middle Atlantic regions) by congestion.[16] In the western states, examples of congested links include power flows between Montana and the Pacific Northwest, and between Utah and Nevada.[17]

- State-level congestion: for example, congestion restricts power flows into and out of southwestern Connecticut.[18]

- Local congestion: These are "load pockets" with limited ability to import power. New York City is an example of a load pocket.

Transmission congestion can increase costs to consumers by forcing utilities to depend on nearby inefficient power plants to meet load instead of importing power from more distant but less costly units. Studies suggest that the annual costs of transmission congestion range from the hundreds of millions to billions of dollars.[19] However, for the purposes of this report the key aspect of transmission system congestion is not the cost impact, but the restrictions it imposes on power flows. Because of congestion, it may not be possible to ship power from an underutilized NGCC plant to a load served by coal power, because the transmission path available to the combined cycle is too congested to carry the electricity.

The solution for congestion is not necessarily massive transmission construction. For example, DOE found that in the Eastern Interconnection "a relatively small portion of constrained transmission capacity causes the bulk of the congestion cost that is passed through to consumers. This means that a relatively small number of selective additions to transmission capacity could lead to major economic benefits for many consumers."[20] However, in the absence of this construction, congestion remains a constraint on the choice of power plants available to meet a load.

Power Plant Proximity Analysis

Transmission system limitations on coal displacement can be rigorously analyzed using sophisticated computer models. Such an analysis is beyond the scope of this report. However, a first approach to the significance of transmission factors can be made by examining how close coal plants are to existing NGCC plants. The assumption behind such a "proximity analysis" is that the closer an NGCC plant is to a coal plant, the more likely that the NGCC plant will connect to the same transmission lines as the coal plant. If the NGCC plant has this comparable transmission access—that is, the combined cycle is "transmission interchangeable" with the coal plant—it potentially could serve the same load as the coal plant and supplant the coal generation.

---

[16] Ventyx Corp., *Major Transmission Constraints in PJM*, 2007, http://www1.ventyx.com/pdf/wp07-transmission-constraints.pdf.

[17] Western Electric Coordinating Council, *2008 Annual Report of the Transmission Expansion Planning Policy Committee, Executive Summary*, March 31, 2009, p.9, http://www.wecc.biz/committees/BOD/TEPPC/Shared%20Documents/TEPPC%20Annual%20Reports/2008/CoverLetter_Exec_Summary_Final_.pdf.

[18] Connecticut General Assembly, Office of Legislative Research, *Factors Behind Connecticut's High Electric Rates*, August 5, 2008, No. 2008-R-0452, http://www.cga.ct.gov/2008/rpt/2008-R-0452.htm.

[19] Bernard Lesieutre and Joseph Eto, *Electricity Transmission Congestion Costs: A Review of Recent Reports*, Lawrence Berkeley National Laboratory, p. 2, http://certs.lbl.gov/pdf/54049.pdf, and U.S. Department of Energy, *National Transmission Grid Study*, May 2002, pp. 16–18, http://www.pi.energy.gov/documents/TransmissionGrid.pdf.

[20] U.S. DOE, *National Electric Transmission Congestion Study*, August 2008, p. 28, http://www.pi.energy.gov/documents/TransmissionGrid.pdf. Emphasis in the original not shown.

CRS performed a proximity analysis for the coal plants and NGCC plants in the study groups defined for this report. The analysis was conducted as follows, in all cases using 2007 data (the most recent pre-recession year for which complete data were available):

(1) Study groups of large coal plants and NGCC plants were defined. The plants in these groups accounted for the great majority of power plant coal generation and NGCC generation in 2007.[21]

(2) The latitude and longitude of each plant (provided by EIA) was entered into a geographical information system (GIS).

(3) The GIS was used to identify all coal plants with one or more existing NGCC plants within a ten mile radius. The hypothetical surplus generation for each NGCC plant within the ten-mile radius was calculated and assumed to displace generation from the coal plant.[22] If one NGCC plant was within ten miles of two or more coal plants, it was allocated first to the coal plant with the largest estimated CO_2 emissions in 2007.[23]

(4) A second version of Step 3 was performed which included all NGCC plants within 25 miles of a coal plant.

The maps in **Figure 7** and **Figure 8** show the locations of the coal plants assumed to have generation displaced by existing NGCC plants.[24]

---

[21] The study group of combined cycle plants includes 314 larger plants that accounted for 98% of combined cycle generation in the electric power sector in 2007. The study group of coal plants includes 298 larger plants that accounted for 95% of coal-fired generation in the electric power sector in 2007. For additional information on the characteristics of the study groups see footnote 11.

[22] Actual generation in 2007 is from the EIA-906/920 database. Capacity factors were computed using this generation data and each plant's capacity as reported in the EIA-860 database. An NGCC plant was assumed to have surplus generation if its annual capacity factor in 2007 was less than 85%; that is, the hypothetical surplus generation available to displace coal was the difference between the NGCC plant's actual generation in 2007 and the electricity it could have produced at an 85% utilization rate. A few NGCC plants had capacity factors of 85% or greater in 2007 and were therefore assumed to have no surplus generation available for coal displacement. The EIA databases are available at http://www.eia.doe.gov/cneaf/electricity/page/data.html.

[23] CO_2 emissions were estimated for each coal plant based on the type and volume of coal consumed. Fuel consumption in MMBtus was taken from the EIA-906/920 database and used to calculate CO_2 emissions using the emission factors in EIA, *Electric Power Annual 2007*, Table A3, http://www.eia.doe.gov/cneaf/electricity/epa/epa_sum.html. The same data sources were used to calculate CO_2 emissions for combined cycles.

[24] The maps only show coal plants assumed to have had generation displaced, and the existing NGCC plants responsible for the displacement. If a coal plant had an NGCC plant with the ten or 25 mile radius, but the NGCC plant was assumed to be unavailable to displace coal (for example, because it had a capacity factor in 2007 of 85% or higher) no coal is assumed to have been displaced and the coal plant is not shown on the map.

Figure 7. Coal Plants with Hypothetical Generation Displaced by a NGCC Plant Within 10 Miles

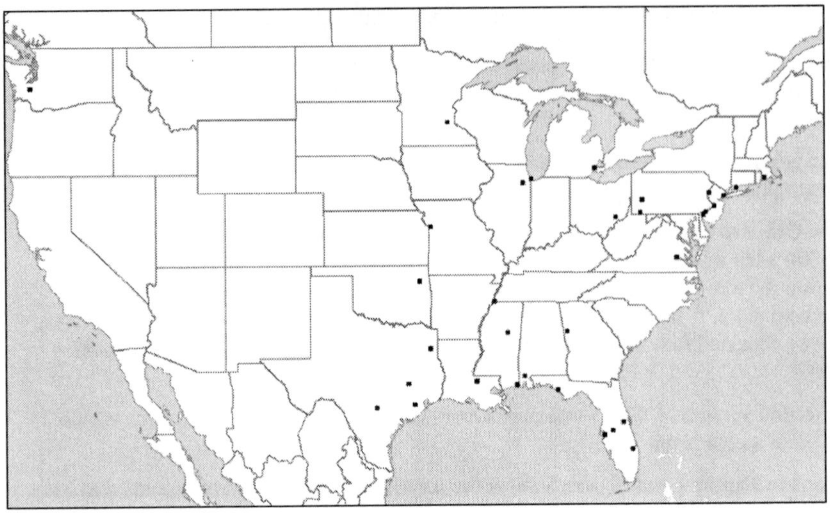

Source: CRS estimates, mapped using the Platts Powermap system.

Notes: The maps only show coal plants assumed to have had generation displaced. If a coal plant has an NGCC plant with the ten mile radius, but the NGCC plant was assumed to be unavailable to displace coal (for example, because it had a capacity factor in 2007 of 85% or higher) the coal plant is not shown on the map.

Figure 8. Coal Plants with Hypothetical Generation Displaced by a NGCC Plant Within 25 Miles

Source: CRS estimates, mapped using the Platts Powermap system.

Notes: The maps only show coal plants assumed to have had generation displaced. If a coal plant has an NGCC plant with the 25 mile radius, but the NGCC plant was assumed to be unavailable to displace coal (for example, because it had a capacity factor in 2007 of 85% or higher) the coal plant is not shown on the map.

This analysis is not a forecast. It is a first approach to estimating coal displacement potential based on one factor, the proximity of coal and existing NGCC plants. Many other factors, including, for example, how utility systems are dispatched, the configuration and capacity of the electric power transmission system, fuel cost and availability, natural gas transportation capacity, and power system reliability requirements, would influence actual coal displacement potential. These other factors could increase or decrease the potential displacement.

Table 5, which gives the results of the proximity analysis, shows in column 4 that existing NGCC plants located near coal plants might be able to achieve 15% to 28% of the potential maximum coal generation and CO_2 emissions displacement. However, the *displaceable* coal generation and emissions (see **Table 3** and **Table 4**) are only a fraction of *total* U.S. coal generation and CO_2. As shown in **Table 5**, column 5, the hypothetical displaced coal generation and emissions are equivalent to 5% to 9% of *total* U.S. coal generation, and 3% to 5% of the associated CO_2 emissions.

Given its limitations, the analysis suggests that existing NGCC plants near coal plants may be able to account for something on the order of 30% or less of the displaceable coal-fired generation and CO_2 emissions. Greater displacement of coal by existing NGCC plants would depend on more distant NGCC plants which would be less clearly "transmission interchangeable" with coal plants. This emphasizes the importance that the configuration and capacity of the transmission system will likely play in determining the actual potential for displacing coal with power from existing NGCC plants.

Table 5. Hypothetical Estimates of the Displacement of Coal Generation and Emissions by Existing NGCC Plants Based on Proximity

Based on 2007 Data

Case	Category	Amount Displaced	Amount Displaced as a % of the Maximum Potential Displacement of Coal by Existing NGCC Plants[a]	Amount Displaced as a % of Total Electric Power Sector Coal MWh and Associated CO_2 Emissions[Error! Reference source not found.]
(1)	(2)	(3)	(4)	(5)
Generation and CO_2 Displaced for Coal Plants within 10 Miles of a NGCC Plant[Error! Reference source not found.]	Generation	101.8 Million MWh	16%	5%
	CO_2 Emissions	58.1 Million Metric Tons	15%	3%
Generation and CO_2 Displaced for Coal Plants within 25 Miles of a NGCC Plant[Error! Reference source not found.]	Generation	181.5 Million MWh	28%	9%
	CO_2 Emissions	104.8 Million Metric Tons	27%	5%

Source: CRS estimates primarily based on EIA data. See the main text of the report for more information. For detailed backup, such as lists of plants, contact the author.

Displacing Coal with Generation from Existing Natural Gas-Fired Power Plants

Notes: This is not a forecast; it is a rough approximation of coal displacement potential based on one factor, the proximity of coal and existing NGCC plants. Many other factors, including, for example, how utility systems are dispatched, the configuration and capacity of the electric power transmission system, fuel cost and availability, natural gas transportation capacity, and power system reliability requirements, would influence actual coal displacement potential. These other factors could increase or decrease the potential displacement. MWh = Megawatt-hours; NGCC = natural gas combined cycle.

a.   The values in this column are calculated using column 3; Table 3, column 3; and Table 4, column 4.

b.   The values in this column are calculated using column 3; Table 3, column 4; and Table 4, column 5.

c.   The study group included 298 coal-fired plants. In the ten-mile radius case, coal is displaced in whole or part at 35 of these plants (11.7% of the plants). In the 25-mile radius case, coal is displaced in whole or part at 60 of these plants (20.1%).

System Dispatch Factors

System dispatch refers to the pattern in which power plants are turned on and off, and their power output ramped up and down, to meet changing load patterns. (For additional discussion, see **Appendix A**.) The concept of displacing coal generation with power from existing NGCC plants assumes that the NGCC plants are underutilized or idle when coal plants are operating. However, this is not necessarily the case. This can be illustrated by examining the monthly utilization of the coal and gas-fired plants in the study groups (**Figure 9**). As shown in the figure, the utilization of coal and combined cycle plants follows a similar pattern: utilization is highest in the summer and, to a lesser degree, in the winter, and lowest in the "shoulder" months of the spring and fall. The figure illustrates that when coal plant operation is at its highest and the most coal power can be displaced, NGCC plant operation is also at its highest and surplus gas-fired generation is therefore at its lowest.

Figure 9. Monthly Capacity Factors in 2007 for Study Group Coal and NGCC Plants

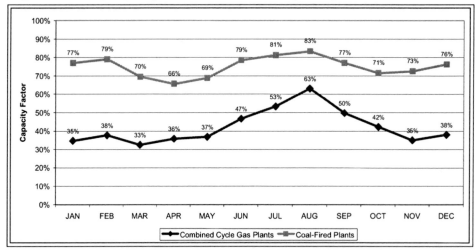

Source: Calculated by CRS from the EIA-906/920 and EIA-860 databases.

Notes: For information on the study groups of coal and NGCC plants, see footnote 11. NGCC= natural gas combined cycle.

Figure 9 is a national, monthly picture of power plant dispatch. System dispatch actually takes place moment-to-moment, and at this level of detail the complexities in displacing coal with gas become further evident. **Figure 10** graphically illustrates *hourly* dispatch at Plant Barry, a power plant in Alabama that has both coal and NGCC units at the same site. The data is for November 2007, the month in which the NGCC units at Plant Barry had their lowest generation for the year and therefore, in principle, the most excess capacity available to displace coal.[25] However, the graphic illustrates that even during this low utilization month for the NGCC units, there are still periods when the units were running near maximum output[26] (e.g., November 6 to 9, and 27 to 30). While there were periods when coal plant output was high and the NGCC units were shut down (e.g., November 4), creating the maximum opportunity to displace coal with gas, there were also periods when the NGCC units were available but potential coal displacement was reduced by limited operation of the coal units (e.g., November 18). These examples illustrate the level of detailed analysis required to realistically estimate the potential for changing plant dispatch to displace coal with natural gas.

Figure 10. Hourly Coal and Combined Cycle Generation at Plant Barry

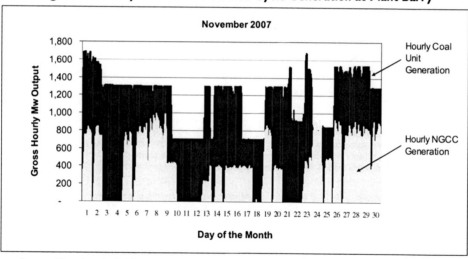

Source: Data downloaded from the EPA website at http://camddataandmaps.epa.gov/gdm/index.cfm?fuseaction= emissions.prepackaged_select.

Natural Gas Supply and Price

Large scale displacement of coal-fired generation by existing NGCC plants could result in a significant increase in U.S. gas demand. **Table 6** compares the actual demand for natural gas for all purposes in 2007 with an illustrative estimate of the additional gas supplies needed if all of the

---

[25] According to U.S. EPA data, the gross output of the NGCC units at Plant Barry was 288,726 MWh in November 2007. In comparison, the highest output was 532,040 MWh in August. The data was downloaded from the EPA website at http://camddataandmaps.epa.gov/gdm/index.cfm?fuseaction=emissions.prepackaged_select.

[26] The NGCC units at Plant Barry have, according to the Platts Powermap database, a nominal total net winter capacity of 1,090 MW. However, the maximum output achievable at any point in time will vary with the ambient air temperature, which affects the density of the air flow into the combustion turbine units of a NGCC.

Displacing Coal with Generation from Existing Natural Gas-Fired Power Plants

displaceable coal-fired generation (see **Table 3**) were actually replaced by existing NGCC plants. As discussed above, this maximum displacement of coal by existing NGCC plants may be unachievable, so results are also shown for a half and a quarter of the maximum.

Table 6. Illustrative Estimates of Increased Natural Gas Demand For Coal Displacement Compared to Total National Demand

Based on 2007 Data

	Hypothetical Maximum Displacement of Coal by Existing NGCC Plants (2007 data and 85% capacity factor)	Half of Hypothetical Maximum Displacement	One Quarter of Hypothetical Maximum Displacement
1. Additional MWh of NGCC Generation Needed to Displace Coal	640,128,780	320,064,390	160,032,195
2. Required Additional Natural Gas in Trillion Btus (Tbtus)	4,775	2,388	1,194
3. Additional Gas as a Percentage of 2007 Gas Consumed for All Purposes in the U.S.ª	20%	10%	5%

Source: Table 3 and EIA, *Annual Energy Review 2008*, Tables 6.1 and A4 (http://www.eia.doe.gov/emeu/aer/contents.html).

Notes: Total gas consumption in 2007 of 23,047 billion cubic feet was converted to TBtus using a conversion factor of 1.028 (see Table A4 in the *Annual Energy Review*, cited immediately above). The MWh of additional gas-fired generation was converted to TBtus using a heat rate of 7.4596 MMBtus of fuel input per MWh. This is the 2007 average annual heat rate for the study group of 314 combined cycle plants, calculated using the generation and fuel input reported in the EIA 906/920 database (http://www.eia.doe.gov/cneaf/electricity/page/eia906_920.html).

a.   Total gas consumption in 2007 for all residential, commercial, industrial, electric power, and transportation purposes was 23,692 Tbtus. The percentages shown in Line 3 are calculated by dividing this number into the values shown on line 2.

Total U.S. natural gas demand in 2007 was the third highest on record. The illustrative estimates of increased gas demand for coal displacement would increase the already high level of demand in 2007 by another 5% to 20% (**Table 6**, line 3).

This increased demand might be met with a combination of increased domestic production, pipeline imports from Canada, Alaskan supplies if the trans-Alaskan gas pipeline is built, and imports of liquefied natural gas by tanker from overseas. For example, one reason for the interest in coal displacement by gas is the recent increase in natural gas available from shale formations and other "unconventional" sources of gas.[27] The combination of higher production (up a projected 3.7% for 2009) and reduced demand due to the 2008-2009 recession has contributed to a sharp decline in gas prices from the peaks experienced earlier in the 2000s (see **Figure 3**).[28] For

---

[27] For additional information see CRS Report R40894, *Unconventional Gas Shales: Development, Technology, and Policy Issues*, coordinated by Anthony Andrews; and FERC, *State of the Markets Report 2008*, August 2009, Section 2, http://www.ferc.gov/market-oversight/st-mkt-ovr/2008-som-final.pdf.

[28] EIA, *Short-Term Energy Outlook*, December 2009, pp. 4 – 6, http://www.eia.doe.gov/emeu/steo/pub/dec09.pdf.

the longer term, there is widespread optimism concerning the gas supply and price outlook. An example is a late 2009 assessment by the Federal Energy Regulatory Commission (FERC):

> The long-term [gas production] story is one of abundance. In June, the Potential Gas Committee, an independent group that develops biennial assessments of gas resources, raised its estimate to over 2 quadrillion cubic feet, one-third more than its previous level and almost 100 years of gas production at current consumption levels. The large increase is almost entirely due to improvements in our ability to harvest gas from shale and get it to markets at a reasonable cost.... As we have indicated before, gas production is becoming more like mining and manufacturing with high probability of production from each well drilled. This environment should have profound effects on the traditional boom and bust cycle of gas production.[29]

EIA's most recent long-term forecasts of natural gas wellhead prices for 2020 and 2030 have dropped, respectively, 13% and 11% from its prior forecast, "due to a more rapid ramping up of shale gas production, particularly after 2015. [The forecast] assumes a larger resource base for natural gas, based on a reevaluation of shale gas and other resources...."[30]

Even with the current optimism concerning natural gas supplies and prices, it is important to note that natural gas markets have historically been exceptionally difficult to forecast. According to an EIA self-assessment of its long-term projections, "The fuel with the largest difference between the projections and actual data has generally been natural gas."[31] In the 1990s gas prices were expected to be low; by 2004 prices were much higher than expected and major gas buyers were reported to be "increasingly critical of the nation's system for forecasting natural gas supply and demand."[32] Subsequently, as shown in **Figure 3**, prices plummeted. In the October 2009 Senate hearing on natural gas, a cautionary note was sounded by the witness for Dow Chemical Company:

> Although increased supply from shale gas appears to have changed the production profile, we have seen similar scenarios occur after past spikes. In 1998, significant new imports from Canada came on line; in 2002-2003, there were new supplies from the Gulf of Mexico and in 2005, new discoveries in the Rockies were brought into play. In each case, the initial hopes were too high and production increases were not as large as initially expected.[33]

> In 2009, as in 2002, 2004 and 2006, drilling has declined dramatically as price has fallen. After each trough, natural gas demand and price rise once the economy turns, signaling the production community to increase drilling. During the lag between the pricing signals and new production, only one mechanism exists to rebalance supply and demand: demand

---

[29] FERC, *Winter 2009/2010 Energy Market Assessment*, November 19, 2009, p. 3, http://www.ferc.gov/EventCalendar/Files/20091119102759-A-3-final.pdf. For additional information on the findings of the Potential Gas Committee, see the press release at http://www.energyindepth.org/wp-content/uploads/2009/03/potential-gas-committee-reports-unprecedented-increase-in.pdf.

[30] EIA, *Annual Energy Outlook 2010 Early Release Overview*, pp. 3, 4, 12, http://www.eia.doe.gov/oiaf/aeo/pdf/overview.pdf.

[31] EIA, *Annual Energy Outlook Retrospective Review: Evaluation of Projections in Past Editions (1982-2008)*, September 2008, p. 2, http://www.eia.doe.gov/oiaf/analysispaper/retrospective/pdf/0640%282008%29.pdf.

[32] Rebecca Smith, "Utilities Question Natural-Gas Forecasting," *The Wall Street Journal*, December 27, 2004.

[33] Statement for the Record of Edward Stones, Director of Risk Management, Dow Chemical Co., before the Senate Energy and Natural Resources Committee hearing on *The Role of Natural Gas in Mitigating Climate Change*, October 28, 2009, p. 4, http://energy.senate.gov/public/_files/StonesTestimony102809.pdf.

---

destruction brought about by price spikes. Demand destruction is an antiseptic economic term for job destruction.[34]

Although multiple options may exist to meet the additional natural gas demand created by a coal displacement policy, the significance of the potential increase in demand should not be underestimated. The lowest level of increased gas demand shown in **Table 6**, 1,194 trillion Btus (TBtus), would raise total demand to 24,886 TBtus. In its most recent Reference Case forecast, the U.S. Energy Information Administration (EIA) does not envision this demand level being reached until after 2028. The middle estimate of increased gas demand shown in **Table 6** would raise total gas demand to 26,080 TBtus, which is larger than EIA's forecast for 2035.[35] A policy of rapid change from coal to gas could therefore involve a significant acceleration of gas demand growth compared to EIA's current estimates.

Natural Gas Transportation and Storage

Gas-fired power plants and other gas consumers receive fuel through a vast national pipeline network. At the end of 2008 the network consisted of 293,000 miles of interstate and intrastate pipelines with the capacity to move up to 215 billion cubic feet (BCF) of gas daily.[36] The capacity of this system is sized to meet peak loads, such as during the winter residential heating season. Peak demands are also supported by a system of natural gas storage facilities connected to the pipeline network. These storage facilities hold gas which is produced during lower demand periods until it is needed to meet peak demand.

It seems unlikely that on a national, aggregate scale, pipeline capacity would be a constraint on coal displacement by existing NGCC plants. The natural gas consumption required for the maximum potential coal displacement by existing NGCC plants (see **Table 3**) equate to about 15 BCF per day of natural gas, or about 7% of existing pipeline capacity.[37] A 7% increase in peak demand would appear manageable given the planned expansions to the pipeline system (see below). But irrespective of national system-wide capacity, a different question is whether increased use of gas-fired plants could overstress the specific pipelines and storage facilities that serve those plants. This may be an important issue because the increase in gas demand from existing NGCC plants for coal displacement could be large relative to the amount of gas currently used for power generation. As shown in **Table 7**, illustrative estimates of this increase range from 16% to 66%, which means that the facilities serving those plants could have to handle a material increase in gas demand.

---

[34] Ibid., p. 3.

[35] EIA's Annual Energy Outlook 2010 backup spreadsheet for Table 13, located at http://www.eia.doe.gov/oiaf/aeo/aeoref_tab.html. Values were converted from cubic feet to Btus using a conversion factor of 1.028. This is the Reference Case forecast, which assumes no changes to current law or regulations.

[36] The interstate portion of the system consists of 217,000 miles of pipeline with a capacity of 183 BCF per day. The interstate portion consists of 76,000 miles of pipeline with a capacity of 32 BCF per day. EIA, *Expansion of the U.S. Natural Gas Pipeline Network: Additions in 2008 and Projects through 2011*, September 2009, p. 3, http://www.eia.doe.gov/pub/oil_gas/natural_gas/feature_articles/2009/pipelinenetwork/pipelinenetwork.pdf.

[37] As shown in **Table 3**, the maximum potential increase in existing NGCC generation to displace coal is 640,128,780 MWh. This number assumes an annual average capacity factor of 85%, but on a given day the existing NGCC plants could be running at full load to displace coal, which is 640,128,780 MWh ÷ 0.85 ÷ 365 days = 2,063,268 MWh per day. The average heat rate for combined cycles in the study group is 7.4596 MMBtus per MWh and the conversion factor from MMBtus of thousands of cubic feet is 1.028, so the daily gas demand can be calculated as 2,063,268 MWh x 7.4596 MMBtus per MWh ÷ 1.028 ÷ 1,000,000 = 15 BCF per day.

Congressional Research Service 22

Displacing Coal with Generation from Existing Natural Gas-Fired Power Plants

A balancing factor is that the natural gas industry has been effective at adding large amounts of capacity to the pipeline system. Capacity additions in 2007 and 2008 were, respectively, 14.9 and 44.6 BCF per day, and as of mid-2009, 31.9 BCF per day was under construction or approved for construction and completion in 2009. Another 62.1 BCF per day of capacity additions are planned for 2010 and 2011,[38] which is equivalent to almost 30% of current capacity. It appears that, given sufficient lead time, the natural gas industry has the ability to install large amounts of additional transportation capacity to meet increased demand.

Table 7. Illustrative Estimates of Increased Natural Gas Demand Relative to Electric Power Demand, Based on 2007 Data

	Hypothetical Maximum Displacement of Coal by Existing NGCC Plants (2007 data and 85% capacity factor)	Half of Hypothetical Maximum Displacement	One Quarter of Hypothetical Maximum Displacement
1. Additional MWh of Existing NGCC Generation	640,128,780	320,064,390	160,032,195
2. Required Additional Natural Gas in Trillion Btus (Tbtus)	4,775	2,388	1,194
3. Required Additional Gas as a Percentage of Actual Gas Used for Power Generation in 2007[a]	66%	33%	16%

Source: Table 6 and EIA, *Annual Energy Review 2008*, Tables 8.4a (http://www.eia.doe.gov/emeu/aer/contents.html).

Notes: The MWh of additional gas-fired generation was converted to TBtus using a heat rate of 7.4596 MMBtus of fuel input per MWh. This is the 2007 average annual heat rate for the study group of 314 combined cycle plants, calculated using the generation and fuel input reported in the EIA 906/920 database (http://www.eia.doe.gov/cneaf/electricity/page/eia906_920.html).

a.   Electric power gas consumption in 2007 was 7,288 Tbtus. The percentages shown in Line 3 are calculated by dividing this number into the values shown on line 2.

Policy Considerations

As discussed in this report, the potential for displacing coal consumption in the power sector by making greater use of existing NGCC power plants depends on numerous factors. These include:

- The amount of excess NGCC generating capacity available;

- The current operating patterns of coal and NGCC plants, and the amount of flexibility power system operators have for changing those patterns;

- Whether or not the transmission grid can deliver power from existing NGCC plants to loads currently served by coal plants; and

---

[38] EIA, *Expansion of the U.S. Natural Gas Pipeline Network: Additions in 2008 and Projects through 2011*, September 2009, Table 2, http://www.eia.doe.gov/pub/oil_gas/natural_gas/feature_articles/2009/pipelinenetwork/pipelinenetwork.pdf.

- Whether there is sufficient natural gas supply, and pipeline and gas storage capacity, to deliver large amounts of additional fuel to gas-fired power plants; and consideration of the environmental impacts of increasing gas production.

All of these factors have a time dimension. For example, while existing NGCC plants may have sufficient excess capacity today to displace a material amount of coal generation, this could change in the future as load grows. Therefore a full analysis of the potential for gas displacement of coal must take into account future conditions, not just a snapshot of the current situation.

There is also the question of cost which, as discussed in the introduction, is beyond the scope of this report. Clearly, the cost of a coal displacement by gas policy is highly uncertain, and depends on such factors as future natural gas and coal prices, any need to build additional pipeline and transmission line facilities, and the cost of carbon (if any). The economic impacts of a coal displacement by gas policy could also spill over to other parts of the economy. For example, increased power sector demand could drive up the price of natural gas, to the detriment of other residential, commercial, and industrial users. Decreased production of coal and increased production of natural gas would pose varying costs and benefits for states and regions.

As a step toward addressing these questions, Congress may consider chartering a rigorous study of the potential for displacing coal with power from existing gas-fired power plants. Such a study would require sophisticated computer modeling to simulate the operation of the power system, to determine whether there is sufficient excess gas fired capacity and the supporting transmission and other infrastructure to displace a significant volume of coal over the near term. This kind of study might also estimate the direct costs of a gas for coal policy, such as the impact on electric rates. Because of the large number of uncertainties, such as the future price of natural gas, the study would have to consider several scenarios. Such a study could help Congress judge whether there is sufficient potential to further explore a policy of replacing coal generation with increased output from existing gas-fired plants.

Congress may also consider chartering an analysis of the potential for directly using gas in existing coal-fired plants, either as a supplemental or primary fuel. As noted in the introduction, large scale use of gas in coal plants raises engineering issues and the question of how many coal plants have adequate pipeline connections. However, burning gas in coal plants would make it possible to displace coal while still using existing transmission lines to meet load, which could be a significant advantage.[39]

---

[39] Many coal plants use natural gas as a startup fuel and for flame stabilization during normal operations. However, this is different from running the plant primarily or largely on natural gas. In addition to the engineering issues, even if a coal plant currently uses natural gas as a startup fuel, its existing natural gas pipeline connection may not have sufficient capacity to provide enough gas for full load (or even large partial load) operation on gas. There are examples of coal units switching to natural gas for environmental reasons ("Marketwatch: Public Service Electric & Gas of New Jersey," *Platts Coal Week*, June 22, 1992; "Ill. Power to Shift Vermilion to Gas; Phase I Decision Kills Coal Solicitation," *Platts Coal Week*, October 10, 1994; "PEPCO Mulls NOx Ozone Season's Effect on Coal, Gas, Oil Use," *Platts Coal Week*, October 25, 1999.

Appendix A. Background on the Electric Power System

This appendix provides background on the components and operation of the electric power system. Readers familiar with these topics may wish to skim or skip this appendix.

Power Plants and Power Lines

Power plants, transmission systems, and distribution systems constitute the major components of the existing electric power system, as briefly described and illustrated below (**Figure A-1**):

- *Generating plants* produce electricity, using either combustible fuels such as coal, natural gas, and biomass; or non-combustible energy sources such as wind, solar energy, or nuclear fuel.

- *Transmission lines* carry electricity from power plants to demand centers. The higher the voltage of a transmission line the more power it can carry and the fewer the line losses during transmission. Current policy discussions focus on the high voltage network (230 kilovolts (kV) rating and greater) used to move large amounts of power long distances.

- Near customers a step-down transformer reduces voltage so the power can be carried by low voltage *distribution lines* for final delivery.

Figure A-1. Elements of the Electric Power System

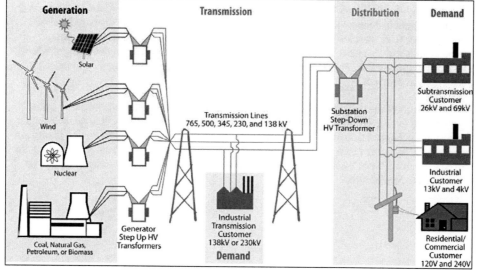

Source: CRS.

Capacity and Energy

Capacity is the potential instantaneous output of a generating or storage unit, measured in watts. Energy is the actual amount of electricity generated by a power plant or released by a storage device during a time period, measured in watt-hours. The units are usually expressed in thousands (kilowatts and kilowatt-hours) or millions (megawatts and megawatt-hours). For example, the maximum amount of power a 1,000 megawatt (MW) power plant can generate in a year is 8.76 million megawatt-hours (MWh), calculated as: 1,000 MW x 8,760 hours in a year = 8.76 million MWh.

Capacity Factor

Capacity factor is a standard measure of how intensively a power plant is utilized. It is the ratio of how much electricity a power plant produced over a period of time, typically a year, compared to how much electricity the plant could have produced if it operated continuously at full output. For example, as shown in the prior paragraph, the maximum possible output of a 1,000 MW power plant in one year is 8.76 million MWh. Assume that during a year the plant actually produced only 7.0 million MWh. In this case the plant's capacity factor would be 7.0 million MWh ÷ 8.76 million MWh = 81%.

Generation and Load

The demand for electricity ("load") faced by an electric power system varies moment to moment with changes in business and residential activity and the weather. Load begins growing in the morning as people waken, peaks in the early afternoon, and bottoms-out in the late evening and early morning. **Figure A-2** shows an illustrative daily load curve.

The daily load shape dictates how electric power systems are operated. As shown in **Figure A-2**, there is a minimum demand for electricity that occurs throughout the day. This base level of demand is met with "baseload" generating units which have low variable operating costs.[40] Baseload units can also meet some of the demand above the base, and can reduce output when demand is unusually low. The units do this by "ramping" generation up and down to meet fluctuations in demand.

The greater part of the daily up and down swings in demand is met with "intermediate" units (also referred to as load-following or cycling units). These units can quickly change their output to match the change in demand (that is, they have a fast "ramp rate"). Load-following plants can also serve as "spinning reserve" units that are running but not putting power on the grid, and are immediately available to meet unanticipated increases in load or to back up other units that go off-line due to breakdowns.

---

[40] Variable costs are costs that vary directly with changes in output. For fossil fuel units the most important variable cost is fuel. Solar and wind plants have minimal or no variable costs, and nuclear plants have low variable costs.

Figure A-2. Illustrative Daily Load Curve

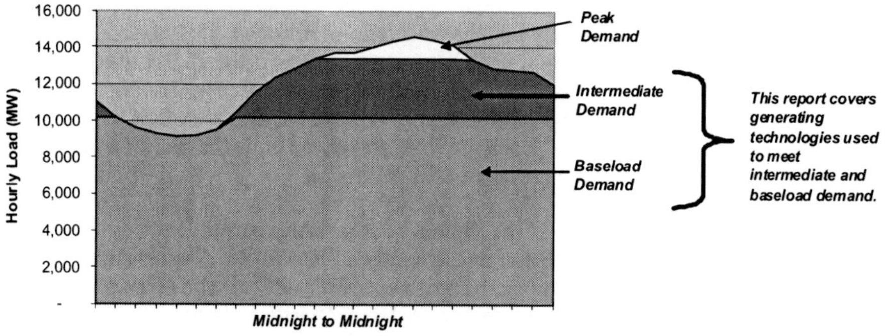

Source: CRS.

The highest daily loads are met with peaking units. These units are typically the most expensive to operate, but can quickly start up and shut down to meet brief peaks in demand. Peaking units also serve as spinning reserve and as "quick start" units able to go from shutdown to full load in minutes. A peaking unit typically operates for only a few hundred hours a year.

Economic Dispatch and Heat Rate

The generating units available to meet system load are "dispatched" (put on-line) in order of lowest variable cost. This is referred to as the "economic dispatch" of a power system's plants.

For a plant that uses combustible fuels (such as coal or natural gas) a key driver of variable costs is the efficiency with which the plant converts fuel to electricity, as measured by the plant's "heat rate." This is the fuel input in British Thermal Units (btus) needed to produce one kilowatt-hour of electricity output. A lower heat rate equates with greater efficiency and lower variable costs. Other things (most importantly, fuel and environmental compliance costs) being equal, the lower a plant's heat rate, the higher it will stand in the economic dispatch priority order. Heat rates are inapplicable to plants that do not use combustible fuels, such as nuclear and non-biomass renewable plants.

As an illustration of economic dispatch, consider a utility system with coal, nuclear, geothermal, natural gas combined cycle, and natural gas peaking units in its system:

(1) Nuclear, coal, and geothermal baseload units, which are expensive to build but have low fuel costs and therefore low variable costs, will be the first units to be put on-line. Other than for planned and forced maintenance, these baseload generators will run throughout the year.

(2) Combined cycle units, which are very efficient but use more expensive natural gas as a fuel, will meet intermediate load. These cycling plants will ramp up and down during the day, and will be turned on and off dozens of times a year.

(3) Peaking plants, using combustion turbines,[41] are relatively inefficient and burn natural gas. They run only as needed to meet the highest loads.[42]

An exception to this straightforward economic dispatch are "variable renewable" power plants—wind and solar—that do not fall neatly into the categories of baseload, intermediate, and peaking plants. Variable renewable generation is used as available to meet demand. Because these resources have very low variable costs they are ideally used to displace generation from gas-fired combined cycle plants and peaking units with higher variable costs. However, if wind or solar generation is available when demand is low (such as a weekend or, in the case of wind, in the evening), the renewable output could displace coal generation.

Power systems must meet all firm loads at all times, but variable renewable plants do not have firm levels of output because they depend on the weather. They are not firm resources because there is no guarantee that the plant can generate at a specific load level at a given point in time.[43] Variable renewable generation can be made firm by linking wind and solar plants to electricity storage, but with current technology, storage options are limited and expensive.

---

[41] A combustion turbine is an adaption of jet engine technology to electric power generation. A combustion turbine can either be used stand-alone as a peaking unit, or as part of a more complex combined cycle plant used to meet intermediate and baseload demand.

[42] This alignment of generating technologies is for new construction using current technology. The existing mix of generating units in the United States contains many exceptions to this alignment of load to types of generating plants, due to changes in technology and economics. For instance, there are natural gas and oil-fired units built decades ago as baseload stations that now operate as cycling or peaking plants because high fuel prices and poor efficiency has made them economically marginal. Some of these older plants were built close to load centers and are now used as reliability must-run (RMR) generators that under certain circumstances must be operated, regardless of cost, to maintain the stability of the transmission grid.

[43] Hydroelectric generation is a special case. Hydro generation is very low cost and is firm, dispatchable capacity to the degree there is water in the dam's reservoir. However, operators have to consider not only how much water is currently available, but how much may be available in upcoming months, and competing demands for the water, such as drinking water supply, irrigation, and recreation. These factors can make hydro dispatch decisions very complex. In general hydro is used to meet load during high demand hours, when it can displace expensive peaking and cycling units, but if hydro is abundant it can also displace baseload coal plants.

Appendix B. Combined Cycle Technology

The combined cycle achieves a high level of efficiency by capturing waste heat that would otherwise be lost in the generating process. As shown in **Figure B-1** for a combined cycle unit fueled by natural gas, the gas is fed into a combustion turbine which burns the fuel to power a generator. The exhaust from the combustion turbine is then directed to a specialized type of boiler (the heat recovery steam generator or HRSG) where the heat in the exhaust gases is used to produce steam, which in turn drives a second generator. In combined heat and power (CHP) applications, part of the steam is used to support an industrial process or to provide space heating, further increasing the total energy efficiency of the system.

Figure B-1. Schematic of a Combined Cycle Power Plant

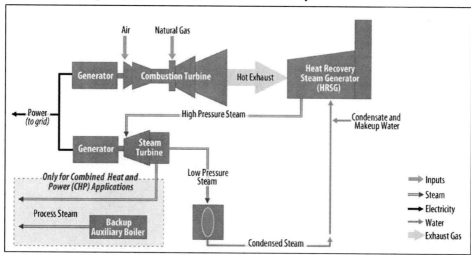

Source: CRS, based on a Calpine Corp. illustration.

Combined cycles are built in different configurations, depending in part on the amount of capacity needed. **Figure B-1** illustrates a configuration in which one combustion turbine feeds one HRSG; this is referred to as "1x1" design. In higher capacity 2x1 or 3x1 designs, multiple combustion turbines feed a single HRSG. These options illustrate the modular (or "building block") nature of combined cycles, which facilitates rapid and flexible construction of new generating units to match changes in demand.

In the United States the predominant fuel used in combined cycle plants is natural gas. Combined cycles can also be designed to use fuel oil as a primary or backup fuel. Gasified coal can also be used as the fuel in an integrated gasification combined cycle (IGCC) plant. There are currently two prototype IGCC plant operating in the United States and a commercial-scale unit is under construction in Indiana.

Displacing Coal with Generation from Existing Natural Gas-Fired Power Plants

Author Contact Information

Stan Mark Kaplan
Specialist in Energy and Environmental Policy
skaplan@crs.loc.gov, 7-9529

Your Partner in Improving Operational Efficiency, Saving Money, and Reducing Emissions

What is Natural Gas STAR?

Natural Gas STAR is a flexible, voluntary partnership that encourages oil and natural gas companies—both domestically and abroad—to adopt proven, cost-effective technologies and practices that improve operational efficiency and reduce methane emissions. Methane is the primary component of natural gas and is emitted as a result of oil production and in all aspects of the natural gas industry, from drilling and production, through gathering and processing to transmission and distribution.

Working collaboratively with the oil and natural gas industry in the United States since 1993, Natural Gas STAR has provided a framework to encourage partner companies to implement methane emissions reducing technologies and practices and document their voluntary emission reduction activities. As a result, EPA has compiled a comprehensive suite of technical information on proven cost-effective methane mitigation technologies and practices that have been successfully implemented by partner companies. In 2006, in support of the Methane to Market Partnership, EPA expanded the Program to include international operations, significantly increasing opportunities to reduce methane emissions from the oil and natural gas sector worldwide.

Why is Reducing Methane Emissions Important?

Oil and natural gas operations are the largest human-made source of methane emissions in the United States and the second largest human-made source of methane emissions globally. Given methane's role as both a potent greenhouse gas and clean energy source, reducing these emissions can have significant environmental and economic benefits. By working through the Natural Gas STAR Program, EPA and the oil and natural gas industry are preventing methane losses and delivering more natural gas to markets around the world. These efforts are not only conserving natural gas resources but also generating additional revenues, increasing operational efficiency, and making positive contributions to the global environment.

"Our mission is simple: to reduce methane emissions collaboratively and in a cost-effective manner using the latest technologies and practices. Reduced methane emissions mean more natural gas to market, greater energy security for our nation, increased revenue for partners, and reduced greenhouse gas emissions."

— Roger Fernandez,
U.S. EPA Natural Gas STAR,
Team Leader

"We are pleased and proud that many of our member companies are part of the Natural Gas STAR Program. Participating in the Program makes sound business sense. The data has clearly shown positive results in reducing greenhouse gas emissions, demonstrating that voluntary, cooperative programs are an effective tool to simultaneously meet environmental goals and put more natural gas into the market for consumers."

—William Whitsitt,
American Exploration &
Production Council, President

NaturalGas
EPA POLLUTION PREVENTER

Join Natural Gas STAR

What are the Benefits to Participating in Natural Gas STAR?

Created in collaboration with industry, the Natural Gas STAR Program serves as a credible and trusted resource for oil and natural gas companies.

Participation in the Natural Gas STAR Program has the following key benefits:

- **Information Sharing and Technology Transfer**—EPA facilitates Technology Transfer and Annual Implementation Workshops and publishes detailed *Lessons Learned Studies* and *Partner Reported Opportunities (PRO) Fact Sheets*; technical reports and studies; and a quarterly newsletter to help partners learn about new and innovative technologies and practices.

- **Program and Technical Assistance**—Natural Gas STAR offers a full range of Program support and technical assistance to partners. Through such services as project- and operational-level analyses, technical workshops, and administrative Program support, EPA provides guidance that helps partners reap the full economic and environmental benefits of reducing methane emissions. The Natural Gas STAR team includes technical experts from all sectors of the oil and natural gas industry, as well as communication and outreach professionals.

- **Peer Networking**—Partners can participate in Technology Transfer Workshops, Annual Implementation Workshops, and Web-based communications to build strong networks with industry peers and keep up on industry trends, initiatives, and the latest technologies.

- **Voluntary Record of Reductions**—Through Program participation and reporting, companies create a permanent record of their voluntary accomplishments in reducing methane emissions. Each year, EPA provides post-reporting feedback to partners through individual detailed summary reports that highlight their participation and accomplishments within the Program.

Every greenhouse gas has a global warming potential (GWP)—the measure of its ability to trap heat in the atmosphere relative to CO_2. Methane is referred to as a potent greenhouse gas because it has a GWP of 23. This means that methane is 23 times more powerful than CO_2 at trapping heat in the atmosphere over a 100-year period.

"Participating in the Natural Gas STAR Program is a simple yet powerful way for Northern Natural Gas to create a permanent record of the cost-effective methods to avoid methane emissions. There are many facets to our program: an implementation plan that guides our participation, an information database that stores the methods of avoiding methane emissions and ensures accurate data, and a reporting plan that allows Northern to communicate its accomplishments to outside sources.

Northern—a MidAmerican Energy Holdings Company—operates under its corporate environmental RESPECT policy of Responsibility, Efficiency, Stewardship, Performance, Evaluation, Communication and Training. Participation in the Natural Gas STAR Program is an extension of its corporate environmental RESPECT policy."

—Rick Loveless,
Northern Natural Gas,
Greenhouse Gas Manager and
Natural Gas STAR
Implementation Manager

592

- **Public Recognition**—EPA provides recognition, honors, and distinctions to highlight partner achievements at an annual awards ceremony, in articles in the Program newsletter and industry journals, public service announcements, and technical studies and fact sheets. EPA also helps partners communicate Program achievements to shareholders, customers, and the public.

How Does the Natural Gas STAR Program Work?

Becoming a Natural Gas STAR partner and participating in the Program involves the following steps:

Step 1 – Sign a One-Page Memorandum of Understanding

This important step initiates the Partnership, demonstrates the company's commitment to the Program, and identifies company points of contact. By signing the MOU, the company is signifying its intent to evaluate current and future technologies and management practices that reduce methane emissions, implement them when cost-effective and report these activities to EPA on an annual basis. MOU forms for each oil and natural gas industry sector and international companies are available online.

Step 2 – Develop an Implementation Plan

Natural Gas STAR Implementation Plans facilitate development of a strategy for how partners will identify non-regulatory methane emission reduction activities they are undertaking, plan new activities, and develop mechanisms for tracking methane emission reduction data and activities. Companies develop this plan within 6 to 12 months of joining. Partner approaches to developing an Implementation Plan vary. To provide guidance to partners and to minimize the administrative burden, Implementation Plan Forms are available online and Natural Gas STAR staff can provide any necessary assistance.

Natural Gas STAR partners are making a difference! In 2008 alone, domestic partners reduced methane emissions by 114 billion cubic feet (Bcf)—equivalent to removing approximately 8.5 million passenger vehicles from the road for one year or 10.5 million acres of pine or fir forests storing carbon for one year. This added nearly $802 million to natural gas sales (based upon an average gas price of $7.00 per thousand cubic feet). Since 1993, the Program has helped realize nearly 822 Bcf of methane emissions reductions domestically. Natural Gas STAR International partners reported 51.1 Bcf in emissions reductions for 2008 and a total of 65.5 Bcf since the inception of the Natural Gas STAR International Program.

"At Devon, we are committed to protecting the environment and being a good neighbor in communities where we live and work. That's why we joined EPA's Natural Gas STAR Program in 2003. Since we began participating in the Program, we have reduced our methane emissions over 27 billion cubic feet. Since 1990, we have reduced methane emissions by over 31 billion cubic feet. To put that into perspective, that is enough natural gas to heat over 450,000 homes for a year. Further, the reduction of greenhouse gases is equivalent to planting 3.8 million trees or taking 2.75 million cars off the road for a year. Emission reduction is an important part of being an environmental steward, and we are proud to be associated with a project of this magnitude."

—Steven O'Connell,
Devon Energy,
Central Division EHS Supervisor
and Natural Gas STAR
Implementation Manager

Step 3 – Execute the Program

The Implementation Plan provides a roadmap for how partners will actually execute the Program within their company. The Natural Gas STAR Program is available to provide assistance in identifying and prioritizing technologies and practices based on company-specific circumstances. However, to reap the full benefits of participation, it is ultimately up to partners to implement these cost-effective technologies and practices and continue to expand on their methane emission reduction activities.

Step 4 – Submit an Annual Progress Report

After one full calendar year of participation in the Program, partners begin submitting annual reports documenting the previous year's emission reduction activities and corresponding methane emissions reductions. Natural Gas STAR offers convenient reporting options. Partners can choose between submitting data via the easy Online Reporting System, using hardcopy annual reporting forms, or using their own custom format. To provide guidance to partners, EPA Natural Gas STAR Program Managers and STAR Service Representatives can assist as necessary.

By participating in the Natural Gas STAR Program, partners demonstrate leadership in their field by implementing cost-effective technologies and practices that improve operational efficiency, reduce the emissions of methane, increase natural gas supply, save money, and protect the environment. Additionally, through Program participation, partners create a credible record of their voluntary accomplishments and receive EPA recognition.

For detailed information on the Natural Gas STAR Program, key components and benefits of participation, and technical resources available, visit epa.gov/gasstar.

EPA430-F-08-011
November 2009

As part of the Annual Natural Gas STAR Implementation Workshop, EPA publicly recognizes partners in the following categories:

Distribution Partner of the Year

Gathering and Processing
    Partner of the Year

Production Partner of the Year

Transmission Partner of the Year

Implementation Manager of the Year

Continuing Excellence

For a complete list of Natural Gas STAR Award Winners, visit epa.gov/gasstar/newsroom/awardwinners.html.

EPA Natural Gas STAR Program Managers:

Jerome Blackman
blackman.jerome@epa.gov
Phone: (202) 343-9630

Carey Bylin
bylin.carey@epa.gov
Phone: (202) 343-9669

Roger Fernandez
fernandez.roger@epa.gov
Phone: (202) 343-9386

Suzie Waltzer
waltzer.suzanne@epa.gov
Phone: (202) 343-9544

Resources from TheCapitol.Net

Live Training
<www.CapitolHillTraining.com>

- Capitol Hill Workshop
  <www.CapitolHillWorkshop.com>

- Understanding Congressional Budgeting and Appropriations
  <www.CongressionalBudgeting.com>

- Advanced Federal Budget Process
  <www.BudgetProcess.com>

- The President's Budget
  <www.PresidentsBudget.com>

- Understanding the Regulatory Process: Working with Federal Regulatory Agencies
  <www.RegulatoryProcess.com>

- Drafting Effective Federal Legislation and Amendments
  <www.DraftingLegislation.com>

Capitol Learning Audio Courses™
<www.CapitolLearning.com>

- Congress and Its Role in Policymaking
  ISBN: 158733061X

- Understanding the Regulatory Process Series
  ISBN: 1587331398

- Authorizations and Appropriations in a Nutshell
  ISBN: 1587330296

Other Resources

Government

- House Committee on Natural Resources, Energy and Mineral Resources Subcommittee
  <http://resourcescommittee.house.gov>

- Senate Committee on Energy and Natural Resources, Subcommittee on Energy
  <http://energy.senate.gov>

- Department of Energy *<http://www.energy.gov>*

- Energy Information Administration (EIA), Department of Energy *<http://www.eia.doe.gov>*

- Country Energy Profiles, from EIA *<http://tonto.eia.doe.gov/country/>*

- Monthly Energy Review (MER), from EIA *<http://www.eia.doe.gov/emeu/mer/>*

- Bureau of Land Management (BLM), Department of the Interior *<http://www.blm.gov>*

- Oil and Gas, Bureau of Land Management (BLM)
  <http://www.blm.gov/wo/st/en/prog/energy/oil_and_gas.html>

- Minerals Management Service (MMS), Department of the Interior *<http://www.mms.gov>*

- Federal Energy Regulatory Commission (FERC) *<http://www.ferc.gov>*

- EPA *<http://www.epa.gov>*

- Annual Energy Outlook, from the from U.S. Energy Information Administration
  <http://www.eia.doe.gov/oiaf/aeo/>

- Natural Gas Independent Statistics and Analysis, from the U.S. Energy Information
  Administration *<http://www.eia.doe.gov/oil_gas/natural_gas/info_glance/natural_gas.html>*

- Natural Gas Prices, from U.S. Energy Information Administration
  <http://tonto.eia.doe.gov/dnav/ng/ng_pri_sum_dcu_nus_m.htm>

- Natural Gas Annual Supply & Disposition by State, from U.S. Energy Information
  Administration *<http://tonto.eia.doe.gov/dnav/ng/ng_sum_snd_dcu_NUS_a.htm>*

- U.S. Department of Energy Natural Gas Import and Export Regulation
  <http://www.fossil.energy.gov/programs/gasregulation/index.html>

- Alternative Fuels and Advanced Vehicles Data Center (AFDC), from the
  U.S. Department of Energy *<http://www.afdc.energy.gov/afdc/>*

- The National Energy Technology Laboratory (NETL) *<http://www.netl.doe.gov/>*

- Clean Cities, from the U.S. Department of Energy *<http://www1.eere.energy.gov/cleancities/>*

- Weekly Natural Gas Storage Report, from the U.S. Department of Energy
  <http://www.eia.doe.gov/oil_gas/natural_gas/ngs/ngs.html>

Associations, Coalitions, News

- American Petroleum Institute (API) <*http://www.api.org*>

- Adventures in Energy, from the API <*http://www.adventuresinenergy.org*>

- American Gas Association (AGA), represents local energy companies that deliver natural gas throughout the United States <*http://www.aga.org*>

- American Public Gas Association (APGA), association for publicly- and community-owned gas utilities <*http://www.apga.org*>

- Coalbed Natural Gas Alliance (CBNGA) <*http://www.cbnga.com*>

- Interstate Natural Gas Association of America (INGAA), the North American association representing interstate and interprovincial natural gas pipelines <*http://www.ingaa.org*>

- Gas Processors Association (GPA), corporate members are engaged in the processing of natural gas into merchantable pipeline gas, volume movement, or further processing of liquid products from natural gas <*http://gpaglobal.org*>

- LNG World Shipping <*http://www.rivieramm.com/publications/LNG-World-Shipping-3*>

- National Alliance for Drilling Reform (NA4DR) <*http://www.na4dr.com*>

- National Association of Regulatory Utility Commissioners <*http://www.naruc.org*>

- NaturalGas.org, from Natural Gas Supply Association (NGSA) <*http://www.naturalgas.org*>

- True Blue—blog from the American Gas Association <*http://www.truebluenaturalgas.org*>

- Natural Gas Supply Association (NGSA), members produce approximately one-third of the U.S. natural gas supply <*http://www.ngsa.org*>

- Society of Petroleum Engineers (SPE) <*http://www.spe.org*>

- Society of Petroleum Evaluation Engineers (SPEE) <*http://www.spee.org*>

- The Center for LNG (CLNG) <*http://www.lngfacts.org*>

- The Gathering Line, from National Alliance for Drilling Reform (NA4DR) <*http://www.actionotsego.org/gatheringline.html*>

- un-naturalgas.org <*http://un-naturalgas.org*>

Books

- *Dictionary of Petroleum Exploration, Drilling & Production,*
  by Norman J. Hyne, ISBN 0878143521

- *Fundamentals of Natural Gas: An International Perspective,*
  by Vivek Chandra, ISBN 1593700881

- *Fundamentals of Natural Gas Processing,*
  by Arthur J. Kidnay and William R. Parrish, ISBN 0849334063

- *Fundamentals of Oil & Gas Accounting,*
  by Charlotte J. Wright and Rebecca A. Gallun, ISBN 1593701373

- *Gas Purification,* by Arthur L. Kohl and Richard Nelson, ISBN 0884152200

- *Handbook of Natural Gas Transmission and Processing,* by Saeid Mokhatab,
  William A. Poe, and James G. Speight, ISBN 0750677767

- *Introduction to Oil Company Financial Analysis,*
  by David Johnston and Daniel Johnston, ISBN 159370044X

- *Liquefied Natural Gas,* by Paul Griffin, ISBN 1905783019

- *LNG: A Level-Headed Look at the Liquefied Natural Gas Controversy,*
  by Virginia Thorndike, ISBN 0892727012

- *LNG: A Nontechnical Guide,*
  by Michael D. Tusiani and Gordon Shearer, ISBN 087814885X

- *Oil & Gas Production in Nontechnical Language,*
  by William L. Leffler, ISBN 1593700520

- *Oil & Gas Pipelines in Nontechnical Language,*
  by Thomas O. Miesner, ISBN 159370058X

- *Oil 101,* by Morgan Downey, ISBN 0982039204

- *Oil: A Beginner's Guide,* by Vaclav Smil, ISBN 1851685715

- *Oil and Gas: A Practical Handbook,* by Geoffrey Picton-Turbervill, ISBN 190578323X

- *Oilfield Processing of Petroleum: Natural Gas,* by Francis S. Manning, ISBN 0878143432

- *Natural Gas: A Basic Handbook,* by J. G. Speight, ISBN 1933762144

- *Natural Gas and Geopolitics: From 1970 to 2040,*
  by David G. Victor, Amy M. Jaffe, and Mark H. Hayes, ISBN 0521082900

- *Natural Gas Engineering Handbook,* by Boyun Guo and Ali Ghalambor, ISBN 0976511339

- *Natural Gas in Nontechnical Language,* by Rebecca L. Busby, ISBN 0878147381

- *Natural Gas Production Engineering,* by Mohan Kelkar, ISBN 1593700172

- *Nontechnical Guide to Petroleum Geology, Exploration, Drilling and Production,*
  by Nomran Hyne, ISBN 087814823X

- *Oil Politics: A Modern History of Petroleum,* by Francisco Parra, ISBN 1848851294

- *Petroleum Economics: Issues and Strategies of Oil and Natural Gas Production,*
  by Rognvaldur Hannesson, ISBN 1567202209

- *Standard Handbook of Petroleum and Natural Gas Engineering,*
  by William Lyons and Gary Plisga, ISBN 0750677856

- *The Prize: The Epic Quest for Oil, Money & Power,*
  by Daniel Yergin, ISBN 1439110123

- *Trading Natural Gas: Cash, Futures, Options and Swaps,*
  by Fletcher J. Sturm, ISBN 0878147098

- *Understanding Today's Global LNG Business,*
  by Bob Shively and John Ferrare, ISBN 0974174424

- *Understanding Today's Natural Gas Business,*
  by Bob Shively and John Ferrare, ISBN 0974174408

Video and Movies

- A Crude Awakening - The Oil Crash, ASIN B000PY52IG

- Blood and Oil, ASIN B001HWCNCI

- Blood and Oil: The Middle East in World War I, ASIN B000HEWH3C

- Crude Impact, ASIN B001N4K6KQ

- Empires of Industry - Black Gold: The Story of Oil (History Channel),
  ASIN B000BKVL8E

- Firing Line Debate: Resolved: The Price of Oil and Natural Gas
  Should Be Regulated by the Fed. Govt., ASIN B001E50RW6

- GasLand <http://www.gaslandthemovie.com/>

- Giant, ASIN B0007US7FI

- Local Hero, ASIN 6305558205

- Mad Max: The Road Warrior, ASIN B00005R2IS

- The Abyss, ASIN B00005V9IL

About TheCapitol.Net

We help you understand Washington and Congress.™

For over 30 years, TheCapitol.Net and its predecessor, Congressional Quarterly Executive Conferences, have been training professionals from government, military, business, and NGOs on the dynamics and operations of the legislative and executive branches and how to work with them.

Instruction includes topics on the legislative and budget process, congressional operations, public and foreign policy development, advocacy and media training, business etiquette and writing. All training includes course materials.

TheCapitol.Net encompasses a dynamic team of more than 150 faculty members and authors, all of whom are independent subject matter experts and veterans in their fields. Faculty and authors include senior government executives, former Members of Congress, Hill and agency staff, editors and journalists, lobbyists, lawyers, nonprofit executives and scholars.

We've worked with hundreds of clients across the country to develop and produce a wide variety of custom, on-site training. All courses, seminars and workshops can be tailored to align with your organization's educational objectives and presented on-site at your location.

Our practitioner books and publications are written by leading subject matter experts.

TheCapitol.Net has more than 2,000 clients representing congressional offices, federal and state agencies, military branches, corporations, associations, news media and NGOs nationwide.

Our blog: Hobnob Blog—hit or miss ... give or take ... this or that ...

TheCapitol.Net is on Yelp.
Our recommended provider of government training in Brazil is
PATRI/EDUCARE <www.patri.com>

**TheCapitol.Net supports the T.C. Williams Debate Society,
Scholarship Fund of Alexandria, and Sunlight Foundation**

TheCapitol.Net

Non-partisan training and publications that show how Washington works.™

PO Box 25706, Alexandria, VA 22313-5706   703-739-3790   www.TheCapitol.Net

Lightning Source UK Ltd.
Milton Keynes UK
175600UK00004B/1/P